FORENSIC PSYCHOLOGY

Jack Kitaeff, Ph.D., J.D.
University of Maryland, University College

Prentice Hall
Boston   Columbus   Indianapolis   New York   San Francisco   Upper Saddle River
Amsterdam   Cape Town   Dubai   London   Madrid   Milan   Munich   Paris   Montreal   Toronto
Delhi   Mexico City   Sao Paulo   Sydney   Hong Kong   Seoul   Singapore   Taipei   Tokyo

Editor in Chief: Vernon R. Anthony
Acquisitions Editor: Tim Peyton
Editorial Assistant: Lynda Cramer
Director of Marketing: David Gesell
Marketing Manager: Adam Kloza
Senior Marketing Coordinator: Alicia Wozniak
Project Manager: Holly Shufeldt
Creative Director: Jayne Conte
Cover Designer: Lisbeth Axell
Cover Image: Shutterstock
Full-Service Project Management: Integra Software Services, Ltd.
Composition: Integra Software Services, Ltd.
Printer/Binder: Hamilton Printing Co.
Cover Printer: Demand Production Center
Text Font: Minion

Library of Congress Cataloging-in-Publication Data

Cataloging-in-Publication Data for this title can be obtained from the Library of Congress.

10 9 8 7 6 5 4

Prentice Hall
is an imprint of

www.pearsonhighered.com

ISBN 10:   0-13-235291-5
ISBN 13: 978-0-13-235291-8

To Tress, Isaiah, Moriah, and Mordechai—my family,
for your never-ending love and support

PREFACE

In many ways, writing a textbook on forensic psychology is like shooting at a moving target. This is due in part to the compartmentalization of the profession into clinical forensic practice, experimental research, and psychology and the law. It is also due to the tremendous growth of forensic psychology generally during the last 30 years, and specifically during the last 10. To complicate matters even further, various areas within psychology can be subsumed within forensic psychology, and none are exclusively dominant. These include clinical, counseling, developmental, social, cognitive, and neuropsychology to name a few.

Forensic psychology is generally defined as the application of the science and profession of psychology to questions and issues related to law and the legal system. The term *forensic* comes from the Latin word *forensis*, meaning "of the forum," where the law courts of ancient Rome were held. Today forensic refers to the application of scientific principles and practices to the legal system. Indeed, forensic psychologists are perhaps best known for their assessment of persons involved with the legal system. Because of their knowledge of human behavior, abnormal psychology, and psychological assessment, forensic psychologists (specifically *clinical* forensic psychologists as they are sometimes called) are well suited to perform court-ordered evaluations and provide an "expert opinion," either in the form of a pscychological report or verbal testimony. These could include offering the court information regarding whether a defendant can understand the charges against him/her and comprehend the judicial process, (i.e., whether the defendant is incompetent to stand trial), whether the defendant was "insane" when the relevant crime was committed, and whether treatment or punishment would be the most logical sentence.

In the civil arena, forensic psychologists may evaluate persons who are undergoing guardianship proceedings, and assist the court in determining whether someone has a mental disorder that could affect his/her ability to make important life decisions (e.g., managing money, making health care and legal decisions). Appropriately trained forensic psychologists also evaluate plaintiffs in lawsuits, involving people who allege that they were emotionally harmed as a result of another party's negligence. Or they may evaluate children and their parents in cases of divorce, perhaps as an aid in making custody determinations and evaluating children for alleged abuse or neglect.

It is a truism that professional forensic psychology can be instrumental in making the law more therapeutic and helping the legal system become more effective in achieving its aims. This approach is heavily influenced by the concept of "therapeutic jurisprudence," which asserts that the legal system should seek to promote the health and emotional well-being of individuals in addition to ensuring justice and social order. This approach frequently embraces multidisciplinary and systemic issues of a psychological nature within a legal context.

The main purpose of this book is to present the clearest picture possible of forensic psychology from its beginnings to the scientifically based profession that it is today. Since it is difficult, if not impossible, to separate "psychological principles" from "legal principles" and still provide an informative text on forensic psychology, no significant attempts were made to draw such distinctions. In fact, wherever possible throughout the text, psychology is linked with legal opinions and actual case law in an attempt to further illustrate their connectivity and mutual reliance in the real world.

This book is divided into five main sections. The first section provides an introduction to the field of forensic psychology. Discussions include the history of forensic psychology; significant past and present applications as a science and a profession; history-changing court decisions in which forensic psychology played a major role; the education of forensic psychologists, their roles and responsibilities, and their duties and obligations from professional, ethical, moral, and legal standpoints. Section Two of the book looks at the criminological aspects of forensic psychology and includes an examination of theories of aggression and violent crime; the definitions and classification of nonviolent crimes; a discussion of mass murder and serial killers; and an analysis of the psychology of terrorism, cults, and extremism. The third section of the book presents an overview of police and law enforcement. This includes the topic of police psychology and the role psychologists have in selecting and assessing police officers, and consulting in areas of law enforcement such as hostage negotiations and critical incident stress debriefing. This section also includes an examination of the tools and techniques involved in the investigation of crime. Section Four looks at the involvement of forensic psychologists in the American criminal justice system and adjudication process, both on a pretrial and trial basis. This includes discussions of eyewitness identification and accuracy; psychology of false confessions; competency; and juries and the courtroom. The final chapter of the book highlights forensic psychology's direct application to five special categories. These are repressed memories; novel syndromes, the workplace, children and families, and issues of treatment and rehabilitation.

Jack Kitaeff
Burke, Virginia
Fall, 2009

ACKNOWLEDGMENTS

I gratefully acknowledge the following reviewers for their insightful comments and suggestions: Bart Abplanalp, South Puget Sound Community College; Ife Alexander-Caines, ECPI College of Technology; Jason Dickinson, Montclair State University; and Annette Nolte, TCC/NW.

I also would like to give special thanks to the students who assisted me with specific research components of this book: Debra Lynch, Zeeyon Walker, Sandra Thomas, and Francean Baxter.

A special debt of gratitude goes to Tim Peyton, Lynda Cramer, Holly Shufeldt, Shiji Sashi, and the many other dedicated publishing professionals for their hard work and support for the first edition of this text.

Dr. Jack Kitaeff

ABOUT THE AUTHOR

JACK KITAEFF, Ph.D., J.D. is a licensed clinical psychologist in the Commonwealth of Virginia specializing in police and forensic psychology. He received his undergraduate education at Brooklyn College, and his graduate education at the State University of New York at Cortland and the University of Mississippi. He received his law degree from the George Mason University School of law, and completed a legal clerkship with the U.S. Attorney's Office, Eastern District of Virginia.

After completing a clinical psychology internship at Walter Reed Army Medical Center, and a psychology residency at U.S. Dewitt Army Hospital, Dr. Kitaeff served as the chief psychologist at Fort Belvoir, Virginia and a Major in the U.S. Army Medical Service Corps. In 1984, he became the first police psychologist for the Arlington County Police Department, where he established a preemployment psychological screening program for police applicants. From 1984 to the present he has been the consulting police psychologist for numerous law enforcement agencies in the northern Virginia area, including the Arlington County Sheriff's Office, the Alexandria Police Department, and the Warrenton Police Department, among many others. Dr. Kitaeff is an adjunct professor of psychology with the University of Maryland, University College. He also holds dual faculty appointments with Walden University in the school of psychology and the school of counseling and social service. He is a Diplomate in Police Psychology from the Society of Police and Criminal Psychology and a member of the American Psychological Association, the Virginia Psychological Association, and the Virginia Academy of Clinical Psychologists.

Dr. Kitaeff has written numerous articles and delivered presentations on police psychology and forensic psychology. His books include *Selected Readings in Forensic Psychology* (2006), *Jews in Blue* (2006), and *Malingering, Lies, and Junk Science in the Courtroom* (2007). He is also the editor of a Handbook of Police Psychology which is slotted for publication in October 2010. Dr. Kitaeff lives in northern Virginia with his wife and three children.

CHAPTER 1

History and Current Issues in Forensic Psychology

CHAPTER OBJECTIVES

After reading this chapter you would:

- Understand the significance of the ability to reason in criminal law.
- Know the basic definition of forensic science and the disciplines that fall under this rubric.
- Appreciate the impact of social learning principles on aggressive behavior.
- Understand the difference between psychological syndromes and psychological profiles.
- Know the general differences between science and law.
- Understand the effects of unsupported scientific concepts in the American legal system.
- Comprehend the psychological and societal significance of *Brown v. Board of Education*.
- Appreciate the roles of the judge and the jury in evaluating **syndrome evidence**.

INTRODUCTION

To the nonscientist, it must seem at times that forensic psychology (as well as forensic psychiatry) harkens back to those instances in history, human behavior, and the law when some person acts unreasonably, unpredictably, violently or is "insane." Indeed, in 1256, English judge Henry de Bracton formulated a **"wild beast test"** to identify insane people who he believed should not be held morally accountable for their actions because they were "beast-like." He wrote, "Such men are not greatly removed from beasts for they lack reasoning" (Platt & Diamond, 1965). They were to be regarded as beasts not criminals.

For centuries, it was considered unjust to label a person as a "criminal" unless his unlawful act was performed with a guilty mind. The English Court of Appeal has stated,

> We all know that both men and women who are deeply in love can, and sometimes do, have outburst of blind rage when discovering unexpected wantonness on the part of their loved ones; the wife taken in adultery is the classical example of the application of the defense of "provocation"; and when death or serious injury results, profound grief usually follows. Jurors do not need psychiatrists to tell them how ordinary folk who are not suffering from any mental illness are likely to react to the stresses and strains of life. (*Regina v. Byrne*, 1960)

HISTORY OF FORENSIC PSYCHOLOGY

In *People v. Schmidt* (1915) the defendant, Hans Schmidt, was charged with killing and dismembering a woman and throwing her remains into the Hudson River. Claiming that God had commanded the killing "as a sacrifice and atonement," he pleaded insanity. The opinion of the court was written by Judge **Benjamin Cardozo**, who later became a Supreme Court justice. In his opinion, he wrote, "[T]here are times and circumstances in which the word 'wrong' . . . ought not to be limited to a legal wrong. For example, if a person has an insane delusion that God has appeared to [the accused] and ordained the commission of a crime, we think it cannot be said of the defendant that he knows that act to be wrong" (p. 915).

This view has not changed much through the years. The 1955 Model Penal Code commented on this situation: "A madman [who believes that God has commanded him] is plainly beyond the reach of the restraining influence of law; he needs restraint but condemnation is entirely meaningless and ineffective" (ALI Model Penal Code, § 4.01, 1955). But this was not the case in every instance. For example, in *Davis v. State* (1999), the court found that the defendant should not be excused of criminal responsibility since on cross-examination of the defendant's psychiatrist it was acknowledged that the defendant's description of an angel's command to commit child sexual abuse seemed tailored specifically to match the legal standard for insanity in effect at the time.

Although the current definitions of "forensic psychology" are discussed in the next chapter, it is safe to say that such definitions go significantly beyond the voyeuristically titillating matters of the extremes of behavior already mentioned. It will be seen that the applications of forensic psychology have been associated with some of the most positive social and legal matters in American history and in the way we live our lives and regard others.

One prominent example is the U.S. Supreme Court's decision in *Brown v. Board of Education of Topeka, Kansas* (1954). *Brown* marked the first time that the results of psychological research were actually cited in a Supreme Court decision. The psychological data cited by the Court effectively forever ended school segregation based on color in the United States and signaled a dramatic change in the role of scientific and psychological evidence in advocacy and judicial decision making. In a similar fashion, in 1961, social learning research conducted by Albert Bandura and his associates was utilized by lawmakers to demonstrate that aggressive behavior seen on television and in the movies can be transmitted to children by imitation if such aggression is seen as being rewarded (Bandura Ross, & Ross, 1961).

But the socially relevant changes resulting in part from psychological input did not lessen the emergence of more peculiar cases. For example, in 1985, newly elected San Francisco city councilman Dan White shot dead fellow councilman Harvey Milk and Mayor George Moscone. At his trial for murder, White's defense team presented psychiatric evidence that White's mental illness caused him to significantly increase his consumption of junk food (such as Twinkies) to deal with his problems and that this made him feel more depressed, contributing to the likelihood of such dramatically violent actions. The jury convicted White of only of two counts of voluntary manslaughter (rather than the much more severe charge of first-degree murder). The public and the media forever dubbed this as the "Twinkie Defense" (Ewing & McCann, 2006).

In 1978, Ted Kaczynski began loading packages with explosives and leaving them in predetermined locations, causing death and disfigurement. In 1982, in a different case, seven people died after ingesting Tylenol capsules that had been laced with cyanide. In the same year, George Banks shot 13 family members and relatives for no clear reason. In October 2002, John Allen Muhammad and Lee Boyd Malvo (the "Beltway Snipers") killed ten people in three weeks in Maryland, Virginia, and Washington, DC. Muhammad was 41 and Malvo 16 (but turned 17 prior to the last murder). The victims appeared to have been randomly shot while going about their everyday lives—mowing the lawn, pumping gas, shopping, and going to school. At his trial, Malvo pleaded not guilty by reason of insanity on the ground that he was being controlled by the older Muhammad.

On June 25, 2005, the sexually motivated serial killer Dennis Rader pled guilty to ten counts of first-degree murder, which beginning in 1974 ran a course of over 20 years. Dubbed the "the BTK killer" for his confessed predisposition to "bind, torture, and kill" his victims, Rader, in a robot-like fashion, devoid of emotion or regret, described his killings (or "projects") in cold and meticulous detail. And on April 16, 2007, Virginia Polytechnic Institute ("Virginia Tech") student Seung-Hui Cho, in the worst school shooting in U.S. history, killed 32 people and wounded 25 others.

Finally, the late twentieth and early twenty-first centuries brought a new kind of belief-based terror to the world—apocalyptic religious groups. Members of such groups engage in terrorism out of a fundamentalist religious ideology. Their doctrinal principles include no negotiation, no dialogue, and no peacemaking. Furthermore, these groups firmly believe that they have been divinely ordained to commit violent acts resulting in mass casualties.

FORENSIC PSYCHOLOGY AND FORENSIC SCIENCE

A discussion and analysis of the issues and scenarios covered in the previous section legitimately falls under the vast rubric of "forensic psychology," and the pages and chapters to come will deal with all of these in greater depth. The science and discipline of forensic psychology as described in this text includes a myriad of topics:

1. Psychology applied to civil law
2. Psychology applied to criminal law
3. Psychology applied to juries
4. Psychology applied to investigative issues
5. Psychology applied to law enforcement
6. Psychology applied to diagnostic and assessment issues
7. Psychology applied to treatment issues
8. Psychology applied to ethical and profession-specific issues
9. Psychology applied to social issues
10. Psychology applied to world issues

But to trace the history of forensic psychology, we must first look back to one of its forerunners, **forensic science**. In the broadest sense, forensic science is the study and practice of applying natural, physical, and social sciences to the resolution of social and legal issues. A number of disciplines exist under the wide umbrella of forensic science. Many of these are simply adaptations of existing disciplines. For example, forensic pathology deals with the investigation of death or injury as a result of violence, or with the cause of unexpected and unexplained death. Forensic odontology (a branch of dentistry) deals with dental evidence, usually involving an examination of dental remains for identification of the victim, injuries to the teeth or jaw, or bite marks for comparison with those of a suspect. Forensic anthropology deals with the identification of skeletal remains through the application of standard anthropological techniques. Forensic toxicology concerns itself with the analyses of tissues and fluids from deceased persons to identify toxic substances that might have caused the death. Forensic engineering deals with the causes of failure of devices and structures. It is the investigation of materials, products, structures, or components that fail to operate or do not function as intended. Forensic economics is the study and interpretation of the economic damage evidence that includes present day calculations of lost earnings and benefits, the lost value of a business, lost business profits, lost value of household service, replacement labor costs and future medical care costs. Forensic accounting, on the other hand, is defined as the study and interpretation of accounting evidence. Forensic entomology deals with the examination of infesting insects in, on, and around human remains to assist in determination of time or location of death.

ISSUES IN FORENSIC PSYCHOLOGY

As will become apparent in the remainder of this text, forensic psychology and psychiatry deal with the legal aspects of human behavior, that is, the application of psychological principles and knowledge to various legal activities such as child custody disputes; child abuse of an emotional, physical, and sexual nature; assessing the personal capacity to manage one's affairs; competency to stand trial; criminal responsibility and personal injury; and advising judges in matters related to sentencing.

Whenever forensic science is brought into a court of law it takes the form of "expert scientific testimony." Such testimony may involve physical or medical sciences, or it may involve the social sciences. Expert opinion based upon social science usually takes one of two forms. First, the research can be applied directly to a case. For example, a forensic psychologist might offer his or her expert opinion that the complaining witness in a criminal case had in fact been raped. This conclusion might be based upon the expert's comparison of characteristics exhibited by the complaining witness with characteristics possessed by other women who reported that they had been raped. On the other hand, such **expert testimony** may be applied in a "generic" fashion, and the psychological expert may simply explain to a jury how the "typical" rape victim reacts after the incident without stating a specific opinion as to whether a rape occurred in the case at hand. Social science expert testimony also usually involves "**syndromes**" or "**profiles**." Examples of syndromes include the rape trauma syndrome and battered wife (or partner) syndrome. Examples of profiles include the battering parent profile, the child sexual abuser profile, and the profile of a defendant as being incompatible with the commission of the crime. But exactly what qualifies for the designation of "syndrome" or "profile" is unclear (Goodwin & Gurulé, 1997).

Another quality of psychological or behavioral evidence (sometimes called "soft" scientific evidence) is that it is much closer to the common understanding of the ordinary juror than are the physical, chemical, and biological sciences (sometimes called "hard" scientific evidence). An example of soft scientific evidencing coming together to form a psychological syndrome is the "battered women syndrome" (McCord, 1997), in which "a woman who could have left but instead chose violence [by killing her abuser] . . . should be excused from criminal liability" (p. 361).

Some of the reasons for the confusion and suspicion regarding the limits of psychological evidence and testimony result from the basic differences between the professions of law and psychology. "Law is normative, while science is descriptive. Law is value-laden, while science is value-free. Legal reasoning is largely deductive, while scientific method is primarily inductive. Legal findings are based on certainties and standards such as proof beyond a reasonable doubt, while scientific findings are based on probabilities and contingencies" (Ancheta, 2006, pp. 19–20).

In 1895, Columbia University psychologist **James McKeen Cattell** conducted one of the earliest research studies in what could be called forensic psychology (Cattell, 1895). Cattell tested the reliability of witness testimony by posing a series of memory questions to students similar to questions that might be asked in a court of law. He was surprised at the degree of inaccuracy of these memory reports, especially when coupled with students' high degree of confidence that they were in fact accurate. Cattell's findings sparked further research by other psychologists. Alfred Binet replicated Cattell's research and examined the results of other experiments related to the suggestibility of witnesses as well as law and criminal justice in general. Many of his findings were reported in his book *La suggestibility* (Binet, 1900). The psychologist **William Stern** also studied witness recall (Stern, 1910). In the earlier study, students were asked to summarize a dispute between two classmates that they had witnessed. Stern discovered that errors were common among the witnesses, concluding that emotions decrease the accuracy of witness recall. Stern also initiated the first specialized journal in the reliability of testimony, *Psychologie der Aussage* (Psychology of Testimony), in 1902. Six years later, the name of the journal was changed to the *Journal of Applied Psychology*.

The first recorded example of actually taking the new forensic psychology into the courtroom was in 1896 when Albert von Schrenck-Notzing (a student of Wilhelm Wundt) testified at a murder trial in Munich. Drawing on research into errors of recall and suggestibility, he argued that pretrial publicity resulted in witnesses not being able to distinguish between what they actually saw and what they had read in the press. He called this kind of perceptual error "**retroactive memory falsification**" (Schrenck-Notzing, 1914). In the world of applied forensic psychology, Karl Marbe, another of Wundt's students, in 1911 was the first psychologist to serve as an expert witness in a civil trial. He demonstrated in court the phenomenon of "reaction time," showing that an engineer (who was assumed to be responsible for a railway accident) could not have stopped his train in time to avert the collision (Slovenko, 2002).

Even Sigmund Freud advocated for the use of psychology in the legal system, most pointedly in the determination of truthfulness and witness accuracy and veracity. In 1906, he delivered a lecture entitled "Psychoanalysis and the Ascertaining of Truth in Courts of Law" to a law class at the University of Vienna. There he advocated for the use of psychological research that would provide judges insight into a defendant's psychological makeup and character.

In 1908, **Hugo Münsterberg**, regarded by many as the father of forensic psychology, advocated for psychology's increased involvement in the courts and legal system. In his book *On the Witness Stand*, he described the psychological factors that can affect a trial's outcome. These include false confessions, the power of suggestion in cross-examination, and the use of physiological measurements (heart rate, blood pressure, and skin resistance) to detect heightened emotional states in suspects and defendants. He also recommended that witnesses be tested for reliability in experimental situations before their testimony is accepted. During one murder trial, Münsterberg administered almost 100 mental tests to the confessed killer of 18 people who had accused a labor union leader of paying for the murders. On the basis of the test results, Münsterberg announced, even before the jury had reached its verdict in the labor leader's trial, that the murderer's confession implicating the labor leader was true. When the jury acquitted the labor leader, the damage to Münsterberg's credibility was substantial (Schultz & Schultz, 2004, p. 250).

In America, in 1922, William Marston, a student of Münsterberg, became the first American professor of "legal psychology." Following through on the work of his mentor, Marston created the first systolic blood pressure test used to detect deception. The test was the forerunner of the modern polygraph. Unfortunately, his expert testimony on the matter was rejected in court as not being "practical" (Jansz & Van Drunen, 2003, p. 208). But it was not until the 1950s that psychologists began to successfully testify in American courts, since such testimony had hitherto been seen as the province of medical experts.

Once social science evidence in general, and psychological evidence in particular, was allowed into court, the result in some instances was nothing less than monumental. As mentioned previously, one of the most salient examples of the power of psychological testimony during the last 100 years was the case of **Brown v. Board of Education of Topeka, Kansas**, in 1954. Moreover, it has a special significance for psychology because it marked the first time that psychological research was cited in a Supreme Court decision and because social science data were seen as paramount in the Court's decision to end school segregation. The Supreme Court's holding in *Brown* signaled a dramatic change in the role of scientific and psychological evidence in advocacy and judicial decision making. Prior to 1954, the constitutional issue of segregation was based upon the Supreme Court's decision in *Plessy v. Ferguson* (1896).

In *Plessy* the court stated, "The object of the [Fourteenth] Amendment was undoubtedly to enforce the absolute equality of the two races before the law, but in the nature of things it could not have been intended to abolish distinctions based upon color, or to enforce social, as distinguished from political, equality, or a commingling of the two races upon terms unsatisfactory to either" (*Plessy v. Ferguson*, Justice Henry Billings Brown speaking for the majority).

In *Brown*, several psychologists testified for both the plaintiffs and the defendants. Two of the plaintiff's psychologists were **Kenneth Bancroft Clark** and his wife, Mamie Phipps Clark. The Clarks designed a test (the "**doll test**") to study the psychological effects of segregation on black children. They used four plastic, diaper-clad dolls, identical except for color. They showed the dolls to black children between the ages of three and seven and asked them questions to determine racial perception and preference. Almost all of the children readily identified the race of the dolls. However, when asked which they preferred, the majority selected the white doll and attributed positive characteristics to it. The Clarks also gave the children outline drawings of a boy and girl and asked them to color the figures the same color as themselves. Many of the children with dark complexions colored the figures with a white or yellow crayon. The Clarks concluded that "prejudice, discrimination, and segregation" caused black children to develop a sense of inferiority and self-hatred.

The Brown Court stated,

> Segregation of white and colored children in public schools has a detrimental effect upon the colored children. The impact is greater when it has the sanction of the law; for the policy of separating the races is usually interpreted as denoting the inferiority of the negro group. A sense of inferiority affects the motivation of a child to learn. Segregation with the sanction of law, therefore, has a tendency to [retard] the educational and mental development of [N]egro children and to deprive them of some of the benefits they would receive in a racial[ly] integrated school system. (Bass & Davis, 1994)

The Court's judgment in *Brown* is broadly recognized as the first serious blow to the comprehensive system of laws collectively referred to as "**Jim Crow**," which codified separation of the races and limited the freedom and options of former slaves in the South following the Civil War. In 1954, the Supreme Court changed the course of American history. Its decision in *Brown v. Board of Education* nullified the concept of "separate but equal," ended legal segregation in public education, and energized the civil rights movement (Alpert, 1995).

IMPACT OF FORENSIC PSYCHOLOGY ON EXPERT EVIDENCE

In the last 60 years, psychologists have continued to provide expert testimony in both criminal and civil courts of law. Topics of such testimony have included, but have not been limited to, dangerousness, criminal and adjudicative responsibility, child custody, psychological damages, malingering and deception, brain injury, post-traumatic stress disorder, eyewitness testimony, jury selection, recovered memories, hypnosis, sexual harassment, child abuse and neglect, partner violence, and involuntary commitment. Furthermore, organized psychology has provided opinions in the form of *amicus curiae* (friend of the court) briefs in cases involving issues of societal importance. The American Psychological Association has filed numerous *amicus* briefs on topics such as abortion, affirmative action, child abuse, civil commitment, competency, the insanity defense, the death penalty, the duty to warn/protect, gay parenting, the right to refuse medication, sexual harassment, and sexual orientation (Terr, 1991). But not all representations by psychologists have been based on adequate science and not all have reflected the profession of psychology in a positive light.

In the 1960s the psychoanalyst Bruno Bettelheim decreed that autistic children were produced by "**refrigerator moms**," mothers who, according to Bettelheim, were not competent to bond emotionally with their children, eventually resulting in a complete incapacity for emotional attachment in the children. Aside from some clinical or anecdotal experiences, Bettelheim presented no supporting evidence whatsoever.

Bettelheim's pronouncement had a significant impact on how society viewed child care. It also had a significant impact on how mothers regarded themselves. Some mothers felt deficient in their child-rearing practices and feared that they could be "refrigerator moms"; low self-esteem and even depression resulted. Although unwittingly, Bettelheim was supplying an explanation and a cause for these "adult children of refrigerator moms" experiencing problems in the future with interpersonal relationships of all sorts. He was also laying the groundwork for a possible future defense to violent crimes. It would not take much imagination to foresee a forensic expert in the future testifying for the defense of such an adult child of a refrigerator mom who was a defendant in criminal case—all this based on an unsupported theoretical concept with no scientific or empirical validation.

Psychologist Margaret Hagen (1997) wrote a telling book, *Whores of the Court: The Fraud of Psychiatric Testimony and the Rape of American Justice*. In it she talks about the wasted resources caused by the business of expert testimony and the ludicrous verdicts due to the testimony of these "experts" injecting fanciful psychological theories into life-and-death settings. Hagen describes modern psychiatry as "**junk science**," overly influenced by faddists who have invented numerous syndromes and dysfunctions and placed them into the American legal system (Salerno, 2005; *see also* Bernstein & Putnam, 1986).

FORENSIC PSYCHOLOGY IN THE SPOTLIGHT

Is Rape Trauma Syndrome Testimony Admissible to Explain Conduct of a Complainant that Would Seem to be Inconsistent with a Rape?

People v. Taylor (1990)

On July 29, 1984, the complainant, a 19-year-old Long Island resident, reported to the town police that she had been raped and sodomized at gunpoint on a beach near her home. The complainant testified that at about 9:00 P.M. she had received a phone call from a friend, asking her to meet him at a nearby market in half an hour. Twenty minutes later, the same person called back and changed the meeting place. The complainant arrived at the agreed-upon place, shut off the car engine, and waited. A man approached her car, and she unlocked the door to let him in. Only then did she realize that the person who had approached and entered the car was not the friend she had come to meet. According to the complainant, he pointed a gun at her, directed her to nearby Clarke's Beach, and once there, raped and sodomized her.

The complainant arrived home around 11:00 P.M., woke her mother, and told her about the attack. Her mother then called the police. Sometime between 11:30 P.M. and midnight, the police arrived at the complainant's house. At that time, the complainant told the police she did not know who her attacker was. She was taken to the police station where she described the events leading up to the attack and again repeated that she did not know who her attacker was. At the conclusion of the interview, the complainant was asked to step into a private room to remove the clothes that she had been wearing at the time of the attack so that they could be examined for forensic evidence. While she was alone with her mother, the complainant told her that John Taylor (the defendant) was her attacker. The time was approximately 1:15 A.M. The complainant had known Taylor for years, and she later testified that she happened to see him the night before the attack at a local convenience store.

Her mother summoned one of the detectives, and the complainant repeated that Taylor was the person who attacked her. The complainant said that she was sure because she had had ample opportunity to see his face during the incident. He was arrested on July 31, 1984, and was indicted by the Grand Jury on one count of rape in the first degree, two counts of sodomy in the first degree, and one count of sexual abuse in the first degree.

The defendant's first trial ended without the jury being able to reach a verdict. At his second trial, the judge permitted Eileen Treacy, an instructor at the City University of New York, Herbert Lehman College, with experience in counseling sexual assault victims, to testify about rape trauma syndrome. The prosecutor introduced this testimony for two separate purposes. First, Treacy's testimony on the specifics of rape trauma syndrome explained why the complainant might have been unwilling during the first few hours after the attack to name the defendant as her attacker where she had known the defendant prior to the incident. Second, Treacy's testimony that it was common for a rape victim to appear quiet and controlled following an attack responded to evidence that the complainant had appeared calm after the attack and tended to rebut the inference that because she was not excited and upset after the attack, it had not been a rape. At the close of the second trial, the defendant was convicted on all counts.

Summary

Forensic science is the study and practice of applying natural, physical, and social sciences to the resolution of social and legal issues. There are many forensic specialties, such as forensic pathology, forensic anthropology, forensic economics, and forensic psychology and psychiatry. Forensic science in courts of law takes the form of expert scientific testimony.

Psychological testimony often takes the form of psychological syndromes or profiles and is often referred to as **soft science**, while the physical sciences are seen as **hard sciences**. There is often a strain between psychology and the law due to fundamental differences in how each field draws conclusions and regards truth. The first real psychological testimony was applied in a court of law in 1896, but it has been since about 1950 that psychological and social science experts have been most visible in the criminal and civil justice systems. Some of the contributions by psychologists have been monumental, such as the psychological testimony in *Brown v. Board of Education*.

During the last 100 years, psychologists and psychiatrists have been advocating for increased involvement in the courtroom and the legal system. This has resulted in a "parade of experts" seeking to testify regarding all kinds of psychological phenomena and syndromes, some of which are unsupported by scientific research. Psychologists and mental health professionals have been injecting their expertise into the criminal justice system in such matters as repressed and recovered memories of childhood sexual abuse.

There have been many novel syndromes during the last 30 years, some of which are based on scientific data and are useful, while many are based on questionable research and developmental methods and are of no value. The latter is particularly true when a "syndrome" is initially developed for the purpose of establishing a legal defense. In addition, there is evidence that applied psychology is inordinately affected by "social fashion" and that social activism is presented to the courts and the public in the guise of science.

A syndrome is a set of symptoms and signs that occur in a regular pattern from patient to patient that collectively indicate or characterize a disease, psychological disorder, or other abnormal condition. Psychological syndrome evidence is extremely important because it can put in the hands of the jury tremendous power to determine the credibility of a witness in a trial. This is a determination that an expert witness would not be permitted to make on his own and would thereby allow such evidence into testimony "through the back door."

Judges in federal courts and those jurisdictions that have adopted the federal rules of evidence or *Daubert* standard must aggressively assume the role of gatekeeper and examine the relevance and reliability of all proffers of expert testimony. The other ways of dealing with questionable techniques and testimony are through the investigation and cross-examination of the experts themselves.

Key Terms

Wild beast test *1*
Forensic Science *3*
Profiles *4*
Expert testimony *4*
William Stern *4*

Hugo Münsterberg *5*
Doll test *5*
Jim Crow Laws *6*
Benjamin Cardozo *2*
Syndromes *4*

Junk Science *6*
Soft versus Hard
    Science *7*
James McKeen
    Cattell *4*

Kenneth Bancroft
    Clark *5*
Refrigerator Moms *6*
Retroactive Memory
    Falsification *4*

Review Questions

1. In the thirteenth century, were insane people generally held criminally responsible for their actions? Why or why not?
2. What are some of the topics included in the scientific study of forensic psychology?
3. What is forensic odontology, and how can it help criminal investigators?
4. What branch of forensic science deals with the examination of insects that may be near and around a crime scene?
5. What is an example of a psychological "syndrome" that may be introduced as evidence by a forensic psychologist?

6. What is the essence of the research performed by James Cattell at Columbia University in 1895?
7. How would Albert von Schrenck-Notzing define retroactive memory falsification?
8. How does organized psychology attempt to influence the outcome of high-profile legal cases?
9. Why does *Brown v. Board of Education* hold a special significance for psychology?

Chapter Resources on the World Wide Web

American Academy of Forensic Sciences
http://www.aafs.org/

Forensic-Evidence.com
http://www.forensic-evidence.com/

Google Web Directory in Forensic Sciences
http://directory.google.com/Top/Science/Science_in_Society/Forensic_Science/

American Journal of Forensic Medicine and Pathology (2001-Present)
http://www.amjforensicmedicine.com/

All about Forensic Psychology
http://www.all-about-forensic-psychology.com/history-of-forensic-psychology-part-one.html

Brown v. Board of Education of Topeka, Kansas
http://www.loc.gov/exhibits/brown/brown-brown.html

The Skeptics Dictionary: False Memory
http://skepdic.com/falsememory.html

Famous American Trials
http://www.law.umkc.edu/faculty/projects/ftrials/sweet/background.htm

A Society of Victims
http://www.arachnoid.com/psychology/victimhood.php

For Further Reading

Ancheta, A. N., *Scientific Evidence and Equal Protection of the Law.* Piscataway (New Jersy: Rutgers University Press, 2006).

Darrow, C. (1927). *Clarence Darrow's Two Greatest Trials: Reports of the Scopes Anti-Evolution Case and the Dr. Sweet Negro.* Gerard, Kansas: Haldeman-Julius Co.

Halpern, D. F., Brooks, A., & Stephenson, C. "How science by media creates false certainties and resistance to conceptual change," in Kitaeff, J., ed., *Malingering, Lies, and Junk Science in the Courtroom* (Youngstown, NY: Cambria Press, 2007).

Jansz, J., & Van Drunen, P. (2003). *A Social History of Psychology.* Malden, MA: Wiley-Blackwell.

Johnston, M., *Spectral Evidence* (Boston, Mass: Houghton Mifflin Company, 1997).

Salerno, S., *SHAM* (New York: Crown, 2005).

CHAPTER 2

Roles and Responsibilities of Forensic Psychologists

CHAPTER OBJECTIVES

After reading this chapter you would:

- Understand the definition of forensic psychology.
- Know the major issues in the education and training of forensic psychologists.
- Appreciate the ethical obligations of forensic psychologists.
- Understand the Frye and Daubert rules related to admitting expert evidence.
- Understand the differences between a lay and an expert witness.
- Appreciate the balance between psychologist privilege and the duty to warn.
- Know the legal and psychological principles related to predicting dangerousness.
- Understand the difference between clinical and actuarial judgments.

INTRODUCTION

Chapter 1 described the nature and history of forensic science and the way in which forensic science enters the criminal justice system. This chapter concentrates on one form of forensic science—forensic psychology. We will look at the meaning of forensic psychology, the making of a forensic psychologist, and the rules used by courts for evaluating psychological testimony. The rights and privileges of the psychologist–client relationship will also be discussed. The assessment of dangerousness, along with its significant limitations, using both clinical and actuarial techniques will also be examined, along with relevant case law.

WHAT IS FORENSIC PSYCHOLOGY?

The field of forensic psychology is notoriously difficult to define. At the very basic level it is the branch of psychology that represents the interaction and comingling of psychological science with the legal system. Some psychologists such as Bartol and Bartol (2004) hold an extremely broad view of forensic psychology and define it as "both (1) the research endeavor that examines aspect of human behavior directly related to the legal process . . . and (2) the professional practices of psychology within, or in consultation with, a legal system that embraces both civil and criminal law" (p. 3). A still broader definition includes the integration of applied and experimental psychology with forensic psychological research. A much narrower definition views forensic psychologists basically as clinical psychologists who are engaged in clinical practice within the legal system. This definition may be too restrictive because it seems to imply a specialty called **forensic clinical psychology**. "The broad definition, on the other hand, includes not only clinicians but also social, developmental, counseling, cognitive, experimental, industrial-organizational, and school psychologists—some but not all of whom are clinicians. The common link is their contribution to the legal system" (Bartol & Bartol, 2004).

For the purposes of this textbook, **forensic psychology** is seen as involving the application of scientific and professional aspects of psychology to questions and issues related to the law and the legal system. Specialty guidelines for forensic psychology were first introduced by the American Psychology-Law Society (AP-LS) in 1991. In 2001, the council of representatives of the American Psychological Association (APA) voted to recognize forensic psychology as a specialty. In 2008, the AP-LS issued new specialty guidelines defining the scope of forensic psychology. These guidelines apply to psychologists providing services to all aspects of the judicial and legal systems, including "examining or treating persons in anticipation of . . . legal, contractual, administrative, or disability determination proceedings; offering *amicus* briefs or testimony to judicial, legislative or administrative bodies; . . . serving as a trial consultant . . . to attorneys, the courts, or others; [or] conducting research in connection with the anticipation of litigation" (AP-LS, § 1.03).

In a practical sense, forensic psychology involves an overlapping relationship between clinical practice, experimental research, and the law. This fluid relationship is expressed in Figure 2.1. The clinical aspects of forensic psychology generally include things such as sanity, competency to stand trial, preemployment psychological screening for law enforcement and other high-risk occupations, fitness-for-duty evaluations, hypnosis, psychological profiling, psychological autopsies, custody evaluations, general clinical psychological assessment, working with violent sexual offenders, and helping people who have been the victims of crimes and trauma.

The research aspects of forensic psychology include conducting studies on the jury decision-making process, the effects of pretrial publicity and expert testimony, the accuracy of eyewitness identification, the evaluation of research and public policy, and the effects of the legal system upon victims, witnesses, and criminals (e.g., Under what conditions will the legal system create or exacerbate psychological distress, and how should legal systems and legal processes be modified to minimize that distress?). The legal aspects include alternate dispute resolution and negotiations, determination of psychological damages in civil cases, trial procedure, techniques of criminal investigation, interrogations and confessions, death penalty trials and appeals, and social issues in litigation (e.g., psychological syndromes, discrimination, and sexual harassment).

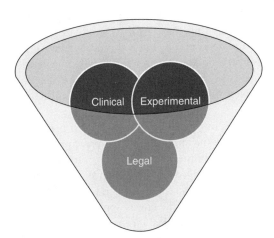

FIGURE 2.1 Components of Forensic Psychology

Relevant Forensic Psychology Associations

As previously mentioned, the AP-LS, Division 41 of the APA, is a primary organization representing many forensic psychologists. The goals of the AP-LS include advancing the contributions of psychology to the understanding of law and legal institutions; promoting the education of psychologists in matters of law; educating legal personnel in matters of psychology; and informing the psychological and legal communities and the general public of current research, educational, and service activities in the field of psychology and law. The AP-LS publishes a journal called *Law and Human Behavior*, as well as a newsletter. Examples of recent articles include "How can we help witnesses to remember more? It's an (eyes) open and shut case," "The effectiveness of opposing expert witnesses for educating jurors about unreliable expert evidence," "Religious characteristics and the death penalty," "Assertions of 'future dangerousness' at federal capital sentencing: rates and correlates of subsequent prison misconduct and violence," and "Cues to deception and ability to detect lies as a function of police interview styles."

Another relevant organization is Division 18 of the APA (Psychologists in Public Service). Members of the Police and Public Safety Section of this division work with law enforcement, fire departments, and other public-safety entities. They are involved in the selection of employees, fitness-for-duty evaluations, mental health programs, criminal investigative analysis (profiling), and hostage negotiations. Division 18 publishes the journal *Psychological Services*. Recent articles include "Developing services for insanity acquittees conditionally released into the community: maximizing success and minimizing recidivism," "A preliminary classification system for homeless veterans with mental illness," and "Timing of post-combat mental health assessments."

The Society for Police and Criminal Psychology is a multidisciplinary professional organization whose members study police and criminal psychology and the application of scientific knowledge to the criminal justice system, law enforcement, the judiciary, and corrections. The society publishes a journal called the *Journal of Police and Criminal Psychology*. Recent articles include "An examination of officer stress: Should police departments implement mandatory counseling?" "Defining the field of police psychology: Core domains & proficiencies," and "Police stress: A structural model."

The Police Psychological Services Section of the International Association of Chiefs of Police (IACP) is made up of psychologists who work with law enforcement as either consultants or employees. The section acts as a resource to the IACP on an array of psychologically related issues such as hiring, assessment, counseling, and police operations.

EDUCATION OF FORENSIC PSYCHOLOGISTS

In 2006, there were 3,629 Doctor of Philosophy (PhD) and 1,573 Doctor of Psychology (PsyD) degrees awarded in psychology, and 54% of these were in clinical or counseling psychology (APA, 2007; Hoffer, Hess, Welch, & Williams, 2007). As of this writing, there are three graduate training programs in the United States that offer pure doctoral degrees (i.e., not a clinical degree with a "concentration" in forensic psychology), but a dedicated doctoral degree specifically in forensic psychology. These programs are Alliant International University in California, John Jay College of Criminal Justice (part of the City University of New York system), and Nova Southeastern University.

Alliant University offers PsyD and PhD programs in forensic psychology. Both programs are accredited by the APA. The PsyD program emphasizes the application of forensic practice in various settings (e.g., prisons, probation, parole, and group homes) and applied to various populations with forensic issues (e.g., substance abuse, sex offending, domestic violence, serial killing, juvenile delinquency, and stalking). The PhD program emphasizes the integration of forensic clinical psychology, forensic and legal research, criminology, and the law as applied to a relevant forensic population. This program offers three tracks. The first, Clinical Licensure Track, prepares the student for licensure and practice. The second, Policy and Justice Track, emphasizes research on the legal and criminal justice system. The third, Police Psychology Track, focuses on working with the police department and law enforcement.

The John Jay College of Criminal Justice offers a PhD in forensic psychology with either a clinical or an experimental track. Its clinical track emphasizes clinical assessment and evidence-based intervention focusing on areas such as risk assessment, legal competencies, and insanity and child-custody evaluations. The school maintains one of the largest databases on police officer suicide, child-molesting priests, and celebrity homicide stalkers (L. B. Schlesinger, personal communication, October 21, 2008). John Jay's experimental track provides research and applied training as well as training in evaluation research and policy development.

Nova Southeastern University offers APA-accredited PhD and PsyD programs in clinical psychology. Both programs offer clinical training in assessment and intervention. One of the major tracks of each program is called Clinical Forensic Psychology and emphasizes psychological skills applicable in the criminal justice system such as competency and criminal responsibility, psychological damages in civil trials, and criminal profiling.

Closely aligned to Alliant University, John Jay, and Nova Southeastern University are at least 25 programs offering a PsyD degree in clinical forensic psychology, a PhD or PsyD degree in clinical psychology with a concentration in forensic psychology or forensics, 13 of which offer degrees in areas closely akin to forensic psychology, such as psychology and law or forensic and behavioral science, and 5 of which grant a combination law (JD or LLB degree) and psychology degree. Two of these joint law–psychology programs offer a degree in clinical psychology with a forensic concentration, while three grant combined law and generic psychology degrees. Although there is a clinical component to most of these programs, a research orientation generally seems more prevalent. A general example is the combined program at Arizona State University that trains students for work in various areas such as academia and government where they can apply their knowledge and skills in the interdisciplinary field of "psychology and the law."

Details from a survey of most of the forensic psychology and forensic psychology-related doctoral programs are displayed in Table 2.1

Some recipients of a doctoral degree in a nonforensic discipline (e.g., clinical, counseling, school or social psychology) may choose to complete a postdoctoral fellowship or certificate program in forensic psychology. A survey of these programs is depicted in Table 2.2. Of course, some psychologists—regardless of how long they have been in practice—may choose to attend law school on their own and not as part of a dual professional training program (this is the path the author of your text chose).

An example of a postdoctoral fellowship in forensic psychology is the program at the University of Southern California, Keck School of Medicine. This is a full-time, one-year program that offers training in performing psychological evaluations and consultation in psycho-legal arenas such as psychiatric hospitals, county jails, state or federal prisons, family courts, and other agencies that interrelate with mental health and law.

Board Certification

Some forensic psychologists with the required training choose to become "Board Certified" by a credentialing body within professional psychology. The oldest and most respected of such bodies is the American Board of Professional Psychology (ABPP), which grants a diploma to forensic psychologists who meet a list of rigorous educational and training requirements. In addition to the diploma in forensic psychology, the board grants diplomas in 12 other areas of psychology: child and adolescent, clinical, clinical health, clinical neuropsychology, cognitive and behavioral, counseling, couple and family, group, organizational and business, psychoanalysis, rehabilitation, and school (American Board of Professional Psychology, 2009). Certification by the ABPP is totally voluntary and not required for professional practice in any of the designated specialties; however, it does give the recipient a certain competitive edge in both private practice and representing himself/herself to the public and third parties.

TABLE 2.1 "Psychology and the Law" and other Forensic Psychology–Related Graduate Programs in 2009

School	Program	Degree offered
Alliant International University	Forensic Psychology	PhD/PsyD
Arizona State University	Law and Psychology	JD/PhD
California State University, Fresno	Forensic and Behavioral Science	PhD
Carlos Albizu University, Mimi	Clinical Psychology with a concentration in Forensic Psychology	PsyD
Chicago School of Professional Psychology	Clinical Psychology with a concentration in Forensic Psychology	PsyD
Drexel University	Clinical Psychology and Law; Clinical Psychology with Forensic concentration	PhD/JD PhD
Florida International University	Legal Psychology	PhD
Fordham University	Clinical Psychology with a concentration in Forensic Psychology	PhD
John Jay College of Criminal Justice	Forensic Psychology, clinical or experimental tracks.	PhD
Massachusetts School of Professional Psychology	Clinical Psychology with a concentration in Forensic Psychology	PsyD
Nova Southeastern University	Clinical Forensic Psychology	PsyD
Pacific Graduate School of Psychology	Clinical Psychology and Law	PhD/JD
Sam Houston State University	Clinical Psychology with Forensic concentration	PhD
Simon Fraser University (Canada)	Clinical Psychology with concentration in Forensics; Law and Forensic Psychology	PhD LLB/JD
University of Alabama	Clinical Psychology with a concentration in psychology and law	PhD
University of Arizona, Tucson	Psychology, Policy, and Law; Clinical Psychology, Forensic Interest	PhD PhD
University of California, Irvine	Psychology with concentration in Psychology and Law	PhD
University of Denver	Psychology with specialty in Forensic Psychology	PsyD
University of Florida	Psychology and Law	PhD/JD
University of Illinois, Chicago	Clinical Psychology with minor in Psychology and Law	PhD
University of Minnesota	Social Psychology and Law	PhD
University of Nebraska	Legal Psychology	PhD
University of Nevada, Reno	Social Psychology with a concentration in Psychology and Law	PhD
University of Texas at El Paso	Legal Psychology	PhD
Widener University	Clinical Psychology with a concentration in Forensic Psychology	PsyD
University of Wyoming	Social Psychology with a concentration in Psychology and Law	PhD

Correctional Psychology

The United States has the highest incarceration rate of any industrialized country in the world (Bartol & Bartol, 2004). And it is an unfortunate truth that prisons are becoming treatment centers of last resort for a substantial segment of our population. The work of a correctional psychologist, or forensic psychologist working in a corrections setting, might include any of the following: psychological screening; violence and suicide risk assessment; psychological testing; crisis

TABLE 2.2 Certificate and Postdoctoral Fellowships in Forensic Psychology

Institution	Program
AA Argosy University, Twin Cities	Certificate in Forensic Psychology
Chicago School of Professional Psychology, Chicago	Certificate in Applied Forensic Psychology
Pacific Graduate School of Psychology, CA	Certificate in Forensic Psychology
Patton State Hospital, CA	Postdoctoral Fellowship in Forensic Psychology
University of Washington, WA	Postdoctoral Fellowship in Forensic Psychology
University of Southern California—Keck School of Medicine, CA	Postdoctoral Fellowship in Forensic Psychology
Aa University of Virginia, VA	Postdoctoral Fellowship in Forensic Psychology

intervention; evaluative and therapeutic services for mentally disordered, developmentally disabled, and disruptive inmates; substance abuse and sex offender treatment; and dealing with the occupational stressors of correctional officers (APAGS, 2008).

Many psychologists who work in prisons or detention centers are members of the Criminal Justice Section of Division 18 of the APA. The International Association for Correctional and Forensic Psychology also represents the interests of many correctional psychologists. The association's goals involve promoting psychological practice in criminal justice and law enforcement settings; teaching of the psychology of crime, delinquency, and criminal justice; effective treatment approaches for individuals in the care of the criminal justice system; and stimulating research into the nature of criminal behavior.

There is a lack of clarity on whether correctional psychology falls under the general rubric of forensic psychology. Some textbooks on forensic psychology do not include corrections at all, some make a passing reference, and some devote considerable space to the topic. (Arrigo & Shipley, 2005). But regardless of whether correctional psychology is part of forensic psychology (or part of psychology and law), courses on the topic are offered in some doctoral programs in clinical and counseling psychology; there are nearly 80 internships that describe themselves as forensic or correctional in nature, and some postdoctoral programs offer further training in correctional psychology as well.

Regardless of how one becomes a forensic psychologist or where one works, the identification as "**forensic expert**" is always pertinent. The next section examines the qualities of being a forensic expert in a legal context as well as the accompanying duties and responsibilities.

THE EXPERT WITNESS

Before discussing forensic experts and their impact on the justice system, it is necessary to examine the kinds of evidence generally presented in courts of law.

Types of Evidence

REAL OR PHYSICAL EVIDENCE   **Real evidence** is an actual thing that is relevant and material to a case. It is "the real thing"—the actual murder weapon, not a mere example of a weapon of the type said to have been used in the alleged crime. Real evidence can be a written contract, fingerprints, a crumpled automobile, etc. Real evidence can usually (but not always) be brought into the courtroom.

DEMONSTRATIVE EVIDENCE   **Demonstrative Evidence** is *not* "the real thing." It is tangible material used for explanatory or illustrative purposes only; it is a visual aid such as an anatomical model, a chart, a diagram, a map, or a film. Because its purpose is to illustrate testimony, demonstrative evidence is authenticated by the witness whose testimony is being illustrated. That witness will usually identify the salient features of the exhibit and testify that it fairly and accurately reflects what he/she saw or heard on a particular occasion, such as the location of people or things on a diagram.

DOCUMENTARY EVIDENCE Documentary Evidence is usually a writing or a sound or video recording. It may be the transcript of a telephone intercept. Authentication of the evidence is usually required along with expert testimony. Some documents, such as certified copies of public records, official documents, newspapers, periodicals, and trade inscriptions, may be considered self-authenticated and do not require an expert to authenticate them.

TESTIMONIAL EVIDENCE Testimonial evidence comes to court through witnesses speaking under oath or affirmation. They could be testifying about something they saw (eyewitnesses), something they heard (hearsay witnesses), or something they know (character, habit, or custom witnesses). Such a **lay witness** usually has *personal* knowledge of the underlying facts of a case and can only testify to perceptions, facts, and data grounded in their own experience. Lay witnesses are prohibited from testifying as to their opinions.

There are numerous realistic exceptions to the rules against opinion testimony. Most of them involve lay "shorthand," where it is next to impossible to express the matter in any other way.

Examples:

Matters of taste and smell—"It smelled like gunpowder."

Another's emotions—"He seemed nervous."

Vehicular speed—"He was going very, very fast."

Voice identification—"I've known Joyce Johnson for 15 years, and I'd recognize her voice anywhere. It was Joyce's voice on the telephone."

A witness's own intent, where relevant—"I was planning on crossing the street."

Genuineness of another's handwriting—"That's my wife's signature."

Another's irrational conduct—"He was acting like a crazy man."

Intoxication—"The man was drunk."

The second type of testimonial evidence is evidence testified to by an **expert witness**. An expert witness has *special* knowledge or skill gained through education, training, or experience and is considered more knowledgeable than ordinary citizens. Some of the common expert witnesses who testify in criminal proceedings are professionals in the medical, mental health, or forensic fields. Expert witnesses can interpret data and information relevant to a case and express their opinion about the facts (Nemeth, 2001).

Admissibility of Evidence

It may be asked, "Are there rules that determine the admissibility of evidence?" The answer is an emphatic "yes." Evidence is admitted into testimony via rules of evidence established by the jurisdiction in which a court sits. These rules of evidence are based on two significant court cases, which will be discussed below.

A 1923 case from the District of Columbia called *Frye v. United States* held that expert scientific opinion was admissible only if the principles on which the opinions were based had gained *general acceptance in the relevant scientific community*. This was an attempt by the court to avoid the testimony of charlatans and quacks. But the common law "*Frye* test" also prevented the fact finder (jury) from hearing expert opinions from accomplished scientists who were intellectually credible and yet novel or cutting-edge (i.e., they had not yet gained general acceptance within the relevant scientific community). Many felt that the *Frye* test was thus unduly restrictive.

Seven decades later came the landmark case of *Daubert v. Merrell Dow* in 1993. In this case two minor children and their parents (the plaintiffs) alleged that the children's serious birth defects had been caused by the mother's prenatal ingestion of Bendectin, a prescription drug marketed by Merrell Dow Pharmaceuticals, Inc. (the defendant). The district court decided for the defendants based on a well-credentialed expert's affidavit concluding, upon reviewing the extensive published scientific literature on the subject, that maternal use of Bendectin has not been shown to be a risk factor for human birth defects.

Although the plaintiffs presented testimony of eight other well-credentialed experts, who based their conclusion that Bendectin can cause birth defects on animal studies, chemical structure analyses, and the unpublished "reanalysis" of previously published human statistical studies, the court determined that this evidence did not meet the "general acceptance" standard for the admission of expert testimony as established in *Frye*. The court of appeals agreed and affirmed, citing the **Frye Rule** for the requirement that expert opinion based on a scientific technique is inadmissible unless the technique is "generally accepted" as reliable in the relevant scientific community.

The U.S. Supreme Court vacated the decision of the court of appeals, ruling that the **Federal Rules of Evidence** (often referred to as the ***Daubert* Rule**), not Frye, provide the standard for admitting expert scientific testimony in a federal trial and that Frye's "general acceptance" test was superseded by the rules' adoption. The Federal Rules of Evidence (28 U.S.C.A. § 702) assign to the trial judge the responsibility of ensuring that an expert's testimony is *reliable and relevant* to the task at hand. In other words, expert testimony can be admitted into evidence if in the judge's opinion (as the trier of law) the testimony would be relevant in assisting a jury (as the trier of fact) in better understanding the case. Under *Daubert* and the Federal Rules of Evidence (Rule 702) the jury is seen as a more capable entity. The judge makes a preliminary assessment of whether some testimony's underlying reasoning or methodology is scientifically valid—*even if not completely accepted by the scientific community*— and may admit such evidence if it can assist the jury in understanding a fact in issue in the case. The standard is a flexible one in contrast to the wholesale exclusion of certain evidence often found under the uncompromising "general acceptance" standard established in *Frye*. Certainly, under *Daubert* and the Federal Rules of Evidence there is the opportunity for new scientific knowledge, devices, and procedures that have not existed long enough to gain general acceptance in the relevant scientific community to be admitted into evidence.

Testimonial Privilege

When a forensic psychologist or other mental health expert testifies in court, two types of privileges are generally relevant: treatment provider–patient and attorney–client (Parry & Drogin, 2007). Where the testifying psychologist serves as a treatment professional, the patient–treatment provider privilege(s) applies; where the testifying professional serves as an expert evaluator, the attorney–client privilege applies. Typically, these privileges belong to the patient or client, but may also be asserted by the mental health professional or attorney who has the protected relationship with the patient or client, unless doing so contradicts the expressed wishes of the patient or client.

Most states recognize a physician–patient privilege. Many states, including some that do not recognize a general physician–patient privilege, recognize a psychiatrist–patient privilege. This may be due to the perception that mental health concerns are considered more sensitive, private, and embarrassing than physical ones. In addition, there is often a need for patients to disclose this sensitive information to effectuate successful mental health treatment.

The **psychologist–patient privilege** exists in all 50 states and the District of Columbia. In Colorado, for example, the privilege was established by statute and provides,

> A licensed psychologist . . . or unlicensed psychotherapist shall not be examined without the consent of such licensee's or unlicensed psychotherapist's client as to any communication made by the client to such licensee or unlicensed psychotherapist, or such licensee's or unlicensed psychotherapist's advice given thereon in the course of professional employment. . . . (Section 13-90-107(1)(g), 5 C.R.S., 2002).

The purpose of the psychologist–patient privilege, like that of the psychiatrist–patient privilege, is to enhance the effective diagnosis and treatment of illness by protecting the patient from the embarrassment and humiliation that might be caused by the psychologist's disclosure of information divulged by the client during the course of treatment. To invoke this privilege, as with the physician–patient and psychiatrist–patient privileges, the patient must usually be communicating with the psychologist for the purpose of receiving professional treatment or advice.

The psychologist–patient privilege may not apply to situations where the psychologist is hired by an attorney to conduct an examination or assessment of a client for the purpose of case preparation. In these circumstances, the information used by and culled from the medical or psychological professional remains protected from discovery through the attorney–client relationship, its privilege, and/or the attorney work-product doctrine rule.

Is there a Psychotherapist–Patient Privilege?

Jaffe v. Redmond (1996)

Police officer Mary Lu Redmond shot and killed an individual to prevent the stabbing of another person. The decedent's family brought suit against the officer alleging constitutional violations of the decedent's rights (under 42 U.S.C. § 1983) and sought damages under a theory of wrongful death. After the shooting, the officer sought psychotherapy from a licensed clinical social worker. The plaintiffs sought to obtain information regarding the contents of the officer's therapy sessions, but the defendant (the officer) refused, citing **psychotherapist–patient privilege**.

The trial court found that the Federal Rules of Evidence (Rule 501) did not provide for a psychotherapist–patient privilege. When the defendant continued to refuse to comply, the trial court instructed the jury that it could draw an adverse inference from this refusal and presume that the contents of these communications would be unfavorable to the defendant. The jury awarded the plaintiffs $545,000 in damages. The Seventh Circuit reversed, finding that the Federal Rules of Evidence did, indirectly, recognize a psychotherapist–patient privilege because all 50 states recognized some sort of psychotherapist–patient privilege. The court reasoned that recognition of the privilege would serve to encourage troubled individuals, as well as those who witness, participate in, and are intimately affected by acts of violence in today's stressful, crime-ridden environment, to seek the necessary professional counseling and to assist mental health professionals to succeed in their endeavors. The plaintiffs appealed to the U.S. Supreme Court.

The American Psychological Association (APA) submitted an *amicus* brief arguing that (1) the Federal Rule of Evidence 501 authorizes the federal courts to recognize a psychotherapist–patient privilege; (2) common law principles, applied in the light of reason and experience, strongly support recognition of a psychotherapist–patient privilege in that (a) psychotherapeutic clients have a strong expectation of confidentiality, (b) confidentiality is essential to the success of psychotherapy, (c) society has a strong interest in fostering the psychotherapeutic relationship and in protecting client privacy, and (d) the benefits of the psychotherapist–patient privilege outweigh its costs; and (3) applying the psychotherapist–patient privilege using a case-by-case balancing approach would substantially undermine the value of the privilege.

The Supreme Court supported the APA's arguments and affirmed the Seventh Circuit decision. In so doing, the Court created an absolute privilege for confidential communications between a licensed psychotherapist and her patients in the course of diagnosis or treatment. In extending the psychotherapist–patient privilege to licensed clinical social workers, the Court concluded that "[t]he reasons for recognizing a privilege for treatment by psychiatrists apply with equal force to treatment by . . . clinical social worker[s]" (p. 15). The Court focused on three main rationales for extending the privilege. First, it pointed out that social workers provide a significant amount of mental health treatment. Second, it explained that social workers often serve the poor and those of modest means who cannot afford a psychiatrist or psychologist, "but whose counseling sessions serve the same public goals" (p. 16). Third, the Court noted that the vast majority of states extend a **testimonial privilege** to licensed social workers.

The **attorney–client privilege** provides that communications between an attorney and a client are privileged with certain exceptions such as where the client threatens to perform illegal acts in the future. Information the lawyer obtains from the client in the course of representation concerning the client's mental health is not subject to discovery. In addition, under the attorney work-product doctrine, materials produced by the attorney in the course of representing that client are also protected.

In 2001, in *Oleszko v. State Comp. Ins. Fund*, the Ninth Circuit extended privileged communication to include unlicensed counselors employed by a state's employee assistance program (EAP) because many of the issues the counselors addressed—substance abuse, depression in the workplace, and domestic violence—are serious national problems, which would be further hidden from view if a privilege was not enforced. Such counselors were seen by the court as playing an important role in increasing access to mental health treatment and that such a gateway was worth protecting.

THE FORENSIC PSYCHOLOGIST AS EXPERT

A psychologist may provide forensic testimony in various ways. These include performing forensic evaluations as a private consultant, serving as a court-appointed evaluator, and being an agent or employee of an attorney. When attorneys hire psychologists as agents or employees, their work falls under the **attorney–client privilege**, and some courts have ruled that the attorneys may, after reviewing the reports or comments of the psychologists, choose not to reveal that information in court. However, when psychologists do appear in court, either as a court-appointed evaluator, an independent consultant, or an employee of an attorney, they typically assume the role of an expert witness.

It is the judge who admits a psychologist as an expert witness based on the psychologist's education, training, and experience and the way in which this experience relates to the specific question before the court. The opposing counsel can object to the admission of an expert witness; however, more often, the witness is accepted and their testimony subjected to cross-examination (Knapp, VandeCreek, & Fulero, 1993).

Many times psychologists and other experts are granted *immunity* from civil claims for their conduct as experts. Expert witnesses have traditionally been considered to be friends of the court, people whose willingness to take time out of their busy professional lives and participate in the judicial process entitled them to absolute immunity from civil liability for anything they said on the witness stand. But lawsuits against experts, while still relatively rare, are multiplying, and many have been meeting with success. Accordingly, psychologists must exercise extreme caution when offering expert testimony. But even more relevant than possible civil liability for a psychologist is the ethical restraints and obligations that must be followed (Hansen, 2000).

The primary sources that guide psychologists doing forensic work are the APA's *Ethical Principles of Psychologists and Code of Conduct* (APA, 2002); the *Specialty Guidelines for Forensic Psychologists (Committee on Ethical Guidelines for Forensic Psychologists (CEGFP), 1991)* of Division 41 of the APA; the *American Board of Forensic Psychology*; and the Society for Law and Psychology. The *Guidelines for Child Custody Evaluations in Divorce Proceedings* (APA, 1994) are further relevant when dealing with child-custody issues and evaluations. In addition, psychologists are responsible for abiding by the laws of their state or province, most notably regarding the duty to protect those at risk and to report suspected child abuse.

The most relevant sections of the *CEGFP* require that forensic psychologists (1) provide competent services in a manner consistent with the standards of their profession; (2) limit their services to the boundaries of their education, training, and competence; (3) be aware of the legal requirements as well as professional standards governing their professional practice and activities; (4) only offer opinions (through reports or verbally) that are based on the appropriate data and available information; and (5) abide by all professional rules, standards, and laws dealing with privacy, confidentiality, and privilege.

Elements of the *APA Ethics Code* that are most relevant to forensic practice require that psychologists (1) limit their services to the boundaries of their competence, education, and supervised experience; (2) base their opinions on information and techniques sufficient to substantiate their findings; (3) obtain informed consent (from the individual or a legally authorized representative) prior to providing assessment or therapy; (4) consider individual ethic and cultural differences that might affect the results of psychological testing and evaluations; (5) clarify their role expectations and extent of confidentiality to their clients, especially when court proceedings are involved; (6) be aware of and understand the different expert opinions in any case they are involved in, and balance the demands of other psychologists, lawyers, judges, and other professionals and professional entities; and (7) be unbiased and forthright when expressing their assessments and opinions and not be obligated to deliver favorable testimony due to contractual relationships with either side of a case (APA, 2002, Principles 2.01a; 9.01a; 3.10a; 3.10b; 9.06; 3.05c).

What the Legal Profession Desires from Mental Health Experts

Redding, Floyd, and Hawk (2001) presented a hypothetical insanity defense case to 59 trial court judges, 46 prosecuting attorneys, and 26 defense attorneys throughout Virginia in order to assess their preferences for types of forensic mental health testimony and for types of mental health experts. Four key findings emerged from the results:

1. Judges, prosecutors, and defense attorneys preferred that psychiatrists conduct forensic evaluations for the court. This preference was closely followed by a preference for doctoral-level psychologists.
2. Judges seemed to want juries to have the benefit of hearing the judgments of mental health professionals.
3. Judges and lawyers were relatively disinterested in statistical or actuarial data as compared with other types of testimony. These findings suggest that judges may not fully understand the relevance of such evidence (Monahan & Walker, 1986, 1987, 1998).
4. Judges seemed to prefer testimony that provided more information, even somewhat speculative testimony such as theorizing about the causes of a defendant's behavior. Prosecutors, on the other hand, were the least interested in theoretical and speculative information, probably because it usually tends to have mitigating effects. Defense attorneys saw more value in clinical diagnosis, theoretical explanations about a defendant's behavior, and testimony speculating about different, possibly exculpatory or mitigating motives for criminal behavior.

Who is an Expert?

Jenkins v. United States (1962)

In a trial for housebreaking, assault, and intent to rape, a defendant presented the testimony of three clinical psychologists in support of an insanity defense. All three psychologists testified, based on their personal contact with the defendant, review of his case history, and standard psychological tests, that on the date the alleged crimes were committed, the defendant had been suffering from schizophrenia. One of the three testified that he could give no opinion concerning the relationship between the illness and the crimes, but the other two gave opinions that the two were related and that the crimes were the product of the illness.

At the conclusion of the trial, the judge instructed the jury to disregard the opinions of the psychologists in that psychologists were not qualified to give expert testimony on the issue of mental disease. The judge stated,

"A psychologist is not competent to give a medical opinion as to a mental disease or defect. Therefore, you will not consider any evidence to the effect that the defendant was suffering from a mental disease or a mental defect on June 10, 1959, according to the testimony given by the psychologists." The jury proceeded to convict the defendant.

The case was appealed to the DC Circuit Court. The American Psychological Association submitted an *amicus* brief arguing that (1) psychology is an established science, (2) the practice of psychology is a learned profession, (3) a clinical psychologist is competent to express professional opinions concerning the existence or nonexistence of mental disease or defect and its causal relationship to overt behavior, and (4) experience is the essential legal ingredient of competence to give an expert opinion.

The DC Circuit reversed the conviction and remanded for a new trial. On the issue of psychologists' expert testimony, the court stated that some psychologists are qualified to render expert testimony on mental disorders, but that this would depend on the nature and extent of their knowledge and not simply on the claim to the title "psychologist" (unlike the case with psychiatrists). The court held that ". . . the lack of a medical degree, and the lesser degree of responsibility for patient care which mental hospitals usually assign to psychologists, are not automatic disqualifications." But the court also saw the issue in terms of ". . . whether *medical* opinions and *medical* diagnoses can be made by and be the subject of expert testimony by a Doctor of Philosophy in Psychology with added clinical experience."

In its decision, the court referred to a 1954 resolution adopted by the American Medical Association, the council of the American Psychiatric Association, and the executive council of the American Psychoanalytical Association to the effect that psychologists and other related professional groups were autonomous and independent in matters where medical questions were not involved, but that where diagnosis and treatment of mental illness was involved, the participation of psychologists "must be coordinated under medical responsibility."

The dissenting justices in this case delivered what amounted to a scathing diatribe against the utilization of psychologists in forensic cases. The dissent called it "sheer folly" to allow a "*lay* psychologist" to testify as to the presence of a mental disease or defect since such a psychologist is not a "doctor of medicine" (emphasis added). The dissent relied, in part, on an *amicus* brief filed by the American Psychiatric Association in which was stated, among other things, "A psychologist, lacking *medical* training and the specialization required of the qualified psychiatrist, is not qualified to make [a] total *medical* diagnosis or to testify as a *medical* expert thereon" (emphasis appears in *amicus* brief).

Since *Jenkins* was decided in 1962, most states have provided by statute or case law that doctoral-level clinical psychologists may offer opinions on insanity as well as on other issues concerning the mentally disordered (Gass, 1979). But some states still refuse to allow psychologists as free a reign as psychiatrists. For instance, in insanity cases, some courts still limit psychologists to interpretations of psychological tests; testimony by psychologists about degree of cognitive or volitional impairment or causes of mental deficiencies is prohibited or limited (*Commonwealth v. Williams*, 1979; *People v. McDarrah*, 1988; *State v. Bricker*, 1990).

And in most states, master's-level psychologists and master's- and doctoral-level social workers are barred entirely from testifying on most issues.

The psychiatric profession continued to adhere to the position it took in 1954 in *Jenkins* for many years. In 1980, American Psychiatric Association President Langsley acknowledged that psychologists, social workers, and others can and should be members of the "treatment team," but asserted that "it is [now] more appropriate than ever that the psychiatrist is the member of the team best equipped to perform triage, make differential diagnosis, [and to] plan and render treatment for a variety of psychological and somatic problems" (Langsley, 1980, p. 25).

CONFIDENTIALITY AND ITS LIMITS

Before addressing the issue of psychologist–client confidentiality and the circumstances in which it might be necessary to breach such confidentiality, certain basic legal tenets and terms of art concerning the concepts of "duty" and "breach" of duty must be established. Under what conditions and circumstances do psychologists (or any mental health professional) owe a duty to persons other than their patients themselves? Generally speaking, if a duty is found, the question is whether there has been a breach of that duty. Accordingly, the concepts of "duty" and "breach" are the very benchmarks of legal liability. Under the law, a *duty* is a "legal or moral responsibility . . . [a]n obligation, recognized by the law, requiring [the] actor to conform to certain standard[s] of conduct for [the] protection of others against unreasonable ricks (Black's Law Dictionary, 1998, p. 505; *Samson v. Saginaw Professional Building, Inc.*, 1973).

In a general sense, a **breach of duty** is some form of violation or omission of a preestablished duty (Black's Law Dictionary, 1998, p. 189). For the purposes of forensic psychology in general, and psychologist–client relationships in particular, breaches concern the neglect or failure to fulfill a duty or obligation in a just and proper manner often as defined with particularity by a professional code of ethics. But legal breaches are certainly not confined to these situations. For example, a "breach of contract" would refer to the failure of one party to perform any promise that forms the whole or part of a contract without legal excuse. A "constructive breach" takes place when the party bound to perform disables himself from performance by some act, or declares, before the time comes, that he will not perform (Black, p. 189); a "breach of prison" is an unauthorized departure of a prisoner from legal custody using force "breach of close" where an individual unlawfully enters another person's soil or land; or "breach of the peace" where the peace or public tranquility is disturbed.

Of all the American courts with all the issued opinions, the one case that is considered seminal and ultimately "on point" (relevant) on "duty to warn" is *Palsgraf v. Long Island R. R. Co.* (1928). The case is standard fare in every law school course on torts. In the law, a **tort** is a private or civil wrong committed by an individual or a group against another individual or group.

Palsgraf v. Long Island R. R. Co

Using *Palsgraf v. Long Island R. R. Co.* as a model, this is an ideal point in this textbook to discuss some rudimentary yet essential elements involved in the referencing, summary, and discussion of law cases that are appealed from a lower court to a higher court. This is generally referred to as the "appellate brief" by practicing attorneys and should be understood by students of forensic psychology. An **appellate brief** is a written argument filed with an appellate ("reviewing") court on why a trial (initial decision-making) court acted correctly or incorrectly. A legal brief filed as to why a trial court's actions were "correct" is referred to as an **appellee's brief**. A legal brief filed as to why a trial court's actions were "incorrect" is called the **appellant's brief**. The terms used to describe the roles and statuses of individuals as they progress up the judicial ladder can be confusing not only to beginning law students but to new lawyers as well. Just imagine how unclear, yet essential, these terms are for students of forensic psychology who may have very little exposure to, or training in, civil and criminal procedure.

At a very basic level, **plaintiffs** sue **defendants** in civil suits in trial courts. In criminal cases it is the government (or "the people") that prosecutes the **defendant**. The losing party in a criminal prosecution or a civil action may ask a higher (appellate) court to review the case on various grounds and in accordance with very strict rules. Basically, the reviewing court must know what happened (or did not happen) in the lower court, the facts that were admitted into evidence, the legal decisions and their rationales, and of course the premise for the appeal. And all this must be done within specific time limits that are jurisdictionally determined. Perhaps Supreme Court Justice Oliver Wendell Holmes best expressed the nature of and requirements for an appeal in 1881, when he said, "In order to know what it is, we must know what has been, and what it tends to become" (Holmes, 1881).

Some of the justifications for an appeal might include incompetent counsel; a tainted jury; jurisdictional issues and defects (e.g., that the court did not have jurisdiction to hear the case to begin with); improper jury instructions; evidentiary matters (vital evidence that was left out of a trial or should not had been let in); hearsay violations (admitting testimony that was clearly hearsay evidence and did not satisfy any of the exceptions to the hearsay rules); inappropriately relying on the expert testimony of an unqualified expert witness; an error in the interpretation of the law; or a reversible error made by a trial court judge. If the law gives the unsuccessful party in a case the right to an appeal, depending on the jurisdiction, there are strict rules that must be met as to the time limits for the appeal to be undertaken, when papers must be filed, the necessity for sending up the precise trial court record, et cetera (Smith, 1996).

Although appeals and *certiorari* are sometimes loosely grouped together as "appeals," there are differences between them. A person who seeks a **writ of *certiorari***, that is, a ruling by a higher court that it hear the case, is known as a petitioner. The person who must respond to the petition, that is, the winner in the lower court, is called the **respondent**. A person who files a formal **appeal** demanding an appellate review as a matter of right is known as the **appellant**. His/her opponent is the **appellee**. The name of the party initiating the action in court, at any level on the judicial ladder, always appears first in the legal papers. In criminal cases, switches in the titles of cases are common, because most reach the appellate courts as a result of an appeal by a convicted defendant. Thus, the case of *Arizona v. Miranda* later became *Miranda v. Arizona* (Pratt, 1993).

An appeal *as of right* is one that is guaranteed by statute or some underlying constitutional or legal principle. For example, death sentences in capital cases are appealed directly to the Supreme Court. This shall occur as a matter of right and shall operate to stay the execution of the sentence of death until further order of the Supreme Court. The appellate court cannot refuse to listen to the appeal. But even in cases such as these, some death-row prisoners may elect to forgo appeals, thus hastening execution. There are many reasons for such a decision, including depression, psychosis, incompetence, and conditions in prison. Due to the gravity of the sentence, and the states' duty to ensure fairness, some jurisdictions impose restrictions on the waiver. An inmate who lacks trial competence may be subject to a *habeas corpus* hearing and the appointment of a "next friend," often a family member. Moreover, the Constitution forbids execution of the "insane." The decision, then, may be taken out of the inmate's hands (*In re Heidnik*, 1997).

Returning to *Palsgraf v. Long Island R. R. Co.*, the basic facts of the case are excerpted below from Benjamin N. Cardozo who was the chief justice of the appellate division of the Supreme Court of New York.

> Plaintiff was standing on a platform of defendant's railroad after buying a ticket to go to Rockaway Beach. A train stopped at the station, bound for another place. Two men ran forward to catch it. One of the men reached the platform of the car without mishap, though the train was already moving. The other man, carrying a package, jumped aboard the car, but seemed unsteady as if about to fall. A guard on the car, who had held the door open, reached forward to help him in, and another guard on the platform pushed him from behind. In this act, the package was dislodged, and fell upon the rails. It was a package of small size, about fifteen inches long, and was covered by a newspaper. In fact it contained fireworks, but there was nothing on its appearance to give notice of its contents. The fireworks when they fell exploded. The shock of the explosion threw down some scales at the other end of the platform, many feet away. The scales struck the plaintiff, causing injuries for which she sues. (Cardozo, 222 App. Div. 166, 1927)

The injured party, 43-year-old Brooklyn janitress Mrs. Helen Palsgraf (the plaintiff), claimed to have been hit on the "arm, hip, and thigh" and sued the railroad and its employees for negligence.

At the initial trial in 1927, the jury determined the acts of the defendant's employees (the guards) to be negligent, causing the bundle to be thrown under the train and to explode. It was not a defense to these negligent acts to say that the employees had no awareness of the contents of the package. The plaintiff was seen as a passenger of the defendant pure and simple and as such was entitled to have the defendant exercise the highest degree of care required of common carriers (such as trains, planes, and busses). The decision was then appealed to the New York State Court of Appeals (the highest court in New York State), where it was dismissed.

Reading for the majority, Justice Cardozo made clear that the conduct of the defendant's employee (the train guard), if wrong or negligent in relation to the holder of the package, was not wrong in relation to the plaintiff, standing far away. There was no liability because there was no negligence toward the plaintiff. Negligence, he noted, must be founded upon the foreseeability of harm, hence duty, to the person in fact injured. The defendant's conduct was not a wrong toward the plaintiff merely because there was negligence toward someone else (Slovenko, 2002). In *Palsgraf*, Judge Cardozo said that the plaintiff must sue in her own right for a wrong personal to her and not as the vicarious beneficiary of a breach of duty to another.

THE DUTY TO WARN OR PROTECT

The *Palsgraf* decision and issues related to duty of care to third parties and remoteness of damages raise many questions that become especially relevant to forensic psychologists and their work. More specifically, in many cases in which the defendant has no notice of the dangerous conditions created by a third party, it may be contended that there is no negligence at all. There are many legal cases that speak to these issues, but the famous *Nitroglycerine Case* (1872) is one of the earliest and best examples. The facts of the case involve an unmarked package containing nitroglycerine that was delivered to the defendant's business establishment located in a building owned by a third party. When some of the defendant's workers tried to open the unmarked package, it exploded, killing them and damaging the building. Two cases resulted—one was a property damage case by the landlord against the defendant's business because there was a clause in the rental agreement stating that the defendant would be responsible for such occurrences without the need to prove negligence (a standard lesser–lessee clause), and the other case was a wrongful death suit filed by the victims' families against the defendant. The Supreme Court denied this claim because, unlike the property damage clause, negligence on the part of the defendant would have been required for the plaintiffs to prevail. But there was no proof of negligence since the package gave no indication or notice of its dangerous contents (see Cardozo, 1939; Epstein, 1995; *Larrimore v. American National Ins. Co.*, 1939).

Judge Cardozo was careful to point out in the *Palsgraf* case that physical injury does not *per se* equate to liability when there is no negligence toward the plaintiff. For there to be negligence, there must be a foreseeability of harm. If there is the foreseeability of harm, then there is a duty to a person who may be injured. The defendant's (the train guard's) conduct in *Palsgraf* did not represent a "wrong" toward the plaintiff (woman at the other end of the tracks) solely because there was negligence toward someone else (the passenger carrying the package). The train guard's behavior was reasonably foreseeable to cause injury to the passenger with the package but not to Palsgraf, who was standing a considerable distance away on the platform. Judge Cardozo's opinion was clearly that the train guard owed a duty to the passenger boarding the train but not to Palsgraf. The fact that the guard's actions led to the plaintiff's injury was irrelevant.

How much have issues of foreseeability of harm, negligence, and duty to take preventive action related to the care and treatment of mentally ill individuals affected the emerging field of forensic psychology during the last 100 years or so? The answer is "plenty."

Certainly the psychotherapy of a patient can result in a foreseeable risk of harm to a third party. From an institutionalized perspective, mental hospitals have long acknowledged their duty to protect not only the patient but third parties as well. This can run the gamut from preventing incompetent clinicians from supervising patients and providing treatment to preventing premature discharges and escapes from psychiatric facilities. For example, as a New York

State court put it 70 years ago, a state mental hospital "has a duty to protect the community from acts of insane persons under its care" (*Jones v. State of New York*, 1943). It has been accepted by many mental institutions across the country that a hospital breaches its duty of care by failing to provide adequate security when a patient has known violent tendencies (*Fair v. United States*, 1956).

Exactly what are the limits of confidentiality when a clinician is faced with a patient or client who threatens to harm others? Such a duty to protect third parties, known preeminently as the "**Tarasoff Duty**," received national attention in the seminal case of *Tarasoff v. Regents of the University of California* in 1974 and 1976. But the limits of confidentiality and the duty to warn third parties was examined in earlier cases such as *Underwood v. United States* (1966) and actually cited by the Tarasoff court in support of the legal requirements in cases in which potential victims could be clearly identified. However, this case did not suggest that therapists had a duty to warn *potential* victims or protect *third* parties.

In *Underwood*, the Federal Appeals Court held the United States liable for the actions of a psychiatrist in negligently releasing a dangerous client. At a U.S. Air Force base in Alabama in 1964, Airman Dunn was admitted to the psychiatric clinic. The admitting clerk was instructed by the psychiatrist on duty to contact Dunn's wife. In so doing, the clerk concluded from the conversation that Airman Dunn was a threat to his wife, and he conveyed this information to the psychiatrist in charge. This psychiatrist instructed the clerk not to make a written note of the discussion with Dunn's wife. Subsequently, another psychiatrist, unaware of the conversation with Dunn's wife, released Dunn. Dunn left the hospital, went to the armory and obtained a gun, and killed his wife.

In the actual *Tarasoff* cases, an Indian graduate student named Prosenjit Poddar was studying naval architecture at the University of California, Berkeley, when he started to date a fellow student named Tatiana Tarasoff. Although he had only kissed her a few times, he felt he had a special relationship with her. He was totally unfamiliar with American customs and had never had a date before. He felt betrayed when he learned that Tatiana had relationships with other men. He became depressed. He went to a psychologist, Dr. Moore, at the University Health Service and in the process of therapy revealed his intention to get a gun and shoot Tatiana Tarasoff. Dr. Moore sent a letter to the campus police requesting them to take Poddar to a psychiatric hospital. The campus police interviewed Mr. Poddar, but he convinced them that he was not dangerous. They released him on the promise that he would stay away from Ms. Tarasoff. When the Health Service psychiatrist-in-charge returned from vacation, he directed that the letter to the police be destroyed and no further action be taken. Mr. Poddar moved in with Tatiana's brother over the summer while Tatiana was visiting her aunt in Brazil. When Tatiana returned, Mr. Poddar stalked her and eventually stabbed her to death.

Tatiana's parents sued the campus police, Health Service employees, and Regents of the University of California for failing to warn them that their daughter was in danger. The trial court dismissed the case because it said there was no cause of action. The appeals court supported the dismissal. An appeal was taken to the California Supreme Court. In 1974, the California Supreme Court reversed the appellate decision. The Court held that a therapist bares a duty to use reasonable care to give threatened persons such warnings as are essential to avert foreseeable danger arising from a patient's condition. This is known as the "Tarasoff I" decision.

Due to great uproar among psychiatrists and police officials, and in an almost unprecedented move, the California Supreme Court reheard the same case in 1976. That decision came to be known as "Tarasoff II." The Court ruled that when a therapist determines, or pursuant to the standards of his profession should determine, that his patient presents a serious danger of violence to another, he incurs an obligation to use reasonable care *to protect* the intended victim against such danger. In essence, there is little practical difference between Tarasoff I and Tarasoff II.

The case was eventually settled out of court for an undisclosed amount of money and never went to trial. Mr. Poddar served four years of a five-year prison sentence for manslaughter, but his conviction was overturned due to faulty jury instructions on the issue of diminished capacity.

A second trial was not held on the promise that Poddar would leave the United States. He was last heard to be happily married in India.

It was unfortunate that the distinction between inpatient and outpatient settings was not addressed in Tarasoff, nor has it been addressed by many of the courts deciding similar cases. But one of the main controversial aspects of the decision was not the imposition of a duty to protect third parties from dangerous clients, but the imposition of a new duty to warn a third party of information obtained in a *confidential* setting. At the time of the case, the American Psychiatric Association filed an *amicus* brief arguing that the client's right to confidentiality was a right essential to the therapeutic relationship. The court, while agreeing that the right to confidentiality was an important consideration, held that this right was subservient to an obligation to protect the public from a known danger.

When the Supreme Court of California ruled that a psychologist had a duty to warn a potential victim of a dangerous client's threat, that ruling became the law in California, and all state and federal courts in that state were bound by that decision. Since the California decision, many other states have enacted Tarasoff-like statutes, limiting confidentiality in cases where an explicit threat has been made by a patient. Under most of these statutes a therapist is required to do a number of things. These include notifying the intended victim and/or law enforcement. It is important to note that most of these states require that a third party be an "identifiable victim" before the therapist can be said to have a duty to this person.

But court decisions are mixed, even within the same state, and no general rule is applicable to every situation. For example, in *Shaw v. Glickman* (1980), the Maryland Court of Special Appeals held that state law forbids a psychiatrist to reveal the violent tendencies of a patient to the patient's estranged wife or his girlfriend. And in *Hopewell v. Adibempe* (1981), a Pennsylvania court held that there was no duty to warn a third party and held a psychiatrist liable for breach of confidentiality when such warning was made. In both cases, courts rejected the duty to warn and held that client confidences to mental health professionals remain privileged.

It may be prudent at this point to explain how the decisions by state courts affect the federal courts. Federal courts often declare that a state statute or procedure violates the U.S. Constitution. Only under these circumstances can a federal court set aside a state law, procedure, or court ruling, including state supreme court decisions. Unless such a constitutional claim is being presented, a federal court is bound by the decisions of the state supreme court regarding interpretation of its own state's law.

A federal court's decision otherwise interpreting state law is given the same value as any other published decision in that state. Many of the following state cases are from federal and state appellate courts that represent the law in that state until the state supreme court addresses the issue. These cases are examples of both Tarasoff-supporting and Tarasoff-limiting decisions that have appeared before state and federal courts during the last 30 years.

Tarasoff-Supporting Cases

In *Jablonski by Pahls v. United States* (1983), a court of appeals stated there was a duty to protect a foreseeable victim even though no specific threats were made. In this case, Ms. Kimball and Mr. Jablonski had been dating. Jablonski was arrested for threatening to rape his girlfriend's mother. A staff psychiatrist at a Veterans' Administration (VA) hospital evaluated him but failed to order his prior medical records. These records documented that Jablonski had made homicidal statements concerning Ms. Kimball in the past. Jablonski was diagnosed as an antisocial personality with explosive features, with the added caution that he was dangerous. However, the psychiatrist found no basis for involuntary commitment and allowed Jablonski to leave the hospital. Two days later, Jablonski attacked and murdered his girlfriend. In *Petersen v. State* (1983), the Washington Supreme Court held that a psychiatrist had a duty to take reasonable precautions to protect any person who might *foreseeably* be endangered by his patient's mental condition.

In *Naidu v. Laird* (1988), the plaintiff, Ann Laird, brought a wrongful death action against Dr. Venkataramana Naidu, a Delaware State Hospital psychiatrist, alleging that he was grossly negligent in releasing a mental patient, Mr. Putney. Five and a half months after release, Mr. Putney, while in a psychotic state, killed Ann Laird's husband in an auto accident.

Mr. Putney had an extensive history of paranoid schizophrenia involving many admissions to VA hospitals and seven admissions to Delaware State Hospital. He also had a history of medication noncompliance. In one of his hospitalizations Mr. Putney was described as being a danger to himself and others, especially if given the opportunity to drive an automobile. His fifth admission to Delaware State Hospital occurred after he intentionally rammed a police vehicle with his automobile. Prior to one VA admission, he cut his wrist and then drove his car off the road. During his seventh psychiatric admission, Mr. Putney requested, and was granted, a discharge against medical advice. He was released on March 22, 1977.

Dr. Naidu testified that he did not personally review the records from the six prior hospitalizations at Delaware State Hospital or the VA medical records. He also did not review the complete records from the March 7–22, 1977, admission; instead he relied on the treatment team for his information regarding the patient.

Upon discharge, Mr. Putney was given a 30-day supply of medication and was told that he had a follow-up appointment at the VA hospital. After discharge, Putney stopped taking his medication and did not appear for his follow-up VA appointment. He moved to New York, and on September 6, 1977, while psychotic, he drove his car into that of Mr. Laird.

At the trial, the plaintiff's expert, Dr. Davis, testified that Dr. Naidu had been grossly negligent in the treatment and discharge of Mr. Putney. This negligent treatment and discharge included discharging Putney without a program of continuing care, failing to address Putney's medical noncompliance, failing to consider alternatives such as referrals to outpatient or day-treatment facilities, and failing to seek involuntary commitment to a Delaware State Hospital. Dr. Davis opined that Putney was sufficiently dangerous on March 22, 1977, to have met the statutory requirements for involuntary commitment. The jury agreed and awarded the plaintiff $1.4 million in damages.

Dr. Naidu appealed the trial court's decision, contending *inter alia* (among other things) that his treatment of Putney was not the proximate cause of Mr. Laird's death. The Delaware Supreme Court held that the trial court correctly instructed the jury concerning the duty of reasonable care, that a breach of duty had occurred, that there was sufficient evidence regarding proximate cause, and that it was not unforeseeable that Putney would stop taking his medication and would again become a danger to others, especially while driving an automobile. Regarding the passage of time between Dr. Naidu's release of Putney and the latter's actions involving Mr. Laird, the court held that in the absence of any proven significant intervening cause, the temporal span in this case was not sufficient to relieve Dr. Naidu of responsibility.

Finally, in its decision, the court looked to the case of *McIntosh v. Milano* (1976) when it said in essence that a psychiatrist has a duty to protect an intended or potential victim when he determines (or should determine) that his patient may present a probability of danger to that person. Such a duty arises from one of two possible legal relationships—that between the therapist and the patient or the more broadly based obligation between a mental health practitioner and the community at large.

Lodged between these two cases were the events of October 1979 when Seth Buckmaster was brought to the Fort Logan Mental Health Center for the fourth time since 1975. He had previously been arrested and sent to Fort Logan for making physical threats toward his family, beating his 70-year-old father, and carrying a concealed weapon. The records revealed that during Buckmaster's third commitment the attending psychiatrist had noted that Buckmaster's condition had deteriorated since his last admission. The note also indicated that Buckmaster's paranoid state had exacerbated to the point that he blamed the police for all his misfortunes, including the nondelivery of his mail, the mechanical problems with his car, and even the blisters on his feet.

Dr. Anders, who interviewed Buckmaster in October 1979, found him to be angry, incomprehensible, seriously disorganized in his thinking, and extremely delusional. After this interview, Dr. Anders filed with the court a certification for short-term treatment on the basis that Buckmaster was gravely disabled as a result of his mental illness.

Pursuant to a court order, in the three-month period from October 18, 1979, to December 11, 1979, Dr. Anders spent a total of 2 hours and 35 minutes with Buckmaster. Based upon these sessions, Dr. Anders released Buckmaster on December 11, 1979, apparently without the benefit of ever reading Buckmaster's file. He concluded in his discharge summary that there were no serious acts of violence in his past, and although he refused to take his medication, he did not pose any risk of violence to others.

On April 1, 1980, approximately four months after his release from Fort Logan, Buckmaster created a disturbance at a Colorado Springs convenience store by talking to himself, muttering profanities, and sitting on the floor near the front door. Despite the clerk's requests that he leave the store, Buckmaster stayed put and continued his bizarre behavior. The clerk flagged down a Colorado Springs police officer who escorted Buckmaster out of the store; they spoke for a few minutes in the parking lot. Buckmaster suddenly produced a handgun and fired several shots at the officer, killing him instantly (see *Perreira v. State*, 1989).

In *Almonte v. New York Medical College* (1994), a federal court held that a psychiatrist had a duty to control a dangerous client to protect a class of victims—a duty that superseded any obligation of confidentiality. In this case, a federal court, interpreting Connecticut law, held that the head of the psychiatric unit at a hospital, who was also the therapist for a resident psychiatrist, had "control" of the resident, and once he learned in a therapy session that the resident was a pedophile, had a responsibility to exercise this control to prevent him from inflicting sexual abuse on patients at the hospital.

In *Shepard v. State* (1997), the Oklahoma Court of Civil Appeals held that a mental hospital had a duty to advise a patient's family that the patient should not have guns in the home. The patient had been evaluated at a psychiatric hospital, and based on the results of this evaluation, it was strongly recommended that the patient not live around guns. But the patient was released from the hospital without this recommendation being communicated to his wife. Four days after his release, the patient shot and killed his wife and two children and then committed suicide with the same gun. The court held the hospital liable for the deaths of the patient's wife and children. In doing so the court did not rely on Tarasoff to support the duty to advise. Rather, it reached this result by finding negligence in the release of a dangerous patient without advising his family that the patient should not have guns in the home.

In *Turner v. Jordan* (1997), the Tennessee Court of Appeals held a psychiatrist liable for failing to protect a psychiatric nurse on the hospital staff from the violent and intentional acts of a hospitalized mentally ill patient. In March 1993, a patient at the psychiatric hospital attacked and severely beat a psychiatric nurse on the hospital staff. The nurse sued the psychiatrist treating the patient for failure to protect her. The court found that the psychiatrist owed a duty of care to the nurse because he knew (or should have known) that his patient posed an unreasonable risk of harm to a foreseeable, readily identifiable third party.

In *Ewing v. Northridge Hospital Medical Center* (2004), a California appeals court extended the *Tarasoff* rule to include threats disclosed by family members.

Geno Colello was in psychotherapy with Dr. David Goldstein and was despondent over the breakup of his long-standing relationship with Diana Williams, who had recently begun dating Keith Ewing. On June 21, 2001, Colello asked his father to loan him a gun. When his father refused, Colello said he would get another gun and "kill" the "kid" who was then dating Williams. Colello's father relayed this threat to Goldstein, who urged him to take Colello to Northridge Hospital Medical Center. Later that evening a hospital social worker evaluated Colello. Colello's father told the evaluator about his son's threat. Colello was admitted to the hospital as a voluntary patient but discharged the next day. The following day he shot and killed Ewing and then himself.

Ewing's parents sued Goldstein and the hospital, alleging that Colello posed a foreseeable danger to their son and that both Goldstein and the hospital were aware of the threat but failed to discharge their duty to warn either Ewing or a law enforcement agency. At trial, Goldstein claimed he was not liable for failure to warn because Colello had never directly disclosed to him any intention to seriously harm Ewing. The hospital claimed that expert testimony was required to prove a psychotherapist's liability for failure to warn and noted that the plaintiffs had no plans to present such testimony. The trial judge agreed with both arguments and granted summary judgment to the defendants.

On appeal, the California Court of Appeals held that the plaintiffs had a right to take their claims to trial. Specifically, the court held that the defendants' duty to warn could have been triggered by the statements Colello's father made to Goldstein and the social worker regarding his son's threats. The court saw no difference between threats conveyed directly by the patient and those related by an immediate family member of the patient. The appeals court also concluded that no expert testimony was required because the issue was not whether the defendants violated a professional standard of care but whether they "actually believed or predicted" that Colello posed a serious risk of inflicting grave bodily injury upon an identifiable victim—an issue that could be decided by a lay jury based upon "common knowledge." The court's decisions in this case extended the reach of *Tarasoff* in California and to the consternation of some have led to further erosion of professional psychotherapeutic confidentiality.

TARASOFF-LIMITING CASES   In *Bellah v. Greenson* (1978), a California appeals court held a psychiatrist not liable for his failure to warn the parents of their child's suicidal tendencies.

In the course of treatment, a young adult woman revealed suicidal tendencies to her psychiatrist. The psychiatrist, feeling that the information was confidential, did not inform the woman's parents of her suicidal tendencies. The young woman committed suicide. Her parents brought suit claiming that the psychiatrist had a duty to warn them of their daughter's suicidal tendencies. The court ruled in favor of the psychiatrist saying that *Tarasoff* required a therapist to disclose confidential information only if "the strong interest in confidentiality was counterbalanced by an even stronger public interest in safety from violent assault." The court recognized that the therapeutic relationship could be compromised if therapists revealed that their patients manifested suicidal tendencies and held that the therapist is not required to reveal such tendencies.

In *Thompson v. County of Alameda* (1980), a California appeals court held that a psychologist was not liable for failure to warn the public of a dangerous client's threat. A juvenile offender in confinement told his psychologist that when they released him, he was going to randomly kill a child in the community. The juvenile was released to the custody of his mother without the police being warned about the threat. Twenty-four hours after his release, the client made good his threat and killed a child in the community. The parents of the dead child sued the detention center for failure to warn. The court ruled in favor of the detention center stating that liability may be imposed only in those instances in which the released offender posed a predictable threat to a named or readily identifiable victim.

In *Brady v. Hopper* (1984), a federal court in Colorado held a psychologist not liable for failure to warn the public of a client's dangerous propensities. John W. Hinckley began outpatient treatment with Dr. John Hopper in October 1980 and continued until February 1981. The evidence showed that Dr. Hooper was aware that Hinckley identified with the assassin in the movie *Taxi Driver*, that he was collecting books and articles on political assassination, and that he possessed guns and ammunition.

On March 29, 1981, Hinckley boarded a bus and traveled to Washington, DC. On March 30, Hinckley left his room and took a cab to the Washington Hilton where President Reagan was scheduled to speak. At 1:30 p.m., Hinckley stepped forward from a crowd of television reporters and fired six shots from a Rohm R6-14 revolver. The bullets from Hinckley's gun struck Ronald Reagan in the left chest, Press Secretary James Brady in the left temple, Officer Thomas Delahanty in the neck, and Secret Service Agent Timothy J. McCarthy in the stomach. Brady, Delahanty, and McCarthy sued Dr. Hopper alleging that Dr. Hopper knew or should have known that his patient Hinckley was a danger to himself or others.

The court ruled that "the bystanders (Brady, Delahanty, and McCarthy) did not state a cause of action against the therapist even assuming that the treatment and diagnosis of Hinckley fell below the applicable standard of care, because it was not foreseeable that Hinckley would attempt to assassinate the President and, in the course thereof, injure plaintiffs, because Hinckley had never made any threats against the President or anyone else."

In *Wofford v. Eastern State Hospital* (1990), the Oklahoma Supreme Court ruled that a psychiatrist was not liable for the release of a mental patient who killed his stepfather more than two years after his discharge. On March 3, 1982, Billy Wofford was released from Eastern State Hospital where he was being treated for schizophrenia. On July 27, 1984, Billy shot and killed his stepfather. The court held that the psychiatrist was not liable for negligent release saying that such a duty arises only when, in accordance with the standards of his profession, the therapist knows or should know that his patient's dangerous propensities present an unreasonable risk of harm to others. The duty extends to such persons as are foreseeably endangered by the patient's release. According to the court, a person harmed more than two years after the patient's release is not a person who is foreseeably endangered by the patient's release.

In *Weitz v. Lovelace Health* (2000), a federal appeals court held that a therapist seeing a dangerous client on an outpatient basis had no duty to control the client. In this case, Edward Gutierrez was an air force staff sergeant stationed at Kirtland Air Force Base in Albuquerque, New Mexico, during the 1990s. Edward and Arlene Gutierrez began having marital problems in the early 1990s. After a series of individual and couple sessions with Edward and Arlene, Dr. Cal Bolinder informed Arlene that she should try to keep herself and her daughter, Loretta, away from Edward.

Soon after, Edward asked Arlene to come to his home—they now had separate residences—to discuss their marital problems. Edward was drunk and pulled a gun on Arlene. Arlene managed to get the gun away from Edward. He then threatened to kill himself. Arlene reported the incident to Edward's commanding officer who asked Edward to turn over his weapons, which he did. Two weeks later Edward asked for his weapons back so that he could do some target practice; they were returned. A week later he shot and killed Arlene and Loretta and then took his own life.

The court, after an extensive examination of the law, held that there is no duty to control a patient in outpatient therapy. The court also ruled that there was no duty to warn the wife since she already knew of her husband's dangerousness.

STATUTORY PROVISIONS   Many states have adopted statutory provisions that, in general, impose a variation of the duty to warn or protect readily identifiable potential victims from a communicated threat and that shield therapists from liability for breach of confidentiality for acting in accordance with the statute. The following states have statutory provisions regarding the duty to warn: Alaska, Arizona, California, Colorado, Florida, Idaho, Indiana, Kentucky, Louisiana, Maryland, Massachusetts, Minnesota, Montana, New Hampshire, New Jersey, Ohio, Tennessee, Utah, Virginia, and Washington (see Beecher-Monas & Garcia-Rill, 2003; Cocozza & Steadman, 1976). These statutes can be helpful in clarifying the scope of the duty to protect in a particular state.

For example, Virginia's legislation states,

A mental health service provider has a duty to take precautions to protect third parties from violent behavior or other serious harm only when the client has orally, in writing, or via sign language, communicated to the provider a specific and immediate threat to cause serious bodily injury or death to an identified or readily identifiable person. . . . (VA Code § 18.2-67.10)

The duty set forth under Virginia law is satisfied if the practitioner takes one or more of the following actions:

1. Seeks involuntary admission of the client.
2. Makes reasonable attempts to warn the potential victim or the parent or guardian of the potential victim if the potential victim is under the age of 18.
3. Makes reasonable efforts to notify a law enforcement official having jurisdiction in the client's or the potential victim's place of residence or place of work or in the place of work of the parent or guardian if the potential victim is under age 18, or both.
4. Takes steps reasonably available to the provider to prevent the client from using physical violence or other means of harm on others until the appropriate law enforcement agency can be summoned and takes custody of the client.
5. Provides therapy or counseling to the client or patient in the session in which the threat has been communicated until the mental health service provider reasonably believes that the client no longer has the intent or the ability to carry out the threat (VA Code § 18.2-67.10).

Virginia law protects a mental health service provider from civil liability to any person for breaching confidentiality when the purpose of such a breach is to protect third parties by communicating threats made to them to potential third-party victims or law enforcement agencies. Providers are also not liable for failing to predict harm to a third party if the threats communicated to them are not made *in the manner* the law describes or if the provider fails to take precautions *other than* those specifically enumerated in the law.

THE IMPLICATIONS FOR PSYCHOLOGISTS AND OTHER MENTAL HEALTH PROFESSIONALS

It has always been a well-settled principle of law that a special relationship exists between a psychiatrist/psychologist and a patient at a mental institution. This special relationship is based upon the awareness that one who takes charge of a third person who is likely to cause harm to others if not controlled is under a duty to exercise reasonable care to control that third person. In an *outpatient* setting, it is usually necessary for a dangerous client to *make an actual threat* before a court will find a mental health professional liable for that client's actions. Court decisions in the 1980s and 1990s extending the Tarasoff duty of warning an identifiable potential victim into a duty to protect the *public at large* have been either superseded by legislation or relegated to a minority position by the courts.

Anfang and Appelbaum (1996) have provided guidelines to help therapists limit potential liability arising from duty to protect cases. These include knowing the law in your state or seeking legal consultation if you are not sure, making a careful and adequate assessment of the risk of violence in accordance with local standards, involving the patient in such decisions where possible and appropriate, consulting with colleagues, keeping up-to-date records, and warning third parties and/or the police when it is necessary and where there is a clear and substantial risk of harm that cannot be avoided through less intrusive means.

Finally, cases such as *Ewing* illustrate that psychologists and psychotherapists must take seriously threats reportedly made by a patient but revealed to them by a relative of the patient. Mental health professionals should also be concerned by the *Ewing* court's conclusion that in some cases, such as this one, jurors may rely solely upon "common knowledge" to determine whether a psychotherapist actually believed or predicted that a patient posed a serious risk to an identifiable victim. The court concluded that reaching such a conclusion was not beyond the ability of most jurors. Where the line is drawn between those cases in which expert testimony is necessary and those where it is not remains a murky, troubling question.

PREDICTION OF DANGEROUSNESS

The Legal Perspective

Legal scholars have not been very confident in the ability of the mental health profession to predict future dangerousness. The following quotes are just samples of this sentiment:

1. "Can psychiatrists predict danger with reasonable accuracy? Are there well-established clinical symptoms which, if present, can be relied upon to indicate potential danger? Can one be reasonably sure that persons who are not dangerous will not be labeled as such and unnecessarily confined? I believe the answer to all these questions is an emphatic 'no.' There are a number of statistical studies which amply demonstrate that the predictions of dangerousness by psychiatrists are unreliable . . ." (Carbone, 2007).

2. "Study shows that psychiatric predictions of dangerousness were as likely to produce false positives as to correctly predict future dangerousness" (Cocozza & Steadman, 1976).

3. "In general, mental health professionals . . . [w]hen predicting violence, dangerousness, and suicide . . . are far more likely to be wrong than right . . ." (Hammond, 1980).

4. "Reliance by the courts on testimony by psychotherapists may be misplaced, since the ability to accurately predict dangerousness has not been demonstrated" (Hammond, 1980).

5. "Predictions of violence have been the subject of extensive literature that consistently criticizes psychiatrists' ability to gauge individuals' long-term future dangerousness" (Texas Defender Service, 2004).

6. "The courts have increasingly relied upon the psychiatrists' and psychologists' predictions in determining an offender's potential for future dangerousness, even though the psychiatric literature stresses the unreliability of these expert predictions" (Skaggs, 1995).

7. "Psychiatric predictions based on hypothetical situations sometimes bear more resemblance to medieval fortune-telling than to modern scientific techniques" (Texas Defender Service, 2003).

8. "Lay people can predict future dangerousness as well as medical experts. . . . Although the testimony of clinicians about future dangerousness offers little more than that of an astrologer, such clinical testimony is pervasive, and courts persist in circumventing any inquiry into the scientific validity of expert future dangerousness predictions. This is an important concern because giving the imprimatur of science to chicanery undermines our justice system" (Beecher-Monas & Garcia-Rill, 2003).

9. "Juries give great credence to expert testimony, and the scientific literature evaluating the predictive value of clinical judgments about future violence has shown that these expert predictions are no better than lay judgments. If courts applied Daubert standards to the kinds of clinical predictions currently offered in our courts, they would not admit the predictions because they do not meet any of the criteria for scientific validity" (Beecher-Monas, 2003).

10. "Predictions of future dangerousness were inaccurate in forecasting serious assaultive behavior in prison 95% of the time" (Texas Defender Service, 2004).

11. "The prediction of dangerousness is arguably the most difficult aspect of the [adjudication] process, largely because of its uncertainty. Research over the past thirty years shows a significant degree of inaccuracy in clinicians' predictions of dangerousness, especially with false positives" (Menninger, 2005).

12. "The courts reasoned . . . that predictability in psychiatric matters is notoriously poor" (Sarno, 2005).

13. "Studies have not been heartening about the ability of psychotherapists to predict dangerousness . . . finding that only one in three predictions of long-term dangerousness among institutionalized population were correct. Even with relatively sensitive tests for dangerousness, a substantial number of false positives occur because of the low base rate of dangerousness among the patient population" (Restatement (Third) of Torts: Liability for Physical Harm, 2005).

Many court decisions have added to the doubts concerning the accuracy of predicting future dangerousness. In *Barefoot v. Estelle* in 1983, the U.S. Supreme Court explicitly stated that a mental health professional could address the future dangerousness of a capital murder defendant at sentencing. The American Psychiatric Association filed an *amicus* brief noting that psychiatric predictions of long-term future dangerousness are deemed unreliable by the profession. The American Psychiatric Association's best estimate was that two out of three predictions of long-term future violence made by psychiatrists are eventually proven to be wrong, even amongst populations of psychiatrically ill individuals who have committed violence in the past. In the 1984 case of *Schall v. Martin*, Justice Marshall, citing several scholarly works on mental health and the law, opined that no diagnostic tools were available that allowed for even the most highly trained professional to predict reliably who would engage in violent crime.

In *Hamman v. County of Maricopa* (1989), a psychiatric patient lived with his mother and stepfather. Following his release from an inpatient unit, the patient attacked and killed his stepfather. The mother sued alleging that a competent psychiatric examination would have revealed that her son was suffering from schizophrenia and was dangerous to others. The state supreme court held that it is next to impossible for the legal system to expect that mental health professionals are able to accurately predict future dangerousness.

In the 1975 case of *People v. Burnick*, a California state court, in opining about experts' opinions of future dangerousness, quoted the American Psychiatric Association's *amicus* brief and stated, "Neither psychiatrists, nor [any other mental health or law enforcement professionals], have reliably demonstrated an ability to predict future violence or dangerousness. Neither has any special psychiatric 'expertise' in this area been established." In *Lindabury v. Lindabury*, a Florida state court held in 1989 that "[psychiatry] represents the penultimate grey area . . . particularly with regard to issues of foreseeability and predictability of future dangerousness."

In the 1982 case of *Johnson v. Noot*, the state supreme court, when faced with a situation calling for a prediction of future dangerousness, held that "many psychiatrists themselves admit that their ability to predict future dangerousness is not reliable; to date, no valid clinical experience or statistical evidence describes psychological or physical signs or symptoms that can be reliably used to discriminate between the harmless and the potentially dangerous individual." The court went on to state that "neither psychiatrists nor other behavioral scientists are able to predict the occurrence of violent behavior with sufficient reliability to justify the restriction of freedom of persons on the basis of the label of potential "dangerousness". Accordingly, the court recommended that lower courts no longer ask such experts to give their opinion of the potential dangerousness of any person (*Johnson v. Noot* at 728).

Finally, the state court in *Boynton v. Burglass* (1991) offered, "When the duty sought to be imposed is dependent upon standards of the psychiatric profession, we are asked to embark upon a journey that will take us from the world of reality into the wonderland of clairvoyance."

THE PSYCHOLOGICAL PERSPECTIVE In a 1969 issue of *Psychology Today* magazine, Alan Dershowitz, then best known as the coauthor of one of the first textbooks in psychiatry and the law, concluded, "[F]or every correct psychiatric prediction of violence there are numerous erroneous predictions. That is, among every group of inmates presently confined on the basis of psychiatric predictions of violence, there are only a few who . . . would actually engage in violence if released" (p. 47). In 1978, a task force of the APA on the role of psychology in the criminal justice system concluded, "It does appear from reading the research that the validity of psychological predictions of dangerous behavior, at least in the sentencing and release situation . . ., is extremely poor, so poor that one could oppose their use on the strictly empirical grounds that psychologists are not professionally competent to make such judgments" (APA, 1978, p. 1110). Echoing these views, as noted earlier, the American Psychiatric Association in its *amicus* brief in the 1983 case of *Barefoot v. Estelle* stated that ". . . psychiatrists simply have no expertise in predicting long-term future dangerousness" (*Barefoot v. Estelle* at 921).

ACTUARIAL VERSUS CLINICAL PREDICTIONS OF DANGEROUSNESS   In 1996, Grove and Meehl reviewed the literature on the efficacy of "subjective and impressionistic" predictions of dangerousness. Litwack and Schlesinger (1999) have correctly pointed out that synonyms for *subjective* are "arbitrary," "biased," "partial," "partisan," and "prejudiced" and argue that clinicians do usually attend to *some* concrete data in their decision-making process. Although many clinicians will admit that there are occasions when their intuition leads them to make further inquiries of a patient or of collateral witnesses or sources and that those intuition-based inquiries lead to the discovery of important, if not critical, information related to their assessment, the information ultimately obtained is nonetheless concrete and apparently relevant (Litwack & Schlesinger, 1999). Indeed, many experienced forensic clinicians argue that when they conduct dangerousness assessments they consider the factors recommended for consideration by structured assessment guides.

The controversy regarding making decisions using clinical judgment versus relying strictly on data begs the question, is the assessment of dangerousness different from other predictive assessments? The most likely answer is that it is. To examine this, it would be helpful to elucidate the differences between clinical and actuarial assessments of dangerousness. This issue is particularly important considering the argument made by some that actuarial methods should completely replace clinical judgments in the assessment of dangerousness (see, e.g., Quinsey, Harris, Rice, & Cormier, 1999).

The idea of predicting future performance is not new. It has been used with respect to graduate school admissions, parole board decisions, offender risk, spousal assault, and even credit risk. In all these areas some sort of an actuarial model is used (Gottfredson & Moriarty, 2006).

Clinical judgments are assessments based on human judgment that consider *clinical* variables that are dynamic. **Actuarial assessments**, on the other hand, are statistical assessments based on validated relationships between measurable predictor and outcome variables and ultimately determined by fixed, or mechanical, and explicit rules. Actuarial variables are defined as variables that are "static or historical" and do not change (Monahan, 1981).

Some of the most popular actuarial risk assessment instruments for adults are the Hare Psychopathy Checklist-Revised (PCL-R) (Hare, 1991, 2003); Violent Risk Appraisal Guide (VRAG) (Quinsey et al., 1998); Sex Offender Risk Appraisal Guide (SORAG) (Quinsey et al., 1998); Rapid Risk Assessment for Sex Offence Recidivism (RRASOR) (Hanson, 1997); STATIC-99/STATIC-2002 (Hanson & Thornton, 1999, 2003); Sex Offender Needs Assessment Rating (SONAR) (Hanson & Harris, 2001); Sexual Violence Risk-20 (SVR-20) (Boer, Hart, Kropp, & Webster, 1997); Workplace Risk Assessment (WRA-20) (Bloom, Eisen, Pollock, & Webster, 2000); and the Minnesota Sex Offender Screening Tool-Revised (MnSORT-R) (Epperson, Kaul, & Hasselton, 1998).

The PCL-R is used to assess likely future recidivism and violent offending. It is a 20-item rating scale, scored on the basis of both semistructured interview and collateral information. It has been validated for use in adult male correctional and forensic psychiatric samples. The VRAG involves a 12-item actuarial scale that is used to predict risk of violence within a specific time frame following release from an institution in violent, mentally disordered offenders. This tool uses the clinical record, particularly the psychosocial history component, as a basis for scoring. The Hare PCL-R score is incorporated into the VRAG calculations of risk. The SORAG is a 14-item instrument that is used to assess the risk of violent and sexual recidivism of previously convicted sex offenders within a specific period of release. It uses the client's clinical record as a basis for scoring and incorporates the PCL-R scores.

The RRASOR is a brief, 4-item screening instrument for risk of sexual offender recidivism among males who have been convicted of at least one sexual offence. It relies on information obtained through client files and has been tested extensively on forensic populations. The STATIC-99 and the updated STATIC-2002 are used to assess the long-term potential for sexual recidivism among adult male sex offenders. The SONAR is designed to measure change in risk level for sexual offenders. The WRA-20 focuses exclusively on environmental and situational variables presumed to assess the risk for violence in the workplace. The MnSORT-R is a sexual violence risk assessment tool that is used to predict sexual recidivism in rapists and intrafamilial child molesters. It uses 16 static and dynamic variables to distinguish three levels of risk category.

Some researchers have expressed that a combination of clinical and actuarial judgments are best for making predictions of future dangerousness (Dawes et al., 1989; Douglas, Yeoman, & Boer, 2006). But in most cases, the literature reveals strong support for the accuracy of actuarial prediction over clinical judgment. In the only meta-analysis performed on this topic, Mossman (1999) reanalyzed findings of 58 data sets from 44 published studies and determined that actuarial instruments significantly outperformed clinical opinions for long-term predictions of dangerousness.

Regardless of the apparent superiority of actuarial data over clinical data in actually predicting dangerousness, many forensic psychologists continue to "feel" that dynamic clinical factors are more important. Werner and Meloy (1992) found that dynamic factors considered important by clinicians include thought disorganization, emotional withdrawal, anxiety, tension, grandiosity, hostility, suspiciousness, uncooperativeness, noncompliance, and absence of social and family support. In addition, factors such as previous violence, consumption of alcohol, and tension are also utilized by psychologists when making violence predictions.

In a recent controlled study, Odeh, Zeiss, and Huss (2006) found two factors used significantly most often by clinicians when predicting future dangerousness: previous assaults and medication compliance. "These make reasonable sense with relation to future violence. That is, a person with serious mental illness who has been violent in the past or is not taking prescribed psychotropic medications is likely to have an increased propensity for future violence" (p. 154). But the same authors found that these clinical predictions on the whole were not significantly related to *actual* violence outcome. This finding is similar to that of other researchers (e.g., Litwack, 2001; Webster, Hucker, & Bloom, 2003).

FORENSIC PSYCHOLOGY IN THE SPOTLIGHT

Is a Jury Influenced more by Clinical Expert Testimony or Actuarial Expert Testimony when Considering Dangerousness?

Krauss & Lee (2003)

The researchers in this study wanted to investigate which form of expert testimony has more of an impact on a jury—clinical or actuarial—when considering the death penalty. The participants were 114 undergraduate "mock juror" college students who took part in a simulated capital-sentencing hearing based on Texas's capital-sentencing procedures and instructions. The Texas Criminal Procedure Code requires that a sentencing jury (the students in this case) in death penalty deliberation must unanimously find, beyond a reasonable doubt, that there is a probability that the defendant would commit criminal acts of violence that would constitute a continuing threat to society in order for the death penalty to be imposed.

The jurors were given the standard jury instructions for capital sentencing based on dangerousness as they appear in the Texas code. They were also provided with a written summary of the case and were free to ask any questions that they had. Subsequently, they rated their beliefs concerning the criminal defendant's dangerousness and their confidence in that belief. Expert testimony (either actuarial or clinical) was then presented via videotape, and the participants reassessed the criminal defendant's dangerousness and their confidence in that rating.

The clinical opinion expert testimony on dangerousness was based on actual testimony from actual trials in Texas where the death penalty was a possibility. The expert's credentials were manufactured by and presented

(continued)

(continued)

by the researchers to be similar to those in actual capital-sentencing cases in Texas. The testimony offered by the "expert" concerned four areas: his education and experience, the interview supposedly conducted with the defendant, the expert's opinion that the defendant was a sociopath, and the expert's belief that the defendant represented a continuing danger to society.

The actuarial expert testimony was presented by the same psychologist as in the clinical condition. In this condition also the "expert" testimony consisted of four factors. The first two were the same as in the clinical condition (i.e., his experience and education and the interview). The third consisted of his description of the Violent Risk Appraisal Guide (VRAG) and his use of the VRAG with the defendant. The fourth factor was the same as that in the clinical condition, that is, it was his belief based on the VRAG that the defendant represented a continuing danger to society.

In the ineffective cross-examination condition, the defense attorney attacked only the credibility of the expert, but not the content of his testimony. In the effective cross-examination condition, the attorney attacked the content of the clinical expert's testimony. This consisted of pointing out that (a) the predictions of dangerousness made by clinicians are often wrong, (b) most experts agree that clinicians are not able to predict dangerousness, (c) the testifying expert had no special training in the prediction of dangerousness, (d) clinical opinions tend to overestimate future violence, (e) the expert did not know the base rates of violence for this criminal population, (f) actuarial techniques for the prediction of dangerousness have shown greater validity than clinical instruments, and (g) the confidence the expert has in his opinion has not been linked to accuracy in making long-term dangerousness predictions.

In the effective cross-examination condition, the attorney challenged the content of the actuarial expert's testimony. This consisted of attacking (a) the use of the VRAG on a population on which it is not validated, (b) the unknown error rate of the VRAG, and (c) the failures and weaknesses of the VRAG.

The study found that mock jurors were influenced by both types of testimony, but that they were significantly more influenced by clinical opinion expert testimony than by actuarial expert testimony in their confidence ratings of the defendant's dangerousness. The jurors in this study seemed to have a preference for clinical opinion expert testimony, and they seemed unable to fully appreciate the weaknesses of clinical opinion estimates of dangerousness even after cross-examination and deliberation. In other words, "jurors may be more influenced by less accurate clinical opinion testimony than they are by more accurate actuarial expert testimony . . ." (p. 121). Accordingly, the researchers cautioned that courts should be especially vigilant in admitting such testimony.

The findings in this study cast a doubt on the validity of the Supreme Court's pronouncement in *Barefoot v. Estelle* that the adversary system will be ". . . competent to, uncover, recognize, and take due account of its [clinical expert testimony's] shortcomings" (*Barefoot*, p. 3398). How true is the Court's holding that jurors are capable with the aid of adversary procedures (i.e., cross-examination and competing experts) ". . . of . . . separating the wheat from the chaff" (*Barefoot*, p. 3398) and of appropriately weighing expert testimony on future dangerousness in capital-sentencing decisions?

Summary

Forensic psychology is the application of scientific psychology to the legal system and legal issues. Within forensic psychology there is an overlapping relationship between clinical practice, research, and the law. There are about eight graduate training programs that offer doctoral degrees in forensic psychology or clinical psychology with a forensic concentration. Thirteen graduate programs offer degrees in a closely related field such as "psychology and law." There are also postdoctoral fellowship and certificate programs in forensic psychology. Some forensic psychologists work in the prison system, but the field of correctional psychology can in many ways be considered a specialty in its own right. What all forensic psychologists have in common is that they are "forensic experts" and in court their testimony is proffered as expert testimony evidence. Various types of evidences are used in court. These include real or physical evidence, demonstrative evidence, documentary evidence, and testimonial evidence. Testimonial evidence can be offered by lay witnesses or expert witnesses. A lay witness may generally only testify to what he/she has personal knowledge of. An expert witness, on the other hand, may offer an opinion. Under the Frye Rule established in the 1923 case of *Frye v. United States*, an expert's scientific opinion was admissible only if the principles on which the opinions were based had gained general acceptance in the relevant scientific community. This was replaced by the Federal Rules of Evidence as established in the 1993 case of *Daubert v. Merrell Dow*. The Federal Rules of Evidence place limits on the admissibility of purportedly scientific evidence by assigning to the trial judge the task of ensuring that an expert's testimony is both *reliable and relevant* to the task at hand.

In addition to rules of evidence and statutory requirements, psychologists are bound by ethical principles. The primary source documents that guide psychologists doing forensic work are the APA's *Ethical Principles of Psychologists and Code of Conduct* (APA, 2002) and the *Specialty Guidelines for Forensic Psychologists* (Committee on Ethical Guidelines for Forensic Psychologists (CEGFP), 1991) from Division 41 of the APA.

Psychologists and other mental health professionals have an ethical and statutory obligation to uphold confidentiality regarding their patients' communications. There are times, however, where this confidential relationship can (and

often must) be breached. These include instances where a dangerous patient threatens an identifiable potential victim. This is generally referred to as a Tarasoff Duty based on the California case of *Tarasoff v. Regents of the University of California* in which the Supreme Court of California ruled that a psychologist had a duty to warn a potential victim of a dangerous client's threat. Psychotherapists should be aware of the laws in their states regarding the actions that must be taken in such instances.

There are times when a forensic psychologist, by way of his/her involvement with the courts and the legal system, is asked to make predictions regarding the future dangerousness of an individual. Such predictions are notoriously difficult (if not impossible) to make with any significant degree of accuracy.

There is some disagreement within forensic psychology regarding the relative efficacy of clinical versus actuarial (statistical) forms of assessments when predicting such dangerousness. The research clearly points to the superiority of actuarial methods, but many forensic psychologists seem comfortable with their clinical judgments, and there is research to support the notion that juries are more influenced by clinical opinion expert testimony over more accurate actuarial opinion expert testimony.

Key Terms

Actuarial assessments *34*
Appeal *23*
Appellant *23*
Appellant's brief *22*
Appellate brief *22*
Appellee *23*
Appellee's brief *22*
Attorney–client privilege *19*
Breach of Duty *22*

Clinical judgments *34*
Daubert Rule *16*
Defendant *22*
Demonstrative evidence *15*
Documentary evidence *16*
Expert witness *16*
Federal Rules of Evidence *17*
Forensic clinical psychology *11*

Forensic expert *15*
Forensic Psychology *11*
Frye Rule *17*
Lay witness *16*
Plaintiff *22*
Psychologist–patient privilege *17*
Psychology *22*
Psychotherapist–patient privilege *18*

Real evidence *15*
Respontent *23*
Tarasoff Duty *25*
Testimonial evidence *16*
Testimonial privilege *18*
Tort *22*
Writ of certiorari *23*

Review Questions

1. What are the two doctoral degrees normally awarded in forensic psychology?
2. What is an expert witness, and how is this different from other witnesses?
3. What are the basic holdings of the Frye and Daubert standards?
4. What is the meaning and significance of relevance and reliability when evaluating expert testimony?
5. In what ways is a psychologist ethically and legally obliged to maintain confidentiality? What are the limits of this confidentiality?

6. What is a "Tarasoff Duty," and how does it affect the practice of forensic psychology?
7. In what ways is clinical prediction different from actuarial prediction?
8. What does the research say about the efficacy of actuarial judgment over clinical judgment?

Chapter Resources on the World Wide Web

History and Overview of Forensic Psychology
http://faculty.ncwc.edu/toconnor/psy/psylect01.htm

The American Psychology-Law Society
http://www.ap-ls.org/

Division 18, American Psychological Association
http://www.apa.org/divisions/div18/homepage.html

American Board of Professional Psychology
http://www.abpp.org/

The Center for Psychology Workforce Analysis and Research
http://research.apa.org/PipelineGraphic.pdf

American Psychological Association for Graduate Students
http://www.apa.org/apags/

John Jay College of Criminal Justice, Department of Psychology
http://www.jjay.cuny.edu/psychology/

Argosy University Twin Cities, PsyD, Clinical Psychology
http://www.argosy.edu/colleges/ProgramDetail.aspx?id=1816

Institute of Psychiatry, Law, and Behavioral Science, Keck School of Medicine
http://www.usc.edu/schools/medicine/departments/psychiatry_behavioralsciences/research/psychiatryandlaw/index.html

American Psychological Association Ethics Code
http://www.apa.org/ethics/

Violence Risk.com: Risk Assessment: Actuarial Instruments & Structured Clinical Guide
http://www.violence-risk.com/risk/instruments.htm#vrag.

For Further Reading

Bartol, C. R., & Bartol, A. M. (Ed.). (2008). *Current perspectives in forensic psychology and criminal behavior* (2nd ed.). Thousand Oaks, CA: Sage.

Carbone, J. (2007). Into the wonderland of clairvoyance: Faulty science and the prediction of future dangerousness. In J. Kitaeff (Ed.), *Malingering, lies, and junk science in the courtroom.* Youngstown, NY: Cambria Press.

Grove, W. M., & Meehl, P. E. (1996). Comparative efficiency of informal (subjective, impressionistic) and formal (mechanical, algorithmic) prediction procedures: The clinical–statistical controversy. *Psychology, Public Policy, and Law, 2,* 293–323.

Monahan, J. (1993). Limiting therapist exposure to Tarasoff liability: Guidelines for risk containment. *American Psychologist, 48*(3), 242–250.

Nemeth, C. P. (2001). *Law & evidence: A primer for criminal justice, criminology, law, and legal studies.* Upper Saddle River, New Jersey: Prentice-Hall, Inc.

Parry, J., & Drogin, E. Y. (2007). *Mental disability law, evidence and testimony.* Chicago, Illinois: American Bar Association.

Quinsey, V. L., Harris, G. T., Rice, M. E., & Cormier, C. A. (1999). *Violent offenders: Appraising and managing risk.* Washington, DC: American Psychological Association.

CHAPTER 3

Aggression and Violent Crime

CHAPTER OBJECTIVES

After reading this chapter you would:

- Know the difference between affective and instrumental aggression.
- Understand the biological and ethological explanations of aggression.
- Appreciate the frustration–aggression hypotheses.
- Understand how imitation, modeling, and reinforcement effect aggression.
- Know why antisocial and narcissistic personalities are prone to aggression.
- Know how *actus reas* and *mens rea* are essential components of all crimes.
- Understand the different kinds and degrees of murder.
- Understand "reasonable provocation" and "heat of passion" killing.

INTRODUCTION

Aggression refers to behavior that has as its goal the infliction of harm upon another person who is in turn motivated to avoid the harm. Accidental harm is not aggression because it is not intended. Harm that is a by-product of helpful actions is also not aggressive because the harm doer believes that the target is not motivated to avoid the action (e.g., pain experienced during a dental procedure). All violence is aggression, but many instances of aggression are not violent. And violence and aggression are not necessarily crimes.

Crimes are of different general classifications. They can be crimes against property, white-collar crimes, insurance crimes, crime against the law of nations, crimes against nature, and crimes against persons. It is this latter type of crime that is addressed in this chapter. Crimes against persons are sometimes referred to as crimes of violence since there is usually the use, attempted use, or threatened use of physical force. Alternatively, it may be behavior which, by its nature, involves a substantial risk to life or limb.

AFFECTIVE AND INSTRUMENTAL AGGRESSION

Affective aggression (or hostile aggression) is impulsive or thoughtless and driven by anger. The ultimate goal of hostile aggression is harming of a target. Hostile aggression has historically been conceived as being impulsive; thoughtless (i.e., unplanned); driven by anger; having the ultimate motive of harming the target; and occurring as a reaction to some perceived provocation. This type of aggression is also referred to as violent or reactive aggression. It is impulsive and usually occurs in a flash or anger. However, sometimes this anger is not expressed immediately but is delayed. This has been referred to as a form of "sentiment" rather than anger in that the feelings of anger toward the other person becomes transformed in time into the sentiment of hatred, which outlives the original anger. Long-term feuds and grudges are examples of such cases.

Instrumental aggression is a premeditated means of obtaining some goal other than just to harm the victim. This type of aggression is simply a means to some other end. One such end is self-defense, which most American courts recognize as a valid justification for violence under certain circumstances. Aggressive military action is another form of instrumental aggression. Instrumental aggression can also occur in response to coercion or threats of violence. In one of the most famous (and controversial) research studies in the twentieth century, social psychologist Stanley Milgram showed how obedience to perceived authority can also be a powerful catalyst for instrumental aggression toward an innocent victim.

It should be noted that affective and instrumental aggression are not mutually exclusive; some acts have both affective and instrumental properties in which intention to harm is only a proximate goal. For example, both robbery and physical assault are acts of aggression because both include intention to harm the victim. However, they typically differ in ultimate goals, with robbery serving primarily profit-based goals and assault serving primarily harm-based goals.

BIOLOGICAL THEORIES

Some of the earliest biological theories of aggression, violence, and criminal behavior focused on body constitution, heredity, and intelligence. In the eighteenth century, researchers were applying the techniques of physiognomy (the study of facial features) and phrenology (the study of bumps on the head) in search of clues to criminal behavior. In *The Criminal Man* published in 1876, Cesare Lombroso offered the premise that certain individuals are "born criminal." He suggested that criminals are atavistic—they are a throwback to an earlier, more primitive evolutionary stage of human development, a notion influenced heavily by Charles Darwin's 1871 treatise, *The Origins of Man*.

Ernst Kretschmer (1921) and William Sheldon (1942, 1954) both attempted to use somato-typing or constitutionalism (i.e., classification of body and physique) to understand criminality in their studies of the biological, psychological, and social factors distinguishing delinquents and nondelinquents. There have also been attempts to link aggression with factors such as food allergies, hormones, sugar, fluorescent lighting, lead exposure, and other environmental contaminants. None of these theories have met with tremendous success.

More recently, there has been some success in showing that various *psychoactive drugs* used to treat depression and attention deficit disorder may trigger violent and even murderous behavior. One example is the mass murder committed by Joseph Wesbecker in 1989 when he opened fire with an AK-47 assault weapon, shooting to death eight of his coworkers and then taking his own life. Another example is purported to be that of 15-year-old Sam Manzie, who on September 27, 1997, raped and strangled to death an 11-year-old boy in his neighborhood. He was being treated with the antidepressant Paxil (Sampson & Lamb, 1993).

Besides Wesbecker and Manzie, there have been many other high-profile killers who were treated with psychiatric medications just before they committed senseless murders. On May 21, 1998, Kip Kinkel, a 14-year-old boy from Springfield, Oregon, who took both Ritalin and Prozac, killed his parents and then launched a shooting spree through his high school. On April 20, 1999, 18-year-old Eric Harris of Littleton, Colorado, who was taking the antidepressant Luvox, teamed up with his friend Dylan Klebold to perpetrate a horrific rampage at Columbine High School, killing 12 students and a teacher.

The possible deleterious effects of antidepressant medications is difficult to prove. These individuals are often depressed loners who may have had personality disorders among other diagnosable conditions. The fact that they were being prescribed antidepressant medication is no surprise. Whatever role Prozac, Paxil, or Luvox may have had in lifting the weight of depression and enabling someone to take action is not clear. But it does affirm the importance of using scientific research to help explain how various elements may be causative factors in violence and murder.

There has been research to suggest that androgenic hormones such as testosterone and cortisol may play a role in a biological predisposition for antisocial behavior (Booth & Osgood, 1993). Researchers in the 1960s claimed that inmates in institutions for the criminally insane were significantly more likely to possess the **XYY syndrome.** They believed that as many as 100,000 men—so-called *Super Males*—were inclined to violence by virtue of an extra Y or male sex chromosome (Gotz, Johnstone, & Ratcliffe, 1999). As stated previously, the XYY syndrome was previously known as the super-male syndrome, in which men with this condition were thought to be overly aggressive and more likely to become criminals.

More recent research does not support the super-male syndrome but does suggest that XYY males have an increased risk of behavior problems such as hyperactivity and temper tantrums during childhood, as well as learning disabilities, lower than average intelligence, and difficulty adapting to stressful situations. There have also been indications that XYY males have higher frequency of antisocial behavior in adolescence and adulthood and of criminal convictions than normal individuals (Archer, 1991; Dabbs, 1991).

There is evidence from animal research that the neurotransmitter serotonin (5-Hydroxytryptamine) plays a key role in mediating aggressive behavior. Mice with a selective knockout of the serotonin 1B receptor show an increase in aggression. Similarly, depleting serotonin in monkeys has been found to increase their aggressive behavior, whereas augmenting serotonin levels reduces aggression and increases peaceable interactions such as grooming (Mann, 1999).

Serotonin has also been implicated in human aggression. For example, pharmacological interventions that augment the body's efficient use of serotonin have been shown to reduce hostile sentiment and violent outbursts in aggressive psychiatric patients. Also, some people with a history of violent behavior, such as arsonists, violent criminals, and suicide victims, show low levels of the serotonin in their cerebral spinal fluid.

One of the structures of the brain thought to be implicated in aggression is the limbic system. The limbic system is a complex set of structures that lies on both sides and underneath the thalamus, just under the cerebrum. It includes the hypothalamus, the hippocampus, and the amygdala. It is essentially the "old" part of the brain as far as evolutionary development and is closely related to emotional experience.

One of the first indications that the amygdala might be important for fear and aggression came from Kluver and Bucy's (1939) descriptions of monkeys who had their temporal lobes removed. They noted that the animals were remarkably tame and showed little fear. Later research indicated that docile behavior associated with the Kluver-Bucy syndrome (a pattern of complex behavioral changes that is induced in several species by bilateral damage to the anterior temporal lobes) is likely mediated by the amygdala, as selective removal of that structure produced similar effects on fear and aggression (Goscinski, Kwiatkowski, Polak, Orlowiejska, & Partyk, 1997).

It is also possible to increase aggression through modulation of the amygdala. In animals, electrical stimulation of the amgydala augments all types of aggressive behavior, and there is evidence for a similar reaction in humans. Sniper Charles Whitman, who killed several people from the University Tower at Texas, left a note behind that begged people to examine his brain for possible dysfunction. His autopsy revealed he had a tumor pressing into his amygdala.

The role played by the amygdala in responding to threat and initiating aggressive behavior is fairly clear. But it is also important to mention the cortical inhibitory mechanisms of the neurobiological system. The prefrontal cortices, particularly the orbital prefrontal cortex and the ventral medial prefrontal cortex, play a significant role in inhibiting limbic regions involved in the generation of aggression. These seem to play a part in evaluating affectively charged stimuli and signaling other critical nodes, such as the hypothalamus, that modulate the body's hormonal internal milieu and cortical regions initiating motor action.

Can the Effects of TV Violence be "Brainmapped"?

Murray (2001)

In children viewing TV violence, the brain systems involved are not presently understood. In this study, eight children viewed televised violent and nonviolent video sequences while brain activity was measured with functional magnetic resonance imaging. The violent video segments consisted of two, 3-minute clips of boxing from *Rocky IV*. The nonviolent video segments were two, 3-minute clips of a National Geographic program on animals at play and *Ghostwriter*, a children's literacy program set in a mystery context. A control clip of an "X" was presented on a blue screen.

Murray and his associates found that both violent and nonviolent viewing activated regions of the brain involved in visual processing and auditory listening. However, viewing TV violence selectively affected areas of the right hemisphere such as the precuneus,

posterior cingulate, amygdala, inferior parietal, and prefrontal and premotor cortex. These are regions of the brain involved in the regulation of emotion, arousal and attention, episodic memory encoding and retrieval, and motor programming. They are also regions involved with threat perception and possible long-term memory storage of the threat events, such as the memory storage of traumatic events in post-traumatic stress disorder.

The results suggest that this pattern of brain activation may explain the finding in many studies that children who are frequent viewers of TV violence are more likely to behave aggressively. The authors conclude that although this research is preliminary, there do seem to be theoretically predictable patterns of neurological response to viewing media violence.

Measures of brain functioning such as the EEG have long suggested that violent criminals have impaired neurological processes, but recent advances in neuroimaging techniques have allowed researchers to examine violent offenders' brains in more detail. Raine, Buchsbaum, and LaCasse (1997) conducted the largest and most thorough study to date, in which they used positron emission tomography (commonly called a PET scan) to compare brain activity in 41 convicted violent offenders to activity in 41 age-matched control subjects. They found that the subcortical regions, such as the thalamus, were implicated. This finding supports previous research showing that damage to the prefrontal cortex impairs decision making and increases impulsive behavior. However, the subjects in some of these studies were at the extreme end of the aggressive spectrum (i.e., violent criminals) and may not be typical of most aggressors. Also, there are examples of people with prefrontal cortex damage who never commit violent acts, so PET scans obviously cannot be used to "predict" violence.

Can aggression be hereditary? Twin studies have been used to examine similarities between members of identical (monozygotic) and nonidentical, or fraternal (dizygotic), pairs. But the evidence from these twin studies on the role of inherited biological factors in human aggression is inconclusive. In a review of 24 studies covering a wide range of methods, Miles and Carey (1997) found that evidence for heritability of aggression depends on several variables, such as the age of the sample and whether aggression is quantified in terms of parent- and self-report or observation of behavior. Outcomes also seem to depend on how aggression is defined. To date, there is still not sufficient evidence from any type of study to draw strong conclusions regarding the heritability of aggression.

ETHOLOGICAL THEORIES

Ethology is the zoological study of animal behavior. Ethologists have a special interest in genetically programed behaviors or **instincts**. The origins of ethology can be traced back to Charles Darwin and his work on the expressive movements of man and animals. According to Darwin, the predictable behavioral programs are inherited by animals from their parents, and portions of the programs are open to natural selection and modification. Thus, these behaviors are phyloge-netic adaptations that have an evolutionary history. This often leads to a comparative approach and has led researchers to search for the biological basis of human behavior by comparing our activities to those of our close relative (other primates, especially chimps).

There are two schools of thought as to how animals acquire their behavior patterns. Some hold the view that animals, including humans, learn all their behavior during the course of onto-genetic development. Ducks, for example, learn how to quack like a duck and don't honk like a goose because they hear their parents while within the egg. Experiments have since shown that these behaviors are built in and not learned. Very complex behavior patterns can be passed on through the genes. A spider's orb web, for example, is built perfectly the first time a spider attempts construction, despite the fact that they may have no prior experience with webs. Female spiders construct egg sacs in the fall and then die. The spiderlings emerge in the spring and have no experience with an orb web before building their own.

Konrad Lorenz (along with fellow scientists Oscar Heinroth, Karl Von Frisch, and Niko Tinbergen) was one of the most influential ethologists of our time. Lorenz's early scientific con-tributions dealt with the nature of instinctive behavioral acts, particularly how such acts come about and the source of nervous energy for their performance. He also investigated how behavior may result from two or more basic drives that are activated simultaneously in an animal. In many ways, Lorenz used a **hydraulic model** to explain instinctive behavior (Lorenz, 1966). Under such a theory, the expression of any fixed action pattern depends upon the accumulation of energy. (In a hydraulic system, the accumulation of energy builds up pressure that forces action or change.) But Lorenz was not the first to discuss instinct using such a mechanistic–hydraulic model. William McDougall envisaged energy held back by "sluice gates" and "bubbling over" under certain conditions. Later he used an analogy in which each instinct was pictured as filling a chamber in which gas was constantly escaping (Lorenz, 1966). To ethologists such as Lorenz and McDougall, release of energy occurs when triggered by some external stimulus.

The concept of "releases" is used by ethologists to explain the relationship between internal factors and external, triggering stimuli. Lorenz documented many cases in which animals respond with aggressive behavior to specific, delimited stimuli. If the male stickleback sees a red spot on the belly of a rival male, it will attack. If the red spot is on the rival's back, it does not attack. But the sign stimulus also has no effect if internal conditions in the potential aggressor are not appropriate. The male stickleback will not attack the appropriately located red spot unless it has an accumulation of reproductive hormones at that time.

Lorenz eventually applied his ideas to the behavior of humans as members of a social species. In his popular book, *Das sogenannte Böse (On Aggression)*, Lorenz referred to aggression as a fighting instinct in beast and man that is directed against members of the same species. He argued that fighting and warlike behavior in man have an inborn basis but can be environmental-ly modified by the proper understanding of and provision for the basic instinctual needs of human beings (Lorenz, 1966).

Lorenz's own work was based largely on his research of a variety of animal species, particu-larly fish and birds, and to a lesser extent, nonprimate mammals. In these varied species, he notes a shared instinct to defend territory from encroachment by an animal of the same species, to defeat a rival for a desired female, and to protect the young and defenseless of the species. He found that such aggression serves the animal kingdom well in that it brings about a balance in the distribution of animals of the same species over the environment (Lorenz, 1966). This assures that the gene pool would continually be modified toward strength and enhances the likelihood of the young of a species growing to adulthood. In these ways, Lorenz saw aggression as preserving the species and regularly improving it to make it more adaptive to the environment. Beyond this, Lorenz attrib-uted to aggression a role in developing the social structure in groups, where members are rank ordered by strength. In fact, he regarded this as a necessity for developing an advanced social life.

But empirical research does not support many of Lorenz's theoretical formulations regard-ing aggression (e.g., that human aggression evolved out of communal defense responses of our prehuman ancestors). Our internal mechanisms for inhibiting aggression may have once been sufficient to assuage our actions when our weapons were limited to our hands, but they were not designed to offset the use of high-tech mechanisms or even something as low-tech as a handgun. The hydraulic model and cathartic effect of aggression (that the expression of aggression discharges aggressive energy) have also not been supported. For example, common sense and experience tell us that individuals who argue the most are also those who are the most likely to escalate. In domestic violence situations, the spouse who is verbally aggressive often moves on to pushing, slapping, punching, and worse. After viewing a particularly aggressive movie, do people tend to feel "discharged" of their aggression? In addition, the best predictor of an individual's likelihood of criminal violence at any time is his/her history of exhibiting such violence in the past. Violence, according to modern theorists, seems to beget violence rather than decrease it.

BEHAVIORAL AND SOCIAL LEARNING THEORIES

One of the earliest and most widely known theories of aggression described aggression as being instigated by frustration. This **frustration–aggression hypothesis** was originally proposed by John Dollard and associates in 1939. According to this view, frustration emerges when environmental (or even internal) circumstances interfere with a desired goal response. Certainly, in some situations, frustration does indeed increase the likelihood of aggression. For example, Buss (1963) had college students experience one of three types of frustration (failure to win money, failure to earn a better grade, or failure on a task). All three groups showed more subsequent aggression than a control group that was not frustrated. The amount of frustration and subsequent aggression depended on how near the individual was to the goal when they were blocked. In studies where researchers purposely cut in front of people standing in line at movie theatres, they were much more likely to elicit verbal aggression if they cut ahead of someone standing second in line than if they cut ahead of someone twelfth in line. Of course, it also needs to be remembered that one person's "aggression" is another's expression of "justice."

The original frustration–aggression hypothesis was revised by Berkowitz. According to this **revised frustration–aggression hypothesis**, frustration does not inevitably result in aggression but creates only a "readiness" for aggressive acts. The actual expression of the aggression depends on an eliciting event in the environment. Aggressive behavior in this model is regarded as a combination of the individual being primed to respond aggressively and cues (or symbols) in the environment that make aggressive responses more or less likely to occur. This model would be consistent with the expression "He's a time bomb waiting to explode."

Under the revised theory, aversive events such as frustrations, provocations, loud noises, uncomfortable temperatures, and unpleasant odors produce negative or uncomfortable affect (feelings). Negative affect produced by unpleasant experiences automatically stimulates various thoughts, memories, expressive motor reactions, and physiological responses associated with both fight and flight tendencies. The fight associations give rise to rudimentary feelings of anger, whereas the flight associations give rise to rudimentary feelings of fear. Furthermore, the theory assumes that cues present during an aversive event become associated with the event and with the cognitive and emotional responses triggered by the event.

The frustration–aggression hypothesis has been extended into a "general strain theory" by social psychologists. According to the theory, aggression, especially criminal violence, is a result of strain (frustration, anger, disappointment, fear, or depression). There are four important sources of strain: (a) the presence of negative stimuli (e.g., child abuse, peer rejection, school failure, and physical punishment); (b) the removal of positive stimuli (e.g., death of a loved one, parents' divorce, and residential mobility); (c) perception of inequity (e.g., peers who make more money or get better grades because they have "connections"); and (d) failure to achieve desired goals (e.g., missing out on success because of a lack of educational opportunities). One important advantage of this theory over the earlier frustration–aggression hypothesis is its emphasis on more than just absolute levels of deprivation. In focusing on the gap between expectations and achievements and between the successes of individuals and their peers, strain theory incorporates "relative deprivation" rather than just absolute deprivation or discomfort.

It has been proposed that aggressive behavior may be controlled to a great extent by "**cognitive scripts**." Cognitive scripts are learned ways of responding that are stored in a person's memory and are used as guides for behavior and social problem solving. A script tells an individual what event in the environment must occur to bring about a certain response. A person's neurophysiological predispositions, mood states, and prior experiences produce such cognitive scripts, which, in turn, determine what cues he will attend to in the environment. Individuals with neurophysiological, cognitive, or learning deficits will be impaired in their ability to focus on the appropriateness of their responses, and this has a negative effect on future behavior (Abelson, 1982).

The social learning theory of aggression emerged in the 1960s, largely as a result of the work done by Albert Bandura and his associates. The approach has undergone several elaborations since it was first presented, and it continues to exert a strong influence. It emphasizes the acquisition and maintenance of aggressive response tendencies through observation, **modeling**, and reinforcement.

Under the social learning model, the normal child observes numerous instances of aggression both in real-life situations at home, in school, and on the streets and on television. By observing the consequences of aggression on the actors, the child gradually acquires a rudimentary knowledge of certain rules of conduct (e.g., that one may sometimes obtain desirable outcomes by using force). In this way an aggressive behavioral repertoire is developed. Whether these behaviors are acted out in real life depends on the rewards or punishments that the child receives for his/her behavior. If suitable incentives for aggression are present, the probability of aggression is likely to be high. In addition, aggressive behaviors acquired through observation of others are likely to be carried out if the child is being rewarded for such actions.

Bandura believed that aggression reinforced by family members was the most prominent source of behavior modeling and that children use the same aggressive tactics that their parents

Can Aggressive Behavior be Transmitted by Imitation?

Bandura, Ross, and Ross (1961)

In this classic study on the effects of modeling on aggression, Bandura and his associates assigned 24 preschool children to one of three conditions. One experimental group observed aggressive adult models; a second observed inhibited nonaggressive models, while subjects in a control group had no prior exposure to the models. Half the subjects in the experimental conditions observed same-sex models and half viewed models of the opposite sex. Subjects were then tested for the amount of imitative as well as nonimitative aggression performed in a new situation in the absence of the models.

Comparison of the subjects' behavior in the generalization situation revealed that subjects exposed to aggressive models reproduced a good deal of aggression and that their mean scores differed markedly from those of subjects in the nonaggressive and control groups. Subjects in the aggressive condition also exhibited significantly more partially imitative and nonimitative aggressive behavior and were generally less inhibited in their behavior than subjects in the nonaggressive condition.

Imitation was found to be differentially influenced by the sex of the model, with boys showing more aggression than girls following exposure to the male model, the difference being particularly marked on highly masculine-typed behavior. Subjects who observed the nonaggressive models, especially a subdued male model, were generally less aggressive than their controls.

Bandura interpreted these results as providing evidence that observational cues of aggressive behavior by adults is an effective means of producing aggressive behavior in children.

display when dealing with others. Children learn to act aggressively when they model their behavior after the aggressive acts of adults, especially family members. Bandura also believed that television provided sources of behavior modeling. This has implications even today where aggression and violence are often expressed as acceptable behavior without negative consequences. For example, homicide rates have been found to increase after a heavy weight championship fight, and John Hinckley attempted to assassinate President Reagan after he watched the movie *Taxi Driver* 15 times (Bandura, 1998; Bettencourt, Tally, Benjamin, & Valentine, 2006; Bushman & Baumeister, 1998). Given these and many other similar findings, Bandura's admonition that the mass media provide positive role models for children and the general public is particularly salient, although not necessarily proven.

PERSONALITY THEORIES

People who experience negative emotional states and psychological distress such as anxiety and depression are apt to be mistrusting, opposing, attacking, and punishing of others. They also tend to be emotionally cold, interpersonally distant, and reveal antagonistic hostility (Bushman et al., 1998). There is also research suggesting that excessively high self-esteem may produce aggression. More specifically, individuals with inflated or unstable self-esteem are prone to anger and are highly aggressive when their high self-image is threatened. Individuals with an inflated sense of self-worth without a strong set of beliefs that support this sense of superiority are often referred to as "narcissists." Because narcissists have unstable self-esteem, they are extremely sensitive to personal slights, such as insults and criticism. That is, narcissism is characterized by a vulnerability to threats to the self-concept, and thus, when ego-threatening situations occur, narcissistic individuals tend to behave aggressively. In this way, narcissism is linked to extreme emotional changeableness and intense reactions, which could include anger and rage (Bettencourt, Tally, Benjamin, & Valentine, 2006).

Several studies have suggested that narcissism predicts aggressive behavior in situations involving some sort of provocation (Hennig et al., 2005). In one experiment, participants who were either high or low in narcissism were either insulted or praised by a confederate of the researcher. Subsequently, participants were given the opportunity to administer noise blasts to a confederate in a competitive reaction time task. The results showed that participants high in narcissism administered more intense noise blasts than those low in narcissism, and the positive relation between narcissism and aggressive behavior was much stronger in the insult condition than in the praise condition (Bushman et al., 1998). Although the number of experiments that focus on narcissism and aggressive behavior is relatively low, the available findings suggest that narcissism and level of provocation interact in their influences on aggressive behavior.

PERSONALITY DISORDERS

A personality disorder, as defined in the *Diagnostic and Statistical Manual of the American Psychiatric Association, Fourth Edition* (DSM-IV), is an enduring pattern of inner experience and behavior that differs markedly from the expectations of the individual's culture, is pervasive and inflexible, has an onset in adolescence or early adulthood, is stable over time, and leads to distress or impairment. Personality disorders are a long-standing and maladaptive pattern of perceiving and responding to other people and to stressful circumstances.

The DSM-IV (soon to be updated to the DSM-V) codifies ten personality disorders into three clusters. It is the *dramatic and emotional (Cluster B)* that is representative of impulsive aggression. Cluster B includes antisocial personality disorder, borderline personality disorder, histrionic personality disorder, and narcissistic personality disorder. But it is the antisocial and narcissistic personality disorders that seem most related to the outward expression of aggression (Twenge & Campbell, 2003). Some of the main characteristics of the **antisocial personality**

disorder include repeated criminal activity, lying, unreliability, irresponsibility, manipulativeness, disregard for the rights of others and the standards of society, lack of remorse, and physical aggressiveness. Individuals with this disorder may appear to be charming at times but their ability to form and maintain deep and long-lasting relationships is just about nil. They use people to suit their momentary needs and generally have the view that "the world is their oyster." Individuals with an antisocial personality disorder may be particularly susceptible to alcohol-related aggression and are prone to meet the DSM-IV criteria for alcohol abuse or dependence. Some researchers have also found that the styles and patterns involved in serial killings (such as domination, control, and humiliation) are consistent with features of the antisocial personality disorder (Geberth & Turco, 1997).

The other personality disorder within Cluster B that appears prone to aggression is the **narcissistic personality disorder**. The essential features of the narcissistic personality disorder include a sense of entitlement, exaggeration of their abilities or accomplishments, lack of empathy, exploitation of others, envy, and an arrogant and haughty attitude. These individuals are grandiose and require extreme amounts of admiration from others. In addition to overt aggression, they are particularly prone to committing verbal and psychological abuse when they feel unappreciated for their self-perceived special talents, humiliated, or "narcissistically injured." They tend to be paranoid and vindictive. It is no surprise that they represent the most frequently occurring diagnosis for individuals incarcerated for violent crimes (Warren et al., 2002).

Another interesting personality construct associated with aggression, which first appeared in psychoanalytic circles in the 1950s and 1960s, is "boredom." One of the primary proponents of this theory was the psychoanalyst Erich Fromm (Fromm, 1973). This is not the kind of boredom one feels in response to external circumstances as when there is a lack of excitement or stimulation. This is the subjective boredom within the person, the inability to respond to things and people around oneself with real interest. The "bored character," as he is sometimes called, shows a lack of appetite for life, a lack of any deep interest in anything or anybody, and a deep sense of powerlessness and resignation.

According to Fromm, most normal people can compensate for internal states of boredom by creating a stimulating external environment or by engaging in compulsive consumption (e.g., cars, sex, travel, alcohol, drugs). However, such efforts are not always subjectively successful, and aggression, violence, and destructiveness are used to fill the psychological void. People, according to Fromm, tolerate boredom badly, and if they cannot feel interested in life, may feel forced to seek violence and destructiveness to sustain themselves.

Are Narcissists More Aggressive than Nonnarcissists?

Girgis (2006)

Girgis used a "noise blast technique" (originally developed by Bushman & Baumeister, 1998) to determine if individuals who scored high on a narcissistic personality inventory (Raskin & Terry, 1988) would react with more aggression than nonnarcissistic individuals. All participants were then given the opportunity to aggress against a simulated competitor who had a negative impression of them based on information they knew was wrong. Narcissistic individuals significantly more often responded with aggression.

The results of the study substantiate the link between narcissistic personality traits and aggression, demonstrating that narcissistic individuals are more likely to respond with aggressive behavior toward others when placed in a situation where their inflated self-perceptions are threatened. The author also concluded from the results that the narcissistic individuals seemed to particularly enjoy the act of hurting others, that is, narcissists appear to not only "love building themselves up," but also "love tearing other people down."

There is some support in the literature for connecting boredom with a host of maladaptive behaviors. Examples of some of these behaviors include aggression, drug use, excessive eating, and pathological gambling. Boredom has also been significantly related to a multitude of negative affective states such as depression, anxiety, loneliness, dissatisfaction, impulsivity, and hostility. In a study of curiosity and boredom, bored children exhibited a significant increase in hostile impulses, and significant and positive relationships have been found between the tendency to experience boredom (i.e., boredom proneness) and the "Hostility" subscale of the Multiple Affective Adjective Checklist (Boyle, Richards, & Baglioni, 1993; Vodanovich, Verner, & Gilbride, 1991).

IMPULSE CONTROL AND MOOD REGULATION

The ability to control and regulate impulses, emotions, desires, and other behaviors is one of the most important and adaptive traits a person can have. Deficiencies and failures in impulse control are associated with many personal and social problems. Included among these problems are violence, addiction, crime, smoking, and obesity.

In general, impulse control requires a person to delay short-term rewards so as to pursue long-term goals and rewards. To achieve the most desirable long-term outcomes, people must avoid reacting to immediate situations in their environment to pursue long-term strategies that produce significant (but delayed) benefits. Impulse control and optimal self-regulation may require a long-range focus on these distant goals. Emotional distress, however, may make such a long-term focus more difficult. When people feel acutely bad, they generally wish to feel better, and this wish is often very strong. The promise of feeling better in one or two years is probably too remote to console most people who are acutely upset here and now. Emotional distress may therefore work against the usual pattern of impulse control because distress promotes a short-term focus, whereas impulse control requires a long-term one. Ample evidence has indicated that self-regulation (especially impulse control) tends to deteriorate during periods of emotional distress. Eating is an example of one important area in which bad moods may lead to an inability to control ones actions and impulses. Overweight people are more likely to report excessive eating when they are anxious or depressed (see, e.g., Sayette, 1993; Schachter, 1977).

Emotional distress also causes people to fail in their efforts at smoking cessation, and smoking behavior tends to increase when people are distressed or upset. People made to feel anxious in the laboratory setting increased their smoking, and during stressful situations, smokers feel better if they smoke. Distress also contributes to drinking behavior, as alcohol is widely believed (by the general public) to reduce anxiety and improve mood (Gustafson, 1993).

Aggression and violence are also influenced by self-control. The immediate causes of much violence may in fact be a breakdown of the internal restraints that normally keep people from acting on their angry impulses. As previously discussed, the revised frustration–aggression hypothesis holds that many forms of negative feelings could contribute to increased aggression, not just frustration, as the early frustration–aggression hypothesis held. Many acts of aggression therefore may reflect a general loss of self-control under the influence of emotional distress.

The control of one's impulses typically entails resisting the desire for something that is expected to make one feel good. In many ways emotional distress intensifies the desire to feel better, and so it many increase the subjective intensity or urgency to act impulsively. In the short run, people may enjoy some escape from emotional distress by giving in to their urges (e.g., by consuming alcohol or by acting aggressively). The temporary gains associated with such behavior, however, may be outweighed by the eventual outcomes (e.g., addiction, arrest). The pursuit of short-term gains despite severe long-term costs may account for much of the aggressive and violent behavior committed by people not normally predisposed to aggression.

Some of the classic research related to aggression could not be easily conducted today due to ethical restrictions involving research with human participants. In one study, male university students received either one or seven electric shocks from a fellow student and were then given

Does the Trigger Pull the Gun or the Gun Pull the Trigger?

Anderson, Benjamin, & Bartholow (1998)

The "weapons effect" is the finding that the presence of a weapon can cause people to behave more aggressively. The investigators in this study hypothesized that the presence of a weapon-word prime (such as "dagger" or "bullet") or the picture of a weapon (such as a gun or sword) would increase the accessibility of an aggressive word (such as "destroy" or "wound") in the same fashion that the presence of an actual weapon may increase aggressive behavior.

In the first of two experiments, undergraduate students were presented with a priming stimulus word (weapon or nonweapon word) for 1.25 seconds, a blank screen for 0.5 seconds, and then a target word (aggressive or nonaggressive word). Each subject named both aggressive and nonaggressive words following both weapon and nonweapon "primes." The experimenter instructed the subjects to read the first word to themselves and then to read the second word out loud as quickly as they could.

The computer recorded response times and computed mean response times for each participant for each of the four conditions. These response times were taken as the measure of the "accessibility" of that word.

Examples of the weapon priming words were shotgun, grenade, and dagger. Examples of the nonweapon priming words were rabbit, fish, withdraw. Examples of the aggressive words were injure, shatter, assault. Examples of the nonaggressive words were consider, relocate, and read.

In the second experiment, the students were presented with 18 black-and-white drawings of nine weapons (guns, swords) and nine plants (trees, flowers) and then a target picture. The response times were recorded as in the first experiment.

The results from both experiments showed that the mere identification of a weapon (by word or picture) primes aggression-related thoughts. The authors concluded that the gun may indeed pull the trigger.

the opportunity to administer shocks in return. For some subjects, a rifle and a revolver were on the table near the shock key; for other subjects, two badminton rackets were on the table, and for a group of control subjects, no object was on the table. More shocks were administered by the strongly aroused subjects (who had received seven shocks rather than one), but equally important was the finding that the presence of weapons significantly increased the average number of shocks administered (Berkowitz & Le Page, 1967).

Carlson and associates conducted a meta-analysis of 56 published experiments involving this so-called **weapons effect**, and the results suggested that the mere presence of weapons in pictures or in the natural environment increases aggressive behavior in both angered and nonangered adults (Benjamin & Bartholow, 1998). Some researchers have gone so far as to conclude that the trigger may actually pull the finger, rather than the other way around.

ALCOHOL AND DRUGS

Numerous studies indicate an association between alcohol consumption and aggressive behavior. Based on a review of many of these studies, Roizen (1997) found that up to 86% of homicide offenders, 37% of assault offenders, 60% of sexual offenders, up to 57% of men and 27% of women involved in marital violence, and 13% of child abusers had consumed alcohol preceding the offense. The National Violence against Women Survey indicated that alcohol is a prominent factor in wife assault. In one-half of all violent partnerships, the perpetrator was usually drinking. The rate of wife assault for women currently living with men who drank regularly (at least four times per week) was triple the rate of those partners who did not drink at all. Women were at six times the risk of violence by partners who frequently consumed five or more drinks at one time compared with women whose partners never drank (National Violence against Women Survey, 1999).

Researchers have presented ideas on the physiological connection between alcohol and aggression. Alcohol may encourage aggression or violence by disrupting normal brain function.

According to the **disinhibition hypothesis**, for example, alcohol weakens brain mechanisms that normally restrain impulsive behaviors, including inappropriate aggression. By impairing information processing, alcohol can also lead a person to misjudge social cues, thereby forcing them to overreact to a perceived threat. Also, a narrowing of attention may lead to an inaccurate assessment of the future risks of acting on an immediate violent impulse (Gustafson, 1993).

The connection between substance abuse and aggression does not seem to be a linear one. A retrospective chart review of 311 consecutive psychiatric emergency room patients indicated that alcohol, cocaine, and/or cannabis were not associated with aggressive behavior. Patients with positive toxicology for cocaine were actually less frequently aggressive than cocainenegative patients. This suggests that aggression is not a common acute manifestation of recent substance abuse. As an example, the generally perceived link of cocaine to aggressive behavior may actually be due to the violence associated with the illicit drug trade (Dhossche, 1999).

However, case reports suggest that **anabolic steroids**, when used in high doses, increase irritability and aggression. Some steroid abusers report that they have committed aggressive acts, such as physical fighting or armed robbery, theft, vandalism, or burglary. Abusers who have committed aggressive acts or property crimes generally report that they engage in these behaviors more often when they take steroids than when they are drug free (Pärlklo, 2002). But additional studies are required to definitively link drug-induced neurochemical changes with the development or display of aggressive behaviors and to better understand the neurobiology of aggression induced by drugs or alcohol.

TABLE 3.1 Summary of Theories of Violence and Aggression

Theory	Theorists	Examples
Biological	Archer (1991); Booth and Osgood (1993); Dabbs (1991); Darwin (1871,1899); Kretschmer (1921); Lombroso (1876); Miles and Carey (1997); Sheldon (1942,1954)	Somatotyping Genetics Hormonal
Structural	Kluver and Bucy (1939); Raine, Buchsbaum, and LaCasse (1997)	Amygdala Hypothalamus Hippocampus Prefrontal Cortex
Behavioral and Social Learning	Abelson (1982); Bandura, Ross, and Ross (1961); Buss (1963); Dollard, Doob, Miller, Mowrer, and Sears (1939)	Frustration–Aggression Hypothesis, Imitation and Modeling, Cognitive Scripts
Ethological	Lorenz (1966)	Instincts Hydraulic Model, Phylogenetic Adaptations
Personality	Fromm (1973); Boyle, Richards, and Baglioni (1993); Geberth and Turco (1997); Bushman and Baumeister (1998)	Five-Factor Model, Boredom, Narcissistic and Antisocial Personality Disorders
Impulse Control	Berkowitz and LePage (1967), Schachter (1977), Gustafson (1993), Sayette (1993), Benjamin and Bartholow (1998), Bushman and Baumeister (1998), Burk and Landt (2005)	Mood Regulation, Provocation Resistance, Weapons Effect
Alcohol & Drugs; Steroids	Gustafson (1993); Sampson and Lamb (1993); Roizen (1997); Dhossche (1999); Pärlklo (2002)	Disinhibition Effect, Impaired Reasoning and Judgment

Would the Government be Justified in Restricting Violent Television Programing?

There has been research presented to Congress by social scientists and antiviolence activists requesting that the presence of violence in the media be restricted. Would this be possible from a legal standpoint? Would such a move survive constitutional scrutiny? The answer is, probably not.

The Supreme Court has repeatedly stressed that "above all else, the First Amendment means that government has no power to restrict expression because of its message, its ideas, its subject matter, or its content" (*Police Department v. Mosley*, 1972, p. 95). The Court has made clear that moral and esthetic judgments are "for the individual to make, not for the Government to decree, even with the mandate or approval of the majority" (*United States v. Playboy Entertainment Group, Inc.*, 2000, p. 818). Indeed, other courts have also maintained, "Material limited to forms of violence is given the highest degree of First Amendment protection" (*Sovereign News Co. v. Falke*, 1980, p. 923). In *Winters v. New York*, the Supreme Court invalidated a law that prohibited the distribution to minors of any publication "principally made up of . . . accounts of criminal deeds, or pictures, or stories of deeds of bloodshed, lust or crime." Even though the Court saw nothing of any possible value to society in these magazines, the justices held that the material was "as much entitled to the protection of free speech as the best of literature" (1948, p. 507).

The First Amendment not only protects expression that depicts violence, it also protects speech that advocates the "use of force or violence" (*NAACP v. Claiborne Hardware Co.*, 1982, p. 527). In cases such as *Walker v. Osbourne* (1991) in which the plaintiffs claimed that the context of song lyrics advocated minors to commit violence, courts have found that such expression enjoys full First Amendment protection. Similar rulings can be found in cases such as *DeFilippo v. National Broadcasting Co.* (1982) and *Olivia N. v. National Broadcast Co.* (1982).

Even defining "violence" presents great constitutional difficulties. The law favors bright lines when regulating speech, so it is clear what is and is not permissible. Assuming the government can provide an objective definition of "violence," it must then proceed to the task of defining what is and is not permissible. For example, *The Magnificent Seven* is a movie about seven men who protect a village from violent marauders. Is their defense of the village "good" violence and thus allowable?

Two other films that pitted "good" violence against "bad" violence and where "talking out their differences" would likely not have been effective were *Universal Soldier* and *Bonnie and Clyde*. In *Universal Soldier*, two soldiers kill each other in Vietnam but are "reanimated" in a secret army project along with a large group of other previously dead soldiers. Later they are called on to dispatch several terrorists by whatever means necessary, including extreme violence. *Bonnie and Clyde* is about Bonnie Parker and Clyde Barrow, bank robbers who roamed the central United States during the Great Depression. The film shows many violent killings, including the final scene where the two bank robbers are riddled with bullets just as they were in real life.

Is the depiction of violence of the marauders, terrorists, and bank robbers in these movies therefore not allowed? If so, then how does one place the violence committed by the Magnificent Seven, the soldiers, and the police in context? Prohibiting showing the violence of the "bad guys" in these films would seem to make the violence shown by the "good guys" unreasonable. Or, can these movies only show a "debate" between the parties with no violence whatsoever?

While proponents of regulating media violence often claim they are only seeking to prohibit "gratuitous" or "excessive" violence, defining that is a lot like "knowing it when you see it," which is insufficiently precise for constitutional purposes.

In *Zamora v. Columbia Broadcasting System* (1979) a father sued three broadcasting companies after his son killed an 83-year-old woman. The father alleged that television violence caused his son to become desensitized to violent behavior, thus leading to the murder. The Zamora court held for the broadcasting companies and found that the imposition of civil responsibility for damages would act as a restraint on the broadcasters' exercise of their asserted First Amendment rights. The Zamora court also communicated the importance of giving viewers and the public access to social, political, esthetic, or moral ideas.

In *Davidson v. Time Warner* (1997), the widow of slain state trooper Bill Davidson brought a suit against Tupac Shakur and Time Warner, claiming that Shakur's rap album *2Pacalypse Now* caused her husband's death. Ronald Howard was driving a stolen car, and Davidson pulled Howard over in an unrelated traffic stop. Howard pulled out a handgun and fatally shot Trooper Davidson

(continued)

(continued)

during the traffic stop. During the shooting, Howard was listening to *2Pacalypse Now,* which contains at least one song advocating violence against police officers. Holding for the defendants, the U.S. District Court for the Southern District of Texas found that although the songs were insulting and outrageous, there was no proof that the artist intended to incite violence.

All in all, the balance between preserving First Amendment rights while protecting the safety of America's youth is a difficult one. It is important to ensure that children are not unduly influenced by excessive violence in the media; however, it is equally important that constitutional rights and guarantees are not violated in the process. A possible solution may be through education in the way of media awareness programs. The American Academy of Pediatricians (1996) suggests that parents become "media-literate" by "watching television with their children and teenagers, discussing the content with them, and initiating the process of selective viewing at an early age" (p. 1220). Similarly, the Recording Industry Association of America (RIAA) (2006) encourages parents to watch television with their children and discuss the content with them. The RIAA works with recording artists to develop public service materials in its "Talking with Kids about Tough Issues Campaign" (Talking Campaign). The Talking Campaign helps parents to better communicate with their children about difficult issues facing their lives. For example, school media literacy programs can help children interpret and analyze what they see and hear in the media. If parents and children became more educated and aware of violence on television, in the movies, and in song lyrics, perhaps Congress would be under less pressure to impose restrictive and even draconian regulations concerning minors and the media.

VIOLENT CRIME

Homicide

Homicide is the killing of a human being caused by another. *Homicide* itself is a neutral term and does not imply criminality. The working definition of homicide is derived from one of two places. The first is the common law. The common law is that law which is handed down from judge to judge and court to court. It represents the decisions that courts have made on a particular issue from one generation to the next. The second is the statutory law, or the law made by the legislature or other law-making body.

Under the common law, and in the absence of a statute, for there to be a homicide there must be a **life in being**, that is, there must be a human being who was born alive and was still alive at the time of the killing. An act causing a child to be born dead was not considered a homicide because the fetus was not "alive." However, if a pregnant woman is injured by a felonious act that causes the child to die after it is born or causes a fatally premature birth, the person inflicting the injury would be guilty of homicide.

The question of homicide at the beginning of the life process is further complicated by U.S. Supreme Court decisions allowing a woman to have a voluntary abortion during the first two trimesters of pregnancy. Abortion and feticide statutes attempt to make criminal the termination of the existence of a fetus; this is not homicide because the victim has not yet attained the status of a human being. Before the fetus is viable, the female may terminate its existence under her constitutional right to privacy. In the third trimester of the pregnancy, the termination may be feticide or abortion but is not homicide unless the baby is born alive in the attempt to terminate its existence as a fetus and then dies.

The shooting of a dead person is not homicide. However, an act that accelerates the process of dying may be homicide. Since no homicide ever does more than "hasten the inevitable," it is homicide to shorten the life of one suffering from an incurable disease or of one dying from a mortal injury. Thus, for example, a doctor who removes a vital organ for transplantation purposes before the donor is legally dead could be subjected to criminal liability.

The second essential element of homicide is that the death of the human being must be caused by another (self-destruction by suicide is not homicide). In addition, the other human's act must be the sole or concurrent substantial "but for" proximate cause of the death, not broken by an intervening superseding factor. Aside from some affirmative act, the proximate cause of the death could be the result of an omission to act, or of negligence. In most jurisdictions, an additional required element of a homicide is that the death of the victim occur within a year and a day of the defendant's act (or omission). For example, if S shoots V and V dies two years following the shooting (even from complications resulting from the shooting), murder has not been committed.

Murder

At common law, if a homicide is not justified or excused, it is criminal homicide. Criminal homicide is divided into two categories: murder and manslaughter. Murder is defined as the unlawful killing of a human being committed with malice. The term *malice* does not imply malevolence to the victim particularly, but rather the general intentional doing of a wrongful act without a just cause or excuse. In cases of homicide, the term means "an intention to kill." This definition, like that for all crimes, contains two components: an **actus reus** and the **mens rea**. The *actus reus* is the physical or external part of the crime; the *mens rea* is the mental or internal ingredient.

The mens rea or "intent" of a person is at times very clear and at other times a difficult thing to establish. The intent to kill established by "express malice" is usually straightforward. For example, a disgruntled and rejected lover desires to kill his former girlfriend. He purchases a handgun and shoots her, successfully causing her death. He had the requisite intent to kill as well as the lethal means. But suppose he wants to kill her but has chosen a method that makes it highly unlikely that he would succeed. For example, he decides to shoot a rock at the woman with a slingshot. For death to occur the rock would have to hit her at precisely the right spot. If he were successful in this scenario, he would be guilty of an intentional homicide, despite the fact that its success was not likely.

In a similar fashion, a person may be guilty of an intentional homicide even if he does not desire the death of another person, but engaged in behavior that made the death substantially certain to occur. For example, if a criminal puts an explosive device on an airplane in an attempt to destroy some incriminating evidence that it is carrying, he is guilty of an intentional homicide of the pilot if the plane crashes, killing the pilot, even though he did not know the name of the pilot and did not desire that that particular individual should die.

Although it is difficult to establish intent in certain situations, there are certain common law doctrines that help to establish such intent. One of these is the **deadly weapon doctrine**. This doctrine states that one who intentionally uses a deadly weapon on another human being and thereby kills her presumably intends to kill her. When a deadly weapon is used, this doctrine permits, but does not compel, a jury to infer that the defendant intended to kill her victim. A deadly weapon is one which, from the manner used, is calculated to produce death or serious bodily injury. It may be a gun, a knife, a rock, an automobile, or even one's fists.

Earlier it was pointed out that the *actus reus* could be an act or "omission" that can comprise the physical elements of a crime. Although an intentional killing is usually committed by some affirmative act on the part of the killer, such as shooting a gun or stabbing with a knife, certain "nonactions" (such as leaving a wheelchair-bound person on railroad tracks) would be an intentional killing if the actor desired the result and the victim died. Indeed, words alone may be used to cause an intentional death, such as when one perjures an innocent person into the electric chair or when one, seeing a blind person at the edge of a precipice, advises him that all is clear. Finally, one may be guilty of murder for failure to act where there is a duty to act, as in the case of a parent's failure to rescue his imperiled infant.

Intent can also be transferred to an individual to whom a defendant bore no malice. Transferred intent can occur when the victim is not the one the defendant meant to kill. A person shooting at one person and accidentally hitting another is guilty of murder nonetheless (in addition to bad aim). Once a shot is fired with intent to kill someone, the shooter is guilty regardless of who is killed. So then, if a would-be terrorist expressly intending to kill a soldier shoots at the soldier but misses and kills a civilian, his express intent to kill is transferred to the new victim and the terrorist is guilty of the murder of the civilian.

A person who acts (or fails to act when a duty to act exists) without the intent to kill but with the intent to do great bodily injury and causes another's death possesses malice aforethought. Thus, in *Director of Public Prosecutions v. Smith* (1961), a conviction of murder was affirmed where a police officer, observing stolen goods in an automobile, directed the driver to pull over, whereupon the driver pulled away and the officer jumped on the outside of the car. The driver accelerated and swerved, causing the officer to fall off and be killed by an oncoming vehicle.

If a person shoots another person in the arm, intending to break his arm and keep him from leaving but not to kill him, it would be murder if the victim died from the wound. The reason for this is that the defendant had the intention to do "great or serious bodily injury." It is not enough that an individual wanted to inflict some minor injury on someone; rather, it would be necessary to inflict an injury likely to result in dangerous or fatal consequences.

The intentional use of a deadly weapon on another will imply the intent to kill or at least the intent to do serious bodily injury. This intent is inferred even though a third person, and not the intended victim, is killed through the use of the dangerous weapon. For example, if A, with intent to do serious bodily injury to B, shoots B but misses and kills C, A has the intention to inflict great bodily harm, possesses malice aforethought, and is guilty of the murder of C through the transferred-intent doctrine previously discussed. Failure to warn or rescue another to whom a duty is owed would also constitute murder if the failure was caused by the intent to inflict serious bodily harm on the victim and death resulted.

As discussed earlier, under some circumstances a defendant may be guilty of murder if he acts in a manner that creates an unusually high risk of death and that actually results in death. Driving over 100 mph in a school zone while young children are present, for example, could establish malice under a "**depraved heart**" theory. A similar situation would exist where a healthy newborn is thrown into a trash bin and covered up or where the defendant fires a weapon into a moving automobile, train, or into an inhabited house or a crowd. In *Commonwealth v. Malone* (1946), the accused was found guilty of murder when he killed the victim while playing a game of "Russian roulette." The game involved loading a pistol with one round and, after spinning the chamber, placing the gun to the victim's head and pulling the trigger. In holding the defendant responsible, the court ruled that the defendant had acted with the awareness that his conduct created an extremely high risk of death to the victim.

This kind of willful and wanton disregard of an unreasonable risk resulting in the death of another shows malice even though there is no intent to kill or do great bodily injury. As a further example, a person wishes to destroy certain property by explosion. He realizes that there is a great risk that someone might be killed, but hopes that this does not happen. He takes certain precautions, but a person is killed in the course of the explosion. Because he has proceeded with a wanton and willful disregard of an obvious human risk, he is guilty of murder.

Felony Murder

A person can be held responsible for murder even if that person wasn't directly involved in the killing. This is generally known as the **felony murder rule** and states that when a death occurs during the process of a felony, murder has been committed. More specifically, in the majority of jurisdictions, the felony must be an inherently dangerous one in order to give rise to felony murder. The common law felonies that most commonly give rise to the felony murder doctrine are mayhem, rape, sodomy, burglary, arson, kidnapping, escape, and robbery. For the purposes of this rule, "escape" refers to the separate crime of escape from official custody, not escape from the scene of the felony.

The commission or attempted commission of the felony must be the proximate cause of the death. If there is an act that intervenes between the defendant's action and the death, the question of proximate cause turns on whether the death was foreseeable as a result of the defendant's actions. For example, if A sets fire to B's house and either B, a visitor, or a firefighter is killed in the fire, then A is guilty of murder. Even if an innocent bystander rushed into the house to save the occupants and was killed, A would be guilty of murder. On the other hand, A would not be guilty of murder if a looter entered the burning building to steal whatever he could or if a firefighter fell off the fire truck while returning to the station house.

The proximate cause requirement is not satisfied merely because the killing occurs while the felony is being committed; there must be a causal relationship. For example, if, while one is setting fire to a building, an occupant, unaware of the arson, dies of a heart attack, the arsonist would not be guilty of felony murder. The situation would be otherwise if the occupant, having a weak heart, died of fright brought on by the fire. This is the essence of the *res gestae* theory, which holds that the death must occur during preparations or attempt to perpetrate the underlying felony, during the perpetration of the felony, or during escape from the underlying felony before reaching momentary safety.

For example, assume that A and B were in the process of burglarizing a gas station at night when a police officer, P, arrived. A and B dropped their loot and fled into the nearby woods. P followed them for about 200 feet, where B shot P to death. Both A and B are guilty of felony murder because the death occurred during the uninterrupted escape attempt; it was part of the process of the felony because it was so closely connected in time and place as to be a part of the occurrence.

A person who conspires to commit a felony may be charged with felony murder if his accomplice committed the murder. A conspiracy is an agreement between two or more persons to engage in a criminal act. It is one of a class of criminal offenses referred to as inchoate or incomplete crimes. For there to be a conspiracy, at least one of the participants must take a step toward the commission of the crime the parties formerly agreed to commit. It is irrelevant whether or not the criminal goal is completed.

Not all jurisdictions recognize the felony murder rule, and most states only apply it to certain felonies. Generally, there are three or more requirements for application of the felony murder rule. These include acts that (1) are inherently dangerous to life or health, (2) are held to be *malum in se*, or (3) were felonies at common law. A malum in se act is "wrong in itself," in its very nature being illegal because it violates the natural, moral, or public principles of a civilized society. In criminal law it is one of the collection of crimes that are traditional and not just created by statute, which are *malum prohibitum*. Examples would include murder, rape, burglary, and robbery, while violations of the Securities and Exchange Act or most "white-collar crimes" are malum prohibitum (not inherently immoral but forbidden due to law).

A number of problems have arisen with respect to the deaths of third persons involved in or at the scene of the felony. If the victim of a robbery is killed by the felon, even accidentally, during the felony, the felon is guilty of murder. Likewise, if the robber kills a police officer or an innocent bystander during the robbery, it is felony murder. It has also been held that if two people commit a felony, and one accidentally kills the other during the course of the felony, this too is felony murder.

If the felon uses the victim as a human shield and the victim is accidentally killed by one attempting to shoot the felon, the felon is guilty of felony murder because the death is foreseeable. Likewise, the felony murder doctrine has been applied when the felons and the victims or police exchange gunfire started by the felons in the course of an escape from the felony and a nonfelon is killed.

Most courts will not apply the felony murder doctrine where one of the cofelons is killed by the police. In the leading case of *Commonwealth v. Redline* (1958), the Pennsylvania court stated what is now referred to as the *Redline view*. In this case, A and B, after robbing X, started to flee. An interceding police officer shot one of the two robbers to death. The court held that the surviving robber was not guilty of felony murder, since murder cannot be based upon a shooting that constitutes a justifiable homicide (where, e.g., the police officer or felony victim shoots the felon to prevent his escape or to prevent the commission of a felony). The failure to apply a felony murder theory to the death of a cofelon can also be justified because the victim was a willing participant in a risky criminal venture.

Degrees of Murder

Most commonly, **first-degree murder** includes murder committed with premeditation and deliberation and, as discussed earlier, murder in the commission of or attempted commission of certain inherently dangerous felonies. In addition, many jurisdictions include as first-degree murder a murder committed with atrocity or cruelty, or one committed by torture, by poison, or by lying in wait.

When used in connection with first-degree murder, "deliberation" implies a cool mind that is capable of reflection. For example, being insulted verbally is usually regarded as insufficient to reduce a killing from murder to a lesser degree of homicide (e.g., manslaughter), but it may arouse enough passion in the person insulted that if she kills the speaker intentionally under the sudden excitement engendered by these words, the homicide will not be "deliberate" and hence not murder in the first degree.

"Premeditation" means that the person with the cool mind did in fact reflect, at least for a short period of time (in some cases a matter of seconds), before the act of killing. It is not necessary that there be any appreciable space of time between the intention to kill and the act; they may be as instantaneous as successive thoughts of the mind. In establishing premeditation and deliberation, it is not enough to show only that the defendant had the time to premeditate and deliberate. One must actually premeditate and deliberate as well as intend to kill to be guilty of this type of first-degree murder.

Premeditation and deliberation, being subjective states of mind, are usually established by circumstantial evidence of the defendant's conduct. There usually must be some affirmative evidence to support a finding that the defendant did in fact premeditate and deliberate. The following facts help to establish premeditation: (1) the defendant's prior possession of the murder weapon, (2) the defendant's surreptitious approach toward the victim, (3) prior threats by the defendant to do violence to the victim, and (4) the deliberate infliction of wounds to vital parts of the victim's body.

The law of most jurisdictions provides that where the intention to kill is carried into effect by extremely cruel means—or by poison, torture, or lying in wait—the killing amounts to first-degree murder, because in each of these situations the means of the homicide shows premeditation and deliberation. For a killing by torture or by another extremely cruel method, the killer must intend to and actually inflict pain on the victim. The specific intent to inflict pain on the victim makes unnecessary proof of additional malice, deliberation, or premeditation. To be first-degree murder, the act that causes the pain must also cause the victim's death.

Many jurisdictions provide that murder by poison is first-degree murder. The poison need not be administered orally, but may be injected or inhaled. A killing perpetrated while *lying in wait* is also first-degree murder. The term generally requires a watching and waiting in a concealed position with the intent to kill. "Concealment" is the important factor in defining the term. The words refer not to the position of the body, but to the "purpose of taking the person unawares" and necessarily imply malice, premeditation, deliberation, and willful intent.

Second-degree murder is typically defined as any murder that is not first-degree murder. Included in the category of second-degree murder are (1) a killing with malice aforethought, but without premeditation and deliberation; (2) a killing that results from an act done with intent to do great bodily harm (regardless of whether done with premeditation and deliberation); (3) a killing that results from an act done with a wanton and willful disregard of an unreasonable human risk; and (4) in some jurisdictions, a murder committed in the course of a felony not listed under first-degree felony murder (e.g., embezzlement, larceny).

A murder with malice but without premeditation is committed when the killer lacks the capacity to deliberate. A killer may be incapable of the cool reflection required when, for example, his capacity to premeditate and deliberate is prevented by intoxication or feeblemindedness short of insanity. The defendant is guilty of second-degree murder, however, if he still had an intention to kill. The majority of jurisdictions reduce murder to second degree on the grounds of diminished mental capacity or voluntary intoxication.

MANSLAUGHTER

Voluntary Manslaughter

Voluntary manslaughter consists of an intentional homicide under extenuating circumstances that mitigate, but do not justify or excuse, the killing. The element of malice aforethought (necessary for murder) is not present. The most common type of voluntary manslaughter involves the intentional killing of another while in the **heat of passion** caused by an adequate provocation, that is, a provocation that causes a reasonable person to lose their normal self-control.

Generally three requirements must be met to reduce an intentional homicide from murder to voluntary manslaughter on the ground of provocation:

1. There must have been legally adequate provocation.
2. The killing must have been in the sudden heat of passion; that is, the killing must have followed the provocation before there had been a reasonable opportunity for the passion to cool and before the slayer's passion had, in fact, cooled.
3. There must have been a causal connection between the provocation, the passion, and the fatal act.

Some of the situations that might normally give rise to voluntary manslaughter include attempted battery, mutual combat, the commission of a crime against a close relative or family member, witnessing one's spouse in an act of adultery, and false or unlawful arrest.

An attempted battery can constitute adequate provocation if its natural result is to arouse the passions of a reasonable person. Such an attempted battery can also give rise to the right of self-defense. But just words, even if they are "fighting words," no matter how abusive, insulting, or scurrilous, do not constitute adequate provocation. Some courts have held that adequate provocation can sometimes be established by a combination of insulting words and some other circumstance that would not of itself be sufficient. For example, insulting words plus a slight blow or insulting words plus an aggravated trespass to property have been held sufficient. It should be noted that although insulting words cannot constitute adequate provocation for voluntary manslaughter, "informational" words can. These words are treated as legal substitutes for the facts they convey. Thus, for example, V relaying information to D that he has raped D's wife or assaulted his child would constitute adequate provocation.

When two persons willingly engage in mutual combat that is not deadly by design and during the fight one kills the other as the result of an intention to do so formed during the struggle, the homicide is manslaughter and not murder. This rule applies where the fight is really "mutual," in the sense that both enter it willingly, as distinguished from the situation in which one is clearly attacking and the other is clearly defending. But there is no such provocation if the intent to kill was formed prior to the mutual combat, or if one, by words or acts, provokes an encounter for the purpose of killing the other and does, in fact, kill him. In these cases, the killer would be guilty of murder. Likewise, there is no provocation where two persons, not in the heat of passion, form an intention to kill one another. For example, a killing that results from a fairly conducted duel is murder and not manslaughter.

A person who discovers his/her spouse in the act of committing adultery may be reasonably provoked, and the killing of the spouse or lover or both is voluntary manslaughter. "Adultery" requires sexual intercourse; any other type of sexual activity will not give sufficient

Are Words alone sufficient Provocation for a Heat of Passion Killing Defense?

Girouard v. State (1991)

Steven S. Girouard and Joyce M. Girouard had been married for about two months on October 28, 1987. They were both in the army. The marriage was often tense and strained, and there was evidence that Joyce was having an extramarital affair. On that night Steven overheard Joyce talking on the phone to her friend, whereupon she told the friend that she had asked her first sergeant for a hardship discharge because her husband did not love her anymore. Steven asked Joyce what she meant by her comments; she responded, "nothing." Angered by her lack of response, Steven kicked away the plate of food Joyce had in front of her. He then went to lie down in the bedroom.

Joyce followed him into the bedroom, jumped on his back, pulled his hair and said, "What are you going to do, hit me?" She continued to taunt him by saying, "I never wanted to marry you . . . I want a divorce . . . this marriage has been a mistake." She also told him that she had seen his commanding officer and filed charges against him for abuse and that she had filed charges against him with the Judge Advocate General's Office (JAG) and that he would probably be court martialed. Steven then left the bedroom, went to the kitchen and procured a long-handled kitchen knife, which he hid behind a pillow he was carrying. She continued with her barrage, telling him that she wanted him out of the apartment but that she would remain there and that she did not want him and that a divorce would be better for her.

Joyce again asked Steven what he was going to do. What he did was lunge at her with the kitchen knife he had hidden behind the pillow; he stabbed her 19 times. Feeling suicidal, Steven went to the kitchen and slit his wrists. When he realized that he would not die from his wounds, he called the police, telling them that he had just murdered his wife.

Steven was convicted of second-degree murder and sentenced to 22 years in prison. He appealed the conviction claiming that he should have been tried for voluntary manslaughter instead of murder based on a theory of provocation and heat of passion killing. The appeals court did not agree. The court noted that voluntary manslaughter is defined as "an intentional homicide, done in a sudden heat of passion, caused by adequate provocation, before there has been a reasonable opportunity for the passion to cool."

The issue for the court was whether the taunting words by Joyce were enough to inflame the passion of a reasonable man so that he would be sufficiently provoked to strike out in hot-blooded blind passion and kill. Although the court acknowledged that there was indeed needless provocation by Joyce, the provocation was not seen as being adequate to mitigate second-degree murder to voluntary manslaughter.

As this case illustrates, words might be enough to inflame someone sufficiently and allow for a reduction of a charge from murder to manslaughter. But the words would have to be of such an extreme nature so as to provoke a reasonable person into killing. In addition, the killing would have to be almost simultaneous with the provocation so as to make cooling off nearly impossible.

provocation. A reasonable though mistaken belief that the spouse is committing adultery may also be sufficient. The provocation formula does not extend beyond the marital relationship. Thus, it does not apply in situations involving engaged persons, divorced couples, or unmarried lovers.

Resisting a lawful arrest by the police or other law enforcement authorities does not provide a defense or an excuse to the use of force. However, in resisting an unlawful arrest, the cases are not in complete agreement. Some courts have held that if an individual is unlawfully arrested, and there are aggravating circumstances (injuries or the use of a dangerous weapon), there may be sufficient justification to arouse the passion of a reasonable person so as to render him guilty of manslaughter only. Other cases, reflecting the modern view that one should submit to the illegal arrest and then take legal means to secure one's release, have held that an illegal arrest is not a provocation sufficient to arouse the passion of a reasonable person. Of course, where the provocation rule is not operative, the killing, under most circumstances, would be murder, unless the arrest is conducted with excessive force giving rise to the independent justification of self-defense.

It is important to note that for "heat of passion" to be an effective basis for reducing an offense from murder to voluntary manslaughter, it must be of a nature that would inflame the passion of a reasonable person and cause that person to act from passion rather than reason. The "reasonable person" standard does not consider innate peculiarities and idiosyncrasies of the individual. For example, in *Bedder v. Director of Public Prosecutions* (1954) the defendant, who was impotent, was jeered at by a prostitute with whom he was attempting to have intercourse. In a rage, the defendant killed the woman. The court held that an infirmity of the body of the assailant is not material in testing whether there has been provocation by the deceased to justify the violence used.

To mitigate a killing from murder to voluntary manslaughter on the ground of provocation, it must also be shown that the killer had not cooled off at the time of the killing, that is, the killing must have been in a sudden heat of passion. The test for whether provocation continued until the time of the act has both objective and subjective components. Even assuming that the slayer was reasonably and actually provoked, there will be no reduction from murder to manslaughter if the time elapsing between the provocation and the death blow was such that a reasonable person thus provoked would have cooled. What constitutes a reasonable cooling time in each case depends upon the nature of the provocation and the circumstances surrounding its occurrence. But a murder that occurs six months after an incident of provocation, for example, would probably not be reduced to voluntary manslaughter in most jurisdictions.

Assuming that a reasonable person might still have been provoked, the second step of the inquiry is subjective: Did this particular person kill in the actual heat of passion? Thus, even if the killer had been actually and reasonably provoked, if he had actually cooled off prior to the killing, the killing is not in the heat of passion and is murder. Since the extent of the cooling time is measured by the reasonableness standard, or the actual cooling off time (whichever is shorter), it is also murder if the slayer has cooled off, even though the reasonable person might still have been enraged. Courts have considered such circumstances as the transaction of business, rational conversations on unrelated subjects, or evidence of preparation for the homicide as indicators that the heat of passion has cooled.

Involuntary Manslaughter

Involuntary manslaughter is an unintentional homicide, committed without malice, which is neither justified nor excused. The two principal types of involuntary manslaughter are *criminal negligence manslaughter* and *unlawful act manslaughter*.

Criminal negligence manslaughter is conduct that involves a high degree of risk of death or serious injury. The following scenarios would be examples of such behavior:

1. A camper leaves a campfire burning, which later burns down a home, killing the occupants.
2. A parent is told by a doctor that his child must obtain competent medical attention the next time he suffers certain symptoms. Those symptoms recur, but the parent fails to get medical attention because he believes that doctors are evil. The child dies.
3. In the presence of other people, an individual attempts to clean a gun that she knows is loaded. The gun accidentally discharges, killing one of the onlookers.
4. The operator of a nightclub permits substantial overcrowding and fails to provide for fire exits as required by law. A fire occurs in the nightclub, killing a large number of people who could not get out because of the violations.
5. A person voluntarily becomes intoxicated and while in that condition drives an automobile at high speed down a busy street and kills a pedestrian.

Unlawful act manslaughter is a killing that occurs in the commission (or attempted commission) of an unlawful act, not amounting to a felony. For an unlawful act to give rise to misdemeanor manslaughter, the unlawful act must be malum in se (an act that is wrong in itself without being made so by the legislature). Many traffic deaths fall into this category, although some states have a special category of homicide called vehicular homicide.

HOMICIDES THAT ARE NOT CRIMES

A homicide is rendered noncriminal in one of two ways—by justification or by excuse.

Justifiable Homicide

Justifiable homicide is homicide that is commanded or authorized by law. These situations include self-defense; defense of others; defense of one's dwelling; and killing done under public authority, or during an attempt to arrest, prevent escape, or prevent crime. Examples would be a soldier who kills in the line of duty, a police officer who shoots and kills a dangerous felon who is escaping from a bank robbery, and a person who engages in self-defense or defense of others.

Self-defense employs either nondeadly or deadly force. Nondeadly force is that type of action that is neither intended nor likely to cause death. Nondeadly force is justified when the defendant is threatened by an assailant whom she reasonably believes is inflicting or is about to inflict unlawful bodily harm. Deadly force is that type of action that is either intended or likely to cause death.

A main prerequisite to the use of deadly force in self-defense is that the defendant must reasonably believe she is in danger of death or great bodily harm and that it is necessary to use deadly force to prevent it. If the defendant unreasonably believes her life is in danger, there is not right of self-defense. On the other hand, there need be no actual danger if the defendant reasonably believes the danger to be real. For example, if an assailant threatened the defendant with a toy pistol that she could not reasonably believe to be genuine, the defendant could not use deadly force. On the other hand, if the toy pistol appeared real to a reasonable person, deadly force would be justified. Another prerequisite to the use of deadly force is that the threat of danger be immediate. If the danger is in the distant future, then there is probably some other way to avoid it, and deadly force is not authorized.

Can Deadly Force be used to Prevent the Escape of an Unarmed Felon?

Tennessee v. Garner (1964)

At about 10:45 P.M. on October 3, 1974, two Memphis police officers answered a "prowler inside call" at a private residence. A man was seen running from the house. One of the officers called out "police, halt," but the suspect continued running and began to climb a fence that would have assured his escape. Convinced that if the suspect made it over the fence he would elude capture, the officer shot him. The bullet hit him in the back of the head, and he later died on the operating table. Ten dollars and a purse taken from the house were found on his body.

In using deadly force to prevent the escape, the officer was acting under the authority of a Tennessee statute and pursuant to police department policy, both of which allowed the use of deadly force in cases of burglary where the suspect flees or resists. The incident was also reviewed by the Memphis Police Firearm's Review Board and presented to a grand jury. Neither took any action.

The deceased's father brought a suit in the Federal District Court for the Western District of Tennessee, seeking damages under 42 U.S.C. § 1983 for violations of his son's constitutional rights. Section 1983 provides, "Every person who, under color of [law] . . . subjects, or causes to be subjected, any citizen of the United States . . . to the deprivation of any rights . . . secured by the Constitution . . . , shall be liable to the party injured in an action at law. . . ." The court entered judgment for the defendants, concluding that the officer's actions were authorized by the Tennessee statute, which was constitutional. The court of appeals reversed the decision of the district court, and the state of Tennessee appealed to the U.S. Supreme Court.

The Supreme Court acknowledged that governments have a legitimate interest in law enforcement. But the Court opined that the use of deadly force to apprehend nonviolent suspects tends to frustrate the interests of the individual, society, and judicial determination of guilt and punishment. The Court also stated that where a suspect poses no immediate threat to an officer and no threat to others, the harm resulting from failing to apprehend him does not justify the use of deadly force to do so. Finally, the Court held the Tennessee statute invalid.

A person is also justified in using reasonable force in defense of another person when he honestly and reasonably believes that the other is in immediate danger of unlawful bodily harm from his assailant. Deadly force is reasonable only when the attack of the assailant upon the third person reasonably appears to the defender to be a deadly attack, that is, that the third person would have a right to defend himself with deadly force.

Excusable Homicides

Excusable homicides are those homicides to which the law does not attach criminal guilt but that are not authorized by the law. Although these defenses excuse homicide, they are not justifications for it. Excusable homicides include duress, necessity, involuntary intoxication, mistake of fact, mistake of law, and incapacity (infancy, insanity).

ASSAULT, BATTERY, MAYHEM, AND RAPE

Assault

As **assault** is generally one of two things. It is either an attempt or a threat to inflict harm (battery) upon a person, or an intentional placing of another person in apprehension of being harmed.

In the "attempted harm" type of assault, a person must take substantial steps toward the actual infliction of harm. For example, someone is guilty of assault if he throws a rock at another, intending to hit her. This is so even if the intended victim was unconscious, asleep, or otherwise unaware of the activity. It is generally required that the wrongdoer come reasonably close to committing the battery to be guilty of assault. For example, if a wrongdoer throws a rock at someone, it would likely have to be shown that he was close enough to actually hit the person. If the victim was clearly out of range, no assault would be committed.

In the "fear-of-harm" type of assault, a person must intend to cause apprehension in the victim and that apprehension must actually exist in order to show assault. So, for example, if A points an unloaded gun at C who knows that the gun is unloaded, A is not guilty of an assault, even though A intended to cause apprehension. The fear engendered in the victim must be a reasonable one. The wrongdoer must have the apparent intent *and* present ability to commit a battery. If it is obvious to the victim that the wrongdoer is unable or unwilling to carry out the threat, no assault is committed.

In addition to these common law elements and definitions, each state has its own definitions of assault. Each state also has unique statutes covering specific kinds of assaults, including the unauthorized administration of an intoxicant that substantially impairs his/her conduct or reasoning ability, **stalking**, assault on a child, gang assault, and menacing behavior. New York also makes "hazing" illegal in the context of initiation into or affiliation with any organization where substantial risk of physical injury is involved (*N.Y. Criminal Code,* § 120.16). *Stalking* is a Class 1 misdemeanor in Virginia (e.g., VA Code § 18.2–60.3) as well as in other states and is usually considered a subdivision of assault.

Battery

A **battery** is the unlawful application of force to the person of another or to an extension of the other. The application of force must be unwanted; a person who consents to such force cannot be the victim of a battery. Thus, in a wrestling match, each contender consents to a certain amount of physical contact. But even in this situation, an intentional punch in the face is beyond the scope of consent and may constitute a battery. The same is true of a medical procedure. The only thing that prevents a surgeon's activities on a patient from being a battery is that there is consent. It would be a different story, however, if the surgeon would go beyond the level of consent and perform a procedure for which consent has not been given.

MAYHEM In 1993 John Wayne Bobbitt and his wife, Lorena Bobbitt, had significant marital problems allegedly stemming from a combination of the couple's financial troubles, John's extramarital affairs, and his intensifying emotional and physical abuse of his wife. Their troubles peaked on June 23, 1993, when John came home to their Manassas, Virginia, apartment intoxicated after a night of partying and allegedly forced his wife to have sex, Lorena later testified during a 1994 court hearing.

Lorena was traumatized by the experience. In a state of shock she got out of bed and went to the kitchen for a drink of water. While there she noticed an eight-inch carving knife on the counter and when she picked it up "memories of past abuse raced through her head," such as the first time he raped her, "the put-downs," and the abortion. Lorena then went to the bedroom with the knife in hand, removed the sheets that covered her sleeping husband, and cut off almost half of his penis, the report further suggested (*Virginia v. Lorena Bobbitt*, 1994).

As John lay in shock losing vast amounts of blood, Lorena left the apartment, got in the car, and drove off. In her panic she hadn't realized that she was still clutching John's penis. Horror struck, she rolled down the window of the moving vehicle and threw it out into a field. When she recovered her senses, she stopped and called 911. John was rushed to the hospital, where he was treated for his horrendous wound. He was informed that he would likely never be able to have sex again because his organ sustained such massive damage. Yet, hours later after an exhaustive search, the police located his penis. They packed it in ice and rushed it to the hospital.

Surgeons operated on John for more than 9 hours to reattach his penis. The procedure was an astounding success, and doctors believed that he would regain full functioning after a yearlong recovery process. Even though they were optimistic about John's physical condition, they realized that the emotional damage would likely last much longer.

Under the common law mayhem refers to the infliction of injury that permanently renders a victim less able to fight or defend himself. This might be accomplished by dismemberment of parts of the body useful in fighting. Today, by statute, permanent disfigurement has been added, and there is no longer a requirement that the body part be of military significance. In many states the crime of mayhem is treated as aggravated assault.

Rape

Under the common law rape is defined as unlawful sexual intercourse with a female without her consent. So then, rape is committed when a man has unlawful intercourse with a woman who has fainted, is drugged, intoxicated, unconscious, or insane. This is because in all these cases the woman is incapable of giving valid consent. There are circumstances where it is rape when a man has sexual intercourse with a woman by the use of some fraud or trickery. This is referred to as *fraud in the factum* and refers to a situation where a woman is having unlawful intercourse but thought she was not having intercourse or she thought she was having intercourse with her husband. For example, if a woman has consented to a gynecological medical procedure and nothing else and the man has unlawful sexual intercourse with her, he is guilty of rape. Similarly, a man is guilty of rape if he somehow impersonates a woman's husband and she believes she is having lawful intercourse.

Many modern statutes have materially changed the common law definition creating an offense known as *statutory rape*, where the offense consists of having sexual intercourse with a female or male under statutory age. For example, Virginia law regards rape as involuntary sexual intercourse by force, threat, or intimidation, or when the victim has a mental incapacity, is physically helpless, or under 13 years of age (see Code of Virginia § 18.2–51.2).

Finally, the issue of "valid consent freely given" for lawful sexual intercourse is somewhat of a slippery slope. How much consent is valid consent? What constitutes "freely given"? The sociological and psychological aspects of this issue are especially poignant considering that for so long the male-dominant female-submissive form of "sexual courtship" was the social norm in this country (for right or for wrong). The court observed in *Deborah S. v. Diorio* (1994) that many men have been conditioned to believe that initial refusals by women are merely part of the mating game ritual, which dictates that women must resist somewhat to make themselves more attractive to men.

FORENSIC PSYCHOLOGY IN THE SPOTLIGHT
Does Fraud in the Inducement Vitiate Consent in a Rape Case?

Boro v. Superior Court (1962)

Ms. R. received a telephone call from a man who identified himself as "Dr. Stevens" and stated that he worked at Peninsula Hospital. He told Ms. R. that the results of her recent blood tests indicated that she has contracted a dangerous, highly infectious, and perhaps fatal disease. "Dr. Stevens" explained that there were two ways to treat the disease. The first was through a painful surgical procedure costing $9,000 and requiring her to remain in the hospital for six weeks (she had no insurance). The other alternative was to have sexual intercourse with an anonymous donor who had been injected with a serum that could cure the disease. This latter procedure could be conducted for a cost of $4,500 but $1,000 would suffice as a down payment. Ms. R. agreed to the nonsurgical procedure and "consented" to have intercourse with the donor.

Ms. R. was instructed to meet the donor at a specified room in the Hyatt Hotel. She then had intercourse with the "donor" after paying the $1,000. At the time of actual penetration, it was Ms. R's belief that she would die unless she consented to the intercourse.

The defendant (Daniel Boro) in this case was subsequently arrested and charged with two counts of rape as follows: Count I: section 261, subdivision (2) of the California Penal Code—rape: sexual intercourse ". . . accomplished against a person's will by means of force or fear of immediate and unlawful bodily injury on the person of another." Count II: section 261, subdivision (4)—rape: "[w]here a person is at the time unconscious of the nature of the act, and this is known to the accused."

The defendant petitioned the California Court of Appeal for a writ of prohibition to halt further prosecution of Count II of the charges, claiming that the victim was fully aware of the "*nature* of the act" in which she voluntarily engaged and that her motivation for doing so was irrelevant. The Attorney General contended the opposite and argued that the victim's agreement to intercourse was predicated on a fraudulent inducement by the defendant under the pretence that intercourse was necessary in order to save her life and that she was hence unconscious of the *nature* of the act within the meaning of the statute.

The court of appeal accepted the defendant's argument and granted the writ to set aside prosecution of Count II. In making this decision, the court relied in part on certain legal authority in the criminal law, which states,

If deception causes a misunderstanding as to the fact itself (fraud in the *factum*) there is no legally-recognized consent because what happened is not that for which consent was given; whereas *consent induced by fraud is as effective as any other consent,* so far as direct and immediate legal consequences are concerned, if the deception relates not to the thing done but merely to some collateral matter (fraud in the inducement). (Perkins & Boyce, 1982)

The court cited other decisions in California as supporting its interpretation of the statute—that in situations such as these, fraud in the *factum* serves to vitiate consent; however, fraud in the inducement does not.

Domestic Violence

Most states do not have a separate category of crime known as "domestic violence." These kinds of situations usually are subsumed under the crimes of assault, battery, aggravated assault, harassment, stalking, and rape. Some states do, however, express an awareness and concern over the phenomenon of spousal abuse and have enacted special procedures and funding to be used for investigating and prosecuting such abuse. Furthermore, in 1993, marital rape became a crime in all 50 states, at least where force is used.

In 1994, Congress also passed the Violence Against Women Act (VAWA), which declared that "all persons within the United States shall have the right to be free from crimes of violence motivated by gender" (title IV, § 40001–40703 of the *Violent Crime Control and Law Enforcement Act of 1994* HR 3355). The law was reauthorized by Congress in 2000 and again in December 2005. The bill was signed into law by President George W. Bush on January 5, 2006. On March 11, 2009, President Barack Obama signed an Executive Order to establish the White House

Council on Women and Girls. The council will provide a coordinated federal response to the challenges confronted by women and girls and to ensure that all Cabinet and Cabinet-level agencies consider how their policies and programs impact women and families. One of the main priorities of the council is to work closely with the vice president, the Justice Department's Office of Violence against Women, and other government officials to prevent violence against women, at home and abroad.

Summary

In this chapter, we defined aggression and violence and differentiated affective from instrumental aggression. We examined some of the classic theories used to explain aggressive and violent behavior, such as the instinctual hydraulic model of Lorenz and others, the XYY syndrome, Sheldon's somatotyping model, and the frustration–aggression hypothesis as proposed by Dollard and Berkowitz. The behavioral and social learning approaches to accounting for aggression were reviewed as well. These included Albert Bandura's model showing how imitation, modeling, and reinforcement are all used to learn and maintain aggressive behavior. The influence of psychoactive medications (such as various antidepressants), neurotransmitters (such as serotonin and 5-Hydroxytryptamine), hormones (e.g., testosterone), and drugs and alcohol on aggressive behavior was discussed. We also examined personality theories that might be related to aggression, such as the **five-factor model**. Disorders of personality were reviewed with specific attention given to the antisocial and narcissistic personalities. The effects of poor impulse control and deficient mood regulation on aggressive behavior were discussed, with special attention on how the presence or image of a weapon may increase aggressive tendencies. Finally, we looked at whether the government's attempts to regulate violence on television, in the movies, and in song lyrics will survive constitutional muster.

For there to be a homicide, the victim must be a "life in being" and the death must be caused by another. Murder was defined as the unlawful killing of a human being committed with malice. Murder, like all crimes, requires an *actus reus*, which is the act (or omission) that comprises the physical elements of a crime, together with a *mens rea*, which is the mental component of the crime or the "guilty mind." *Mens rea* is sometimes a difficult thing to establish. But it is clearly established when a deadly weapon is used in the commission of a crime. It is also clearly established when the defendant's conduct creates an extremely high risk of death to the victim.

First-degree murder includes murder committed with premeditation and deliberation. A killing perpetrated while "lying in wait" is also first-degree murder. This requires a watching and waiting in a concealed position with the intent to kill. The "felony murder rule" states that when a death occurs during the process of a felony, murder has been committed. This is particularly true in those felonies that are inherently dangerous to life or health and are *malum in se*. *Malum in se* crimes are crimes that by their very nature violate the natural, moral, or public principles of a civilized society.

Second-degree murder includes killing with malice aforethought, but without premeditation and deliberation; killing that results from an act done with intent to do great bodily harm (regardless of whether done with premeditation and deliberation); and killing that results from an act done with a wanton and willful disregard of an unreasonable human risk.

Voluntary manslaughter consists of an intentional homicide under extenuating circumstances, such as killing in the "heat of passion." For such an extenuating circumstance to be effective, however, the situation must be one that would arouse the passions of a reasonable person. Involuntary manslaughter is an unintentional homicide, committed without malice, which is neither justified nor excused. An example would be where a person plays with a loaded weapon in the presence of others and it goes off, killing one of those present.

A homicide is rendered noncriminal in one of two ways—by justification or by excuse. Justifiable homicide is homicide that is commanded or authorized by law. These situations include self-defense, defense of others, or a police officer using deadly force in the legal execution of his official duties. Excusable homicides are those homicides to which the law does not attach criminal guilt. These include homicides done under duress, necessity, involuntary intoxication, mistake of fact, mistake of law, and incapacity (infancy, insanity).

An assault was defined as an attempt or threat to inflict harm upon a person, or intentionally placing another person in apprehension of being harmed. A battery was defined as the unlawful application of force to the person of another or to an extension of that person. And mayhem was defined as the infliction of permanent disfigurement on a person.

Under the common law rape is unlawful sexual intercourse with a female without her consent. An essential element of this definition is that any consent must be "valid and freely given." Statutory rape is a state-defined alteration of the common law definition, in which a person is guilty if sexual intercourse takes place with a person under statutory age.

Most states do not have a separate category of crime known as "domestic violence," but these offenses are usually handled through existing laws. Child abuse and neglect is defined as "any recent act or failure to act on the part of a parent or caretaker which results in death, serious physical or emotional harm, sexual abuse or exploitation." In every state, the following people are required by law to report suspected abuse: doctors, nurses, dentists, mental health professionals, social workers, teachers, day-care workers, and law enforcement personnel.

Key Terms

Actus Reus 53
Affective aggression 39
Aggression 39
Anabolic steroids 50
Antisocial personality disorder 46
Assault 61
Battery 61
Cognitive scripts 45
Deadly weapon doctrine 53

Depraved heart killing 54
Disinhibition hypothesis 50
Felony murder 54
First-degree murder 56
Five-factor model 64
Frustration–aggression hypothesis 44
Heat of passion killing 57

Hydraulic Model 43
Instincts 42
Instrumental aggression 40
Involuntary manslaughter 59
Justifiable homicide 60
Life in being 52
Mens rea 53
Modeling 45

Narcissistic personality disorder 47
Revised frustration– aggression hypothesis 44
Stalking 61
Voluntary manslaughter 57
Weapons Effect 49
XYY Syndrome 41

Review Questions

1. How does aggression differ from "violence"? Differentiate affective aggression from instrumental aggression.
2. What is the frustration–aggression hypothesis? How is it similar to the revised frustration–aggression hypothesis?
3. According to Bandura, what group is the most prominent source of behavior modeling for children?
4. Why are antisocial and narcissistic personalities prone to aggressive behavior?

5. What is the "weapons effect"?
6. What is the common law definition of homicide?
7. What are the two essential ingredients of all criminal offenses?
8. What is the legal term for "heat of passion" killing?
9. What is the common law definition of rape? How has this definition been statutorily modified in many states?

Chapter Resources On The World Wide Web

A Web resource on the Science of the Brain
http://www.brainconnection.com/topics/?main=fa/aggression

A Web site of thought-provoking News Articles
http://www.pbs.org/wgbh/pages/frontline/

A Non-profit Publisher's cite of Scientific works
http://arjournals.annualreviews.org/

An On-Line Encyclopedia of Genetic Disorders
http://health.enotes.com/genetic-disorders-encyclopedia/

A Psychology and Crime News Cite
http://crimepsychblog.com/?cat=47

A Cite of Forensic Science terms
http://www.forensiceducation.com/sourcebooks/glossary/b.htm

The National Institute of Mental Health Web Site
http://www.nimh.nih.gov/nimhhome/index.cfm

An Overview of the Court System in the United States
http://library.thinkquest.org/2760/intro.htm

Famous criminal murder trials
http://library.thinkquest.org/2760/

The Legal Information Institute
http://www.law.cornell.edu/wex/index.php/Main_Page

The Journal of Criminal Law and Criminology
http://www.law.northwestern.edu/jclc/

title 18 of the U.S. Code: Crimes and Criminal Procedure
http://www4.law.cornell.edu/uscode/html/uscode18/usc_sup_01_18.html

For Further Reading

Allen, L., & Santrock, J. (1993). *The contexts of behavior psychology.* Madison, WI: Brown & Benchmark Press.

Bandura, A. (1972). *Aggression: a social learning analysis.* Englewood Cliffs, New Jersey: Prentice-Hall.

Bandura, A. (1975). *Social learning & personality development.* NJ: Holt, Rinehart & Winston.

Brownmiller, S. (1975). *Against our will: Men, women, and rape.* NY, NY: Simon & Schuster.

Capote, T. (1994). *In cold blood: A true account of multiple murder and its consequences.* New York, NY: Vintage Books.

Cleckley, H. (1964). *The mask of sanity.* St. Louis, MO: Mosby.

Dressler, J. (1990). Hating criminals: How could something that feels so good be wrong? *88 Michigan Law Review 1448: Michigan Law Review Association.*

Fromm, E. (1973). *The anatomy of human destructiveness.* New York, NY: Holt, Rinehart and Winston.

Green, E. (1993). *The intent to kill: Making sense of murder.* Baltimore, MD: Clevedon Press.

Jacobs, S. (2006). *Case studies in criminal procedure.* Upper Saddle River, NJ: Pearson Prentice-Hall.

Kaplan, J., & Weisberg, R. (1991). *Criminal law: Cases and materials,* 2nd ed. Boston, MA: Little, Brown.

Reisner, R, Slobogin, C., & Rai, A. (2004). *Law and the mental health system.* St. Paul, Minn: West Publishing Company.

Schmalleger, F. (2002). *Criminal law today.* Upper Saddle River, NJ: Pearson Prentice-Hall.

CHAPTER 4

Nonviolent Crimes

CHAPTER OBJECTIVES

After reading this chapter you would:

- Be able to differentiate between the concepts of possession, custody, and title.
- Know the components of the common law crime of robbery.
- Be able to explain the different forms of white-collar crime.
- Understand the definition of common law burglary.
- Know some of the major crimes against the administration of justice.
- Know what constitutes crimes against the public order.
- Understand how obscenity laws are limited by the U.S. Constitution.
- Understand the motivations of Americans who commit espionage.

INTRODUCTION

Much of the American legal system originates from the *common law* of England. The term *common law* is derived from the medieval theory that the law as administered by the king's courts represented the common custom of the realm, as opposed to the custom of local jurisdictions that was applied in local or "manorial" courts. In its early development, common law was largely a product of three English courts: the King's Bench, the Exchequer, and the Court of Common Pleas. The common law tradition recognizes private property rights as an important part of the rules that govern society. An important holdover from English common law in the United States, and clearly incorporated into our Constitution, is the right accorded to citizens in the protection of one's property, both real and personal.

As American government has expanded, so has the need for regulation; out of this was born the modern *statutory law,* or laws enacted by authorized powers of the state. These laws serve the purpose of combining common law offenses into distinct crimes. As our society and system of government have become more complex, there has developed the need for laws protecting their own integrity, the public order, and the administration of justice. Some of these statutory laws are discussed below.

THEFT CRIMES

Larceny

Common law **larceny** is defined as the trespassory taking and carrying away of the tangible personal property of another with the intent of depriving the other person of the property permanently or for an unreasonable period of time.

What is a reasonable period of time under the above definition depends on the nature of the property. For example, the use of an automobile for one day would probably not qualify as theft, but the use of a bouquet of freshly cut roses for the same time probably would. If a person takes the personal property of another with the intent of returning it within a reasonable period of time, the property must be returned to a place where the owner is substantially certain to find it, but not necessarily to the exact place from which it was taken. Whether or not taken property qualifies as larceny depends on how the owner was deprived, not on how a potential thief may use it. A person who takes the property of another with the intent of destroying it, selling it, or giving it away has the intent to steal under the law.

The concept of possession is important to understand within the framework of larceny. **Possession** means the legal right to control an object physically for a reasonably long period of time. This must be distinguished from **title**, which connotes legal ownership. A person who has title to property does not have possession if he/she has leased the property to another, or has given another a possessory lien on the property. Possession is also to be distinguished from **custody**, which is a momentary physical control subject to the right of another person to regain physical control at any time. So, for example, J, the owner of an automobile, takes it to a garage for repair of a broken radiator. The mechanics repair the car. J, without paying the bill and without permission of the garage owner, goes onto the garage lot and takes the car. J is guilty of larceny because, although he still has title to the vehicle, the garage has a possessory lien on the car.

Embezzlement

Embezzlement is the fraudulent conversion of tangible personal property of value from another person after the wrongdoer has already obtained lawful possession. Unlike the crime of larceny, which requires the taking and carrying away, embezzlement involves the conversion of property in a way that seriously interferes with the owner's rights to the property. This can be accomplished by using the property for an extended period of time, selling it, damaging it, or somehow unreasonably withholding possession.

If the property in question is a deposit in a checking account on which the wrongdoer is an authorized signatory, conversion has occurred if he draws a check without authorization payable to himself or to another person. Conversion (and embezzlement) also occurs if one forges the endorsement on a check or draws an unauthorized check to pay his own expenses or for his own uses.

Receiving Stolen Property

The crime of *receiving stolen property* essentially requires both receiving the stolen property and knowing that the property is stolen. To be guilty of receiving stolen property, one only needs to control its disposition or act as a broker in selling it even without ever physically receiving it. For there to be a crime, the goods must in fact be "stolen." If someone receives goods that he/she believes are stolen, but are not, no crime has been committed. The test of "knowledge" is a subjective one that involves what the receiver of the goods actually knew, not what a reasonable person "should have known" under the circumstances. But the fact that a recipient had actual knowledge that goods were stolen may be inferred from the circumstances. For example, if the recipient paid a price for the goods that were way below the going price, or the transaction was conducted with much secrecy, the inference that the buyer had guilty knowledge may be raised.

Is there a Difference between "Possession" and "Custody"?

United States v. Mafnas (1983)

Mafnas was employed with the Guam Armored Car Service that was hired by the Bank of Hawaii and the Bank of America to deliver bags of money. On three occasions Mafnas opened the bags and removed money. As a result he was tried and convicted of three counts of stealing money from two federally insured banks (a federal crime) in violation of 18 U.S.C. § 2113(b). The Ninth Circuit (which includes Hawaii) had in the past ruled that § 2113(b) applies only to common law larceny, which requires a possessory taking. Mafnas argued that there was no possessory taking in this case since he had lawful possession of the bags, with the consent of the banks, when he took the money.

The appeals court pointed out that the law distinguishes between "possession" and mere "custody." Mafnas was given only temporary custody to deliver the money bags to various destinations. His later decision to take the money was larceny, because it was beyond the consent of the owner, who retained constructive possession until the custodian's task was completed.

The central concept here is that if a person receives property for a limited or temporary purpose, only *custody* is acquired. Accordingly, if a person receives property from the owner with instructions to deliver it to the owner's house, he is acquiring custody and nothing more. But if he decides to keep the property for himself, it would be *larceny* (Torcia, 1980). This was the legal reasoning behind the appeals court upholding Mafna's conviction for the crime of larceny.

Robbery

The common law felony of **robbery** consists of larceny from a person by violence or intimidation. For there to be a robbery, the essential elements of larceny must be present (i.e., there must be a trespassory taking and carrying away of someone's tangible personal property with the specific intent of depriving him of it permanently), plus there must be the use of force or intimidation or the threatened use of force. Since robbery is an intent crime, an intoxicated person cannot commit the offense if he is too intoxicated to form the required intent. Likewise, if a person's personal property was intentionally destroyed by another under threat or intimidation, but there was no carrying away, there would be no robbery.

When property is taken by actual force, the force must be greater than the amount necessary to permit the taking and carrying away of property. For example, if a wrongdoer stealthily removes an expensive watch from a victim almost without being noticed, larceny has been committed but not robbery. On the other hand, if the victim is held down or his arm twisted in order to effectuate the crime, it is robbery.

When property is taken by intimidation, the words, gestures, or actions of the wrongdoer must create an apprehension of danger in the victim. It is the fear instilled in the victim that is the controlling factor in robbery. For example, if a holdup is committed with a toy gun (no real danger present) but the victim believes the gun is real and is in fear, there is a robbery. On the other hand, if there is indeed an actual threat but no realization by the victim, then there is no robbery. For example, if a pickpocket armed with a loaded pistol approaches someone from behind and takes his wallet without his knowledge, the crime committee is larceny, not robbery.

White-Collar Crime

The term **white-collar crime** was originally used to refer to a crime committed by a person of respectability and high social status. Although there has been some debate as to what qualifies as a white-collar crime, the term today generally encompasses a variety of nonviolent crimes usually committed in commercial situations for financial gain. Many white-collar crimes are especially difficult to prosecute because the perpetrators are sophisticated criminals who have attempted to conceal their activities through a series of complex transactions. The most common white-collar offenses include:

1. *Antitrust Violations*—Infractions of the Sherman Antitrust Act (15 U.S.C. § 1–7) and the Clayton Act (15 U.S.C. § 12–27). The goal of antitrust laws is to shelter trade and commerce from price fixing, monopolies, et cetera, and to foster competition.

2. *Computer and Internet Fraud*—Fraud of this type includes using or applying for credit cards online under false names, unauthorized use of a computer, manipulation of a computer's files, and computer sabotage.

3. *Credit Card Fraud*—The unauthorized use of a credit card to obtain merchandise.

4. *Phone and Telemarketing Fraud*—According to the U.S. Department of Justice, telemarketing fraud is any scheme to defraud in which the perpetrators use the telephone as the primary means of communicating with the potential victims of the scheme. Typical fraudulent telemarketers use multiple aliases, telephone numbers, and locations. They frequently change their product line, sales pitch, and recently many have moved their operations to Canada in response to effective U.S. law enforcement efforts.

5. *Health Care Fraud*—Types of fraud include kickbacks, billing for services not rendered, billing for unnecessary equipment, and billing for services performed by a less-qualified person. The health care providers who engage in these fraud schemes encompass all areas of health care, including hospitals, home health care, ambulance services, doctors, chiropractors, psychiatric hospitals, laboratories, pharmacies, and nursing homes.

6. *Insurance Fraud*—A variety of fraudulent activities committed by applicants for insurance, policy holders, third-party claimants, or professionals who provide insurance services to claimants. Such fraudulent activities include inflating or "padding" actual claims and fraudulent inducements to issue policies and/or establish a lower premium rate.

7. *Mail Fraud*—Using the U.S. Mail in furtherance of a criminal act.

8. *Securities Fraud*—Theft from manipulation of the market, theft from securities accounts, and wire fraud.

9. *Cellular Phone Fraud*—The unauthorized use, tampering, or manipulation of a cellular phone or service. This can be accomplished by either use of a stolen phone or where an actor signs up for service under false identification or where the actor clones a valid electronic serial number (ESN) by using an ESN reader and reprograms another cellular phone with a valid ESN number.

Although white-collar criminal charges are usually brought against individuals, corporations may also be subject to sanctions for these types of offenses. The penalties for white-collar offenses include fines, home detention, community confinement, costs of prosecution, forfeitures, restitution, supervised release, and imprisonment. However, sanctions can be lessened if the defendant takes responsibility for the crime and assists the authorities in their investigation. Any defenses available to non-white-collar defendants in criminal court are also available to those accused of white-collar crimes. Many individuals or organizations facing white-collar criminal charges claim the defense of *entrapment,* in which they are somehow "induced" by law enforcement to commit the crime. For instance, in *United States v. Williams* (1983), one of the cases arising from Operation Abscam, Senator Harrison Williams attempted unsuccessfully to argue that the government had induced him into accepting a bribe.

Both state and federal legislation enumerate the activities that constitute white-collar criminal offenses. The Commerce Clause of the U.S. Constitution gives the federal government the authority to regulate white-collar crime, and a number of federal agencies, including the Federal Bureau of Investigation (FBI), the Internal Revenue Service, the Secret Service, U.S. Customs, the Environmental Protection Agency, and the Securities and Exchange Commission, participate in the enforcement of federal white-collar crime legislation. In addition, most states employ their own agencies to enforce white-collar crime laws at the state level.

CRIMES AGAINST PROPERTY

Burglary

The idea that "a man's castle is his home" runs deep in Anglo-American culture. Many of the early settlers in America came from the English town of Colchester, where in 1575, armed townspeople first challenged the queen's soldiers from entering homes without a warrant. Lord Pitt's famous speech in the House of Commons expressed these sentiments:

> The poorest man may in his cottage bid defiance to all the forces of the Crown. It [his home] may be frail, its roof may shake, the wind may blow through it, the storm may enter, but the King of England himself cannot enter. All the King's forces dare not enter, nor cross the threshold of the tenement. (Samaha, 1999)

Common law **burglary** is the breaking and entering of the dwelling of another in the nighttime with the intent to commit a felony therein. Under the common law it was required that the breaking and entering occur at night in a place where people live and sleep. One also is "breaking" if he enters a dwelling with consent through an open door, if such consent was procured through fraud or trickery. For example, if a wrongdoer gained entry to a home by posing as a telephone repairperson, there would be a breaking. Force or intimidation used to gain entry is likewise a breaking. Furthermore, if someone enters a house without breaking, burglary will still have been committed if that person, once inside, then opens a door to gain entry to another part of the house.

Upon breaking, if any part of the wrongdoer's body crosses into the dwelling through the opening made by the breaking, then there has been an entry. It does not have to be the person himself who enters the dwelling to constitute burglary; his instrumentality, such as an accomplice, tool, or child, will suffice. Under most modern statutes, the definition of "breaking and entering" has been modified by statute so as not to require a dwelling house, but can be any enclosure used for living, even including mobile homes.

Legally, "nighttime" is defined as whenever it's too dark to discern a person's face or to recognize them. This element is intended to get at the characteristics of stealth, disguise, or cover-up common to burglaries. But only about half of all burglaries are committed at night, and all states today recognize daytime burglaries with nighttime intrusions as an *aggravating* circumstance. Some states have eliminated the nighttime element completely. Burglary also does not require a one-night action; a person can commit a "breaking" on one night and an "entering" on another night.

Arson

Arson is another crime that has been significantly expanded in scope by state legislatures. Under the common law, **arson** is defined as the malicious burning of the dwelling of another. There must be an actual burning to constitute arson. The burning need not be extensive to constitute arson, and the building need not be destroyed. However, mere scorching (blackened change in appearance) will not suffice. The common law requires that the burning in arson involve the very structure of the building; however, modern statutes have extended the crime to burning the personal property (including vehicles) of another. The requirement that a dwelling be that of "another person" has also been repealed in most jurisdictions and replaced with "the property of himself or of another."

In many modern statutes arson is typically graded into first degree (homes, schools, churches), second degree (unoccupied structures, vehicles), and third degree (personal property). As arson is a crime against possession, not ownership, it's possible for a person to be charged with burning their own house, or committing an arson against themselves. Some states reserve their harshest punishments for arson with intent to defraud (arson for profit or arson for hire). Some states also have the offense of aggravated arson, which is similar to felony murder, but carries additional penalties if a firefighter gets injured while trying to put out the fire. Making a false bomb threat or false fire alarm is also a separate, but related offense in most states.

Can a Federal Arson Charge be applied to Private Residences?

Jones v. United States (2000)

Jones threw a Molotov cocktail into the home of his cousin, causing severe damage to the building. He was convicted under 18 U.S.C. § 844(i), which makes it a federal crime to maliciously damage or destroy by means of fire or an explosive any building used in interstate or foreign commerce or in any activity affecting interstate or foreign commerce. The government argued that the private residence in question was used in interstate commerce in three ways. First, it was used as collateral to secure a mortgage from an out-of-state (Oklahoma) lender. Second, it was used to obtain casualty insurance from another out-of-state (Wisconsin) insurer. Finally, the house also was used to receive natural gas from sources outside Indiana. Jones appealed his conviction, arguing that 18 U.S.C. § 844(i), as applied to the arson of a private dwelling, exceeded Congress's Commerce Clause powers. The court of appeals affirmed the conviction.

The U.S Supreme Court overturned the conviction holding that an owner-occupied residence not used for any commercial purpose does not qualify as "property used in commerce" or "commerce-affecting activity" and therefore damaging it is not a federal offense. The Court also expressed that Congress did not define the crime described in the statute to cover the explosion of a building whose damage or destruction "might" affect interstate commerce, but rather that the "function of the building" under ordinary circumstances affected interstate commerce. In addition, the Court noted that a house used for everyday living is not the same as a house with commercial value (such as renting apartments).

Finally, the Court noted that if Congress wanted to make arson (as traditionally handled by the states) a federal crime, it would do so.

CRIMES AGAINST THE ADMINISTRATION OF JUSTICE

Crimes against justice are common law misdemeanors that hinder, corrupt, or impede the functioning of the judicial branch of government. Crimes such as bribery, subornation of perjury, and tampering with witnesses or evidence are typical examples, but then there are crossover crimes, like tax evasion, where taxes support not only the judicial branch, but the whole government. Some of these "crossover" crimes include *counterfeiting* (the making of false money, bonds, postage stamps, and postal money orders) and *tax evasion* (paying less in taxes than the law permits or committing fraud in filing or paying taxes. Also included in this category would be *money laundering* (the investment or other transfer of money flowing from illegal sources into legitimate channels so that its original sources cannot be traced); *resisting arrest* (evading, resisting, or escaping from a lawful detention by police officers acting in their official law enforcement capacity); *obstruction of justice* (impeding or obstructing those who seek justice in a court, or those who have duties or powers of administering justice); *perjury* (the willful taking of a false oath in a judicial proceeding with regard to material matter at issue before the court); *subornation of perjury* (procuring or inducing another to commit the crime of perjury); *barratry* (exciting and stirring up lawsuits between people); *bribery* (the tender or receipt of anything of value to (or by) a public office holder with the intent that the public office holder will be influenced in the performance of his/her official duties); and *contempt* (the willful disregard of the authority of a court or legislative body).

CRIMES AGAINST THE PUBLIC ORDER

Public order crimes are those that disturb the public peace and tranquility. These offenses include such things as disturbing the peace; disorderly conduct; affray (fighting in public); vagrancy; illegal loitering; carrying weapons; public intoxication; inciting a riot; unlawful assembly; criminal nuisance; harassment; falsely reporting an incident; disturbance of a religious service; drug offenses (opiates, heroin, cocaine, crack, marijuana); driving while intoxicated; cigarette smoking by minors; prostitution; precocious sex (underage sex); pornography; gambling; gang activities; adultery and fornication; bigamy; keeping a house of ill fame (bawdy house); cruelty to animals; urinating in public; sleeping in public; and appearing nude in public. A final category, deviant sex (paraphilias), will be discussed separately in another chapter.

Laws regarding crimes against public order and morals are generally ways of upholding minimum standards of decency and civility. Most such laws have ancient roots, but in modern times they have come to be associated with efforts to improve the quality of life or with the legislation of morality. These crimes have in the past been known as "consensual crimes" or "**victimless crimes**"; however, this is a misnomer in that they involve acts that interfere with the operations of society and the ability of people to function efficiently. Moreover, as there are frequently secondary victims (family, friends) to these crimes, their status as victimless crimes is questionable.

At common law, the mutual combat of two or more persons in a public place is termed an *affray*. This is an unpremeditated event that occurs spontaneously in a public place to the terror of the people there. When three or more persons assemble by design in a public place for any unlawful purpose or under such circumstances as to endanger the public peace, the common law classifies it as an *unlawful assembly* (Black, 1990). At common law, an unlawful assembly becomes a *rout* when four or more persons take steps toward the performance of their purpose. If they put their design into actual execution, it is a *riot*.

Vagrancy and Loitering

In this country, as in England before it, vagrancy and loitering laws have been used to protect society from vagabonds, paupers, and beggars who wandered about from place to place without any visible means of support. Vagrancy laws are much broader than disorderly conduct laws. Some states use the term *loitering* rather than *vagrancy,* which is often defined as being in a place at a time and in a manner not usual for law-abiding individuals and under circumstances that warrant alarm for the safety of persons or property in the vicinity.

Most vagrancy and loitering laws (with the exception of curfew and truancy laws) have been held to be too broad, in violation of the due process requirements of the Fourteenth Amendment to the U.S. Constitution, that is, individuals were not adequately warned of what conduct was forbidden, and the police had too much discretion in deciding whether to make an arrest. Enforcement of such laws often violated the protections of the **First Amendment**, especially when police used them against political demonstrators and unpopular groups. U.S. vagrancy laws generally punish the status of being a vagrant and not some overt act. This approach derives from English laws of the sixteenth century that generally failed to distinguish between the indigent and the criminal and that set harsh punishments, including whipping and transportation to the colonies. England gradually modified its poor laws and today punishes only overt acts dangerous to the community (Ribton-Turner, 1887).

Prostitution

Prostitution is generally defined as the act or practice of engaging in sexual activity for money or its equivalent. Except for parts of Nevada, it is a criminal act in the United States. The greatest health consequences of prostitution are drug abuse, violence, and sexually transmitted infections, including HIV/AIDS, gonorrhea, pelvic inflammatory disease, and syphilis. The risk for HIV infection has increased because of multiple partners and limited safe sex practices—some customers are willing to pay more for a sexual encounter if they do not have to use a condom.

Prostitutes are often victimized by the person for whom they work and by their customers. Other health issues related to prostitution are early pregnancy for juveniles, rape, tuberculosis, post-traumatic stress disorder, assault, and other acts of violence—including murder. There are also negative consequences besides those related to health issues. In places where it is common, prostitution lowers the value of property and the attractiveness of communities.

Obscenity

Any prohibition on the use or sale of obscene material must not fly afoul of the Constitution's First Amendment safeguards. In 1957, in *Roth v. United States* (1957), the Supreme Court distinguished between "sex" and "**obscenity**." The Court ruled that the latter was not constitutionally protected speech under the First Amendment. Then in 1973, in *Miller v. California* (1973) the Court specifically held that to be obscene (and thus not protected as free speech) objectionable material must meet all of the following requirements:

1. The average person, applying contemporary community standards, would find that the work, taken as a whole, appeals to the **prurient interests**.
2. The work depicts or describes, in a patently offensive way, sexual conduct specifically defined by the applicable statute.
3. The work, taken as a whole, lacks serious literary, artistic, political, or scientific value.

Building on the *Roth* and *Miller* cases, the Model Penal Code states that "material is obscene if, considered as a whole, its predominant appeal is to prurient interest, that is, a shameful or morbid interest in nudity, sex, or excretion, and if in addition it goes substantially beyond customary limits of candor in describing or representing such matters" (Model Penal Code § 251.4).

But First Amendment restrictions on censorship are relaxed when it comes to **child pornography**. To protect children from being exploited by producers of child pornography, the U.S. Supreme Court has allowed the government to ban visual sexually explicit material that does not even rise to the level of obscenity. Unlike the case with obscenity, to be banned, child pornography does not have to be as hard core as obscenity and is limited to visual material involving real minors. Such statutes are aimed at protecting children from being exploited and abused by attempting to dry up the demand for such materials.

All states prohibit child pornography. Child pornography may encompass either the creation or reproduction of materials depicting minors engaged in actual or simulated sexual activity or the publication or distribution of obscene, indecent, or harmful materials to minors. All such laws require actual knowledge, or reason to know, that the person portrayed or the recipient of the obscene, indecent, or harmful material is a minor. A few states also penalize the distribution, with reckless disregard, of obscene or indecent materials to minors. The states generally provide defenses to the publisher or distributor where some reasonable attempt has been made to discern the age of the recipient of the obscene, indecent, or harmful material.

Public Intoxication

Being drunk in public constitutes being intoxicated while in a public place. The legal standard for public intoxication almost always requires that a person be so drunk as to be a danger to themselves or others. California's drunk in public law is typical of those around the country. It provides that it is illegal to be in any public place under the influence of intoxicating liquor (or combination of liquor and drugs), in such a manner as would constitute a threat or danger to the person or others, or interfere with the use of sidewalks, streets, or roads (California Penal Code § 647 (f)).

Can a Law against Distributing Nonobscene Child Pornography be Valid?

New York v. Ferber (1982)

A New York bookstore proprietor was selling films depicting young boys masturbating. He was convicted under a state statute prohibiting persons from knowingly promoting a sexual performance by a child under the age of 16 by distributing material that depicts such a performance. The statute defines "sexual performance" as any performance that includes sexual conduct by such a child, and "sexual conduct" is in turn defined as actual or simulated sexual intercourse, deviate sexual intercourse, sexual bestiality, masturbation, sado-masochistic abuse, or lewd exhibition of the genitals.

The defendant (bookstore proprietor) asserted that the statute violated the First Amendment by being both underinclusive and overbroad. The trial court held that, in light of the explicit inclusion of an obscenity standard in a companion statute banning the knowing dissemination of similarly defined material, the statute in question could not be construed to include an obscenity standard and therefore would prohibit the promotion of materials traditionally entitled to protection under the First Amendment. The appellate division of the New York Supreme Court affirmed.

The New York Court of Appeals (the highest state court) reversed, holding that the statute in question does not violate the First Amendment as applied to the states through the Fourteenth Amendment.

The court of appeals reasoned that the states are entitled to greater leeway in the regulation of pornographic depictions of children for the following reasons: (1) the legislative judgment that the use of children as subjects of pornographic materials is harmful to the physiological, emotional, and mental health of the child; (2) the advertising and selling of child pornography provide an economic motive for, and are thus an integral part of, the production of such materials, an activity illegal throughout the nation; and (3) recognizing and classifying child pornography as a category of material outside the First Amendment's protection is not incompatible with previous decisions dealing with what speech is unprotected. The court stated, that when material, such as that covered by the New York statute, drastically and pervasively impacted on the welfare of children engaged in its production, the balance of competing interests is clear, and it is permissible to consider these materials as not having First Amendment's protection.

CRIMES AGAINST THE STATE

Treason

In designing the Constitution, the Framers adopted two of the three formulations of the English Statute of Treason enacted in 1350. But they conspicuously omitted the phrase defining treason as including "imagining the death of our lord the King," under which most of the English law of "constructive treason" had been developed.

Treason is the only crime specifically defined in the Constitution. It is one of those crimes that is sometimes also referred to as "crimes against the government" and "firing squad offenses." Similar and related crimes would be *espionage* (spying or being a party to spying); *insurrection* or *rebellion* (arming oneself or one's group to the point that makes it creates a reasonable expectation that force or violence would be used against the U.S. government); *mutiny* (unlawfully taking over command of the U.S. government, any part of the U.S. government, or any part of the armed forces); *sabotage* (damaging or tampering with any national defense material or national defense utilities); *sedition* (communication intended to stir up treason or rebellion against the government); *subversion* (transmitting blatantly false information in hopes of helping the enemy); *syndicalism* (organizing a political party or group advocating the violent overthrow of the U.S. government); and *terrorism* (the systematic use of violence or threats of violence to intimidate or coerce the government or whole societies by targeting innocent noncombatants).

Article III, Section 3, Paragraph 1 of the U.S. Constitution says,

Treason against the United States, shall consist only in levying War against them, or, in adhering to their Enemies, giving them aid and comfort. No Person shall be convicted of treason unless on the Testimony of two Witnesses to the same overt Act, or on Confession in open Court (Article 3, U.S. Constitution).

The case of *United States v. Haupt* (1942) further clarified the definition of treason to mean any act that strengthens or tends to strengthen the ability of the enemies of the United States or that weakens or tends to weaken the power of the United States to resist such enemies.

Not until World War II did the Supreme Court of the United States further review a treason conviction. Two cases in the Supreme Court and five in the U.S. Courts of Appeal established that for a successful prosecution under the "aid and comfort" provision of treason, four points must be proven beyond a reasonable doubt. First, there must be an overt act; second, there must be testimony by two witnesses; third, the behavior of the accused must manifest an intent to betray the United States (which can be inferred from the overt act itself); and fourth, the act must provide aid and comfort to the enemy.

The first three elements of the crime of treason are generally not difficult to prove because they are objective in nature. More specifically, selling goods to enemies of the United States, statements made that praise the enemy, residing in the country of an enemy, delivery of a prisoner to the enemy, surveillance of a nuclear plant, broadcasting of enemy propaganda, and torturing American prisoners of war are all manifestly overt acts. The requirement for two witnesses is also objective in nature, as is the intent to betray. It is the final element of the crime of treason that has been the most difficult to prove, that is, providing "aid and comfort" to an enemy of the United States.

There has been recent disagreement whether a "levying war" charge requires that the United States actually be at war. For example, Were the activities of the American John Walker-Lindh with the Taliban and al-Qaeda in Afghanistan treasonous even though the United States was not formally at war? The answer is probably no. But neither the constitutional law pertaining to treason nor the legal commentary interpreting that law seems to suggest that a formally declared war is a necessary element of the crime of treason. Accordingly, this is not a settled question.

The U.S. Code further clarifies the definition of treason:

Whoever, owing allegiance to the United States, levies war against them or adheres to their enemies, giving them aid and comfort within the United States or elsewhere is guilty of treason and shall suffer death, or be imprisoned for not less than five years, and fined not less than $10,000; and shall be incapable of holding office under the United States. (18 U.S.C. § 2381)

The modern treason statute basically follows the language of the constitutional provision. Other provisions of Title 18 criminalize various acts of war making and adherence to the enemy. These include destruction of aircraft or aircraft facilities (Section 32), use of weapons of mass destruction (Section 2332a), acts of terrorism transcending national boundaries (Section 2332b), providing material support to terrorists (Section 2339A), providing material support to certain terrorist organizations (Section 2339B), misprision of treason (Section 2382), rebellion or insurrection (Section 2383), seditious conspiracy (Section 2384), enlistment to serve in armed hostility against the United States (Section 2390), and prohibiting the making or receiving of any contribution of funds, goods, or services to terrorists (31 FR Section 595.204).

Espionage

Espionage is spying for a foreign government. The Federal Espionage Act states,

Whoever, when the United States is at war, shall willfully make or convey false reports or false statements with intent to interfere with the operation or success of the military or

Does Dual Nationality Alter Allegiance to the United States?

Kawakita v. United States (1952)

Kawakita was a native-born citizen of the United States and also a national of Japan by reason of Japanese parentage and law. While a minor, he took the oath of allegiance to the United States, went to Japan for a visit on an American passport, and was prevented by the outbreak of war from returning to this country. During the war, he turned 18 in Japan, changed his registration from American to Japanese, showed sympathy with Japan and hostility to the United States, served as a civilian employee of a private corporation producing war materials for Japan, and brutally abused American prisoners of war who were forced to work there. After Japan's surrender, he registered as an American citizen, swore that he was an American citizen and had not done acts amounting to expatriation, and returned to this country on an American passport.

In 1952 he was charged and convicted of treason. Claiming that he had renounced his American citizenship in Japan during the war, he appealed his conviction to the U.S. Supreme Court. The Court ruled that the evidence of whether Kawakita had intended to renounce his American citizenship was one for the jury, and their verdict that he had not intended to do so was based on sufficient evidence. In sustaining the conviction, the Court stated that an American citizen owes allegiance to the United States wherever he may reside, and dual nationality does not alter the situation.

naval forces of the United States or to promote the success of its enemies and whoever, when the United States is at war, shall willfully cause or attempt to cause insubordination, disloyalty, mutiny, or refusal of duty, in the military or naval forces of the United States, or shall willfully obstruct the recruiting or enlistment service of the United States, to the injury of the service or of the United States, shall be punished by a fine of not more than $10,000 or imprisonment for not more than twenty years, or both. (18 U.S.C. § 793)

Why would a hitherto loyal American commit espionage against the United States? According to the Defense Personnel Security Research Center there are certain conditions that make it likely that a disaffected or troubled employee would actually commit a serious betrayal of trust like espionage. These conditions are as follows:

1. An opportunity to commit the crime. "Opportunity" is of two types: (a) access to information or material that can be exchanged for money or used to achieve some other goal, and (b) personal acquaintance with, or easy access to, persons expected to be interested in obtaining such valuable information or material.
2. A motive or need to be satisfied through the crime.
3. An ability to overcome natural inhibitions to criminal behavior, such as moral values, loyalty to employer or coworkers, or fear of being caught.
4. A trigger that sets the betrayal in motion.

Technological advances, such as the widespread use of the Xerox copiers in the 1950s, have made it increasingly difficult to control the distribution of sensitive information. It is now also possible to commit crimes while sitting at one's computer engaged in what appears to casual observers as normal activity. In June 1996, the FBI had 800 open investigations of economic espionage involving 23 different countries (Geide, 1996).

When considering motives for espionage, it is useful to remember that the real motive may be different from the surface appearance. Although financial motivation is important, many people who commit espionage for money have more pressing *emotional needs* than financial needs. The true motivation is almost always deeper than what may appear on the surface—money, ideology, or revenge. For example, spies value money not just for what it can buy, but for what it symbolizes—success, power, and influence. It helps to sooth for injured self-esteem. People commit espionage not just for money, but in a desperate attempt to fulfill complex emotional needs. Espionage may also be an expression of power to influence events (satisfy a frustrated sense of self-importance), an outlet for anger (restore damaged self-image by outsmarting or punishing the bosses who failed to recognize one's talents), a means of revenge, or a source of excitement.

A government survey of the 98 Americans who were arrested for espionage (i.e., "being spies") since the start of the cold war revealed certain commonalities. One of the most surprising outcomes of the study is that many Americans who became spies volunteered their services to a foreign government. They were not enticed or coerced into treasonous activity (Gelles, n.d.). The study also indicated that spies are often emotionally disturbed or suffer from a personality disorder. Of the personality disorders found in spies, the two most common are antisocial personality disorder and narcissistic personality disorder. The traits inherent to these disorders that are associated with a predilection to espionage include rejection of the standards of society, lack of guilt feelings or remorse, manipulative and self-serving attitudes, deficient ability to form close personal attachments, undeserved and grandiose feelings of self-importance, and tendencies to react to criticism or failure with disdain and rage.

One thing that almost all spies have in common is an inability to accept responsibility for their own actions. They tend to blame others for their problems and minimize or ignore their

FORENSIC PSYCHOLOGY IN THE SPOTLIGHT
Who was one of the most Damaging Spies in U.S. History?

United States v. Robert Philip Hanssen (2001)

Robert Philip Hanssen had been an FBI agent for 27 years when he was charged in 2001 with spying for Russia for more than 15 years. He was arrested in a park near his home in Vienna, Virginia, as he dropped off a bag containing seven secret documents at a covert location. For most of his FBI career Hanssen had worked in counterintelligence, and he made use of what he had learned in his own espionage career. He was charged with espionage and conspiracy to commit espionage. Specifically, Hanssen provided first the Soviets and then the Russian government over 6,000 pages of classified documents and the identities of three Russian agents who were actually working for the United States. Two of these agents were tried in Russia and executed. According to court documents, Hanssen provided information on "some of the most sensitive and highly compartmented projects in the U.S. intelligence community" as well as details on U.S. nuclear war defenses. In return, the Russians paid him $1.4 million over the period of his espionage activities, including over $600,000 in cash and diamonds and $800,000 deposited in a Russian bank account. Hanssen was finally identified after the United States obtained his file from a covert source in the Russian intelligence service.

However, the Russians never knew Hanssen's true name. To them, he was known only as "Ramon" or "Garcia."

It is believed that Hanssen was involved with the Soviets beginning in 1979, broke off the relationship in 1980, but again volunteered to engage in espionage in 1985 by sending an unsigned letter to a KGB officer at the Soviet Embassy in Washington, DC. Although Hanssen's motives are unclear, they seem to have included ego gratification, disgruntlement with his job at the FBI, and a need for money. He and his wife struggled to provide for his large family on an agent's salary and by 1992 had incurred debts of over $275,000. Hanssen exploited the FBI's computer systems for classified information to sell, and he kept tabs on possible investigations of himself by accessing FBI computer files. As is often the case in these situations, friends and coworkers could not explain how this supposedly deeply religious father of six and ardent anticommunist could have been leading a double life. A large part of his illegal income is believed to have been used to buy expensive gifts and a car for a local stripper. In July 2001, a plea agreement was reached by which Hanssen would plead guilty to espionage, fully cooperate with investigators, but avoid the death penalty. On May 11, 2002, the former FBI agent was sentenced to life in prison.

The government's sentencing memorandum stated in part that "Robert Philip Hanssen is a traitor. For all the words that have been written about him, for all the psychological analyses, . . . at the end of the day, [that is] all that really warrants being said about [him]. . . ."

own mistakes or faults. One example of blaming others comes from the reports by convicted spies when they say that stealing information was too easy, because physical security was too lax. They argued that if tighter security had been in place it would have been more of a deterrent and they might not have got into trouble. They blamed the organization for their problems because it didn't do enough to protect secret information (Weiner, 1994).

Summary

This chapter dealt with crimes that are generally not considered to be violent. Some of these are common law crimes that have been codified by local statutes and ordinances. Others are federal constitutionally derived offenses.

At common law, the offense of larceny consists of the trespassory taking and carrying away of the tangible personal property of another. Larceny is an intent crime where the wrongdoer must have the intent of depriving the other person permanently of their property. Possession refers to the legal right to control an object physically for a reasonably long period of time. Title connotes legal ownership. A person may have title to property yet not possession. This may occur if the property has been leased to another person. Custody is the momentary physical control of property subject to the right of another person to regain physical control at any time.

Common law robbery consists of larceny from another person by violence or intimidation. For there to be a robbery all the elements of larceny must be present in addition to violence or the threat of violence. White-collar crime is a nonviolent crime usually committed in commercial situations for financial gain.

Common law burglary is the breaking and entering of the dwelling of another in the nighttime with the intent to commit a felony therein. Under most modern statutes, the breaking and entering does not have to be a dwelling house, but can be any enclosure used for living, including mobile homes. Under most statutes, the intent to commit any crime has replaced the felony requirement. Arson is a crime that has been significantly expanded in scope by state legislatures but almost always involves malicious burning.

Crimes against justice are common law misdemeanors that hinder, corrupt, or impede the functioning of the judicial branch of government. Crimes such as bribery, perjury, subornation of perjury, and tampering with witnesses are

typical examples, but then there are also crossover crimes, like tax evasion, counterfeiting, and bribery, which would fit into this category.

Public order crimes are those that disturb the public peace and tranquility of a community. These offenses include disturbing the peace, disorderly conduct, vagrancy, public intoxication, inciting a riot, unlawful assembly, and others. Some crimes in this category are referred to as consensual or victimless crimes (e.g., prostitution). Prohibition on the sale of obscene material falls into this category, and such laws must comply with the First Amendment (free speech) as elucidated in the Supreme Court cases of *Roth v. United States* and *Miller v. California*, where legal distinctions were made between "sex" (protected speech) and "obscenity" (nonprotected speech), with obscenity being that which appeals to prurient interests by contemporary community standards. Free speech restrictions on prohibiting sexual images are relaxed, however, when it comes to child pornography.

Treason is the only crime specifically defined in the Constitution. Similar and related crimes would be insurrection, mutiny, sabotage, sedition, subversion, and espionage. Espionage consists of spying for a foreign government. Although financial motivation is usually a factor in this crime, many people who commit espionage have more pressing emotional needs such as revenge, success, power, and influence. Espionage may also be an expression of power to influence events (satisfy a frustrated sense of self-importance), an outlet for anger (restore damaged self-image by outsmarting or punishing the bosses who failed to recognize one's talents), a means of revenge, or a source of excitement. There is also evidence that such individuals are often emotionally disturbed or suffer from a personality disorder.

Key Terms

Arson *71*
Burglary *71*
Child pornography *75*
Custody *68*

Embezzlement *68*
Espionage *76*
First Amendment *73*
Larceny *68*

Obscenity *74*
Possession *68*
Prurient interests *74*
Public order crimes *72*

Robbery *69*
Title *68*
Victimless crime *73*
White-Collar Crime *69*

Review Questions

1. What is the common law definition of larceny?
2. What is the difference between title, custody, and possession?
3. What is the common law definition of robbery?
4. List some examples of white-collar crimes.
5. How has the common law definition of burglary been modified by modern statutes?
6. Why have public order crimes such as prostitution been referred to as "victimless" crimes?

7. Under the common law, differentiate "riot" from "rout"?
8. What is the only crime expressly defined in the Constitution?
9. What are the three essential elements of the crime of treason?
10. Aside from money what are some of the motivations for espionage?
11. What one personality trait do almost all people who commit espionage share?

Chapter Resources on the World Wide Web

Cornell University Legal Information Institute
http://www.law.cornell.edu/wex/index.php/White-collar crime

U.S. Supreme Court Cases—OYEZ
http://www.oyez.org/

New York State Law
http://ypdcrime.com/index.htm

Find Law for Legal Professionals
http://caselaw.lp.findlaw.com/data/constitution/article03/24.html#f1286

Code of Virginia
http://leg1.state.va.us/000/src.htm

Web Journal of Current Legal Issues
http://www.webjcli.ncl.ac.uk

Stanford Law & Policy Review
http://www.stanford.edu/group/SLPR

California Court and Judicial System
http://www.courtinfo.ca.gov

Exploring the Mind of the Spy
http://www.usda.gov/da/ocpm/Security%20Guide/Treason/Mind.htm

For Further Reading

Blount, E. C. (2002). *Occupational crime: Deterrence, investigation, and reporting in compliance with federal guidelines.* Baco Raton, FL: CRC Publications.

Podgor, E. S. (2004). *White collar crime in a nutshell (nutshell series).* St. Paul, MN: Thomson West.

Bruce, J. W., & Ely, Jr., J. W. (1994). *Cases and materials on modern property law* (American Casebook Series). St. Paul, MN: West Publishing Co.

Maxim, P., & Whitehead, P. (1998). *Explaining crime, fourth edition.* St. Louis, MO: Butterworth-Heinemann.

Ronczkowski, M. R. (2003). *Terrorism and organized hate crime.* Baco Raton, FL: CRC Publications.

Stoebuck, W. B., & Whitman, D. A. (2000). *The law of property.* St. Paul, MN: West Publishing Company.

Ziff, J., & Sarat, A. (1999). *Espionage and treason (crime, justice, and punishment).* New York: Chelsea House Publications.

CHAPTER 5

Mass Murders and Serial Killers

CHAPTER OBJECTIVES

After reading this chapter you would:

- Know the five types of mass murders.
- Understand the kind of mass murder Andrea Yates is associated with.
- Know the kind of mass murder Charles Whitman and James Huberty are associated with.
- Understand what kind of mass murder Seung-Hui Cho is associated with.
- Understand the meaning of spree murder.
- Know the meaning of serial murder.
- Understand the various motive-based typologies of serial killers.
- Know the difference between organized and disorganized types of serial killers.

INTRODUCTION

The concept of multiple murder (also referred to as multicide) is both frightening and fascinating. High-profile cases of mass murder, spree murder, and serial murder have been exceptionally newsworthy for many years, and there is no sign of this appeal letting up. Even the film media has reflected society's morbid curiosity with this subject dating back to the 1960s with films such as *Psycho, Helter Skelter, Bonnie and Clyde, The Boston Strangler, Summer of Sam, The Red Dragon,* and many more.

The killing of multiple victims is classified according to variables such as time intervals between killings, location(s) of the killings, and the number of people killed. The three categories of multiple murder are (1) mass murder, (2) spree murder, and (3) serial murder. Each of these groups can be further divided into subcategories dependent upon factors such as the killer's motivation, relationship to the victims, the types of weapons used, and degree of organization of the crime. This chapter will explore these various types of multiple murders, examine possible explanations for the acts, and provide in-depth case examples.

MASS MURDER

Typically, **mass murder** is a single episodic act of violence, occurring at one time and in one place. Most authorities have stipulated three as the minimum number of victims necessary for an event to be classified as a mass murder. Mass murder is defined then as the killing of three or more persons at a single location with no **cooling-off period** between the killings (Bartol & Bartol, 2004).

Mass murderers are generally divided into the following types: disciple killers, family annihilators, pseudocommandos, school shooters, disgruntled employees, and set-and-run killers. In addition, the term *rampage killer* is often used to describe an individual who sets out, typically with an arsenal of guns, to kill as many people as he can, sometimes randomly and sometimes those against whom he has a grievance (Dietz, 1982).

The **disciple killer** follows the dictates of a charismatic leader. In 1969 Leslie Van Houten, Lynette Fromme, Tex Watson, Bobbie Beausoleil, and others fell under the spell of their charismatic leader, Charles Manson. The motivation for mass murder for the disciple killer is usually external to the killer; it is the leader of the group who orders the killing and the followers who obey in order to achieve a degree of psychological gain, that is, acceptance by the leader, who must be obeyed at all costs. The process is akin to "brainwashing." The victims, typically strangers, are selected by the leader, and the orders are carried out by the dispatched disciple or dicsciples (Holmes & Holmes, 2001).

The **family annihilator** is a person who kills an entire family at one time. The killer is usually a male who is depressed (often psychotically) and often with a history of alcohol abuse. The motivation for the killing typically lies within the internal psychological world of the individual. He often feels alone, helpless, and hopeless when he decides to kill his family. His primary motivation may be suicide, and he kills his family to save them from the resulting remorse and embarrassment. In 1982, George Banks shot 13 family members and relatives for unknown reasons, and in 1988, David Brown in Minnesota axed four family members to death for no clear reason.

These killers certainly do not have to be men. In 1994 Susan Smith drowned her children by pushing her car into a lake while they were strapped in child restraint seats. In 2002 Andrea Yates systematically drowned her five children in the bathtub. More recently, in Washington, DC, in 2008, U.S. marshals were enforcing an eviction notice on one Banita Jacks when they encountered more than they bargained for. The home had no furnishings on the entire first floor, which was spray painted with bizarre writing, and a foul stench permeated the house. When the marshals went upstairs they found the corpses of Jacks's four daughters, ranging in age from 5 to 17, in an advanced state of decomposition. Ms. Jacks reportedly told investigators that the children were "possessed by demons" and died in their sleep. They had been dead for at least four months.

The **pseudocommando** is preoccupied with weaponry of all sorts. He often keeps semiautomatic pistols, sniper rifles, assault weapons, and even machine guns in his house. When he kills, it is usually after a long period of deliberation and careful planning. Motivation for killing usually rests in the internal world of the killer. He may wish to "teach the world a lesson" in a generalized way, call attention to one issue or another, or exact revenge against individuals or systems that have "done him wrong." The majority of pseudocommando mass murderers are driven by revenge, and their victims seem to be chosen because of their actions or because of what they represent to the killer (Fox & Levin, 1998). Sometimes the motivation relates to the desire of the killer or killers to live on in history. Colorado students Eric Harris and Dylan Klebold, who killed 12 fellow students and a teacher in a commando-style attack at Columbine High School in Littleton, Colorado, in April 1999, are considered pseudocommando killers. Likewise, Virginia Tech shooter Cho Seung Hui, who systematically killed 32 people on April 16, 2007, is seen as a pseudocommando killer.

Although there are individualized personality, environmental, and cultural factors at play in each stereotypic mass murderer, there are surprisingly uniform factors present as well. For example, the pseudocommando killer, almost always a male, is usually a loner and has been since childhood. Growing up in a broken and dysfunctional home, he feels rejected and alone and cannot form close or lasting relationships. He consequently becomes obsessed with *power* at its most basic level. He may seek early entry into the armed forced or dress in battle dress uniforms and be attracted to activities suggesting power and bravado, such as martial arts and weapons. He develops a hatred for groups of people whom he can blame for his own weaknesses and misfortune. These may include certain ethnic groups, past employers, or government officials.

Over time the future killer becomes more and more frustrated with the world and his own inability to achieve or obtain what he believes others have. He wants people to know who he is, to make a name for himself. His grasp on what is real decreases until something occurs that triggers his final separation from reality. This may be a rejection by a woman, a reprimand or demotion at work, a termination, or a slight by a person on the street or a merchant. At this point he may spontaneously erupt or make the final decision to make his place in history by going out in a homicidal blaze of glory (Fox, Levin, & Quinet, 2005; Lane & Gregg, 2004; Newton, 2000).

Table 5.1 provides a survey of mass murders in the United States beginning in 1857. **School shooters** reveal additional idiosyncratic personality features and reactionary patterns to

TABLE 5.1 Survey of Mass Murders, 1857 to Present

Date	Location	Name	Number Killed	Notes
1857	Mountain Meadows, Utah	John D. Lee	120	Entire families shot down as they traveled from Arkansas to Utah
1866	Philadelphia, Pennsylvania	Anton Probst	8	Lured eight people into a barn and axed them to death
1927	Bath, Michigan	Andrew Kehoe	45	A discontented school board member blew up the school
1928	Butler, Kansas	Owen Oberst	7	Killed entire family, said, "I just got mad at them and shot them"
1942	Chatsworth, Georgia	Mark Pulliam	6	Killed family, burned down house, possibly for insurance payoff
1943	Purcellville, Virginia	Thomas Clatterbuck	5	A debtor kills man who lent him money, along with his family
1949	Camden, New Jersey	Howard Unruh	13	Shoots neighbors out of retaliation for perceived slights
1950	Yuma, Arizona	William Cook	5	After being released from prison, he shot entire family and the dog
1953	Chicago, Illinois	Vincent Ciucci	4	Shoots wife and three children
1954	Colorado	Frank Archina	3	Heated argument with in-laws resulted in mass murder
1955	Denver, Colorado	John Graham	44	Planted a bomb in mother's suitcase before she boarded a plane
1958	Wolcott, Kansas	Lowell Andrews	3	Shot his family dead then faked a burglary and went to see a movie
1959	Halcomb, Kansas	Richard Hickock & Perry Smith	4	Stabbed and shot an entire family
1959	Houston, Texas	Paul Orgeron	4	Man used a bomb to kill two teachers and two children in a school
1963	Green Bay, Wisconsin	Harry Hebard	5	Following a quarrel with his stepmother, boy killed his family
1966	Austin, Texas	Charles Whitman	16	From an observation deck at the University of Texas, he sniped at people below

(continued)

TABLE 5.1 Continued

Date	Location	Name	Number Killed	Notes
1966	Mesa, Arizona	Robert Smith	5	Left a beauty salon, told police "I just killed five women in there"
1967	Lock Haven, Pennsylvania	Leo Held	6	Shot coworkers and neighbors who "annoyed him"
1969	Beverly Hills, California	Charles Watson, Patricia Krenwinkel, Linda Kasabian, and Susan Adkins	9	Brutally and ritualistically stabbed nine people for Charles Manson
1970	North Carolina	Jeffrey MacDonald	3	Stabbed three members of his family
1971	Westfield, New Jersey	John List	5	Shot his entire family, was apprehended 18 years later
1971	Jacksonville, Florida	James Edward Pough	12	After his car was repossessed, shot many people at car finance office
1972	Cherry Hill, New Jersey	Edwin Grace	6	With two sawed-off rifles, he entered an office and opened fire
1973	New Orleans, Louisiana	Mark Essex	7	Stormed into a Howard Johnson's motel "to kill white people
1973	Seminole County, Georgia	Carl Isaacs	5	During a burglary, methodically shot an entire family
1974	New Orleans, Louisiana	Mark Essex	9	Hatred for whites caused a shooting spree, mostly police were killed
1974	Amityville, New York	Ronald DeFeo	6	Shot an entire family, claimed he was possessed by Satan
1975	Wintergarten, Florida	Bill Ziegler	4	Shot customers in a store
1975	Hamilton, Ohio	James Ruppert	11	Methodically guned down every member of his immediate family
1975	Lincoln, Nebraska	Erwin Simants	6	While drunk, he sexually assaulted his neighbor, then killed her family
1976	Fullerton, California	Edward Allaway	7	A janitor at Cal State shot students at close range in the library
1976	Montvale, New Jersey	Harry De La Roche	4	Young man bludgeoned family rather than return to the Citadel
1977	New Rochelle, New York	Frederick Cowan	6	Shot coworkers, self-professed Nazi
1977	Prospect, Connecticut	Lome J. Acquin	9	Stabbed, bludgeoned, and burned entire family
1978	Casa Grande, Arizona	Gary Gene Tison & Randy Greenawalt	4	Kidnapped a family for their car, killed them all with a shotgun
1978	Rockford, Wisconsin	Simon Nelson	6	Stabbed and bludgeoned entire family over pending divorce
1980	Reno, Nevada	Priscilla Joyce Ford	6	Goes on a five-block-rampage in her 1974 Lincoln
1982	Miami, Florida	Carl Brown	8	Unhappy with work done on his lawnmower, he killed eight in store
1982	Pennsylvania	George Banks	13	Shot family and guests

TABLE 5.1 Continued

Date	Location	Name	Number Killed	Notes
1982	Los Angeles, California	Humberto de la Torre	25	Set fire to an apartment building after a dispute with the manager
1982	Tarrant County, Texas	Larry Keith Robison	5	He decapitated his roommate and killed four others as well
1982	Marrero, Louisiana	Leslie Lowenfield	5	He barged into girlfriend's home and killed everyone present
1982	Mitchelville, Maryland	Edward Mann	2	A masked man drove a car into an office building shooting people
1983	New Orleans, Louisiana	Michael Perry	5	Shot entire family
1983	Seattle, Washington	K. Mak, Tony & Banjamin Ng	14	Shot members of a gambling club in Chinatown
1983	McCarthy, Alaska	Louis Hastings	12	Killed a dozen residents of a small Alaska town
1984	San Ysidro, California	James Huberty	21	Shot patrons at a McDonald's, dubbed "McMurder" by the press
1984	Dallas, Texas	Abdelkrim Belachheb	6	Shot dance partner and then opened up on nightclub
1984	Los Angeles, California	John Orr	4	Former fire department captain used arson to commit his murders
1985	Philadelphia, Pennsylvania	Sylvia Seegrist	3	Paranoid schizophrenic woman shot people randomly at a mall
1986	Edmond, Oklahoma	Patrick Sherrill	14	Shot coworkers at a Post Office
1987	Dover, Arkansas	Ronald Gene Simmons	16	Strangled entire extended family one at a time as they arrived at his house
1987	Tacoma, Washington	Daniel Patric Lyman	7	Killed entire family then killed himself
1987	Elkland, Missouri	James Schnick	7	Killed family and blamed 14-year-old nephew for the crime
1987	Palm Bay, Florida	William B. Cruse	6	Thought that neighbors were taunting him, so he killed them
1987	San Luis Obispo, California	David Burke	43	Vengeful fired employee shot boss on plane then blew it up
1988	Noble, Illinois	Christopher Churchill	5	Killed his family with hammer to "relieve stress"
1988	Sunnyvale, California	Richard Farley	7	Used shotgun to kill former boss and coworkers
1988	Davidson, North Carolina	Michael Hayes	4	Mentally ill man starting shooting at neighbors
1988	Algona, Iowa	Robert Dreesman	6	Killed family because he was jealous of his sister
1988	Winnetka, Illinois	Laurie Dann	2	Shot six students, killed one, then she shot a passerby
1988	Greenwood, So. Carolina	James Wilson	2	He shot seven students and two teachers; two 8-year-old girls died
1989	Stockton, California	Patrick Purdy	5	Used AK-47 to kill 5 children and wound 30 others at a school

(continued)

TABLE 5.1 Continued

Date	Location	Name	Number Killed	Notes
1989	Louisville, Kentucky	Joseph Wesbecker	7	Killed coworkers at a printing plant where he worked
1989	Glen Ellen, California	Ramon Salcido	6	Killed five family members and then his supervisor at work
1990	Lincoln Park, Michigan	Lawrence DeLisle	4	Drowned his four children in the Detroit River
1990	Bronx, New York	Julio Gonzalez	87	Rebuffed by girlfriend, he set fire to night club she was attending
1991	Phoenix, Arizona	M. McGraw, L. Bruce, and M. Nunez	9	Went on a shooting spree in a Buddhist Temple
1991	Columbus, Ohio	Kim Chandler	3	Shot her children while suffering from postpartum depression
1991	La Grange, Kentucky	Michael Brunner	3	Shot girlfriend and her two children
1991	Ridgewood, New Jersey	Joseph Harris	4	A fired postal employee killed supervisor and other coworkers
1991	New York, New York	Andrew Brooks	4	Shot father and three other men
1991	Honolulu, Hawaii	Orlando Ganal	4	Shot four people including his wife's parents
1991	Belton, Texas	George Hennard	22	Shot 22 people in cafeteria while yelling "This is payback day"
1991	Harrodsburg, Kentucky	Robert Daigneau	4	Shot wife and three strangers
1991	Iowa City, Iowa	Gang Lu	5	After not receiving an academic award, he shot five in physics lab
1991	Concord, New Hampshire	James Colbert	4	Shot wife and three children, said "If I can't have them nobody can"
1992	Huntsville, Alabama	Robert Coulson	5	Systematically killed his family for "spending his inheritance"
1992	Morro Bay, California	Lynwood Drake	6	Killed six, left note saying "I have been persecuted my whole life"
1992	Olivehurst, Ca	Eric Houston	4	Killed four students and wounded ten at his former high school
1993	Long Island, New York	Colin Ferguson	6	Shot and killed six passengers on the Long Island Railroad
1993	San Francisco, California	Gian Luigi Ferri	8	Rampaged through a law firm shooting lawyers
1995	Harlem, New York	Ronald Smith	7	Barricaded seven people in a store and set fire to it
1995	Bronx, New York	Michael Vernon	5	An argument with a shoe store employee prompted this mass slaying
1995	Potomac, Maryland	Bruman Alvarez	5	A house painter bludgeoned the family in the house he was painting
1996	Jackson, Mississippi	Kenneth Tornes	5	After killing wife, he went to fire department to "hunt his bosses"
1996	Chicago, Illinois	Richard Speck	9	Killed nine nurses in a university dormitory
1996	Glendale, California	Jorjik Avanesian	7	Killed his wife and six children by torching their apartment

TABLE 5.1 Continued

Date	Location	Name	Number Killed	Notes
1996	Albuquerque, New Mexico	Shane Harrison & Esther Beckley	5	A store robbery turned deadly and five were gunned down
1996	Lawrence County, Ohio	Todd Hall	8	Ignited a box of fireworks inside a fireworks store, killing 8
1996	Portland, Oregon	Ray Martin DeFord	8	Eleven-year-old boy set fire to his apartment complex killing eight
1996	Bandon, Oregon	Girley Logsdon Crum	5	Slashed five people to death in a trailer park
1997	Fort Wayne, Indiana	Joseph Corcoran	4	Believed family members were talking about him, killed them all
1997	Wheeling, West Virginia	Mark Storm	5	Left mental hospital and proceeded to kill family
1997	Holton, Tennessee	Daryl Keith	4	Killed four family members with a semiautomatic weapon
1997	Shelbyville, Tennessee	Daryl Keith Holton	4	In an attempt to "resolve" a custody dispute, he killed entire family
1997	Wilmington, Delaware	Richard Herr	3	Opened fire at work killing three
1997	Oklahoma City, Oklahoma	Danny Keith Hooks	5	Bound, gagged, and stabbed to death five women
1998	Arkansas, Kansas & Florida	Daniel Remeta	5	Went on a robbing and killing spree in three states
1998	Dallas, Texas	Reginald Sublet	4	Put ex-girlfriend and three others into a garage and gassed them all
1998	Santa Clarita, California	Sandi Nieves	4	During a bitter custody dispute she asphyxiated her four daughters
1999	Abilene, Texas	Arthur Goodman	4	Killed girlfriend and three of her friends
1999	Kansas City, Kansas	Richard Gary Beach	5	Killed family members and hid bodies in his house
1999	Las Vegas, Nevada	Zane Michael Floyd	4	Opened fire in a supermarket with a pump-action shotgun
1999	Brier, Washington	Lonnie Davis	4	Killed four neighbors in a shooting spree, but spared the dogs
1999	Memphis, Tennessee	Alan Eugene Miller	3	A man who "kept to himself" shot three office coworkers
1999	Sidney, Ohio	Lawrence Michael Hensley	4	Involved with devil worship, he shot members of a rival cult
1999	Fort Worth, Texas	Larry Gene Ashbrook	7	Opened fire in Baptist Church while shouting anti-Baptist rhetoric
1999	Jefferson County, Arkansas	Clay Smith	5	Shot four family members plus the baby sitter
1999	St. Louis, Missouri	Nevelyn Stokes	6	Bent on revenge over a fight, he burned down the man's house
1999	Atlanta, Georgia	Mark Barton	12	After killing his ex-wife and two children, he shot nine coworkers
1999	Honolulu, Hawaii	Byron Uyesugi	7	Shot and killed seven coworkers at Xerox building

(continued)

TABLE 5.1 Continued

Date	Location	Name	Number Killed	Notes
1999	Baton Rouge, Louisiana	Shon Miller	4	Shot four people to death in a church
1999	Aurora, Calorado	Nathan Dunlap	4	At Chuck E Cheese, his former employer, he shot four coworkers
2000	Lawrence, Minnesota	Larry Dame	5	Killed family, later said "I better kill them before they kill me"
2000	Colville, Washington	William Lembcke	4	Killed family after having argument with his father
2000	Pittsburgh, Pennsylvania	Baumhammers, Richard	5	Neo-Nazi went on a shooting spree at two shopping centers
2000	Tampa, Florida	Dexter Alonzo Levingston	5	Killed a family of five in a suburban Tampa neighborhood
2000	Boston, Massachusetts	Michael McDermott	7	Using a semiautomatic weapon he killed seven coworkers
2001	Rifle, Colorado	Mike Stagner	4	Angered over growing Hispanic population, went on shooting spree
2001	Sioux City, Iowa	Adam Moss	7	Murdered girlfriend, her mother, and associates
2001	Sacramento, California	Joseph Ferguson	5	Killed former coworkers stating, "It's time to feed the news media"
2001	Sacramento, California	Nikolay Soltys	6	Stabbed to death six members of his family
2002	Mesa, Arizona	Kemp Crowley	5	Allegedly shot his family dead
2002	Detroit, Michigan	John Wolfenbarger	5	Shot entire family during robbery, execution-style
2002	Yamhill County, Oregon	Robert Bryant	6	Shot family and self
2003	Marion, Mississippi	Douglas Williams	5	Shot and killed five coworkers before killing himself
2005	Red Lake, Minnesota	Jeff Weise	9	Killed grandfather and friend, then a teacher and students at school
2006	Lancaster, Pennsylvania	Charles Carl Roberts	5	Took hostage and killed five girls in a one-room Amish school
2007	Salt Lake City, Utah	Sulejmen Talovic	5	In a six minute rampage, he shot 5 people in a shopping mall
2008	Dekalb, Illinois	Steven Kazmierczak	5	Five dead, 19 wounded, gunman was described as a "quiet person"
2009	Alabama countryside	Michael McLendon	10	Killed 10 people on a rampage across Alabama seeking revenge on former employers and co-workers he believed had wronged him
2009	Carthage, North Carolina	Robert Stewart	8	Fatally shot eight people and injured three others at a nursing home before a confrontation with a police officer ended the attack
2009	Binghamton, New York	Jiverly Wong	14	Entered a New York State Immigration office shooting clients before turning the gun on himself

Sources: Fox, J. A., & Levin, J. (2005). *Extreme killing: Understanding serial and mass murder*. Thousand Oaks, CA: Sage; Fox, J. A. & Levin, J. (1998). Multiple homicide: Patterns of serial and mass murder. *Crime and Justice, 23*, 407; Bartol, C. R. & Bartol, A. M. (2004). *Introduction to forensic psychology*. Thousand Oaks, CA: Sage Publications, p. 147; Fox, J. A., Levin, J., & Quinet, K. (2005). *The will to kill*. Upper Saddle River, NJ: Pearson, p. 136; Lane, B., & Gregg, W. (2004). *The encyclopedia of mass murder*. New York, NY: Carroll & Graf Publishers; Leyton, E. (1986). *Hunting humans: The rise of the modern multiple murderer*. Toronto, Ontario: McClelland and Stewart.

campus life. American society is steeped in beauty, attraction, popularity, and social status. Males who are unattractive and who have few or no compensatory skills are continuously subjected to frustration, social isolation, and rejection, especially from women and others who appear to be part of certain social cliques found on campus. Students who are seen as being unattractive can be socially ostracized, rejected by members of the opposite sex and not invited to become a part of the social order. In both high school and college settings these disenfranchised young men are unsympathetically called geeks, gangly, skinny, dorks, and/or ugly.

There are other factors that often distinguish adolescent from adult mass murderers. First, as mentioned above, adolescent killers experience a high rate of bullying compared with a baseline of most students, who report being bullied at least once. About 14% of both boys and girls have experienced trauma from bullying abuse. When the killer reciprocates with lethal violence, he/she shows identification with the aggressor, now reversing roles and assuming the aggressive posture. A second difference between adolescent and adult mass murderers is that one out of four mass killings by adolescents involves killings in pairs. This may be a means of seeking approval from a peer, which is part of adolescent development. Almost always, one perpetrator is dominant (Meloy et al., 2001). Table 5.2 provides a sample of school shootings in the United States from 1979 onward, in cases where the shooters were students.

Disgruntled Employees

Disgruntled employees are often former employees of a company who have been counseled, disciplined, dismissed, or placed on some form of medical leave or disability. The individual retaliates for this perceived injustice by going to the place where he once worked and killing former fellow employees either randomly or selectively. In November 1991, Thomas McIlvane, dismissed from his job as a mailman, entered the loading dock of the post office in Royal Oak, Michigan, and walked around the building spraying fire from a Ruger semiautomatic carbine, killing three supervisors and wounding 14 onlookers, before shooting himself. The same year, Joseph M. Harris, a former mail sorter in Ridgewood, New Jersey, stabbed his former supervisor to death with a samurai sword, he then visited his former workplace and shot dead two more postal workers. In a note left at his home, he evoked the 1986 murder by another disgruntled post office employee, of 14 people in a post office in Edmond, Oklahoma. Similarly, on July 8, 2003, in Lauderdale County, Mississippi, an employee of a Lockheed Martin plant armed with a shotgun and a semiautomatic rifle went through the entire facility and shot workers randomly. Five workers were killed, and eight others were injured. The shooter committed suicide. And on July 2, 2004, in Kansas City, Kansas, a former employee shot and killed four people at the ConAgra Foods Inc. meatpacking plant. The gunman walked into the cafeteria shortly after 5:00 P.M. and began firing; then he killed himself. At least three other people were injured.

Although the average age of murderers in general is 29 years, a notable exception exists with workplace avengers, where the average age is 38 years. Nearly 93% of these killers are male, and 75% are white. As is the case with pseudocommando killers, there are also various uniform factors present in disgruntled employee workplace killers. He is usually a middle-aged white male who has been overinvested in his job and devastated by problems at work, which he sees as a harbinger of the end of existence as he knows it. It is a sobering fact that despite the changing gender roles in this society during the last 35 years, men still tend to evaluate their self-worth based on what they do rather than who they are. "If they aren't doing anything, then what good are they?" (Fox et al., 2005. p. 137).

Almost all workplace avengers feel somehow "justified" in their actions and perceive themselves as the victim. They believe they have been treated unfairly by the boss and by coworkers. They feel that management and the system are corrupt and must be taught a lesson. Finally, for many isolated workers who may already live on the edge of society, termination from a job means much more than a loss of income and self-esteem; it also means the loss of companionship by not having his coworkers anymore.

TABLE 5.2 Survey of School Mass Murders Committed by Students, 1979 to Present

Date	Location	Name	Number Killed	Notes
1979	San Diego, California	Brenda Spencer, age 16	2	Said she "didn't like Mondays"
1983	St. Louis, Missouri	David F. Lawler, age 14	2	Angry over remarks made about his older brother
1988	Oakland, South Carolina	William Wilson, age 19	2	He was angry at being ridiculed for being overweight
1993	Grayson, Kentucky	Scott Pennington, age 17	2	Shot English teacher in the head, then shot the janitor
1996	Moses Lake, Washington	Barry Loukaitis, age 14	3	Opened fire in algebra class
1997	Lynnville, Tennessee	Jamie Rouse, age 19	2	Went on a shooting rampage over poor grades
1997	Bethel, Alaska	Evan Ramsey, age 16	2	Opened fire with a shotgun, killed principal and classmate
1997	Pearl, Mississippi	Luke Woodham, age 16	2	Shot fellow students, stated that he worshiped Satan
1997	West Paducah, Kentucky	Michael Carneal, age 14	3	Opened fire at prayer circle in the hallway of his high school
1998	Jonesboro, Arkansas	Andrew Golden, age 11, and Mitchell Johnson, age 13	5	Shot at classmates from woods after pulling the fire alarm
1998	Springfield, Oregon	Kip Kinkel, age 15	4	Killed parents, then two students, and wounded 20 at school
1999	Littleton, Colorado	Dylan Klebold, age 17, and Eric Harris, age 18	13	Went on shooting spree at Columbine High School, then killed themselves
2000	Savannah, Georgia	Darrell Ingram, age 19	2	Shot and killed two girls leaving a high school dance
2001	Santee, California	Charles Andrew Williams, age 15	2	Killed two students and wounded 13
2003	Red Lion, Pennsylvania	James Sheets, age 14	2	Began shooting with two handguns in his school cafeteria
2003	Cold Spring, Minnesota	Jason McLaughlin, age 15	2	Shot fellow students because of being teased
2005	Red Lake, Minnesota	Jeff Weise, age 16	9	Shot grandfather and friend, then seven others at his school
2007	Blacksburg, Virginia	Cho Seung-hui	33	In a shooting rampage, killed 33 at Virginia Tech

Sources: Lane, B., & Gregg, W. (2004). *The encyclopedia of mass murder*. New York, NY: Carroll & Graf Publishers; McBride, D. *Recent school shootings*. Geocites.com. Retrieved January 12, 2009 from http://www.geocities.com/dtmcbride/hist/mass_murderers.html#school; *Preventing school shootings*. A summary of a U.S. Secret Service school initiative report. Retrieved May 18 from http://www.ncjrs.gov/pdffiles1/jr000248c.pdf; *School shootings*. Holology by Freydis. Retrieved March 13, 2009 from http://www.holology.com/shooting.html

It is sometimes assumed that suicide is a motive of many classic mass murderers, that is, the individual plans on taking as many innocent people with him before dying either by his own hands or by the police. But this does not seem to be the case. Duwe (2000) examined 495 mass murders over a 21-year time span and discovered that only 24% of mass murderers either committed suicide or were killed by police (a phenomenon referred to as "suicide by cop"). In reality, of all mass murderers, only *family annihilators* are most likely to take their own lives.

Set-and-Run Killers

Set-and-run killers are also usually motivated by a need for revenge. But extortion, insurance fraud, and ideological motives are also frequent motives. In contrast to some mass murderers (especially family annihilators) who commit suicide at the scene or force police to kill them, these individuals will employ techniques to allow escape before the act itself occurs. For example, a set-and-run killer might plant a bomb in a building, setting a time device so that he is far away from the crime scene when the explosion occurs. In other cases, the killer tampers with a food product or a medicine, places the container back upon the shelf, and leaves. The killer, then, does not directly observe the consequences of his act. He may be in another part of the city or even in another country when the results of his actions become evident. While the offender may have particular victims in mind, he considers the death of bystanders to be unimportant.

An example of set-and-run killings would be the Tylenol poisonings, when seven people died of cyanide poisoning between September and October 1982 after ingesting Tylenol capsules. No one has ever been charged with the murders. Another example would be the case of Theodore John Kaczynski (the "Unabomber"), who sent 16 bombs through the U.S. mail between 1978 and 1995, injuring 23 people and killing 3. Before Kaczynski's identity was known, the Federal Bureau of Investigation (FBI) had used the term UNABOM (university and airline bomber) to refer to his case; hence the media latched on to this name.

Another example of set-and-run killings occurred during the course of several weeks beginning on September 18, 2001, when letters containing anthrax spores were mailed to several news media offices and two U.S. senators, killing 5 people and infecting 17 others. In the summer of 2008, the FBI was very close to making an arrest in the anthrax killings when on July 29, 2008, their prime suspect, 62-year-old Bruce E. Ivins, committed suicide. Ivins had been a scientist with the army's biological warfare labs at Fort Detrick for 18 years. He was an expert in anthrax who had complained about the limits of testing anthrax drugs on animals. The Justice Department's theory was that he allegedly released the toxin to test his treatment regimen on humans.

In what may be the most powerful piece of evidence to be released, lab records show that in September and October 2001 Ivins worked much later than usual on the nights leading up to the days on which the anthrax letters were mailed. In December 2001, he allegedly wrote a very disturbing e-mail that was released by the Justice Department. In it he stated, "I made up some poems about having two people in one (me the person in my dreams) . . . I'm a little dream-self, short and stout. I'm the other half of Bruce—when he lets me out. When I get all steamed up, I don't pout. I push Bruce aside, them [*sic*] I'm Free to run about!" (Ripley, 2008). Ivins also allegedly had a history, extending back to his graduate school days, of making homicidal threats and had been described by his former psychiatrist as "homicidal and sociopathic."

Since Ivins's death, his attorney, Paul Kemp, has repeatedly claimed he was innocent. He said Ivins cooperated fully with the FBI during two dozen interviews and passed at least two lie-detector tests. Kemp claims the FBI harassed his client for months, driving him into a spiral of alcohol and depression (*Worcester Telegram & Gazette*, 2008).

There have been numerous copycat murders using the set-and-run technique to cover up other murders. One such event took place in 1986 when Stella Nickell of Washington State killed her husband, Bruce, with cyanide-laced Excedrin to collect on his life insurance. In an attempt to cover her tracks, she also killed a complete stranger by placing three packages of tampered Excedrin and Anacin capsules on the shelves of three stores. One of the packages was purchased by Sue Snow, who became Nickell's other victim. Nickell was sentenced to 90 years in prison. Another copycat scenario took place in 1993, when Joseph Meling, also of Washington State, was convicted of murdering two people and trying to poison his wife. Meling tampered with capsules in six Sudafed packages, five of which he placed on store shelves. The sixth he gave to his wife, Jennifer, who survived the poisoning. Unfortunately, Kathleen Daneker and Stan McWhorter did not survive taking the tampered-with capsules they had purchased. The other three packages were recovered without incident (Manning, 2000).

CASE EXAMPLES OF MASS MURDERERS

Charles Joseph Whitman

Charles Joseph Whitman was born on June 24, 1941, in Lake Worth, Florida, to Margaret and Charles A. Whitman. Charles had two younger brothers. His father, a plumber turned successful contractor and businessman, was a strict disciplinarian who was known to use belts, paddles, and his fists on his wife and children. He later looked back on his treatment of his wife and children without remorse or regret. He told *Newsweek* shortly after the massacre, "With all three of my sons it was 'yes, sir' and 'no, sir.' They minded me. The way I looked at it, I am not ashamed of my spankings. I don't think I spanked enough, if you want to know the truth about it. I think they should have been punished more than they were punished" (Douglas & Olshaker, 1999, p. 278). Whitman's mother, Margaret, on the other hand, was reported by Douglas and Olshaker to be an elegant, gracious, and devoutly religious individual. At the age of six, Charles Whitman scored 138 on a test of intelligence. He was a gifted student, accomplished pianist, and reportedly the youngest Eagle Scout in the world. He was also a gun fanatic from an early age.

Despite these accomplishments, Whitman still endured his father's harsh discipline. In June 1959, shortly before Whitman's eighteenth birthday, he came home drunk from a night out with friends, whereupon his father beat him and threw him into the pool, where he nearly drowned. A few days later Charles enlisted in the U.S. Marine Corps. He quickly excelled at the use of a rifle, and the records of his scores on shooting tests show that he scored 215 out of 250 possible points, that he excelled at rapid fire from long distances, and that he seemed to be more accurate when shooting at moving targets. He was a good Marine and won a navy scholarship to attend the University of Texas in Austin where he would be expected to earn an engineering degree and follow that with Officer's Candidate School.

In 1962 Whitman married Kathy Leissner, who was also a student at the University of Texas. But it was not long before Whitman's behavior turned increasingly odd. He was arrested after poaching a deer and skinning it in his dormitory shower. In addition, his grades were poor, and he accumulated gambling debt, which he refused to pay. His scholarship was withdrawn in 1963, and he had to leave school. Back on active duty in 1963, Whitman received a court martial for threatening another soldier, gambling, and possession of a nonmilitary pistol. He was sentenced to 30 days confinement and 90 days of hard labor; he was also reduced in rank. He was discharged from the Marine Corps in December 1964 (MacLeod, 2007).

Shortly after being discharged, Whitman returned to the University of Texas where he pursued a degree in architectural engineering. To pay his tuition, he held a number of jobs: a bill collector for Standard Finance Company, a bank teller at Austin National Bank, and as a traffic surveyor for the Texas Highway Department. But he had intense marital problems and became physically abusive toward his wife. During this same time his parents divorced. He became anxious and depressed and saw a psychiatrist one time at the University Health Center where he mentioned "climbing to the top of a tower with a deer rifle and shooting people." He was prescribed Valium, which he abused. He never returned for another session. He also abused the prescription amphetamine Dexedrine, which he used to stay awake for long periods of time (Douglas & Olshaker, 1999, p. 280).

On July 31, 1966, Whitman made his final plans for what was about to happen. At 6:45 P.M., he began typing a letter of explanation and farewell. "I don't quite understand what it is that compels me to type this letter," he wrote. "Perhaps it is to leave some vague reason for the actions I have recently performed." He went on to say he'd increasingly been a victim of "many unusual and irrational thoughts" and that his attempt to get help with his problems had failed. He expressed a wish that his body be autopsied after his death to see if there was a physical cause for his mental anguish and desires to kill. He then outlined his plan for the coming 24 hours. "It was after much thought that I decided to kill my wife, Kathy, tonight after I pick her up from work at the telephone company," he revealed. At about midnight he went to his mother's apartment, strangled and stabled her to death. He then returned to his home and stabbed his wife, Kathy, five times in the chest as she slept. He also called his wife's and mother's employers telling each that they would not be at work that day. In his letter he had stated, "The prominent reason in my mind is that I truly do not consider this world worth living in, and am prepared to die, and I do not want to leave her [his wife] to suffer alone in it." He offered a similar explanation for killing his mother (Macleod, 2007).

On August 1, 1966, Whitman rented a dolly from Austin Rental Company so he could cart supplies up to the tower of the University of Texas administration building. His supplies included:

- 12 gauge shotgun
- Remington 700 rifle with scope
- ammunition box with gun-cleaning kit
- M1 Carbine
- .357 Magnum pistol
- Galesi-Brescia pistol
- Luger pistol
- machete with scabbard

- Channel Master 14 transistor radio
- .35 Caliber Remington Rifle
- 3.5 gallon jug full of water
- hatchet, hammer, canteen,
- compass, binoculars
- locking pocketknife
- hunter's body bag
- hunting knife, with scabbard

Using the badge he had from his job as a research assistant, Whitman was able to get past security checkpoints on campus. He entered the main administrative building of the university a little after 11:30 A.M. and made his way to the twenty-seventh floor. Here he encountered receptionist Edna Townsley who he knocked down to the floor with a rifle butt. A group of tourists then got out of the elevator and Whitman fired three rapid blasts from his sawn-off shotgun, killing Marguerite Lamport and teenager Mark Gabour and seriously injuring Mark's mother and brother. He barricaded the door, shot Mrs. Townsley in the head, and went out on to the observation deck.

The first shots rang out from the outer deck of the tower at approximately 11:48 A.M. Alex Hernandez, the first victim, was shot through the leg. Three more students were hit one after the other, before police officer Billy Speed responded to reports of a gunman on the roof of the administrative building. He arrived at the campus and was approaching the tower when Whitman shot him. Whitman used the tower's waterspouts as turrets, which protected him from gunfire. As an ex-Marine sharpshooter, he shot most of his victims in or around the heart. Claudia Rutt was walking up one of the malls when she clutched at her chest and fell. As her boyfriend, Paul Sonntag, reached down to her, he too was shot—both dying instantly. Harry Walchuk was 200 yards away, browsing at a newsstand, when he was hit in the throat and collapsed on to the magazine rack (Lane & Gregg, 2004, p. 353).

Police and civilians as well fired at Whitman unsuccessfully from the ground for over 90 minutes as the death toll mounted. Three policemen on the ground managed to cross the plaza to the tower. Here they picked up Allen Cram, an experienced ex-serviceman, deputized him on the spot and gave him a rifle. The four men took the elevator to the twenty-sixth floor and entered the observation deck. Crum encountered Whitman first, firing a rifle shot that sent Whitman backing up to where Officer Ramiro Martinez was positioned. Whitman managed to fire one more shot before Martinez emptied his service weapon into him. It was 1:20 P.M. Whitman's killing spree left 15 dead and 30 injured (Lane & Gregg, 2004, p. 353).

Whitman had been convinced that he had a medical problem with his brain that caused his violent impulses. Upon autopsy, doctors did discover a temporal lobe **glioblastoma** multiforme brain tumor the size of a walnut, erupting from beneath the thalamus, impacting the hypothalamus, extending into the temporal lobe and compressing the amygdaloid nucleus. It has been speculated that this brain tumor could have been at least partially responsible for the violent personality changes seen in Whitman (Rhawn, 2008).

There is further evidence for the possible impact of a brain tumor on Whitman's symptoms and behavior. He suffered terrible headaches. He also had frequent bouts of anger and on one occasion lost his temper in class, pulling a male student bodily from his chair and tossing him from the classroom. He had difficulty concentrating and was beginning to overeat. Such increased food consumption is often associated with a disturbance of the hypothalamus. He also experienced difficulty sleeping, and there were periods where he couldn't sleep for days at a time. This too has been shown to be a disturbance associated with the hypothalamus, a major sleep center (Rhawn, 2008).

There is also research suggesting that amygdaloid activation (such as might have been the case with Whitman's brain tumor) causes patients and animals to react defensively and with anger, irritation, and rage, which seem to gradually build up until finally the animal or human attacks (Azevedo, Hilton, & Timms, 1980; Egger & Flynn, 1963; Ursin, 1960). There have been reported instances of patients suddenly lashing out and even attempting to attack those close by while in the midst of a temporal lobe seizure. Indeed, in those situations where the amygdale overwhelms the neocortex and the rest of the brain, the person not only forms emotional ideas but responds to them, sometimes with vicious, terrifying results (Rosen & Schulkin, 1998)

Fear and rage reactions have also been triggered in humans following depth electrode stimulation of the amygdala (Chapman, 1960). One female patient, following amygdaloid stimulation, became irritable and angry and then enraged. Her lips retracted, there was extreme facial grimacing, threatening behavior, rage, and then attack—all of which persisted well beyond stimulus termination (Mark, Ervin, & Sweet, 1972).

Similarly, Schiff et al. (1982) described a man who developed severe aggression following a head injury and damage (determined by depth electrode) to the amygdala. Subsequently, he became easily enraged, sexually preoccupied (although sexually hypoactive), and developed hyper-religiosity and psuedo-mystical ideas. Similarly, patients with tumors invading the amygdala have been reported to exhibit extreme rage attacks (Vonderache, 1940). But many theorists discount the physiological explanation for the violence exhibited by Charles Whitman. The consensus of their view is that although a certain number of people have brain tumors, they don't all go up in towers and start shooting because of it.

James Oliver Huberty

"I'm going to hunt humans."

—James Oliver Huberty

James Oliver Huberty was born in Canton, Ohio, in 1942 to Icle and Earl Huberty. He was described by his father and boyhood neighbors as a withdrawn, moody youth, whose one passion was for guns (Holusha, 1984). As he grew, his love of guns grew. In his teen years Huberty was a gangly teen with flat top hair and square glasses. He tried out for the basketball team but didn't make the cut. After high school James attended Pittsburg Institute of Mortuary Sciences in Pennsylvania, then returned to Canton for an apprenticeship with a funeral director. But this was the first of many failures for Huberty. His employer, Don Williams, is reported to have said that although Huberty was good at embalming, he had difficulties relating to people and could not deal with clients. After leaving the funeral business, Huberty obtained work as a welder, married Etna Markland, and bought a house 10 miles outside of town.

Very few people were allowed inside the Huberty home. Those who were, reported seeing guns in every corner of the house. He was stated to have kept meticulous records on what he defined as "debts"; these included any perceived offense or slight against him or his family. He called the police often complaining about his neighbors; if he didn't get satisfaction, he would threaten the neighbors directly. He frequently complained about the communist threat, Soviet spies, and that the CIA was following him and preventing him from getting jobs. He had complained about President Jimmy Carter, and then he complained about President Ronald Reagan.

When the plant where he worked as a welder shut down and Huberty found himself out of work, he told a coworker that if he couldn't support his family any longer, he would kill himself and take a lot of people with him. He did find another job, but in a little over a month that plant closed, too. At this point Huberty fervently believed that people were out to get him. Etna Huberty reported that this resulted in Huberty having a "nervous breakdown" and that he threatened suicide, but she pried his fingers from the pistol and took and hid it in another room.

Huberty decided to move to Mexico where the cost of living would be cheaper. It is reported that Huberty had the belief that by going somewhere far away and exotic, he could make a lot of money and show up all the people who had been unfair to him (Douglas & Olshaker, 1999). But he could not speak Spanish, was not making enough money, and decided to move back to California. They moved into a two-bedroom apartment in San Ysidro, where they were the only non-Hispanics in the apartment complex. At times he was known to have fired shots from the balcony at night. In 1984, he landed a job as a security guard for a condominium complex, but lost this when his supervisors decided he was too unstable to carry a weapon. He believed that the Department of Defense was somehow behind his losing this job.

Etna Huberty reported that on Tuesday July 17, 1984 (the day before the shooting), Huberty called a mental health center, seeking help, but that for some reason an appointment was never made. The next day Huberty had to appear in traffic court. After court he and Etna had lunch at a downtown McDonald's, after which they walked around the zoo. When they returned home, Huberty told his wife "I'm going to hunt humans," just before he left the apartment. He then drove the short distance to McDonald's, entering around 4:00 P.M., dressed in a black T-shirt and military camouflage fatigues. He entered the restaurant and shouted, "Everybody down" or "I'll kill somebody." He then moved up and down the aisles, cursing and shooting 41 people, 21 of whom died. After about 90 minutes, he himself was taken down by a police sniper.

Why did Huberty choose a McDonald's? The answer to this question will never be known for sure. But it was certainly a target of convenience, filled with people, many of whom were "foreigners" he disdained. Etna Huberty later filed an unsuccessful lawsuit against McDonald's, on the ground that her husband's rampage was due to eating too many hamburgers and Chicken Mc'Nuggets. She claimed that the high levels of monosodium glutamate in the food interacted with Huberty's confirmed levels of lead and cadmium built up from his years as a welder.

Does Exposure to Cadmium Affect Aggression?

Davis, Arb, and Huss (1995)

Davis and colleagues surveyed the research literature, which indicated that some forms of violence may be caused by medical conditions and metabolic disorders (e.g., limbic and hypothalamic brain tumors, encephalitis, Wilson's and Huntington's diseases), as well as by medical conditions associated with hormones, vitamins, and toxins (Raine, 2002; Tardiff, 1998). A relationship between lead and cadmium levels and hyperactivity, behavioral problems, and aggression had already been suggested by prior research (e.g., Arito, Sudo, & Suzuki, 1981; Davis, Armstrong, & Huss, 1993).

To further assess the effects of toxins such as cadmium, Davis, Arb, and Huss conducted experiments using 36 male Holtzman rats. The animals that had been exposed to cadmium demonstrated significantly more frequent aggressive responses than animals exposed to saccharin. The presence of cadmium was confirmed using atomic absorption spectrophotometry procedures and tissue analyses. The researchers also found that cadmium-exposed rats were more resistant to partial reinforcement and extinction effects than saccharin-exposed rats. The results of these experiments suggest that cadmium exposure may indeed result in heightened emotionality, reactivity, and behavioral changes.

Seung-Hui Cho

> I didn't have to do this . . . I could have fled. You had a hundred billion chances . . . but you decided to spill my blood. You forced me into a corner and gave me only one option. The decision was yours. Now you have blood on your hands that will never wash off.
>
> —Seung-Hui Cho

Seung-Hui Cho was a college student at Virginia Polytechnic Institute and State University (Virginia Tech) when he committed the worst nonterrorist mass murder in U.S. history, killing 32 people and wounding 25 others.

Seung-Hui Cho was born in South Korea on January 18, 1984. His father, Seung-Tae Cho, worked in oil fields and at construction sites in Saudi Arabia before his arranged marriage to Seung-Hui's mother, Kim Hwang-Im. They lived a frugal existence before moving to America in 1984 where they finally settled in Centreville, Virginia, a suburb of Washington, DC. Cho was eight years old. In the United States, from the beginning, Seung-Hui did not talk much; he was quiet, withdrawn, and avoided eye contact.

In the summer before Cho started seventh grade, his parents were advised by an elementary school teacher that Cho be evaluated by a mental health professional. In July 1997, the Chos took their son to a psychiatrist who diagnosed Cho as having severe social anxiety. Two years later, in 1999, the murders at Columbine High School occurred. Shortly thereafter, Cho wrote a disturbing paper in English class in which he expressed generalized thoughts of suicide and homicide, even indicating that he had a desire to repeat what happened in Columbine. Cho received another psychiatric evaluation and was diagnosed with "selective mutism" and "major depression: single episode." He was prescribed the antidepressant Paroxetine (Paxil), which Cho took from June 1999 to July 2000. He seemed to respond to these medications and in the fall of 1999 he began Centreville High School. The following year he was transferred to a new school, Westfield High School, one of the largest schools in Fairfax County, Virginia. But he did not fit in. He was skinny and looked younger than his age. He did not participate in class discussions and at times refused to speak at all. Some classmates reported that he had a "haunted" look on his face. He was the victim of teasing by classmates for his strange ways, poor English, and deep-throated voice.

After graduating from high school Cho attended VA Tech in Blacksburg, Virginia. At Tech he continued being a loner. He was said to be obsessed with violent video games and music lyrics. The students who shared his dorm suite said he rarely spoke and that they were afraid to push the issue out of fear of making him angry. In his junior year (2005) Cho began to show signs of mental deterioration. He became known to many students and faculty not only for his extremely withdrawn personality and complete lack of interest in responding to others in and out of the classroom, but also for hostile, violent writings, and threatening behavior.

Later on, after the Virginia Tech shootings, an official report to the governor, called the "Mental Health History of Seung Hui Cho," would state that the odd statements made by Cho disgusted other students in his college creative writing class. Cho chastised other students for eating meat and stated that such practices made him want to "barf all over my new shoes." He allegedly stated in one paper that people who ate meat were despicable cannibals who will "burn in hell" for their behavior (Leyton, 2005). An investigation conducted by the FBI revealed that Cho had written a play entitled *Richard McBeef*, which featured a 13-year-old boy who accuses his stepfather of pedophilia, and how the teenager desired to kill the man and how his mother threatened the stepfather with a chainsaw. The play ends with the man striking the child with "a deadly blow." Some students were reportedly fearful of attending classes with Cho. Aside from his bizarre remarks, he was also known to take pictures of other students, allegedly even under the desk, without their permission, using his cell phone.

On December 12, 2005, the Virginia Tech Police Department (VTPD) received a complaint from a female sophomore regarding Cho's taking a knife to her dorm room and stabbing the carpet. The following day, a campus police officer met with Cho and instructed him to cease any further contact with the female complainant. Following the visit from the police, Cho sent an instant message to a roommate stating that he wanted to kill himself. This message was reported to the campus police and resulted in an order by a local magistrate to attend a mental health hearing at St. Albans Hospital, which Cho did on December 14. Cho was evaluated by a licensed clinical psychologist who completed the state-mandated evaluation form certifying that Cho was mentally ill but did not present an imminent danger to himself or others and did not require involuntary hospitalization. He was, however, court ordered to follow up with outpatient treatment.

Around the spring of 2007, Cho became more isolated. He began wearing reflector sunglasses with his hat pulled low over his face. One roommate reported that Cho was "totally alone" every day and never spoke to family or friends on the phone or via the Internet. But he spent an inordinate amount of time on the computer, writing. Then, in February and March Cho ordered the weapons that he was to use in the shootings in April. Cho's first purchased was a .22-caliber Walther P22 semiautomatic pistol. On March 13, 2007, he purchased his second handgun—a Glock 19 semiautomatic pistol. Cho passed the background check for both weapons by presenting his U.S. Permanent Residency Card, his Virginia driver's license to prove his legal age and length of time as a Virginia resident, and a checkbook to verify his Virginia address. He neglected to disclose on the gun applications that he was court-ordered for psychiatric treatment, and there was apparently no electronic record of this fact. As per Virginia law at the time, he waited the required 30 days before taking possession of the weapons. On March 22, 2007, Cho purchased two 10-round magazines for the Walther P22. He also purchased hollow point bullets, which are known for causing substantial tissue damage due to their expansion upon entering a human body.

Around 7:00 A.M. on April 16, 2007, Cho began his murderous rampage when he killed two students, Emily J. Hischer and Ryan C. "Stack" Clark, on the fourth floor of West Amber Johnston Hall, a high-rise coeducational dormitory. During the 2 hours after killing these students, Cho returned to his room to rearm himself and to mail a package to NBC News. The package contained photographs, digital video files, documents, and his personal "manifesto." In Cho's room police later found a note criticizing "rich kids," "debauchery," and "deceitful charlatans." In the note Cho also stated, "You caused me to do this." The package to NBC had a return address of "A. Ishmael." The words "Ismail Ax" were also scrawled on Cho's arm in red ink. In the videos, Cho posed with guns pointing toward the camera, a hammer in his hands, and in some dressed like a warrior.

Close to 9:45 A.M., Cho returned to campus and walked to Norris Hall. In a matter of 9 minutes he shot dozens of people, killing 32, before killing himself. Investigators found that Cho had fired a total of 170 rounds.

SPREE KILLING

Spree murder normally refers to the killing of three or more individuals without a **cooling-off period**, usually at two or three different locations. A spree killer does not stop and wait for recognition of his crimes. The amount of time between killings is sporadic; spree killers can kill five people in one day and ten the next, often putting fear into communities or even across states. An example of a spree killer was Howard Unruh, who in 1949 killed 13 victims in the space of 20 minutes while walking through his neighborhood in Camden, New Jersey. Another infamous example of a spree killer was Andrew Phillip Cunanan, who murdered five people, including fashion designer Gianni Versace, in a cross-country spree from Minnesota to Miami Beach, Florida, during a three-month period in 1997. Some of these killings were particularly grizzly, involving bondage and torture followed by a brutal death. Cunanan's killing spree finally ended with his suicide.

Some spree killers are known to operate in pairs. One infamous couple was Clyde Barrow and Bonnie Parker, who were believed to have committed 13 murders and several robberies and burglaries across America from 1932 to 1934. In 1958, 19-year-old Charles Starkweather and his

14-year-old girlfriend, Caril Ann Fugate, went on an eight-day killing spree in Nebraska, during which they murdered ten people, including Fugate's parents. The Starkweather–Fugate spree killings formed the basis for Oliver Stone's 1994 film, *Natural Born Killers.*

More recently, John Allen Muhammad and Lee Boyd Malvo (the "Beltway Snipers") killed ten people during a three-week period in October 2002 in Maryland, Virginia, and Washington, DC. Muhammad was 41 years old, and Malvo was 16 (but turned 17 prior to the last murder). Victims appeared to be randomly shot while going about their everyday lives—mowing the lawn, pumping gas, shopping, and going to school. The spree of shootings actually began in February 2002 in Tacoma, Washington, before the killers slowly migrated to Virginia. The possible motivations of the DC snipers are reviewed in Chapter 6 in the discussion on the psychology of terrorism. Table 5.3 presents the timeline of the shootings linked to Muhammad and Malvo.

Some theorists have expressed doubt whether spree killings should exist as a separate and distinct category within the classification of mass (or multiple) murders. It is the "cooling off period" that differentiates spree murder from serial murder—the latter has one and the former does not. But this is somewhat of an arbitrary guideline. Is 2 hours too little time for sufficient cooling off? Is two days too much time? In 2008, the FBI eliminated spree murder as a category of multiple murders, indicating that it does little to aid law enforcement in the investigation of multiple murders.

TABLE 5.3 DC-Area Sniper Shootings of 2002

Date	Place	Victim	Action
February 16, 2002	Tacoma, Washington	Keenya Cook, age 21	Killed in front of her mother's home
March 21, 2002	Tucson, Arizona	Jerry Ray Taylor, age 61	Killed playing golf
May 18, 2002	Clearwater, Florida	Albert Michalyczyk, age 76	Injured playing golf
May 27, 2002	Denton, Texas	Billy Dillon, age 37	Killed in his yard
September 20, 2002	Atlanta, Georgia	Million Woldemarian, age 41	Killed at a liquor store
September 21, 2002	Montgomery, Alabama	Claudine Parker, age 52	Killed at a liquor store
September 23, 2002	Baton Rouge Louisiana	Hong Ballenger, age 45	Killed walking to car
October 2, 2002	Wheaton, Maryland	James D. Martin, age 55	Killed in a parking lot
October 3, 2002	White Flint, Maryland	James L. Buchanan, age 39	Killed cutting grass
October 3, 2002	Rockville, Maryland	Premkuma A.Walekar, age 54	Killed pumping gas
October 3, 2002	Silver Spring, Maryland	Sarah Ramos, age 34	Killed in front of Post Office
October 3, 2002	Kensington, Maryland	Lori Lewis-Rivera, age 25	Killed at gas station
October 3, 2002	Washington, DC	Pascal Charlot, age 72	Killed walking down street
October 4, 2002	Fredericksburg, Virginia	Caroline Seawell, age 43	Injured in parking lot
October 7, 2002	Bowie, Maryland	Ira Brown, age 13	Injured being dropped off at school
October 9, 2002	Manassas, Virginia	Dean H. Meyers, age 53	Killed pumping gas
October 11, 2002	Fredericksburg, Virginia	Kenneth H. Bridges, age 53	Killed pumping gas
October 14, 2002	Falls Church, Virginia	Linda Franklin, age 47	Killed in a store parking lot
October 19, 2002	Ashland, Virginia	Jeffrey Hopper, age 37	Injured leaving a restaurant
October 22, 2002	Aspen, Hill, Maryland	Conrad Johnson, age 35	Killed boarding bus

Sources: CNN.com. *Sniper Victims sent to Virginia for Trial* (2008); Leyton, E. (2005). *Hunting humans: The rise of the modern multiple murderer;* Federal Bureau of Investigation, *The Beltway Snipers* (2007).

SERIAL KILLING

What's one less person on the face of the earth, anyway? We serial killers are your sons, we are your husbands, we are everywhere. And there will be more of your children dead tomorrow.

—Ted Bundy

Serial murder usually refers to incidents in which an individual (or individuals) separately kills a number of people (usually a minimum of three) over time. The cooling-off period for serial killers may be days or weeks but more likely months or years. It was first distinguished from other forms of multiple murders by the American criminologist James Reinhardt when he coined the phrase "chain killers" in his 1957 book, *Sex Perversions and Sex Crimes*. Chain killers were those who left a "chain" of victims behind them. Such crimes were elaborated further in Reinhardt's 1962 book, *The Psychology of Strange Killers*.

But the first person to actually use the term *serial killer* in the criminal justice nomenclature is not clear. The British author John Brophy referred to the term in his book *The Meaning of Murder* in 1966. Apparently independent of Brophy, FBI agent Robert K. Ressler claims to have used the expression in the mid-1970s metaphorically to refer to the "serial movie" motif in which each installment increased rather than lessened the tension (Ressler & Shachtman, 1992). Film historian and professor of comparative literature Akira Lippit sustained the analogy between serial movies and serial killings by arguing, "Like each episode of a serial movie, the completion of each serial murder lays the foundation for the next act which in turn precipitates future acts, leaving the serial subject always wanting more, always hungry, addicted" (Lippit, 1997).

History and Definition

Serial murder is neither a new phenomenon nor uniquely American. Dating back to ancient times, serial murderers have been chronicled around the world. In nineteenth century Europe, Richard von Krafft-Ebing conducted some of the first documented research on violent sexual offenders and the crimes they committed. Best known for his 1886 textbook, *Psychopathia Sexualis*, Krafft-Ebing described numerous case studies of sexual homicide, serial murder, and other areas of sexual proclivity.

There has been at least one attempt to formalize a definition of serial murder through legislation. In 1998, Congress passed the Protection of Children from Sexual Predator Act. This law includes a definition of serial killings as "[A] series of three or more killings, not less than one of which was committed within the United States, having common characteristics such as to suggest the reasonable possibility that the crimes were committed by the same actor or actors" (Title 18, U.S.C. Chapter 51, § 1111). But this definition was limited to setting forth criteria establishing when the FBI could assist local law enforcement agencies with their investigations of serial murder cases. It was not intended to be a generic definition for serial murder. In 2008 the FBI formally defined serial murder as "The unlawful killing of two or more victims by the same offender(s), in separate events" (Federal Bureau of Investigation, National Center for the Analysis of Violent Crime Critical Incident Response Group, 2008, p. 9).

Up into about the second half of the twentieth century, murder was either a relationship crime or a means to an end. More specifically, in 1965 only 5% of murders were committed by strangers. Most murders involved someone known by the victim (e.g., spouse, acquaintance, romantic rival, bitter enemy) or involved individuals seeking to gain something (e.g., business competitor, robber, arsonist). The first group frequently, although certainly not always, involved "crimes of passion," while the second group often were more deliberate. By 1994, murder by strangers represented 23% of all murders in the United States where the murderer was known and where the crimes were reported to the FBI. Forty-nine percent of all murders for 1994 were committed by *unknown* people (i.e., where the murderer was not discovered or where no determination of a relationship could be established one way or the other) (U.S. Department of Justice,

TABLE 5.4 Stranger/Unknown murder by relationship to victim		
Year	By Stranger[a]	By Unknown[b]
2006	28	45
2005	25	45
2004	23	44
2003	22	45
2002	24	43
2001	24	45
2000	23	43
1999	20	40

[a] Percentage of total number of murders where the relationship was known.
[b] Percentage of total number of murders where the relationship was not known.

Source: U.S. Department of Justice, Office of Justice Programs, Bureau of Justice Statistics. *Crime Characteristics* (2007).

2004). Stated another way, for 1994, murders by strangers could theoretically fall anywhere in the 23–49% range of all murders for that year. These ratios have remained fairly constant during the last decade as indicated in Table 5.4. All in all, from 1976 to 2005, 21% of all murders were committed by strangers where the killer was known, 49% of all murders were committed by unknown or undetermined people, and the true "stranger murder" figure lies somewhere between these two figures.

Myths Regarding Serial Killers

There are some common misconceptions concerning serial killers. The first myth is that serial killers are all "dysfunctional loners." According to the FBI, most serial killers are not reclusive misfits who live alone. They do not appear as monsters and may live and work in plain sight within their communities. They often have families and homes and generally appear to be "normal." The fact that many serial murderers can blend in so effortlessly makes it difficult for them to be regarded as possible suspects by law enforcement and the public. For example, the BTK killer, Dennis Rader, killed ten victims in and around Wichita, Kansas. He sent 16 written communications to the news media over a 30-year period, taunting the police and the public. He was married with two children, was a Boy Scout leader, served honorably in the U.S. Air Force, was employed as a local government official, and was president of his church.

The second myth is that serial killers are all white males. The truth is that serial killers span all racial groups. There are white, African-American, Hispanic, and Asian serial killers. The racial diversification of serial killers generally mirrors that of the overall U.S. population. The third myth is that serial killers are motivated only by sex. But not all serial murders are sexually motivated. There are many other motivations for serial murders, including anger, thrill, financial gain, ideology, psychosis, and attention seeking. An example is Richard Angelo, who working as a nurse, was responsible for the deaths of 25 patients when he intentionally caused them to have respiratory distress so he could prove his medical prowess at resuscitation—which he often failed to do. Herbert William Mullin heard voices commanding him to kill people to prevent earthquakes and other catastrophic events. A final myth is that serial killers cannot stop killing. But there are serial killers who stop murdering altogether before being apprehended. For example, as previously mentioned, the BTK killer murdered ten victims from 1974 to 1991. He did not kill any other victims prior to being captured in 2005.

Developmental Aspects of Serial Killers

A vast majority of future serial killers grew up in dysfunctional families with histories of abuse, neglect, and domestic violence (Cook & Hinmn, 1999; Fox & Levine, 1994). But as pointed out previously, this is not always the case. Many, but certainly not all, serial killers grew up in situations of poverty and unemployment. Paternal abandonment before the child turned 12 is commonly a factor, or if the father was present, he was usually domineering and physically violent. Many children who are raised in an abusive household are more likely to respond to stressors in life with violence, and such violence can sometimes lead to homicide. A child who is not taught to value himself or his family is likely to find it difficult to value the lives of others (Sears, 1991).

Many would-be serial killers are extremely isolated and lonely in childhood and adolescence. This social isolation serves to increase the child's reliance on fantasy and feeds his anger and resentment toward society. With no experience in caring or being cared for, the child never develops the ability to love. Rejection and abuse by parents and scorn by other children prevent the future killer from developing a basis for pleasure seen in normal people, and he is thus forced into the extensive use of fantasy and solo sexual activities (Fox & Levine, 1994). Many of these sexual fantasies have significant themes of aggression, power, and control. In addition, there is a heavy emphasis on visual stimuli, with 81% of serial killers using pornography extensively. Forms of media such as detective magazines, with lurid tales of sex and murder, are often an additional source of arousal for the future serial killer, further linking sex and violence (Geberth, 1990).

The developing serial killer's fantasies of power often lead to a fascination, or even an obsession, with police work. Several such killers had posed as law enforcement officers to lure their victims; some held positions as security guards, and some actually worked as auxiliary police. Alex Henriquez, for example, often masqueraded as a DEA agent or an undercover police officer, carrying a small handgun and badge (Dubner, 1992). Ted Bundy worked for the King County Crime Commission in Washington; child killer Wayne Williams often photographed crime scenes and carried a badge; John Wayne Gacy had a police radio in his home; Edmund Kemper frequented a bar near police headquarters and questioned off-duty officers about the murders he himself had committed; and Dennis Rader was known to impersonate a police detective in order to gain access to his victims (Fox & Levin, 1994; Ressler, Burgess, & Douglas, 1988; Singlular, 2006). For the serial killer, the fascination with the police is an extension of the serial killer's pathological need for dominance, and the impersonation of law enforcement officials is an extension of the killer's fantasy life into the real world.

The serial killer usually needs to be in complete control. If he is not in complete control, he feels helpless and powerless. Fantasy, acting like other forms of addiction, often leads to feelings of temporary self-control. But for the serial killer, fantasy alone only works for so long. Often the urge to kill becomes unbearable. Each murder results in further refinement of the fantasy period. Every time the serial killer murders, the fantasy feeds off itself and becomes more structured (FBI, 1985). Just as the fantasy improves, so does the murder. Ted Bundy was known to refer to this as a "learning curve": The more murders the serial killer commits, the better the serial killer becomes (Holmes & DeBurger, 1988).

Serial Killer Phases

The psychological "phases" that many serial killers experience both prior to and following their actual murders do not always fall in a particular order, nor do all serial killers exhibit these phases in the same manner, if at all. But there are common enough elements to the actions and maneuvers of enough serial killers to allow for a general description of modes of activity that appear to be phases. These phases have been described as the aura phase, the trolling phase, the wooing phase, the capture phase, the murder phase, the totem phase, and the depression phase (Norris, 1988; Ressler et al., 1988).

The aura phase consists of a withdrawal from reality and a heightening of the senses. This may last anywhere from several moments to several months and can begin as an extended and prolonged fantasy. The killer-to-be may also abuse or attempt to self-medicate with alcohol or drugs during this phase. In the trolling phase, the killer begins to stalk his potential victim. The wooing phase refers to the killer's attempts to win the confidence of his victim, often by luring them into a trap. For example, Ted Bundy strapped his arm in a sling and asked for help with carrying books or packages to lure many of his victims into his car. Some victims escaped and said he never seemed out of control until the moment he actually attacked them.

The capture phase is when the victim is rendered helpless without the possibility of escape. This may be accomplished by external means such as locking a door or placing a victim in a pit or a box, by violently assaultive means such as a blow to the head, or even by chemical means using drugs, intoxicants, or poisons. Jeffrey Dahmer induced his victims to have a drink, which was actually a drug-laced cocktail. The murder phase is the actual ritualized killing of the victim, which can take place in many forms depending on the nature of the killer's fantasies, needs, and even physical location. The next phase is the totem phase in which many, but not all serial killers seek a memento of their kill by taking artifacts belonging to the victim, removing or eating part of the body, removing and wearing the skin, or taking photographs. The totem is often a means of "reliving" the gratification and sense of power he experienced at the time of the actual killing. A depression phase sometimes occurs after a kill when the satisfaction achieved from the killing begins to wane (explaining to some extent the need for the totem).

Serial Killer Typologies

Holmes and DeBurger (1985, 1988) have classified serial killers into a typology based on their *motives*. Such a classificatory system is not, however, universally accepted. According to this typology, serial killers can be visionary, mission oriented, hedonistic, or power seekers.

The **visionary** type of serial killer is psychotic. He/she often hears voices or sees visions and is driven to kill by these hallucinations or by delusions. David Berkowitz (the "Son of Sam" killer) is an example of a visionary who claimed that his delusional persecutions by demons were responsible for the shootings and killings of his 17 victims. "I am the demon from the bottomless pit here on Earth to create havoc and terror. I am War, I am death. I am destruction" (Leyton, 2005, p. 151).

The **mission-oriented** type of serial killer is not usually psychotic. He/she feels a powerful need to rid the world of those regarded as immoral or unworthy. These undesirables may include prostitutes, homosexuals, women, or members of certain racial or religious groups. Two common subgroups of this category are the *God-mandated* serial killers (who are told to kill by a hallucinated God-like figure) and the *demon-mandated* serial killers (who are forced to kill by the "devil" or other hallucinated demonic figures).

The **hedonistic** type of serial killer gains pleasure from the pure act of killing. To this group, even more than other serial killer, people are mere objects to use for the killer's own enjoyment. Based on their primary motive, hedonistic killers may be further classified as lust, thrill, or comfort killers (Holmes & Holmes, 1998). The *lust killer* is motivated primarily by sex, whether the victim is alive or dead. These killers also tend to exhibit an inordinate degree of bizarre aspects to their killings which defy any degree of rational understanding. Jerry Brudos kept the foot of one of his victims in the deep-freeze to periodically take out and dress up with his collection of black stiletto-heeled women's shoes. Douglas Clark kept a victim's head, which he cleaned and made-up with cosmetics in order to use it in sex acts.

The *thrill killer* kills for the pure fun of it. The thrill of killing is made greater by inducing pain or terror in the victim, and these killers are often considerably sadistic and brutal. Ted Bundy asserted that murder was a "need" and produced such a psychological high that it needed to be repeated again and again (Holmes & DeBurger, 1988, p. 135). The *comfort* killer enjoys what killing can get for him in a material sense. This can be money, business opportunities, or elimination of competition. The main objective of comfort killers is a comfortable lifestyle and the "good life."

The **power seeker** desires complete control over the life and death of others. Jeffrey Dahmer practiced cannibalism to have ultimate control over his victims by bringing them alive in him. "My consuming lust was to experience their bodies. I viewed them as objects" (Lane & Gregg, 1994, p. 129). Ed Kemper described the thrill of taking life from his victims "and then having possession of everything that used to be theirs" (Drukteinis, 1992, p. 533).

Ressler et al. (1988) have formed a classificatory system based on the method of killing, apparent intellect of the killer, degree of emotion expressed during the crime, and the condition of the crime scene. **Organized** killers are of at least average intelligence and are socially competent. They are able to control their emotions during the actual crime and tend to be methodical and well planned in their actions. They often use restraints to gain power and control over their victims, and if a weapon is used, it is not left at the crime scene. When sex takes place as part of the crime, the victim is usually still alive. Such killers understand right from wrong and realize the pain they are causing, but this does not deter them from continuing in their actions. After the killing has taken place, they enjoy following their crimes in the news.

Disorganized killers often have below average intelligence and are not socially proficient. They are anxious while committing the crime and often leave evidence and weapons at the crime scene. Sex with the victim, when it occurs, usually takes place after death. This type of killer does not follow his crimes in the news.

Serial killers, especially of the organized type, are often regarded to be *psychopaths.* Such individuals use a mixture of charm, manipulation, intimidation, and occasionally violence to control others and to satisfy their own needs. People with an antisocial personality disorder tend to be glib, superficially charming, and grandiose in their sense of self-worth. They chronically lie and manipulate others and have no remorse or guilt for their actions. They show shallow affect, a lack of empathy, and a failure to accept responsibility. Such individuals are impulsive, irresponsible, and have a "parasitic" orientation to the world. But not all psychopaths become serial killers.

It should be noted that the organized/disorganized typology of serial murder as proposed by Ressler et al. (1988) and others, for example, Douglas et al. (1992), is not accepted by all forensic psychologists, criminologists, or criminal investigators. For example, Canter, Alison, Alison, and Wentink (2004) tested the organized/disorganized dichotomy by the multidimensional scaling of the cooccurrence of 39 aspects of serial killings derived from 100 murders committed by serial killers. They found no distinct subsets of offense characteristics reflecting such a dichotomy, suggesting that all serial killers are likely to exhibit some aspects that are organized and some that are disorganized. Organized and disorganized crime scenes may not be the opposite to each other; rather, each may represent a dominant style of one or the other.

CASE EXAMPLES OF SERIAL KILLERS

Jeffrey Dahmer

Jeffrey Dahmer was born on May 21, 1960, in Milwaukee, Wisconsin, and the family soon moved to Ohio. He was considered an introverted child and a young adolescent who spent excessive amounts of time engaged in fantasy. It is reported that by age ten, Dahmer was "experimenting" with dead animals, decapitating rodents, and once mounted a dog's head on a stake (Newton, 2000). At the age of 13, Dahmer began drinking alcohol, and by 17 was using marijuana excessively. He also had homoerotic fantasies involving raping and assaulting other men. His fantasies usually involved submissive male lovers who would never leave him, were dead, disemboweled, or dismembered (Simon, 1996). During his high school years, Dahmer had a few homosexual experiences but was essentially a loner.

In June 1978, Dahmer crossed the line from "experimentation" to murder. His first victim was hitchhiker Steven Hicks, whom Dahmer took to his parents' old house in Bath for drinking and marijuana. Dahmer did not want Hicks to leave so he hit him in the head with a barbell and strangled him to death. He left the body in a crawlspace under the rear of house for two days, then dismembered it with a large hunting knife and placed the parts into large trash bags. Dahmer was almost caught by police when he was pulled over for driving erratically, with the bags in the trunk but was able to convince the officer that the bags contained trash. He returned the bags to his house and used Hicks's decomposing head for "satisfying fantasies." Dahmer hid the rest of the remains in a drainage pipe in the woods behind the house and threw Hicks's clothing, identification, jewelry, and the hunting knife into the Cuyahoga River. Three years later he returned to Bath, recovered Hicks's skeletal remains, smashed each bone with a sledgehammer, and scattered the pieces in the deep brush near the house (Flaherty, 1993).

The murder of Steven Hicks seemed to have a sobering effect on Dahmer. He tried to attend college and moved in with his grandmother Catherine, with whom he was very close. He lived with her from 1981 until 1988. He even tried to give up drinking and his violent homosexual fantasies. He attended church and Bible study with Catherine. But any changes did not last long, and Dahmer was drinking again within two years after a man offered him sex in a library bathroom. He had no friends and felt lonely, empty, and depressed. He spent time going to bars, adult bookstores, peep shows, and bathhouses in Milwaukee. He would eventually be kicked out of the bathhouses because of complaints that he was drugging his sexual companions with sleeping pills in their drinks. Dahmer later explained that he "wanted to be in control of the relationship" and he could easily do this when his partner was unconscious. He held jobs at a blood bank and a chocolate factory. He kept the job at the chocolate factory for seven years, but was eventually fired because of poor attendance.

On September 15, 1987, Dahmer met 28-year-old artist and short order cook Steven Tuomi at "Club 219"—a gay bar in Milwaukee's warehouse district. He enticed Tuomi to the Ambassador hotel and offered him one of his cocktails (rum, coke, and five or six crushed sleeping pills). Dahmer drank heavily but did not take the sleeping pills. He later claimed that he "blacked out" and woke up naked, lying on top of Tuomi's corpse with which he had had sex (**necrophilia**). He then stuffed the body into a very large suitcase, taking it to his grandmother's house and hiding it the fruit cellar for a week. After the week he dismembered the body, putting large chunks of flesh into plastic bags and leaving them for the trash collector. He kept the skull but crushed the remaining bones with a hammer. Dahmer's third victim was 14-year-old James "Jamie" Doxtator who accepted Dahmer's offer for a drink in January 1988. Soon after arriving at his grandmother's house, Dahmer gave Doxtator a sleeping pill cocktail and waited for him to become unconscious. He then strangled him, had sex with the corpse, and dismembered the body in the fruit cellar. He also killed Richard Guerrero the same year in a similar fashion, followed by Anthony Sears in 1989. In 1990 he murdered, had sex with, and dismembered four more young men. Around this time he began to cannibalize his victims (**necrophagia**). He took one victim's heart and biceps, treated them with meat tenderizer, fried them, added seasoning, and ate them. By eating these parts, Dahmer felt he was making the victim a part of himself and acquiring their strength. He also began performing lobotomies on his unconscious victims in order to create "zombies" who would be his ever-obedient sex slaves. In February 1991, he killed 17-year-old Curtis Straughter in the usual fashion, then drilled holes in his head and injected acid into the brain using a turkey baster (Newton, 2000).

On May 24, 1991, Dahmer paid 31-year-old deaf mute Tony Hughes $50 to come back to his apartment for sex. They went back to apartment 213 where both men eventually passed out but only Dahmer woke up. He left the body of Hughes in his bed for two days before dismemberment and disposal. Two days later, Dahmer invited 14-year-old Konerak Sinthasomphone to his apartment to pose for photographs. After the boy passed out from a drug-spiked cocktail, Dahmer had sex with him, drank beer, and watched pornographic videos. Dahmer drilled two small holes in the boy's head and injected acid into his brain cavity. He left the unconscious boy to go buy beer and upon returning found him sitting outside naked. Neighbors called the police, but Dahmer was able to convince them that the boy was actually his drunk adult lover. The police escorted the men up to Dahmer's apartment where Tony Hughes still lay dead on the bed. But the police determined that Dahmer was being honest when they saw almost nude photographs of the boy. After the police left, Dahmer strangled the boy, followed his fantasy rituals, and dissolved the corpse in acid. Hughes' remains were also dissolved in the acid vat. Both skulls were kept and added to his collection (Flaherty, 1993; Hickey, 1997).

July 1991 saw the disappearance of several more young men to Dahmer's attacks. Then on July 22, 1991, Dahmer slipped 32-year-old Tracy Edwards a drug-laced cocktail, but it was not strong enough to completely incapacitate the young man. Edwards managed to hit Dahmer in the head with his fist, kick him in the chest, and escape. He ran down the street until he found police officers a few blocks away and explained the best he could what had happened to him. The police went to Dahmer's apartment to investigate. Dahmer answered the door smiling and calm as he attempted to explain the quarrel between him and his "lover." But the officers found photographs of dismembered bodies in the apartment. They also found a skeleton hanging from the shower-head, seven skulls, four heads with flesh still on them in the refrigerator, and the torsos of three victims in a large drum of acid. They also discovered a kettle containing decomposed hands and genitals, a filing cabinet with three skulls and assorted bones, a box holding two skulls, a photographic diary of Dahmer's killings, and three heads in garbage bags.

At his trial in January 1992 Dahmer plead not guilty by reason of insanity. But he was convicted on 15 counts of first-degree murder and sentenced to 15 consecutive life sentences. In 1994, Dahmer was murdered in prison by a delusional schizophrenic named Christopher Scarver, who referred to himself as "Christ." Dahmer was 34 years old.

Dennis Rader (the "BTK" killer)

Dennis L. Rader was born on March 9, 1945, in Pittsburg, Kansas, to William and Dorothea Rader. His father had been a military man but was working at a Wichita power plant, and his mother was employed as a bookkeeper at a grocery store. He and his three younger brothers were raised in a somewhat strict environment that valued honesty and hard work. The children were taught to be thrifty, humble, and religious. Sex was a forbidden topic in the family.

Rader became fascinated with death after watching chickens get slaughtered. Once he killed a cat and was filled with a sense of power and control. He continued killing local animals in the barn, wrapping and strangling them with barbed wire. Around age eight or nine, Rader came across a magazine that contained detective photos of women tied up in bondage positions. He immediately felt that he could relate to these photos because he had always felt out of control, or tied down. He had a desire to create similar pictures, and in grade school he cut photos out of magazines and drew lines on them, recreating the bondage images that he was fascinated with from the detective magazines.

Throughout school, Rader was generally consumed with fantasies about killing animals and binding women. After graduating high school he enlisted in the air force and achieved the rank of sergeant. Soon after being honorably discharged he began working at ADT home security, which enabled him to learn who had security systems in their homes and who did not. On May 22, 1971, Rader married Paula Dietz. They had two children, a boy in 1975 and a girl in 1978. He was active in his Wichita community and became the president of the congregation council at the Christ Lutheran Church where he attended church for 30 years. He attended Wichita State University, graduating in 1979 with a degree in the administration of justice. He began working as a compliance supervisor for Park City, Kansas, and in this capacity he was able to give citations for minor public nuisances such as improper lawn care, improper disposal of appliances (such as leaving appliances on the lawn), and violation of dog laws. He was known to react more harshly toward women who violated the dog and lawn laws, often threatening to have animals put down and using a ruler to measure grass length. For whatever reasons, Rader began killing on January 15, 1974, and stopped on January 19, 1991. He had killed ten people (Singlular, 2006). The dates, victims, and methods of killing are summarized in Table 5.5.

Only Rader's first killings will be described here, as they are typical of his "style" yet stand apart as being particularly heinous.

TABLE 5.5 BTK Killer's Victims

Date	Victim(S)	Method of Killing
January 15, 1974	Joseph Otero, 38; Julie Otero, 34; Josephine Otero, 11; Joseph Otero, Jr., 9	Suffocation and strangulation using plastic bags and rope
April 17, 1974	Kathryn Bright, 21	Stabbing and gunshot
March 17, 1977	Shirley Vian, 26	Strangulation
December 8, 1977	Nancy Fox, 25	Strangulation
April 27, 1985	Marine Hedge, 53	Strangulation
September 16, 1986	Vicki Wergle, 28	Strangulation
January 19, 1991	Dolores Davis, 62	Strangulation

On January 15, 1974, around 7:00 A.M., Rader approached the Otero home at 803 Edgemoor in Sedgwick County, Wichita, Kansas. He cut the phone lines and forced himself into the house as Joseph, Jr., was letting the dog out in the yard. Rader pulled out a pistol and made up a story about needing money and a car. He forced them into the bedroom where he tied the four family members up, binding their feet and hands. The family complained about being tied up, and Rader loosened the bonds and placed a jacket underneath Joseph, Sr., to make him more comfortable (the man had a cracked rib from a car accident). He realized that he had to kill them because he was not wearing a mask and could easily be identified.

Rader placed a plastic bag over Joseph, Sr.'s, head, placed cords around his neck, and tightened them. He left the man and began strangling Julie Otero, Josephine, and Joseph, Jr. Joseph, Sr., managed to tear a hole in the bag, so Rader placed a T-shirt or cloth and two additional bags over the man's head and tied them down. Mr. Ortero subsequently died on the bedroom floor. Julie and Josephine became unconscious after Rader first strangled them. He went over to Joseph, Jr., who was on the floor, and placed a bag on his head and tied it on with a cord. He strangled Julie with a cord again, killing her on this second attempt. Josephine was still alive, so Rader took her to the basement and hung her with a rope tied to a sewer pipe. She was found hanging with her feet and knees bound and a white cloth tied around her mouth. After she was hung, he masturbated and then quickly cleaned the house. He stole Mr. Otero's watch, a radio, and the car. Rader drove the Oteros' car to Dillon's parking lot and walked to where he had parked his car.

During the initial 12 years Rader was killing, he was also bragging, albeit cryptically, to the police and the media. He first made contact in April 1974 by calling the *Wichita Eagle* and giving information about where details of the Otero murders could be found. When a document was found, it contained a statement of responsibility, information regarding the motivation behind the murders, and a detailed account of the Otero crime scene. At the end of the document, he wrote, "[t]he code words for me will be . . . bind them, toture [sic] them, kill them, B.T.K." He continued sending various messages until February 1978.

Rader resurfaced after 27 years by sending a letter to the *Wichita Eagle* that included photos of one of his murder victims from 1986 and a photocopy of her driver's license. Rader followed up this cryptic package with several other messages and packages, one of which contained a diskette that led police to Rader's church. Police swiftly traced the diskette to Rader, and he was arrested on February 25, 2005.

On June 25, 2005, Dennis Rader pled guilty to ten counts of first-degree murder. At his trial, Rader discussed his killings in depth and politely answered all the questions put to him. In an account utterly devoid of emotion, Rader described how he used a "hit kit" consisting of guns, rope, handcuffs, and tape in a briefcase or a bowling bag. He described his killings as "projects" and his victims as "targets." He referred to the murder of the Otero family as if talking about animals, saying he decided to "put them down." When the judge asked Rader what his motivation was for killing the Otero family, he replied that it was all part of his sexual fantasy (Hickey, 2004). He remained courteous and even helpful as he corrected the judge on some matters and at one point began what appeared to be a scholarly discourse on the mentality of serial killers. He talked about the phases that serial killers go through, including stalking and "trolling." Rader was sentenced to ten consecutive life sentences without the possibility of parole.

The Number of Serial Killers

There have been approximately 400 serial killers in the United States in the past century, with anywhere from 2,526 to 3,860 victims (Hickey, 2005). Table 5.6 presents a survey of serial killers in the United States since 1885.

TABLE 5.6 Survey of Serial Killers, 1885 to Present

Year(s)	Locations	Name	Number Killed	Notes
1885–1901	Massachusetts	Jane Toppan (AKA Honora Kelley)	31	As a nurse, she used her patients as guinea pigs in "experiments" with morphine and atropine; she would later kill outside the hospital as well
1920–1947	Nationwide	Jake Bird	44	Stabbed and hacked women across the country
1926–1927	California, Oregon, Pennsylvania, Canada	Leonard Earle Nelson	22	Known as the "The Gorilla Murderer" he raped and bludgeoned to death a series of older women
1927–1954	Alabama, Kansas, North Carolina, Oklahoma	Nanny Hazel Doss	11	This "Jolly Black Widow" poisoned four husbands, two children, her two sisters, her mother, a grandson, and a nephew
1928–1935	New York, Delaware, Wyoming, and others	Albert Fish	15–400	Claimed that he was ordered by God to castrate young boys, he also engaged in cannibalism and coprophagia—the consumption of human excrement
1938	Texas	Joe Ball	5–12	Called "The Alligator Man," he hunted women, chopped them up and fed them to his hungry alligators
1947–1954	Wisconsin	Edward Theodore Gein	2–15	A killer who cannibalized his victims, he confessed to 2 murders but is suspected of scores more due to recovered body parts
1949–1974	Alaska, Washington, Minnesota	Harvey Louis Carignan	5	Used personal ads to attract victims and a claw hammer to kill them
1953–1970	California	Mack Ray Edwards	6	Abducted girls from their homes, molested and killed them
1957–1959	Maryland, Virginia	Melvin David Rees	13	Known as "The Sex beast" he used force to coerce women to have oral sex, then savagely beat them to death
1960–1983	Ohio, Maryland, Florida, New Mexico, Texas	Henry Lee Lucas	81–500	Lucas boasted of brutally killing and mutilating over 500 people

(*continued*)

TABLE 5.6 Continued

Year(s)	Locations	Name	Number Killed	Notes
1961–1984	Florida, Colorado, Maryland	Ottis Elwood Toole	25–133	A practicing cannibal and Satanist, he admitted killing and mutilating victims in 11 states, sometimes killing together with fellow serial killer Henry Lucas
1962–1964	Massachusetts	Albert DeSalvo	13	Sexually assaulted and strangled women from 19 to 85 years of Age
1963–1978	Elkhart, Indiana	Rudy Bladel	7	A lover of trains, he sniped people at stations and near tracks
1966–1981	California	"Zodiac" (unsolved)	6–40	As a means of killing, he used shooting, stabbing, beating, strangulation, drowning, and poisoning. He wrote regular letters to the press and the police calling himself the "Zodiac." The case has never been solved
1967–1969	Ypsilanti, Michigan	John Norman Collins	7	Savagely killed young women
1968–1975	South Carolina	Donald Henry Gaskins, Jr.	110	A sadistic killer who tortured and mutilated his victims
1969–1973	Florida	Gerald Schaefer	34	Known as "The Butcher of Blind Creek," he molested, shot, and butchered as many as 110 women in Florida
1969	Oregon	Jeffrey Brudos	4	He began with knocking women down to steal their clothing, then turned to rape, then to murder and hanging the bodies in his house
1969–1980	New Jersey, Florida	Gerald Eugene Stano	41	Used guns, knives, and strangulation, he killed women ranging in age from 13 to 35. He told police "I hate a bitchy chick"
1970s	Martin County, Florida	Gerard John Schaeffer	2–30	A deputy sheriff, he lured young women off the road, tortured, mutilated and murdered them
1970–1971	London, Kentucky	Donald Harvey	12–34	Working as an orderly, he killed patients to "relieve their suffering"
1971	California	Juan Vallejo Corona	25–26	A labor contractor, he hired down-and-out and homeless men as migrant workers. He also used many workers to satisfy his sexually sadistic needs, after which he stabbed and hacked them to death and buried the bodies in the orchards
1971–1972	Queens, New York	Joseph Baldi	4	Invaded homes at night slashing women in their beds
1972–1973	California	Herbert William Mullin	13	A psychotic, he heard voices "commanding" him to kill people in order to prevent earthquakes and other catastrophic events
1972–1978	Illinois	John Wayne Gacy, Jr.	33	Often flashing a badge and a gun, he would troll the streets of Chicago "arresting" runaways or inviting young males to his house. Once there, he would have sex with them, strangle them and dump their bodies in a crawl space under his house
1972–1973	California	Edmund Emil Kemper, III	8	Stabbed, bludgeoned, and decapitated many of his victims

TABLE 5.6 Continued

Year(s)	Locations	Name	Number Killed	Notes
1972–1980	California	William Bonin	14–44	Responsible for 14 to 44 "freeway murders" of young men and boys in southern California
1972–1990	New York State	Arthur John Shawcross	11	Praying on prostitutes and young women, he usually strangled and battered his victims to death, mutilated them, and dumped their bodies along the Genesee River
1973–1981	Toledo, Ohio	Anthony & Nathaniel Cook	9	Killed couples usually in the victims' cars
1973–1983	Alaska	Robert C. Hansen	17	Raped and killed prostitutes and "exotic dancers" in the Alaskan wilderness
1974	Florida, Texas, Georgia, Ohio	Paul John Knowles	18	Raped, and stabbed or shot his victims, usually hitchhikers
1974–1975	New Jersey, Maryland, Pennsylvania	Joseph Michael Kallinger	6	Raped, stabbed, and mutilated his victims, sometimes by cutting off the penis. Referred to by a judge as "an evil man . . . utterly vile and depraved"
1974–1975	Northern New Jersey	Robert R. Reldan	8	Abducted and killed his victims in pairs
1974–1978	Washington, Oregon, Utah, Colorado, Florida	Ted Bundy	28–100	Raped, killed and viciously mutilated his victims
1974–1982	Michigan, Texas	Coral Eugene Watts	13–80	A paranoid schizophrenic with an IQ of 75, he was dubbed the "Sunday Morning Slasher" because he claimed several of his victims on quiet, peaceful Sunday mornings
1974–1986	Kansas	Dennis Rader	10	From 1974 to 1986, the "BTK Killer" (Bind—Torture—Kill), motivated by sexual fantasies, sadistically murdered his victims and taunted the police with letters and packages to the media. After 18 years he re-emerged sending new material to the press which lead to his arrest. He was sentenced to nine life terms in prison with no chance of parole
1975–1977	California	Patrick W. Kearney	32	Stating that killing "excited him" and gave him a "feeling of dominance," he killed gay men leaving their dismembered bodies in trash bags along the highway
1976	National	Allen Leroy Anderson	8	Robbed and murdered across 20 states
1976–1977	Santa Barbara, California	Thor Nis Christiansen	4	"Look-alike" murders, in that all the women he killed closely resembled one another
1976–1977	New York City	David Berkowitz	9	Known as the Son of Sam Killer, he terrorized New York by prowling for young women and couples and shooting them
1977	New York City	Paul Bateson	6	After having sex with gay prostitutes, he bludgeoned them to death, dismembered them, and dumped their remains in the Hudson River

(continued)

TABLE 5.6 Continued

Year(s)	Locations	Name	Number Killed	Notes
1977–1978	Georgia	William Henry Hance	6	Dubbed the "Stocking Strangler" he beat, strangled, and also decapitated many of his victims
1977–1978	California	Richard Trenton Chase	6	Nicknamed "The Vampire of Sacramento," he drank his victims' blood and cannibalized their remains. He claimed that this was done to prevent Nazis from turning his blood into powder via poison they had planted beneath his soap dish
1977–1979	California, Washington	Angelo Buono, Jr. and Kenneth Alessio Bianchi	10	The pair worked a "white-slave" racket in Los Angeles. They then began procuring first prostitutes and later other women to satisfy their murderers desires
1978	Washington	Stanley Bernson	30	Stabbed and killed women across the state
1978–1982	Missouri, Nebraska, California, Iowa	Charles Ray Hatcher	16	Molested, beat and strangled children
1978–1995	Illinois, Utah, Tennessee, California, Washington, Michigan, Connecticut, New Jersey,	Theodore Kaczynski	3	The "Unabomber" killed 3 and wounded 20 using letter bombs
1979–1980	California	David Joseph Carpenter	10	Shot and stabbed people as they knelt and pled for their lives
1979–1983	Utah	Arthur Gary Bishop	5	Molested and murdered young boys
1980	California	Doug Clark and Carol Bundy	9	Stabbed or shot their victims, practiced necrophilia, and left most decapitated
1980s	Florida	Frank A. Canonico	25	Killed "loose women" whom he met in bars
1980–1981	New York, Georgia	Joseph G. Christopher	13	A vicious racist, he killed African-Americans across two states
1980–1981	Oregon, Washington, California	Randall Brent Woodfield	5	Known as the "I-5 Killer," he shot his victims in the head along Interstate 5 which runs through three west coast states
1982	Florida, Mississippi	Donald William Dufour	5–12	Killed gay men
1982–1984	Washington	Gary Leon Ridgway	48–71	Known as the "Green River Killer," he abducted and killed mostly prostitutes, dumping their bodies near Washington's Green River or on the side of the road
1983	San Francisco, California	Anthony Scully	7	Murdered prostitutes in the San Francisco bay area
1983–1985	California	Richard Leyva Ramirez	14	Known as "The Night Stalker" he broke into women's homes, and raped, battered, mutilated, and killed them

TABLE 5.6 Continued

Year(s)	Locations	Name	Number Killed	Notes
1984	Kansas, Missouri	John Edward Robinson, Sr.	8	Lured victims with personal ads on the Internet, practiced sexual sadism, left bodies in chemical barrels and a storage locker on his farm
1985–1986	Oklahoma, California	Billy Ray Waldon	6	Robbed, beat, burned and shot his victims
1986–94	California, Texas	William Lester Suff	13	Raped, mutilated, and stabbed prostitutes
1985–97	New York, Florida, Massachusetts	Wesley Gareth Evans	8	Obsessed with the idea that girls and women were laughing at his facial scares, he hunted them down and killed them
1987	New York State	Richard Angelo	25	Working as a nurse, he wanted to impress coworkers with his expertise by causing patients to have respiratory distress and then saving them. His efforts at revival, however, often fell short
1987–1991	Wisconsin	Jeffrey Lionel Dahmer	15	Had sex with, cannibalized, and attempted to make "sex zombies" out of his (mostly gay) victims
1989–1990	Florida, Louisiana	Danny Harold Rolling	8	Raped, stabbed, and mutilated his female victims
1989–1991	Florida	Aileen Carol Wuornos	7	A prostitute, she claimed her killings were in self-defense
1989–1993	New York City	Joel David Rifkin	17	Killed prostitutes, sometimes dismembering their bodies and dumping them in the East River
1989–1997	Glendale, California	Efren Saldivar	50	A respiratory care practitioner, he used lethal injections to "help patients die fast"
1990–1991	Alabama, Georgia, California	Joseph Dewey	18	A male nurse, he killed victims with overdoses of Lidocaine
1990–1991	Texas	Charles Albright	4	Shot his victims and surgically removed their eyes
1990–1994	North Carolina	Henry Louis Wallace	10	Raped, robbed, and murdered women in the Charlotte area
1990–1994	Oregon	Keith Hunter Jesperson	4–160	Bragged of killing over 160 people whom he referred to as "piles of garbage"
1990–1996	Massachusetts	Kristen Heather Gilbert	3–300	Dubbed the "Angel of Death," during her seven year tenure as a nurse at a Veterans Administration Hospital, 350 deaths had occurred during her shift, mostly of cardiac arrest. She had caused at least three (and likely many more) of the deaths by administering high doses of ephinephrine. Her motive was allegedly to receive the attention of her security guard boyfriend
1990–1999	Washington, Utah, California	Charles T. Sinclair	12	Robbed, raped, and killed across several western states
1991–1992	New York State	Nathaniel White	6	He stated that his manner of killing was influenced by the movie Robocop 2

(continued)

TABLE 5.6 Continued

Year(s)	Locations	Name	Number Killed	Notes
1991–1997	South Dakota, New York	Michael Joseph Swango	4–60	As a medical intern, he began killing his patients with lethal injections and overdoses
1992–1994	California	Jack Baron	4	His wife, two children, and his mother all mysteriously died in their sleep during a two-year period, but it wasn't accidental
1993–1995	Terre Haute, Indiana	Orville Lynn Majors	7–160	A male nurse who killed elderly patients in his care
1993–1996	Indiana	Herbert Richard Baumeister	20	A wealthy person, he would pick up men from gay bars, take them back to his mansion where he would strangle them and dispose of their bones in the woods behind his home
1996–1998	Washington	Robert Lee Yates, Jr.	16	Picked up prostitutes, murdered them, and buried many of them around his house
2001–1906	Michigan	Shelly Andre Brooks	7	This homeless man raped, beat, and killed prostitutes using stones

Sources: Egger, S. A. (2002). *The killers among us: An examination of serial murder and its investigation*. Upper Saddle River, NJ: Prentice Hall; Fox, J. A., & Levin, J. (2005). *Extreme killing: Understanding serial and mass murder*. Thousand Oaks, CA: Sage; Lane, B., & Gregg, W. (2004). *The encyclopedia of mass murder*. New York, NY: Carroll & Graf Publishers; Vronsky, P. (2004). *Serial killers: The method and madness of monsters*. New York, NY: Penguin Group/Berkley; Vronsky, P. (2007). *Female serial killers: How and why women become monsters*. New York, NY: Penguin/Berkley; Schechter, H., & Everitt, D. (2006). *The A to Z encyclopedia of serial killers*. New York, NY: Simon and Schuster; *Serial killer hit list*. Retrieved October 21, 2008 from http://www.mayhem.net/Crime/serial.html

Serial murders appear to have increased over the past 60 years, with 80% of the 400 serial killers of the past century appearing since 1950 (Knight, 2007). However, there's no way to really know how many serial killers are active at any point in time—experts have suggested numbers ranging from 50 to 300, but there's no hard evidence to support these figures.

Quinet (2007) has expressed that serial killers might be responsible for up to ten times as many U.S. deaths as previously estimated. There are several explanations for this. One of these is the fact that many serial killers' victims are members of marginalized groups, such as prostitutes, transients, gay street hustlers, illegal aliens, foster children, and runaway teens living on their own, many of whom have never been reported missing. Members of such marginal populations have been referred to as the "less-dead" (Egger, 2002). Along these lines, a survey of prostitutes found that 34–46% do not have households; rather, they stay in hotels, motels, halfway houses, and homeless shelters (Potterat et al., 2004).

Other factors that may account for the underreporting of these homicides is that serial killers may dispose of bodies in such a way that the cause of death and the victim's identity are unknown. Furthermore, many of these deaths are not attributed to murder because such people were "expected" to die. This group would include hospital patients and nursing home residents. For example, certain "medical murderers" have killed dozens of people whose deaths were misconstrued as resulting from natural causes. Fox, Levin, and Quinet (2005) have estimated these victims to be about 500–1,000 a year. Of the 2.5 million deaths in the United States each year, in excess of 860,000 occur in hospitals and over 500,000 occur in nursing homes. "The opportunities for foul play are staggering" (Quinet, 2007, p. 332).

FORENSIC PSYCHOLOGY IN THE SPOTLIGHT
Are Serial Killers "Evil"?

Knight (2007)

There is ample evidence from human history suggesting that a dark and destructive side of human nature may exist which is violent, sadistic, and murderous. Cross-cultural evidence of humanity's aggression against one another is ubiquitous. Some may call this dark side of human nature "evil." Lu (2004) asserts that "the concept of evil is indispensable for identifying acts and states of affairs that violate our most basic moral ideals and expectations" (p. 498). There is no single clear definition of evil. But generally, evil may be described as the intentional infliction of unimaginable physical or psychological harm on a person or persons and the experience of intense pleasure by the evildoer from doing so (Knight, 2007; Wilson, 2003).

But is evil a *behavior* or a *trait*? Are actions evil, or are people evil? Can even the best and most moral of us become "evil" under certain sets of circumstances? Freud (1930) viewed mankind as being imbued with powerful and destructive capabilities toward aggressiveness, which must be reckoned with and inhibited. When these inhibitory counterforces are weakened it "reveals man as a savage beast" (pp. 111–112). Indeed, if

powerful aggression is innate and cannot be inhibited, controlled, or sublimated (channeled into constructive endeavors), it is understandable that some serial killers describe a "force within them" that urges them to kill (Schlesinger, 2000, p. 12).

Evidence from social psychology (e.g., Milgram's 1963 study on obedience) and from distant and recent world history (e.g., the Inquisition, the Crusades, the Holocaust, and Darfur) suggest that people can do monstrous things under the cloak of religion, politics, fear, or the general zeitgeist (spirit of the times). There do seem to be dark impulses we are all capable of succumbing to (Kitaeff, 1972). We may be capable of unimaginable aggressive fantasies of torture, sadism, and murder, but we are not all serial killers. Fortunately, most of us are not disconnected from humanity in a way that leaves us immune from empathy, sympathy, understanding, and concern for what is right and what is wrong. Most serial killers know right from wrong (as we do) but for whatever reasons, they choose the evil road—to make no distinction between what is "good" and what is "bad". The choice not to resist aggressive, savage, and murderous impulses make them "bad not mad," and the vast majority are not psychotic or insane.

Summary

Mass murder is defined as the killing of three or more persons at a single location with no cooling-off period. Accordingly, most mass murders take place in a matter of minutes or hours. Depending on their motive, mass murderers are classified in one of the following groups: disciple killers, family annihilators, pseudocommandos, school shooters, disgruntled employees, or set-and-run killers.

Disciple killers follow the commands of a charismatic leader. Such was the case with the followers of Charles Manson. Family annihilators kill an entire family (usually their own) at one time. Pseudocommandos usually seek revenge and desire to teach the world a lesson. One infamous example is the sniper Charles Joseph Whitman, who left 15 dead and 30 injured in Texas in 1966. Another example is James Oliver Huberty, who used automatic weapons to kill 21 and wound 20 patrons at a California McDonald's in 1984.

School shooters are usually socially isolated students who are often depressed and may or may not be mentally ill. Most have felt rejected and ridiculed by other students for a long period of time. The most deadly example of a school shooting occurred in 2007 when Seung-Hui Cho shot and killed 32 people and injured another 25 at Virginia Tech in Blacksburg, Virginia. Disgruntled employees are often former employees of a company who retaliate after being disciplined or dismissed. Set-and-run killers may also be motivated by revenge but kill from a distance by planting a bomb or setting a time device so that he or she is far away when the explosion occurs.

Spree murder refers to the killing of three or more individuals *without* a cooling-off period, usually at two or three different locations. John Allen Muhammad and Lee Boyd Malvo (the "Beltway Snipers") are a prime example of such killers; they shot down ten people during a three-week period in October 2002 in Maryland, Virginia, and the District of Columbia.

Serial murder is when a minimum of three people are killed by the same individual(s) over a period of time ranging from days to years, with an obvious cooling-off period. A vast majority of serial killers come from dysfunctional families and have experienced abuse, neglect, and domestic violence. There are four types of serial killers based on motive. These types are called visionary, mission oriented, hedonistic, and power seekers. Regardless of type, many (but not all) serial killers experience "phases" in their planning, hunting, capturing, murdering, and postkill experiences. These phases are called the aura phase, trolling phase, wooing phase, capture phase, murder phase, totem phase, and depression phase. In the actual killing of their victims, serial murderers are frequently further classified as "organized" or "disorganized" based on factors such as the method of killing, apparent intellect of the killer, degree of emotion expressed during the crime, and condition of the crime scene. Two examples of serial killers are Jeffrey Dahmer, who murdered 15 young boys from 1978 to 1991, and Dennis Rader (the "BTK" killer), who killed 10 people during the period from 1974 to1991. Both were sexually motivated power-seeks.

Serial murders appear to have increased over the past 60 years, but it is difficult to know with certainty how many serial killers are active at any point in time. Recently, some researchers have expressed the opinion that serial killers might be responsible for up to ten times as many U.S. deaths as previously estimated. One of the reasons for this is that many serial killers' victims are members of marginalized groups who may not be adequately counted as homicides.

Key Terms

Cooling-off period *82*
Disciple killer *82*
Disgruntled employee *89*
Disorganized serial
  killer *103*
Family annihilator *82*

Glioblastoma *93*
Hedonistic serial killer *102*
Mass murder *81*
Mission-oriented serial
  killer *102*
Necrophagia *104*

Necrophilia *104*
Organized serial killer *103*
Power-seeker serial
  killer *103*
Pseudocommando *82*
Rampage killer *82*

School shooter *83*
Serial murder *99*
Set-and-run killer *91*
Spree murder *97*
Visionary serial
  killer *102*

Review Questions

1. How is mass murder differentiated from spree and serial murders?
2. About how long would you expect the cooling-off period to be in serial murder?
3. When a charismatic cult leader influences members to kill a group of people, what kind of mass murder would this be?
4. A man kills his entire family then flees to another part of the country. What kind of mass murder has been committed?
5. A worker is fired from his job and returns with a shotgun, killing his boss and several former coworkers. What kind of mass murder is this?
6. What kind of mass murderer sends poison-laced letters through the mail?
7. Name two kinds of brain dysfunctions possibly linked to violence and murder.
8. What is the worst nonterrorist mass murder in U.S. history?
9. Explain some of the common misconceptions about serial killers.
10. When a serial killer attempts to win the confidence of a potential victim, in what killer phase might he be?
11. Removing a body part of a victim by a serial killer in order to preserve his "success" is indicative of what killer phase?
12. What are the four motive-based typologies of serial killers?
13. Explain some of the differences between organized and disorganized serial killers.

Chapter Resources on the World Wide Web

The Mass Murder Website
http://www.fortunecity.com/roswell/hammer/73/

The Mass Murderer Hit List
http://www.mayhem.net/Crime/murder1.html

The Mass Murderer Charles Whitman
http://www.crimelibrary.com/notorious_murders/mass/whitman/index_1.html

Crime Library on TruTV: School Shooters
http://www.trutv.com/library/crime/serial_killers/weird/kids1/index_1.html

National Institute of Justice: Preventing School Shootings
http://www.ncjrs.gov/pdffiles1/jr000248c.pdf

Court TV: The Unabomber
http://www.courttv.com/trials/unabomber/chronology/chron_7882.html

Federal Bureau of Investigation Report on the Beltway Snipers
http://www.fbi.gov/page2/oct07/snipers102207.html

The Serial Killer Database
http://www.serialkillerdatabase.net

U.S. Department of Justice: Bureau of Justice Statistics
http://www.ojp.usdoj.gov/bjs/welcome.html

Crime Magazine: An Encyclopedia of Crime
http://www.crimemagazine.com/serial.htm

For Further Reading

Douglas, J., & Olshaker, M. (1999). *The anatomy of motive.* New York: Scribner.

Egger, S. (2002). *The killers among us: An examination of serial murder and its investigation.* Upper Saddle River, NJ: Prentice Hall.

Fox, J. A., Levin, J., & Quinet, K. (2005). *The will to kill.* Upper Saddle River, NJ: Pearson.

Hickey, E. (2002). *Serial murderers and their victims* (3rd ed.). Belmont, CA: Wadsworth Group.

Holmes, R. M., & Holmes, S. T. (2001). *Murder in America.* Thousand Oaks, CA: Sage Publications.

Lane, B., & Gregg, W. (2004). *The encyclopedia of mass murder.* New York: Carroll & Graf Publishers.

Leyton, E. (2005). *Hunting humans: The rise of the modern multiple murderer.* New York: Carroll & Graf Publisher.

Newton, M. (2000). *The encyclopedia of serial murder.* New York: Checkmark Books.

Ressler, R., & Shachtman, T. (1992). *Whoever fights monsters.* New York: St. Martin's.

Singlular, S. (2006). *Unholy messenger: The life and times of the BTK serial killer.* New York: Scribner.

CHAPTER 6

The Psychology of Terrorism, Cults, and Extremism

CHAPTER OBJECTIVES

After reading this chapter you would:

- Understand how lone terrorists differ from other classifications of terrorists.
- Be aware of the connection between terrorism and mental illness.
- Know how terrorism may be related to antisocial and narcissistic personalities.
- Understand depluralization, self-deindividuation, and other-deindividuation.
- Understand dehumanization and demonization.
- Know how diffusion of responsibility is related to terrorist groups.
- Appreciate how shame and humiliation play a part in religious terrorism.
- Know how authoritarianism contributes to religious terrorism.

INTRODUCTION

Terror has been practiced by state and nonstate actors throughout history and throughout the world. The ancient Greek historian Xenophon wrote of the effectiveness of psychological warfare against enemy populations. Roman emperors such as Tiberius and Caligula used banishment and execution to incite fear and discourage opposition to their rule. The term *terrorism* itself was first coined in the 1790s to refer to the terror used during the French Revolution by the revolutionaries against their opponents (Alexander & Musch, 1991).

In the U.S. federal system, each state determines what constitutes an offense under its criminal or penal code. In general, state laws appear under various headings that relate to terrorism. These include civil defense, destructive devices, terrorist threats, enhanced criminal penalties, victim compensation, street terrorism, and ecological terrorism. At the federal level, there has never been a consensus on what constitutes terrorism. Since the 1980s, for instance, the Federal Bureau of Investigation (FBI) has defined terrorism as "the unlawful use of force or violence against persons or property to intimidate or coerce a government, the civilian population, or any segment thereof, in the furtherance of political or social objectives" (U.S. Department of Justice, Terrorism in the United States, 1988).

The Department of State has adopted a definition, stating that "the term 'terrorism' means premeditated, politically motivated violence perpetrated against noncombatant targets by subnational groups or clandestine agents, usually intended to influence an audience" (USC § 2656f(d)).

Moreover, the term *international terrorism* means "terrorism involving citizens of the territory of more than one country" and the term *terrorist group* means "any group practicing, or that has significant subgroups that practice international terrorism."

The United Nations defines terrorism as "Criminal acts intended or calculated to provoke a state of terror in the general public, regardless of the political, philosophical, ideological, racial, ethnic, religious, or other reasons that may be invoked to justify them" (UN General Assembly Resolution 54/109, 1999).

Although there appears to be no consensus of what terrorism is, there does seem to be agreement among nations and states as to the components of terrorism. These include the nature of the act (e.g., that it is unlawful); perpetrators (e.g., individuals, groups, states); objectives (e.g., political); intended outcomes and motivations (e.g., fear and frustration); targets (e.g., innocent victims); and methods (e.g., hostage taking, bombing). On the basis of these elements, is it reasonable to adopt the following working definition: Terrorism is defined as the calculated employment of violence, or the threat of violence by individuals, subnational groups, or state actors to attain political, social, and economic objectives in the violation of law, and intended to create an overwhelming fear in a target area greater than the one actually attacked or threatened (Alexander & Brenner, 2001).

Since the twentieth century, ideology and political opportunism have led a number of countries to engage in transnational terrorism, often under the guise of supporting movements of national liberation. (Hence, it became a common saying that "One man's terrorist is another man's freedom fighter.") The distinction between terrorism and other forms of political violence became blurred—particularly as many guerrilla groups often employed terrorist tactics—and issues of jurisdiction and legality became similarly obscured.

CLASSIFICATION OF TERRORISTS

The Lone Terrorist

In the United States and elsewhere, isolated individuals have employed terrorism to send a message, seek revenge, extort money, or simply because they lacked any other means to pursue their objectives. These are the "lone gunmen" of terrorism—people such as Ted Kaczynski (the Unabomber) and Timothy McVeigh (one of the Oklahoma City bombers).

TED KACZYNSKI (THE UNABOMBER)   **Ted Kaczynski** was born Theodore John Kaczynski on May 22, 1942. He was apparently intelligent with an assessed IQ of 170. In 1962, he graduated from Harvard and went on to receive a Ph.D. from the University of Michigan in mathematics. After a short career as a professor and researcher, he began to psychologically deteriorate. He apparently showed characteristic signs of schizophrenia such as an almost total absence of interpersonal relationships coupled with paranoid and delusional thinking involving being controlled by modern technology.

In 1978, Kaczynski began loading packages with explosives and leaving them in various locations. On May 26, 1978, a package was found in a parking lot of the University of Illinois in Chicago. The package was addressed to an engineering professor at Rensselaer Polytechnic Institute (RPI) in New York State. It was brought to the individual on the return address, Professor Buckley Crist, but he said that he hadn't sent it and turned it over to the university police. It exploded when they opened it, slightly injuring a campus police officer. The device was a pipe bomb constructed of match heads and packed in a carved wooden box.

His second bomb consisted of a cigar box, taped shut and left on a table between study cubicles on the second floor of Northwestern Technological Institute. A student opened the box, and it exploded causing him to sustain cuts and burns. The debris suggested a device composed of match heads, wires, and flashlight batteries; it was crude and simple.

The third case occurred on November 15, 1979, and targeted American Airlines flight 444 from Chicago to Washington, DC. A bomb was hidden in a package mailed from Chicago and was rigged to detonate when cabin pressure reached a predetermined level. The resulting explosion started a fire in the cargo hold, and the plane made an emergency landing. Twelve passengers were treated for smoke inhalation.

The fourth bomb was placed in a classroom at the University of Utah in Salt Lake City but was defused without injuries. It was with this bomb that an FBI task force was created with the code name "UNABOM" (Douglas & Olshaker, 1999). The unknown suspect was dubbed the "Unabomber" since his bombings were so far directed at universities and airlines. It would be six bombings, and six years later in the Unabomber's steady escalation in sophistication and lethality, that the first life was lost. It occurred on December 11, 1985, when the owner of a computer store in Sacramento, California, was killed as he opened a paper bag that he found in the parking lot behind his store. For the next six years the Unabomber was quiet.

In 1993, the Unabomber mailed a bomb to David Gelernter, a computer science professor at Yale University. The blast left Gelernter with one hand torn off and with the loss of sight in one eye and loss of hearing in one ear. On December 10, 1994, Thomas Mosser, vice president of an advertising agency in New Jersey, was killed instantly when a package bomb exploded at his residence. Kaczynski justified the killing by stating that advertising executives were responsible for brainwashing people.

In 1995, Kaczynski demanded that his 35,000 word paper titled "Industrial Society and its Future" be published in various newspapers. The work became known as the "Unabomber Manifesto" and was eventually published in the *New York Times* and *Washington Post* in the interest of public safety. In the Manifesto, he declared that the progression of technology was a threat to humanity and that it should be stopped to allow humans to live naturally. He stated that a "social crash" was necessary to prevent the domination of the wealthy upper class over the working class. The Manifesto also clearly stated his beliefs that every human should have the power to control his/her own life instead of by governments and corporations.

Recognizing his handwriting, Kaczynski's younger brother eventually notified the FBI of his suspicions. A team of forensic linguists compared the Manifesto handwriting to other samples provided by Ted's family and confirmed that they were indeed written by the same person. On April 3, 1996, a team of FBI agents surrounded his shack in Lincoln, Montana, and arrested him. Among the items the agents found were notebooks filled with detailed sketches of explosive devices, handwritten notes describing chemical compounds that could be used to create explosive charges, logs of previous experiments, pipes for making pipe bombs, containers of bomb-making chemicals, batteries, and wiring. Kaczynski kept a journal in which he detailed all his activities. He made clear that he was not acting out of altruistic motives, but simply out of "revenge" (Dunder, 2003). At his trial Kaczynski did not want to pursue a mental illness defense that would portray him as being schizophrenic. Instead he plead guilty to 13 counts of bombing and murder, and is now serving several consecutive life sentences without the possibility of parole.

TIMOTHY JAMES McVEIGH (THE OKLAHOMA BOMBER)   On April 19, 1995, a yellow Ryder Rental truck drove quietly and unobtrusively through the streets of downtown Oklahoma City toward the Alfred P. Murrah federal building. The driver parked in front of the building, stepped out, and walked away. A few minutes later, at 9:02 A.M., the truck's 4,000-pound cargo blasted the government building with enough force to shatter one-third of the seven-story structure to bits. One hundred and sixty-eight people were killed in the blast, and more than five hundred others were injured.

The man who drove the truck that day was 27-year-old **Timothy James McVeigh**, who was convinced he acted to defend the Constitution, for he saw himself as a hero. McVeigh had long been obsessed with books like *The Turner Diaries* by former American Nazi Party official William Pierce. Writing under the name Andrew Macdonald, Pierce preached venomous hate through the main character, Earl Turner. In the book Turner demonstrated his contempt for gun control laws by truck bombing the Washington FBI headquarters. He also worshipped Adolf Hitler and regarded African-Americans and Jews as unworthy to live. Movies such as *Red Dawn* helped convince McVeigh it was also time to become a survivalist. In the movie, the lead character heads into the woods with his followers where they prepare to fight the communist invaders.

McVeigh had entered the military in 1990 and was accepted into a program to evaluate his potential for Special Forces, but was shipped to the Persian Gulf in Operation Desert Storm in January 1991. It seems that as long as he was in a structured environment and was appreciated for what he was doing, he was relatively stable. After leaving the Persian Gulf he went to Fort Bragg, North Carolina, for another shot at Special Forces but dropped out after a few days saying he wasn't physically prepared. He returned home with decorations but disillusioned. It was around this time that McVeigh gave up his interest in the American system and embraced the role of a lonely, suspicious, and disenfranchised young man.

In March 1993, McVeigh traveled to Waco, Texas, during the government standoff with self-proclaimed prophet David Koresh's cult, the Branch Davidians. McVeigh became incensed and convinced that the group's rights to bear arms were being violated. In fact, he sold bumper stickers at Waco that said, "A Man with a Gun is a Citizen. A Man without a Gun is a Subject." Waco provided McVeigh with the rationale he had been looking for to vent his anger, and the venting would be violent. Waco also convinced McVeigh and accomplice Terry Nichols that it was time to send a dramatic message to the federal government. They sent the message via the Alfred P. Murrah federal building on April 19, 1995.

After being arrested, McVeigh considered himself as a prisoner of war and took no responsibility for his actions. After three days of deliberation, a trial jury returned a guilty verdict, and he was sentenced to death. After a series of appeals lasting more then three years, he was executed on June 12, 2001. The trial of his accomplice, Terry Nichols, began on March 11, 2004, and on May 27 of the same year he was found guilty as well and sentenced to life in prison.

JOHN ALLEN MUHAMMAD AND LEE BOYD MALVO (THE BELTWAY SNIPERS) Lee Boyd **Malvo** (aka John Lee Malvo and Malik Malvo) was born on February 18, 1985, to Una James and Leslie Malvo, in the slums of Kingston, Jamaica. His parents were never married, and his father left when Malvo was an infant. He and his mother settled in Antigua where Malvo became attached to his mother's new friend, **John Allen Muhammad** (aka John Allen Williams), and apparently looked up to him as a father figure. The two later traveled across the United States, staying with Muhammad's friends and family members. While Malvo was in school, Muhammad passed Malvo off as his son. He also reportedly told his cousin in Louisiana that they both were participating in a secret government mission and gave Malvo the nickname "Sniper."

Muhammad indoctrinated the 17-year-old Malvo with racist and anti-American rhetoric. He kept him isolated from other people, exposed him to violent videos and games, and controlled other aspects of his life. Muhammad trained Malvo to be a "child soldier" and taught him to shoot various weapons. He also persuaded Malvo to convert to Islam.

Malvo and Muhammad first killed in February 2002 in Tacoma, Washington. In May 2002, they allegedly used a .44 Magnum revolver to fire two shots into a synagogue. That same month a 76-year old man was shot in the chest while playing golf in Clearwater, Florida, and a 37-year-old man was shot in the head and killed while he worked in his yard in Denton, Texas. Both were the work of Malvo and Muhammad.

September 2002 saw three more homicides. The first two occurred in Baton Rouge, Louisiana, and the second took place in Clinton, Maryland, where a man was shot six times while closing his pizzeria. On September 21, 2002, in Montgomery, Alabama, a woman was killed and another was shot in the head and wounded during a robbery attempt. Evidence tied this robbery attempt to Malvo and Muhammad because Malvo's fingerprints were left at the crime scene. But in October 2002 the pair began a particularly deadly killing spree in the Washington, DC–Maryland–Virginia metropolitan area that would claim the lives of 14 more innocent victims. During their spree they sent a letter to authorities demanding $10 million, they provided a stolen credit card account number where the money should be transferred. Their letter created even more fear because it threatened the lives of children in Virginia.

After unprecedented law enforcement action involving the FBI, state police, and local agencies, Lee Boyd Malvo and John Allen Muhammad were caught on October 24, 2002, while sleeping in their blue 1990 Chevrolet Caprice at a rest stop in Meyersville, Maryland. A truck driver noticed the car, boxed it in, and notified the police. A search of the car revealed a .223-caliber weapon, and the men were arrested on federal weapons charges. Later, ballistic tests linked the weapon to 11 of the bullets that were found at earlier crime scenes.

At his trial, Malvo pleaded not guilty by reason of insanity on the grounds that he was under the total control of John Allen Muhammad. One of Malvo's psychiatric witnesses testified that Muhammad, a member of Louis Farrakhan's Nation of Islam, a radical black separatist movement, had indoctrinated Malvo into believing that the proceeds of the extortion attempt would be used to begin a new nation of only pure black young people somewhere in Canada. Malvo would later testify at Muhammad's trial that Muhammad had intended to bomb schools, school buses, and children's hospitals following the shooting spree (Ahlers, 2006; Montaldo, 2006; Mount, 2006).

On December 18, 2003, after nearly 14 hours of deliberation, Malvo was found guilty and sentenced to life in prison without parole. Virginia prosecutors had hoped to bring further capitol charges against Malvo in the future but the Supreme Court's decision in *Roper v. Simmons* (2005) made such charges impractical. The Court held that the Eighth Amendment prohibits execution for crimes committed by individuals under the age of 18—Malvo was 17 when he committed the crimes. He was, however, convicted of the six murders in Maryland and sentenced to six more consecutive life sentences without the possibility of parole.

In May 2004, a Virginia court found John Allen Muhammad guilty of the death of one of ten people killed during the October 2002 shootings. Muhammad received the death penalty. What was particularly fascinating about the trial was the testimony of Lee Boyd Malvo and the revelations about the true motivations behind the sniper shootings. Part of the duo's plan was to extort several million dollars from the U.S. government, travel north to Canada, stopping along the way at YMCAs and orphanages to recruit other impressionable young boys with no parents or guidance. John Allen Muhammad thought he could act as their father figure as he did with Lee Boyd Malvo. Once he recruited a large number of young boys and made his way up to Canada, he would begin their terrorist training. After their training was complete, John Allen Muhammad would send them out across the United States to carry out mass shootings in many different cities, just as he had done in Washington, DC, Virginia, and Maryland. These attacks would be coordinated and would be intended to send the country into chaos. The underlying cause for the terrorist plan was not directly addressed at the trial; however, a series of trial exhibits indicated that Malvo and Muhammed were motivated by an affinity for Islamic jihad and a desire to destroy the Western world (Horwitz & Ruane 2004; Mount, 2006).

The Unabomber, the Oklahoma City bombers, and the Beltways snipers were all "terrorists." But their actions were motivated by factors well beyond the desire to inflict terror alone. The Unabomber wanted to make a statement for the whole world to hear. The Oklahoma City bombers desired revenge, and the Beltway snipers wanted to extort money to fund the construction of a religiously based terrorist army.

The Revolutionary Terrorist

Revolutionary terrorists seek the complete abolition of a political system and its replacement with new structures. Modern instances of such activity include campaigns by the Italian Red Brigades, the German Red Army Faction (Baader-Meinhof Gang), the Basque separatist group ETA, and the Peruvian Shining Path (Sendero Luminoso), each of which attempted to topple a national regime.

The Irish Republican Army (IRA) was formed in 1969 as the clandestine armed wing of the political movement *Sinn Fein*. It was devoted to both removing British forces from Northern

Ireland and unifying Ireland as a whole. Northern Ireland came into existence with the British Government of Ireland Act (1920), which divided Ireland into two areas: the Irish Free State, made up of the 26 southern counties, and Northern Ireland—comprising the counties of Antrim, Down, Armagh, Londonderry, Tyrone, and Fermanagh. Roman Catholics, who made up around one-third of the population of Northern Ireland, were largely opposed to the partition.

Traditional IRA activities included bombings, assassinations, kidnappings, punishment beatings, extortion, smuggling, and robberies. Before the cease-fire in 1997, the group had conducted bombing campaigns on various targets in Northern Ireland and Great Britain, including senior British government officials, civilians, police, and British military targets. The group's refusal in late 2004 to allow photographic documentation of its decommissioning process was an obstacle to progress in implementing the Belfast Agreement and stalled talks. The group previously had disposed of light, medium, and heavy weapons; ammunition; and explosives in three rounds of decommissioning. However, the IRA is believed to have retained the ability to conduct paramilitary operations. The group's extensive criminal activities reportedly provided the IRA and the political party Sinn Fein with millions of dollars each year, and the IRA was implicated in two significant robberies in 2004, one involving almost $50 million.

The Establishment (or State-sponsored) Terrorist

This type of terrorist is employed by a government or by factions of a government and acts against that government's citizens, against factions within the government, or against foreign governments or groups. The Soviet Union and its allies allegedly engaged in widespread support of international terrorism during the cold war. The military dictatorships in Chile and Argentina committed acts of state terrorism against their own populations. The violent police states of Joseph Stalin in the Soviet Union and Saddam Hussein in Iraq were examples of countries in which one organ of the government engaged in widespread terror against not only the population but also other organs of the government, including the military.

Ecoterrorists

The FBI defines ecoterrorism as "the use or threatened use of violence of a criminal nature against innocent victims or property by an environmentally oriented, subnational group for environmental-political reasons, or aimed at an audience beyond the target, often of a symbolic nature." But **ecoterrorists** will tell you that they are committed to saving nature.

One such group is the *Animal Liberation Front* (ALF) and is the nation's most active extreme animal rights movement. Composed of anonymous underground cells that oppose any form of animal experimentation and perceived mistreatment, it aims to rescue animals from places of abuse and to inflict economic damage upon those profiting from the exploitation of animals. ALF cells have claimed responsibility for hundreds of crimes that include freeing animals from their owners, and destruction of property. By 2002, several ecoterrorist groups in addition to ALF were active in the United States, and the total number of direct actions had reached about 1,000, including more than 600 criminal acts since 1996.

Another ecoterrorist group is *Green Anarchy*, which contends that humans were better off thousands of years ago, before the advent of farming. Based on an ideology devised by John Zerzan and centered in the Eugene, Oregon, the group views technology and civilization as an unnecessary evil and believes humanity would be much happier and healthier outside the modern industrial world.

The sometimes violent activities of these kinds of groups include criminal trespass on the property of logging companies and other firms and obstruction of their operations, sometimes through the sabotage of company equipment or the environmentally harmless "modification" of natural resources in order to make them inaccessible or unsuitable for commercial use. Examples of this practice, known as "monkey wrenching," are the plugging of factory-waste outlets and driving spikes into trees so that they cannot be logged and milled. Other activities described as ecoterrorist include protest actions including the destruction of property in stores that sell products made of fur and the bombing of laboratories that perform experiments on animals.

Extremist Groups in the United States

An obscure religious ideology has arisen in the United States during the last 30 years known as "Christian Identity." Adherents have committed hate crimes, bombings, and other acts of terrorism. Christian Identity's influence ranges from Ku Klux Klan and neo-Nazi groups to antigovernment militia and sovereign citizen movements. Christian Identity's origins can be traced back to the nineteenth century in Great Britain, where a small circle of religious thinkers advanced the idea, known as *British-Israelism* or Anglo-Israelism, that modern Europeans were biologically descended from the ancient Israelites of the Old Testament, specifically from the "Lost Tribes" scattered by invasions of Hittites, Assyrians, and Babylonians. The Lost Tribes had purportedly made their way to Europe and from them descended the modern European nationalities. The group's racist and apocalyptic qualities helped lead to several well-known incidents of domestic terrorism during the past quarter century. In North Dakota in 1983, Gordon Kahl demonstrated how radical Identity adherents could be when he killed two deputy U.S. marshals who had come to arrest him for a parole violation. A four-month manhunt ended in another shootout in Arkansas, where Kahl killed a local sheriff before he himself was killed. That same year, the white supremacist terrorist group known as *The Order* began its series of armed robberies (to which it would add additional crimes ranging from counterfeiting to assassination). Several members of the gang were Christian Identity, including David Tate, who in 1985 killed a Missouri State Highway patrol officer attempting to reach an Identity survivalist compound called the *Covenant, the Sword, and the Arm of the Lord* (CSA). An ensuing standoff resulted in the demise of the CSA and the arrest of its leadership.

During the 1980s, several Identity groups attempted to follow in the footsteps of The Order, including *The Order II* and the *Arizona Patriots*, who committed bombings and an attempted armored car robbery, respectively. In the 1990s, Identity criminal activity continued, including efforts by an Oklahoma Identity minister, Willie Ray Lampley, to commit a series of bombings in the summer of 1995 in the wake of the Oklahoma City bombing by Timothy McVeigh. The following year, the *Montana Freemen*, whose leaders were Identity, made headlines for their "paper terrorism" tactics and their 81-day standoff with the federal government. In 1998, Eric Rudolph, who had been associated with Identity ministers such as Nord Davis and Dan Gayman, became a fugitive after allegedly bombing gay bars, the Atlanta Summer Olympics, and an abortion clinic.

One of the most chilling manifestation of Identity terrorism can be found in the concept of the *Phineas Priesthood,* set forth by Richard Kelly Hoskins in his 1990 book, *Vigilantes of Christendom*. The Priesthood is based on the concept of the obscure biblical character Phinehas, an Israelite who used a spear to slay a "race-mixing" fellow Israelite and the Midianite woman with whom he had sex. Hoskins conjured up the idea of an elite class of "Phineas Priests," self-anointed warriors who would use extreme measures to attack race-mixers, gays, or abortionists, among other targets.

Over the years, Phineas warriors have committed crimes including bombings and bank robberies in the Spokane Washington area in 1996 (four of whom were caught and sentenced to lengthy prison terms). In 2002, two Aryan Nations splinter groups openly adopted Phineas Priest names or symbols. The *Vigilantes of Christendom* and other Christian Nationalist groups have inspired and influenced several incidents of violence. In 1994, Paul Hill, an antiabortion activist who advocated "Phineas actions," shot to death a doctor and his escort outside a Florida woman's clinic.

After the 1996 arrest of *Aryan Republican Army* members Peter Langan and Richard Guthrie (members of a group that tried to finance a white revolution by committing two dozen bank robberies), authorities found a recruiting video in which Langan, wearing a mask, held a copy of *Vigilantes* and referred to it as "an effective handbook for revolution." In what is considered one of the major domestic terrorism cases of the 1990s, four men identifying themselves as Phineas Priests were arrested in 1996 and later convicted of bank robbery and bombings at a newspaper office and abortion clinic in Spokane Washington. In 1999, former Aryan Nations member Buford Furrow fired on children at a Jewish Community Center in Los Angeles and murdered a Filipino-American postal worker. Among Furrow's personal effects, authorities found copies of Phineas Priest documents, along with a copy of *War Cycles, Peace Cycles*.

Christian Identity is strongest in the Pacific Northwest and the Midwest, but Christian Identity groups or churches can be found in virtually every region of the United States (outside the United States, it is much weaker, but there are Identity groups in Canada, Ireland, Great Britain, Australia, and South Africa). Yet while spread far it is also spread thin. Estimates of the total number of believers in North America vary from a low of 25,000 to a high of 50,000; the true number is probably closer to the low end of the scale.

In 2006, the Southern Poverty Law Center criticized the Southern Baptist Convention (an evangelical Christian group) for electing a second vice president whose name appears on a "Declaration of Support for James Kopp," a man convicted of killing a doctor because he provided abortions. Already serving 25 years to life on a 2003 state murder conviction in New York, Kopp was also convicted of violating the *Freedom of Access to Clinic Entrances Act* by assassinating the physician as he talked with his wife and children in the family's kitchen. Kopp, who was on the FBI's "Ten Most Wanted" list before his capture in March 2001, has admitted to the shooting but claims he was only trying to wound the physician, and not kill him, to prevent him from performing abortions. The Southern Poverty Law Center has reported that in the last 30 years, abortion clinics have been bombed 41 times according to law enforcement statistics compiled by the National Abortion Federation. Many of the crimes directed at abortion providers, including 93 attempted bombings and arson, were committed during times that abortion issues were prominent in the news.

Similar examples include the 1998 killing of Officer Robert Sanderson during a clinic bombing in Birmingham, Alabama. Eric Robert Rudolph is serving a life sentence for this bombing as well as for bombings at a gay bar and another abortion clinic. In 1994, Shannon Lowney and Leanne Nichols were shot and killed by John Salvi at two clinics in Brookline, Massachusetts. Five others were injured in the attacks as well. Salvi was sentenced to two life terms but committed suicide in prison in November 1996. In 1993, Dr. George Tiller was shot and injured by Rachelle Shannon at his clinic in Wichita, Kansas. Shannon is serving an 11-year sentence for attempted first-degree murder. She is serving additional prison time for six arsons and two butyric acid attacks. In the same year, Dr. David Gunn was shot to death by Michael Griffin in Pensacola, Florida. Griffin is serving a life sentence for the murder.

Butyric acid has been used by extremists as a weapon against abortion facilities beginning in early 1992. The goal of introducing butyric acid into a clinic is to disrupt services, close the clinic, and harass patients and staff. Depending on the amount used and how it is introduced into the clinic, butyric acid can cause thousands of dollars of damage, requiring clinics to replace carpeting, furniture, and conduct extensive cleanup of the facility. In addition, even after cleanup, butyric acid's smell leaves a reminder of the incident for months, and often years, to come. There have been about 100 butyric acid attacks throughout the United States and Canada, causing in excess of $1 million in damages (National Abortion Federation, 2007).

The Ku Klux Klan

The Ku Klux Klan is a racist, anti-Semitic movement with a commitment to use violence to achieve its goals of racial segregation and white supremacy. More than 40 different Klan groups exist, many having multiple chapters, or "klaverns," with an estimated membership of around 5,000 in the United States. After a period of relative quiet, Klan activity spiked in 2006, as issues of gay marriage and immigration energized them and threatened their idiosyncratic conception of Christianity (*Anti-Defamation League*, 2007).

The Ku Klux Klan first emerged following the Civil War as America's first true terrorist group. Since its inception, the Ku Klux Klan has seen several cycles of growth and collapse, and in some of these cycles the Klan has been more extreme than in others. In all of its incarnations, however, the Klan has maintained its dual heritage of hate and violence. At first, the Ku Klux Klan focused its anger and violence on African-Americans, on white Americans who stood up for them, and against the federal government that supported their rights. Subsequent incarnations of the Klan, which typically emerged in times of rapid social change, added more categories to its enemies list, including Jews, Catholics (less so after the 1970s), homosexuals, and different groups of immigrants.

The Ku Klux Klan was overshadowed in the late 1990s and early 2000s by growing neo-Nazi activity; however, by 2005 neo-Nazi groups had fallen on hard times, with many groups collapsing or fragmenting. This collapse has helped create a rise of racist skinhead activity, but has also provided new opportunities for Klan groups. In addition, in the early 2000s, many communities in the United States began to experiences a significant influx of immigrants, especially Hispanics, for the first time in their histories. A single-issue movement opposing immigration has helped create fear and anxiety about immigration in the minds of many Americans.

The Militia Movement

The militia movement is a right-wing extremist movement consisting of armed paramilitary groups, both formal and informal, with an antigovernment, conspiracy-oriented ideology. Militia groups began to form not long after the deadly standoff at Waco, Texas, in 1993; by the spring of 1995, they had spread to almost every state. Many members of militia groups have been arrested since then, usually on weapons, explosives, and conspiracy charges.

The fact that both the Ruby Ridge and Waco incidents involved illegal firearms added considerable fuel to the fire that fueled the militia movement. Many militia members and leaders were radical gun-rights advocates, people who believed that, in fact, there could be no such things as illegal firearms and whose antigovernment attitude was formed in large part because of fear and suspicion of imminent gun confiscation. In the early 1990s, several prototype militias had emerged in Connecticut and Florida on the basis that members of the "militia" were exempt from federal gun laws. In 1992, a leader of a radical gun-rights group and an advocate of the formation of militias issued a statement in the wake of the Rodney King riots urging the Los Angeles Police Department to take advantage of what the Founding Fathers called the unorganized militia in order to forestall further unrest.

Many people initially joined the fledgling militia movement largely as a way to protect more aggressively their right to bear arms; even today, gun-related issues dominate many of the newsletters published by militia groups. Some militias planned attacks on military installations. The first planned attack would occur against Fort Hood, Texas, on July 4, 1997, which is the day the post hosts an annual "Freedom Festival" attended by 50,000 people. But the Missouri State Highway Patrol and the FBI detected the plans and prevented a tragedy. Some militia groups used the strategy of identifying a perceived "victim of government" and came to their rescue. Militia members viewed events such as Ruby Ridge and Waco as opportunities to present themselves as a defensive army standing between the average citizen and the "tyranny" of the government.

Considering the views and concerns of some of these groups, it is not surprising to find that as of this writing, there has been an increased radicalization of their activities. This may be due to the economic recession, the election of America's first black president (who is pro-choice and pro-gun control), and the return of a number of disgruntled Persian Gulf war veterans. As one example, there is evidence that a recently arrested alleged spree killer named Keith Luke may actually be a Neo-Nazi who was infuriated by the election of a black president. Luke is a 22-year-old white supremacist accused of carrying out a racially motivated rape and murder spree in Brockton, Massachusetts, the day after Barack Obama was inaugurated. He appeared in court in May with a jagged swastika freshly carved into his forehead. Luke stands accused of killing two immigrants from Cape Verdean and attempting to murder a third. He allegedly told police that he was "fighting for a dying race" and that he decided to kill blacks, Latinos, and Jews after reading about "the demise of the white race" on websites such as *PodBlanc*, which is particularly virulent in its anti-Semitic and racist propaganda (Beirich & Potok, 2009; Flint, 2003).

The Black Panther Party

The "New Black Panther Party for Self Defense" takes its name from the original Black Panther Party, formed by Huey Newton and Bobby Seale in Oakland, California, in 1966. The original Panthers combined militant black nationalism with Marxism and advocated black empowerment and self-defense, often through confrontation. By 1969, the group had an estimated 5,000 members spread throughout 20 chapters around the country. In the early 1970s, however, the group lost momentum and most of its support due to internal disputes, violent clashes with police, and infiltration by law enforcement agencies. Despite the collapse, the group's mystique continued to influence radicals, and by the early 1990s a new generation of militant activists began to model themselves after the original Panthers.

The roots of the New Black Panthers can be traced to Michael McGee, a former member of the original Panthers, who was elected to the Milwaukee City Council in Wisconsin in 1984. In 1987, in response to what he viewed as a crisis in the city's black community, McGee threatened to disrupt "Summerfest" events "and other white people's fun" throughout the city unless more jobs were created for black people. He eventually backed off, instead leading demonstrations to call attention to black unemployment. In 1990, at a "state of the inner city" press conference at city hall, McGee—then a Milwaukee alderman—announced his intention to create the Black Panther Militia unless the problems of the inner-city improved. He sought to enlist street gangs in the militia and provide them with weapons training. "They can fight and they already know how to shoot," he said. "I'm going to give them a cause to die for." By 1995, McGee threatened, the militia would carry out violent attacks in the city against "the government, the big private interests, and the multi-millionaires" (Anti-Defamation League, 2007).

TOOLS OF TERRORISM

Bombings

Bombings are the most common type of terrorist act. Typically, improvised explosive devices are inexpensive and easy to make. For example, on August 7, 1998, two American embassies in Africa were bombed. The bombings claimed the lives of over 200 people, including 12 innocent American citizens, and injured over 5,000 civilians. Terrorists can also use materials that are readily available to the average consumer to construct a bomb. Such bombs include:

1. Roadside and hidden bombs
2. Letter bombs sent through the mail
3. Car bombs hidden in vehicles, designed to ignite when a car is started
4. Remote-triggered bombs
5. Suicide bombs

For example, on October 23, 1982, simultaneous suicide truck bomb attacks were made on the American and French compounds in Beirut, Lebanon. A 12,000-pound bomb destroyed the U.S. compound killing 242 Marines, while 58 French troops were killed when a 400-lb bomb destroyed the French base. Islamic Jihad claimed responsibility. On April 18, 1983, 63 people were killed and 120 were injured when a 400-pound suicide truck bomb was detonated at the U.S. Embassy in Beirut, Lebanon. Islamic Jihad again claimed responsibility. On August 1, 1998, a

500-lb car bomb planted outside a store in Banbridge, North Ireland, by the Real IRA injured 35 persons and damaged at least 200 homes. On July 27, 1996, a bombing of Centennial Olympic Park killed 2 and wounded 112. Eric Robert Rudolph was charged with the bombing as well as bombings of numerous women's clinics. And on August 15, 1998, a 500-pound car bomb planted by the *Real IRA* exploded outside a local courthouse in the central shopping district of Omagh, Northern Ireland, killing 29 persons and injuring over 330.

Furthermore, the United States has suffered several terrorist attacks by Puerto Rican nationalists (such as the FALN), antiabortion groups, and foreign-based organizations. The 1990s witnessed some of the deadliest attacks on American soil, including the bombing of the World Trade Center in New York City in 1993 and the Oklahoma City bombing two years later, which killed 168 people. In addition, there were several major terrorist attacks on U.S. government targets overseas, including military bases in Saudi Arabia (1996) and the U.S. embassies in Kenya and Tanzania (1998). In 2000, an explosion triggered by suicide bombers caused the deaths of 17 sailors aboard a U.S. naval ship, the USS *Cole*, in the Yemeni port of Aden.

Kidnappings and Hostage-Takings

Terrorists use kidnapping and hostage-taking to establish a bargaining position and to elicit publicity. Kidnapping is one of the most difficult acts for a terrorist group to accomplish, but, if a kidnapping is successful, it can gain terrorists money, release of jailed comrades, and publicity for an extended period. Hostage taking involves the seizure of a facility or location and the taking of the individuals living or working there as hostages. Unlike a kidnapping, hostage taking provokes a confrontation with authorities. It forces authorities to either make dramatic decisions or comply with the terrorists' demands. It is overt and designed to attract and hold media attention. The terrorists' intended target is frequently the audience affected by the hostage's confinement, not the hostage.

As an example, on February 17, 1988, LTC W. Higgins was kidnapped, tortured, and murdered while serving with the United Nations Truce Supervisory Organization in Southern Lebanon. And January 23, 2002, *Wall Street Journal* reporter Daniel Pearl was kidnapped. Pearl was held captive for several weeks before his captives slit his throat and released the video to the media.

Armed Attacks, Assassinations, and Arson

Armed attacks include raids and ambushes. Historically, terrorists have assassinated specific individuals for psychological effect. Arson and firebombings are easily conducted by terrorist groups that may not be as well-organized, equipped, or trained as a major terrorist organization. An arson or firebombing against a utility, hotel, government building, or industrial center portrays an image that the ruling government is incapable of maintaining order.

Hijackings and Skyjackings

Hijacking is the seizure by force of a surface vehicle, its passengers, and/or its cargo. Skyjacking is the taking of an aircraft that creates a mobile, hostage-barricade situation. It provides terrorists with hostages from many nations and draws heavy media attention. Skyjacking also provides mobility for the terrorists to relocate the aircraft to a country that supports their cause and provides them with a human shield, making retaliation difficult.

For example, on June 14, 1985, a Trans-World Airlines was hijacked on route to Rome from Athens by two Lebanese Hezbollah terrorists and forced to fly to Beirut. The 8 crewmembers and 145 passengers were held for 17 days, during which an American hostage, a U.S. Navy sailor, was beaten to death. After being flown twice to Algiers, the aircraft was returned to Beirut after Israel released 435 Lebanese and Palestinian prisoners. And on June 27, 1976, in the Entebbe hostage crisis, members of the *Bauder-Meinhof Group* and the *Popular Front for the Liberation of Palestine*

(PFLP) seized an Air France airliner and its 258 passengers. They forced the plane to fly to Uganda, where on July 3, 1976, Israeli commandos successfully rescued the passengers.

Weapons of Mass Destruction

This includes using nuclear, biological, and chemical weapons to induce destruction and mass panic. In 1984, the *Animal Liberation Front* (ALF) claimed to have poisoned MARS Bars in the United Kingdom. Every MARS candy bar in the United Kingdom was removed from the shelves at a cost of over £3 million. Again, in 1988, ALF terrorists poisoned a lot of confectionary sugar at a Swiss chocolate factory with rat poison and sent the results to the media. As a result the company had to halt production and clean the factory at a cost of over $30 million. In 1995, the Japanese doomsday cult "AUM Shinrikyo" released nerve gas into a Tokyo subway. In a similar fashion, after the September 11, 2001 attacks on the United States, a number of letters contaminated with anthrax were delivered to political leaders and journalists leading to several deaths.

Suicide Attacks

Some groups, including the *Liberation Tigers of Tamil Eelam* and *Hamas*, adopted the tactic of suicide bombing, in which the perpetrator would attempt to destroy an important economic, military, political, or symbolic target by detonating a bomb on his person. In the latter half of the twentieth century the most prominent groups using terrorist tactics were the Red Army Faction, the Japanese Red Army, the Red Brigades, the Puerto Rican FALN, Fatah and other groups related to the Palestine Liberation Organization (PLO), the Shining Path, and the Liberation Tigers.

The deadliest terrorist strikes to date were the September 11 attacks (2001), in which suicide terrorists associated with al-Qaeda hijacked four commercial airplanes, crashing two of them into the twin towers of the World Trade Center complex in New York City and the third into the Pentagon building near Washington, DC; the fourth plane crashed near Pittsburgh, Pennsylvania. The crashes destroyed much of the World Trade Center complex and a large portion of one side of the Pentagon and killed more than 3,000 people.

ECOTERRORISM Ecoterrorism or "environmental warfare" consists of the deliberate and illegal destruction, exploitation, or modification of the environment as a strategy of war or in times of armed conflict (including civil conflict within states). Modification of the environment that occurs during armed conflict and is likely to have widespread, long-lasting, or severe effects is proscribed by the Convention on the Prohibition of Military or Any Other Hostile Use of Environmental Modification Techniques, adopted by the United Nations General Assembly in 1976. Nevertheless, such destruction has occurred with some regularity. In the 1960s and 1970s, the U.S. military used the defoliant Agent Orange to destroy forest cover in Vietnam, and in 1991 Iraqi military forces retreating during the Persian Gulf War set fire to Kuwaiti oil wells, causing significant environmental damage.

Cyberterrorism

Cyberterrorism is the convergence of terrorism and cyberspace. It is the unlawful attack or threat of attack against computers, computer networks, or information stored on computers, with the intent to intimidate or coerce in order to achieve political or social objectives (Denning, 2000). As an example, in 1996, a computer hacker allegedly associated with a White Supremacist movement temporarily disabled a Massachusetts ISP and damaged part of the ISP's record keeping system. The ISP had attempted to stop the hacker from sending out worldwide racist messages under the ISP's name. The hacker signed off with the threat, "you have yet to see true electronic terrorism. This is a promise" (Denning, p. 2).

In 1998, Spanish protestors bombarded the Institute for Global Communications (IGC) with thousands of bogus e-mail messages. E-mail was tied up and undeliverable to the ISP's users, and support lines were tied up with people who couldn't get their mail. IGC finally had to pull the site because of the mail attacks. During the Kosovo conflict in 1999, NATO computers were bombarded with e-mail bombs and hit with denial-of-service attacks by "hacktivists" protesting the NATO bombings. In addition, businesses, public organizations, and academic institutes received highly politicized virus-laden e-mails and web defacements from various Eastern European countries.

In addition to cyberattacks against digital data and systems, many people are being terrorized on the Internet today with threats of physical violence. Online stalking, death threats, and hate messages are profuse, relatively uncontrolled, and growing. Furthermore, with the advent and proliferation of cell phones equipped with cameras, the ability to send any and all kinds of text messages and digital images has expanded exponentially both the ability for communication and enjoyment, but also the opportunities to embarrass, harass, and extort innocent people. One recent phenomena is that of *sexting*, which is the act of sending a sexually explicit photo/video message via a cell phone. These are increasingly more situations in which preteens, teens, and even adults are taking inappropriate pictures of themselves or friends and then sharing them via cell phones. Sometimes this has disastrous consequences. In 2007, for example, Jessica Logan, a Cincinnati, Ohio, teen, hanged herself after her nude photo, meant for her boyfriend, was sent to teenagers at several high schools.

The National Campaign to Prevent Teen & Unplanned Pregnancy, a private nonprofit group whose mission is to protect children, and CosmoGirl.com, surveyed nearly 1,300 teens about sex and technology. The results indicated that one in five teens say they've sexted even though the majority knew it could be a crime. Phillip Alpert found this out the hard way. Alpert's 16-year-old girlfriend had taken a naked photo of herself and given it to him. Following an argument with the girlfriend, and soon after turning 18, Alpert sent the photo to dozens of her friends and family in an apparent act of revenge. But sexting is treated as child pornography in almost every state, and Alpert became a registered sex offender (and will be labeled as a sex offender until the age of 43 years). He has been expelled from college, lost most of his friends, cannot travel out of the country without making prior arrangements with his parole officer, and cannot find a job due to being a convicted felon (Feyerick & Steffen, 2009).

RELIGIOUSLY BASED INTERNATIONAL TERRORISM

The connection between religion and terrorism is not new. In fact, some of the English words we use to describe terrorists and their acts today are derived from the names of Jewish, Muslim, and Hindu religious groups active centuries ago. The etymology of the word "zealot," for example, is traceable to an ancient Jewish sect that fought against the Roman occupation of what is now Israel between 66 and 73 C.E. The Zealots waged a ruthless campaign against the Romans, which included assassination and mass killings. Similarly, the word *assassin* is derived from a radical offshoot of the Muslim sect called Shi'a, who, between 1090 and 1272 C.E., fought the Christian crusaders attempting to conquer present-day Syria and Iran. The assassin, literally "hashish-eater," would ritualistically use hashish before committing murder, a sacramental act or divine duty designed to hasten the new millennium. Finally, the designation *thug* comes from an Indian religious association of professional robbers and murderers who, from the seventh century until their suppression in the mid-nineteenth century, ritually strangled wayward travelers as sacrificial offerings to Kali, the Hindu goddess of terror and destruction.

Terrorism motivated in whole or in part by religious imperatives often leads to more intense acts of violence producing considerably more fatalities than the relatively discriminating acts of violence perpetrated by secular terrorist organizations. In the year 1995, religious terrorists committed only 25% of the recorded international terrorist incidents, but their acts were responsible for 58% of the terrorist-related fatalities recorded during that year. The attacks that caused the greatest numbers of deaths in 1995—those that killed eight or more people—were *all* perpetrated by religious terrorists. The reasons why religious terrorism results in so many more deaths than secular terrorism may be found in the radically different value systems, mechanisms of legitimization and justification, concepts of morality, and worldviews embraced by religious terrorists. The late twentieth and early twenty-first centuries brought a new kind of religiously based terrorism to the world—that based on apocalyptic and extreme Islamist teachings. Such terrorists engage in terrorism out of a fundamentalist religious ideology that is not amenable to reason or negotiation, dialogue, or pacification. Only capitulation or death is possible. These groups firmly believe that they have been divinely ordained to commit violent acts resulting in mass casualties. This is the terrorism that presents the greatest risk to both the United States and the civilized world, including most other Muslims who do not adhere to such violent ideology.

PSYCHOLOGICAL EXPLANATIONS FOR TERRORISM

What makes a person be a terrorist? It is generally accepted that terrorism results from multiple causations such as psychological, economic, political, religious, and sociological factors. Hubbard (1983) has theorized that physiological factors are prominent in terrorist activities in that stress-produced substances such as norepinephrine, acetylcholine, and endorphins may agitate a person's basic physiology and that such stress is relieved in the form of committing aggressive acts. But this view has understandably not received much support.

The Frustration–Aggression Hypothesis

The frustration–aggression hypothesis, discussed in Chapter 3, has also been used to explain terrorist behavior. Under this theory, such behavior is a response to frustrated attempts to meet various political, economic, and personal goals or objectives (Margolin, 1977). Others have dismissed the frustration–aggression hypothesis as an explanation for terrorism as being overly simplistic and based on the naïve assumption that aggression is always a consequence of frustration. Other theorists point to a *narcissism–aggression hypothesis* as an explanation for terrorist behavior. This hypothesis holds that terrorism is a form of **narcissistic rage**, or an intense overreaction to not being able to acquire or maintain power or control by intimidation, thus resulting in shame (Pearstein, 1991; Post, 1990).

Mental Illness

Are terrorists mentally ill? Borum (2004) points to the difficulty of making any such determination because researchers have little, if any, direct access to terrorists, even imprisoned ones. But a recent review of the scientific literature does conclude that terrorists are not dysfunctional or pathological; rather, their actions are basically another form of politically motivated violence (Ruby, 2002). Israeli psychology professor Ariel Merari has collected empirical data on an extremely large number of suicide bombers in the Middle East and found none of the risk factors traditionally associated with suicide, such as severe depression, bipolar disorder, schizophrenia, substance abuse, or history of suicide attempts. He points out that this may not be surprising since suicide attackers view their acts as expressions of martyrdom, whether for their faith, their people, or their cause (Martens, 2004).

It is an understandable stereotype that someone who commits such abhorrent acts as planting a bomb on an airliner, detonating a bomb on a crowded bus, or flying an airplane into a building full of innocent people must be psychologically "abnormal." Jerrold Post (1990), a leading advocate of the terrorists-as-mentally ill approach, argues that "political terrorists are driven to commit acts of violence as a consequence of psychological forces, and that a special form of 'psychologic' is constructed to rationalize acts they are psychologically compelled to commit"(p. 25).

There has no doubt been instances where mentally ill individuals have committed acts that induced a sense of terror in others. Hubbard (1971), for example, concludes that these people have been especially attracted to airplane hijacking. He conducted a psychiatric study of airplane hijackers in 1971 and concluded that this technique was used by psychiatrically ill patients as an expression of their pathology. His study revealed that skyjackers shared several common traits: a violent father who was often an alcoholic, a deeply religious mother, personal overreligiosity, shyness, timidity, poor academic achievement, and limited earning potential. But the world has changed substantially in the 40 years since this study was conducted. Although terrorists may certainly be extremely alienated from society, there is no solid data to indicate that mental illness is a critical factor in terrorist behavior (Heskin, 1984; McCauley & Segal, 1987).

Personality Disorders

But the psychological literature *does* suggest that although many terrorists may not suffer from a classical and diagnosable mental illness such as schizophrenia, they are more likely to have psychopathic tendencies indicative of **antisocial personality disorders**. The major indicator for this assumption stems from the brutal and dehumanizing acts often committed by these people. But terrorists typically do have some connection to principles or ideology as well as to other people (including families and other terrorists). Psychopaths, however, do not form such connections, nor would they be likely to sacrifice themselves or die for a cause. In addition, in contrast to the terrorist, the purposefulness, if any, of a psychopath's actions are personal and not for the "greater good" as he/she may view it. Psychopaths are also too unreliable and incapable of being controlled to be of use to terrorist groups. But there are some shared characteristics between people with antisocial personality disorders and individuals who become terrorists. These include social alienation, hostility, arrogance, intolerance of criticism, primitive defenses regarding shame, fear of dependency, and a tendency to dehumanize others (Borum, 2004).

Antisocial personalities generally divide the world into three groups: (1) those whom they want something from, (2) their victims, and (3) everybody else in the world. The terrorist's world can similarly be described as consisting of three categories of people: (1) the terrorist's idealized heroes, (2) the terrorist's enemies or targets, and (3) people he encounters in everyday life, whom the terrorist regards as shadow figures of no consequence (Fried, 1982).

Narcissistic Rage Hypothesis

Generally speaking, individuals with narcissistic personality disorders tend to be grandiose and may become physically abusive when feeling humiliated, rejected, or otherwise narcissistically injured. They are frequently perpetrators of domestic violence and wind up incarcerated for violent crimes more than any other diagnostic classification (Warren, Burnette, South, Chauhan, & Bale, 2002). Advocates of a narcissism–aggression hypothesis are concerned with the early development of the terrorist. Basically, if primary narcissism in the form of the "grandiose self" is not neutralized by reality testing (what goes on in the real world), the grandiose self produces individuals who are arrogant, power seeking, and lacking in regard for others. In this manner, some degree of terrorism can be seen as an attempt to acquire or maintain power or control by intimidation, and the "high ideals" of the terrorist group serve to protect the group members from experiencing shame (Pearlstein, 1991).

A particularly striking personality trait of people who are drawn to terrorism is the reliance placed on the psychological mechanisms of "**externalization**" and "**splitting**." These are primitive psychological mechanisms usually found in individuals with narcissistic and borderline personality disturbances. Splitting is a mechanism characteristic of people whose personality development is shaped by a particular type of psychological damage (narcissistic injury) during childhood. Those individuals with a damaged self-concept have failed to integrate the good and bad parts of the self, which are instead split into the "me" and the "not me." Such individuals need an outside enemy to blame for their own inadequacies and weaknesses. There is research to show, for example, that many terrorists have not been successful in their personal, educational, and vocational lives (Post, 1990). Thus, they are drawn to terrorist groups, which have this us-versus-them outlook. Externalization and splitting are purely psychological mechanisms that usually operate independently of intellectual factors. This may account to some extent for these primitive defenses operating in the increasing number of terrorists who are well-educated professionals, such as chemists, engineers, and physicists.

In fact, many terrorist leaders are increasingly well educated and capable of sophisticated, albeit highly biased, political analysis (Hudson, 1999). The new generation of Islamic terrorists, such as Ramzi Yousef, or leaders such as Osama bin Laden, are well educated and motivated by their religious ideologies. As indicated previously, **religiously motivated terrorists** are more dangerous than politically motivated terrorists and are more likely to develop and use weapons of mass destruction in pursuit of their messianic or apocalyptic visions.

Cognitive Distortions

In an attempt to examine the thinking patterns of terrorists, the psychologist Aaron T. Beck has developed a model of terrorist ideologies describing their cognitive distortions, which occur as either individuals or members of a group. An example of such a cognitive distortion is *overgeneralization* where the entire world is guilty of supposed sins or evil. **Dichotomous thinking** is another example of such a distortion where people are seen as either totally good or totally bad but never in between. As with splitting, dichotomous thinking is well known to occur in individuals with borderline personality disorders. Beck sees terrorists as also demonstrating *tunnel vision*, where once they are engaged in their mission (e.g., jihad), their thinking and consequently their actions focus exclusively on the destruction of the target (Beck, 2002).

RELIGIOUS CULTS

Unfortunately, **cults** are nothing new in the world of extreme religiosity. One of the most infamous (and deadly) of these in recent times was the *People's Temple* led by James Warren (Jim) Jones. The People's Temple was initially structured as an interracial mission for the sick, homeless, and jobless. Jones assembled a large following of over 900 members in Indianapolis, Indiana, during the 1950s. He preached a "social gospel" of human freedom, equality, and love, which required helping the least and the lowliest of society's members. Later on, however, this gospel became explicitly socialistic. When a government investigation began into his bogus cures for cancer, heart disease, and arthritis, Jones decided to move the group to Ukiah in Northern California. After another move to San Francisco and Los Angeles, he relocated the Temple to Jonestown, Guyana.

Once in Guyana, the Temple leased almost 4,000 acres of dense jungle from the government. They established an agricultural cooperative there, called the *Peoples Temple Agricultural Project*. They raised animals for food and assorted tropical fruits and vegetables for eating and selling. Jones developed a belief, which he called *Translation*, in which he and his followers would all die together and move to another planet for a life of bliss. The group "practiced" mass suicides in which his followers pretended to drink poison and then all fell to the ground.

During the late 1970s, Jones had been abusing prescription drugs and appeared to become increasingly paranoid. Rumors of human rights abuses circulated. Former members claimed that Jonestown was being run like a concentration camp and that people were being held there against their will. These concerns motivated Leo Ryan, a congressman, to visit Jonestown in November 1978 for a personal inspection. At first, the visit went well. Later, about 16 Temple members decided that they wanted to leave Jonestown with the visitors. This came as quite a blow to both Jones and the rest of the project. While Ryan and the others were waiting at Port Kiatuma airfield, the local airstrip, some heavily armed members of the Temple's security guards arrived and started shooting. Congressman Ryan and four others were killed; three were members of the press; the other was a person from Jonestown who wanted to leave. Eleven people were wounded.

Fearing retribution for the slaughter, the project members discussed their options and reached a consensus to commit group suicide. Most appear to have committed suicide by drinking a grape drink laced with cyanide and a number of sedatives, including liquid Valium and chloral hydrate. Some sources say it was Kool-Aid. Other victims appear to have been murdered by poison injection. The Guyanese coroner said that hundreds of bodies showed needle marks, indicating foul play. Still other victims were shot. A very few fled into the jungle and survived. In all, 914 died: 638 adults and 276 children. Their bodies were in a state of extensive decay when the authorities arrived. There was no time to conduct a thorough investigation (see Layton, 1998; Maaga & Wessinger, 1998; Wessinger, 2000).

Another bizarre and disaster-destined religious group was *Heaven's Gate* led by Marshall Herff Applewhite (aka Bo and Do) and Bonnie Lu Nettles (aka Peep and Ti). Applewhite and Nettles met after he had been dismissed from St. Thomas University as the result of a scandal involving a male student. The dismissal plunged Applewhite into depression and bitterness.

In 1973, Applewhite claimed to have a revelation. He divined that He and Nettles were the two prophets of the eleventh chapter of the Book of Revelations and that after 1,260 days of bearing witness to the truth, they would be killed by their enemies. This event would be followed by their ascension to heaven in a cloud. The cloud, he believed, would be a spacecraft. With a belief system that combined elements of Christian scripture and various metaphysical teachings, along with delusions regarding UFOs, Applewhite and Nettles began to preach their space-age gospel. They came to believe that they themselves were extraterrestrials who offered humans one last chance to move to a higher level of salvation through death and reincarnation. The Heavenly Kingdom that Applewhite and Nettles talked about was more than just spiritual, it was literal, and as previously pointed out, the means of getting to this Kingdom was via a spacecraft. But a boarding pass for the spacecraft was not free; it required payment in the form of a disciplined life according to their rules. These rules appear to have changed during the life of the group, but included celibacy, abstinence from drugs and alcohol, limited contact with the outside world, and the abandonment of worldly connections (the changing of one's name, cutting of hair, and disposal of possessions).

To Applewhite and his believers, the coming of the comet Hale-Bopp signaled that a heavenly spacecraft was positioned behind the comet, waiting to take them to the next level. They did not see themselves as committing suicide; they were merely abandoning the physical "vehicles" that they regarded as no longer necessary. Their deaths were acts of faith.

CULT-LIKE GROUP DYNAMICS IN RELIGIOUSLY MOTIVATED TERRORISM

Terrorist groups often operate like cults in their use of conditioning techniques to transform members into remorseless and robot-like killers. These conditioning techniques and psychological mechanisms include depluralization, moral disengagement, obedience, diffusion of responsibility, self-deindividuation, other-deindividuation, dehumanization, and demonization.

Depluralization

Depluralization is the process whereby terrorist recruits and cult members give up all their former ties and affiliations. To help accomplish this, training camps are frequently located in isolated environments. In these isolated settings it becomes easier for new members to give up membership in any of their previous group affiliations, often including their families. Old group affiliations and identities detract from the total commitment required by the cult. Terrorist groups cannot effectively condition joiners unless the terrorist group is the joiners' only group affiliation. Such an individual's self-concept and self-esteem become totally dependent on retaining membership in the group. Once dependent, the individual is willing to do whatever it takes to retain membership in the group. This process can take days or years to complete (Morgan, 2001; Robbins, 1988).

Moral Disengagement

The social psychologist Albert Bandura studied individuals who participate in activities that prove harmful to others while furthering their own personal interests. He called this process **moral disengagement.** Usually, most normal people do not engage in destructive behaviors unless they have created a way in which to morally justify their actions. In essence, people need to experience a cognitive reconstruction, which allows them to view certain concepts previously thought of as immoral as justifiable. Terrorist organizations and cults recognize this process; thus, through extensive training, recruits are desensitized and morally disengaged in small doses so as not to fully recognize their personal transformation. At the same time part of this process of moral disengagement is recognizing that it is much easier to hurt others when suffering is not clearly evident (i.e., setting off a bomb from a distance) (Bandura, 1990).

Diffusion of Responsibility

Diffusion of responsibility is the process by which people feel less responsible (or less culpable) when, either in the presence of, or on behalf of a group, they engage in harmful or even heinous behavior. In this way the individual mitigates his own culpability by maintaining that he acted under the mandate of some authority and so absolves himself of intent or guilt because he acted "under orders". In turn, the individual giving the orders attempts to absolve himself because he is merely "issuing directives" (Grossman, 1995). When responsibility is diffused, people lose their sense of self-awareness and consequently their inhibitions and restraints (Darley & Latane, 1968).

Self-deindividuation

Self-deindividuation takes away an individual's personal identity, both externally and internally. Externally terrorist, group and cult members may dress in a completely new way. Internally, members are expected to give up any values, beliefs, attitudes, or behavior patterns that deviate from the groups values and expectations. Deindividuated joiners give up their personal sense of right and wrong if it is different from that of the group's leader. Furthermore, the joiners' broader view of reality—their view of how the past, present, and future fit together to create the modern social world—becomes aligned with that of the leader. Deindividuated persons stop thinking about their own unique qualities. They absorb the concept that they are simply anonymous parts of the greater whole (Akhtar, 1999).

Research by Zimbardo (1969) supports this hypothesis of deindividuation as a process in which a series of conditions (social, environmental, behavioral) lead to a change in perception of self and others, and thereby to a lowered threshold of normally restrained behavior. Some of these hitherto restrained behaviors (or output behaviors as Zimbardo calls them) are irrational, impulsive, and regressive, and difficult to terminate once begun. According to this model, deindividuation can also result in perceptual distortions, hyperresponsiveness, and a tendency to become "autistic" in the search for impulse gratification (Zimbardo, 1969).

Other-deindividuation

People tend to categorize their worlds into those who are in the same groups and those who are not in the same groups (Aronson, Wilson, & Akert, 2002). Many terrorist organizations identify certain "outside" groups as enemies. New members are then conditioned to deindividuate members of the enemy group. Enemy deindividuation includes giving up any personal relationships with enemy group members, not referring to enemies by individual names, and not distinguishing any individual "person" attributes or characteristics among enemy members. All enemies become a homogeneous, faceless mass that look alike, think alike, and act alike (see Zimbardo, 1969).

Numerous studies have demonstrated that deindividuation increases aggression against members of enemy groups, a finding that is apparently related to the fact that killing is less traumatic if the victim is further away from the killer. The further away and less individually identifiable the victim is, the easier it is to deindividuate that person and therefore to kill him or her.

Dehumanization

In the **dehumanization** process, all positive characteristics (e.g., moral virtue, intelligence, honesty, God fearing) are attributed to members of the terrorist group and all negative characteristics (moral degeneracy, stupidity, dishonesty, and atheism) are attributed to members of any other group (Grossman, 1995; Zimbardo, 1969).

This type of dehumanization occurs when the enemy and the enemy's characteristics are associated with nonhuman entities, such as animals, vermin, filth, and germs. Nazi propaganda in the 1930s compared Jews to rats and cockroaches, with the perverse and twisted implication that they all shared the same traits (Tajfel, 1982). More recently, radical Muslim fundamentalists have referred to Jews using similar dehumanizing absurd terms (e.g., pigs, swine, and apes). These terrorist group members are constantly encouraged to use these labels when referring to the enemy (Jews, Israel, and the Western world). Even school children receive the same dehumanizing indoctrination. Once these labels are consistently applied to the enemy group, members are conditioned over time to think of the enemy group members as distinctly nonhuman (Waller, 2002).

The dehumanization phase separates extremist hate groups and terrorist groups from nonviolent cults, which do not dehumanize out groups. This predilection also separates terrorist groups from organized militaries of democratic and civilized nations. Although democratic militaries may use depluralization (stripping away of a soldier's membership of all other groups and isolating his allegiance in his military branch and unit), this does not include deindividuation and dehumanization, which are types of conditioning practiced by armed terrorist combatants only. Democratic militaries have strict rules of engagement that preclude killing innocent noncombatants. Terrorist groups have no such restrictions, and their dehumanization conditioning applies to all members of the enemy group (Holmes, 1986).

Demonization

Although dehumanization rationalizes the mass killing of innocents by terrorist group members, an additional phase of conditioning helps prevent the occurrence of after-action killing remorse. **Demonization** is the social psychological conditioning process whereby group members become convinced that the enemy is in league with the devil or represents some kind of cosmic evil. Since most cultures define "good" in comparison to "evil," demonization is practiced regularly. Referring to the United States as the "Great Satan" is an example of cultural demonization. Since many cultures forgive and even glorify those who fight evil, demonization is simply channeled and intensified by terrorist groups. If a terrorist group member believes that Jews, old people, women, or Americans are evil, then killing them is not only easy but is honorable, and rewarded by others in the group (Festinger, Pepitone, & NewComb, 1952). Or the reward can come in heaven if the group member takes his own life in the process of killing those who are "evil."

OBEDIENCE

People generally have a strong respect for authority, and in some cultures this is particularly strong. Add to this the desire to feel safe, and have a leader who will take control and relieve members of "responsibility" for their actions, and a dangerous combination is created. Terrorist leaders exploit this phenomenon (Staub, 2004). Research by Andersen and Zimbardo suggests that this kind of socialization is similar to mind control and encourages an unquestioning **obedience**, which can have horrific consequences (Zimbardo & Anderson, 1993; Zimbardo, et al., 1974). The social psychologist Stanley Milgram sees obedience as one of the most relevant (and potentially dangerous) determinants of behavior in modern times. "It has been reliably established that from

1933 to 1945 millions of innocent people were systematically slaughtered on command. Gas chambers were built, death camps were guarded, daily quotas of corpses were produced with the same efficiency as the manufacture of appliances. These inhumane policies may have originated in the mind of a single person, but they could only have been carried out on a massive scale if a very large number of people obeyed orders" (Milgram, 1974, p. 1).

Milgram has noted that there are extreme instances where people will do what they are told to do, irrespective of the content of the act and without limitations of conscience, so long as they perceive that the command comes from a legitimate authority. For example, before becoming a citizen of a Muslim commune (called "Fuqra"), an adherent must sign the following oath: "I shall always hear and obey, and whenever given the command, I shall readily fight for Allah's sake" (Williams, 2007, p. 201). It is a sad fact that such blind obedience overrides ethics, sympathy for others, and basic moral conduct. English author and physicist C.P. Snow expressed this when he stated, "more hideous crimes have been committed in the name of obedience than have ever been committed in the name of rebellion. . . . The events of the Third Reich and the resulting holocaust illustrated beyond any doubt that obedience to authority resulted in the most wicked large scale actions in the history of the world" (Snow, 1961, p. 24).

How far will ordinary people go in obeying the commands of an authority?

Milgram (1963)

Two people come to a psychology laboratory to take part in a study of memory and learning. One of them is designated as a "teacher" and the other a "learner." The experimenter explains that the study is concerned with the effects of punishment on learning. The learner is taken into a room, seated in a chair, his arms strapped to prevent excessive movement, and an electrode attached to his wrist. He is told that he is to learn a list of word pairs and that whenever he makes an error, he will receive electric shocks of increasing intensity.

The real focus of the experiment is the teacher. After watching the learner being strapped into place, he is taken into the main experimental room and seated before an impressive shock generator. Its main feature is a horizontal line of 30 switches, ranging from 15 volts to 450 volts, in 15-volt increments. There are also labels, which range from SLIGHT SHOCK to DANGER—SEVERE SHOCK. The teacher is told that he must administer the learning test to the man in the other room. When the learner responds correctly, the teacher moves on to the next item; when the man gives an incorrect answer, the teacher is to give him an electric shock. He is to start at the lowest shock level (15 volts) and increase the level each time the man makes an error, going through 30 volts, 45 volts, and so on.

The "teacher" is a genuinely naive subject who has come to the laboratory to participate in an experiment. The learner, or victim, is a confederate of the experimenter

who actually receives no shock at all. The point of the experiment was to see how far a person will proceed in a concrete and measurable situation in which he is ordered to inflict increasing pain on a protesting victim. At what point will the subject refuse to obey the experimenter?

Conflict arises when the man receiving the shock begins to indicate that he is experiencing discomfort. At 75 volts, the "learner" grunts. At 120 volts he complains verbally; at 150 he demands to be released from the experiment. His protests continue as the shocks escalate, growing increasingly vehement and emotional. At 285 volts his response can only be described as an agonized scream. Each time the subject hesitates to administer a shock, the experimenter orders him to continue. To extricate himself from the situation, the subject must make a clear break with authority.

Results showed that many subjects obeyed the experimenter no matter how vehement the pleading of the person being shocked, no matter how painful the shocks seemed to be, and no matter how much the victim pleaded to be let out. Despite the fact that many subjects experienced stress, despite the fact that many protested to the experimenter, a substantial proportion (37 of 40 adults) continued to the highest shock level on the generator. The conclusion drawn from the study was that ordinary people show an extreme willingness to go to almost any lengths based on the commands of authority.

(*continued*)

(continued)

In 2006, Mel Slater and his associates at University College London replicated Milgram's original study. Concerned about the ethical implications of having subjects experience the supposed real-life pain of others (and suffer the resulting psychological distress), the researchers carried out an "ethical" replication experiment in virtual reality. The results of the study were similar to those found by Milgram years earlier as far as the willingness of subjects to administer electric shocks to helpless individuals. There was a clear behavioral difference between subjects ("teachers") depending on whether they could see the virtual human ("learner"). When subjects could not see the learner, they administered all 20 shocks. However, when they could see the learner, only 17 of the 23 subjects gave all 20 shocks (Slater et al., 2006).

RELIGIOUSLY BASED FACTORS

Shame and Humiliation

There are several studies linking conditions of **shame and humiliation** with corresponding increases in violence and crime, especially for males (Feldman & Stenner, 1997; Jones, 2006; Williams, 2007). Psychologists working in prisons know that many acts of violence are preceded by some humiliating event. In the United States, increases in crime follow increases in the number of unemployed men. Feelings of humiliation on the part of Arab populations have been one of the most frequently cited "root causes" of their turn to fundamentalist Islam (Jones, 2006). Like many new religious movements, the Japanese cult Aum Shinrikyo regularly engaged in rituals of shaming and humiliation of its members.

Terrorist groups based on religion create and reinforce feelings of shame and humiliation, which in turn appears to increase the likelihood of violent outbursts. While much of the humiliation that fuels certain acts of terrorism might begin in social and cultural conditions, fanatical religions build upon that and establish a cycle where their teachings and practices increase feelings of shame and humiliation, which intensifies aggressive feelings and then in turn provides religiously sanctioned targets for that aggression.

Sanctifying Violence

Another way in which religion promotes terrorism and genocide is by directly sanctioning violence and killing and by providing a moral justification for terrorists' actions done in the name of God. Jones (2006) reports a series of interviews between psychologists and would-be suicide bombers where their acts were seen both as a defense of their faith and as commanded by their faith. In fact, they received religious absolution for their planned acts. For radical Muslims, such martyrdom is often seen as the highest level of jihad, where bombers are regarded as holy fighters who carry out important articles of faith. Major martyrdom actions are at times the subject of sermons in the mosque, glorifying the attack and the attackers. In other words, those who carry out the attacks are sees as doing Allah's work.

In May, 2003, Saudi cleric Nasir Bin Hamd Al-Fahd signed what amounts to a "Nuclear Fatwa" in which justification and permission was given to al-Qaeda to kill millions of Americans with nuclear weapons. The Fatwa declares, "If the infidels can be repelled from the Muslims only by using [weapons of mass destruction], their use is permissible . . ." (Williams, 2007, p. 215) and ". . . if those engaged in jihad establish that the evil of the infidels can be repelled only by attacking them at night with weapons of mass destruction, they may be used even if they annihilate all the infidels" (p. 222). In a similar fashion a book by a Christian clergyman in the United States uses biblical and theological arguments to justify killing physicians at reproductive health clinics and is titled *A Time to Kill*. One of the killers influenced by this book reported that, on the way to commit a murder, he opened his Bible and found a verse in the Psalms that he interpreted as justifying his actions (Jones, 2006; Williams, 2007).

Authoritarianism

Authoritarianism has long been understood to encompass a set of personality traits strongly associated with (1) aversion to differences in people, (2) a desire for conformity to prevailing social norms and proper authority, (3) strict morality, (4) political and social intolerance, (5) an aversion to ambiguity, (6) and a desire for clear and unambiguous authority. Empirical research has found correlations between certain types of religions and such indicators of authoritarianism (Feldman & Stenner, 1997; Victoroff, 2005). Right-wing authoritarians also tend to "speak for their deity" and demand that others avoid the transgressions their deity demands of them. Expressions of violence can be seen as reactions against those who are imagined to have neglected their obligation to submit to the omnipotent deity that one worships. Fanatic believers must enforce the obligation to submit to their deity. But what is more frightening is that they must destroy those who do not share their faith (Crouse & Stalker, 2007; Juergensmeyer, 2000).

It is important to note that religious orthodoxy is not the same as fundamentalism or fanaticism. Nonfanatical religions, no matter how traditional they are in their beliefs and practices, do not generally think they are the only true religion, do not demand authoritarian submission, and are open to dialogue. It is the rigid and intolerant fundamental religious sects and groups who have these traits, and they are also the most dangerous.

RELIGIOUSLY MOTIVATED TERRORISM AS CRIME

There are many who feel that psychological, sociological, environment, and political explanations for terrorists are moot and that they should simply be regarded as criminals. Shaykh Ali Gomaa, the Grand Mufti of Egypt, has expressed the sentiment that terrorists are the products of troubled environments and their aim is purely political and has no religious foundation. Thus, terrorists are criminals, not Muslim activists (Crouse et al., 2007; Williams, 2007). Should international terrorists be seen as criminals? This may be the best way to describe them as the two groups have much in common. Like the criminal, the terrorist can distort reality to suit his needs. As psychologist Stanton Samenow (author of *The Criminal Mind*) states, "The criminal can make anything wrong right and anything right wrong" (Samenow, 2004, p. 166).

Many naive people see the acts of Osama bin Laden and his ilk as acting in the name of a holy war inspired by the teaching of religion. But others see his actions as a perversion of religion and a blatant fraud. In an article in *USA Today*, author Dinesh D'Souza pointed out that the 911 terrorists, who were reportedly pure and religious, spent their last days in bars and strip joints (D'Souza, 2002). It is a fact that under the pretense of advancing some cause, an ordinary criminal can conceal his true motives, which likely have more to do with power, consolidation of authority, and self-aggrandizement than with bringing about any real political or social change. Most terrorists share these characteristics with the criminal (Samenow, 2004).

THE PSYCHOLOGICAL EFFECTS OF TERRORISM

According to the National Center for Post Traumatic Stress Disorder, in the United States the prevalence rates for post-traumatic stress disorder (PTSD) are about 5% from natural disasters, 28% from mass shootings, 29% from a plane crash into a hotel, and 34% from a bombing. Depression, anxiety, and panic symptoms often accompany a disaster such as a terrorist attack. For example, six months after the bombing of the Federal Building in Oklahoma City, North (2001) interviewed 182 injured adults. One-third (34%) of the sample met criteria for PTSD, and 45% had some postdisaster disorder.

In 2002 Shalif and Leibler wrote, "Every municipality in Israel employs school psychologists who specialize in counseling, testing, group interventions, and crisis intervention. News broadcasts that inform the population about a mass civilian disaster are most often accompanied by the announcement of available services provided by school psychologists in the area" (p. 62). The authors stressed the importance of involving community support to those affected by terrorism as a foundation of crisis intervention in Israel. Debriefing groups are very common, and mental health professionals act as consultants to the community. This ability to face trauma with a positive outlook is an important key to adaptive coping. Culture and religion are important components of this process of making sense out of tragedy. Those who experience the trauma associated with terrorism can have a wide variety of reactions. Notwithstanding the reaction (e.g., fear, anxiety), it should be normalized in an effort to avoid marginalizing individuals, given their unique responses to the trauma.

Strous, Stryjer, Keret, Bergin, and Kotler (2003) examined the effects of terrorism in Israel as it is manifested in the subjective mood and behavior of medical caregivers and patients. The results indicated that the level of worry in response to security instability in the region was the highest in clinical staff and lower in medical patients. This study highlighted the need to assist mental health caregivers in order to facilitate the provision of optimal care to others under conditions that affect the emotional (and traumatic) needs of clinical personnel. Other studies have indicated that nearly two-thirds of Israeli adults who have been victimized by terror attacks feared for their lives and for the lives of their friends and family.

Following a traumatic event, people typically describe feeling things like relief to be alive, followed by stress, fear, and anger. They also often find they are unable to stop thinking about what happened, experience flashbacks, nightmares, intrusive memories, and exaggerated emotional and physical reactions to triggers that remind the person of the trauma. Many people also report feeling detached, feeling a lack of emotions, loss of interest in activities, difficulty sleeping and concentrating, irritability, hypervigilance (being on guard), and having an exaggerated startle response. Such symptoms may be severe enough to warrant a diagnosis from the *Diagnostic and Statistical Manual of the American Psychiatric Association* (DSM-IV-TR) of *Acute Stress Disorder* or *Post-traumatic Stress Disorder*. Acute stress disorder (ASD) was introduced as a diagnostic category into the DSM-IV to help identify those at risk of developing PTSD. ASD is defined as a reaction to traumatic stress that occurs up to four weeks after the trauma and includes mostly dissociative symptoms (e.g., emotional numbing, detachment, derealization and depersonalization) rather than the flashbacks, avoidance, and hyperarousal that are more characteristic of PTSD.

A terrorist attack can expose people to death and the presence of dead bodies and human remains. One component of this is the raw intensity of the exposure—for example, sights, smells, and sounds of the wounded and dying; proximity to the bodies; or actual physical contact with the dead. Personalization, and identification, with the dead victims—"that could have been me"—appears to be a particular risk factor for later psychological disability. Survivors may also feel an intense need to "do something." Or a justifiable anger toward the killers may develop, which may last for years. A common coping mechanism for dealing with these feelings of rage consists of ruminating on fantasies of revenge (Ursano, Fullerton, Bhartiya, & Kao, 1995).

Even more common than anger and rage is a pan-phobia or "fear of everything" that begins to take over the individual following a terror attack. Survivors' heightened sense of their own vulnerability may spur them to change daily routines, install house and car alarms, carry weapons, refuse to go out after dark, or to shun certain locales. A phobic avoidance of anything related to the terror event may develop, including people, places, and so on. They may experience true physiological and aversive reactions to ordinary stimuli such as loud noises, violence on TV, crashing sounds, or shouting. One of the most distressing aspect of survivors' ordeal is the shattering of their fundamental beliefs about themselves, the world, and other people that had previously shaped their lives. Concerns about death and questions about the meaning and purpose of their lives remain in many survivors forever (Difede et al., 1997).

The terrorist attacks that took place on September 11, 2001, in both New York City and Washington, DC, produced 135,800 mental health and grief contacts during the first eight weeks after the attacks across the United States, according to the American Red Cross alone (Taylor, 2002). The World Trade Center terrorist attacks in New York City affected all Americans way beyond ground zero with symptoms of stress, fear, depression, and the feeling that things were somehow "not the same."

Jordan (2003) discussed the emotional reactions to the first-year anniversary of the September 11 attacks in New York. She described the need to deal with anniversaries of trauma proactively to help minimize the potential escalation of stress responses or other emotional reactions and to help the individual move toward closure and to move forward in the grieving process. The first anniversary was described as the most difficult for individuals who had (1) a group affiliation with a victim; (2) shared characteristics, interests, or attributes with a victim; (3) previously demonstrated poor coping skills; (4) exhibited extreme or atypical reactions; and (5) a personal history of trauma and concurrent adverse reactions (e.g., family problems, health problems, psychiatric history).

Mental health professionals should reassure those clients affected by an anniversary of a trauma that the intensity and duration of the experience varies from person to person and that their reactions are normal insofar as they are not "(a) contemplating harming themselves or others, (b) resorting to using alcohol and other substances to numb the pain, and (c) abusing or being abused" (p. 112).

Many victims of terror attacks and disasters also experience "secondary stressors." Such stressors tend to revolve around troubled interpersonal relationships, family strains, and conflicts. Some secondary stressors are work related, such as occupational stress and financial stress, whereas others emerge from transactions between persons and their physical environment, such as environmental worry, ecological stress, and continued disruption during any rebuilding. Such disasters also tend to remove significant supporters from victims' networks through death. Temporary or permanent relocation disrupts neighborhood patterns and engenders interpersonal strains and conflict. Declines in social participation and embeddedness in the community have also been observed.

CONTRIBUTIONS OF FORENSIC PSYCHOLOGISTS

Psychologists must insure that terrorist-related disaster mental health management is humane, competent, and compassionate. Some survivors who have lost loved ones, especially in the early stages, may have difficulty expressing their pain; for them, speaking about the victim's death out loud solidifies it and symbolically makes it real. For such people, Spungen (1998) recommends keeping a daily diary or journal and writing down their thoughts and feelings about the disaster and about their deceased loved one. This notebook should be portable enough to carry around so that patients can jot down their thoughts as they occur. The only caveat is that this exercise should not become a prolonged obsessive preoccupation to the exclusion of other therapeutic strategies and participation in life generally.

Some survivors may also benefit from ongoing psychological intervention or treatment. But it is recommended that this occur after basic safety and comfort needs have been met, the rescue efforts completed or well underway, or even later, when survivors have salvaged what they can, settled insurance claims and other practical matters, and perhaps moved and resettled in a different locale. Treatment may be particularly appropriate for survivors with a history of previous traumatization (e.g., survivors of the current trauma who have a history of childhood physical or sexual abuse) or those who have preexisting mental health problems.

Throughout the course of any therapy, the supportive nature of the clinical intervention and the therapeutic relationship are vital. The nature of the therapeutic relationship may serve to buffer the effects of the trauma, increase self-esteem, and alter the individual's functioning, thereby helping to mitigate the traumatic impact of the event. Some of the therapeutic interventions that are appropriate in trauma situations include cognitive–behavioral therapy, exposure therapy, stress-inoculation training, eye movement desensitization and reprocessing, relaxation training and desensitization, and pharmacotherapy.

Cognitive–behavioral therapy (CBT) focuses on helping patients identify their trauma-related negative beliefs (e.g., guilt or distrust of others) and change them to reduce distress. It often includes exploring personal history as well as history of the event, challenging beliefs and thoughts that lead to distress, and learning to recognize and manage "triggering" episodes. This kind of therapy usually involves *stress-inoculation training*, in which patients are taught skills for managing and reducing anxiety (e.g., breathing, muscular relaxation, self-talk). The efficacy of cognitive–behavioral interventions for chronic PTSD has been demonstrated in a number of different studies with various trauma populations. These include sexual assault victims, adult survivors of childhood abuse, motor vehicle accident survivors, and combat veterans (Bryant, Harvey, Dang, Sackville, & Basten, 1999; Foa, 1998; Foa et al., 1991).

Exposure Therapy is a behavioral approach to traumatic stress that treats PTSD symptoms through a combination of imagined "reliving" of traumatic events during sessions, and "in vivo" confrontation of traumatic triggers in the outside world. In exposure therapy patients are asked to close their eyes, return to and visualize the traumatic event and tell their story. But the telling must be first person and present tense, as if it were happening at that moment. In this manner patients reexperience, rather than simply recount, events. They are encouraged to paint as detailed a portrait of the trauma as possible, including not only facts, but accompanying thoughts, feelings, and physical sensations. The more powerfully the experience is recreated, the more the fear system is activated, the more effective the therapy is likely to be. After each exposure, there is a short debriefing. The story is often taped, and they are instructed to listen to it at home, daily if possible (Echeburua, de Corral, Sarasua, & Zubizaretta, 1996; Kuch, 1989). Between sessions, patients are asked to construct a desensitization hierarchy of items associated with the trauma. Alone or with a trusted other, they put themselves into these feared, but objectively safe situations and remain there until their anxiety begins to subside. Over time, all the traumatic triggers are confronted. Throughout treatment, the therapist is an encouraging, soothing, and supportive presence. Some of the success of this regimen is likely due to habituation, the principle under which any stimulus, with sufficient repetition, will eventually lose its power to elicit a response (Miller, 1998a, 1998b).

Another type of therapy that has achieved some success dealing with traumatized clients is *Eye Movement Desensitization and Reprocessing* (EMDR). In EMDR the client is instructed to focus on the image, negative thought, and body sensations of a traumatic event while simultaneously moving his/her eyes back and forth following the therapist's fingers as they move across his/her field of vision for 20–30 seconds or more. In this dual attention process the client is instructed to just notice whatever happens. After this, the clinician instructs the client to let his/her mind go blank and to notice whatever thought, feeling, image, memory, or sensation comes to mind. Depending upon the client's report the clinician will facilitate the next focus of attention. In most cases a client-directed association process is encouraged. This is repeated numerous times throughout the session. If the client becomes distressed or has difficulty with the process, the therapist follows established procedures to help the client resume processing (Miller, 1998; Shapiro, 2002).

When the client reports no distress related to the targeted memory, the clinician asks him/her to think of the preferred positive belief that was identified at the beginning of the session, or a better one if it has emerged, and to focus on the incident, while simultaneously engaging in the eye movements. After several sets, clients generally report increased confidence in this positive belief. The therapist checks with the client regarding body sensations. If there are negative sensations, these are processed as above. If there are positive sensations, they are further enhanced. As a closure phase, the therapist asks the client to keep a journal during the week to document any related material that may arise and reminds the client of the self-calming activities that were previously mastered (Miller, 1998; Shapiro, 2002).

There are also certain anti-anxiety medications which may help reduce PTSD if given promptly after a traumatic incident. In two French emergency rooms, doctors offered the anti-anxiety drug *Propranolol* to patients within two to 20 hours after a traumatic injury. These patients were medically stable but had tachycardia—an elevated heart rate and known indicator of a panic reaction. If, after lying down for 20 minutes, the heart rate remained higher than 90 beats a minute, the patients were offered the drug. Two months later, patients who had declined drug treatment experienced stress symptoms that were twice as severe. Three out of those eight patients developed full-blown cases of PTSD. Of those who took Propranolol, only one person in 11 was diagnosed with the disorder. The study suggests that PTSD occurs most often in patients who have an especially robust and prolonged negative reaction to trauma. Normally, the stress response—the fight or flight reaction—lasts only a few minutes. Yet for a quarter of the population, it can last for hours or days, which can greatly increase the odds of developing a stress disorder. But quickly calming such patients seems to prevent PTSD from developing (Allen, 2003).

Psychologists and other mental health professionals, recognizing that the effects of successive traumas are often cumulative, may also have to deal with unresolved traumatic material from the past, which may be re-evoked by the more recent trauma. In addition, other aspects of life cannot automatically be put on hold when trauma occurs, so any therapy must address coexisting issues such as school and job problems, marital conflict, substance abuse, or other preexisting family stresses (Alarcon, 1999; Catherall, 1998).

Lastly, forensic psychologists can be of value in the fight against terrorism itself. This can occur on at least four levels. The first is by helping to prevent the occurrence of attacks themselves (through understanding the psychology of individuals prone to these extreme actions, teaching and consulting about the mind-set and techniques used by terrorist groups, and also the mechanisms of conflict resolution which can at times have a positive impact). The second is by mitigating the adverse impact of terrorist attacks when they do occur. The term *psychological counterterrorism* (Everly, 2003) is used in this regard to describe the importance of using psychology to understand terrorism and as a foundation for rebuilding a community devastated by its effects, not only structurally but psychologically as well. This can also include assisting law enforcement personnel with psychological profiling of possible terrorists when appropriate. Third, psychologists can continue to develop through research, psychological methods for the treatment of PTSD and the fears that people have about the reoccurrence of attacks. Fourth, psychologists can utilize research-based treatment regimens as clinicians when the need arises.

FORENSIC PSYCHOLOGY IN THE SPOTLIGHT
The Right-Wing Authoritarian Survey

Altemeyer (1998)

The following 32 statements come from the *Right-Wing Authoritarian Scale* as developed by Altemeter (1998). In theory, these statements express beliefs and attitudes favoring submission to authority, aggression against noncompliers to authority, and adherence to social conventions endorsed by established authority. The higher the score, the greater the likelihood the person taking the survey has authoritarian attitudes.

Only items 3–32 are scored. Respondents respond to each item from very strongly disagree (−4) through neutral (0) to very strongly agree (+4). A −4 is scored as a 1 and a +4 is scored as a 9. Neutral is scored as a 0. *NOTE*: Numbers 4, 6, 8, 9, 11, 13, 15, 18, 20, 21, 24, 26, 29, 30, and 31 are scored in reverse. This means that the lowest possible right-wing authoritarian score is 30 (30 × 1) and the highest is 270 (30 × 9). The true or false statements used in the study and originating from the Right-Wing Authoritarian Scale include:

1. The established authorities generally turn out to be right about things, while the radicals and protesters are usually just "loud mouths" showing off their ignorance.
2. Women should have to promise to obey their husbands when they get married.
3. Our country desperately needs a mighty leader who will do what has to be done to destroy the radical new ways and sinfulness that are ruining us.
4. Gays and lesbians are just as healthy and moral as anybody else.

(*continued*)

(*continued*)

5. It is always better to trust the judgment of the proper authorities in government and religion than to listen to the noisy rabble-rousers in our society who are trying to create doubt in people's minds.

6. Atheists and others who have rebelled against the established religions are no doubt every bit as good and virtuous as those who attend church regularly.

7. The only way our country can get through the crisis ahead is to get back to our traditional values, put some tough leaders in power, and silence the troublemakers spreading bad ideas.

8. There is absolutely nothing wrong with nudist camps.

9. Our country *needs* free thinkers who will have the courage to defy traditional ways, even if this upsets many people.

10. Our country will be destroyed someday if we do not smash the perversions eating away at our moral fiber and traditional beliefs.

11. Everyone should have their own lifestyle, religious beliefs, and sexual preferences, even if it makes them different from everyone else.

12. The "old-fashioned ways" and "old-fashioned values" still show the best ways to live.

13. You have to admire those who challenged the law and the majority view by protesting for women's abortion rights, for animal rights, or to abolish school prayer.

14. What our country really needs is a strong, determined leader who will crush evil, and take us back to our true path.

15. Some of the best people in our country are those who are challenging our government, criticizing religion, and ignoring the "normal way things are suppose to be done."

16. God's laws about abortion, pornography, and marriage must be strictly followed before it is too late, and those who break them must be strongly punished.

17. It would be best for everyone if the proper authorities censored magazines so that people could not get their hands on trashy and disgusting material.

18. There is nothing wrong with premarital sexual intercourse.

19. Our country will be great if we honor the ways of our forefathers, do what the authorities tell us to do, and get rid of the "rotten apples" who are ruining everything.

20. There is no "ONE right way" to live life; everybody has to create their own way.

21. Homosexuals and feminists should be praised for being brave enough to defy "traditional values."

22. This country would work a lot better if certain groups of troublemakers would just shut up and accept their group's traditional place in society.

23. There are many radical, immoral people in our country today, who are trying to ruin it for their own godless purposes, whom the authorities should put out of action.

24. People should pay less attention to the Bible and the other old forms of religious guidance, and instead develop their own standards of what is moral and immoral.

25. What our country needs *most* is discipline, with everyone following our leaders in unity.

26. It's better to have trashy magazines and radical pamphlets in our communities than to let the government have the power to censor them.

27. The facts on crime, sexual immorality, and the recent public disorders all show that we have to crack down harder on deviant groups and troublemakers if we are going to save our moral standards and preserve law and order.

28. A lot of our rules regarding modesty and sexual behavior are just customs which are not necessarily any better or holier than those which other people follow.

29. The situation in our country is getting so serious, the strongest methods would be justified if they eliminated the troublemakers and got us back on our true path.

30. A "woman's place" should be wherever she wants to be. The days when women are submissive to their husbands and social conventions belong strictly in the past.

31. It is wonderful that young people today have greater freedom to protest against things they don't like, and to make their own "rules" to govern their behavior.

32. Once our government leaders give us the "go ahead," it will be the duty of every patriotic citizen to help stomp out the rot that is poisoning our country from within.

Interpretation of Scores

A high score in this study would suggest that the person gains a sense of power by aligning his/her beliefs with leaders (authoritarian). It suggests a need to control fear by giving others power and command to augment ones' own life.

Summary

Terrorism has roots that are psychological, economic, political, religious, and sociological, and no one area holds a satisfactory explanation for it. Some terrorists act alone, while many others operate as part of a group or network. There are different classifications of these groups such as Revolutionary terror groups, Establishment terror groups, and Eco terror groups. Religious and social extremist groups and cults have much in common with terror groups, especially religiously motivated ones as they are the most dangerous. There are psychological explanations for what makes a person vulnerable to becoming a terrorist. One of these deals with personality disorders. Although there are distinct similarities in personality characteristics of many terrorists with both antisocial and narcissistic personalities (e.g., social alienation, hostility, and intolerance of criticism), this is not conclusive, and does not exist in all instances. There is also no evidence that the incidence of mental illness in global terrorist groups is higher than in the general population. This finding includes suicide attackers, which is not surprising since such people view their acts as expressions of martyrdom and as commanded by their faith.

The actions of murderous terrorists are shaped in part by the cult-like attributes of terrorist groups and leaders. These include depluralization, moral disengagement, obedience, diffusion of responsibility, self-deindividuation, other-deindividuation, dehumanization, demonization, and unquestioned obedience. Research by Stanley Milgram has illustrated the powerful effect that obedience to authority can have on people. Would-be terrorists view themselves as morally correct and as adherents to the only real religion, and outsiders (targets) as being subhuman. Authoritarian attitudes, perceived shame and humiliation in the context of their religion, and an official sanctification of violence, all play a role in the formation of a terrorist.

Forensic psychologists can play a valuable role in the prevention of terrorist attacks, mitigating their adverse effects, apprehending perpetrators, rebuilding, and treating victims.

Key Terms

Antisocial personality disorders *130*
Authoritarianism *137*
Cult *131*
Dehumanization *134*
Deindividuation *133*
Demonization *134*

Depluralization *132*
Dichotomous thinking *131*
Diffusion of responsibility *133*
Disengagement *133*
Ecoterrorist *121*
Externalization *130*

John Allen Muhammad *119*
Lee Boyd Malvo *119*
Narcissistic rage *129*
Obedience *134*
Religiously motivated terrorist *131*

Self-deindividuation *133*
Shame and humiliation *136*
Splitting *130*
Ted Kaczynski *117*
Timothy James McVeigh *118*

Review Questions

1. In what ways does the lone terrorist differ from a terrorist who is part of a network?
2. What were Ted Kaczynski and Timothy McVeigh's motivations for their respective actions?
3. What are the goals of a revolutionary terrorist? Ecoterrorist?
4. How are extremist groups and cults related to terror groups?
5. How does the frustration–aggression hypothesis attempt to explain terrorist actions?
6. How does the mental health of terrorists compare with the general population's?
7. What elements of the narcissistic and antisocial personalities seem to be present in many terrorists?
8. How are the psychological mechanisms of externalization and splitting involved in terrorism dynamics?
9. What kinds of group dynamics are shared by cults and terror groups?
10. What did Stanley Milgram's research contribute to the understanding of terrorism?
11. What is authoritarianism, and how does it relate to terrorism?
12. Why is religiously motivated terrorism particularly dangerous?
13. What are the deleterious psychological effects of terrorism?
14. How can psychologists help the victims of terrorism?

Chapter Resources on the World Wide Web

History of the Unabomber Case
http://www.courttv.com/trials/unabomber/

Extremism in America
http://www.adl.org/main_Extremism/default.htm

Cyberterrorism
http://www.cs.georgetown.edu/~denning/infosec/cyberterror.html

The Psychological Roots of Religion and Terrorism
http://home.att.net/pcr-aar/2005/jones.htm

Homepage of Philip G. Zimbardo
http://www.zimbardo.com/current.html

Psychology Today: Stanley Milgram
http://psychologytoday.com/articles/pto-20020301-000037.html

All about Criminal Motivation
http://www.crimelibrary.com/criminal_mind/psychology/
crime_motivation/1.html

Belfer Center for Science and International Affairs
http://bcsia.ksg.harvard.edu/

US Nuclear Regulatory Commission
http://www.nrc.gov

The Sociology and Psychology of Terrorism
http://www.loc.gov/rr/frd/

The Department of Homeland Security
http://www.homelandsecurity.org

Psychology Today: A Treatment for PTSD?
http://psychologytoday.com/articles/pto-20031027-000002.html

For Further Reading

Bandura, A. (1990). Mechanisms of Moral Disengagement. In W. Reich (Ed.), *Origins of terrorism: Psychologies, ideologies, theologies, states of mind* (pp. 161–191). Cambridge: Cambridge University Press.

Borum, R. (2004). *Psychology of terrorism*. Tampa: University of South Florida.

Corbett, J. M. (2000). *Religion in America* (4th ed.). Upper Saddle River, NJ: Prentice Hall.

Festinger, L., Pepitone, A., & Newcomb, T. (1952). Some consequences of deindividuation in agroup. *Journal of Abnormal and Social Psychology, 47*, 382–389.

Hoffman, B. (1998). *Inside terrorism*. New York, NY: Columbia University Press.

Juergensmeyer, M. (2000). *Terror in the mind of God*. Berkeley: University of California Press.

Lewis, J. (2003). Legitimizing suicide: Heaven's gate and new age ideology. In C. Partridge (Ed.), *UFO religions*. London: Routledge.

Milgram, S. (1974). *Obedience to authority*. New York: Harper & Row Publishers.

Miller, L. (1998). *Shocks to the system*. New York: W.W. Norton & Company, Inc.

Post, J., Sprinzak, K., & Denny, L. (2003). The terrorists in their own words: Interviews with 35 incarcerated middle eastern terrorists. *Terrorism and political violence, 15*(1), 178.

Samenow, S. E. (2004). *Inside the criminal mind* (2nd ed.). New York: Crown Publishers.

Waller, J. (2002). *Becoming evil: How ordinary people commit genocide and mass killing*. Oxford, England: Oxford University Press.

Williams, P. I. (2007). *The day of Islam*. Amherst, NY: Prometheus Books.

CHAPTER 7

Law Enforcement and Police Psychology

CHAPTER OBJECTIVES

After reading this chapter you would:

- Know the historical roots of police psychology.
- Appreciate the sources and nature of stress prevalent in police work.
- Understand the basic elements of preemployment psychological screening.
- Appreciate the circumstances when a fitness-for-duty evaluation is needed.
- Be aware of the legal cases relevant to police hiring and evaluations.
- Understand the roles that psychologists play in training and consultation.
- Appreciate cultural competence and multiculturalism in law enforcement.
- Know the role of the police in the enforcement of bias and hate crimes.

INTRODUCTION

The profession of policing, like that of psychology, has grown geometrically in this country during the last 100 years. When the American colonist Asser Levy and his brothers-in-arms served on the **Burgher Guard** in New Amsterdam (New York City) in 1657, they in essence became this country's first policeman. Levy and his brethren could never have imagined the current levels of technology and professionalism of modern police work. Similarly, when the experimental psychologist **Hugo Munsterberg** advocated in 1908 for the entry of psychologists into the arena of the law, he set the stage for psychology's ever increasing contribution to law enforcement and the legal system as a whole (Kitaeff, 2006).

Variously referred to as "applied psychology," and "occupational psychology," *police psychology* has been the preferred term to describe psychologists' involvement with law enforcement. This officially began when **Martin Reiser** was hired by the Los Angeles Police Department in 1968 as the nation's first full-time police psychologist, and Harvey Schlossberg became the first actual police officer to earn a doctorate in psychology and go on to establish the psychological services section for the New York Police City Department in 1971.

Police psychology can broadly be defined as the application of psychological principles and methods to law enforcement. This broad and growing area can include topics such as screening and hiring of police officers, fitness-for-duty evaluations (FFDE), investigations, hostage negotiations, and training and stress counseling.

The history of psychology applied to the assessment of public safety officers in this country can be traced back to the psychologist **Lewis Terman**, who, in 1917, administered the Stanford-Binet intelligence test to 30 police and fire applicants in an attempt to set minimum standards for making hiring decisions. He published the results of his efforts in the first issue of the *Journal of Applied Psychology*, finding that the average IQ score of this group of applicants was 84. Terman therefore recommended that no police or fire applicant with an assessed IQ score of less than 84 be hired.

In the 1950s the Los Angeles Police Department was the first police department to begin performing preemployment psychological screening on a routine basis. Personality testing by the LADP consisted of assessment instruments such as the Humm–Wadsworth Temperament Scale. In 1955 only 14 cities with populations over 100,000 had officially adopted psychological screening as part of their police hiring processes. By 1985, 11 states had passed statutes requiring police departments to psychologically screen their applicants. By 1990, 64% of state police departments and 73% of municipal police departments required psychological screening. Today most large and many medium-sized police departments have a full-time police psychologist on staff or utilize part-time psychologists as consultants.

THE NATURE OF POLICING

What makes a *good* police officer? Hogan (1971) reported that supervisors described their best officers as being functionally intelligent, sociable, and self-assured. A decade later, using the *Inwald Personality Inventory* and the MMPI, Inwald and Shusman (1984) found that patrol officers who exhibited heightened awareness and discernment tended to receive better supervisory ratings. Having conventional attitudes and being free of "neurosis" (excessive anxiety, worry, self-doubt, and phobias) have also been shown to predict fewer serious job problems among police officers (Hiatt & Hargrave, 1988). A certain level of guardedness and circumspection appears to be a desirable personality characteristic for effective policing as well (Detrick & Chibnall, 2002).

The police in this country are the major representatives of the government and the legal system in their transactions with citizens. They are responsible for enforcing the criminal laws, keeping the peace, and responding to calls for service. They are also required to exercise discretion in determining whether or not a violation of the law has taken place and whether someone should be arrested and charged with a particular criminal offense. They are put in the position of mediating disputes between people from all walks of life and making immediate decisions on who might be in the wrong or the right. Indeed, for better or worse, police officers, at least when they are working on the street, are possessors of inordinate amounts of power. Furthermore, the average officer is continuously exposed to temptation and opportunities for corruption with only limited likelihood of getting caught.

Police officers regularly deal with the most violent, impulsive, and predatory members of society. They put their lives on the line and confront miseries and horrors the rest of can't even imagine. In addition, officers are always in the spotlight and open to complaints and criticism from citizens, the media, and the judiciary. This may skew the officer's opinions on the character of the average human being and create a cynicism, isolation, and difficulty trusting people in general. Although the stress of viewing many horrific events, violence, and trauma can be substantial in police work, it is exacerbated by its intermittent nature interspersed with periods of boredom and calm. Officers cannot usually control entrance into most traumatic and dangerous situations they face; they have to react to problems and typically do so without sufficient warning or preparation.

Officers are also required to always be in emotional control and must show extreme restraint even under highly emotional circumstances. They must wear a social mask, which they put on with the uniform. A former president of the International Association of Chiefs of Police has said, "What our society expects from police officers is a perfect blend of robot and person. In any confrontation, no matter the potential for violence, we're not supposed to display emotion or the human characteristics that result from adrenalin. . . . People realize officers are human, but they don't understand that we can't train them to a point where we override every human emotion" (Miller, 1998b).

The police are expected to be conscientious, agreeable, emotionally stable, self-controlled, honest, and morally upright (Berry, Ones, & Sackett, 2007; Marcus & Schuler, 2004; and Ones, Viswesvaran, & Schmidt, 1993, 2003). As will be indicated in this chapter, there have been controlled experiments designed and conducted to identify the personality traits, or degrees of traits, that are correlated with or significantly predict discrete aspects of successful police performance in the future. As forensic psychologists trained in research, empiricism, and the scientific method, we appreciate the importance of these studies and try to incorporate their findings into our daily work in the selection of police recruits, the evaluation of present officers, and in consultation with police administration. As any practicing clinician will also disclose, however, years of experience and observation "on the firing line" have allowed them to also develop certain working hypotheses that are perfectly appropriate to be used as one part of their clinical armamentarium. This author is no different. Table 7.1 presents some of the personality attributes I have found to be important in police work. Of course, complete reliance on these without also using empirically derived personality traits and standardized psychological inventories and tests, would be less than appropriate.

During the 2008 presidential campaign, the debates between candidates Barack Obama and John McCain were subjected to a "lexical analysis." Such an analysis consists of dissecting the words and phrases of each candidate for the types of nouns, verbs, adjectives and adverbs used, the noun/verb/adjective/adverb ratio, and types and complexity of phrases. When words exclusive to a candidate are considered, Obama's more frequent use of verbs and much more frequent use of adjectives and adverbs, compared with McCain's, suggests that he is more of a fluid and contextual thinker who, unlike McCain whose language metrics suggest a categorical approach, does not seek to fit issues into preexisting categories. Obama's greater use of modifiers suggest an outlook that is more open to nuance and interrelatedness of events and issues (Krzywinski, 2008).

TABLE 7.1 Positive Personality Attributes in Police Work

Personality Trait	Interpretation 1	Interpretation 2
Emotional Warmth	Attentive to others	Appropriately distant from others
Dominance	Assertive	Cooperative
Seriousness	Restrained	Spontaneous
Conscientiousness	Rule conscious and dutiful	Individualized thinker
Social Boldness	Venturesome	Cautious
Sensitivity	Feeling for others	Objective
Trusting	Accepting	Vigilant
Forthright	Genuine and honest	Discreet
Self-Assured	Confidence	Accepts mistakes
Traditional	Model social values	Open to change
Self-Reliant	Be independent	Team oriented
Organized	Self-disciplined	Tolerates disorder
High Energy	Driven	Patient

Source: Adapted from Cattell, E., & Tatsuoka, M. M. (1970). *Handbook for the sixteen personality factor questionnaire.* Champaign, ILL: Institute for Personality and Ability Testing, Inc.; Conn, S. R., & Rieke, M. L. (1994). *The 16PF fifth edition technical manual.* Champaign, IL: Institute for Personality and Ability Testing, Inc.; Kitaeff, J. (2006). Psychological assessment services for law enforcement. In J. Kitaeff (Ed.), *Selected readings in forensic psychology.* Boston, MA: Pearson Custom Publishing; Russell, M. T., & Karol, D. (2002). *The 16PF fifth edition administrator's manual.* Champaign, IL: Institute for Personality and Ability Testing.

Such differences between people, as expressed in language, are broadly indicative of five factors or dimensions of personality known in psychology as the "Big Five" personality traits, which include openness, conscientiousness, extraversion, agreeableness, and neuroticism (Digman, 1996; Goldberg, 1993; John, 1990).

What separates the five-factor model of personality from all others is that it is not based on the theory of any one particular psychologist, but rather on language, the natural system that people use to communicate their understanding of one another. The system was originally codified into a personality inventory in the 1970s called the **Neuroticism-Extroversion-Openness Inventory (NEO-I)**, which only measured three of the Big Five personality traits. It was later revised to include all five traits and renamed the **NEO Personality Inventory (NEO PI)**. The last incarnation of the inventory was named the *NEO PI-R Five-Factor Personality Inventory* (Costa & McCrae, 1992; McCrae & Costa, 1983; McCrae & John, 1992; McCrae et al., 1998, 1999). This test will be discussed in somewhat greater detail in the section on preemployment psychological screening later in this chapter.

The plain truth of the matter is that effective police officers need to be intelligent. One important reason for this is that intelligence has been suggested to possess an inhibitory effect with regard to deviant behaviors, in that individuals of above average and high intelligence possess enough foresight to consider possible consequences of their actions and subsequently choose those most beneficial to them (Terman, 1916; White, Moffitt, & Silva, 1989). Engaging in the most beneficial or advantageous behavior involves a considerable amount of judgment on the part of the individual. Police officers high in cognitive ability have the foresight to adjust their behavior and restrain impulses in order to prevent the long-term negative consequences to their careers that would result once their deviance was detected.

Decades of research have shown that cognitive ability is a valuable predictor of performance at work (Dilchert, Ones, Davis, & Rostow, 2007, Ones et al., 2005). Compromised cognitive abilities (e.g., impairment of executive functions such as abstract reasoning, anticipating and planning, and self-monitoring one's behavior) produce impulsive individuals who have difficulties envisioning the implications of their acts (Lynam, Moffitt, & Stouthamer-Loeber, 1993). It is true that individuals in the lower ranges of the ability distribution often suffer from "a deficit in foreseeing temporally remote consequences of actions" (Lubinski, 2000, p. 430). In police work, this lack of foresight will be expressed in a number of behavioral consequences including, but certainly not limited to, impaired moral reasoning behavior, and other consequences that can be quite serious (Gottfredson & Hirschi, 1990; Herrnstein & Murray, 1994; Palmer, 2003a; Wilson & Herrnstein, 1985).

Does Police Work "Change People"?

There are many indications that being a police officer does in fact change people. Despite some popular beliefs that individuals who desire to be police officers are naturally authoritarian, have exaggerated needs to control both people and situations, are inordinately conservative, or are naturally prone to dehumanizing others, the research is not supportive of these contentions. If these traits do exist in current officers, they are more likely to have developed while on the job than to have existed beforehand (Anson & Bloom, 1988; Arrigo & Shipley, 2005). Some of these changes may have something to do with the very nature of the job itself. The working conditions in police work can be atrocious, including the need to work in every possible weather, climate, geographic area, and time of day or night. Work assignments can be miserable, monotonous, routine, and devoid of challenge or chance to utilize one's abilities, skills, ingenuity, or creativity. Although many people enter police work with the hope of "being their own boss" (at least in everyday discretionary matters), this is usually not the case due to micromanagement, intense supervision and paperwork, or the second guessing, frustration, and ambiguity that come with relative autonomy and the exercise of discretionary power when it occurs (Blau, 1994; Miller, 2006; Toch, 2002).

Officers who are generally interested in being part of a "helping profession" may become disillusioned when they feel unappreciated, disrespected, or even despised by the very people they are trying to help. Those officers who are committed to the notion of solving crimes may feel stifled when they are not allowed to see a case through to the end because this is often the province of the detectives. Chances for promotion or participation in special assignments such as undercover work, emergency response units, narcotics, or K-9, may be very limited especially in larger departments. It comes as little surprise that cynicism, emotional distancing and hardening, the development of an "us versus them mentality," and the physical, psychological, and social symptoms of stress may easily develop. It also comes as no surprise that the officer may become in so many ways "changed" by the experience of being a police officer.

POLICE STRESS

Stress and frustration in police work result from the very nature of the job but even more so from internal, bureaucratic rules and procedures that can seem to make no sense, organizational turf battles, and excessive and meaningless paperwork, rules, unnecessary and excessive discipline, shift work, inadequate support by supervisors and administrators, incompatible patrol partners, and insufficient personnel. In fact, 7 of the top 20 stressors on police officers have been found to be purely organizational or administrative (Abdollahi, 2002; Violanti & Aron, 1994).

Aside from the internal stress of police work, it is undeniable that the very nature of the job can be responsible for frustration, tension, strain, anxiety, depression, isolation, burnout, family problems, substance abuse, resignation, and even suicide (Anshel, 2000; Solomon & Horn, 1986). Every officer has his breaking point. For some, it may come in the form of a particular dramatic event, such as a gruesome accident or homicide, a vicious crime against a child, a close personal brush with death, the killing or wounding of a partner, the mistaken shooting of an innocent civilian, or an especially grisly accident or crime scene. Consider, for example, what officers witnessed on April 16, 2007, at the Virginia Tech campus in Blacksburg Virginia. The horrific events of that day left 33 dead and 15 wounded. Most of the victims were young college students in their 20s. It was the deadliest non-terrorist mass murder in U.S. history. The carnage and tragedy of that day is beyond imagination, but for police responding to the campus, it was a scene that was all too real. But for other officers, there may be no single major trauma, but the identified mental breakdown occurs under the cumulative weight of a number of more moderate stresses over the course of the officer's career.

Carter and Radelet (1999) explain that stress is inherent in all police work, but it is the "cumulative interactive stressors" that do the most damage. Life-threatening stressors such as those related to critical incidents are cumulative in nature and may cause many officers to react in an unprofessional manner. For example, a pilot test of the Police–Public Contact Survey (administered as a supplement to the Bureau of Justice Statistics National Crime Victimization Survey) provides the results of more than 6,000 interviews with U.S. residents age 12 or older, which were representative of the U.S. population as a whole. That survey revealed that about 21% of the residents age 12 or older (about 44.6 million) had at least one face-to-face encounter with a police officer in 1996. Of these people, an estimated half million were threatened with use of force or had force used against them by an officer.

Additional stressors exist for homicide detectives, who are involved in the investigation of particularly brutal crimes, such as multiple murders or serial killings (Sewell et al., 1988). A multiple murder investigation forces an officer to project strength and to respond stoically to the demands of the public and his superiors. In addition, the violence, mutilation, and sadistic brutality associated with many serial killings, sometimes involving children, often exceed the defense mechanisms and coping abilities of even the most seasoned and hardboiled investigator. Furthermore, as the investigation continues for longer and longer periods of time, the inability to solve the crime further demoralizes the assigned officers. This is exacerbated by the possibility that the suspect will kill again.

In addition to the stress associated with the basic patrol duties of a police officer, there are special work assignments within police work that have their own, unique stress qualities associated with them. This would include police officers assigned to work in an undercover or covert capacity. There have always been stories of undercover officers losing their perspective or even "going over to the other side" (Daley, 1981; Love, Vinson, Tolsma, & Kaufmann, 2008). High ratings of loneliness, isolation, tension, role diffusion, depersonalization, memory loss, alcohol abuse, and family problems have been found in officers working undercover (Farkas, 1986). Despite the additional strain on undercover police officers, these officers are even more likely than most to deny problems until the cumulative stress takes its toll (MacLeod, 1995).

Whether stress is singular or cumulative, all too often the officer feels unsupported by the department and that there is nowhere else to vent distress. So feelings are bottled up, and the officer becomes isolated and alienated. Couple this behavior with the officer's belief that no civilian or outsider could possibly understand what he goes through on a daily basis, and the result is a breeding ground for stress, illness, and even suicide. It is no wonder that 70% of officers involved in a fatal line-of-duty shooting leave the force within seven years of the incident. Police officers are also admitted to general hospitals in significantly higher numbers than the general population and have significantly high rates of premature death, ranking third among occupations in death rate. Police officers also experience divorce twice the rate of individuals in other occupations and have a suicide rate two to six times greater than the national average (Carter & Radelet, 1999; Kitaeff, 2006; Sewell, Ellison, & Hurrell, 1988).

When police officers carry their job stress home with them, it adversely affects their interactions with their spouses and children. The physiologically aroused states induced by high-stress days make it difficult for police officers to think clearly and to solve problems effectively. This can lead to even more defensive and self-protective behaviors that may have been needed during the workday, but not at home. The resulting emotional detachment, blunting, and suppression of feelings in response to the environment in which they work leads to lack of intimacy, withdrawal, difficulty communicating, and problems showing empathy at home (Roberts & Levenson, 2001; White & Honig, 1995). In addition, many officers lack control over many decisions involved in routine patrol activities. This experience too can have a negative effect on family members. Some officers overcompensate at home, given this perceived lack of control at work. Officers become authoritarian, rigid, demanding, and unapproachable to his/her spouse and children. It is a sad commentary that the traits and dispositions that make exceptional police officers, unfortunately also seem to make very poor spouses, parents, and friends.

Suicide

In 1994, 11 New York City police officers committed suicide. However, only two officers were actually killed by criminals in New York City that same year (Baker & Baker, 1996). This statistic is tragic; however, it must be understood within the totality of suicide rates. For example, the suicide rates of New York City police officers from 1977 to 1996 was almost 15% per 100,000 residents, while the suicide rates of New York's general population was 18% per 100,000 residents (Marzuk, Nock, Leon, Portera, & Tardiff, 2002).

An article by Arrigo and Garsky (1997) investigated a police officer's decision to commit suicide. The authors stated that a combination of occupational stress, nonsupportive family structure, and alcoholism might contribute to suicidal ideation in the police officer. The inherent and chronically stressful nature of police work accumulates in the form of such feelings as helplessness and hopelessness. Also, organizational stressors such as those described earlier lead to feelings of suppressed hostility, frustration, and a sense of having little influence in one's work. Shift work and disabling injuries occur regularly in police work. These and other factors have a tremendous impact on the officer's family, who must deal with these issues daily. A police officer's job requires a large amount of time and energy in order to ensure that he/she is performing properly and "by the book." As a result, the spouses of police officers are often neglected in the process. Also, police officers' training typically instills such psychological coping techniques as detachment from emotional situations. All too often this detachment is reflected in the personal lives of the officers, resulting in a breakdown of family communication and a lack of emotional attachment. The final component described by Arrigo and Garsky (1997) is the officer's use of alcohol and its effects on a decision to commit suicide.

Arrigo and Garsky advocate for three main policies that might help officers cope with the realities of the job. The first of these includes stress management and stress-reduction techniques. The authors recommend that a special class explaining how to cope with anxiety and stressors, in addition to reducing them, needs to be incorporated into all police training programs. Special aspects of the course could focus on such themes as nutrition and dieting, physical health, fitness, the use of humor and play, and amusement strategies. Since abuse of substances such as drugs and alcohol is used as a means for police officers to avoid the discomfort associated with their occupation and to escape its harsh realities, policy implications surrounding the use/abuse of alcohol and/or drugs within the police force must deal with the very root of the problem in addition to the abusive substances themselves. Helping the officer to utilize more effective coping mechanisms and encouraging a more open discussion of one's concerns will, in effect, reduce likely reliance on alcohol or drugs.

Training and other preventive measures provided by forensic or police psychologists are an excellent way to minimize the effects of stress on an officer later on. Counseling, critical incident debriefing, organizational consultations, and other forms of psychological intervention are powerful tools to help reduce the deleterious effects of stress. But another contribution that psychologists can make is to help insure the psychological fitness of new police recruits before they are ever hired. This comes under the rubric of preemployment psychological screening, which will be addressed now.

PSYCHOLOGICAL SCREENING OF POLICE APPLICANTS

Legal Guidelines

In general, psychologists have designed **preemployment psychological screening** programs by attempting to "screen out" those candidates who are psychological inappropriate for police work, and to "screen-in" candidates with positive characteristics, attitudes, and traits known to be associated with highly functioning officers. The screening-out method is based upon the hypothesis that an officer who is "psychologically unstable" is more likely to violate the civil rights of citizens and contribute to community unrest than is a "stable" officer. Most psychologists who work with law enforcement agencies employ a screening battery composed of an interview, at least one cognitive test, and two or more personality tests.

There are legal and liability-related reasons why the preemployment screening of police applicants is necessary. Suing the police is very popular in this country. It can also be very profitable, as the average jury award is over $2 million. This does not take into account the hundreds of cases settled out-of-court likely amounting to hundreds of millions of dollars. Lawsuits against the police may be filed in state court as a tort law claim. This is the preferred method since a "tort" (a "wrong" in the legal sense) can usually only be settled by monetary awards for "damages" done to the plaintiff. In addition, courts may impose punitive damages against the police department as punishment if the wrong done to the plaintiff was particularly severe in the eyes of the court. Under the law, the failure of a police department to properly select police officers can be considered a form of **negligent hiring**. A department may be liable for a charge of negligence by employing an individual who possesses personality attributes or prior conduct that would create an undue risk of harming others in carrying out his/her official responsibilities. Furthermore, the standard of proof in these civil cases is by a preponderance of the evidence and is much easier to meet than the criminal standard of beyond a reasonable doubt.

Is the Need for Psychological Screening of Police Officers Supported by the Courts?

Bonsignore v. City of New York (1982); *Geidel v. City of Bradenton Beach* (1999); *Hild v. Bruner* (1980)

In the case of *Hild v. Bruner* (1980), a federal district court in New Jersey upheld a jury finding of municipal liability for excessive force during an arrest. The reasons for the court's decision was that although the city required its officers to carry guns both on and off duty, it had no consistent psychological testing program in place to help ensure the officers' fitness to carry these weapons. Based on the city's failure to implement an effective psychological testing program to identify officers unfit to carry guns, the court held the city liable for the injuries one of its officers inflicted. In a similar case, *Geidel v. City of Bradenton Beach* (1999), the court held that the city could be liable for any intentional tort by a police officer if it could be shown that the municipality had been negligent in its duty to select, train and supervise the officer. In *Bonsignore v. City of New York* (1982), the failure to adopt a meaningful psychological testing procedure resulted in the award of $300,000 in compensation and $125,000 in punitive damages when an off duty officer, known generally to have emotional problems, wounded his wife and killed himself. In another case, the court concluded that periodic psychological screening is constitutional provided that management provides for the privacy of officers' files and records, and respects their right of Due Process.

Tort liability associated with lawsuits against police departments may include wrongful death, assault & battery, false arrest, and false imprisonment. **Gross negligence** may be assumed by a department's failure to conduct full background investigations and screening of applicants. Police departments can also be charged with negligent retention (keeping employees on the job when they clearly should have been disciplined, demoted, or dismissed) and **negligent entrustment** (inadequately preparing officers prior to entrusting them with police responsibilities).

The risk to municipal government (and to the public) is considerable when a potential employee is a police officer. This increased risk stems from the privileges granted to commissioned police officers to take "life and liberty" under special circumstances. In our society, this privilege to exert lawful, sometimes deadly force and restraint is why the hiring of police applicants known to possess destructive characteristics can make a department legally liable. "Deliberate indifference" may be said to apply when a police department should have had the ability to foresee a risk to the public, but for some reason, did not take the possible steps to minimize that danger. In instances such as these a lawsuit may be filed in federal court as a violation of *Title 42 of the United States Code*. This is a legal claim, which alleges that there has been a violation of someone's **civil rights** under the U.S. Constitution.

Although individual states cannot be sued in federal court under a civil rights claim, municipalities (and their employees), police departments (and their employees), and sheriffs' departments (and their employees) can be sued if it could be shown that they were acting "under color of law" and violated a specific Amendment of the Constitution. The standards used in federal courts in this regard are "custom or policy" and "deliberate indifference," both of which are loosely defined concepts but similar to "totality of circumstances." Although such suits can result in monetary awards, the amounts are usually not great since the purpose of civil rights suits filed under 42 U.S.C. 1983 is essentially injunctive (i.e., to force the municipality or department to change its procedures or behaviors), rather than compensatory or punitive in nature.

A lawsuit against a police department by a present employee or police applicant may be filed in federal court stemming from a complaint filed with the U.S. Equal Employment Opportunity Commission (EEOC). Such complaints could be based on race, age, or sex discrimination in hiring, retention, or promotions. The complaint may also be based on alleged violation of the **Americans with Disabilities Act** (ADA). The provisions of the ADA state that individuals who believe they have been discriminated against on the basis of their disability can file a charge with the EEOC at any of its offices located throughout the United States. The commission will investigate and initially attempt to resolve the charge through conciliation following the same procedures used to handle charges of discrimination filed under Title VII of the **Civil Rights Act of 1964**. A charging party may file a lawsuit within 90 days after receiving a notice of a "right to sue" from EEOC. The ADA also incorporates the remedies contained in Title VII. These remedies include hiring, promotion, reinstatement, back pay, and attorney's fees.

Reasonable accommodation (making changes in the nature of the employee's job) is also available as a remedy under the ADA. Under most EEOC-enforced laws, compensatory and punitive damages also may be available where intentional discrimination is found. Damages may be available to compensate for actual monetary losses, for future monetary losses, and for mental anguish and inconvenience. Punitive damages (used to "punish" an agency for wrongdoings) also may be available if an employer acted with malice or reckless indifference. Punitive damages are not available against the federal government, state or local governments, however.

Certainly there are numerous reasons from legal, psychological, safety, and common sense standpoints why police departments and other law enforcement agencies should perform preemployment psychological screening. Perhaps an Indiana appellate court said it best when it opined that a "policeman frequently works alone, wields great authority, carries lethal weapons" and "it is not an occupation for . . . a person with questionable emotional stability" (*City of Greenwood v. Dowler*, 1986).

THE COMPONENTS OF PREEMPLOYMENT PSYCHOLOGICAL SCREENING

The Interview and Background Information

It is assumed that prior to the psychological screening of a police applicant, all law enforcement agencies, whether they are city, county, state, or federal, will complete a background investigation on the potential recruit. Such an investigation will assess the applicant's competency, motivation, and personal ethics, and cover his/her employment record, credit history, criminal history, and any alcohol or drug use. References and people who have known the applicant will also be interviewed. This will include places of residence, educational institutions, jobs, family members, friends, and neighbors. The investigation may also include an interview conducted by a background investigator or detective. Some departments may also administer a polygraph examination and compare these results with the information obtained from the background investigation.

Interviews performed by a psychologist usually covers information about an applicant's childhood, adolescence, family life, work history, military history, education, and interpersonal relationships. Specific attention should be paid to how well the individual deals with stress and pressure both in work settings and in the personal arena. The applicant's motivation for police work should be pursued with the aim at screening out those individuals who excessively crave excitement or power. The interview is also used to screen for blatant psychopathology.

The applicant's history with drug use is also explored during the interview. Different police departments have their own policies regarding the use of drugs. Some agencies may have a strict drug policy whereby an applicant is rejected if he/she has used marijuana more than 30 times in a lifetime. Some departments may require that no drugs at all should be part of an applicant's history. Other departments have no specific drug policy but instead assess each applicant as an individual in the context of their particular social and cultural background. As with drugs, departments have differing policies regarding problems with alcohol, or how any past arrests or criminal convictions will or will not disqualify them for a police position.

Regardless of departmental policies concerning drug and alcohol use and criminal history, the psychologist will carefully evaluate the circumstances that led up to such involvement, determine whether an addictive pattern is present, and see what the person has learned from such past behavior. Overall, most psychologists make a point of assessing a police applicant's judgment and common sense, communication ability, and interpersonal skills during the interview. But the interview as a selection device has not been free of problems. Interviews have not usually been used as a predictive technique for job performance, and there is no strong research suggesting that interviews by themselves provide a valid indication of future job performance.

Another concern regarding interviews is that there is no agreement among psychologists as to the format that an interview should take. Some psychologists believe that the interview should be formalized and structured to the point that each police applicant is presented with precisely the same questions in precisely the same order. Other psychologists feel that the interview should be used to explore particular areas of concern relative to that individual. For example, there may be questions or concerns raised on the psychological testing, which can be clarified during the interview. Fortunately, most psychologists who perform preemployment psychological screening use the interview as only one part of the total assessment process, not relying on any one part (e.g., interview, cognitive testing, or personality testing) excessively and without some corroboration from the other components of the process.

The interview section of the report should certainly address the applicant's motivation for the police position as well as what aspects of the job he/she finds attractive and unattractive. Biographical data regarding the applicant's education, work record history, and family background (and associated problems) should also be reported. Specific attention should be paid to any "red flags" in the applicant's background. These would include such things as arrests, drug or alcohol abuse, stealing, dishonesty, being fired from jobs, interpersonal conflicts, poor judgment, impulsivity, excessive passivity or overaggressiveness, and any behaviors that could suggest inadequate stress tolerance. The results from clinical observation of the applicant should also be reported. These would include his/her general attitude, cooperativeness, motivation, energy level, verbal and interpersonal skills, affect, mood, and social judgment. The results from the psychological testing (e.g., the cognitive and personality tests) should be carefully examined for possible confirmation of any concerns raised during the interview. All told then, the psychological report should ideally represent a "total picture" of the individual in regards to his/her appropriateness for a law enforcement position.

The Psychological Services Section of the International Association of Chiefs of Police recommends that psychologists provide statements regarding an applicant's strengths and weaknesses for a police position as well as a final rating. Such ratings are usually reported on a relative scale such as from "1 to 5" with 1 indicating "poor" candidate, 3 indicating "average" candidate, and 5 indicating "excellent" candidate. An exception to such a rating scale is where state law requires a strict "pass or fail" determination.

Cognitive Tests

Psychologists make use of a variety of tests to help assess an applicant's cognitive ability. One such test is the **Wechsler Adult Intelligence Scale (WAIS)**, which has been an integral part of clinical and educational Psychology since 1939 with the introduction of the original Wechsler-Bellevue Intelligence Scale. Since the original version, the Wechsler Scales has been restandardized four times, with the latest revision published in 2008. Up until this latest version (the WAIS-IV), the test has consisted of "verbal" scales and "performance" scales, each assessing specific primary abilities. The WAIS is useful in assessing general intelligence as well as various forms of psychological disturbance. This is because brain damage, psychotic deterioration, and emotional difficulties seem to affect some intellectual functions more than others, and an analysis of the pattern of WAIS scores may assist in differentiating between specific disorders.

The WAIS-IV is composed of 10 core subtests and five supplemental subtests, with the 10 core subtests comprising the Full Scale IQ. With the new WAIS-IV, the verbal/performance subscales from previous versions were removed and replaced by the index scores. The General Ability Index (GAI) was included, which consists of the Similarities, Vocabulary, and Information subtests from the Verbal Comprehension Index and the Block Design, Matrix Reasoning, and Visual Puzzles subtests from the Perceptual Reasoning Index. The GAI is clinically useful because it can be used as a measure of cognitive abilities that are less vulnerable to impairment.

Although the WAIS is certainly recognized as a valid and reliable test of intelligence, it has not been researched to a great extent regarding its ability to predict law enforcement performance. But certain researchers have found a strong correlation of earlier version WAIS scores with police academy grades, and with performance ratings of officers after one year on the job. The main drawback of the WAIS is the time it takes to correctly administer (about 1 hour and 40 minutes).

The **Wonderlic Personnel Test (WPT)** is one of the most frequently used cognitive testing devices in both law enforcement and private industry. The test publishers describe the WPT as a short-form test of general cognitive ability, which is often referred to as "g" and is a measure of the level at which an individual learns, understands instructions, and solves problems. The test consists of 50 questions, which include word comparisons, disarranged sentences, sentence parallelism, following directions, number comparisons, number series, analysis of geometric figures, and story problems requiring either mathematical or logical solutions. Questions are arranged in order of difficulty and takes 12 minutes to complete before being stopped by the proctor. Both computerized and large print versions of the test are available as are 11 alternate language versions. The WPT provides a measurable and quantitative look into how easily an individual can be trained, how well they can adjust and adapt to changing situations and demands, how easily they can solve problems on the job, and how well satisfied they are likely to be with the demands of their careers.

Two other cognitive tests used by psychologists performing psychological screening are the *Nelson–Denny Reading Test* and the *Shipley Institute of Living Scale*. The Nelson–Denny is a 118-item test designed to measure reading comprehension and vocabulary and takes about 45 minutes to complete. The Shipley Scale consists of 60 items and measures vocabulary and abstract thinking and takes about 20 minutes to complete.

There is recent speculation that the importance and relevance of cognitive and intelligence tests has not been fully appreciated in the preemployment psychological screening process, and researchers such as Dilchert, Ones, Davis, and Rostow (2007) stress the importance of cognitive ability in the prediction of counterproductive work behaviors (CWB). CWB can range from relatively mild problems such as lateness, abuse of sick leave or work avoidance or misuse of resources, to severe behavioral aberrations such as theft, at-fault car accidents, overaggressiveness, violence, and substance abuse (Ones, 2002). Most of the research over the last 30 years targeted to improve prehire decision making has been aimed at identifying personality traits in an attempt to predict and reduce the occurrence of these kinds of negative police behaviors (Bennett & Robinson, 2000; Fortmann, Leslie, and Cunningham, 2002; Sackett, Burris, & Callahan, 1989; Sackett & DeVore, 2001).

Using the Shipley Institute of Living Scale as a measure of cognitive ability, Dilchert, Ones, Davis, and Rostow (2007) found a negative and substantial relationship between cognitive ability and observed CWB. The Institute of Living Scale was intentionally utilized for the study since other research has suggested that this test assesses reasoning ability "traditionally considered to be at or near the core of what is ordinarily meant by intelligence" (Carroll, 1993, p. 196). The authors conclude that cognitive ability predicts the extent to which individuals engage in CWB, and that in law enforcement jobs, the benefit to be gained from using a test of cognitive ability to select applicants lies not only in enhanced task performance, but also in a reduction of detected CWB among those who are hired. Thus, both improvements in task performance and reductions in CWB contribute to the overall value of personnel selection systems that include measures of cognitive ability.

Can Someone be Too Intelligent to be a Police Officer?

Jordan v. City of New London (2000)

On March 16, 1996, Robert Jordan took a series of written tests to become a police officer in New London Connecticut. One of the tests administered was the Wonderlic Personnel Test (WPT), which measures cognitive ability. He scored a 33 on the test, which is well above the normative or median score for police applicants established by the test publisher of 21. Mr. Jordan's score of 33 was the equivalent of an I.Q. score of 125 and represented the ninety-third percentile of the general population. This was part of the reason Mr. Jordan was shocked when he discovered that he was not being interviewed for the position.

Suspecting age discrimination (he was 46 years old), Jordan filed an administrative complaint with the Connecticut Commission of Human Rights and Opportunities. The city responded stating that it removed Jordan from consideration due to his high score on the WPT, and their concern that applicants who were too intelligent would become easily bored with the job and resign. In order to prevent frequent turnover, they did not interview applicants who scored over 27 on the test.

To justify their policy, the city relied on the Wonderlic Personnel Test & Scholastic Level Exam Manual, which states on page 17,

Higher scores . . . indicate the ability to learn more quickly. . . . Employers are naturally eager to . . . seek new employees who will become immediately productive on the job. A conflict arises when . . . the new employee finds the job itself a bore—and quits. The reduced cost of training is replaced with the high cost of losing, and having to replace, productive employees. *Simply hiring the highest scoring employee can be self-defeating.* [italics added].

Mr. Jordan brought a civil rights action in district court alleging that the city denied him equal protection in violation of the Fourteenth Amendment of the Connecticut Constitution. The court did not agree, finding that Jordan was not a member of a suspect class (a legitimate minority group under the law), and thus his claim must receive a "rational basis" of scrutiny. Under a rational basis analysis, a statutory classification that does not involve a member of a minority group (or suspect class) and that does not involve a fundamental right (such as freedom of speech or freedom of religion) must be upheld if there is a reasonable governmental need. Keeping turnover at a minimum is such a reasonable governmental need.

Jordan appealed the court's holding to the Connecticut Supreme Court, which upheld the lower court's decision. The Court concluded that "Applying [a] lenient standard of review . . . even absent a strong statistical correlation between high scores on the Wonderlic and turnover . . . it is enough that the city *believed*—on the basis of material prepared by the test maker . . . that there was such a connection." (italics added).

The Court added, "Even if unwise, [this] was a rational policy instituted to reduce job turnover and thereby lessen the economic cost involved in hiring and training police officers who do not remain long enough to justify the expense."

The Court in *Jordan* certainly did not say it was a logical practice to reject a police applicant who scores too high on an intelligence test (or a wise one for that matter), but it is a *justifiable* practice if based on a reasonable and documented governmental need.

Personality Tests

One of the most widely used personality tests employed in police psychological screening is the **Minnesota Multiphasic Personality Inventory (MMPI and MMPI-2)**. First published in 1937, the test consists of 566 true or false questions that are related to various forms of clinical psychopathology. The scales of the MMPI are divided up into "validity" scales and "clinical" scales. The validity scales consist of scales *L*, *F*, and *K*, which detect an individual's inconsistency in response style, admission to extremely pathological symptoms, and defensiveness, respectively. The ten clinical scales are *1* (Hypochondriasis), *2* (Depression), *3* (Hysteria), *4* (Psychopathic Deviate), *5* (Masculinity–Femininity), *6* (Paranoia), *7* (Psychesthenia), *8* (Schizophrenia), *9* (Hypomania), and *0* (Social Affiliation).

In response to concerns that the original MMPI contained dated, objectionable (e.g., religious, sexual, and intrusive) items it was republished in 1989 addressing these issues and increasing its face validity as well. The new version was a vast improvement over the older one as it satisfied the criticisms leveled against it yet also maintained the test's usefulness. The MMPI, and later the MMPI-2, has been and remains the most commonly used psychological test in the assessment of police officer applicants. As Blau observed, it has been the workhorse of paper-and-pencil personality assessment for more than half a century (Blau, Super, & Brady, 1993).

Police officers as a group tend to fall within the "normal" MMPI range on clinical scales and present an emotionally healthy image. Hargrave and Hiatt (1987) found that the *L* (Lie) Scale and the *F* (Frequency) Scale tended to distinguish between satisfactory and unsatisfactory officer criterion groups. Herndon (1998) found that elevations on the *L* scale of the MMPI-2 appeared to be related to subsequent poor behavior of police officers after being hired.

Scale *4* (Psychopathic Deviate) of the MMPI is generally thought to have particular relevance in the selection of police officers because the scale was developed to assist in identifying persons with psychopathic personality disorders. A psychopathic personality pattern involves the repeated and flagrant disregard for social customs and mores, an inability to profit from experience, emotional shallowness, and the strongly held belief (whether verbalized or not) that "the world is my oyster." Males who score high on this scale are described by clinicians as being hostile, aggressive in their interpersonal relationships, sarcastic, cynical, ostentatious, exhibitionistic, moody, resentful, and thrill seeking. High-scoring women are described as aggressive, emotionally changeable, and high strung.

Overall, various studies have suggested that officers rated as unsatisfactory by their supervisors tend to score higher on scales *4* (Psychopathic Deviate), *6* (Paranoia), and *9* (Hypomania) than do satisfactory officers (Hargrave & Hiatt, 1987). Bartol (1991b) followed 600 police officers from 34 small-town police departments over 13 years to determine which officers would eventually be terminated for cause. He concluded that an "immaturity index" consisting of a combination of scales *4, 9,* and *L* was a strong predictor of termination.

The **California Psychological Inventory (CPI)** is similar in format to the MMPI and includes such general personal traits as dominance, sociability, and flexibility. Answers to the 434 items yield scores on 20 dimensions in four primary areas. These primary areas (or "measures") are "*poise*" (dominance, capacity for status, sociability, social presence, self-acceptance, independence, and empathy); "*normative orientation and values*" (responsibility, socialization, self-control, good impression, communality, well-being, and tolerance); "*cognitive and intellectual functioning*" (achievement via conformance, achievement via independence, and intellectual efficiency); and "*role and interpersonal style*" (psychological mindedness, flexibility, and femininity).

Scale scores on the CPI have been found to be related to police trainees' academy performance, and Hargrave and Hiatt (1987) found that CPI profiles distinguished between those suitable and unsuitable for training. The **Sixteen Personality Factor Questionnaire (16PF)** is a 187-item personality inventory that usually requires about 1 hour to complete. The test was originally published in 1949 by R. B. Cattell and yields 16 scores on such traits as *reserved versus outgoing, humble versus assertive, shy versus venturesome,* and *trusting versus suspicious* (Cattell, 1969, 1970, 1971; Cattell, Schroder, & Wagner, 1969). Since 1949, the 16PF has been revised six times with the most recent revisions (1993, 1998) being used by many law enforcement agencies today.

The 16 primary factors of the 16PF consist of "*A*" (Interpersonal warmth), "*B*" (Abstract reasoning), "*C*" (Emotional stability), "*E*" (Dominance), "*F*" (Enthusiasm), "*G*" (Conscientiousness), "*H*" (Social boldness), "*I*" (Sensitivity), "*L*" (Vigilance), "*M*" (Imagination), "*N*" (Forthrightness), "*O*" (Apprehensiveness), "*Q1*" (Openness), "*Q2*" (Self-reliance), "*Q3*" (Perfectionism), and "*Q4*" (Tension). Results of one meta-analysis suggests that two of the 16 scales, dominance and conscientiousness, were significantly related to police performance (Aamodt, 2004). Individuals scoring high on these scales are described as being assertive, competitive, conscientious and responsible.

The **Inwald Personality Inventory (IPI)** differs from the MMPI and the CPI in that it was designed specifically to assess the suitability of personality attributes and behaviors of police applicants (Inwald, 1992). The IPI is a 310-item, true–false questionnaire consisting of 25 original scales and one validity scale, designed to measure attributes such as stress reactions, negative behaviors such as lateness for work, interpersonal difficulties, antisocial behavior, and drug and alcohol use. In addition, the scales also measure personality traits such as suspiciousness, anxiety, and rigidity of character. There has been research to suggest that the IPI predicts police functioning better than the MMPI, and it is particularly interesting, that combining the IPI and MMPI scales increased the overall accuracy of classification (Shusman, Inwald, & Knatz, 1987).

As referred to earlier in this chapter, the **NEO Personality Inventory-Revised (NEO PI-R)** is one of the psychological inventories often used by police and forensic psychologists as part of their preemployment psychological screening process for law enforcement applicants. The inventory is the result of the emergence of the five-factor model of personality (Digman, 1996; Goldberg, 1993). It is composed of *Neuroticism* (N; the tendency to experience negative affects such as sadness, anxiety, guilt, fear, anger, embarrassment, irrationality, impulsivity, poor coping); *Extraversion* (E; tendency toward assertiveness, high activity/energy level, sociability, optimism, positive emotions); *Openness* (O; tendency to be open to new experiences, intellectually curious, and aesthetically imaginative and sensitive); *Agreeableness* (A; tendency toward trust, cooperation, altruism, sympathy/empathy); and *Conscientiousness* (C; tendency toward self-control, organization, purposefulness, motivation, and reliability (Costa & McCrae, 1992). To easily remember the five-factor model, use the acronym of OCEAN or CANOE.

For each of the factors of the five-factor model, there are six subordinate dimensions (also known as "facets"). The five factors and facets are illustrated in Table 7.2.

Moderate correlations have been found between Emotional Stability, Conscientiousness, and Extraversion with good work ethic and motivation across various job categories (Barrick & Mount, 2001). Behaviorally, employees who are emotionally stable, extraverted, and conscientious seem to be happier at work and to find their work more satisfying. Accordingly, at least in reference to police work, preemployment psychological screening should ideally include an assessment of these personality features, and the NEO PI-R seems like one way to accomplish this (Barrick & Mount, 1991; Borman, White, Pulakos, & Oppler, 1991; Sarchione, Cuttler, Muchinsky, & Nelson-Gray, 1998). All told, a combination of personality assessment devices (e.g., the MMPI, CPI, 16-PF, IPI, NEO) together with a test of cognitive ability (e.g., the WAIS-IV, Wonderlic, Nelson–Denny, Shipley), and an interview, likely best suits the needs of

TABLE 7.2 Five-Factor Model of Personality

Neuroticism	Extraversion	Openness to Experience	Agreeableness	Conscientiousness
Anxiety	Warmth	Fantasy	Trust	Competence
Hostility	Gregariousness	Aesthetics	Straightforwardness	Order
Depression	Assertiveness	Feelings	Altruism	Dutifulness
Self-Consciousness	Activity	Actions	Compliance	Achievement Striving
Impulsiveness	Excitement Seeking	Ideas	Modesty	Self-Discipline
Vulnerability to Stress	Positive Emotion	Values	Tendermindedness	Deliberation

Source: Adapted from Barrick, M. R., & Mount, M. K. (1991). The big five personality dimensions and job performance: A meta-analysis. *Personnel Psychology, 44*, 1–26; Costa, P. T., Jr., & McCrae, R. R. (1992). *Revised NEO personality inventory and new five factor inventory: Professional manual.* Odessa, FL: Psychological Assessment Resources; Digman, J. M. (1990). Personality structure: Emergence of the five-factor model. *Annual Review of Psychology, 41*, 417–440; Goldberg, L. R. (1993). The structure of phenotypic personality traits. *American Psychologist, 48*, 26–34.

police psychologists, law enforcement administrators and hiring authorities when it comes to hiring personnel who are most suited for the job (Cortina, Doherty, Schmitt, Kaufman, & Smith, 1992; Inwald & Shusman, 1984; Shusman, Inwald, & Landa, 1984).

FITNESS FOR DUTY EVALUATIONS

A **fitness-for-duty evaluation** (FFDE) is an ordered evaluation performed by a psychologist or psychiatrist on a current officer to determine his/her present suitability for law enforcement functioning (e.g., to carry a weapon). The evaluation usually involves an extensive interview and mental status examination, review of background information (including relevant internal affairs files), speaking with third parties if needed, and possibly the administration of psychological tests. Ideally the evaluation should be performed by a psychologist who is familiar with police work and who has had experience dealing with police officers. A FFDE is not a substitute for supervision, and it is definitely not discipline. In any request for a FFDE the police department should clearly state why the examination is being ordered and should insure that all of the officer's problematic behaviors have been documented. The department should also state on the referral to the psychologist any remedial measures that have been attempted but failed.

Guidelines for these purposes have been published by the International Association of Chiefs of Police (IACP), Psychological Services Section, the American Psychological Association (APA), and by established professional and statutory requirements regarding psychological practice.

A FFDE may be requested due to "positive" symptoms or behaviors or due to "negative" symptoms or behaviors. Positive symptoms are those behaviors that the officer is showing and should not be, while negative symptoms are those behaviors that the officer is not showing and should be. Examples of positive behaviors or symptoms would include rudeness, overaggressiveness, abuse of sick leave, repeated instances of insubordination, interpersonal conflicts with coworkers, inappropriate use of alcohol or drugs, domestic violence, excessive anxiety, panic, depression, or mental confusion. Some examples of negative behaviors or symptoms would include lack of needed assertiveness, unwillingness to take action when it is required, failure to maintain order, and inattention to basic officer safety.

After the FFDE is performed the psychologist will send a report to the chief of police. At this point various things can happen. If the officer is found to have a psychological problem but is able to perform his/her duties, a referral for treatment may be made. If the psychological problem is a diagnosable condition under the *Diagnostic and Statistical Manual of the American Psychiatric Association* (DSM-4) and the officer in not capable of performing his/her duties, temporary restricted duty (i.e., light duty) may be considered. Examples of a diagnosable condition would include major depression, panic disorder, and adjustment reaction. Individuals with diagnosable conditions usually qualify for "disability" status pursuant to the requirements of the **American with Disabilities Act (ADA)** and possible work accommodations will be sought. Following any period of treatment, a reevaluation will be required prior to the officer returning to full duty.

If an officer is found to have a psychological problem that is not protected by the ADA (e.g., antisocial personality disorder) he/she may be handled through disciplinary channels, possibly referred for counseling, or terminated if he/she cannot behaviorally conform to the requirements of being a police officer. If no psychological problem is found than the officer may be cleared for duty with a recommendation that the problem be handled administratively or by other means.

U.S. courts at all levels have generally been supportive of a police department's right to order FFDEs and for making the necessary and appropriate recommendations based on these evaluations. Police departments have an affirmative "duty" to take reasonable precautions in only retaining those police officers who are not psychologically disturbed.

Can Fitness-For-Duty Evaluations be Mandatory?

Conte v. Harcher (1977); *P.B.A. Local 319 v. Township of Plainsboro* (1998); *Miller v. City of Springfield* (1998); *Risner v. U.S. Dept of Transportation* (1982)

In *Conte v. Harcher* (1977), a court held that, in order to protect the public interest, insure the efficiency of the police department, and be kept informed about an officer's ability to perform his/her duties, a chief has the authority to order a fitness-for-duty evaluation.

In *P.B.A. Local 319 v. Township of Plainsboro* (1998), a "legitimate government interest" was found in the periodic psychological testing of all police officers. In *Miller v. City of Springfield* (1998), a Florida police commander observed that a patrol officer showed "unusually defensive and antagonistic behavior" toward his coworkers and supervisors. The officer was relieved from duty pending a fitness-for-duty examination when he brought suit under the ADA. The trial judge dismissed the action, and the appellate court affirmed, stating that no disability was implicated as management did not perceive the officer as psychological disabled, and that characterizations such as "oppositional," "suspicious," "threatening," and "difficult to interact with" merely suggested "serious personality conflicts" with coworkers and that "such conflicts do not rise to the level of a mental impairment under the ADA."

In *Risner v. U.S. Dept of Transportation* (1982), the court stated that "the fitness-for-duty examination is a useful procedure to determine an employee's competency to perform his duties . . . [and] failure to submit to such an examination, when there are good reasons for directing an employee to submit to it, is insubordination and can justify discharge."

TRAINING AND CONSULTATION

All law enforcement agencies have training programs. Probably the first structured training situation that a recruit experiences as a new police officer or federal agent, is the academy. There are two major ways that a psychologist can assist in designing a training program at the academy level. The first is in the *method* of training. As experts in learning theory and human factors, most psychologists can offer significant input on the use of effective teaching techniques that academy instructors can use to effectively teach required courses.

Some of the police training programs that psychologists can help design or implement as far as teaching *methodology* include, but are certainly not limited to, the Criminal Justice System, Law, Abnormal Behavior, Patrol and Investigations, Traffic, Report Writing, Proactive Patrol, Vehicle Stops, Searches, Community Policing, Driving Techniques, Firearms, Use of Deadly and Nondeadly Force, Disability Awareness, Cultural Awareness, Physical Training and Tactics, First Aid, CPR, ID Theft, Media Relations, Terrorism and Terrorist Indicators, Mass Gatherings, Fraudulent Documents, Suspected Explosive Devices, Citywide and National Incident Management.

Another way that psychologists can assist with training programs is by designing their *content*. As experts in human behavior, personality, and abnormal psychology, psychologists themselves can teach recruits in relevant subject areas within professional psychology. A relevant sample of areas within psychology can include Wellness Training and Burnout Prevention, Stress Management, Organization and Team Building, Assertiveness Training, Parenting Skills, Coping with Bereavement and Loss, Evaluation and Preparation for Special Assignments, Counseling and Psychotherapy, and Hostage Negotiations (Templin, 1990).

It is an unfortunate reality that training in **hostage negotiations** is relevant now and will continue to be in the future. The historical development of this specialized area of training is of considerable interest.

In the summer of 1972, Assistant Chief Inspector Simon Eisdorfer of the New York Police Department, watched as a hostage drama unfolded on TV. What became known as the "Munich massacre" occurred at the 1972 Summer Olympics in Munich Germany, when members of the

Israeli Olympic team were taken hostage by the Palestinian terrorist organization Black September. The attack, miserable and failed attempts at negotiations, and botched rescue attempt, eventually led to the deaths of 11 Israeli athletes and one German police officer.

As the commanding officer of the New York Police Department's special operations division, Eisdorfer realized that such an event could actually happen in New York City. He also knew that the police department was not prepared to deal with it. Accordingly, he developed the operational plans for the nation's first Hostage Negotiation Team. The team became reality in the spring of 1973, months after a high-profile standoff in January in which armed robbers seized a dozen hostages at a Brooklyn sporting goods store and one police officer was killed.

Eisdorfer knew that by putting fresh cops into a hostage situation he could wear down hostage takers. He realized that negotiators could subtly turn a siege into a waiting game that played out in their favor. Police officers could change shifts but the suspects could not, and would become tired and hungry and more likely to surrender.

Psychologists such as Dr. Harvey Schlossberg (the first full-time police officer in this country to earn a Ph.D. in psychology) were used to "profile" hostage takers; determine their motivation, vulnerabilities, and dangerousness; and suggest dialogue strategies or psychological tactics that could defuse the situation. Dr. Schlossberg also helped the police determine if a hostage taker might be mentally ill. This was seen as being particularly important since some hostage takers may be out of touch with reality and attempting to commit "suicide by cop." Based on Eisdorfer's and Schlossberg's pioneering work, a special hostage negotiations team became a permanent fixture of the New York Police Department and was eventually incorporated within the Emergency Service Unit (ESU).

Psychologists are often involved in various phases of any hostage negotiations process. There are specific areas of training or modules that are necessary to develop a fully trained hostage negotiations team which psychologists can and should have input in developing. These are as follows:

1. *Basic Hostage Negotiations:* Based on the Federal Bureau of Investigation (FBI) training program, this includes classes on barricade situations; face-to-face negotiations; diagnosis of hostage takers; handling of demands; and dealing with deadlines.
2. *Equipment:* Dealing with and managing team equipment such as the hostage phone, notebooks, and checklists and personal equipment such as extra clothing, snack food, personal hygiene items, and personal first aid kits.
3. *Policy:* Knowledge of police policy concerning negotiations; team organization; mobilization of teams; relationship with the tactical team; role of commanders; and "green light" considerations.
4. *Team Duties:* The individual responsibilities of each team member such as the primary negotiator, secondary negotiator, coach, intelligence coordinator, and departmental liaison.
5. *Penal Code:* Knowledge of the penal code and case law relative to hostage situations.
6. *City/Community Interface:* Outside agencies who might be asked to participate and interface with the hostage negotiation's team. These include telephone and cellular carriers, electric and gas companies, schools, and news networks.
7. *Practical Exercises and Command Post Practical Problems:* This brings together all job functions on the team and creates practical exercises involving different scenarios.
8. *Negotiator Stress Survival:* This provides the negotiators with specific suggestions and procedures for dealing with their own stress encountered before, during, and after a hostage incident.
9. *Knowledge and Review of Previous Hostage Situations:* This training program involves the review of hostage situations handled by their own and other departments or agencies.
10. *Simulations with Tactical Team Interface:* These are simulations of hostage situations with involvement of the negotiations team and the tactical (SWAT) team (Greenstone, 1995; McMains, 1995).

Most police departments' hostage negotiations teams consist of at least five people. These include the primary negotiator (who does most of the active negotiations); a secondary negotiator (who monitors negotiations and makes suggestions); an intelligence officer (who seeks and organizes incoming information); a psychologist (who serves as a consultant, advisor, actual negotiator); and a tactical liaison (who maintains communications with command) (Greenstone, 1995).

Psychologists have found that the first 15–45 minutes of a hostage situation are the most dangerous. This is because the hostage takers are still going through a panic reaction. This is when most hostages get injured or killed, either because they tried to be a hero, made some remark or suggestion, stood out in some symbolic way, or were just picked at random to make a point. Unless the hostage takers are under the influence of some chemical stimulant, they are likely to calm down after awhile, appear to be exhausted, and tell everyone to get some rest.

There are several communication techniques to keep in mind when dealing with hostage takers and barricaded subjects:

1. Give yourself a lot of leeway to negotiate.
2. Focus on the hostage taker and not the hostages.
3. Do not be afraid of silences.
4. Avoid becoming defensive.
5. Allow the hostage taker to vent feelings.
6. Do not become angry unless you have planned such a response and it is part of your strategy.
7. Make the hostage taker(s) work for everything he/she gets. Don't solicit demands, don't give anything not explicitly asked for, and don't deliver more than absolutely necessary to fulfill the request.
8. Ensure that the hostage taker(s) make concessions before you give something or respond affirmatively to a demand. If there are multiple hostages involved, let the hostage taker make the first offer of how many hostages he's willing to release. It's better to get one or two people out safely now, rather than risk having the hostage taker change his mind because he feels you're pressuring or manipulating him for more. If there is only a single hostage or very few hostages, and the hostages are personally known to the hostage taker (such as in family arguments or workplace disputes), the situation is more dangerous because the hostages have a particular personal or symbolic value to the hostage taker.
9. Use time to your advantage whenever possible. Use the passage of time to allow the hostage taker to expend adrenalin and become fatigued, however, be aware that total exhaustion can sometimes lead to heightened agitation and impulsive action.
10. Do not try to manipulate or intimidate the hostage taker into surrendering as this may have the opposite effect because he/she may see this as a sign of weakness. If at all possible, convince the hostage taker to come out "voluntarily" with as much dignity preserved as possible (Greenstone, 1995; McMains & Mullins, 2006; Miller, 2006).

CRITICAL INCIDENT DEBRIEFING

Every year, hundreds of officers experience intense, traumatic events that can have serious long-term consequences for them, their families, and their departments. It is incumbent upon police administrators to ensure that their officers and their departments have the tools at hand to cope with such critical incidents. In the past, most studies of stress in law enforcement focused exclusively on postshooting trauma. Recently the research has expanded to encompass stress induced by other traumatic events, collectively known as critical incidents.

A *critical incident* has been defined as any event that has a stressful impact sufficient to overwhelm the usually effective coping skills of an individual. It is also seen as an event that lies outside the realm of normal human experience and could be expected to produce significant emotional reactions in anyone. A critical incident is a situation that reminds the officer of his own limits and overwhelms the individual's capacity to cope (McMains, 1995). This can be a sudden death in the line of duty, serious injury from a shooting, a physical or psychological threat to the safety or well being of an individual regardless of the type of incident. Such an incident can involve any event faced by emergency or public safety personnel that causes a distressing, dramatic or profound change or disruption in ones physical or psychological functioning (Copes, 2005; Davis & Rostow, 2003).

To help police officers in dealing with such symptoms that are generally associated with exposure to trauma, psychologists have developed *critical incident stress debriefing (CISD)* techniques. Such debriefing allows the officer to process the event, ventilate emotions, and talk about its impact. The debriefing itself can be conducted on or near the site of the event or at another location. Debriefing should ideally occur as soon as possible following the critical event but certainly within the first 24–72 hours. As the length of time between exposure to the event and debriefing increases, the less effective it becomes.

But providing the needed stress debriefing or any therapeutic services for law enforcement is not always easy to do and presents unique challenges. There is a natural inclination by police officers to resist psychological intervention for many reasons. These include a strong sense of independence and self-sufficiency, a need to appear "invincible," and a skepticism and distrust of "outsiders." Accordingly, a psychologist who provides services for the police should be somewhat familiar with the police culture and the police job. The psychologist should be familiar with the organization of the police department and its power and rank structure as well.

Debriefing can be done in large or small groups or one-to-one depending on the situation. But most such approaches are done in a group setting. The approaches to CISD (e.g., Bohl, 1995; Mitchell & Everly, 1993) incorporate some combination of the following aspects:

1. Encourage participants to talk about what happened during the incident.
2. Allow participants to ventilate their thoughts, emotions, and experiences associated with the event.
3. Assess the impact of the critical incident on police personnel and survivors.
4. Identify the immediate issues involving safety and security.
5. Allow for validation of thoughts, emotions, and experiences associated with the event.
6. Encourage participants to express what they are *still* experiencing from the event, and to discuss the presence of any "unfinished business."
7. Educate participants regarding how to deal with their families and their children. This is especially important for police as their family may have heard that the officer killed someone during the incident.
8. Bring in support personnel and survivors as community resources to encourage the healing and rebuilding process.
9. Assist in the "reentry" process back into the police department and community.
10. Predict reactions that may arise in the aftermath of the event.

It is important to note that any model of critical incident stress debriefing is designed for short-term assistance and is not psychotherapy. After debriefing is over, brief follow-up meetings may be necessary. Sometimes issues persist or symptoms are not alleviated with debriefing and more formalized counseling or psychotherapy is required. A referral for such additional assistance should then be made for the officer. Such a referral could be made to an employee assistance counselor, the local mental health center, or a private psychologist, social worker or psychiatrist.

Does critical incident stress debriefing work? McMains (1995) as well as Mitchell and Everly (1993) found that there are fewer resignations in police departments that have critical incident stress debriefing programs than in departments that do not have such programs. Case reports and anecdotal evidence of debriefing suggest that they may indeed lead to symptom mitigation. However, there has not been rigorous, controlled investigation on this point. It may be the case that certain types of debriefing procedures (i.e., pharmacotherapy, behavior therapy, cognitive therapy, psychodynamic and hypnotherapies) may be well suited to one individual but not another and that certain treatments may be more suitable for certain symptoms (Solomon, Gerrity, & Muff, 1993).

There is also some evidence to suggest that certain "person" characteristics are important in determining who is likely to develop stress reactions and post traumatic stress disorder in the future. For example, Thompson (1993) found that a police body recovery team had lower psychological symptom scores compared to other similar teams. In addition to debriefing sessions and ongoing management support, this result was likely due to the careful selection and training of the individuals on the team.

Some of the important person variables that have been found to be related to resistance to traumatic stress include higher intelligence, hardiness of personality, extraversion, solid coping skills, advanced educational level, the lack of other life stressors, and the absence of psychological premorbidity (Thompson, 1993).

MULTICULTURALISM IN LAW ENFORCEMENT

Policing in the twenty-first century requires a whole new and refined set of skills, tools, and cultural knowledge. In contrast to the past, today law enforcement must pay significantly more attention to race, class, ethnicity, religion, sexual orientation, gender, and other demographics in our complex multicultural society. In an effort to become more responsive to our new diverse citizenry, the police are working to become more closely connected in direct relationships with all aspects of the community. These attempts have created a "cultural competence" on the part of the criminal justice system as a whole. For law enforcement in particular, the effects of cultural competence and multiculturalism can be seen in such areas as recruitment, retention, and promotion; cross-cultural awareness; and responding to hate crimes.

Recruitment, Retention, and Promotion

Law enforcement agencies are obliged to actively and energetically recruit a diverse workforce. The "business as usual" tactics of recruitment will no longer suffice in this regard. A study commissioned by the International Association of Chiefs of Police in 1998, called The Future of Women in Policing: Mandates for Action, concluded that "unfocused, random, recruiting is unlikely to attract diversity. Targeted programs are more likely to do so." Recruiting minority and women applicants requires commitment, planning, and effort by police and sheriff departments and federal agencies. A strategic recruitment plan should target diverse populations where they live and work. Advertising should also be aimed at minority colleges and universities, military bases, and places of worship.

Furthermore, in the applicant selection process, in addition to background investigations, interviews, polygraph examinations (where allowed by law), and psychological and medical examinations, police applicants should also be assessed for racial, ethnic, gender, sexual orientation, and cultural biases. An agency whose hiring procedures screen for unacceptable biases demonstrates to the community that it seeks police officers who will discharge their duties and authority with fairness, impartiality, and respect for the civil rights and dignity of all the people they protect.

Recruiting a diverse population of police applicants who respect all citizens is one important challenge for law enforcement. But retention and promotion are equally as important. Failure to promote qualified candidates representative of the diverse population served by the agency can result in distrust of the police by the community, and in aggravation of the tension that may already exist between these two entities.

Police chiefs and other executives must determine if minority and women officers are applying for supervisory positions, and if their numbers are at least proportional to their numbers on the department. Does the promotional process tend to inappropriately screen out female and minority officers? Is the promotion process too subjective? Many agencies find that by making promotional processes more objective, using "hands-on" tasks such as assessment centers, and selecting board members who are representative of both sexes and different races, women and minorities are more likely to be fairly assessed.

Cross-Cultural Awareness

Across the United States, changing demographics have resulted in the need for police to deal increasingly with a multicultural population whose primary language is not English and who may not speak any English at all. Some officers are noticeably impatient (if not angry) when dealing with non-English-speaking people. Citizens are aware when an officer does not understand what they are trying to say or does not grasp their side of a story.

Perhaps most difficult is the situation in which a person with limited English skills is traumatized, further affecting the victim's ability to speak English. Officers need to be aware of the potential for inadvertent discrimination based on a citizen's language background, which could fall under "language and national origin discrimination." In addition to sensitivity to those who do not speak English, the hiring and training of bilingual officers, and the use of translators is needed. Many police departments offer language classes on the job with tuition reimbursement for classes and incentive pay for second-language proficiency.

Officers also need to be aware of the special styles of communication, semantics, and sensitivities within cultures and they should receive training in these. Nonverbal attributes of communication are also essential to understand as they often convey as much as words. These would include things such as physical distance between officer and citizen, hand gestures that may be insulting in some cultures, facial expressions, eye contact, and other aspects of body language.

For example, the "OK" gesture is considered obscene in Latin America, the good luck gesture is offensive in parts of Vietnam, and the "come here" gesture (beckoning people to come with the palm up) is very insulting in most of Asia and Latin America. A police officer sitting at a desk with his feet up, baring the soles of his shoes, would most likely offend a Thai or Saudi Arabian citizen coming into the office. And for a person from Southeast Asia, a smile or giggle can be covering up pain, humiliation, or embarrassment.

Hate crimes are especially injurious forms of offenses that the police must investigate. One of the reasons for this is that the victim(s) often feel traumatized and terrified. Furthermore, victims are often hesitant to report attacks to the police because of fear of becoming victims again, fear of retaliation, fear of reduced privacy, fear of the police themselves and the criminal justice system, cultural and language barriers, and humiliation or shame about being victimized.

The families of the victims often feel frustrated and powerless to prevent additional attacks and may be reluctant to report the incidents at all. Members of the community who share the victim's characteristics may also feel victimized and vulnerable, which may result in community unrest. A swift and strong response by law enforcement can help stabilize and calm the community as well as aid in a victim's recovery. Failure to respond to hate crimes within departmental guidelines may jeopardize public safety and leave officers and departments open to increased scrutiny and possible liability.

It is important that police agencies accurately and comprehensively report all incidences of hate crimes so that the prevalence and patterns of these crimes both locally and nationally can be further determined. The Federal Hate Crimes Statistics Act of 1990 (Public Law 102–275, April 23, 1990) encourages states to report hate crime data to the FBI. Twenty-three states and the District of Columbia require the collection of hate crime data. In 1997, 11,211 state and local law enforcement agencies voluntarily reported 9,861 hate crime offenses to the FBI. Some of the things that a police department can do to prevent and help investigate hate crimes include:

1. Establish a policy of "zero tolerance" for prejudice throughout the agency for both internal and external matters, and convey a commitment to unbiased policing.
2. Ensure that police are trained to recognize and respond appropriately to hate crimes.
3. Provide officers with user-friendly hate crime incident report forms that comply with state and national reporting standards.
4. Sponsor and participate in community events and activities that promote diversity, tolerance, bias reduction, and conflict resolution.
5. Track the criminal activities of organized hate groups.
6. Collaborate with community organizations, schools, and other public agencies to develop coordinated approaches to hate crime prevention and response.
7. Appoint police officials to be liaison officers with targeted groups.
8. Engage the media as partners in restoring victimized communities and preventing bias-motivated incidents and crimes.
9. Document the positive outcomes of hate crime prevention and response strategies.

FORENSIC PSYCHOLOGY IN THE SPOTLIGHT

Should Officer Counseling be *Mandatory*?

Carlan & Nored (2008)

Police officers run a greater risk than the general population of developing many stress-related conditions such as hypertension, heart disease, stomach disorders, psychosomatic illnesses, and alcohol and substance abuse. They also experience divorce twice the rate of individuals in other occupations, and have a suicide rate two to six times greater than the national average (Abdollahi, 2002; Carter & Radelet, 1999; Woody, 2005).

Officers are also expected to always be in emotional control and show extreme restraint even under highly emotional circumstances. Stress prevention is usually preferable to poststress intervention (Stinchcomb, 2004). Unfortunately, officers continue to report a perceived stigma regarding the use of mental health services. Such stigma includes the fear of being labeled as weak or unfit, a fear of job loss or reassignment, and a concern that confidentiality would not be maintained (Baker & Baker, 1996; Church & Robertson, 1999).

One way to circumvent these problems is to require periodic counseling for all officers. Such an "early warning system" was recommended as far back as the 1970s by police psychologist Dr. Harvey Schlossberg for the New York City Police Department. But the idea was rejected by police administrators because of the number of people hours required for such a system to be implemented (H. Schlossberg, personal communication, February 1, 2006).

The periodic psychological *testing* of police officers has survived various court challenges. For example, in *PBA L-319 v. Township of Plainsboro* (1998), the court ruled that periodic psychological screening is constitutional, provided that management provides for the privacy of officers' files and records, and respects their right of Due Process. No appeal was taken. In *Spades v. City of Walnut Ridge* (1999), the court articulated that a police department's potential civil liability on grounds of negligent hiring, supervision, and retention, help to validate the need for the mandatory counseling or even termination of certain troubled officers.

Carland and Nored (2008) conducted a study to empirically test the hypothesis that police departments offering (or at least promoting) psychological counseling would see a corresponding reduction in officer stress, as well as decreased resistance to the potential benefits of counseling.

The researchers found that officers working in departments where counseling opportunities were made available reported diminished levels of stress and need for counseling compared to officers working in departments that did not offer counseling. Officers in departments offering counseling also expressed a greater willingness to use such services. All in all, departments promoting counseling in the work environment benefited from officer stress reduction. The authors concluded that police departments should consider requiring mandatory and periodic counseling for all officers.

Summary

This chapter has presented the historical development of **police psychology** from Hugo Munsterberg in 1908 through the present. This includes the nature of police work and the stressors that are inherent in the job. The potential legal liability faced by police departments due to negligent hiring and negligent entrustment was discussed. Preemployment psychological screening most often consists of the administration of cognitive and personality assessment instruments, and an interview with a psychologist. Almost all departments also make use of a background investigation and medical examination. Some agencies also utilize a polygraph and situational testing.

Fitness-for-duty evaluations are conducted by psychologists at the request of police administrators when faced with officers experiencing apparent psychological difficulties or multiple disciplinary actions. Psychologists also contribute to the training of police officers, and are valuable consultants in hostage negotiations, critical incident stress debriefing, and officer counseling. Finally, there is an ever-present need for modern police work to be sensitive and responsive to the multiculturalism of our society. This includes being culturally competent in areas such as recruitment, hiring, retention, and promotion, and in the investigation of bias and hate crimes.

Key Terms

Americans with Disabilities Act *152*

Burgher Guard *145*

California Personality Inventory *157*

Civil Rights Act of 1964 *153*

Fitness-for-duty evaluation *159*

Gross negligence *152*

Hostage negotiations *160*

Hugo Munsterberg *145*

Inwald Personality Inventory *158*

Lewis Terman *146*

Martin Reiser *145*

Minnesota Multiphasic Personality Inventory *156*

Negligent entrustment *152*

Negligent hiring *151*

Neo Personality Inventory *148*

Police psychology *167*

Preemployment psychological screening *151*

Sixteen Personality Factor Questionnaire *157*

Wechsler Adult Intelligence Scale *154*

Wonderlic Personnel Test *155*

Review Questions

1. What is "police psychology," and who were some of the psychologists involved in its origin?
2. Why do police officers tend to suffer from stress-related conditions such as hypertension, heart disease, stomach disorders, psychosomatic illnesses, and alcohol and substance abuse?
3. What are some of the ways a citizen can pursue legal action against a law enforcement agency?
4. Discuss some of the plusses and minuses of a police department having a specific drug policy when it comes to hiring new officers.
5. In what ways is Scale 4 of the MMPI a good predictor in police selection?
6. What is the Five-Factor Model?
7. What are some of the personality traits found to be important for effective police officers to possess?
8. What are some of the behaviors exhibited by a police officer that might require a fitness-for-duty evaluation?
9. In what areas could a psychologist be most effective in the design of training programs for police recruits and police officers?
10. What takes place in Critical Incident Stress Debriefing?
11. What is meant by "cultural competence," and why is it so important in a modern law enforcement agency?

Chapter Resources On The World Wide Web

Psychology and the Law
http://www.ap-ls.org

Types of Jobs in Law Enforcement
http://www.bls.gov/oco/ocos160.htm

Employment Law and Public Safety
http://www.aele.org/law/Digests/emplmenu.html

Case Law and State and Federal Codes
http://caselaw.lp.findlaw.com/scripts/getcase.pl?court=US&vol=508&invol=476

Forensic Glossary
http://www.forensiceducation.com/sourcebooks/glossary/b.htm

Society of Consulting Psychology of the American Psychological Association
http://www.apa.org/divisions/div13/InsideIndex.htm

Critical Incident Stress Debriefing
http://www.ncptsd.va.gov/publications/cq/v4/n2/hiley-yo.html

Hostage Negotiations: Psychological strategies for resolving crises
http://www.policeone.com/standoff/articles/1247470-Hostage-negotiations-Psychological-strategies-for-resolving-crises/

Hostage Negotiations
http://www.questia.com/library/sociology-and-anthropology/criminology-and-crime/hostage-negotiations.jsp

For Further Reading

Aamodt, M. G. (2004). *Research in law enforcement selection*. Boca Raton, FL: Brown Walker Press.

Brooks, L. W. (2001). Police discretionary behavior: A study of style. In R. G. Dunham & G. P. Alpert (Eds.), *Critical issues in policing: Contemporary readings* (4th ed., pp. 117–131). Prospect Heights, IL: Waveland Press.

Claussen-Rogers, N. L., & Arrigo, B. A. (2005). *Police corruption and psychological testing*. Durham, NC: Carolina Academic Press.

Copes, H. (2005), *Policing and stress*. Upper Saddle River, NJ: Pearson Prentice-Hall.

Inwald, R. E. (1987). *Use of psychologists for selecting and training police*. Springfield, IL: Charles C. Thomas.

Kitaeff, J. (2006). *Jews in blue*. Youngstown, NY: Cambria Press.

Kitaeff, J. (2006). *Selected readings in forensic psychology*. Upper Saddle River, NJ: Pearson Prentice-Hall.

McMains, M. J., & Mullins, W. C. (2006). *Crisis negotiations: Managing critical incidents and situations in law enforcement and corrections* (rev. ed.). Cincinnati, OH: Anderson.

Miller, L. (2006). *Practical police psychology: Stress management and crisis intervention for law enforcement*. Springfield, IL: Charles C. Thomas.

Shusta, R. M., Levine, D. R., Wong, H. Z., & Harris, P. R. (2005). *Multicultural Law Enforcement*. Upper Saddle River, NJ: Pearson Prentice-Hall.

Toch, H. (2002). *Stress in policing*. Washington, DC: American Psychological Association.

CHAPTER 8

Investigations

CHAPTER OBJECTIVES
After reading this chapter you would:

- Know how modern fingerprint analysis is used in the identification of suspects.
- Know the mechanics and accuracy levels of voice identification techniques.
- Know the basic approaches to using the polygraph test.
- Understand the limits of accuracy when using the polygraph teachique.
- Know the two main uses of forensic hypnosis.
- Understand the basics of the cognitive interview, its strengths and weaknesses.
- Know the meaning of *modus operandi*, signature, ritual, and staging, when referring to offender behavior at crime scenes.
- Know the difference between nonscientific and scientific models of criminal profiling.

INTRODUCTION

One of the major ways forensic psychologists are involved in criminal investigations is by the identification of suspects. This identification process can take various forms. One form is to apply psychological principles and analyses to a *specific* crime in an attempt to gather information and narrow down the categories and lists of possible suspects. This can be accomplished by applying psychological science to interviewing witnesses and suspects (e.g., interrogations), obtaining confessions, and structuring lineups and showups for visual identification. This can also be done by accumulating psychological and personality data from past crimes and applying the resulting information to help categorize suspects, motives, and *modes operandi* to the present criminal investigation. Some of these forensic psychological applications are discussed in the chapters on mass murders and serial killers, eyewitness identification and accuracy, and psychology of false confessions and repressed memories. In this chapter, we will examine the remaining significant method for the application of psychological principles to current criminal cases—psychological profiling. But before discussing this somewhat controversial method of suspect description and identification, it is necessary to review some of the other more traditional means of suspect identification. These include fingerprint analysis, voice identification, the polygraph, and forensic hypnosis.

FINGERPRINTS

History of Fingerprint Analysis

Fingerprints have been discovered on ancient Babylonian clay tablets, seals, and pottery. They have also been found on the walls of Egyptian tombs and on Minoan, Greek, and Chinese pottery. On some pottery, fingerprints were impressed so deeply that they were likely intended to serve as the equivalent of a brand label (Ashbaugh, 1999; Åström, 2007; Laufer, 1912). Fingerprints have traditionally also been used as substitutes for signatures. In Babylon from 1885 to 1913 B.C.E., in order to protect against forgery, parties to a legal contract impressed their fingerprints into the clay tablet on which the contract had been written. In addition, there are indications from the age of the Babylonian king Hammurabi (1792–1750 B.C.E.) that legal officials fingerprinted people who had been arrested, and in China around 300 C.E. that handprints had been used as evidence in trials for theft since "no two individuals have fingers exactly alike" (Cole, 2001, pp. 60–61).

By 246 B.C.E., Chinese officials impressed their fingerprints in clay seals, which were used to seal documents. With the advent of silk and paper in China, parties to a legal contract impressed their handprints on the document. All told, even in the first century it was recognized that fingerprints are unique to each person and cannot be imitated. This is not always the same with physical appearances or handwriting. In addition, fingerprints do not change naturally over time. Furthermore, despite the attempts of modern day criminals to efface their prints with sandpaper or acid, they cannot be disguised or permanently altered.

In the Western world, the first practical application using fingerprints was utilized in 1858 when an English administrator in India, Sir William Herschel, began placing the inked palm impressions and, later, thumb impressions of some members of the local population on contracts. These prints were used as a form of signature on the documents because of the high level of illiteracy in India and frequent attempts at forgery. Herschel also began fingerprinting all prisoners in jail. As the locals felt more bound to a contract through the use of palm and thumb prints, the practice became permanent. Later, only the prints of the right index and middle fingers were required on contracts. In time, after viewing a number of fingerprints, Herschel noticed that no two prints were exactly alike, and that even in widespread use, the fingerprints could still be used for personal identification purposes.

In 1880, Dr. Henry Faulds, a British surgeon and superintendent of Tsukiji Hospital in Tokyo, published an article in the scientific journal *Nautre* (Nature). In the article he described how fingerprints could be used as a means of personal identification, and how printers' ink could be used as a method for obtaining such fingerprints. Faulds had begun his study of what he called "skin-furrows" during the 1870s after looking at fingerprints on pieces of old clay pottery. He is also credited with the first fingerprint identification: a greasy print left by a laboratory worker on a bottle of alcohol. Soon, Faulds began to recognize that the distinctive patterns on fingers held great promise as a means of individual identification. He further developed a classification system for recording these inked impressions. Faulds described the pattern formations on the fingers, referred to as "loops" and "whorls," and stated how good sets of fingerprints may be obtained by the use of "a common slate or smooth board of any kind, or a sheet of tin, spread over very thinly with printer's ink." Faulds correctly concluded that fingerprints do not change and that "fingermarks" (i.e., latent prints) left on objects by bloody or greasy fingers may lead to the scientific identification of criminals (Adelmann, 1966).

Expanding on the foundation established by Henry Faulds, in 1892 **Sir Francis Galton** published his book *Finger Prints*, which represented the results of his collection of over 8,000 sets of prints through the work in his anthropological laboratories. The cover of the book actually contained a full set of Galton's own prints. Galton's primary interest in fingerprints was as an aid in determining heredity and racial background. While he soon discovered that fingerprints offered no firm clues to an individual's intelligence or genetic history, he was able to scientifically prove that no two finger-prints are exactly the same and that fingerprints do not change over the course of an individual's lifetime. According to his calculations, the odds of two individual fingerprints being the same were 1 in 64 billion.

Galton classified fingerprints by general shape (arch, loop, or whorl); position in finger; and relative size. The *arch fingerprint* shape is formed by ridges entering from one side of the pattern, rising in the center (in an archlike fashion), and flowing out the other side of the pattern. In the *loop fingerprint* shape, ridges enter one side of the pattern, recurve (turning back to the direction of entry), and exit the pattern. If the ridges of the pattern area slant toward the thumb, the pattern is termed *radial loop*. If the ridges of the pattern area slant toward the little finger, the pattern is termed *ulnar loop*. The *whorl fingerprint* shape consists of a pattern of ridges that encircle a central circular pattern (Galton, 1892). Galton discovered that his arch, loop, and whorl details are not continuous, but rather, contain numerous detailed interruptions. These are known as "minutia" and are to an extent still in use today, often referred to as **Galton's Details**. These details are more commonly called "characteristics" or "points of identity" and consist of various types: ridge endings, bifurcations (a ridge that divides), dots, short ridges, and enclosures (an island).

About the same time of the publication of Galton's book, an Argentinean police officer named Juan Vucetich (who had been corresponding with Galton) devised his own system of fingerprint classification, which he called "Icnofalangometría or Galtonean Method." This system consisted of 101 types of fingerprints that Vucetich personally classified based on Galton's incomplete taxonomy. This new method was used successfully in 1892 in the case of a Buenos Aires resident Francisca Rojas. Rojas claimed that she had been brutally attacked and her two children murdered by a neighboring ranch worker named Velasquez. Velasquez was arrested but refused to confess to the murder of the two children. Nine days after the crime, a search of the crime scene was carried out and a number of fingerprints in blood were found on a door post of the woman's hut. The inked fingerprint impressions did not match Velasquez's but were identical with those of Rojas. When confronted with this evidence, Rojas confessed to the murder of her children and was found guilty and sentenced to life imprisonment (Vucetich, 2008).

In 1897, British official Sir Edward Richard Henry devised a workable fingerprint classi-fication system, which he used to classify prisoners in India. In 1901, he was appointed assistant commissioner of police at New Scotland Yard and began to introduce his fingerprint system into that institution. Within a few years, the Henry Classification System was in use around the world, and fingerprints had been established as the uniform system of identification for the future. The Henry Classification System is still in use today in English-speaking countries around the globe (Fido & Skinner, 1999; Tewari & Ravikumar, 2000).

Procedures for Collecting Fingerprints

The study of fingerprint patterns for the purpose of making identifications is called **dactyloscopy**. Latent fingerprints are the result of contact of the sweat pores located on the ridge surface of a suspect's finger. When a fingertip comes in contact with a surface, an oily deposit or residue of perspiration is transferred to that surface. The first step in fingerprint detection at a crime scene is to examine all surfaces and objects and photograph or collect all visible fingermarks. There are various means of collecting latent prints. One of the oldest and most widely-used methods is *dusting* a surface with a fine powder of contrasting color. Fingerprint powder is applied at the crime scene on smooth, nonabsorbent surfaces and, in general, only to objects that cannot be transported back to a laboratory. The powder adheres to the humid, sticky, or greasy substances in the latent fingerprint deposit. The application of powder is relatively simple and inexpensive and little experience is necessary to obtain satisfactory results. The ideal powder has good adherence properties and sensitivity, and possibly incorporates some sort of luminescent material. Magnetic powders, generally made by mixing iron grit with either aluminum or copper flake powder, are applied using a magnetic wand. Their use avoids the brushing, and hence destruction, of fragile prints; however, the technique is difficult to apply on vertical surfaces.

Fingerprint lifting tape is the most common method of collecting latent fingerprint evidence after powdering. After a surface is dusted with fingerprint powder, adhesive tape is placed over the print and smoothed down with the finger. Particles of fingerprint powder adhere to the sticky surface of the tape and thereby transfer a mirror image of the fingerprint pattern. The tape is finally placed onto a card of suitable color, contrasting with the powder used. Latent fingerprints on smooth, nonporous surfaces, such as glass, plastic, and polished metal, can also be detected using *episcopic coaxial illumination*. This technique involves the use of a semitransparent mirror to observe the reflection of light perpendicular to the surface. The light is diffused by the fingerprint deposit but specularly reflected by the surface; the print is therefore visible as dark ridges against a light background. Sometimes fingerprint development from absorbent surfaces, such as paper, requires the use of more complicated procedures. These include the use of iodine, silver nitrate, **ninhydrin**, and lasers. Sometimes the amino acids (naturally present in perspiration) remain unchanged for an extremely long time. For example, if a paper specimen has remained in dry conditions, it is not unusual for latent fingerprints to be detected using ninhydrin 30 or 40 years after they were deposited (Lyman, 2008, p. 142).

A laser is sometimes used in the forensic setting to detect fingerprints that could not be detected through the use of powders, iodine, silver nitrite, or ninhydrin. In this process, a laser beam is used to luminesce perspiration, body oils, and other substances found on a latent print. The three principal types of lasers in use today are *argon ionic laser*, the *copper vapor laser*, and the *neodymium (Nd):YAG laser*. Positive results have been obtained using these lasers with prints left on many different surfaces, including metal, human skin, and even polystyrene foam. Yet for some applications, such as the search for visible fingerprints or for the detection of footwear marks on smooth surfaces, strong white light is also a useful tool, and a number of nonlaser light sources, or "alternative" light sources (ALS), have been developed specifically for fingerprint applications (Beavan, 2001).

Integrated Automated Fingerprint Identification System (IAFIS)

When analyzing fingerprints, the expert attempts to conclude whether the latent print is from the same origin as another impression through a careful comparison of the ridge impressions of both prints. Indentable ridge characteristics, such as ridge endings, bifurcations, ridge islands, and ridge crossings, are noted and compared with regard to appearance and location in the pattern. In the past, this process could take considerable time because fingerprint cards had to be physically transported and processed. A fingerprint check could often take three months to complete even when conducted by the Federal Bureau of Investigation (FBI).

In 1999, the FBI and the law enforcement community developed the **Integrated Automated Fingerprint Identification System (IAFIS)**, which maintains the largest biometric database in the world, containing the fingerprints and corresponding criminal history information for more than 55 million subjects in the Criminal Master File. The fingerprints and corresponding criminal history information are submitted voluntarily by state, local, and federal law enforcement agencies. The IAFIS provides automated fingerprint search capabilities, latent searching capability, electronic image storage, and electronic exchange of fingerprints and responses, 24 hours a day, 365 days a year. When a law enforcement agency submits fingerprints electronically to IAFIS, it can usually expect to receive electronic responses within 2 hours of submission and within 24 hours for civil (non-criminal) fingerprint submissions.

The Limits of Fingerprint Evidence

Despite the obvious benefits of fingerprint analysis on the identification of suspects and the solving of crimes, these are not infallible. For example, suppose that after studying a latent print from a crime scene, an examiner concludes that "only one person in the world could be the source of the print." This assertion is problematic because of the difficulty in determining the basis for such a statement. Is it the examiner's general knowledge or his experience that allows for such an extreme conclusory statement? Suppose an examiner is wrong in saying that there is a unique "match" in two sets of prints. Instead it turns out that 1 in 1,000,000 persons have fingerprints bearing as great a degree of similarity to a particular latent print as the particular fingerprint in question. How could the examiner distinguish between these two scenarios based on his knowledge and experience? Stated more precisely, How much correspondence between two fingerprints is sufficient to conclude that each print was made by the same finger? (Stoney, 2001; Zabell, 2005).

David Stoney, a forensic scientist and distinguished expert on fingerprints, asserts that the best answer to the question, "How much correspondence between two fingerprints is *enough* to determine a match," is that "this is up to the individual expert fingerprint examiner to determine, based on that examiner's training, skill, and experience" (Stoney, 2001, p. 329). In other words, the criterion for establishing fingerprint identification is based to some degree on subjective criteria with limited standards. Overall, contrary to popular belief, fingerprint matching is not infallible and occasionally does lead to false matches (Cole, 2006; Pankanti, Prabhakar, & Jain, 2002; Saltzman, 2004; Thomas, 2004).

A dramatic illustration of the limits of fingerprint evidence is the *Mayfield Affair*. On March 11, 2004, a terrorist bomb attack on a Madrid train station resulted in 191 deaths and some 2,000 people injured (Sciolino, 2004). The Spanish authorities found a bag of detonators near the site of the explosion with a fingerprint on it that did not match any in their databank. The authorities forwarded the print to several investigative organizations, including the FBI. After searching its fingerprint database, the FBI located a possible match in the prints of Mr. Brandon Mayfield, an attorney in Portland, Oregon (Schmidt & Harden, 2004). The FBI examiners concluded that the print was a "100% positive identification" and so informed the Spanish authorities on April 2, 2004 (Stacey, 2004, p. 710). The Spanish disagreed and reported in a memorandum to the FBI that the match was "conclusively negative" (Kershaw, 2004 at A1). Where the FBI found 15 points of agreement for the fingerprint, the Spanish found only 7.

Mr. Mayfield was arrested on May 6, 2004, on a material witness warrant. Shortly after Mayfield's arrest, the Spanish authorities announced that they had matched the latent print to an Algerian named Ouhnane Daoud (Schmidt, 2004 at A2) and "found traces of Daoud's DNA in a rural cottage outside Madrid where investigators believe the terrorist cell held planning sessions and assembled the backpack bombs used in the attack" (Schmitt, Tizon, & Rotella, 2004 at A13). Mr. Mayfield was finally released after spending two weeks in jail. This case illustrates how the process of comparing latent and inked prints can be subjective and may fall victim to human error (Dror, 2006).

Part of the reason for an uncertain match being reported as a true match may be **confirmation bias**. Confirmation bias refers to a type of selective thinking whereby one tends to notice and to look for what confirms one's beliefs and to ignore, not look for, or undervalue the relevance of what contradicts one's beliefs (Carroll, 2007). Modern psychological research supports the contention that much of human observational measurements are prone to such bias (Risinger, Saks, Thompson, & Rosenthal, 2002). More specific to errors in fingerprint analysis, there is research to show that such errors result from the way the brain processes information and makes decisions (Cole, 2005; Stacey, 2004).

Are Fingerprint Experts Vulnerable to Extraneous Contextual information?

Dror and Charlton (2006); Dror, Charlton, and Peron (2006)

In one study, Dror et al. (2006), five experts were shown fingerprints that they had assessed in a previous case as being from a common source (i.e., a positive I.D.). They were told that the prints represented the falsely matched prints from the Mayfield case. Although the subjects were all familiar with the particulars of this case, none had actually seen the prints. The prints were presented as having been ruled out with "100% certainty" by other experts as having come from a common source. The experts were instructed to ignore all the contextual information and to focus solely on the actual prints. The results were striking. Only one of the five subjects remained consistent with his/her original conclusion and insisted that the prints were from a common source.

In another study, Dror and Charlton (2006) utilized six fingerprint experts, representing more than 35 years of experience in examining fingerprints (each with a minimum of 5 years' experience in latent prints), as subjects. The expert participants were not only highly experienced, but were highly trained, certified by a nationally recognized independent authority, and had successfully completed proficiency testing. They were approached by the director or head of their respective laboratory or bureau and asked to provide opinions on a variety of latent prints (which they had actually done in the past within the context of other cases). They were told that the conclusions they reached after the examination would be used for an assessment project. They were further told that the project was intended to look at problematic prints and assessments. During the comparison process all of the participants were allowed to evaluate the prints as they would do routinely (handling the prints, using magnifying and lighting equipment, and so forth). The participants were allowed an unlimited amount of time and all normal resources (e.g., comparators) to make their evaluations. The results indicated that from 48 experimental trials, the fingerprint experts changed their past decisions on six pairs of fingerprints. Only two of the six experts remained entirely consistent across all the experimental trials.

These studies demonstrate that fingerprint and other forensic experts are not immune to the psychological and cognitive factors which are characteristic of human intelligence and decision making. "Experts" are vulnerable to extraneous contextual information, and the conclusions they make are malleable and susceptible to bias.

VOICE IDENTIFICATION

Historical Factors

Bruno Richard Hauptmann was executed in the electric chair on April 3, 1936, for the kidnapping and murder of the young son of the famous aviator Charles Lindbergh. In the murder trial Lindbergh identified Hauptmann's voice as that of his son's kidnapper. Lindbergh had heard the voice of his son's kidnapper three years earlier. Still hoping to get his child back alive, Lindbergh had accompanied Dr. John Condon to St. Raymond's Cemetery in the Bronx to deliver ransom money. Condon handed off $50,000 in marked gold certificates while Lindbergh waited nearly 100 yards away in a car. Out of the darkness came the words, "Hey, doctor! Over here, over here" (Kennedy, 1985).

The question of how well lay witnesses like Lindbergh can recognize voices arises regularly in legal cases. When a woman is sexually assaulted by a man wearing a ski mask or when a government official receives a bomb threat, the case may hinge on how well the victim can identify the perpetrator's voice. But at the time of Hauptmann's trial, no experts were available to assess the accuracy of Lindbergh's account. In fact, research on how well people can identify speakers by their voices was actually initiated by Hauptmann's trial.

One year after Hauptmann's execution, a psychology professor at the University of Illinois named Frances McGehee had students listen to a person read a 56-word passage from behind a screen. The students were then tested at various times to see whether they could pick the reader out from a group of five voices. They did so with 83% accuracy the next day. Three weeks later,

TABLE 8.1 Effect of Delay on Accuracy of Identification

Delay	Correct Responses (%)
1 day	83
2 days	83
3 days	81
7 days	81
2 weeks	69
3 weeks	51
3 months	35
5 months	13

Source: McGehee, F. (1937). The reliability of the identification of the human voice. *Journal of General Psychology, 17,* 249.

however, their success rate had declined dramatically to 51%. Five months later they were down to a dismal 13% accuracy rate—well below chance (Yarmey, Yarmey, & Todd, 2008). McGehee's 1937 results are depicted in Table 8.1.

Although the Lindbergh case is probably one of the most famous uses of "earwitness testimony," voice identification has frequently been used as evidence in the courtroom. The forensic science of voice identification has come a long way from when it was first introduced in the American courts back in the mid-1960s. In the early days of this identification technique there was little research to support the theory that human voices are unique and could be used as a means for identification. There was also no standardization of how an identification was reached or even training or qualifications necessary to perform the analysis. Voice comparisons were made solely on the pattern analysis of a few commonly used words.

The Mechanics of Voice Identification

The fundamental theory for voice identification rests on the premise that every voice is individually characteristic enough to distinguish it from others. There are two general factors involved in the process of human speech. The first factor in determining voice uniqueness lies in the sizes of the vocal cavities, such as the throat, nasal and oral cavities, and the shape, length, and tension of the individual's vocal cords located in the larynx. The vocal cavities are resonators, much like organ pipes, which reinforce some of the overtones produced by the vocal cords, which produce formats or voiceprint bars. The likelihood that two people would have all their vocal cavities the same size and configuration and coupled identically is very remote (Caine et al., 1990).

The second factor in determining voice uniqueness lies in the manner in which the articulators or muscles of speech are manipulated during speech. The articulators include the lips, teeth, tongue, soft palate, and jaw muscles whose controlled interplay produces intelligible speech. Intelligible speech is developed by the random learning process of imitating others who are communicating. The likelihood that two people could develop identical use patterns of their articulators is also very remote. Overall, the chance that two speakers would have identical vocal cavity dimensions and configurations coupled with identical articulator use patterns is likewise extremely remote (Caine et al., 1990).

Today the process of voice identification is much more sophisticated than that used in the Lindbergh case and involves the use of both aural and visual senses. In the typical voice identification case the examiner is given several recordings—one or more recordings of the voice to be identified and one or more recorded voice samples of one or more suspects. It is from these recordings that the examiner must make the determination about the identity of the unknown voice.

The first step is to evaluate the recording of the unknown voice, checking to make sure the recording has a sufficient amount of speech with which to work and that the quality of the recording is of sufficient clarity in the frequency range required for analysis. The volume of the recorded voice signal must be significantly higher than that of the environmental noise. The greater the number of obscuring events, such as noise, music, and other speakers, the longer the sample of speech must be. Some examiners report that they reject as many as 60% of the cases submitted to them with one of the main reasons for rejection being the poor quality of the recording of the unknown voice. Once the unknown voice sample has been determined to be suitable for analysis, the examiner then turns his attention to the voice samples of the suspects. Here also, the recordings must be of sufficient clarity to allow comparison, although at this stage, the recording process is usually so closely controlled that the quality of recording is not a problem. The examiner can only work with speech samples that are the same as the text of the unknown recording. Under the best of circumstances the suspects will repeat, several times, the text of the recording of the unknown speaker, and these words will be recorded in a similar manner to the recording of the unknown speaker. For example, if the recording of the unknown speaker was from a bomb threat made over a recorded telephone line, then each of the suspects would repeat the threat, word for word, on a recorded telephone line. This will provide the examiner with not only the same speech sounds for comparison but also with valuable information about the way each speech sound completes the transition to the next sound. These are all components of the aural process of voice sample comparisons.

The visual process of voice sample comparisons involves a spectrographic analysis of the recorded samples. The sound spectrograph is an automatic sound wave analyzer with a high quality, fully functional tape recorder. The speech samples to be analyzed are recorded on the sound spectrograph. The recording is then analyzed in 2.5 second segments. The product is a spectrogram, a graphic display of the recorded signal on the basis of time and frequency with a general indication of amplitude. The spectrograms of the unknown speaker are then visually compared to the spectrograms of the suspects. Only those speech sounds that are the same are compared. The comparisons of the spectrograms are based on the displayed patterns representing the psychoacoustical features of the captured speech. The examiner studies the bandwidths, mean frequencies, and trajectory of vowel formants; vertical striations, distribution of formant energy, and nasal resonances; stops, plosives (speech sound produced by complete closure of the oral passage and subsequent release accompanied by a burst of air, as in the sound (p) in *pit* or (d) in *dog*), and fricatives (a consonant, such as *f* or *s* in English, produced by the forcing of breath through a constricted passage); and interformant features, the relation of all features present as affected during articulatory changes, and any peculiar acoustic patterning. The examiner looks not only for similarities but also for differences. The differences are closely examined to determine if they are due to pronunciation differences or if they are indicative of different speakers.

When the analysis is complete the examiner integrates his findings from both the aural and spectrographic analyses into one of five standard conclusions: a positive identification, a probable identification, a positive elimination, a probable elimination, or no decision. To arrive at a positive identification the examiner must find a minimum of 20 speech sounds that possess sufficient aural and spectrographic similarities. There can be no differences (either aural or spectrographic) for which there is no accounting (McDermott, Owen, & McDermott, 1996).

Research and Admissibility

Despite the importance of such evidence, research into earwitness performance has been much less than prolific (Baddeley, 1990; Clifford, 1983; Deffenbacher et al., 1989). Several studies have been published evidencing the ability to reliably identify voices under certain conditions, and an FBI survey of its own performance in the examination of 2,000 forensic cases revealed an error rate of 31% for false identifications and 53% for false eliminations (Koenig, 1986). Among the variables known to affect the ability to recognize a voice after a relatively brief exposure are the subject's preparedness at the time of study for a later memory test, voice sample duration, retention interval, and changes in the content and form of speech between the initial encounter and the subsequent recognition test. People who are unprepared for a voice memory test during a study perform more poorly than when they are prepared.

In a study by Saslove and Yarmey (1980), participants first heard an angry outburst that lasted for 11 seconds and later attempted to identify the voice of the person making the outburst. At recognition, participants heard five test recordings—the original target recording and four other voices uttering the same words—and judged whether each recording was old or new. In one group, the target voice was represented by the recording presented in the study, whereas the remaining participants heard a changed "normal" voice. Some of the participants were prepared for a recognition test before hearing the voice, and others were not. Unprepared participants were less likely than prepared ones to recognize the speaker, even when the voice was unchanged.

As might be expected, research indicates that voice recognition improves as the presentation duration of the initial voice sample increases. Legge, Grosmann, and Pieper (1984) had participants study voice samples that varied in duration from 6 to 120 seconds and then attempted to recognize the same voices saying different things (although using the same tone of voice) at delays ranging from 15 minutes to 10 days. Recognition of voices studied for 6 seconds was not significantly better than chance. Other studies also showed that recognition of voices heard only briefly is very poor, providing that the content of their utterances changes (Clifford, 1983). Thus, it appears that, for practical purposes, memory for brief voice samples is quite poor. Voice samples presented for longer durations are remembered with more accuracy; however, this effect is dramatically reduced if the target speaker's tone is changed from the first presentation to the second (Clifford, 1983; Clifford, Rathborn, & Bull, 1981; Saslove & Yarmey, 1980).

As far as admissibility of voice identification evidence into court is concerned, it is primarily those jurisdictions utilizing the *Daubert* standard that allow such evidence into testimony. As discussed in Chapter 2, under this standard a judge may admit such evidence if it will assist the finder of fact (the jury) in better understanding the case as a whole. Many of the courts that have upheld the admission of voice identification evidence have done so because the trial courts set up a number of precautions to insure the evidence was viewed in its proper light (see, e.g., *United States v. Williams*, 1978; *United States v. Baller*, 1975; *United States v. Franks*, 1975; *United States v. Tanya Smith*, 1989; *United States v. Maivia*, 1990; *Alaska v. Coon*, 1999). These precautions include allowing the jury to see the spectrograms of the voices in question, hear the recordings from which the spectrograms were produced, view the expert's qualifications and opinions, and learn about the reliability of the equipment and techniques utilized. As a further precaution, these matters are all subject to scrutiny by the other side in the case. All in all, juries are instructed that they are free to assign whatever weight, if any, to the evidence they feel it deserves. One particular such case came before the Supreme Court of Alaska in 1999. In *Alaska v. Coon* (1999) a superior court found George Coon guilty of making terroristic telephone calls. Three messages threatening David Rudolph's life were left on Deborah Rudolph's telephone answering machine. Deborah, Coon's former daughter-in-law, recognized the recorded voice as Coon's. The state charged Coon with terroristic threatening. The state retained a voice analysis expert, Steve Cain, who compared the voice on the answering machine with verbatim voice exemplars provided by Coon. The jury then heard Cain state his opinions that Coon made the first telephone call and that there was a "high probability" Coon also made the second and third calls. Cain described for the jury the scientific foundation for his opinions. The jury found Coon guilty of terroristic threatening. The Alaska Court of Appeals held that Cain's expert testimony should not have been admitted at the trial because the voice spectrographic analysis did not meet the standards of the *Frye* Test (only scientific testimony that is "generally accepted by the relevant scientific community" can be admitted into evidence).

In its review of the original 1992 trial, the Alaska Supreme Court noted that the superior court held a hearing outside the jury's presence to determine whether Cain's testimony would be admissible under the strict general acceptance standard articulated in *Frye*. Although not admissible under these standards, the superior court did acknowledge that Cain's testimony would have assisted the jury in understanding the case. The Alaska Supreme Court therefore held that the "more flexible" standards as articulated in *Daubert* should be the new standard for admitting expert testimony under the Alaska Rules of Evidence. Coon's judgment and conviction were therefore affirmed.

POLYGRAPHS

Polygraph History

The modern **polygraph** has been used in one form or another for nearly a century, and much cruder versions of its components existed as far back as 300 B.C.E. The Bedouins of Arabia, for example, required the authors of conflicting statements to lick a hot iron. The one whose tongue was not burned was considered truthful. The common principle underlying this primitive test as well as others (e.g., spitting drier rice powder than another person or being less able to swallow a "trial slice" of bread) is that the tense, nervous person (the one who is lying) has less saliva (dry mouth and tongue) and thus is more likely to have their tongue burned, spit dry rice, or have difficulty swallowing a piece of bread (Smith, 1967). As indicated previously, in modern times, the admissibility of voice identification evidence into court is usually evaluated utilizing the *Daubert* standard, which allows such evidence into testimony if the judge assesses that such evidence will assist the jury in better understanding the case as a whole.

In 1878, the Italian physiologist Angelo Mosso used an instrument called a plethysmograph (an instrument for measuring changes in volume within an organ or the whole body, usually resulting from fluctuations in the amount of blood or air it contains) in his research on emotion and fear in subjects undergoing questioning. He studied, in particular, the effects of emotion such as fear on subjects' cardiovascular and respiratory activity. He also studied blood circulation and breathing patterns and how these changed under specified conditions. The use of the plethysmograph revealed periodic waves in a subject's blood pressure caused by changes in the respiratory cycle in response to certain stimuli. Mosso was the first scientist to report on experiments in which he observed that a person's breathing pattern changed under certain stimuli and that this change, in turn, caused variations in their blood pressure and pulse rate. Although not for the purpose of detecting deception, Sir James Mackenzie constructed the first *clinical polygraph* in 1892, an instrument to be used for medical examinations with the capability to simultaneously record undulated line tracings of the vascular pulses (radial, venous and arterial), by way of a stylus onto a revolving drum of smoked paper. Until the end of the nineteenth century, no measuring device for the detection of deception had ever been used. The first use of a scientific instrument designed to measure physiological responses for this purpose came in 1895 when Italian physician, psychiatrist, and pioneer criminologist Cesare Lombroso modified an existing instrument called a *hydrosphygmograph* and used this modified device in his experiments to measure the physiological changes that occurred in a crime suspect's blood pressure and pulse rate during a police interrogation.

In 1914, Italian psychologist Vittorio Benussi invented a method to calculate the quotient of the inhalation to exhalation time as a means of verifying the truth and detecting deception in a subject. Using a *pneumograph*—a device that recorded a subject's breathing patterns—Benussi conducted experiments regarding the respiratory symptoms of lying. He concluded that lying caused an emotional change within a subject that resulted in detectible respiratory changes that were indicative of deception. William Moulton Marston, an American attorney and psychologist, is credited with inventing an early form of the *lie detector* when, in 1915, he developed the discontinuous systolic blood pressure test that would later become one component of the modern polygraph. Dr. Marston's technique used a standard blood pressure cuff and a stethoscope to take intermittent systolic blood pressure readings of a suspect during questioning for the purpose of detecting deception (Lykken, 1988).

The idea of "lie detection" caught on rapidly in the United States during the 1920s and 1930s after John Larson was asked by the chief of police in Berkeley, California, to develop a "lie detector" to solve a case under investigation (Larson, 1969). This instrument, to many, became the first true polygraph used for lie-detection purposes (Bartol & Bartol, 2004). In the 1930s, the increasing demand for polygraph examiners resulted in at least 30 polygraph schools opening across the United States (Barland & Raskin, 1976; Lykken, 1988).

Polygraph Procedure

What exactly is a modern polygraph machine? A polygraph is an instrument that simultaneously records changes in physiological processes such as heartbeat, blood pressure, respiration, and electrical resistance (galvanic skin response or GSR). The underlying theory of the polygraph is that when people lie they also get measurably nervous about lying. The heartbeat increases, blood pressure goes up, breathing rhythms change, perspiration increases, et cetera. A baseline for these physiological characteristics is established by asking the subject questions whose answers the investigator knows. Deviations from the baseline for truthfulness are usually taken as signs of lying (Iacono & Patrick, 1999).

There are three basic approaches to the polygraph test: (1) The **Control Question Test** (CQT) (also referred to as the relevant–irrelevant technique), (2) The **Directed Lie Test** (DLT), and (3) the **Guilty Knowledge Test** (GKT).

The *CQT* compares the physiological response to relevant questions about the crime with the response to questions related to neutral matters. For example, comparing responses (in a case involving alleged child sexual abuse) to the question, "Did you insert your finger in Susan's vagina?" with responses to irrelevant questions covering inconsequential topics for which the correct answer is readily apparent ("Is today Tuesday?"). This technique is seldom used in forensic settings because even innocent people are more reactive to the threatening accusation contained in the relevant question than to the innocuous content covered by the irrelevant question (Horowitz, Kircher, Honts, & Raskin, 1997). The CQT is actually more of a collection of procedures that have in common the inclusion of relevant and control questions, than it is a single test. Basically it is a polygraph-assisted interview during which the examiner must convince the subject that the control questions are just as important as the relevant questions. Without ever making a distinction between the control and relevant questions, the examiner then introduces possible control questions that the subject also agrees are reasonably worded and can be answered unambiguously; for example, "Have you ever lied to a person in a position of authority?" Because the examiner admonishes the subject that the test will only work if the subject is completely truthful, many subjects, when confronted with a control question like this, will indicate that they have in fact lied to an authority figure—for example, to a parent or teacher. At this point, the control question is reworded so that it begins with this question, "Other than what you have told me about, have you ever lied to a person in a position of authority?" If the subject says, "yes," then the examiner leads the subject to believe that making such admissions is somewhat incriminating thereby hoping that the subject will refrain from revealing any additional misdeeds (Iacono, 2008).

Another phase of the CQT involves asking questions while the physiological reactions are recorded. Because the inflated blood pressure cuff becomes uncomfortable and about 20 seconds must elapse between each question to provide ample time for the physiological response to register and recover, a typical 10-question CQT lasts about 3 minutes. Each run through the question list produces a chart (or the computer equivalent of a chart) recording of the physiological reactions to the questions. Often, three such charts are obtained with the order of questions altered for each. Between each pair of charts, the subject is given the opportunity to alter the wording of questions that, with additional reflection, may seem unclear or confusing. Some examiners also include a procedure designed to convince subjects they will be caught if they lie. The subject may be asked to choose a card from a marked deck or to write down a number between 1 and 10 and place it face up so both the subject and examiner can see it. The examiner then asks the subject if he has selected any of a series of cards or numbers, including the chosen one, to see if the physiological reactions are strongest to the subject's pick. This test, sometimes called a *stim test* (intended to stimulate the subject to increase detectability) or acquaintance test (acquainting the subject with the inevitability of detection), is interpreted such that the subject's pick is always "detected" (Iacono, 2008).

The *DLT* tries to detect lying by comparing physiological responses when the subject is told to deliberately lie to responses when they tell the truth. The *GKT* compares physiological responses to multiple-choice type questions about the crime, one choice of which contains information only the crime investigators and the criminal would know about. In a typical GKT, a suspect is exposed to guilty knowledge information as well as other types of information with similar thematic content. If pictures of weapons are flashed on a computer screen, the perpetrator would be expected to recognize the weapon used in the crime, and the picture of this weapon, when processed by the brain, is supposed to produce a recognition response evident in autonomic nervous system reactivity and cerebral electrical responses. This technique actually does have a legitimate scientific foundation as it is based on brain processes underlying memory (Allen, 2002; Allen & Iacono, 2001; Lefebvre, Marchand, Smith, & Connolly, 2007).

Evaluation of the Polygraph Technique

The justification for using the polygraph as a lie detector derives from the observation that many people do indeed reveal increased physiological arousal at the moment they tell a lie. From a theoretical standpoint at least, truthful responses are accompanied by relatively flat reaction lines, whereas untruthful responses are hypothesized to cause significant fluctuations in physiological measures such as heart rate, perspiration, and respiration. In addition, there is some evidence that the accuracy of polygraphs can even be increased through intensive training of the examiner and by using computerized systems (Kircher & Raskin, 2002). But the majority of the scientific evidence indicates that whatever accuracy the polygraph examination does provide seems to come from the conclusions made by individual examiners of factors such as the subject's general demeanor rather than his/her actual chart responses. Most experienced examiners would even concur that the key ingredient for a competently administered polygraph is the examiner regardless of whether a computerized scoring procedure is utilized (Iacono, 2008).

Supporters of the polygraph technique, such as Honts and colleagues, point to studies already showing that polygraph results are about as sound as other, admissible forms of forensic evidence, such as ballistics and hair fiber analysis (Honts, Kircher, & Raskin, 2002; Honts & Perry, 1992). Honts suggests that even the most pathological liars (who may even convince themselves that they are truthful) aren't likely to pass a polygraph. He points to psychopaths and killers who he himself has tested, who, when lying, fail the polygraph (Honts & Raskin, 1988; Iacono & Lykken, 1997; Raskin, 1990). But he is in the minority in the scientific community, where even the most ardent advocates of the polygraph are obliged to admit that good liars (and psychopaths) can fool the test.

Indeed, some of this country's most prolific and dangerous spies, such as Aldrich Ames and Robert Hanssen, repeatedly passed the polygraph, and many researchers continue to be very wary of relying on the polygraph for national security reasons. Although some professional field polygraphers have claimed extraordinary accuracy rates, ranging from 92% to 100%, their objectivity must be questioned since their livelihood depends on such inflated figures. Not withstanding this built-in bias, a number of factors—such as the specific technique used, the nature of the population tested, the issues to be resolved, the context of the examination, whether one is trying to detect truth or deception, the training of the examiner, what cues the examiner considers besides the polygraphic data, or even whether one is examining the victim or the suspect—must be considered before any conclusions can be made. Currently, the research conducted under laboratory or controlled conditions indicates that the correct classification of truthful and deceptive examinees ranges between 70% and 80% at best (Krapohl, 2002).

One of the problems with polygraphs is their susceptibility to **countermeasures** used by examinees to fool the machine and the examiner (Bartol & Bartol, 2004). Countermeasures can be physical or psychological. The most common countermeasures utilized are either pain or muscle tension. For example, in an effort to deceive the polygrapher, "biting one's lip or tongue or subtly jabbing oneself with a pin may induce enough pain to promote a physiological response that masks the subject's response to questions from the polygrapher" (Bartol, p. 86). Mental countermeasures include deliberate attempts at distortion using techniques such as counting backward from 100 or thinking of a peaceful or arousing scene. In this way the examinee tries to either minimize or maximize the emotional impact of questions. Although physical countermeasures can often be detected by experienced polygraphers, mental countermeasures are far more difficult to detect (Shakhar, 1996).

Overall, it is generally recognized that there is no physiological response that is uniquely associated with lying. Moreover, the brain mechanisms involved in lying are unknown, rendering it difficult to develop techniques that can distinguish liars from truth tellers. Indeed, a person's physiological reactions in response to lying are likely to be similar in nature to those resulting from the passionate denial that occurs when false charges are leveled against him. The fear of detection is indistinguishable from the fear of false detection, and the physiological reactions recorded by the polygraph under these two circumstances cannot be discriminated one from the other. Scientists with no direct involvement in the polygraph profession have repeatedly reviewed the scientific literature and concluded that the accuracy claims of the polygraph profession are exaggerated and indefensible. Carroll (2005) summarized the results of a series of laboratory experiments on the polygraph using mock crimes and blind scoring (where examiners had no knowledge of guilt or innocence). The results suggested a "staggering high rate of false positives and a dearth of contribution to the process of establishing innocence" (p. 27). These opinions are reflected in reviews spanning several decades (Lykken, 1974; Saxe, Dougherty, & Cross, 1985) as well as in more recent evaluations of the literature carried out for texts in polygraphy and forensic psychology (Ben-Shakar, 1996; Iacono & Patrick, 2006; Oksol & O'Donohue, 2003), and on behalf of the German legal system (Fiedler, Schmod, & Stahl, 2002).

In a 1997 survey of 195 psychologists from the Society for Psychophysiological Research, most respondents answered that polygraphic lie detection is not theoretically sound, that the lie detector test can be beaten by easily learned countermeasures, and that test results should not be admitted in courts of law (Iacono & Lykken, 1997). The issue was settled for real in 1998 with the U.S. Supreme Court case of *U.S. v. Scheffer* where in an 8–1 decision the Court emphasized the poor reliability of polygraph evidence as a whole. Justice Thomas, writing for the majority, stressed that a fundamental premise of the criminal justice system is that jurors are the ultimate and most reliable evaluators of credibility and truthfulness (*U.S. v. Scheffer* at 313). Since 1998 almost all courts reject polygraph results or only allow them if their admissibility is stipulated by both parties prior to the polygraph examination taking place. Only a few courts leave their admissibility up to the judge.

HYPNOSIS

History

In the late eighteenth century, **Franz Anton Mesmer** experimented with "magnetic healing" and articulated his research in his *Mémoire sur la découverte du magnétisme animal*. Concurrent with Mesmer was the work of Marquis de Puységur who further developed the theory of "mesmerism" and who coined the term *artificial somnambulism*—a peaceful, sleep-like trance, which later came to be known as a *hypnotic trance*. In Europe in 1819, Abbé José Custodio de Faria, inspired by the work of Mesmer and Puységur, discovered what he called the "perfect crisis," which was a somnambulistic sleep state in which patients carried out the commands of the "magnetizer" and upon reawakening exhibited no memory for having done so. De Faria developed a trance induction ("fixation") technique that emphasized the importance of the will of the subject rather than that of the magnetizer, thereby stressing the collaborative effort of the process rather than simply something "done to" the subject.

In 1843, James Braid published *Neurypnology; or, the Rationale of Nervous Sleep, Considered in Relation with Animal Magnetism*. In it, he described a state of nervous sleep as "hypnotism" and substituted fixation of a luminous object, for the "magnetic process" used by his predecessors. In another 50 years, the young profession of psychoanalysis, especially through the work of Jean-Martin Charcot, Josef Breuer, and Sigmund Freud, employed hypnosis in the study of hysteria and discovered that, under hypnosis, one could reproduce hysterical phenomena such as amnesia (loss of memory), mutism (loss of ability for speech), and anesthesia (lack of feeling and/or sensation of pain). Breuer and Freud also applied hypnosis to patients' symptoms of paralysis, which sometimes resulted from railway accidents at that time. (Today, this kind of mental compartmentalization resulting from severe trauma is known as **dissociation**.) In 1893, Breuer and Freud published a preliminary communication in *Neurologische Centralblatt* describing their use of the "cathartic" method of bringing a trauma to consciousness and allowing it to discharge through affect, words, and guided associations. Their case example of treatment using the cathartic method was that of the infamous "Anna O."

Applications and Problems

Hypnosis, or "forensic hypnosis" as it is also called, is generally used today in two broad areas. The first of these areas involves *memory enhancement*. Memory enhancement is the use of hypnosis (usually by law enforcement and prosecutors) to uncover memories often associated with criminal trauma (Gruzelier, 2000; Killeen & Nash, 2003). Interrogations and interviews using hypnosis in the criminal justice system in this way are often referred to as *hypnoinvestigations*. The heyday of the use of hypnosis in investigations was in the late 1970s and early 1980s when it was being used relatively frequently as a memory enhancement procedure by the police in the United States and a number of other countries as well (Haward, 1988; Haward & Ashworth, 1980; Hibbard & Worring, 1981; Kleinhauz, Horowitz, & Tobin, 1977; Reiser, 1980).

The rationale underlying the use of hypnoinvestigations is that when an individual suffers severe trauma, certain thoughts, emotions, sensations, and memories are compartmentalized (separated into isolated, unconscious compartments), resulting in **dissociation** (partial or complete disruption of the normal integration of a person's conscious or psychological functioning). Dissociation is a mental process that severs a connection to a person's thoughts, memories, feelings, actions, or sense of identity (Butler, Duran, Jasiukaitis, Koopman, & Spiegel, 1996).

Can hypnosis be effective in the face of compartmentalization and dissociation? Erdelyi (1994) reviewed the psychological literature on memory facilitation using hypnosis and found that in some cases, hypnosis did result in increases in correct responses; however, when they occurred, such increases were more or less confined to situations that require free recall of high-sense materials (e.g., filmed crimes, staged incidents). Significantly also, in such cases, hypnosis also tended to increase the number of incorrect responses such that overall accuracy, as determined by the proportion of correct to incorrect responses, was not improved. In fact, there is a large body of research indicating that hypnotic procedures do not improve the accuracy of memory to a level greater than that achievable in motivated nonhypnotic conditions (Kebbell & Wagstaff, 1998; McConkey & Sheehan, 1996; O'Connell, Shor, & Orne, 1970; Sanders & Simmons, 1983; Smith, 1983; Steblay & Bothwell, 1994; Wagstaff, 1989; Webert, 2003).

Hypnosis and Approaches to the Admissibility Question

Echoing much of the scientific research, state and federal courts have identified the following problems with the reliability of hypnotically refreshed recall:

1. A person undergoing hypnosis becomes more susceptible to suggestion. The subject may be influenced by verbal and nonverbal cues, intentionally or unintentionally planted by the hypnotist. This suggestibility may be enhanced by the perception that hypnosis will refresh one's memory and by a wish to please the hypnotist (*State v. Hurd*, 1981).

2. A hypnotized person may confabulate, that is, fill in the gaps in his/her memory to make it seem comprehensible. The added details of the confabulation may be derived from irrelevant facts or even from one's imagination. As with suggestibility, confabulation can occur as a result of the subject's desire to please the hypnotist by coming up with complete and coherent memories (*Pearson v. State*, 1982).

3. Hypnotically refreshed individuals often show "memory hardening," in which the subject adopts enhanced confidence in the facts remembered, whether they be true or false (*People v. Hughes*, 1983). Such courts point to scientific research indicating that a person being interviewed using hypnotically induced techniques is very susceptible to suggestion and "may be subsequently unable to separate actual memories from 'suggested' ones" (Melton, Petrila, Poythress, and Slobogin, 2007, p. 66). Under this view, subjects and witnesses who have been interviewed under hypnosis also tend to incorporate more misleading information into their reports and present an "aura of confidence" in their statements that is nondeserved (Slovenko, 2002).

4. After undergoing hypnosis to refresh memory, individuals may lose the ability to assess their memory critically and be more prone to speculation than if they had relied only on normal memory recall (*Little v. Armontrout*, 1988).

As of this writing, two-thirds of all states (including California) consider hypnotically refreshed testimony as *per se inadmissible* and bars its use altogether (see, e.g., *People v. Shirley*, 1982, and *People v. Hughes*, 1983). The second major group of states regard such testimony as *per se admissible* and allow its use under most circumstances (see, e.g., *Kline v. Ford Motor Co.*, 1975, and *United States v. Waksal*, 1983). But more and more states are adopting a middle-ground approach requiring the use of procedural safeguards that tend to reduce the potential inaccuracies of posthypnotic testimony (see, e.g., *State v. Hurd*, 1981, and *Rock v. Arkansas*, 1987).

In *State v. Hurd* (1981), a middle-ground, case-by-case, or totality-of-the-circumstances approach to the evaluation of testimony of previously hypnotized criminal defendants was most clearly articulated. Other cases adopting such an approach include *State v. Weston*, 1984; *House v. State*, 1984; *McQueen v. Garrison*, 1987; *Wicker v. McCotter*, 1986; and *Sprynczynatyk v. General Motors Corp.*, 1986. In *Hurd* the court stated,

> First, a psychiatrist or psychologist experienced in the use of hypnosis must conduct the session. This professional should also be able to qualify as an expert in order to aid the court in evaluating the procedures followed. Although we recognize that there are many other people trained to administer hypnosis and skilled in its use for investigative purposes, we believe that a professional must administer hypnosis if the testimony revealed is to be used in a criminal trial. . . .
>
> Second, the professional conducting the hypnotic session should be independent of and not regularly employed by the prosecutor, investigator or defense. This condition will safeguard against any bias on the part of the hypnotist that might translate into leading questions, unintentional cues, or other suggestive conduct.
>
> Third, any information given to the hypnotist by law enforcement personnel or the defense prior to the hypnotic session must be recorded, either in writing or another suitable form. This requirement will help the court determine the extent of information the hypnotist could have communicated to the witness either directly or through suggestion.
>
> Fourth, before inducing hypnosis the hypnotist should obtain from the subject a detailed description of the facts as the subject remembers them. The hypnotist should carefully avoid influencing the description by asking structured questions or adding new details.

Fifth, all contacts between the hypnotist and the subject must be recorded. This will establish a record of the pre-induction interview, the hypnotic session, and the post-hypnotic period, enabling a court to determine what information or suggestions the witness may have received during the session and what recall was first elicited through hypnosis. The use of videotape, the only effective record of visual cues, is strongly encouraged but not mandatory.

Sixth, only the hypnotist and the subject should be present during any part of the hypnotic session, including the pre-hypnotic testing and the post-hypnotic interview. Although it may be easier for a person familiar with the investigation to conduct some of the questioning, the risk of undetectable, inadvertent suggestion is too great, as this case illustrates. Likewise, the mere presence of such a person may influence the response of the subject. (*Hurd v. State*, at 96–97)

In *Rock v. Arkansas* (1987), the Supreme Court again endorsed such a middle-ground safeguard approach in its review of the strict Arkansas rule that a criminal defendant's hypnotically refreshed testimony was per se inadmissible. The Court held that such a complete prohibition implicated the Sixth Amendment's guarantee to call witnesses in the defendant's favor (see *Rock* at 52–53), and the Fifth Amendment's guarantee against compelled testimony (see *Rock* at 52). The Court concluded that the rule of per se inadmissibility was an "arbitrary restriction on the [criminal defendant's] right to testify in the absence of clear evidence by the State repudiating the validity of all post-hypnosis recollections" (p. 61). But the Court refused to express an opinion as to the appropriate rule of admissibility "of testimony of previously hypnotized witnesses *other* than criminal defendants" (p. 58, note 15) (italics added).

Hypnosis as a Means of "Inducing" Criminal Behavior

The notion that hypnotized persons can be induced to commit immoral, criminal, or self-injurious acts of which they would normally be incapable has not received empirical support. One of the most famous cases of supposed hypnotic coercion is that of Palle Hardrup in 1951, when he committed two bank robberies in Copenhagen, during which he shot dead two bank tellers. Hardrup claimed that his hypnotist, Bjorn Nielsen, instructed him to do so. Nielsen allegedly admitted to have convinced Hardrup to commit the crime as a test of his own hypnotic prowess. But there were indications that Neilsen actually told Hardrup that he needed the money to fund a new Danish Nazi Party (Janus, 2005).

At the trial, evidence was presented to this effect and the defense claimed that Hardrup was therefore not responsible for his actions. After being committed to an institution for the insane, he changed his story, stating that he was never successfully hypnotized at all (Reiter, 1958). One of the leading authorities on hypnosis in the 1940s, psychologist George Estabrooks, claimed that one in five adults are capable of being placed in a trance so deep that they will have no memory of it (Estabrooks, 1972). Such individuals could be, according to Estabrooks, hypnotized secretly by using a disguised technique and given a posthypnotic suggestion. Estabrooks also suggested that a dual personality could be "constructed" with hypnosis, thereby creating the perfect double agent with an unshakable cover (Brandt, 2002).

There is evidence from the social psychological literature that hypnosis may not even be necessary to coerce or influence people to adopt extreme views or commit antisocial or harmful acts. Experiments conducted by Solomon Asch in the 1950s, demonstrated that expressed opinions can be easily manipulated by social pressure, even in obvious cases, such as whether Line A is longer than Line B on a particular card (Asch, 1956). Stanley Milgram showed that many unwitting research subjects would administer a series of escalating electric shocks to another, even to the point of an apparent heart attack, simply because a white-coated authority figure asked them to continue (Levitt, Aronoff, Morgan, Overley, & Parrish, 1975; Milgram, 1974; Orne, 1962, 1966, 1971, 1971).

HYPNOSIS AND THE MULTIPLE PERSONALITY DEFENSE

Late in 1977, eight women were found murdered and dumped along roadways around Los Angeles, California. A ninth victim was soon found naked on the side of a hill. Then on February 17, 1978, a police helicopter spotted a car off a highway, and locked inside the trunk was victim number ten— strangled. Almost a year after the last Los Angeles victim was discovered, in Bellingham, Washington, college roommates Diane Wilder and Karen Mandic were reported missing. On January 12, 1979, a security officer said one of them had indicated they were going to do a job for **Ken Bianchi**, a goodlooking man with a girlfriend and an infant son who worked at the security company. Police questioned him, and although he denied any knowledge of the girls, he remained a suspect. Then they found the girls' bodies inside a car parked in a cul-de-sac. They picked up Bianchi for questioning and collected trace evidence, which turned up carpet fibers on the bodies that matched those from inside the house Bianchi had sent them to. Police also found a lint brush in Bianchi's home with fibers from the same house, hairs from one of the girls, and a pubic hair on one girl consistent with Bianchi's own pubic hair.

Upon questioning, Bianchi gave a history of repeated spells of amnesia since childhood. His defense attorney called in psychology professor John G. Watkins who interviewed Bianchi under hypnosis. What emerged was an apparent alter-personality named "Steve" who claimed responsibility for two killings and involvement in nine others (Allison, 1984; Schwarz, 1981). As was described in Chapter 5, many serial killers' histories reveal nonachievement, erratic academic and work performance, and a bizarre fascination with police and security work; Bianchi was no exception. In 1970 at age 19, Kenneth Bianchi enrolled at Monroe Community College to be trained to work as a police officer. But he was rejected by various law enforcement agencies including the Los Angeles Police Department, Los Angeles Police Reserves, and the Glendale Police Department (Boren, 2000). He even posed as a psychologist after buying a fake degree and rented office space from a real psychologist. He had also falsely represented himself as a marriage counselor, a sex counselor, a movie talent scout, and a professional photographer (Boren, 2000).

Bianchi underwent three psychological evaluations. It was on the third, when he was questioned by psychologist Martin Orne, that Bianchi was revealed as a fake. Orne explained to Bianchi that multiple personalities usually involve more than just two personas. In the next hypnosis session Bianchi produced a third persona, Billy, and two others emerged as well. After being exposed, Bianchi agreed to testify against his cousin and accomplice, Angelo Buono, so as to be spared the death penalty in Washington State (Wilson & Seaman, 1997). In 1982 Bianchi was convicted of all nine murders, and is presently serving a life sentence. Buono died of a heart attack on September 21, 2002, while serving a life sentence in Calipatria State Prison. He was 67 years old.

A technique frequently used by hypnoinvestigators to enhance memory recall is called the **cognitive interview**. A cognitive interview is designed to fully immerse a subject in a partially recalled situation using "freedom of description" rather than hypnosis. The subject or witness is instructed to report everything he/she can think of no matter how trivial it may seem. Instructions may also be given to recount the incident in more than one order. This can also involve recalling events from different visual perspectives, such as from that of the perpetrator (Geiselman, Fisher, MacKinnon, & Holland, 1985, 1986). The cognitive interview method relies on a four-step process during which the subject is guided back to the criminal event (Gilbert, 2007). The first step of the questioning reconstructs the incident. Aside from various minutia regarding the physical scene, subjects are encouraged to recall how they were feeling and what their reactions were during the crime (Geiselman & Fisher, 1985). The second phase encourages free recall. The third phase instructs the subject to recall the events in various orders, and during the fourth stage, the subject is asked to change perspectives.

The major intent of the cognitive interview is to allow for a much deeper level of recollection than the traditional interview (Wagstaff, 1982b, 1989). This technique also encourages the use of open-ended questions (such as "describe your attacker") rather than closed questions (such as "Was your attacker wearing a hat?"). Closed questions often used in traditional interviews, tend to result in short, truncated answers, and the only information elicited is that which is requested. In contrast, cognitive interviews encourage less interruption and give the witness an opportunity to elaborate freely when giving his/her account.

Following the four general phases of the cognitive interview, there is a series of questions designed to elicit items of information commonly encountered in criminal cases but easily forgotten by many subjects. These include:

1. Physical appearance: Did the suspect remind the subject of anyone? If so, can the subject state who and why?
2. Names: If the subject thinks a name was spoken but cannot remember, one can try going through the alphabet to determine the first letter of the name. Can the subject think of the number of syllables in the name?
3. Speech: Did the suspect's voice remind the witness of someone else's voice? If so, why? Was there anything unusual about the voice?

It is not unusual for subjects to recall important information hours or even days following a cognitive interview. Information may come to conscious memory as a result of the stimulating effect of the questioning. Thus, investigators should always close the interview by explaining this possibility and the importance of contacting the investigator quickly with any additional information. Although the cognitive interview approach seems to elicit significantly more accurate information than a standard police interview, its efficacy has been seriously questioned. Some theorists have noted that under some circumstances, the increase in the amount of correct information recalled has been associated with a significant increase in errors and confabulations as well (Bekerian et al., 1994; Mantwill, Köhnken, & Aschermann, 1995; Mello & Fisher, 1996; Memon & Higham, 1999). The main argument against the cognitive interview is similar to one that has been made regarding the effect of hypnosis on memory reports. Generally speaking, the more a person reports, whether due to hypnosis or a particular interviewing technique, the more likely it is that correct information will be elicited. However, if the person is reporting more because of a liberal criterion, the report is likely to contain many errors and confabulations as well. Some instructions that are given to participants during the cognitive interview render this interpretation likely. For example, the "report-everything" instruction, although intended to ensure that the interviewee retrieves all accurate memories, may be interpreted by some interviewees to mean that they should be reporting information about which they have low confidence (Higham & Roberts, 1996; Memon & Higham, 1999).

Even trained investigators place an overabundance of confidence in interviews (Kassin, 2008). Indeed, many long-held beliefs regarding the behavior of suspects during interviews (e.g., gaze aversion, frozen posture, slouching, and fidgeting) have little empirical support (DePaulo et al., 2003), and there is no real evidence that liars and truth tellers can be distinguished from one another (Inbau et al., 2001; Vrij et al., 2008). For example, Kassin and Fong (1999) randomly trained some college students, but not others, in the use of behavioral cues cited by the "Reid technique" (Horvath, Jayne, & Buckley, 1994; Inbau, Reid, Buckley, & Jayne, 2001). All students then watched videotaped interviews of mock suspects, some of whom committed one of four mock crimes and others who did not. On questioning, all suspects denied their involvement. The results indicated that observers were generally unable to differentiate between the two groups of suspects. Moreover, those who underwent training were significantly less accurate, more confident, and more biased toward seeing deception. Other research, including research using experienced police detectives, found that police tend to make prejudgments of guilt, with confidence, that are frequently in error (Elaad, 2003; Garrido, Masip, & Herrero, 2004; Leach, Talwar, Lee, Bala, & Lindsay, 2004).

PSYCHOLOGICAL PROFILING

Historical Roots

The Italian physician Cesare Lombrosos is generally credited with launching the scientific era in criminology. In 1872 he differentiated five types of criminals—the *born criminal,* the *insane criminal,* the *criminal by passion,* the *habitual criminal,* and the *occasional criminal*—all of which were primarily based on Darwin's theory of evolution (Lindesmith & Dunham, 1941). Lombrosos noticed that many of those whom he considered to be born criminals shared particular physical characteristics. These included receding hairlines, forehead wrinkles, bumpy face, broad noses, fleshy lips, sloping shoulders, long arms, and pointy fingers. Lombroso associated these features with the physical attributes of primitive man. He felt strongly that the criminals of his time were immoral persons who had not developed to the same level as noncriminal man. He regarded the born criminal as being the result of a family history of insanity, feeblemindedness, syphilis, epilepsy, and alcoholism (Bartol, 1991a).

As more and more studies were conducted on criminals and criminal behavior in the early twientieth century, it became apparent that psychological and personality difficulties were more significant factors than feeblemindedness in the development of criminal personalities. As an example of this new understanding, building upon the recent insights gained from psychoanalysis and descriptive psychiatry (the study of observable symptoms and behavioral phenomena), in 1932 the Psychiatric Clinic of the Court of General Sessions in New York began to classify each offender according to a personality evaluation consisting of four categories: (1) presence or absence of psychosis, (2) intellectual level, (3) presence of psychopathic or neurotic features and/or personality diagnosis, and (4) physical condition (Guttmacher, 1933; Wertham, 1954). A project at the Bellevue Psychiatric Hospital in New York City, spanning from 1932 to 1965, indicated that personality and "the external realities of mental life" (e.g., social pressures, cultural emphases, physical needs, subcultural patterns of existence) were more involved in criminal behavior than psychoses or defective intelligence (Guttmacher, 1955; Pinizzotto, 1984; Webster, et al., 1994). Also in the 1960s, several research-based classification typologies for offenders were developed. Irrespective of the causes of crime, it became obvious in the 1960s and 1970s that a system must be put in place for the description, classification, and cataloging of the behavioral elements of criminal offenders as exhibited at crime scenes themselves.

History and Classification of Crime

There are three basic types of offender behavior at a crime scene—***modus operandi***, **signature** (or "personation" or "calling card"), and **ritual** (Douglas, Burgess, Burgess, & Ressler, 1992; Hazelwood & Warren, 1990; Keppel & Birnes, 1997).

The term ***modus operandi*** (**MO**) represents the functional components that are necessary for an offender to be successful in committing a crime. These can include such things as the time of day chosen by an offender, preferred location, the type of victim, points or techniques for gaining entry, as well as tools used for committing the crime. Generally, the "MO" can be used to link cases because these elements often remain constant. But this is not always the case. An MO may be *static* or *dynamic.* A look at the case of a common burglar helps illustrate this issue. The novice burglar shatters a locked basement window to gain access to a house. Fearing that the sound of a window breaking will attract attention, he rushes in his search for valuables. Later, during subsequent crimes, he brings tools to force open locks, which will minimize the noise. This allows him more time to commit the crimes and to carry away more valuables from the house. As he commits more burglaries, the burglar refines his breaking-and-entering techniques to lower the risk of capture and to increase profits. This exemplifies how an MO can be learned in a dynamic and malleable fashion. The victim's response also influences the dynamics of the MO. If a rapist has problems controlling a victim, he will modify the MO to accommodate resistance. He may use duct tape, other ligatures, or a weapon on the victim. Or, he may blitz the victim and immediately incapacitate her. If such measures are ineffective, he may resort to greater violence or he may kill the victim. In this manner, criminals continually tweak their MO to meet the changing demands of their crime (Douglas, 2003).

A more in-depth example is that of Nathaniel Code, Jr., who killed a total of eight people on three separate occasions. The first homicide occurred on August 8, 1984, and involved a 25-year-old black female. Code stabbed her nine times in the chest and slashed her throat. One year later, on July 19, 1985, Code killed four more people—a 15-year-old girl, her mother, and two of their male friends. Code cut the throat of the girl, asphyxiated the mother, shot one of the males in the head, and shot the other male twice as well as cutting his throat. Code's final killings occurred on August 5, 1987. The victims were Code's grandfather and his 8-year-old and 12-year-old nephews. The boys died of ligature strangulation. Code stabbed his grandfather five times in the chest and seven times in the back. The changes in Code's MO, exhibited from case to case, show how the MO is refined as needed. More specifically, in the first murder, he gagged the victim with material found at the scene; the next time, he brought duct tape. In the second killings, Code brought a gun to the scene to dispose of the males, who posed the greatest threat to him. Since the last victims were an elderly man and two children, Code perceived little threat and did not use a gun on them.

Signature aspects of a crime, also referred to as *personation* or *calling card*, are behaviors that go beyond what is necessary to commit the crime to the fulfillment of a psychological need of the offender. Unlike MO, signature aspects are stable over time and will be witnessed at each crime scene throughout a series. Although there may be subtle differences from crime to crime, there will be an evident theme. As this theme represents a psychological need of the offender, signature seems to be based heavily upon, and reflect the offender's fantasies. Signature aspects are symbolic and hold special significance to the offender and may not be understood by anyone other than the offender. If over a series of murders the victims' arms are left crossed upon their chests, this is significant to the offender and goes beyond what is necessary to commit the crime. The actual reason or meaning may not be understood by investigators, but there is a clear indication that each of these crimes were committed by the same offender for whom the crossing of the arms does have a significance.

One example of the signature aspect of a crime would be the Unabomber Ted Kaczynski's apparent fascination with wood. One of his victims, president of United Airlines at the time, was named Percy A. Wood. Wood received the bomb hidden inside a book published by Arbor House. Another intended victim was named LeRoy Wood Bearnson. Perhaps most intriguing, in June 1995, Kaczynski sent a letter to the *San Francisco Chronicle* bearing the return address of Frederick Benjamin Isaac (which, interestingly, would be abbreviated FBI) Wood of 549 Wood Street in Woodlake, California. His final target was the headquarters of the California Forestry Association (Douglas, 2003).

The following scenario further helps illustrate the difference between the MO and signature aspects of crimes. A rapist enters a dormitory residence and takes a woman and her roommate captive. He orders one student to lie face down on the floor and then balances a glass on her back and another glass on the back of her head. He tells her, "If I hear the glass move or hit the floor, your roommate dies." The offender then takes the other young woman into the next room and rapes her. In another situation, a rapist enters the dormitory, orders the woman to phone her roommate, and tells her to use some ploy to get her to return to the dorm. Once the roommate arrives, the rapist ties her to a chair and forces her to watch the assault on her friend. The rapist who used the two glasses employed a specific MO to control the roommate. However, the other rapist went beyond just committing the rape. He satisfied his fantasies fully by not only raping the woman but also by frightening and exhibiting his actions to the roommate. His personal needs compelled him to perform this signature aspect of the crime (Bennell & Jones, 2005; Douglas, 2003: Hicks & Sales, 2006).

Ritual indicates a combination of fantasy and motivational factors that are psychologically based and fulfill a need of the offender but which may not be necessary for the successful commission of the crime. Ritual may be indicated at a crime scene with bindings on the victim, posing of victims, unique markings on victims, or any other behaviors that are symbolic and fulfill a psychological need of the offender. Together, MO, ritual, and signature are important aspects of a crime scene (especially a violent crime scene) that provide clues enabling investigators to link together crime scenes and determine if they are looking for one or more offenders (Douglas, 2003).

When offenders display rituals or peculiar behaviors at a crime scene, a "calling card" or signature aspect is left behind. Douglas and Munn (1992) give the example of a rapist who demonstrates his signature by exhibiting domination, manipulation, or humiliation using verbal, physical, or sexual acts. The use of exceptionally vulgar or abusive language, or preparing a script for the victim to repeat, represents a verbal signature. When the rapist prepares a script for a victim, he dictates a particular verbal response from her, such as "Tell me how much you enjoy sex with me," or "Tell me how good I am." The use of specific physical behavior also shows a subject's signature. One example of signature sexual behaviour involves the offender who repeatedly engages in a specific order of sexual activity with different victims (Douglas, Burgess, Burgess, & Ressler, 1992).

Understanding and recognizing the signature aspects of criminal behavior is vital in the apprehension and prosecution of an offender, especially a serial offender. The case of David Vasquez in Arlington, Virginia, is a prime example of this importance. In 1984, Vasquez pled guilty to the murder of a 34-year-old Arlington, Virginia, woman. The woman had been sexually assaulted and died of ligature strangulation. The killer left her lying face down with her hands tied behind her back. He used unique knots and excessive binding with the ligatures, and a lead came from the wrists to the neck over the left shoulder. The body was openly displayed so that discovery offered significant shock value. The offender spent considerable time at the crime scene. He made extensive preparations to bind the victim, allowing him to control her easily. His needs dictated that he move her around the house, exerting total domination over her. It appeared that he even took her into the bathroom and made her brush her teeth. None of this behavior was necessary to perpetrate the crime; the offender felt compelled to act out this ritual.

Vasquez had a borderline I.Q. Believing this would make it difficult to prove his innocence, his lawyers convinced him that he would probably receive the death sentence if the case went to trial. Instead, Vasquez opted for life imprisonment by pleading guilty. Three years later, in 1987, police discovered a 44-year-old woman lying nude and face down on her bed. A rope bound her wrists behind her back, and a ligature strand tightly encircled her neck with a slip knot at the back. It continued over her left shoulder, down her back, and then was wrapped three times around each wrist. Forensics revealed that she died of ligature strangulation and that she had been sexually assaulted. The offender left the body exposed and openly displayed. He appeared to have spent a considerable amount of time at the crime scene. This homicide occurred four blocks from the 1984 murder.

David Vasquez had been imprisoned for three years when the 1987 murder occurred. At the request of the Arlington, Virginia, Police Department, the National Center for the Analysis of Violent Crime (NCAVC) conducted an extensive analysis of these two murders, a series of sexual assaults, and several other killings that occurred between 1984 and 1987. Eventually, the NCAVC linked these offenses through analogous signature aspects of another local suspect. Physical evidence later corroborated this connection and determined that the "calling card" left at the 1984 homicide did not belong to David Vasquez. As a result of this finding, the Commonwealth of Virginia released Vasquez from prison and exonerated him of the crime. The events of the Vasquez case were depicted in the book *Stalking Justice* (Mones, 1995).

Staging

Sometimes investigators confront crime scenes that are baffling and contain peculiarities that serve no apparent purpose in the perpetration; this may be the result of **staging**. Staging occurs when someone purposely alters the crime scene prior to the arrival of the police usually in order to obscure the underlying motive of the crime. For example, the offender may not just happen to come upon a victim, but is someone he has some kind of association or relationship with him. This person, when interacting with the police, will consciously attempt to steer the investigation away from himself, perhaps by being overly solititious or inordinately extremely distraught. Staging may also occur when someone desires to protect the decedent or the decedent's family. This can occur in rape–murder cases, domestic homicide, or "autoerotically induced accidental deaths." Or the killer who was actually known to the victim may try and make the crime scene appear disorganized or carried out in a manner that would imply no previous relationship (Dietz & Hazelwood, 1982; Saferstein, 2001; Wade, 2006).

MODERN PROFILING

Criminal psychological profiling, or more simply profiling, is the technique of analyzing behavior patterns of a crime or series of crimes to construct a descriptive template of the probable offender and the identification of an offender's biographical characteristics, such as his/her age, sex, and marital and employment status (Rossmo, 2000; Wilson, Lincoln, & Kocsis, 1997). Hicks and Sales (2006) divide the models of **criminal profiling** currently in use by forensic psychologists and law enforcement into two groups—*nonscientific* and *scientific*. According to Hicks and sales, nonscientific profiling relies on intuition, investigative experience, and professional judgment. Scientific profiling relies on empirical and scientific methodology.

Nonscientific models of Criminal Profiling

This group includes the models developed by Douglas, Ressler, Burgess, and Hartman (1986), Holmes and Holmes (1996), Turco (1990), and Turvey (1999). These models provide primarily an intuitive analysis of crime scene evidence where proficiency is a "gift reserved to certain individuals who can reach inside the criminal mind and understand it" (Holmes & Holmes, 1996, p. 166). The basic approach of the Holmes and Holmes model is to match case evidence to various criminal typologies (e.g., disorganized asocial versus organized nonsocial offenders).

Both the Holmes and Holmes model and the Douglas, Ressler, Burgess, and Hartman models of profiling emphasize the importance of *victim* profiling, which is related to the offender's (usually serial killers') choice of victims. Examples of victim attributes include physical traits, marital status, personal lifestyle, occupation, education, geographical demographics, medical history, psychosocial history, and previous involvement with the criminal justice system. Both models also divide serial killers into various typologies as previously discussed in Chapter 5 of this text. These typologies are based on killers' psychological state, pathology, motive, needs, and social orientation and acclamation. Resler, Burgess, and Douglas's typologies include the *visionary serial killer* (induced to kill because of psychotic visions or voices), the *mission-oriented serial killer* (a nonpsychotyic type who kills to eradicate certain groups or types of people), the *hedonistic serial killer* (who desires sexual pleasure or some personl gain from killing and often utilizes mutilation, torture, dismemberment, and even necrophilia/necrophagia in his killings), and the *power/control serial killer* (who achieves sexual pleasure mostly from exercising power, control, and domination over a helpless victim and who uses "hands-on" methods of killing (Holmes & Holmes, 1996, p. 67).

The Turco model of profiling advocates for the use of psychoanalytic principles, stating that profiling should be oriented "around the basis of Borderline and Narcissistic Personality Disorders" (Turco, 1990, p. 149). The Turco model views the crime scene as the manifestation of a projection of the offender's underlying personality and developmental experiences (e.g., maternal bonding). This would be similar to the type of projection that takes place in the Rorschach inkblot test (Hicks & Sales, 2006; Turco, 1990). The Turvey model places emphasis on the MO and signature behaviors exhibited by the offender during the commission of the crime, which may change as the offender gains confidence or experience, or as his emotional needs change over time.

Scientific models of Criminal Profiling

Hicks and Sales state, "Without scientific inquiry, models or profiling provide only speculation. Science is needed to help the profiling field move from the realm of conjecture to the possibility of truths" (Hicks & Sales, 2006, p. 70). They view the **Cantor model** of profiling (Cantor, 1994, 1995, 2000) as the only current model that satisfies the designation of "scientific" (p. 71). Cantor's model stresses the importance of linking behaviors, personalities, and other human characteristics to the commission of crime. For Cantor, the concept of linking offense actions and offender characterisc-itcs is represented with the following equation:

$$F_1A_1 + \ldots F_nA_n = K_1C_1 + \ldots K_mC_m$$

The left side of the equation contains the kinds of information about a crime that would be available to law enforcement (e.g., actions of the offender). The right side represents the individual characteristics that would be useful to the investigation of the crime (e.g., personality attributes and psychological state of the offender). For there to be an empirically based model of profiling, there must be a reliable relationship between actions and offender characteristics. More specifically, it would have to be true that there are some psychologically important variations *between* crimes that relate to differences in the people who commit them (Cantor, 2000).

To apply a scientific model of profiling, one must be able to use information from a particular crime to correctly make inferences about the perpetrator (Hicks & Sales, 2006). But for this to be done, Cantor's *offender consistency hypothesis* and *offender specificity hypothesis* must be understood. The offender consistency hypothesis assumes that there are consistencies between the manner in which an offender carries out a crime on one occasion and the way he carries out crimes on other occasions. These similarities are attributable to characteristics of the offender himself rather than to features of the situation where the crime was committed (Hicks and Sales). The offender specificity hypothesis holds that offenders' crimes become specialized to the situation due to various factors such as social processes, preparedness, impulsiveness, and reactionary idiosyncratic personality features. This interplay between offender consistency and offender specificity can be viewed in terms of a hierarchy and is illustrated in Figure 8.1.

As of this date very little scientific scrutiny has been given to the topic of psychological profiling, and much supportive material consists of largely anecdotal accounts (Britton, 1997; Douglas & Olshaker, 1999) or publications in nonacademically peer-reviewed journals (Douglas & Burgess,

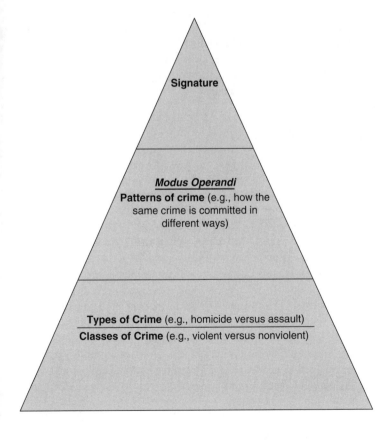

FIGURE 8.1 Interplay between Offender Consistency and Offender Specificity

1986). When empirical indicators are used, the results do not often inspire confidence. For example, Pinizzotto and Finkel (1990) provided the details of a closed rape and murder case to small groups of trained profilers, police detectives, clinical psychologists, and students. Each group was assigned the same profiling exercises and asked to identify the likely offender. The details of the perpetrators of both offenses were known, thus providing the "correct" profile as a criterion for quantitative analysis. Multiple-choice questionnaires were administered as a means of gathering predictions regarding the probable offender for both the rape and murder case. No significant differences were found among any of the groups involving the number of correct predictions in the murder case. The sampled profilers were unable to predict the characteristics of the murderer any better than any of the compared groups, and indeed, their mean score was found to be the lowest among the four groups. Similarly, Smith and Alison (2001) demonstrated that police officers were unable to discern any difference in the amount of accurate information in two profiles that differed substantially in their descriptions of the offender. Independent of the contents of the profile, police officers perceived the profiles as generally accurate.

Along similar lines, Canter, Alison, Alison, and Wentink (2004) examined whether 100 murders committed by serial killers could be categorized as "organized or disorganized" based on a major classification system discussed in the FBI's *Crime Classification Manual*. In contrast to what would be predicted from the typology, the analysis did not reveal any distinct subsets of organized and disorganized behaviors, thus making it difficult to see how serial homicides may be categorized easily in this way.

What is needed? Hicks and Sales conclude that for psychological profiling to be "scientific," it must be accurate, valid, reliable, comprehensive, and not be based on anecdotal evidence or subjective investigative experience (Hicks & Sales, 2006). Rather, such a model must be based on empirical testing and research in areas such as crime scene evidence, crime scene reconstruction, motive, personality, situational factors, and behavior. The theory must allow for the generation of predictions about offender behavior that will substantively assist law enforcement in identifying and apprehending criminal offenders.

Despite the meager scientific evidence to support its practice, psychological profiling continues to be used by law enforcement agencies around the world. Snook (2008) expresses that this is not a bad thing. For one, psychological profiling may actually work, albeit not to the level made by some profilers' extraordinary claims. Second, by disseminating information on its use, further scientific research is encouraged. Indeed, more empirical investigation into the validity and underlying skills of psychological profiling is sorely needed.

FORENSIC PSYCHOLOGY IN THE SPOTLIGHT

Does the Perceived Accuracy of a Psychological Profile Depend on the Supposed Author?

Kocsis and Hayes (2004)

In this study, police officers read a profile labeled as being written by either a professional profiler or "someone the investigator consulted" in response to a case file of a closed homicide case. Unknown to the participating police officers, the author of the profile, as labeled in the instructions, was determined randomly. The participants were shown a particular profile and asked to indicate their expectations as to how useful they regarded the profile likely to be. In this examination no differences were found concerning the perceived utility of the profile as related to the author label. Next, the participants were given a description of the actual perpetrator of the crime and were asked to make a side-by-side comparison of the profile and the actual perpetrator and then judge the accuracy of the profile in comparison to the actual perpetrator. In a side-by-side comparison between the profile and the actual perpetrator, police officers rated the profile ostensibly written by a professional profiler as more accurate than one ostensibly written by someone the investigator consulted even though they contained the same information and the author label was merely randomly assigned to the profile. These studies suggest that perception of the accuracy of a profile is quite likely to be associated with the reader's perception regarding the identity of its author.

Summary

Fingerprints have been discovered on ancient Babylonian seals as well as on the walls of Egyptian tombs and were apparently used as substitutes for signatures. One of the first great contributors to the study of fingerprints was Sir Francis Galton, who published his book *Finger Prints* in 1892, presenting his collection of over 8,000 sets of prints. Galton classified fingerprints by general shape (arch, loop, or whorl); position in finger; and relative size. One of the oldest and most common methods for the development of latent fingerprints is that of *dusting* a surface with a fine powder of contrasting color. In modern times latent fingerprints are collected using lifting tape, powder, silver nitrate, ninhydrin, and lasers. The benefits of fingerprint analysis include the identification of suspects and the solving of crimes. But the method is not infallible as the process of comparing latent and inked prints is inherently subjective and subject to error. One of the main reasons for an uncertain fingerprint match is confirmation bias, or a form of selective thinking whereby one looks for what confirms one's beliefs and ignores that which contradicts one's beliefs.

The technique of voice identification was first introduced in the American courts in the mid-1960s and has frequently been used as evidence in the courtroom. For practical purposes, memory for brief voice samples is quite poor, and its admissibility into court is limited to the jurisdictions utilizing the *Daubert* standard, which allows a judge to admit evidence if it will assist the jury in better understanding the case as a whole.

The first practical use of a scientific instrument designed to measure physiological responses for the purpose of determining truth telling was in 1895 when Cesare Lombroso modified an existing instrument called a hydrosphygmograph and used this modified device in his experiments to measure the physiological changes that occurred in a crime suspect's blood pressure and pulse rate during a police interrogation.

At its basic level, a polygraph is an instrument that simultaneously records changes in physiological processes such as heartbeat, blood pressure, respiration, and electrical resistance (galvanic skin response or GSR). The underlying theory of the polygraph is that when people lie they also get measurably nervous about lying. The heartbeat increases, blood pressure goes up, breathing rhythms change, perspiration increases, et cetera. A baseline for these physiological characteristics is established by asking the subject questions whose answers the investigator knows. Deviations from the baseline for truthfulness are usually taken as signs of lying. One of the problems with polygraphs is their susceptibility to "countermeasures" used by examinees to fool the machine and the examiner. The most common countermeasures utilized are either pain (e.g., biting one's lip or tongue) or muscle tension. Almost all courts reject polygraph results or only admit them if their admissibility is stipulated by both parties prior to the polygraph examination taking place. Only a few courts leave their admissibility up to the judge.

In the late eighteenth century, Franz Anton Mesmer experimented with "magnetic healing" and "mesmerism," which served as the basis for modern hypnosis. Hypnosis is used in modern investigations in two main arenas—interviewing (e.g., refreshing memory) and as legal defense (e.g., that a defendant had been coerced to perform criminal acts, or hypnosis is utilized to uncover dissociated states that might mitigate criminal responsibility). Another use of hypnotic-like procedures is the cognitive interview where a subject or witness is instructed to use certain measures (e.g., to report memories no matter how trivial they may seem). But the more a person reports, the more likely it is that both correct and incorrect information will be elicited.

There are three basic types of offender behavior that may be exhibited at a crime scene—*modus operandi* ("MO"), signature (or "personation" or "calling card"), and ritual. The term *modus operandi* represents the functional components that are necessary for an offender to be successful in committing a crime. Signature aspects of a crime, also referred to as personation or calling card, are behaviors that go beyond what is necessary to commit the crime and fulfill a psychological need of the offender. Ritual is a combination of psychologically based fantasy and motivational factors used to fulfill a need of the offender but which may not be necessary for the successful commission of the crime.

Criminal psychological profiling is the technique of analyzing behavior patterns of a crime or series of crimes to construct a descriptive template of the probable offender and the identification of an offender's biographical characteristics. Current models of criminal profiling may be divided into two groups—nonscientific and scientific. Nonscientifc profiling relies on intuition, investigative experience, and professional judgment. Scientific profiling relies on empirical and scientific methodology. There has been a dearth of empirical scrutiny given to psychological profiling, and the bulk of material cited in support of the process consists of largely anecdotal accounts. But it is known that for psychological profiling to be "scientific" it must be accurate, valid, reliable, and comprehensive. A true scientific model must be based on empirical testing and research in areas such as crime scene evidence, crime scene reconstruction, motive, personality, situational factors, and behavior.

Key Terms

Cantor model *190*	Directed Lie Test *179*	Ken Bianchi *185*	San Francisco
Cognitive interview *185*	Dissociation *182*	*Modus operandi 187*	Chronicle *188*
Confirmation bias *173*	Franz Anton Mesmer *181*	Ninhydrin *172*	Scientific model of
Control question test *179*	Galton's Details *171*	Nonscientific model of	criminal profiling *190*
Countermeasures *180*	Guilty knowledge test *179*	criminal profiling *190*	Signature *188*
Criminal profiling *190*	Hypnosis *182*	Polygraph *178*	Sir FrancisGalton *170*
Dactyloscopy *171*	IAFIS *172*	Ritual *188*	Staging *189*

Review Questions

1. What are the three basic shapes that Galton used to classify fingerprints?
2. What is "dactyloscopy"?
3. What is the oldest and most common method for the development of latent fingerprints?
4. What is the main goal of the forensic expert when analyzing fingerprints?
5. What is "IAFIS"?
6. What does the 2001 case of *Commonwealth v. Cowans* stand for?
7. How does the *Mayfield Affair* in 2004 demonstrate the limits of fingerprint evidence?
8. What is conformation bias, and how does it sometimes result in an uncertain match being reported as a true match?
9. What is the general technique used in voice identification?
10. What is the sound spectrograph, and how is it used?
11. Which jurisdictions are most likely to admit voice identification into evidence?
12. What is the underlying theory of the polygraph?
13. What kinds of individuals have been known to "fool" the polygraph test?
14. What are "countermeasures," and how are they used?
15. What is the significance of the U.S. Supreme Court case of *U.S. v. Scheffer* (1998) regarding polygraph admissibility?
16. What are the two broad areas in which hypnosis is used in investigations?
17. How is the totality of circumstances approach of admissibility different from the per se exclusionary rule regarding hypnosis?
18. How was hypnosis used with Ken Bianchi of the Hillside Strangler case?
19. What is a cognitive interview, and what is it designed to accomplish? How?
20. What are the three basic types of offender behavior at a crime scene?
21. What is "staging," and when is likely to occur?
22. What is the definition of criminal (or psychological) profiling?
23. What are the differences between nonscientific and scientific models of profiling?

Chapter Resources on the World Wide Web

American polygraph association
http://www.polygraph.org/

Automated fingerprint identification systems
http://www.printquest-afis.com/?gclid=CPC3pIrb6pYCFQHHGgodTjyxPA

Brief History of the Polygraph
http://www.galianospolygraphe.com/html/brief_history_of_the_polygraph.html

Crime scene investigation
http://science.howstuffworks.com/csi.htm

Criminal profiling research
http://www.criminalprofiling.ch/

DNA and forensic science criminal investigations
http://www.karisable.com/crdna.htm

Electronic crime scene investigation
http://www.ncjrs.gov/pdffiles1/nij/187736.pdf

Fingerprinting
http://www.cyberbee.com/whodunnit/fp.html

Forensic hypnosis in famous court cases
http://lifeloom.com/II1Ritzel.htm

Forensic science: Psychological profiling
http://library.thinkquest.org/04oct/00206/nts_psychological_profiling.htm

Functional Nervous Disorders and the Subconscious Mind
http://serendip.brynmawr.edu/Mind/Trance.html

Francis Galton and fingerprints
http://galton.org/fingerprinter.html

Glossary of fingerprint terms
http://www.crimescene-forensics.com/Fingerprint_terms.html

History of police fingerprinting
http://www.policensw.com/info/fingerprints/finger01.html

Historical review of fingerprinting
http://www.onin.com/fp/

How lie detectors work
http://people.howstuffworks.com/lie-detector.htm

Integrated automated fingerprint identification system
http://www.fbi.gov/hq/cjisd/iafis.htm

"Mind control," LSD, the CIA and the American people
http://www.mindcontrolforums.com/lsd-mc-cia.htm

Offender profiling
http://student-guide-to-forensic-psychology.blogspot.com/2008/
09/offender-profiling.html

Personality and psychological profiling instruments
http://wilderdom.com/tools/ToolsPersonality.html

Psychological profiling: An introduction
http://www.csbsju.edu/uspp/CrimPsych/CPSG-1.htm

The Hillside Stranglers: Kenneth Bianchi & Angelo Buono
http://www.karisable.com/skazbianchi.htm

The Hillside Strangler Trial
http://llr.lls.edu/volumes/v33-issue2/boren.pdf

Scientific validity of polygraph testing
http://www.fas.org/sgp/othergov/polygraph/ota/index.html

Some principles of criminal typology
http://www.trutv.com/library/crime/criminal_mind/psychology/
crime_motivation/4.html.]

The forensic examiner
http://www.theforensicexaminer.com/?gclid=CJTx4uDc6pYCFQE
TGgodjjGDO

The strange tale of Dr. Jekyll and Mr. Hyde
http://www.bartleby.com/1015

U.S. Department of justice: Crime scene investigation
http://www.ncjrs.org/pdffiles1/nij/200160.pdf

Violent crime scene analysis: Modus operandi, signature, and staging
http://www.criminalprofiling.ch/violent-crime.html.

For Further Reading

Baddeley, A. (1990). *Human memory: Theory and practice.* Boston, MA: Allyn & Bacon.

Bartol, C. R. (1991). *Criminal Behavior.* Upper Saddle River NJ: Prentice Hall.

Douglas, J. E., Burgess, A. W., Burgess, A. G., & Ressler, R. K. (2006). *Crime classification manual: A standard system for investigating and classifying violent crimes.* San Francisco, CA: Jossey-Bass.

Gale, A. (Ed.). (1988). *The polygraph test: Lies, truth and science.* London: Sage.

Gilbert, J. N. (2007). *Criminal investigation* (7th ed.). Upper Saddle River, NJ: Prentice Hall.

Harris, T. (1986). *The red dragon.* New York: Heineman.

Heaton, A. A., Shepherd, E., & Wolchover, D. (Eds.). (1999). *Analyzing witness testimony.* London: Blackstone.

Hicks, S. J., & Sales, B. D. (2006). *Criminal profiling: Developing an effective science and practice.* Washington, DC: American Psychological Association.

Holmes, R., & Holmes, S. (1996). *Profiling violent crimes: An investigative tool.* Thousand Oaks, CA: Sage.

Inbau, F. E., Reid, J. E., Buckley, J. P., & Jayne, B. C. (2001). *Criminal interrogation and confessions* (4th ed.). Gaithersberg, MD: Aspen.

Keppel, R. D., & Birnes, W. J. (1997). *Signature killers: Interpreting the calling cards of the serial murderer.* New York, NY: Pocket Books.

Lee, H. C., & Gaensslen, R. E. (Eds.). (2001). *Advances in fingerprint technology* (2nd ed.). Boca Raton, FL: CRC Press.

Lyman, M. D. (2008). *Criminal investigation: The art and the science.* Upper Saddle River, NJ: Prentice Hall.

Melton, G. B., Petrila, J., Poythress, N. G., & Slobogin, C. (2007). *Psychological evaluations for the courts: A handbook for mental health professionals and lawyers* (3rd ed.). New York: The Guilford Press.

Schwarz, T. (1981). The Hillside Strangler: A murderer's mind. Garden City, NY: Doubleday.

Turvey, B. (1999). *Criminal profiling: An introduction to behavioral evidence analysis.* San Diego, CA: Academic Press.

Wilson, C., & Seaman, D. (1997). *The serial killers: A study in the psychology of violence.* London: Virgin Publishing.

CHAPTER 9

Eyewitness Testimony and Accuracy

CHAPTER OBJECTIVES

After reading this chapter you would:

- Understand the importance of eyewitness testimony in a criminal trial.
- Know the history of psychological research into eyewitness accuracy.
- Know how eyewitness accuracy, perception, and memory are related.
- Be aware of the estimator variables in eyewitness accuracy.
- Appreciate the system variables in eyewitness accuracy.
- Understand what is meant by a cognitive interview.
- Know what a lineup is and how it should be constructed.
- Know the difference between simultaneous and sequential presentation.

INTRODUCTION

It is estimated that approximately 4,500 innocent people are convicted each year in the United States because of mistaken eyewitness identification (Cutler & Penrod, 1995). In fact, errors in eyewitness identifications are responsible for more wrongful convictions than all other cases combined (Borchard, 1932; Brandon & Davies, 1973; Huff, Rattner, & Sagarin, 1986; Loftus, 1979). Yet it is ironic that eyewitness testimony is also the most powerful incriminating evidence that can be presented in court next to an actual confession (Brandon & Davies, 1973). Prosecutors have learned through their experience that there is almost nothing more valuable than an absolutely positive and credible eyewitness. Eyewitness testimony is so powerful that individuals often change their verdict from nonguilty to guilty based on the introduction of such testimony, and jurors tend to over believe, or at least rely heavily on, such evidence.

A case on point is that of Kirk Bloodsworth, who in March 1985 was convicted of the 1984 sexual assault and slaying of a nine-year-old girl in Maryland (*State of Maryland v. Kirk N. Bloodsworth*). Five eyewitnesses identified Bloodsworth at trial, and he was sentenced to death. He spent two years on death row before he received a new trial based on the prosecution's withholding of information about other suspects. This time he received a life sentence. Bloodsworth maintained his innocence but it was not until 1993 that he was released from prison on the basis of DNA testing that proved he was not the source of semen found on an item of clothing belonging to the victim. In September 2003, DNA testing got a hit on the actual murderer, Kimberly Shay

Ruffner. The Bloodsworth case illustrates the profound effects of mistaken eyewitness testimony: not only can an innocent person be convicted but the guilty may remain free and pose a danger to society (Kennedy & Haygood, 1992; Wells, Memon, & Penrod, 2005).

EYEWITNESS PSYCHOLOGY IN HISTORICAL PERSPECTIVE

Thucydides was a Greek historian and author of the *History of the Peloponnesian War*, which recounts the fifth-century B.C.E. war between Sparta and Athens to the year 411 B.C.E. Thucydides has been called the "father of scientific history" due to his strict standards of evidence gathering and analysis in terms of cause and effect without reference to divine intervention, which was so common for that time in history. In his writings, he discussed the unreliability of eyewitnesses when he noted a "want of coincidence between accounts of the same occurrences by different eyewitnesses, arising sometimes from imperfect memory, [and] sometimes from undue partiality for one side or the other" (cited in Levine & Tapp, 1973; see also Cochrane, 1929; Connor, 1984.)

Two centuries ago, a legal scholar writing in a handbook of criminal law and criminal politics stated,

> [An] identification procedure has to be preceded by a comprehensive interrogation of the witness, wherein he is to describe the characteristic features which could facilitate recognition of the persons or objects to which his testimony or statements refer . . . He should be urged to point out, for example, the identified object, without hesitation, and also to give the reasons why he had identified this one as the real one instead of any of the others . . . On the one hand, the investigator has to take care, to the best of his ability, to remove any changes that may have occurred in the object to be recognized and that may thus impair recognition: therefore, for example, he must not present the accused in his prison clothes, or with a distorting beard, etc." (Henke, 1838, pp. 705–706; translation by Sporer, 1992).

During the first decade of the twentieth century several psychologists (Binet, 1900; Münsterberg, 1908; Stern, 1910; Whipple, 1909, 1910) scientifically investigated the foundations and application of cognitive processes to legal issues. They conducted applied experimental studies on perception and memory, suggestibility, confessions, lie detection, and hypnotism. Alfred Binet (1900) was one of the first psychologists to advocate for the scientific study of testimony based on eyewitness observation. Binet felt strongly that eyewitness' reports were affected by suggestive questioning. In 1908, in his book *On the Witness Stand*, Hugo Münsterberg continued the critical examination of the relationship between eyewitness certainty and accuracy. But it was not until the 1970s that cognitive psychologists and social psychologists showed a heightened interest once again in the experimental research of eyewitness testimony and identification.

WHAT PSYCHOLOGY TELLS US ABOUT EYEWITNESS IDENTIFICATION AND ACCURACY

In the 1970s Robert Buckhout of Brooklyn College was one of the first social psychologists to perform research on eyewitness recall, memory for people, and **unconscious transference.** Unconscious transference refers to the generation of memory that is related to an incident, but is not relevant to that actual incident. For example, a convenience store worker who has been robbed may mistakenly identify one of his regular customers as a suspect in the robbery. This phenomenon was demonstrated by Buckhout in 1974 when he staged a mock assault in front of 141 unsuspecting college students. Seven weeks later, these students were asked to pick the perpetrator from a group of 6 photographs. Of the 60% who did not correctly identify the assailant, two-thirds incorrectly chose an innocent bystander who was at the crime scene (Buckhout, 1974). In one study, Buckhout arranged for a New York City television station to broadcast a staged mugging followed by a six-person lineup. Of the 2,145 viewers who called in, nearly 2,000 were mistaken in their identification of the mugger (Buckhout, 1980).

Buckhout reported several factors in addition to unconscious transference that are likely to cause an unreliable identification based on psychological factors of a witness. These factors include stress, the physical condition of the witness, suggestive identification procedures, and conformity. Buckhout emphasized that juries in any criminal case must be aware of these factors when assessing the credibility of identifications, and that research on perception and memory suggests strongly that any eyewitness report should be evaluated cautiously and skeptically. Over time, Buckhout's findings have been reaffirmed by studies of mistaken identifications that contributed to known wrongful convictions. The research into eyewitness identification continued, and by 1995, there were well over 2,000 peer-reviewed research articles on eyewitness identification and memory (Cutler & Penrod, 1995).

Over the years it became increasingly more apparent to law enforcement, that eyewitness descriptions of events cannot always be trusted. The potential unreliability of eyewitness accounts was a major reason why the Federal Bureau of Investigation discounted the theory that the July 1996 explosion of TWA Flight 800 over New York was caused by a missile fired from the ground. The accuracy of at least 20 eyewitnesses was doubted when they all reported seeing a streak of light shooting toward the sky moments before the plane exploded killing all 230 passengers. And many crimes have only one eyewitness. A robbery, for example, is usually witnessed only by the victim; the same is true for the sexual abuse of children. But eyewitness testimony, even from one person, can still be very convincing to a judge or jury.

Are Jurors Aware of Factors That Influence Eyewitness Memory?

Cutler, Penrod, and Dexter (1990)

Legal experts are of the belief that jurors often need expert psychological testimony concerning the limitations of eyewitness memory in order for them to make sound decisions regarding eyewitness testimony. It is assumed that jurors are insensitive to the factors that influence eyewitness memory, and that this lack of sensitivity threatens the effectiveness of traditional safeguards, such as direct and cross-examination and judicial instructions, which are designed to protect the defendant from mistaken identifications.

In the present study, a videotaped mock trial concerned a defendant accused of the armed robbery of a liquor store. A positive identification of the defendant by the robbery victim was the crucial source of trial evidence. The two prosecution witnesses followed by two witnesses for the defense were examined and cross-examined in the trial. Testifying first, the clerk of the liquor store and victim of the robbery described the witnessing conditions and the conditions under which she identified the defendant as the robber. Next, the police officer in charge of the investigation described

the conditions under which the identification was made. Third, a character witness—a friend of the defendant—provided him with a relatively weak alibi. The defendant was the last witness. He denied all allegations against him yet offered little concrete evidence to support his case. Examination (direct and cross) of the two prosecution witnesses served as a vehicle for disclosure of the approximately 20 witness and identification factors that were discussed in the trial.

The two primary dependent measures were verdict (not guilty or guilty) and the subject's estimate of the probability that the identification was correct. The independent variables included:

1. *Disguise of Robber.* The witness testified that, during the robbery, the robber either wore a knit cap fully covering his hair or wore no hat.
2. *Weapon Presence.* The witness testified that throughout the robbery a handgun was either outwardly brandished and pointed at her or hidden in the robber's jacket.

3. *Violence.* According to the witness, the robber either threatened to kill her, manhandled her, fired his handgun into the floor, and pushed her to the floor before leaving or calmly and quietly demanded the money and then left.
4. *Retention Interval.* The witness testified that the identification was made either 2 days after the robbery or 14 days after the robbery.
5. *Mugshot Search.* During the interval between the robbery and the identification, according to eyewitness testimony, the witness either searched through mugshot books for the robber or searched no mugshot books.
6. *Lineup Instructions.* The police officer who had conducted the lineup procedure testified that the witness was instructed to either "choose the suspect from the lineup who you believe is the robber or indicate that the robber was not in the lineup" or"choose the suspect from the lineup who you believe is the robber."
7. *Lineup Size.* The witness testified that there were a total of either 6 persons or 12 persons in the lineup from which the defendant was identified.
8. *Similarity of Lineup Members.* This manipulation addressed the fairness of the lineup. In half of the videotapes the witness testified that there were several lineup members who resembled the robber in physical appearance. To complement this testimony, the police officer added that, in constructing the lineup, he had provided another officer (not involved with the case) with the witness's

original description of the robber and asked him to select foils who matched that description. In the other trial the witness testified that very few of the lineup members looked like the robber. Added to this, the officer testified that, foil selections included anyone who was available at the time.

9. *Voice Samples.* The witness testified that she either was allowed to hear the lineup members speak before making a decision or did not hear the lineup members speak.
10. *Witness Confidence.* The witness testified that she was either 80% or 100% confident that she had correctly identified the robber.

The study demonstrated (among other things) that jurors are generally insensitive to the factors that influence eyewitness memory such as the effects of disguise, weapon presence, retention interval, suggestive lineup instructions, and procedures used for constructing and carrying out a lineup. The authors concluded that the unawareness of jurors to these factors, which can distort eyewitness testimony, provides justification for admitting expert psychological testimony on eyewitness identification to assist jurors in understanding these issues. Traditional safeguards designed to protect a defendant from mistaken identification therefore remains in question without such expert testimony. The authors recommend that further research explore how the content of expert testimony would influences jurors' decisions, and how alternative methods for educating jurors about eyewitness memory could be employed.

Perception and Memory

People make perceptual errors all the time. This includes over or underestimating the height or weight of others, their distance from people or objects, speed of movement, the durations of events and when they occurred, and even the time of day. The process of the acquisition of new information, keeping it in memory, and then using this information at a later time, consists of encoding, storage, and retrieval.

Encoding refers to the acquisition of information. Many aspects of a stimulus can affect how it is encoded; stimuli that are only briefly seen or heard are not encoded fully, of course. The complexity of a stimulus also affects its encoding, but the relationship is not a straightforward one. As the complexity of an event increases, some portions of the event probably will be wrongly remembered, whereas other aspects of the event will be accurately recalled. Despite what some people believe, a stressful situation does not enhance the encoding of events. Although mild stress or arousal may indeed heighten alertness and interest in the task at hand, extreme stress usually causes the person to encode the information incompletely or inaccurately. This principle reflects an application of the **Yerkes–Dodson law**, which describes the effects of arousal on learning. Under extremely low levels of external stress, a person may be so relaxed and un-alert that little learning takes place. On the other hand, if a person is facing an excessively stressful situation, perception is narrowed, information is funneled, and less learning occurs than under mild levels of stress. Performance on many tasks is best when the level of arousal is moderate enough to ensure adequate attention but not so high as to disrupt accuracy (Gorenstein & Ellsworth, 1980).

Characteristics of the witness also affect encoding. We all differ in visual acuity and hearing ability. If we have more experience perceiving a given kind of stimulus, we will usually notice its details better than when it is a novel experience. This is why experienced judges notice flaws in an ice-skater's performance that the rest of us can only detect in a slow-motion replay. Different expectancies about upcoming events also influence how they are subsequently perceived; in general, we have a tendency to see what we expect to see (Cutler, Penrod, & Dexter, 1990).

Storage is the second step in building memory. The experimental psychologist Hermann Ebbinghaus showed that early memory loss is rapid. Lipton (1977) illustrated this phenomenon by showing subjects a film of an armed robbery and shooting without any prior knowledge that they would be serving as eyewitnesses. Those who were questioned after one week generated 18% less memory information than those who were questioned immediately after viewing the film.

A second phenomenon also occurs during the storage phase. Activities that eyewitnesses carry out or information they learn after they observe an event can alter their memory of the event. For example, an eyewitness to a crime who views mugshots or photographs of suspects can alter his/her capacity to recognize faces that he/she viewed before the mug shots, that is, the new activity can interfere with memory of the old. In a similar fashion, simply providing an eyewitness with information about what other witnesses have already said influences the first witness's recollection. Moreover, questions that eyewitnesses are asked after the crime have been found to interfere with information that eyewitnesses acquired during the crime. In one study, subjects were shown a film of an automobile accident and then asked a series of follow-up questions about the accident. A misleading follow-up question contained information about a barn, which was actually not present in the film. One week later, 17% of subjects erroneously reported seeing a barn in the film. In effect, the misleading question incorporated new and inaccurate stimulus information in the memory store (Loftus & Palmer, 1974).

Retrieval, the final stage in the memory process, involves the recall of information from the memory store. Yet, recall may be influenced by the types of questions that eyewitnesses are asked. One study found that language can influence the retrieval of stimulus information. In this study, subjects were shown a film of an automobile accident and then asked a series of follow-up questions. Those subjects who were asked how fast the cars were going when the cars "smashed", reported an average speed of 40.8 mph. However, participants who were asked how fast the cars were going when the cars "contacted" reported an average speed of 31.8 mph. Suggestive questioning procedures, therefore, should be eliminated as much as possible to minimize their effect on eyewitness accuracy (Loftus, 1979).

Eyewitness testimony that is based on human perception, memory, and the processing of information is affected by **estimator variables** (attributes of the person and the environment), and system variables (those things inherent to the justice system). For example, cross-race versus within-race identifications, fatigues, lighting, or stress, are estimator variables (Loftus & Palmer, 1974). How eyewitnesses are interviewed by police and how eyewitnesses are instructed prior to viewing a lineup are **system variables.**

Estimator Variables

Gary L. Wells et al. (2005) have provided an excellent overview of the estimator variables in eyewitness identification The researchers consider the following as among the most important.

Cross-race identification refers to the phenomenon of people being less accurate in their identification of subjects of another race than of their own. Meissner and Brigham (2001) analyzed data from 39 research articles and reported that the chance of a mistaken identification

Are Jurors' Decisions Affected By Race?

Abshire & Bornstein (2003)

Racial differences appear in civil trials, where black mock jurors are more likely to reach a verdict for the plaintiff. This pattern seems to reflect a belief among the majority of black persons that the justice system (i.e., law enforcement and the courts) is discriminatory and biased (Ellsworth, 1989). The purpose of this present study was to assess if similar tendencies are present in criminal trials.

The independent variables in the present experiment were the race of the eyewitness (black or white) and the race of the mock juror (black or white): The race of the defendant was held constant.

The participants were 145 undergraduates, 80 of whom were white and 65 of whom were black. An audiotape of a murder trial was played on a tape player. The 22-minute trial consisted of normal courtroom proceedings: judge's instructions, opening arguments, witness testimony (with direct and cross-examination), closing arguments, and jury instructions. The victim was killed following an argument at night outside a gym. The prosecution called an eyewitness, who identified the defendant in court as having committed the crime, and a police detective, who described how he found the gun used in the murder at the defendant's house and how he conducted the lineup. The defense argued that the eyewitness lineup was biased and that the eyewitness was unreliable, because he observed the crime from 75 ft away, in poor lighting, and without his glasses. Finally, the defense called an alibi witness, who testified that she saw the defendant at his house (where she was visiting the defendant's roommate) both before and after the time at which the crime occurred; she believed that at the time of the murder, the defendant was upstairs alone.

The prosecution argued that the defendant could have snuck out of the house, committed the crime, which occurred only a couple of blocks away, and returned to the house, all without this witness's knowledge. During the trial, a picture of each trial participant was projected on a screen. The trial was pretested to ensure that the evidence of guilt was evenhanded and to select photos for the black and white eyewitness.

The results indicated that white participants found the prosecution witnesses including the eyewitness) more credible, and the defense witness less credible, than did black participants; they were also more likely to find the defendant guilty. The black eyewitness was perceived as more credible than was the white eyewitness, but eyewitness race had no effect on verdict. These results were consistent with the literature indicating that jurors of different races reach different verdicts, and also that jurors are relatively insensitive to factors that affect eyewitness testimony, such as the cross-race effect.

The authors state that their findings support the notion that, "race matters." For example, they suggest that black criminal defendants should prefer to have black jurors. Also, they suggest that the race of the eyewitness in relation to the defendant may have an effect on the jurors' perceptions of the eyewitness's credibility, but this effect does not appear strong enough to influence their verdicts.

is 1.56 times greater in other-race than in same-race conditions and that the witnesses were 1.4 times more likely to correctly identify a previously viewed own-race face as they were to identify an other-race face. Participants were more than 2.2 times as likely to accurately categorize own-race faces as new versus previously viewed as they were to accurately categorize other-race faces.

Stress has also been found to affect the accuracy of identification. There has been research to show that increased violence in videotaped reenactments of crimes leads to decrements in both identification accuracy and eyewitness recall, but this finding is not true in all cases. Morgan et al. (2004) examined the eyewitness capabilities of more than 500 active-duty military personnel enrolled in a survival-school program. After 12 hours of confinement in a mock prisoner-of-war camp, participants experienced both a high-stress interrogation with real physical confrontation and a low-stress interrogation without physical confrontation. Both interrogations were 40 minutes long; they were conducted by different persons. A day after release from the camp, and having recovered from food and sleep deprivation, the participants viewed a 15-person live lineup, a 16-person photo spread, or a sequential presentation of photos of up to

16 persons. Regardless of the testing method, memory accuracy for the high-stress interrogator was much lower overall than for the low-stress interrogator.

The **weapon effect** or weapon focus, refers to the visual attention eyewitnesses give to a perpetrator's weapon during the course of a crime. It has customarily been assumed that the attention the eyewitness focuses on the weapon will reduce his/her ability to later recall details about the perpetrator or to recognize the perpetrator. Researchers have assessed eyewitness recall of various crime details in an attempt to establish the parameters of weapon-focus effects on perception and memory. Various researchers have substantiated the weapon effect but others have found that any surprising object can draw attention away from the perpetrator and that novelty, rather than threat, may be the critical ingredient in the effect (Mitchell, Livosky, & Mather, 1998; Pickel, 1998; Steblay, 1992).

It seems logical that the exposure duration (or amount of time available for viewing a perpetrator) is positively associated with the witness's ability to subsequently identify him or her. Various researchers have found these results as did Shapiro and Penrod (1986) when they had mock witnesses view a realistic videotaped crime in which the target/perpetrator was visible for 12 versus 45 seconds. Witnesses were tested with target-present and target-absent arrays 40 minutes later. The proportion of correct identifications in target-present arrays and correct rejections in target-absent arrays increased substantially when exposure time increased from 12 seconds to 45 seconds (from 32% to 90% for correct identifications and from 15% to 59% for correct rejections), although mistaken identifications in target-absent arrays remained high even with longer exposure (85% at 12 seconds and 41% at 45 seconds). In a similar vain, the retention interval (the time between the crime and the identification test) leads to fewer correct identifications.

A disguise is when criminals use face masks, stockings, hats, and hoods to diminish their facial-feature cues and reduce the likelihood of accurate recognition. In one study, subjects viewed a videotaped liquor store robbery and later attempt an identification from a videotaped lineup. In half of the robberies, the robber wore a knit pullover cap that covered his hair and hairline. In the other half, he did not wear a hat. The robber was less accurately identified when he was disguised: 45% of the participants identified the robber in the lineup test if he wore no hat during the robbery; only 27% identified him if he wore a hat during the robbery (Memon, Hope, & Bull, 2003). Similar results have been obtained by other researchers (e.g., Cutler, Penrod, & Martens, 1987).

If a witness is intoxicated while observing people or events, is he less likely to make accurate identifications later on? Some researchers have answered this question in the affirmative. By testing identification accuracy one week after a staged event using a six-person lineup, it was found that alcohol intoxication while witnessing the event was associated with a lower rate of correct identifications when the level of arousal (manipulated by varying the participants' perceptions of the probability of getting caught stealing an item from an office) was low during the event. Higher blood-alcohol levels have been found to be associated with a higher likelihood of false identification than were lower blood-alcohol levels, but this result was only found in a target-absent situation (where the suspect was shown along with fillers) (Dysart, Lindsay, MacDonald, & Wicke, 2002; Read, Yuille, & Tollestrup, 1992).

System Variables

Law enforcement officers frequently discover that eyewitnesses seldom provide sufficient information to break a case (Kebbell & Milne, 1998). One of the variables in the criminal justice system that may determine whether or not a case is solved, is the manner in which eyewitnesses are interviewed. The **cognitive interview** (CI), as discussed in the chapter on investigations, is an example of a prime system variable allowing for accurate eyewitness statements. The cognitive interview was initially developed by psychologists R. Edward Geiselman and Ronald P. Fisher in the early 1980s (Geiselman et al., 1984; Geiselman, Fisher, Mackinnon, & Holland, 1985) and has resulted in more than two decades of research. Through various adaptations and revisions, the CI in its present form incorporates the social–psychological aspects of face-to-face verbal interaction with what psychologists knew about the way people remember things. A revised CI comprises several phases during which the interviewer engages with and establishes rapport with the witness, asks the witness to provide a narrative account of the witnessed event, and then probes with questions relating to the details the witness has provided. Throughout the process, the interviewer interrupts as little as possible, allows the witness to dictate the subject matter and sequence of questioning, and listens actively to what the witness has to say. As previously indicated, one of the primary aims of the CI is to facilitate the exchange of information between the witness and interviewer through effective communication.

Once the witness has provided an open-ended account, the CI interviewer can probe for details using **open-ended questions** and, when appropriate, can ask follow-up questions to clarify what the witness has said. The interviewer should be guided by the interviewee's pattern of recall rather than adhering to a rigid protocol or predetermined checklist. For example, if an interviewee is describing a suspect's face, this indicates that the mental image of the perpetrator's face is currently active and details about the face are accessible (Pecher, Zeelenberg, & Barsalou, 2003). At this point, the interviewer asks questions relating to the suspect's appearance and not switch to another topic, such as the suspect's car. The interviewer exhausts the content of each image by asking the witness to form an image and then describe it in as much detail as possible.

LINEUPS

At its simplest level, a **lineup** involves placing a suspect among distracters (called fillers or foils) and asking the eyewitness if he/she can identify the suspect (or target). The use of lineups by law enforcement to make identifications can often be troublesome because police officers sometimes give unintentional clues as to the identity of a suspect—whether it's a verbal cue, body language or even an encouraging word to the eyewitness. They may unwittingly make witnesses feel like they've done a good job and picked the "right" guy.

Why does this happen? One reason is that when a victim of a serious crime is placed together with a police investigator wanting to find a suspect and make an arrest, there is a unification of goals. Both have a desire to solve the crime, but if the victim has a very strong desire to solve that crime—as most victims of serious crimes do—they become especially sensitive to any feedback they may receive. And so, if the investigator has a suspect in mind, there remains the possibility that they may communicate that idea to the victim without being aware they are even doing it.

Another reason for this kind of investigator–witness interaction is suggestibility. Suggestibility is defined as the tendency of an individual to accept uncritical information during questioning, or merely complying with what they believe the interviewer wants to hear. There have been studies to suggest that suggestibility depends on a variety of factors, including the questioning techniques utilized by the person posing the questions, and assertiveness of the interviewee (Sadava & McCreary, 1997).

For the reasons mentioned, there are researchers and criminal justice professionals who maintain that all lineups should be conducted on a double-blind basis. The idea of the **double-blind lineup** is straightforward: The person who administers the lineup should not be aware of which lineup member is the suspect and which members are fillers. This recommendation does not presume any intention or awareness on the part of the lineup administrator to influence the eyewitness but only that he/she may unintentionally signal a certain choice or expectation. The signal need not be blatant, even subtle changes in body posture can be enough to tip off the witness. For example, a slight lean forward while the eyewitness views a picture can be enough to indicate approval (Bothwell, Deffenbacher, & Brigham, 1987).

How important are lineups? The case of James Newsome is an example. Newsome served 15 years for a murder he did not commit. His case is an extreme example of an eyewitness making a positive identification from a lineup, even though his memory told him that the man he identified was not the man who committed the murder. After Newsome was proved innocent and the actual perpetrator was found through physical evidence, eyewitness Anthony Rounds came forward and described how Chicago police had forced him to identify Newsome from the lineup, even though he knew that Newsome was not the man he saw commit the murder. According to Rounds, the lineup administrators told Rounds whom to identify; when he resisted, their intimidating insistence led him to identify Newsome and give confident identification testimony at the trial. A lawsuit in 2002 yielded strong evidence to support Rounds's claim, and a jury awarded damages to Newsome; the finding was upheld by the U.S. Seventh Circuit Court of Appeals (*Newsome v. McCabe et al.*, 2002).

In a typical lineup or **photo spread**, the eyewitness sees the suspect and the foils simultaneously. (In a photo spread, the six photos are typically arrayed on a single page. In a live lineup, the suspect and foils are shown together, standing in a line.) This procedure is termed *simultaneous presentation*. In a simultaneous presentation of individuals in a lineup or photo spread, eyewitnesses tend to identify the person who, in their opinion, looks most like the culprit *relative to* other members of the group. In other words, they make a relative judgment. But what happens when the actual culprit is not shown? Under this condition, the relative judgment process will still yield a positive identification because someone in the group will always look *most* like the culprit (Wells et al., 1998).

Contrast this situation with a lineup or photo spread in which the members are presented *sequentially*, one at a time. Here, the eyewitness compares each member in turn to his/her memory of the perpetrator and, on that basis, decides whether any person in the lineup is the individual who committed the crime. This is an absolute judgment process. The value of sequential presentation is that it decreases the likelihood that an eyewitness will make a relative judgment in choosing someone from the lineup or photo spread. A meta-analysis by Meissner and associates supported the observation by other researchers of lower mistaken identification rates for the sequential than for the simultaneous lineup. The characteristics of the fillers used in a lineup also have a strong influence on the chances that an innocent suspect will be identified. In general, if the innocent suspect fits the description of the target and the fillers do not, the innocent suspect is likely to be mistakenly identified (Meissner & Brigham, 2001).

What are some of the structural aspects of a lineup that can be considered to be "suggestive" and therefore increase the likelihood of a positive identification? The research suggests these are (1) the heterogeneity of the lineup, (2) the instructions administered to the witness prior to viewing the lineup, and (3) the manner in which the individuals in the lineup are presented to the witness.

Heterogeneity of Lineup (Foil Bias)

Lineups that do not contain propitious heterogeneity are biased. Propitious heterogeneity exists if foils match the description of the perpetrator as given by the witness but vary on characteristics not mentioned in the witness's description. Researchers have reliably demonstrated that biased foils increase the rate of false identifications made by eyewitnesses (Luus & Wells, 1991). The size of a lineup (when it contains too few people) can also have deleterious effects on accurate identification. It is common practice in the United States to use five or six persons (a suspect plus four or five fillers) in a live lineup, and six or eight photos in a photo lineup (see Lindsay & Wells, 1980; Wells, 1993; Wells & Lindsay, 1993). But the opposite does not seem to hold true, that is, the research on eyewitness identification has not shown that increased lineup size after a certain point is related to in accurate identification. There does not seem to be a drop in accurate-identification rates when lineup sizes were increased from 10 to 40 persons. In fact, the literature includes reports of eyewitnesses being able to view up to about 300 photos with little reduction in the chances of an accurate identification (see Levi, 2002).

Instructions Administered to the Witness (Instruction Bias)

Instructions given a witness by the police to the effect that the culprit is definitely in the lineup, or strongly implying this by not advising the witness that the perpetrator may not be in the lineup at all, increases the rate of false identifications and is representative of bias (Cutler, Penrod, & Martens, 1987; Malpass & Devine, 1981; Paley & Geiselman, 1989).

Manner in which Individuals in the Lineup are Presented (Presentation Bias)

As previously indicated, simultaneous lineups present all the members of the lineup at the same time, thus requiring the witness to compare them with one another before making an identification decision. Sequential lineups present one lineup member at a time to the witness, which allows the witness to make an identification decision independently, before viewing the next lineup member, and without the need for comparing members. Rather, the witness is comparing the presented member only with his/her own memory. During a sequential lineup, the witness is not informed regarding how many lineup members he/she will be viewing, seeing and is instructed that she or he may not go back to view a previously viewed lineup member (Wells, 1993). As mentioned above, research comparing simultaneous to sequential lineup presentation have found fewer false identifications when suspects are sequentially presented, as opposed to simultaneously presented (Cutler & Penrod, 1988; Lindsay, Lea, & Fulford, 1991; Lindsay & Wells, 1985; Lindsay et al., 1991).

WHAT THE LAW TELLS US ABOUT EYEWITNESS IDENTIFICATION AND ACCURACY

In 1967, the U.S. Supreme Court decided three cases (*United States v. Wade, Gilbert v. California,* and *Stovall v. Denno*) reinforcing the critical importance of information obtained from lineups in the suspect identification process. But the Court's decisions and recommendations were made without any substantial contribution from psychological science (Brigham et al., 1999).

In *Wade,* the Court declared that a suspect has the constitutional right to the presence of counsel during a live lineup. This decision was reversed five years later in *Kirby v. Illinois* (1972), however, when the right to counsel during identification proceedings was limited to after an indictment had been formally laid down. A direct result of this revision, was that police began conducted their identification procedures before arresting suspects and without the presence of counsel. One year later in *United States v. Ash* (1973), the Supreme Court ruled that there was no right to counsel at any identification procedure, including photo identification. The Court reasoned that because the identification procedures could be reconstructed at trial and analyzed for suggestibility, there was no need for counsel at the identification stage. In reaching their decision, the Court may have relied to some extent on psychological research suggesting that the effectiveness of these legal safeguards were limited in that attorneys are insensitive to factors that influence the suggestiveness of lineups (Stinson, Devenport, Cutler, & Kravitz, 1996) and that most attorneys were not even present at these identification sessions (Stinson et al., 1996).

In *Neil v. Biggers* (1972) and *Manson v. Braithwaite* (1977) the Court established a total of five factors that determine the reliability of an identification: (1) the witness's opportunity to view the criminal during the crime, (2) the length of time between the crime and the subsequent identification, (3) the level of certainty demonstrated by the witness at the identification, (4) the accuracy of the witness's prior description of the suspect, and (5) the witness's degree of attention during the crime. As in previous decisions, these criteria were established without the consultation of psychological experts on perception and memory. Subsequent research has shown that only two of the factors listed in these cases are actually related to the estimation of the accuracy of identification (opportunity to observe and the length of the retention interval). However, research has also shown that even these factors are affected by other variables, such as race or stress.

A quarter of a century after *Neil v. Biggers* and *Manson v. Braithwaite,* Attorney General Janet Reno commissioned a report based on Barry Scheck and Peter Neufeld's **Innocence Project** in New York City, which used DNA evidence to examine claims of innocence by people who were convicted by juries based primarily on eyewitness testimony. In fact, the commission discovered that 52 of the first 62 DNA exonerations were mistaken-identification cases (Wells et al., 1998). At the urging of Attorney General Reno, a National Institute of Justice report, *Eyewitness Evidence: A Guide for Law Enforcement*, suggested specific guidelines for the conduct of initial reports, the composition of mug books, witness interviews, field identification procedures, and lineups. In her introduction to the published guidelines, Reno stated that it was absolutely essential that eyewitness evidence be accurate and reliable. She also acknowledged the growing body of research in the field of eyewitness identification as support for the guidelines.

Among the recommendations adopted by the Justice Department were the following:

1. When obtaining information from the witness(es), the investigating officer should ask open-ended questions (e.g., "What can you tell me about the car?") and avoid leading questions (e.g., "Was the car red?").
2. The investigator conducting the photo spread or lineup should instruct the witness that the person who committed the crime may or may not be present. This rule is aimed at reducing the tendency for eyewitnesses to pick the person in a lineup who looks most like the culprit relative to the others, a judgment that encourages false identifications when the actual culprit is not included in the lineup.
3. In composing a photo spread or lineup, the investigator should select fillers who generally fit the witness's description of the perpetrator. It would not be fair to create a photo spread or lineup in which only the suspect fit the prior description of "a man with a beard." In such circumstances, if a nonwitness was simply told the description of the culprit and then saw the photographs showing only one man with a beard, the nonwitness would be able to pick out the suspect.
4. After conducting an identification procedure, the investigator should record the witness's own words regarding how sure he/she is of any identification. This recommendation is based on the fact that eyewitnesses often express increased confidence in their identifications after they are told by the police that they picked out the real culprit or after they learn additional information that implicates the person they identified.

AMELIORATIVE METHODS TO PROBLEMS ASSOCIATED WITH EYEWITNESS IDENTIFICATION AND LINEUPS

Trial Simulation

Trial simulation have been designed to assess, among other things, juror sensitivity to factors that affect eyewitness memory. In these experiments, some testimony and evidence are systematically varied, whereas other evidence and testimony are held constant (e.g., Bell & Loftus, 1985; Cutler, Penrod, & Dexter, 1990; Lindsay, Lim, Marando, & Cully, 1986). In trial simulations, participants are asked to assume the role of jurors while reading a written summary of a trial, hearing an audio simulation, or viewing a video simulation, after which they report their verdicts and other reactions to the trial. Juror sensitivity is indicated by significant effects of factors that are known to influence identification accuracy and by nonsignificant effects of factors that are known to not predict identification accuracy (e.g., Cutler, Penrod, & Dexter, 1990).

One trial simulation study conducted by Cutler, Penrod, and Stuve (1988) examined juror sensitivity to ten factors that varied in the extent to which they influence eyewitness identification performance. Factors included in the design were the presence or absence of instruction bias and foil bias, as well as the level of witness confidence. Participants were 321 students who each viewed a version of a videotaped trial simulation and who served as mock jurors. The results indicated that jurors were not sensitive to the importance of information that affected eyewitness accuracy. In fact, they appeared to pay little attention to such factors when evaluating evidence and rendering verdicts. A replication study by the same authors in 1990 found similar results.

Motion to Suppress

Counsel who feel they may be adversely affected by prejudiced evidence resulting from eyewitness identification, may request to be present at postindictment lineups, or they may file a Motion to suppress identifications. Motions to suppress are legal devices used to prevent evidence from entering a trial that has been secured illegally, or in violation of a constitutional right. For eyewitness identification issues, the rights most likely to be implicated would be the Fourth Amendment (search and seizure), or the Sixth Amendment (right to confront witnesses, etc.) (Black, 1990; Federal Rules of Criminal Procedure, 12(b) and 41(f)).

Voire Dire

The lawyers for each side of a case can survey and inform the jury regarding knowledge about sources of eyewitness unreliability, the ability of jurors to differentiate accurate from inaccurate eyewitnesses, and the probabilistic nature of factors that influence perception, storage, and retrieval of information in general. Several studies using survey methodology have administered the *Knowledge of Eyewitness Behavior Questionnaire* (Deffenbacher & Loftus, 1982) to assess juror knowledge about the factors that influence eyewitness identification accuracy (Deffenbacher & Loftus, 1982; McConkey & Roche, 1989; Noon & Hollin, 1987). Although these studies examined prospective jurors' knowledge about the factors that influence eyewitness identification accuracy, they did not assess which factors jurors attend to when evaluating eyewitness testimony in court and when rendering verdicts. Research that is conducted using postdiction methodology (prediction after the fact) has found that laypersons often predict higher identification accuracy rates than are generally found among participants in eyewitness research (Brigham & Bothwell, 1983; Wells, 1984). Of course, the presence of juror bias or personal experiences that might influence their decision making in a case should be evaluated as in any trial.

Expert Witness

An expert witness, if accepted by a court, may be asked to comment on the reliability of eyewitness testimony in general, the construction and composition of lineups and photo arrays in particular, and many other topics as well. The expert witness should be prepared to discuss the strengths and weaknesses of the data on which he/she bases an opinion. Research has shown that if done correctly and with sincerity, expert testimony does enhance juror sensitivity to factors influencing witnessing and identification conditions (Cutler, Penrod, & Dexter, 1989; Wells, 1986). Chapter 13 will present more information on how to deal with the expert witness. Suffice it to say, depending on the rules of evidence in effect in the trial's jurisdiction, the judge must determine whether this evidence would be of assistance to the court or is scientifically reliable within that particular discipline.

Cross-Examination

It has been established that an expert witness can be used to a limited extent for explaining to the judge and jury (or the judge alone in a bench trial) the factors associated with eyewitness accuracy and credibility. But this is only the beginning for such a witness. Although direct examination is utilized to provide a venue for the expert to express the relevant research and current state of scientific knowledge on these issues, cross examination is the means by which opposing counsel will attack these assessments and opinions to the greatest extent possible. In fact, cross-examination, more than other trial technique, is the most commonly implemented safeguard against erroneous conviction resulting purely from mistaken identification. Its use is essential. There is nothing worse than allowing an expert witness to state opinions without challenge. The jury (or jury) may believe that failure to cross-examine an expert witness is the equivalent of the other side in a case simply "accepting" the expert's opinion.

Cross-examining an expert witness should never be taken lightly, or conducted without sufficient preparation by counsel. Thorough preparation on the subject that will be the basis of a lawyer's questioning is the sine qua non of any good cross-examination. A trial attorney preparing to cross-examine an expert witness should first read and summarize the deposition taken of the expert witness in the case or read and summarize prior depositions given by that same expert in other cases (Cantor, 2009). Additionally, a trial attorney is well advised to research whether a particular expert has written any articles, books or editorials that may contradict his opinion in the case at hand. Determining what schools or universities the expert graduated from is helpful, as professors may be found that taught the expert and who have different opinions regarding eyewitness testimony. This information may be introduced and compared to the expert's opinion at trial (Sylvester, 2007). But it is always more advisable to undermine an expert's qualifications than the expert's theory or conclusions, and this should never seem like an "attack" since this can arouse sympathy from the jury toward the expert, and hostility toward the lawyer conducting the cross-examination (and his/her case).

All told, research on eyewitness testimony and accuracy has made considerable progress in convincing a number of jurisdictions in the United States to improve their identification procedures. The state of New Jersey, for example, has adopted an entire package of reforms for how it conducts lineups. These reforms are based explicitly on the eyewitness literature and include the adoption of recommendations for selecting lineup fillers, instructing eyewitnesses before the lineup, using double-blind lineup administrators, using the sequential procedure, and obtaining a confidence statement from the eyewitness before external factors can influence the person's confidence. Other jurisdictions—including the states of Wisconsin and North Carolina and the cities of Boston and Minneapolis—have also adopted these reforms.

Forensic psychologists are playing a central role in explaining the psychological literature and helping translate the findings into practical reforms of eyewitness identification procedures. Increasingly, forensic psychology researchers are publishing their findings in actual law enforcement, legal, and judicial journals to make their findings more directly accessible to these entities. As just one example, police investigators are being educated on basic procedures for obtaining reliable and accurate information from eyewitnesses, conducting identification procedures, avoiding leading or suggestive questions, and instructing witnesses that the actual perpetrator may or may not be present during lineup procedures. Psychologists are also educating judges about eyewitness testimony's unreliability and why eyewitnesses make errors. One of the major goals here is to prevent witness biases and false identifications from occurring in the first place.

FORENSIC PSYCHOLOGY IN THE SPOTLIGHT

Do Older Adults Make Poor Eyewitnesses?

Dodson and Krueger (2006)

Researchers at the University of Virginia found through a series of experiments that when younger and older adults were matched on their overall memory for experienced events, both groups showed comparable rates of suggestibility errors in which they claimed to have seen events in a video that had been suggested in a subsequent questionnaire. However, older adults were "alarmingly" likely to commit these suggestibility errors when they were most confident about the correctness of their response. Younger people were more likely to commit these errors when they were uncertain about the accuracy of their response.

Previous studies by other investigators have shown that older adults are more likely than younger people to "remember" events that did not occur, and to misremember events that did occur. The study further suggests that this occurs because older adults are more inclined to miscombine details of events, which results in a high degree of confidence that they are remembering these details accurately.

Participants in the study were shown a 5-minute video clip reenacting a burglary and police chase. They were then asked to answer 24 yes/no questions about what they had witnessed in the video. Eight of those questions referred to details that never actually happened in the video, such as suggesting the presence of a gun when in fact no gun ever appeared in the video itself.

Prior to completing the memory test, the participants were told that some of the test questions would refer to details that had not actually occurred in the video. They were asked to indicate for each test question whether it had occurred in the video only, in the questionnaire only, or neither. They were also asked to judge the likely accuracy of their response, essentially whether they were guessing or certain. It was here that the confidence level, even when wrong, was much higher among older adults than younger adults.

"This finding suggests that this is not simply a case of poorer memory among older adults, but that there may be some other mechanism leading to the high rate of confidence," Dodson said. "We believe the high confidence comes from the detail that they believe they remember. Because the detail seems sharp, they are highly confident that they are correct in their recollection, even when the recollection has been suggested to them rather than actually witnessed. This pattern of behavior is particularly worrisome, given the influence of eyewitness confidence on jury decision making."

The older study participants were 60–80 years of age, while the younger participants were college students. There were three study groups: the older participants who all took the questionnaire immediately after seeing the video, a young group who also took the questionnaire immediately after seeing the video, and a group of younger participants who answered the questionnaire two days after seeing the video to replicate the memory differences between older and younger adults.

Chad Dodson, the study's lead researcher, stated, "Given that older adults will constitute an increasing proportion of the U.S. population, there may be a corresponding increase in the occurrence of wrongful convictions based on the testimony of highly confident but mistaken eyewitnesses."

Summary

This chapter emphasized the importance of eyewitness testimony as a means of influencing jurors at trial. Despite the tremendous impact that such testimony can have, it is unfortunately fraught with errors that have resulted in innocent people being sent to prison or even executed.

The research suggests numerous factors that account for the unreliability of eyewitness identification. These include factors relating to the eyewitness such as stress, perceptual problems, faulty memory, conformity behavior, cross-race issues, the weapon effect and intoxication. There are also numerous situational factors that affect accuracy of identification. These include suggestive identification procedures and questioning by police, faulty lineups construction using inappropriate fillers, and employing the less reliable simultaneous presentation method (where members of the lineup are presented all together) instead of the more reliable sequential method (where members are presented one by one). The latter method allows for absolute judgments while the former encourages relative (and less accurate) judgments.

Department of Justice recommendations for conducting lineups were presented and include such factors as asking open-ended questions and informing witnesses that the suspect may or may not be present in the lineup. Finally, the importance of educating the criminal justice system to the frailties of eyewitness identification was stressed, as was the need for implementing positive changes that make it more likely that only the guilty are punished.

Key Terms

Cognitive interview *202*

Cross-race identification *200*

Double-blind lineup *204*

Encoding *199*

Estimator variables *200*

Innocence Project *206*

Instruction bias *205*

Lineup *203*

Open-ended questions *203*

Photo spread *204*

Presentation bias *205*

Retrieval *200*

Storage *200*

System variables *200*

Unconscious transference *197*

Weapons effect *202*

Yerkes–Dodson law *199*

Review Questions

1. Why is eyewitness testimony often considered the most important kind of evidence next to an actual confession?
2. What parts did Albert Binet and Hugo Munsterberg play in the history of eyewitness identification issues?
3. What role does memory encoding, storage, and retrieval play in eyewitness accuracy?
3. What does the Yerkes–Dodson law say?
4. What are estimator variables, and how are they related to eyewitness accuracy?
5. What are system variables, and how are they related to eyewitness accuracy?

6. What is meant by a "cognitive interview"?
7. What is the "cross-race effect"?
8. What are some of the factors in lineups that determine their effectiveness?
9. What is the "weapons effect"?
10. What is the difference between simultaneous and sequential presentation in a lineup? Which is generally considered to be superior?
11. What are some of the ways psychologists and the legal system attempt to ameliorate the deleterious effects of false identifications?

Chapter Resources on the World Wide Web

Investigator-Witness Interactions
http://www.pbs.org/wgbh/pages/frontline/shows/dna/interviews/loftus.html

Lineups and Eyewitness Identification
http://www.psy.unsw.edu.au/~kipw/Lectures/3rdYearPsychLaw/PL7-Eyewitness_files/v3_document.htm

Crime Statistics in the United States
www.fbi.gov/ucr/cius_04/offenses_reported/violent_crime/index.html

Forensic Psychology and Eyewitness Recall
http://www.campsych.com/eyewitness.htm

Psychology and Crime News
http://crimepsychblog.com/?p=1382

Social Psychology and Eyewitness Testimony
http://www.uplink.com.au/lawlibrary/Documents/Docs/Doc51.html

Academy of Criminal Justice Sciences
http://www.acjs.org/

The Innocence Project
http://www.innocenceproject.org/

For Further Reading

Buckhout, R. (1974). Eyewitness testimony. *Scientific American, 231*, 23–31.

Loftus, E. F. (1979). *Eyewitness testimony.* Cambridge, MA: Harvard University Press.

Penrod, S. D., Loftus, E. F., & Winkler, J. (1982). *The reliability of eyewitness testimony: A psychological perspective.* In N. L. Kerr & R. M. Bray (Eds.), *The psychology of the courtroom.* Orlando, FL: Academic Press.

Brewer, N., Weber, N., & Semmler, C. (2005). Eyewitness identification. In N. Brewer & K. D. Williams (Eds.), *Psychology and law: An empirical perspective.* New York: Guilford.

Kassin, S. M., & Gudjonsson, G. H. (2004). The psychology of confessions: A review of the literature and issues. *Psychological Science in the Public Interest, 5*, 33–67.

Wells, G. L., & Luus, E. (1990). Police lineups as experiments: Social methodology as a framework for properly conducted lineups. *Personality and Social Psychology Bulletin, 16*, 106–117.

CHAPTER 10

Psychology of False Confessions

CHAPTER OBJECTIVES

After reading this chapter you would:

- Understand how confessions play a role in religion and psychotherapy.
- Appreciate why confessions are such a powerful form of evidence.
- Know the three types of false confessions.
- Understand the factors that make a person vulnerable to forced confessions.
- Know the difference between minimization and maximization.
- Know the impact of *Miranda* rights on false confessions.
- Know how police interrogations can be improved.
- Understand the definition of false memories and confabulation.

INTRODUCTION

In 1989, a female jogger was severely beaten, raped, and left for dead in New York City's Central Park. She had multiple skull fractures, a crushed eye socket, and bled profusely. She survived the attack but had no memory of the incident. Within two days of the attack five African-American and Hispanic boys, 14–16 years old, were arrested. They were interrogated by police and ultimately confessed to the crime. At their trials, four of the videotaped confessions were presented, which described the role of each defendant in the attack in graphic detail. All the boys were convicted and sentenced.

In 2002, Matias Reyes, already in prison for three rapes and a murder committed subsequent to the Central Park attack, confessed to the crime. He stated that he had raped the Central Park jogger and that he had acted alone. The district attorney's office questioned Reyes and discovered that he had accurate, privileged, and independently corroborated knowledge of the crime and crime scene. In addition, DNA testing revealed that the semen samples originally recovered from the victim belonged to Reyes. These DNA samples had originally excluded the boys as the donors but prosecutors at the time argued that the police may not have captured all the perpetrators in the alleged gang rape, but this did not mean they did not get some of them. Yet in December 2002, the defendants' convictions were vacated after it became clear that their detailed confessions were false. Unfortunately, this was not a new phenomenon.

As a result of technological advances in forensic DNA typing—which now enables investigators to review past cases in which blood, hair, semen, skin, saliva, or other biological material has been preserved—many new cases of wrongful convictions have emerged. Reliable estimates, such as those from the Innocence Project, suggest that at least 25% of innocent defendants (especially in homicide cases) who confess to the crimes would be exonerated by DNA evidence (White, 2003).

CONFESSIONS IN HISTORICAL PERSPECTIVE

Throughout history, confessions have been pivotal in three arenas: religion, psychotherapy, and criminal law.

Confession in Religion

Confession in religion is usually a mechanism by which adherents acknowledge and disclose their transgressions. The purposes served by these confessions are to cleanse the individual's soul and to deter further wrongdoing in the religious community.

In the Jewish faith a penitent sinner must give verbal expression of his remorse: He must confess his sin before God pardons him. But confessing to God is only appropriate for sins committed against God. For sins committed against other people, forgiveness must be asked directly from them. Confessing sins and making amends are possible at any time but are most evident during the high holy day of Yom Kippur. The Yom Kippur confession is a public and communal act, recited in the plural.

For Catholics, confession is the popular name for the Sacrament of Penance or Reconciliation recognized by the Roman Catholic and Orthodox churches. The rite consists in the acknowledgment of sins to a priest, who grants absolution in the name of God. Buddhist teaching (dharma) stresses that to successfully walk on the eightfold path it is necessary to observe a strict moral discipline, not commit evil, and purify one's mind by mental discipline. Hindus do not practice formal confession, but many gurus, monks, and swamis give an ear to the devotees, thereby reducing their pain in times of trouble.

Confession in Psychotherapy

Confession is an ancient medicinal practice. Natives of North and South America believed that physical and mental purity was achieved in part through elaborate confession ceremonies involving shamans and witch doctors. In the early stages of the psychoanalytic movement, Freud observed that patients often felt better after purging the mind of material buried beneath consciousness. For Freud and other psychoanalysts this was called "catharsis." The idea of catharsis is traceable to Greek tragedies in which incidents in plays arousing pity and fear would vicariously purge, purify, or morally reeducate those watching the tragedy. Catharsis has been used as a cleansing or purification process worldwide through healing rituals and confession.

The idea that expressing feelings is healing and restorative, while bottling up or suppressing them is unhealthy, became a widely held belief in certain prevailing periods of psychological thought (or "zeitgeist") in this country as well as Europe. It is still relatively common for psychologists to provide relief to patients by having them unearth, talk about, and "relive" previously suppressed hurts and traumas. Some forms of therapy have traditionally emphasized the discharge of emotions. Others emphasize the importance of "understanding" the events associated with emotional expression, and still others focus on the restructuring of thoughts, cognitions, and beliefs associated with emotions. Although psychologists may not agree on why emotional recall is curative, most endorse or encourage such expression.

There is recent research confirming the therapeutic effects of opening up and "letting go" rather than keeping confessional secrets (Smyth, 1998). In a study of women who had undergone an abortion, those who talked about it to an experimenter—compared with those who did not—were later less disturbed by intrusive thoughts of the experience. Other studies have found that recently infected men with the Human Immunodeficiency Virus showed a more rapid spread of infection and greater rate of mortality in those men who kept their orientation and life styles a secret compared with those who were open about their sexual orientation and identity (Major & Gramzow, 1999).

Confession in the Criminal Law

Confessions play a vital role in law enforcement, crime control, and the criminal justice system. But they also raise reoccurring questions as to whether a statement is authentic and voluntary and was procured without undue pressure and with a knowing waiver of rights. Because of this, American courts have developed guidelines for the admission of confession evidence at trial. Typically, in any case involving a disputed confession, a preliminary hearing is held so that a judge can determine whether the confession was voluntary and, hence, admissible as evidence. A judge will admit confessions deemed voluntary either without special instruction or with directions to the jury to make an independent judgment of voluntariness and disregard statements they find to be coerced.

In the landmark case of **Brown v. Mississippi** (1936) three black men were arrested on a charge of murder. The men were not allowed to consult with an attorney and were subsequently threatened, beaten, and tortured. Each of the three men eventually signed a police written "confession" to the murder. Each defendant was convicted and then sentenced to death. The Supreme Court reversed the convictions on the grounds that the police had violated the defendants' constitutional rights to due process of law. It was ruled that evidence procured through physical torture cannot be admitted into evidence in trial and that "[a trial] is a mere pretense where the state authorities have continued a conviction resting solely upon confessions obtained by violence" (p. 287).

In the *Brown* case, the precedent was thereby established that a state court conviction based upon an extorted confession by brutality violates a defendant's due process rights under the Fourteenth Amendment. And in **Miranda v. Arizona** (1966), the Supreme Court ruled that unless the accused is advised by the police of his constitutional rights to remain silent and to obtain counsel, all **self-incriminating** statements are inadmissible in court.

Coerced or not, the reality of the situation regarding confessions is that most are not spontaneously made but rather are the result of negotiations with the prosecution. In addition, 20% of all confessions are later recanted. Most surprising, however, is how often confessions are made by individuals who are absolutely innocent.

THE PSYCHOLOGY OF FALSE CONFESSIONS

Aside from the use of torture or extreme measures, why would an innocent person confess to a crime he did not commit? From a psychoanalytical perspective, some theorists such as Theodor Reik believed that false statements originate from an unconscious need to confess and be punished (Conti, 1999).

Some criminal investigators follow a step-by-step process by which to elicit a confession from a suspect by using deceit and psychological manipulation. Suspects are told that the police have evidence linking them to the crime where none exists or try to minimize the seriousness of the offense suggesting that anyone else under similar conditions or circumstances might have done the same thing (Inbau, Reid, Buckley, & Jayne, 2001). Hugo Munsterberg was probably the first psychologist to express a view on untrue confessions in his book **On the Witness Stand** (1908). He expressed the belief that in some instances the innocent confessing person actually believes himself to be guilty and that such confessions (called "pseudo-confessions") occurred even in defendants who were psychologically normal.

Three Types of False Confessions

1. **Voluntary false confessions** are self-incriminating statements that are purposefully offered in the absence of pressure by the police (Bedau & Putnam, 1996). Sometimes false confessions are offered to protect a friend or relative, a fact often revealed in interviews with juvenile defenders. There are several possible reasons for why people give voluntary false confessions. A pathological need for fame and recognition is one, or as Note (1953) described it, a morbid desire for notoriety.

A case on point concerns the 1996 murder of six-year-old JonBenet Ramsey who was found dead in the basement of her parents' home in Boulder, Colorado, nearly 8 hours after she was reported missing. The case drew attention throughout the United States when no suspect was charged and suspicions turned to possible family involvement. On August 16, 2006, the case returned to the news when John Mark Karr, a 41-year-old school teacher living in Bangkok, confessed to her murder. Karr seemed eager to implicate himself in the crime yet also professed love for the child.

Waiving extradition, Karr was flown from Thailand back to Boulder, Colorado. He received legal assistance from a public defender, despite the fact that dozens of lawyers had offered to represent him (for free in many cases). But on August 28, 2006, the Boulder County District Attorney's Office announced that the case of *People v. John Mark Karr* has been vacated. The reason for this was that the DNA taken from Karr's hair and saliva after his arrest, and tested by the Denver Police Department's crime lab, did not match the DNA found on JonBenét Ramsey's body. The actual motive for Karr having made the false confession is not known, although possibilities include notoriety, pervasive guilt over past transgressions (he allegedly had a history of involvement with child pornography), or even a deliberate tactic to avoid jail in Thailand on other charges.

There is also no clear answer to why someone like Karr would proclaim that his involvement in a crime merited a charge of "second-degree murder," as Karr is reported to have told police in Thailand, without being told by police that a lesser charge might be possible. Most suspects do not come to the police and say "I committed second-degree murder." There is research indicating that aggressive interrogation can cause people to admit to crimes they did not commit for a host of reasons, including a desire to escape punishment (e.g., for crimes committed in another jurisdiction or even another country) or, as will be explored in the following sections, suggestibility and misunderstanding of the consequences of a confession, or even the actual belief by the individual that he did in fact commit the crime. The circumstances surrounding John Mark Karr's confession continue to be troubling to this day.

2. Coerced-compliant false confessions occur when suspects confess, despite the knowledge of their innocence, due to extreme methods of police interrogations. Numerous false confessions elicited through the use of torture, threats, and false promises were presumed to be of this type, as in the Salem witchcraft confessions in the seventeenth century. The technique of "brainwashing," commonly used on prisoners of war (POWs), falls into this category. During the Korean War, for example, a number of captured American military men had confessed to a number of treasonable acts and expressions of disloyalty to the United States (Bem, 1966; Wrightsman & Kassin, 1993).

Some American POWs in the Vietnam War also made coerced-compliant false confessions. More recently, during the Persian Gulf War captured American airmen made similar statements on Iraqi television, and in 2007, members of the British Royal Navy also made forced statements implicating Great Britain in negligently entering Iranian waters.

One of the most infamous cases of false confession was that of Jessie Misskelley, Jr., who was convicted of participating in the sex murders of three boys in West Memphis, Arkansas, in 1993, and whose confession may have been false. Misskelley was 17 at the time of the confession and had an IQ of 72 (considerably below the average IQ of 100). After the trial had ended, an independent investigator studied the autopsy photographs with particular attention to the images of bite marks on the face of one of the murder victims. Their pattern did not match Misskelley's teeth or those of the other two teenagers who were also convicted of the murders. Although a polygraph test suggested he was telling the truth, Misskelley was interrogated for over 5 hours before he confessed. He retracted his confession afterwards, claiming that he had caved in under police pressure. An expert testified at the trial that Jessie was a prime candidate for a false confession because of his young age and low IQ level. The Arkansas Supreme Court in its ruling in the Misskelley case noted that the voluntariness of a confession is judged on many factors, including the age, education, and intelligence of the accused; the advice or lack of advice on constitutional rights; the length of detention; the repeated or prolonged nature of questioning; or the use of mental or physical punishment (*Misskelley v. State*, 1996).

There are many more cases where individuals with borderline levels of intelligence may have given false confessions. One of these is Girvies Davis, who in 1979, at age 20, confessed to 11 crimes, including the murder of an 89-year-old man in Belleville, Illinois. Davis was an alcoholic with a childhood history of brain damage and suicide attempts. During his teen years, he was diagnosed with "organic brain dysfunction," which doctors believe was induced by a bicycle accident when he was ten years old. There was no evidence linking him to the murder other than the confession, which, because of Davis's intellectual deficiency and likely suggestibility, could have been erroneously given or coerced. Nevertheless, the police say he "freely confessed," and the state of Illinois executed him on May 18, 1995.

But what constitutes "brutality" or "pressure" for the purposes of a coerced confession? In *Chambers v. Florida* (1940), the Supreme Court ruled that five days of prolonged questioning and other factors that fell just short of physical violence elicited concerns that the confessions given by the defendants could be false. In such a case, an investigation into the "totality of the circumstances" surrounding a confession is required. In the case of *Haynes v. Washington* (1963), the defendant was refused telephone contact with his family and attorney and was told by police that these requests might be granted as soon as he made a statement. Here the Supreme Court ruled that the defendant's confession was coerced by the fact that the defendant's "will" was subverted in an atmosphere of substantial coercion and inducement created by promises made by interrogators.

3. Coerced-internalized false confessions occur when suspects who are innocent actually come to believe that they committed a crime. This may be due to anxiety, fatigue, pressure, confusion, or highly suggestive methods of police interrogation. The interesting quality of these false confessions is that the innocent person's memory is actually altered so that original memory contents can become irretrievable. Recent studies have found that misleading postevent information can indeed alter actual or reported memories of observed events and that it is even possible to "implant" false memories of childhood experiences (Kassin & Sukel, 1997; Kassin & Wrightsman, 1985).

A famous case of a coerced-internalized false confession is that of Paul Ingram in 1988. Ingram was married with five children, and a deputy sheriff for 17 years (one of the top three law enforcement officers in the Thurston County Sheriff's Department). He was chairman of the Thurston County Republican Party, and he and his wife were active members of the Church of Living Waters, a fundamentalist Pentecostal congregation.

While attending a church retreat, Ingram's oldest daughter, Ericka, was told by a spiritual healer (a former stand-up comic) that she was influenced by God with information regarding Ericka, specifically that Ericka had been sexually abused as a child. She further informed Ericka that the abuse was by her father and that it had been happening for years. Ericka later made a statement to the police that her father had been molesting both her sister and her for years. In addition, she claimed that her father had presided over hundreds of satanic rituals in which some 25 live babies were slaughtered and sacrificed (Loftus & Ketcham, 1994).

Ingram was arrested and subjected to numerous police interrogations. He was also hypnotized by his minister and told by a "police psychologist" that sex offenders often repress memories of such events, which supports the likelihood that he was guilty of the offense. After five months Ingram confessed to sexually assaulting his two daughters and killing the infants in satanic rituals. He even claimed to "remember" these events in graphic detail.

Dr. Richard Ofshe, an expert on how the social organization of some cult groups can cause the exploitation of members, was called in as an expert witness in the case. He is also an expert in the areas of interrogations, false confessions, and the creation of "**pseudo-memories**" in patients at the hand of unscrupulous, incompetent psychotherapists. Ofshe was not convinced that Ingram's memories were genuine and was suspicious that the memories could have been implanted in Ingram. He decided to test his theory by telling Ingram completely false information (e.g., that his children disclosed that he had forced them to engage in sexual activities with each other). After repeated questioning Ingram began to "remember" these events and even wrote a three-page confession detailing the events. But this did not change the outcome of the case. His request to change his plea to not guilty was denied, and he was sentenced to 20 years in prison for crimes he did not commit and that likely never even took place. He was finally released from prison on April 8, 2003.

Does Giving False Evidence lead Vulnerable People to Confess to an Act They Did Not Commit and then Internalize the Confession?

Kassin & Kiechel (1996)

Researchers asked 79 students to participate in a supposed reaction time experiment. After being warned not to touch the "ALT" key because the computer would crash, a confederate (a person who is actually part of the experiment) dictated letters to the participants in two different speeds as a means of manipulating their vulnerability by controlling their belief that they might make a mistake. They were all asked to type these letters using the computer keyboard. After 60 seconds, the computer was purposefully crashed by the experimenters. None of the participants were actually responsible for causing the computer to crash; however, each was blamed for doing so.

Half of the participants were told that the confederate had seen them hit the "ALT" key. Participants were then asked to sign a handwritten confession that they had hit the "ALT" key causing the computer to crash. Overall, 69% of the subjects signed the confession, 28% internalized their guilt (believing they had hit the wrong button), and 9% confabulated details to fit with their false belief that they had caused the computer to crash. The most vulnerable group was the fast typing/false evidence (having been "seen" hit the key); 100% of this group signed the confession.

This study by Kassin & Kiechel supported the idea that when presented with false evidence, people can be induced to internalize guilt for an event with which they had no involvement.

Why do False Confessions Occur?

Some researchers and theorists have compared the generation of internalized false confessions to hypnosis (see, e.g., Gudjonsson & Clark, 1986; Ofshe & Watters, 1994). Foster (1969) has referred to such trance-like states of heightened suggestibility in suspects being interrogated by police as the "station house syndrome" (pp. 690–691). Other researchers have proposed that certain individuals are more prone to **interrogative suggestibility** due to social isolation and high anxiety levels during interrogations, generalized poor self-esteem, unassertiveness, and especially low levels of intelligence.

An example of oversuggestibility due to low intelligence can be found in the case of **Delbert Ward**, an introverted 59-year-old farmer with an IQ of 69 (placing him at the upper end of the mentally retarded range). Ward lived with his four brothers in a two-room shack without electricity or running water for over 60 years. On June 6, 1990, the brother who shared a bed with Delbert was found dead, and Delbert was suspected as having suffocated his chronically ailing and suffering brother as an act of mercy. Following long hours of questioning by state troopers, Delbert eventually signed a false confession. At his trial for murder, after 9 hours of deliberation, the jury acquitted Delbert. Many forensic psychologists and psychiatrists agreed at the time that Delbert would have been so nervous and confused at the time of his interrogation that he would have agreed with anything and that his goal would likely be just to free himself from the threatening and uncomfortable situation of the interrogation more than anything else (Wecht, 1994). The events of this case were later turned into a movie titled *My Brother's Keeper*.

Along these lines, **rational choice theory** posits that some suspects falsely confess because interrogation convinces them that confessing is the most rational choice. This can occur when an innocent suspect believes that the police have strong evidence and that confessing is the only way to avoid severe punishment. Or, it can occur if an innocent suspect, wanting to end a stressful interrogation, believes that it will be impossible to shake the interrogator's belief in his guilt but that proof of his innocence will emerge later.

There is also the theory that false confessions could result from a process of **self-perception**. According to the theory, making a false confession could alter the recollection of a person's past behavior if the confession is given in the presence of cues previously associated with telling the truth (e.g., reassurance that one need not admit to wrongdoing). Under conditions normally associated with telling the truth, subjects can come to believe the lies they had been induced to tell (Bem, 1966).

In addition to **person characteristics** explaining false confessions, there are also certain **demand characteristics** of interrogations that increase the probability of a suspect making a confession. Certainly the length of an interrogation may influence its outcome. One study of proven false confessions found that, of those cases in which the length of the interrogation was recorded, the average length was 16.3 hours (Drizin & Leo, 2004). As discussed in reference to Delbert Ward, a long interrogation causes fatigue and stress, exacerbates hopelessness, and may contribute to a false confession from a suspect who wants the interrogation to end. In *Chambers v. Florida* (1940), the suspect was subjected to five days of prolonged questioning before a confession was obtained. This technique actually consists of detaining and wearing down a suspect for a lengthy period of time so that the suspect begins to focus on short-term gratifications (such as removing himself from the situation or being allowed to sleep) while losing sight of long-term consequences such as conviction and sentencing.

Police interrogators base numerous techniques for wearing subjects down on psychological research done on false confessions. For example, interrogation rooms are intentionally unfamiliar to the suspect, free of extraneous sounds, without windows, and contain only a table and a couple of chairs. Police interrogators sometimes try to establish a superficial friendship with suspects as well as exhibit unexpected kindness while seeming to appeal to the best interest of the suspect. Or they may note inconsistencies in a suspect's statements, confront the suspect with (real or faked) incriminating evidence, and even use trickery and deceit to gain a confession (Inbau & Reid, 1967; Leo, 1996; Macdonald & Michaud, 1987; Tousignant, 1991).

Building on the sense of hopelessness that suspects begin to feel, the interrogator may employ strategies designed to convince the suspect that, given the irrefutable evidence, confessing is the best option available. One of these strategies is referred to as **minimization**, in which the interrogator offers some moral justification for the suspect's actions, minimizes the seriousness of the situation, or shifts blame onto others. This is a process of reattribution of the implications of the alleged crime whereby the interrogator might say things such as "It's understandable why you behaved that way" or "It was really something you did impulsively without thinking." Or the blame might be shifted away from the suspect and onto an accomplice or even the victim (e.g., "She really seemed to be asking for it, didn't she?"). In the alternate tactic of **maximization**, the interrogator tries to frighten the suspect by exaggerating the evidence available, the legal consequences, or stating that the interrogator knows the suspect is guilty.

The stress inherent in any police interview combined with isolation and confinement, minimized sensory stimulation, and complete control and domination by the interrogator result in an increased likelihood of a wide range of behavioral and physiological disturbances, including loss of contact with reality (Zimbardo, 1967). Faced with these kinds of circumstances, almost anybody could be worn down enough to say almost anything (Brandon & Davies, 1973).

THE STATUS OF CONFESSIONS IN THE SUPREME COURT

As stated at the beginning of this section, in the 1936 case of *Brown v. Mississippi* the Court set aside a conviction based solely on confessions of the defendants that had been extorted from them through repeated whippings with ropes and studded belts. The Court stated,

> [T]he question of the right of the State to withdraw the privilege against self-incrimination is not here involved. The compulsion to which the quoted statements refer is that of the processes of justice by which the accused may be called as a witness and required to testify. Compulsion by torture to extort a confession is a different matter. . . . It would be difficult to conceive of methods more revolting to the sense of justice than those taken to procure the confessions of these petitioners, and the use of the confessions thus obtained as the basis for conviction and sentence was a clear denial of due process. (pp. 285–286)

Many Supreme Court cases in the first half of the twentieth century revealed clear instances of coercion that no doubt produced involuntary confessions. For example, as previously mentioned, in 1940, in *Chambers v. Florida*, the Court held that five days of prolonged questioning following arrests without warrants and incommunicado detention made a subsequent confession involuntary, and in *Ashcraft v. Tennessee* (1944), the Court held inadmissible a confession obtained near the end of a 36-hour period of practically continuous questioning, under powerful electric lights, by relays of officers, experienced investigators, and highly trained lawyers.

Similarly, in 1948 the Court in *Ward v. Texas* voided a conviction based on a confession obtained from a suspect who had been arrested illegally in one county and brought some 100 miles away to a county where questioning began and who had then been questioned continuously over the course of three days while being driven from county to county and being told falsely of a danger of lynching. Further recognizing the harmful effects of psychological pressure, the Supreme Court in *Blackburn v. Alabama* (1960) stated, ". . . this Court has recognized that coercion can be mental as well as physical and that the blood of the accused is not the only hallmark of an unconstitutional inquisition" (p. 206).

For some 30 years following the original decision in *Brown v. Mississippi*, the Supreme Court attempted to determine whether a confession was "voluntary" and admissible or "coerced" and inadmissible through a consideration of the "totality of the circumstances" approach. During this time, the Court was balancing the view that police questioning of suspects was indispensable in solving many crimes, on the one hand, with the conviction that the interrogation process is not to be used to overreach persons who stand helpless before it. Accordingly, in 1961, in *Culombe v. Connecticut*, the Court reasoned,

> "The ultimate test remains that which has been the only clearly established test in Anglo-American courts for two hundred years: the test of voluntariness. Is the confession the product of an essentially free and unconstrained choice by its maker? If it is, if he has willed to confess, it may be used against him. If it is not, if his will has been overborne and his capacity for self-determination critically impaired, the use of his confession offends due process." (*Culombe v. Connecticut*, p. 602)

The Court's **voluntariness standard**, which had been its guidepost for evaluating confessions in criminal trials, was changed to a "self-incrimination standard" with its 1966 decision in *Miranda v. Arizona*, where the Court held,

> The prosecution may not use statements, whether exculpatory [tending to prove that a defendant is free of guilt] or inculpatory [tending to prove a defendant's guilt], stemming from custodial interrogation of the defendant unless it demonstrates the use of procedural safeguards effective to secure the privilege against self-incrimination. By custodial interrogation, we mean questioning initiated by law enforcement officers after a person has been taken into custody or otherwise deprived of his freedom of action in any significant way. As for the procedural safeguards to be employed, unless other fully effective means are devised to inform accused persons of their right of silence and to assure a continuous opportunity to exercise it, the following measures are required.
>
> Prior to any questioning, the person must be warned that he has a right to remain silent, that any statement he does make may be used as evidence against him, and that he has a right to the presence of an attorney, either retained or appointed. The defendant may waive effectuation of these rights, provided the waiver is made voluntarily, knowingly and intelligently. If, however, he indicates in any manner and at any stage of the process that he wishes to consult with an attorney before speaking there can be no questioning. Likewise, if the individual is alone and indicates in any manner that he does not wish to be interrogated, the police may not question him. The mere fact that he may have answered some questions or volunteered some statements on his own does not deprive him of the right of refrain from answering any further inquiries until he has consulted with an attorney and thereafter consents to be questioned. (p. 445)

The basis for the Court's conclusion was the determination that police interrogations were inherently coercive *by their very nature*. Therefore, the clause requires that police interrogation practices be so structured as to secure to suspects that they are not stripped of the ability to make a free and rational choice between speaking and not speaking. Under *Miranda*, a person questioned while in custody must be warned that anything he says can be used against him in a court of law, that he is entitled to the presence of a lawyer before questioning is begun, and that if he cannot afford counsel he is entitled to an appointed attorney. This applies to questioning initiated by law enforcement officers after a person has been taken into custody or otherwise deprived of his freedom of action in any significant way. Finally, once a warned suspect asserts his right to silence and requests counsel, the police must scrupulously respect his assertion of that right.

Furthermore, *Miranda* requires that if a suspect indicates he wishes the assistance of counsel before interrogation, the questioning must cease until he has counsel. This also applies to situations where the police reinitiate interrogation with a suspect who had requesting counsel in a previous questioning. Thus, in ***Edwards v. Arizona*** (1981), the Court ruled that *Miranda* had been violated when police reinitiated questioning after the suspect had requested counsel. Questioning had ceased as soon as the suspect had requested counsel, and the suspect had been returned to his cell. Questioning had resumed the following day only after different police officers had confronted the suspect and again warned him of his rights; the suspect agreed to talk and thereafter incriminated himself. Nonetheless, the Court held that "when an accused has invoked his right to have counsel present during custodial interrogation, a valid waiver of that right cannot be established by showing only that he responded to further police-initiated custodial interrogation even if he has [again] been advised of [his] rights [and] . . . that an accused . . . , having expressed his desire to deal with the police only through counsel, is not subject to further interrogation by the authorities until counsel has been made available to him, unless the accused himself initiates further communication, exchanges, or conversations with the police" (pp. 484–485). The *Edwards* rule bars police-initiated questioning stemming from a separate investigation as well as questioning related to the crime for which the suspect was arrested.

The Court has created a *public-safety exception to the Miranda warning requirement*, but has refused to create another exception for misdemeanors and lesser offenses. So, for example, in *New York v. Quarles* (1984), the Court held admissible a recently apprehended suspect's response in a public supermarket to the arresting officer's demand to know the location of a gun that the officer had reason to believe the suspect had just discarded or hidden in the supermarket.

WHAT DO FORENSIC PSYCHOLOGISTS HAVE TO OFFER?

How can forensic psychologists assist both the police and the accused in dealing with the issue of possible false confessions? At the very least they should educate police investigators, interrogators, judges, and lawyers as to the factors (personality and situational) that make suspects more vulnerable to making false confessions. As we have seen, such personality factors include diminished capacity, mental impairment, deficient intelligence, fear, confusion, suggestibility, low self-esteem, anxiety, and being a juvenile. Situational factors include the use of duress, coercion, isolation, lengthy interrogations, deception, and questionable interview techniques (e.g., continually interrupting the suspect, asking questions in a rapid manner, inappropriate sequencing of questions, negative phrasing of questions, nonneutral wording of questions, inappropriate language, and judgmental comments).

As a means of limiting the deleterious effects of high-pressured interrogations particularly with vulnerable suspects, many forensic psychologists have been advocating for the mandatory electronic recording of interrogations, which has been shown by the research to decrease the number of false confessions and increase the reliability of confessions as evidence. Although there is presently no federal policy, some individual states have created guidelines to require the recording of interrogations. In 2003, Illinois became the first state to mandate recording of interrogations. Maine and Washington, DC statutes also require the electronic recording of custodial interrogations in homicide investigations, and the supreme courts of Alaska and Minnesota have declared under their state constitutions that defendants are entitled to have their interviews taped as a matter of due process.

The judicial system as a whole needs to be more educated on the dangers of employing inappropriate approaches of eliciting confessions from suspects in custody. Interrogations should be centered around eliciting the *truth* rather than attempting to secure a confession. When questioning

FORENSIC PSYCHOLOGY IN THE SPOTLIGHT

Will a Confession stand if *Miranda* Rights are given Half-Heartedly?

United States v. Taddy Jackman (2007)

Taddy Jackman was arrested by the Salt Lake City police pursuant to a gang-related shooting that injured three people. The resulting interrogation and confession were videotaped. Just prior to reading Jackman his **Miranda** rights, the police officer conducting the interview stated, "So, before we get too far into it, though, [we have] a couple of formalities, . . . since obviously, you're not free to leave after we read you your rights." Jackman's *Miranda* rights were then read, and he verbally acknowledged his rights before eventually confessing.

Jackman filed a motion to suppress his confession on the grounds that he did not knowingly and voluntarily waive his *Miranda* rights, that the officers "down played" and misrepresented the purpose of his *Miranda* warning to give the impression that the rights were mere formalities, or rights that should not be taken seriously. According to Jackman, the officer's remark led him to believe that he was agreeing only to being placed in custody, but not to waiving his rights. He also contends that his two-week long attempts to avoid the police, during which he abused cocaine and methamphetamine,

left him sleep deprived and unable to knowingly and voluntarily consent to waiving *Miranda*. The district court denied Jackman's motion, and he appealed. The appeals court agreed with the lower court.

The appeals court viewed Jackman's confusion over the meaning of the *Miranda* warning to be minimal because he had been taken into custody at a residence, transported to the police station, and questioned. Throughout this period he expressed his willingness to talk. He asked only to speak with his mother, not an attorney. He recounted the history of animosity between certain gang members that led to his shooting of the three individuals. His lengthy story required minimal prompting by the officer. Indeed, the officer asked relatively few questions. Jackman even asked for paper to better illustrate the interrelation of all the various gang members involved. The court also saw as significant that Jackman had been arrested on numerous occasions and had been convicted of several felony charges in matters where he was represented by legal counsel. The concepts encompassed by *Miranda* were not foreign to him as he was represented by counsel during a prior conviction. The court ruled that Jackman knowingly and voluntarily waived his *Miranda* rights.

a potential suspect, the investigator should assume a disinterested role rather than an adversarial one. Using the psychological research on confessions as an educational tool, forensic psychologists need to explain to police, prosecutors, and judges the problems associated with tactics they may currently be employing (or allowing to be employed) to persuade suspects to confess or supply information associated with a criminal case (Baldwin, 1993; Conti, 1999; Fisher, Geiselman, & Raymond, 1987).

Prosecutors in particular should carefully evaluate a confession's trustworthiness prior to deciding to go forward with a criminal charge and possible trial. They need to be cognizant of the factors that contribute to how much trust can be placed in a confession (such as the age, IQ, general mental state, and vulnerability of the confessor and the inducement and interrogation methods used by the police).

Summary

Confessions have been present in many religions for centuries. It has also been a part of psychotherapy in the process of letting out bad feelings and experiencing the resulting catharsis. But it is confession in criminal law that has been the focus of this chapter. The psychological and the legal literature have revealed a history of excessive and inappropriate interrogations in this country leading to false confessions. One of the first law cases involving forced confessions was *Brown v. Mississippi* in which coerced confessions were deemed to have violated the Constitution. Similarly, *Miranda v. Arizona* and other cases have mandated that confessions be voluntarily given in order

to be admitted into evidence, that a suspect's rights against self-incrimination be provided, and that these rights can only be waived knowingly before questioning begins.

Even in the absence of force or coercion, there are numerous instances of suspects making false confessions. Some of these are voluntary false confessions, others are coerced-compliant false confessions, and still others are coerced-internalized false confessions. The research has revealed certain "person factors" that make someone vulnerable to making such confessions. These include suggestibility, low intelligence, young age, anxiety, fear, and intoxication.

There are also "demand characteristics" which make false confessions more likely. These include isolation, confinement, excessive length of interrogations, the use of interrogation techniques of minimization and maximization, and the use of trickery and deceit. Forensic psychologists can play a role in reducing the number of false confessions by educating the criminal justice system as to these person and demand factors that create the atmosphere for individuals to erroneously confess. The practice of video-recording interrogations is also helpful in insuring that only the guilty are punished.

Key Terms

Brown v. Mississippi 213
Coerced-compliant false
    confession *214*
Coerced-internalized false
    confession *215*
Delbert Ward *216*
Demand characteristics
    relating to false
    confessions *217*

Edwards v. Arizona 219
Interrogative
    suggestibility *216*
Maximization *217*
Minimization *217*
Miranda warning *220*
Miranda v. Arizona 213
On the Witness
    Stand *213*

Person characteristics
    relating to false
    confessions *217*
Pseudo-memories *215*
Rational choice
    theory *216*
Self-incrimination *213*
Self-perception
    theory *216*

Voluntary false
    confession *213*
Voluntariness
    standard *218*

Review Questions

1. What role does confession play in many religions?
2. How is the use of confession involved in some forms of psychotherapy?
3. What is a voluntary false confession, and why might it occur?
4. What is a coerced-compliant confession, and why does it occur?
6. Under what circumstances might a coerced-internalized confession occur?

7. What are the facts surrounding the Paul Ingram case of 1988?
8. What role did Dr. Richard Ofshe play in the Ingram case?
9. In what ways might an individual be particularly vulnerable to the effects of an interrogation?
10. What is meant by the "demand characteristics" of an interrogation?
11. What are "minimization" and "maximization," and how are they used in interrogation techniques?

Chapter Resources on the World Wide Web

Religious Confession and Confessions of Faith
http://mb-soft.com/believe/txo/confes.htm

Catharsis Reconsidered
http://robertmasters.com/Work_Section/catharsis.htm

False Confessions
http://www.justicedenied.org/false.htm

National Association of Criminal Defense Lawyers
http://www.nacdltapes.com/index.html?loadfile=item2020-06.html

Investigative Interviewing Research
http://iilab.utep.edu/confession.htm

Psychology and Crime News
http://crimepsychblog.com/?p=1382

The Role of False Confessions in Illinois Wrongful Murder Convictions Since 1970
www.law.northwestern.ed/depts/clinic/wrongful/FalseConfessions2.htm

The Skeptics Dictionary: False Memory
http://skepdic.com/falsememory.html

Famous American Trials
http://www.law.umkc.edu/faculty/projects/ftrials/sweet/background.htm

The Price of Bad Memories
http://faculty.washington.edu/eloftus/Articles/price.htm

For Further Reading

Conti, R. P. (1999). The psychology of false confessions. *The Journal of Credibility Assessment and Witness Psychology, 2*(1), 14–36.

Geller, W. A. (1993). Videotaping interrogations and confessions. *National institute of justice: Research in brief.* Washington, DC: U.S. Department of Justice.

Gudjonsson, G. H. (2003). *The psychology of interrogations and confessions: A handbook.* Chichester: John Wiley & Sons.

Inbau, F. E., Reid, J. E., Buckley, J. P., & Jayne, B. C. (2001). *Criminal interrogation and confessions* (4th ed.). Gaithersberg, MD: Aspen.

Kassin, S. M. (2005). On the psychology of false confessions: Does innocence put innocents at risk. *American Psychologist, 60,* 215.

Williamson, T. (Ed.). (2006). Towards greater professionalism: Minimizing miscarriages of justice. *Investigative interviewing: Rights, research and regulation.* Portland, OR: Willan Publishing.

CHAPTER 11

Capacity and Incapacity

CHAPTER OBJECTIVES

After reading this chapter you would:

- Know how the mentally ill were treated in America from the colonial period onward.
- Understand the meaning of competency in the American legal system.
- Know some of the essential features of a psychological competency evaluation.
- Know why the case of *Jackson v. Indiana* is so important in the criminal justice system.
- Understand the concepts of criminal responsibility and insanity.
- Know under what circumstances competency may be restored against a defendant's will.
- Understand the origins and implications of the *M'Naughten Test* to the insanity defense.
- Know how the *Durham Test* and the *Model Penal Code* are related to the insanity defense.

INTRODUCTION

The Greek philosophers recommended that people with a mental disability be cared for in a comfortable, sanitary, well-lighted place. The Romans appointed a "curator" (guardian) to safeguard the property of these people ("wards") and debated the legal effect of decisions made by the ward during lucid moments (Melton, Petrila, Poythress, & Slobogin, 1997).

During the Middle Ages, definitions of mental disorder were influenced by theories of possession by demons, and exorcism and even torture became primary therapies. In England, the *De Praerogativa Regis* (the "Prerogative of the King") was enacted in the thirteenth century dividing people with mental disability into two classes, "idiots" and "lunatics." The former was defined as a person who "hath no understanding from his nativity." The latter was "a person who hath had understanding, but hath lost the use of his reason" (Brakel & Rock, 1971, p. 36). In this country, the ability to reason and understand the significance of one's actions has always had special significance. The term **competency** appears in the laws of evidence, contract law, wills and estates, domestic and family law, as well as criminal law. In the most general of terms, a competent person is one who has sufficient mental or physical capacity, or has legitimate authority to engage in some legally significant act.

COMPETENCY IN THE CIVIL JUSTICE SYSTEM

In the civil justice system competency may involve the ability to make a contract, understand the terms of a will, competency to decide medical treatment, and competency to consent to research. In addition, lack of sufficient competency may give rise to the associated legal inventions of **guardianship** and **conservatorship**.

Competency to Make a Contract

For a contract to be valid and enforceable the parties must be capable of understanding their mutual obligations. Minors for example, are deemed by the law to have a diminished capacity to contract. A person is legally a minor (or infant under the law) until the age of majority. The law over the centuries has considered this age to be 21. Legislatures in almost all states have lowered this age to 18. A contract entered into by a minor is not necessarily *void*, but is *voidable*.

Persons who are so disabled by mental illness that they are unable to understand the nature of a transaction in a reasonable manner, usually also lack the legal capacity to enter into a contract, but this is not always true and must be evaluated on a case by case basis. Persons who are under the influence of a temporary incapacity such as intoxication, can usually (but not always) void a contract. One of the determining factors is whether the other party was aware of the incapacity but proceeded with the agreement nonetheless, thereby taking advantage of another's known incapacity.

Competency to Make a Will (testamentary capacity)

When a will is contested (i.e., its validity is officially doubted), it is usually because of one of two possible factors. The first is that that the **testator** (i.e., the person making the will) lacked **testamentary capacity**. This would be the case if the testator was somehow mentally incompetent at the time of signing the will. The second reason is that the testator was subject to undue influence such as coercion, manipulation, deception, compulsion, intimidation, et cetera.

Since wills are usually contested after the testator's death, forensic evaluations can obviously not be made of the testator him/herself. Rather, a forensic autopsy of sorts is performed to determine testamentary capacity at the time the will was executed (signed). This would require a careful review of medical, psychiatric, nursing home, pharmacy, and other relevant records in an attempt to "reconstruct" the mental state of the testator at the time of making the will. Friends, family members, caregivers, and anyone who interacted with the testator around the time of making the will are usually interviewed if available as part of the forensic autopsy process.

In general, the forensic examiner performing such an evaluation should determine whether or not the testator, at the time of making the will, had a mental disorder or a cognitive impairment, which could affect the testator's ability to make the will. The evaluator should address the issues of whether the testator had the capacity to understand, know, or recognize: (1) that a will is being made; (2) the extent of his/her estate or property; and (3) potential heirs (beneficiaries) of the estate. A testator with addiction to drugs or alcohol, if making a will during a period of lucidity, does not generally lack testamentary capacity. However, chronic use of drugs or alcohol may result in medical and psychiatric conditions that can impact a testator's mental state or make him/her susceptible to undue influence (Scott & Leslie, 1993).

Competency to Decide Regarding Treatment (informed consent)

Informed consent is the process by which a fully informed patient can participate in choices about his/her health care. Some of the elements involved in informed consent include reasonable alternatives to the proposed intervention, risks and benefits of the intervention, and the patient's understanding of the proposed treatment or intervention. The patient must be considered competent in order for any consent to be held as being valid. To encourage voluntariness, health care providers attempt (or should attempt) to make clear to patients that they are participating in a decision, not merely signing a form. Consider the example of weight loss surgical interventions (e.g., gastric bypass surgery). Greenberg et al. (2005) reviewed 198 abstracts and 17 papers for the period from 1980 to 2004, and found a high incidence of depression, negative body image, eating disorders, and low quality of life in severely obese patients. The researchers recommended that all weight loss surgery candidates be evaluated by a mental health professional experienced in the treatment of severely obese patients prior to surgery. They also recommended developing pre- and postsurgical treatment plans addressing contraindications for surgery and barriers to postoperative success.

Competency to Consent to Research

Are psychiatric inpatients more likely than nonpatients to consent to research, and therefore be more needy of protection? Cohen et al. (2004) found that psychiatric inpatients currently being treated for depression and schizophrenia were not more likely to volunteer to participate in research than were community control subjects. Rather, the opposite proved to be the case. Depressed subjects were six times more likely to decline participation in a pharmacology trial (60% versus 10%) and 1.4 times more likely to decline participation in a functional neuroimaging study involving the administration of a "pharmacologic challenge" (75% versus 55%) than were control subjects.

Subjects with schizophrenia were even more likely to decline participation in research generally, with 96% of the patients that were approached declining any type of research involvement altogether. Furthermore, depressed individuals who agreed to participate in a research protocol were not found to be more impaired in their decision-making capacity than depressed individuals who declined to do so, and they were no more likely to agree to participate in higher risk studies offering no potential for direct medical benefit than were control subjects. The authors therefore found no support for the contention that individuals with mental illness are at greater risk for inappropriate research recruitment (and corresponding coercion) than are individuals without mental illness.

In the civil justice system there are two primary means of protecting individuals who are incompetent to make vital decisions for themselves—guardianship and conservatorship. **Guardianship** is one of the most ancient aspects of mental health law. Under English common law, the sovereign possessed the power and duty to "guard" the estate of incompetent persons. Guardianship is a legal relationship between a competent adult or "guardian" and a person who is no longer able to make responsible decisions. A minor child under legal guardianship appointed by a court is referred to as a ward of the court. The guardian is authorized to make legal, financial, and health care decisions for the ward. The guardian must regularly report to the court and may be removed if he/she does not adequately take care of the ward and adhere to the guardianship law.

A **Conservatorship** is a court-appointed relationship in which the conservator becomes the surrogate decision maker for matters concerning the property and/or income of a person deemed incapable of administering his/her own financial affairs because of physical, mental, or other incapacity.

COMPETENCY IN THE CRIMINAL JUSTICE SYSTEM

In criminal cases, the capacity to comprehend legal proceedings and communicate with an attorney, and to understand and waive certain rights, such as the right to remain silent may be at issue in the determination of competency.

The rule that an individual must be competent in order to undergo the criminal process can be traced back at least to seventeenth-century English law when defendants, rather than making a plea, stood mute. In such a case, the court would then seek to ascertain whether the defendant was "mute of malice" or "mute by visitation of God." If the individual fell into the first category, the court sought to force a plea by ordering increasingly heavier weights to be placed upon the individual's chest. If the individual fell into the latter category, he/she was spared this ordeal. The category "mute by visitation from God" initially included the literally deaf and mute, but over time was expanded to include the "lunatic" (Reisner, Slobogin, & Rai, 1999).

Early American courts, which relied heavily upon English common law, also recognized the incompetency plea. In 1835, for instance, the man who attempted to assassinate President Andrew Jackson was declared unfit to stand trial. In 1899, a federal court of appeals held that "It is not due process of law" to subject an insane person to trial upon an indictment involving liberty or life" (Reisner et al., at 963). Since that time, the U.S. Supreme Court has on several occasions stated that the right of an incompetent defendant to avoid trial is "fundamental to an adversary system of justice" (*Drope v. Missouri*, 1975).

The authority of the government to control its citizens and even incarcerate them when necessary originates from three places. The first two are primarily entities of the criminal law, the third is part of the civil law. The government's *police power* authorizes the state to protect the community and to incarcerate individuals who are threats to the public or who have committed crimes. The *criminal justice system* punishes, rehabilitates, and deters crime. It usually oversees the incarceration of individuals brought to it by the police. The state's ***parens patriae*** authority operates as the general guardian of all those who cannot care for themselves. Originally reserved for "infants, idiots, and lunatics" (i.e., children, the mentally retarded, and the insane), this power deals with the safety and needs of the individual rather than society as a whole. When a person is incarcerated for a crime, there are constitutional protections that automatically take effect. These include various procedural protections, including the right to counsel, cross-examination, an open hearing, and forcing the state to carry the burden of proof "beyond a reasonable doubt." In contrast, the civil commitment process utilizing the parens patriae power demands proof of the lesser standard of "clear and convincing evidence," perhaps reflecting the notion that society is not as troubled by false commitment as it is by false conviction.

The question of whether a defendant is competent to stand trial is one of the most commonly assessed issues in the criminal justice system. **Competence to stand trial** refers to a defendant's ability to function in a meaningful fashion in a legal proceeding. Defendants who are impaired in their ability to understanding legal proceedings, communicate with their attorneys, appreciate their own role in the proceedings, and make legally relevant decisions, are often assessed as being incompetent, and a person who cannot understand the nature and purpose of criminal proceedings should not be the subject of such actions. Although most often raised in pretrial hearings, a defendant's competence is relevant at every stage of the criminal justice process and can be raised at any point.

Why is it so important that a criminal defendant be competent in order to stand trial and make a plea? Because it helps makes legal proceedings more accurate and just. Punishment is morally acceptable only if defendants understand the reasons they are being punished, and the perceived fairness of our adversary system of justice requires participation by defendants who have the capacity to defend themselves against charges levied by the state.

But the *primary* reason competence is so important in the American legal system is based squarely on the Fifth and Six Amendments of the Constitution. Both are applicable to the states through the Due Process Clause of the Fourteenth Amendment. The Fifth Amendment states,

> No person shall be held to answer for a capital, or otherwise infamous crime, unless on a presentment or indictment of a grand jury, except in cases arising in the land or naval forces, or in the militia, when in actual service in time of war or public danger; nor shall any person be subject for the same offense to be twice put in jeopardy of life or limb; nor shall be compelled in any criminal case to be a witness against himself, nor be deprived of life, liberty, or property, without due process of law; nor shall private property be taken for public use, without just compensation. (U.S. Const. Amend. V).

With a guilty plea, defendants waive their right to remain silent and not incriminate themselves. The Sixth Amendment states,

> In all criminal prosecutions, the accused shall enjoy the right to a speedy and public trial, by an impartial jury of the State and district wherein the crime shall have been committed, which district shall have been previously ascertained by law, and to be informed of the nature and cause of the accusation; to be confronted with the witnesses against him; to have compulsory process for obtaining witnesses in his favor, and to have the assistance of counsel for his defense. (U.S. Const. Amend. VI).

With a guilty plea, defendants waive their rights to be clearly informed of the nature and cause of the charges against them, to prepare an adequate defense with the assistance of counsel, have a jury trial, confront accusers, and call defense witnesses in their defense (see *Sheppard v. Rees*, 1990).

In **Dusky v. United States** (1960) the Supreme Court set forth a definition of competency to stand trial that has since come to be the standard in federal court and most state jurisdictions as well. The Court stressed that the important questions that must be answered when evaluating competence. Does a defendant have sufficient ability to consult with his attorney in a rational manner? Does a defendant reasonably understand the proceedings against him? There are five central components to *Dusky*, all of which are vitally important to understand.

1. A competency test rests on *two prongs*: the defendant's capacity to understand the criminal process, including the role of the participants in that process; and the defendant's ability to function in that process, primarily through consulting with counsel in the preparation of a defense.
2. Competency focuses on the defendant's *present* ability to consult with counsel and to understand the proceedings. This differs fundamentally from the test for **criminal responsibility**, which is a *retrospective* analysis on the defendant's state of mind at the time of the offense.
3. A defendant's *capacity* to relate to counsel and understand courtroom proceedings is paramount to his *willingness* to actively participate in these proceedings when determining competency. The defendant who refuses to talk to his attorney (even though capable of doing so) is making a rational choice knowing the consequences. Unless the lack of motivation is based on irrational factors such as delusional beliefs, thereby calling into question one's capacity to assist in one's defense, it is not ground for an incompetency adjudication.
4. A defendant is required to possess a *reasonable* degree of understanding of the criminal process and courtroom proceedings, which suggests that the test applied to a particular case is a flexible one. A "perfect" or complete understanding on the part of the defendant is not required.
5. The final component of the *Dusky* standard is its emphasis on the presence or absence of a "rational" and "factual" understanding, which suggests an emphasis on cognitive *functioning*. The mere fact that a defendant has psychotic symptoms or has a particular IQ does not ipso facto mean that the defendant is incompetent to stand trial. Likewise, neither mental illness per se nor the defendant's need for treatment is sufficient for an incompetency finding. The presence of mental illness is relevant only insofar as that illness affects one's rational understanding as one consults with counsel and undergoes the criminal justice process.

Is the competency standard for pleading guilty or waiving the right to counsel the same as the competency standard for standing trial? The Supreme Court ruled in *Godinez v. Moran* (1993) that it is. The Court reasoned that the decision to plead guilty, though profound, is no more complicated than the sum total of decisions that a defendant may have to make during the course of a trial, such as whether to testify, whether to waive a jury trial, and whether to cross examine witnesses for the prosecution. Nor does the decision to waive counsel require an appreciably higher level of mental functioning than the decision to waive other constitutional rights. A higher standard is not necessary in order to ensure that a defendant is competent to represent himself, because the ability to do so has no bearing upon his competence to *choose* self representation.

CONSTITUTIONAL ISSUES AND STANDARDS OF CARE

Right to Liberty

The right to liberty is at the center of all the rights relating to patients in state confinement. This may be the legal rationale for lawsuits claiming false imprisonment, negligence, or intentional infliction of harm. These actions may also be based on a violation of U.S. Code Title 42, Section 1983 dealing with violations of an individual's civil rights. Section 1983 states in part,

> Every person who, under color of any statute, ordinance, regulation, custom, or usage, of any State or Territory or the District of Columbia, subjects, or causes to be subjected, any citizen of the United States or other person within the jurisdiction thereof to the deprivation of any rights, privileges, or immunities secured by the Constitution and laws, shall be liable to the party injured in an action at law, suit in equity, or other proper proceeding for redress, except that in any action brought against a judicial officer for an act or omission taken in such officer's judicial capacity, injunctive relief shall not be granted unless a declaratory decree was violated or declaratory relief was unavailable. . . . (U.S. Code Title 42 § 1983)

For example, in *Anaya v. Crossroads Managed Care Sys., Inc.* (1999), a group of individuals who had been committed on an emergency basis to a detoxification center successfully brought a federal suit claiming that they had not been committed due to their dangerousness as the law required. The only allegations were that one plaintiff slammed a door, and the other was found asleep in a public place.

Right to Safety

Involuntarily committed residents of state mental retardation institutions have a constitutional right to reasonably safe conditions of confinement, freedom from unreasonable bodily restraints, and habilitation. For example, in *Youngberg v. Romeo* (1982), a profoundly retarded man was involuntarily committed to a Pennsylvania state hospital, where he was injured repeatedly and placed in restraints for long periods of time. His mother filed suit on his behalf against institutional officials claiming that her son had constitutional rights to safe conditions of confinement, freedom from bodily restraint, and habilitation (training), and that the officials knew, or should have known, that her son was suffering injuries and failed to take appropriate preventative measures, thereby violating his rights under the Eighth and Fourteenth Amendments. The jury returned a verdict for the defendants under that Amendment, and the plaintiff appealed. The Third Circuit Court of Appeals reversed and remanded for a new trial holding that the Fourteenth Amendment involved liberty interests in freedom of movement and personal security that individuals involuntarily committed retained. The defendants appealed.

The American Psychological Association submitted an amicus brief arguing that mentally retarded people can learn and can respond positively to instructional programs. It was also argued that where the state has assumed custody of a noncriminal mentally retarded person, it has a constitutional obligation to protect him from harm by meeting his fundamental needs, including his needs for personal security and appropriate habilitation. The Supreme Court agreed, holding that residents of an institution who are mentally retarded and involuntarily committed, have a constitutional right to safety, protection, and to be free from the use of unreasonable bodily restraints.

Right to Treatment

Prior to 1975, there had never been a clearly delineated constitutional "**right to treatment**" in this country. However, the Constitution has been held to guarantee that individuals in custody or confined are entitled to something more than just custodial care, or worse yet, "storage." The 1975 case of *O'Connor v. Donaldson* exemplifieds this right. In *O'Connor*, Kenneth Donaldson was committed to Florida's Chattahoochee State Hospital in 1956 for having, among other things, paranoid delusions. Donaldson denied he was ill and refused treatment; yet he remained in the institution for 15 years. But he was very motivated, persistent, and intelligent, and through the years persistently petitioned the courts for his release. He brought an action for damages under 42 U.S.C. 1983 against the hospital's superintendent, and other staff members, alleging that they had intentionally and maliciously deprived him of his constitutional right to liberty. The evidence showed that Donaldson, whose frequent requests for release had been rejected by the hospital notwithstanding undertakings by responsible persons to care for him if necessary, was dangerous neither to himself nor others, and, if mentally ill, had not received the needed treatment.

At the trial court level, the jury found for Donaldson and awarded compensatory and punitive damages. The court of appeals affirmed the district court's verdict and held that Donaldson had a constitutional right to such treatment as would help him to be cured or to improve his mental condition. The case was appealed to the U.S. Supreme Court. The Supreme Court affirmed saying,

> We hold that a person involuntarily civilly committed to a state mental hospital has a *constitutional right to receive such individual treatment* as will give him a reasonable opportunity to be cured or to improve his mental condition. In reaching this result, we begin by noting the indisputable fact that civil commitment entails a "massive curtailment of liberty" in the constitutional sense . . . the due process clause [of the Constitution] guarantees a right to treatment. . . . (*O'Connor v. Donaldson*, 1975). (Emphasis added)

The right to treatment established in *O'Connor* has since been expanded to an "individualized right to treatment" geared to the particular patient.

The 1970 case of **Wyatt v. Stickney** dealt with Bryce State Hospital in Tuscaloosa, Alabama, which had 5,200 patients living in inhumane conditions and receiving woefully inadequate treatment. Few members of the public knew about the horrible living and treatment conditions at these facilities; patients were out of sight and out of mind. The resulting lawsuit presented a federal question regarding the minimum standards required for treatment of people who were involuntarily committed to a state institution. Filed in 1970, the case was finally dismissed in 2003, and created minimum standards for the care and rehabilitation of people with mental illness and mental retardation. These standards included (1) a humane psychological and physical environment, (2) qualified staff in numbers sufficient to administer adequate treatment, and (3) individualized treatment plans.

Right to a Least Restrictive Alternative

In *Wyatt*, discussed above, the Court's "individualized right to treatment" included movement of residents of mental institutions from (1) more to less structured living arrangements, (2) larger to smaller facilities, (3) larger to smaller living units, (4) group to individual residences, (5) segregation from the community to integration into the community, and (6) dependent to independent living.

In O'Connor, the Supreme Court embraced the limited right of being allowed to live safely in the community with the assistance of family and friends. Then in the 1999 case of *Olmstead v. L.C., ex rel. Zimring*, the Court ruled that the unjustified institutionalization of persons with mental disabilities violated Title II of the Americans with Disabilities Act, and that patients have a right to integrated services under less restrictive conditions including limited rights to community-based treatment.

Right to Refuse Involuntary Medication

Until the 1970s people who were civilly committed or criminally insane could be forcibly medicated regardless of their competency to make treatment decisions. Apparently, the assumption was that since these people were subject to involuntary institutionalization, they were not competent to veto a particular treatment decision. Virtually every court that has considered the matter now recognizes a right to refuse psychotropic medication for institutionalized populations under the doctrine of **informed consent**.

In the 1990 case of ***Washington v. Harper***, the Supreme Court tackled the question of whether a prisoner in a correctional facility has the right to refuse the administration of psychotropic medication. The American Psychological Association submitted an amicus brief arguing that due process requires that a prisoner receive an impartial hearing before he can be forced to take psychotropic medication, and that forcible administration of medication, and significant changes in conditions of confinement implicate basic liberty interests and prisoners usually have a right to refuse invasive and dangerous therapies.

The Court held that although Harper had a substantive liberty right under the Due Process Clause to be free of unwanted medication, the state also had a legitimate interest in reducing the danger a mentally disordered, violent inmate poses. The Due Process Clause permits the state to treat a prison inmate who has a serious mental illness with antipsychotic drugs against his will, if he is dangerous to himself or others and the treatment is in his medical interest. It noted that medical authorities are better able than judges to determine the necessity of the administration of medication and that the policy under which the prisoner was to be treated was a proper accommodation between an inmate's interest in avoiding the forced administration of antipsychotic medication and the state's interest in providing appropriate treatment to reduce the danger that an inmate suffering from a mental disorder represents to himself or others.

THE COMPETENCY EVALUATION

Between 25,000 and 39,000 competency evaluations are conducted in the United States annually (Hogue et al., 1997). Stated somewhat differently, between 2% and 8% of all felony defendants are referred for competency evaluations. Traditionally, forensic psychologists and psychiatrists have focused on the presence or absence of psychosis when assessing a defendant's competency. McGarry (1965) found a 100% correlation between diagnoses of psychosis and findings of incompetence. But this equation of psychosis with incompetency may merely reflect the ability of clinicians to agree when someone is severely mentally ill (Cooke, 1969; McGarry, 1965). There has been research that suggests, however, that the presence of psychosis is not sufficient by itself for a finding of incompetency (Reisner, Slobogin, & Rai, 2004; Roesch, & Golding, 1980). And many courts have held that someone who is quite mentally ill might be able to meet the requirements of the competency standard (i.e., they might be able to demonstrate an understanding of the legal process and proceedings, as well as a capacity to relate relevant facts and the names of witnesses) despite their mental disability (see, e.g., *Swisher v. United States*, 1965).

Relying on a psychiatric diagnosis alone is a common error of clinicians who are helping to determine trial competence. The reason for this is that there is virtually no such diagnosis that always renders a defendant incompetent. People with schizophrenia or bipolar illness are not incompetent per se, and those with less serious diagnoses are not necessarily competent. In addition, the question of malingering (faking illness) is always relevant in competency cases.

Furthermore, the profession of forensic psychology has seen the development of better training programs, some of which offer cooperation of graduate psychology programs and law schools (Roesch, Grisso, & Poythress, 1986). The past few decades have also witnessed the development of a number of instruments specifically designed for assessing competence as well as malingering. As in the case of psychosis, a defendant with amnesia is not per se incompetent to stand trial. In several cases, defendants with memory problems due to brain damage did not present a sufficient reason to bar the trial when the defendant was otherwise competent (*Missouri v. Davis*, 1983; *Ritchie v. Indiana*, 1984). In *Morrow v. Maryland* (1982), the court held that, because of the potential for fraud, amnesia does not justify a finding of incompetence. The court also specifically stated that everyone has amnesia to some degree since the passage of time erodes memory. Similarly, a defendant may be psychotic and still be found competent to stand trial if the symptoms do not impair the defendant's functional ability to consult with his/her attorney and otherwise rationally participate in the legal process.

As noted previously, the issue of competency may be raised at any point in the adjudication process. If a court determines that a bona fide doubt exists as to a defendant's competency, it must formally consider the issue, which normally means ordering a forensic evaluation. Such an evaluation may take place in the jail, an outpatient facility, or in an institutional setting.

The Assessment Process and Report

Even before meeting with a defendant (the examinee) for the first time, the forensic psychologist should speak with both the prosecution and the defense as a means of discovering the reasons behind the request for the forensic evaluation. Every effort should be expended to obtain all the relevant aspects of the examinees family, developmental, mental health, social, and criminal history. If prior mental health treatment did occur, clinical and hospital records should be obtained for review. Similarly, complete police reports of the alleged crime as well as all other adjudications should be obtained. The psychologist should maintain a record of when and from whom information was made available, as well as all contact with members of the criminal justice and mental health systems. With proper permission from the defendant and defense attorneys, attempts should also be made to make an audiovisual or at least audio record of the evaluation. The examining psychologist should certainly be aware of any statutory requirements relevant to the evaluation (e.g., some states require Miranda-like warnings be given that inform the defendant of the limitations of confidentiality). Regardless of statutes, the defendant (or his legal representative's) written permission must be obtained.

Finally, any examining forensic psychologist should conduct the highest quality of evaluation, including interviews and relevant psychological testing. Reports should be professional written with special attention to separating factual information from inference or from even the *appearance* that the psychologist may be tainted, or worse yet biased due to a contractual or financial relationship with one side of the case or the other. The psychologist must not lose track of the likelihood that the psychological report will be admitted into evidence, and that the psychologist will almost certainly be exposed to possible virulent cross-examination by opposing counsel whose main agenda may be to discredit his/her authoritativeness, knowledge, and credibility. "A poorly written report may become, in the hands of a skillful lawyer, an instrument to discredit and embarrass its author" (Melton, Petrila, Poythress, and Slobogin, 1997, p. 523).

SAMPLE FORENSIC REPORT

The following is an actual forensic report (with all names and identifying information obviously altered) on the issue of competency to stand trial. The report is provided courtesy of Anita Boss, Psy.D., ABPP, a forensic psychologist in Alexandria Virginia. The report is one example of a standard competency evaluation and does not necessarily reflect how all forensic psychologists construct their reports procedurally or quantitatively.

Jane Smith, Psy.D., ABPP Board Certified in Forensic Psychology
Psychological Evaluation of Competence to Stand Trial; State Code § 271-2.3

Name: JONES, Bruce M.

Case Numbers: JJ000000-05, 06, 07

D.O.B.: 5/14/1987

Date of Evaluation: June 1 and 8, 2007

Date of Report: June 16, 2007

In response to a Court Order, I evaluated Mr. Bruce M. Jones at the Mason County Adult Detention Center. This examination was requested to assist the Court in determining the defendant's competence to stand trial. The defendant is a 20-year-old African-American man currently facing charges of murder in commission of a robbery, murder of more than one person in a three-year period, and burglary. Mr. Jones was notified of the nature and purpose of this evaluation, as well as the limits of confidentiality. Specifically, he was informed that I had been appointed by the Court for an examination of his competence to stand trial, and that I would file a summary report with the Court, the state's attorney, and defense counsel. He expressed his understanding of this notification and his willingness to cooperate with the examination. The conclusions contained in this report are based on the sources of information listed below. Additional information may or may not affect the conclusions of this evaluation.

Sources of Information for this Examination

1. Clinical interview at the Mason County Adult Detention Center (ADC) on June 1, 8, 2007.
2. Psychological testing sessions with the defendant on the same dates where Mr. Jones completed the Personality Assessment Inventory (PAI).
3. Order for Psychological Evaluation; May 9, 2007.
4. Telephone interview with Luna Davis, R. N., of the ADC; June 9, 2007.
5. Telephone interview with Loretta Jones, defendant's mother; June 10, 2007.

From the State's Attorney

1. Comprehensive Psychiatric Evaluation and Discharge Summary; David Morris, M.D.; March 4, 2007.
2. Physician's Progress Notes from defendant's admission to Middleton State Hospital February 15–17, 2007.

3. Synopsis of events from Assistant State's Attorney Timothy M. Parker, prepared for defendant's evaluation at Middleton State Hospital; February 10, 2007.
4. Telephone conversation with Mr. Parker; May 31, 2007.

From Defense Counsel

1. Psychological test data from evaluation of defendant by David King, MSW, Ed.D. (Wide Range Achievement Test, Test of Nonverbal Intelligence, Patient Self-Evaluation)
2. Letter to The Honorable James S. Robertson from Dennis Singer, M.D. of Central State Hospital; February 18, 2007.
3. Court Ordered Psychological Evaluation by Ernest Brooks, Ph.D.; June 1, 2007; completed for Case Numbers CR01001-00 and 01.
4. Records from defendant's admissions to Middleton State Hospital; December 19, 2005, to January 16, 2006, and February 15–17, 2007.
5. Mason County Adult Detention Center (ADC) Booking File.
6. ADC Classification File.
7. ADC Mental Health records.
8. Telephone conversations with Ms. Barker, defense counsel; May 16, June 10 and 15, 2007.

Background Information

The defendant is the older of two children born in Danville, South Carolina to married parents. Mr. Jones said both of his parents retired from the army. The father left the family when Mr. Jones was about 18 months old; his brother was an infant. The defendant rarely saw him afterward. He said that in 1999, he and his brother were sent to stay with their father for the summer in California; he added, "my brother just got a beating," and he called his mother, who came to retrieve them. Records indicate that the father had left them to fend for themselves during the day; they were about 11 and 12 years old.

Mr. Jones believes his father still lives in California; he has had no recent contact with him. His mother, who worked as a nurse for years, currently lives in Smithtown, South Carolina. She is now on disability due to multiple physical problems. While the records state that the family moved frequently as a function of her job, Mr. Jones said he did not

(continued)

(*continued*)

understand why she moved them so often. He thought she had been trying to get a job and "trying to be happy." His mother said they had lived in North Carolina from 1991 to 1998, then the nursing company that she worked for promoted her and they moved to Georgia for two years, then Arkansas for three years, before returning to North Carolina. In 2003, it was clear that her younger son was suffering from asthma so severely that she needed to find a different climate for him. They moved to Florida. That year, she overheard her sons talking about how they did not like Florida, but they were willing to stay there for her. This prompted her to move the family back to North Carolina the same year.

When they arrived in North Carolina, their U-Haul trailer was stolen, and they lost everything they owned. Mr. Jones's mother said the defendant had been extremely distraught about this, yet took on the role of trying to take care of her. In addition, because the school credit hour system was different in Florida, Mr. Jones was a few credits short to be placed in the tenth grade in the North Carolina school he was to attend. His mother said the school system insisted on placing him in ninth grade, which he had nearly finished in Florida. School records were not available at the time of this evaluation; his mother said he had been a good student until age 16. Mr. Jones was angry and humiliated about having to repeat a grade, to the point that he began to refuse going to school. It was during this same time period that Mr. Jones began exhibiting subtle symptoms of mental disorder, which will be discussed in a later section of this report. Mr. Jones's mother took her children back to Florida in an attempt to restore some order and help her oldest son get back into the appropriate grade level at school. He ultimately quit school in tenth grade.

In contrast to his mother's account, Mr. Jones blamed his mother for holding him back in two grades for reasons unknown to him, and he added that he had been doing well in his classes. He also reported having been expelled once in sixth grade for fighting, allegedly after another boy had been "messing with" his younger brother. He confirmed a high school expulsion for drinking alcohol in class. When asked about this incident, he attributed it to "being stupid." Records from a previous evaluation estimate his reading level to be within the eleventh grade level, with substantially lower spelling and arithmetic skills (fifth and seventh grade, respectively).

Given his age at the time of his arrest, Mr. Jones has a limited work history. He worked at a fast food restaurant for a short time at age 15, but quit the job abruptly when he "got tired of it." He was not employed afterward and has been incarcerated since age 17.

Mr. Jones reported infrequent use of alcohol prior to his incarceration. When he did consume alcohol, it was typically in large quantity, though he reportedly did not do this often. He has reported smoking marijuana from age 15 until the time he was incarcerated. The frequency and intensity of his marijuana use has varied from almost daily use to weekend use. There were no indications that he has been using illegal drugs since his incarceration in the records reviewed for this examination. Mr. Jones has consistently denied any other illegal drug use.

Medical History

Records do not indicate any significant medical issues. Mr. Jones recalled having been stung on the back of the head by an insect when he was six years old. Frightened and in pain at the time, he ran off into a nearby field, where he suffered an asthma attack and required hospitalization. He initially described this as having caused problems with his "head," meaning that he attributed his previous mental health problems to this incident.

The only other medical treatment that Mr. Jones reported was having his stomach pumped after he was "playing with my mother's drugs, trying to get high." He had taken eight or nine Ativan tablets. His mother recalled him saying that he had taken the medication to try to stop the disturbed thoughts that he had been struggling with. When one pill did not work, he took another and another. He was hospitalized for a short time at the Regional Naval Medical Center.

Psychiatric History

Mr. Jones's mother said he began exhibiting "subtle" symptoms of mental disorder after the family's belongings were stolen. She remarked that he had never used "ghetto language" in the past, but started speaking differently and using unusual hand gestures during that time, which she placed around the year 2003, age 16. He started to withdraw from the family, closing the blinds in the house and isolating himself in his room. Next, he became preoccupied with body hair, and she said he would shave his head two or three times a day until it bled. He also shaved his body. He started talking to himself and became paranoid. She added that he would place little strips of paper or string around his door to determine if anyone had been in his room when he was out. He also became violent, which had not been a prominent behavior in his past; she recalled only two fights until he became mentally ill.

After the family returned to Florida in 2003, Mr. Jones's behavior became more erratic, bizarre, and unpredictable. Ultimately, he attacked a child in a restaurant; when asked about it afterward, he reasoned that the child had assaulted him in the bathroom. This incident took place in the restaurant, in front of several other people. He was hospitalized at Edgewater Recovery Center in Florida. From that point, Mr. Jones became what could be described as a "revolving door" patient. He was admitted to the same hospital four times in rapid succession, each time with psychotic symptoms and violent behavior. He continued to shave to the point of bleeding. He was given medication in the hospital to control his aggression, but quickly became bizarre and violent after discharge, hence the rapid readmissions.

At home, Mr. Jones's behavior continued to be erratic and bizarre, and both his mother and brother were fearful of his violent behavior. His mother made several attempts to find a residential treatment setting for him, all to no avail. She had heard that the Regional Naval Medical Center might have a residential treatment facility to which he could be referred, so she and her children moved back to the area. After an admission to Bethesda Naval, Mr. Jones was again discharged, with no additional residential treatment. His mother opted to move the family to a city further south to attempt to get him into an established program there.

Mr. Jones was arrested for Murder on November 13, 2004. He was found incompetent to stand trial in November 2005 and was transferred to Benson Forensic Unit for restoration. Records indicate that he was cooperative with treatment, but reveal little else about him other than basic history that was already documented in previous records. There are no descriptions or information regarding his competence to stand trial at the end of this period of treatment in December 2005. His final diagnosis was Mood Disorder Not Otherwise Specified and Personality Disorder Not Otherwise Specified. It is important to note that he was treated with antipsychotic, antidepressant, and mood stabilizing medications; his mental state was stable at the time while on medication and he was found to be competent for trial.

Mr. Jones was convicted and sentenced to life plus 20 years for that offense. An evaluation prepared a year ago by Dr. Ernest Brooks for sentencing predicted that Mr. Jones was likely first to be perceived as a behavior problem, rather than mentally ill, in Department of Corrections (DOC) facilities. He also anticipated that the defendant's symptoms were likely too subtle to be detected in the prison system. He noted Mr. Jones's clear history of psychosis, even though he did not opine that the defendant was psychotic at the time of the offense in November 2004. As Dr. Brooks projected, Mr. Jones was indeed thought to be a behavior problem; he was involved in violence after his transfer to the DOC, and his mental disorder was not adequately treated. He spent a great deal of time in segregation without taking medication. Information reviewed for this evaluation suggests his medications were discontinued prior to his arrival at State Central Prison, and he also has a history of occasional noncompliance with medication. (Noncompliance is not unusual with people who lack insight into having a mental disorder, particularly when they are young.) Mr. Jones's mother noted that when she attempted to visit with him in prison, he went into the visitation booth but stared blankly when she pleaded with him to pick up the telephone receiver to talk with her. She said he had been batting at insects or something that she was unable to see, did not acknowledge her presence, and had lost a substantial amount of weight. In fact, Mr. Jones had been diagnosed with obesity during his first admission to Central State, and he was unable to provide a reason for his weight loss during the current evaluation, when he appeared to be of appropriate weight.

After the current charges were brought against him, the defendant was transferred to the ADC. For reasons that were not clear from the records, he had a "Do Not Treat" order. Mental health professionals were limited to inquiring about his condition through his cell door due to his history of violence and threats toward custody staff. Records are quite clear that the defendant appeared to be psychotic, and also uncooperative, upon his arrival at the ADC. He was placed on a special segregation unit that housed defendants with serious mental disorders or special protection needs. He remained in his cell, and was observed smearing feces on the window and walls; attempting to insert a hamburger into his anus; putting his food and clothing into the toilet, which also contained urine and feces; talking to himself; and staring into space. It was noted that he had a significant preoccupation with the toilet, and was often observed sitting or lying on the floor next to it. He was typically unresponsive to others. The mental health professionals involved in his care checked on him repeatedly, often observing him through the window when he did not realize they were watching, and his bizarre behavior was highly consistent. It would be most unusual for someone trying to fake a mental disorder to maintain highly

(continued)

(*continued*)

consistent bizarre behavior in seclusion for months. Typically, malingerers attempt to draw attention to their reported symptoms, while at the same time expecting the same liberties afforded to others in the hospital or jail setting. The records did not indicate that Mr. Jones ever complained about his sustained segregation.

Mr. Jones was ultimately transferred to Middleton State Hospital for two days in February. For the majority of time he was there, he was uncooperative. The nursing admitting note indicated his behavior was "very bizarre, Pt [was] aggressive, threatening bodily harm to staff;" however, on the day he was admitted, an order was written stating, "Patient is to receive no antipsychotic medications—please page attending [psychiatrist] if ordered by MOD." The psychiatry admitting note diagnosed malingering and indicated that medications were not to be given; no alternative diagnoses were noted, though Mr. Jones had just arrived and did not cooperate with the examination. Due to his threatening behavior and attempts to spit, Mr. Jones was in restraints and in a hood for the majority of his stay. While he was diagnosed with Malingering, he was never fully evaluated due to his uncooperative behavior, and similarly did not complete any psychological tests. Notes from nursing observations indicate that he was often quiet while in restraints, but he was also observed mumbling to himself. Physical restraint, rather than attempts to use the less restrictive alternative of psychotropic intervention, was the only treatment ordered, even though Mr. Jones had a history of compliance and nonviolence while treated with medications at the Benson Forensic Unit.

Mr. Jones was returned to the ADC in two days, and his behavior continued at the jail as it was before. Finally, in March 2007, he was prescribed Risperdal by the consulting psychiatrist at the jail, which has resulted in a dramatic change. Custody and mental health professionals alike have commented on how Mr. Jones has changed from exhibiting bizarre, uncommunicative or uncooperative behavior to being quite pleasant, cooperative, and compliant with jail routines. While documentation of this was available from the mental health staff, additional comments from different members of the custody staff regarding this change of behavior came unsolicited by this examiner at the time of the evaluation sessions. The frequency of commentary from custody staff has been most unusual, illustrating the degree of disturbance and dramatic change in Mr. Jones since he has been taking medication.

Defense counsel described her past attempts to work with Mr. Jones, noting that he seemed to have a "fog" over his eyes and was typically unresponsive. She had been unable to have a productive conversation with him about his case until recently, when he started taking medications. Mr. Jones's mother remarked that when she recently visited him at the ADC, he said, "Hi Mom" to her for the first time in months, and she was relieved to find he could actually hold a conversation with her after so many months of being bizarre and uncommunicative. His mother expressed her concern that Mr. Jones has been telling her he will be released from prison and will come home to take care of her.

While Mr. Jones has been described as exhibiting psychotic symptoms, such as hallucinations, combativeness, and intense paranoia, as well as obsessive–compulsive symptoms, records indicate he tends to underreport problems. His self-report typically includes comments that his mother had him admitted to hospitals "for a break," or that she did not understand that he liked to have a shaved head. Though he has often been observed talking to himself and appearing to be hallucinating, records reviewed for this examination established his long-standing pattern of denying this problem, even though multiple observers have seen him having conversations or attending to internal stimuli. This pattern continued during the current evaluation, as Mr. Jones adamantly denied any history of mental disorder, psychotic symptoms, or related issues.

Clinical Evaluation

For both evaluation sessions, Mr. Jones's hygiene and attire were appropriate. He was dressed in prison-issued clothing, with a clean-shaven face and very close-cut hair. Though he was no longer obese, he was unable to account for the weight loss. He was alert and fully oriented, smiling easily and presenting a pleasant and cooperative demeanor. His eye contact was good, and he appeared to be motivated to complete the interview and testing. At no time was he argumentative or oppositional. There were times during the evaluation when he seemed to lose his attention, and at such times, he stared blankly for just a moment before recovering and acting as though nothing had happened. He occasionally giggled immaturely, and his emotional expression was at times less serious than his current situation might evoke. In contrast, he also demonstrated an ability to focus keenly on his current predicament and respond appropriately. His demeanor fluctuated in this way throughout both sessions.

On mental status examination tasks, Mr. Jones's performance was similarly variable. He was able to complete the assessment of his recent memory functions, which includes attention and concentration, without error. His performance on tasks specifically designed to assess attention and concentration was poor. His abstract verbal reasoning and judgment revealed an unusual approach to ideas; his judgment was somewhat impaired on these tasks.

Mr. Jones denied having ever suffered from any type of hallucination. When descriptions of his behavior at the jail were read to him, he replied, "I'm just playin' . . . I'm off in my own little world, playing with things." He was informed that he had appeared to be responding to voices on several occasions when observed by mental health staff, to which he replied, "I be off in little communities with other people, having conversations with myself." He would only describe being "somewhere else" while at the jail, and would not divulge much else about his mental state. He avidly denied having a mental disorder, even when confronted with ample documentation of his behavior that suggested the contrary. When asked why he had been unresponsive to mental health staff, he replied, "I'm just in there daydreaming." Mr. Jones said he could not recall his other bizarre behaviors, such as trying to insert a hamburger in his anus. He offered, "I don't remember the hamburgers. I remember the feces." Regarding the smeared feces, he said, "I don't even know why I did it. Probably in there playing. Not playing, probably in there just acting stupid." He said it was not a ploy to get attention, but rather, "Just in there playing around, ended up throwing that shit on the wall." He had similar responses in explanation for his bizarre behavior in the past. For example, he said his mother had found him in his room "swinging my stereo cords around," and she had been afraid he was trying to hurt himself. He explained, "Man, I'm trying to tie my body up head to toe." He said he was doing this because he was bored. Regarding shaving several times a day until he bled, he explained that his mother "just don't understand her baby boy," and that he liked to be clean shaven. He minimized the observations by hospital staff in Florida that he had cuts on his body from shaving.

Neither Mr. Jones's interview behavior nor his psychological test data indicated malingering. In fact, his minimization and denial of past psychotic symptoms was profound and indicated not only an extreme lack of insight, but also the unlikelihood that he would draw attention to psychiatric problems if he needed help.

Currently, Mr. Jones is compliant with taking his antipsychotic medication. He noted that he is "taking the medicine 'cause they keep throwing it at me, but I'm saying I don't need to take it." At an earlier point, he claimed they were "experimenting" on him with the medication, and so he had considered refusing it. Again, it must be noted that multiple observers at the ADC remarked about the change in his behavior and demeanor since he started taking antipsychotic medication last March, and he recently has been returned to the general population at the jail for the first time in many months.

Competence to Stand Trial

Mr. Jones was able to communicate his factual knowledge of the legal system effectively and articulately. He correctly described the functions of a judge, jury, prosecutor, and defense attorney. He demonstrated his understanding of the three plea options (guilty, not guilty, not guilty by reason of insanity), as well as the rights that are forfeited with a guilty plea. In a discussion of the concept of jury versus bench trial, the defendant was able to provide logical reasons for choosing either one. Mr. Jones clearly understood the adversarial nature of legal proceedings, as well as his rights in such proceedings.

During the first session, Mr. Jones said he had "heard about" being charged with another homicide and did not seem to understand how this came about. This was initially viewed with some skepticism; however, before the second session, Mr. Jones engaged in a productive conversation with his attorney for the first time. He was much better informed about his situation at the second meeting with this examiner and was able to hold an intelligent conversation about the new information. He was able to discuss the charges against him and their gravity, and demonstrated his understanding of capital, felony, and misdemeanor charges. He expressed confidence in his attorney and a strong motivation to work with her.

Of concern in this case is a quality that Dr. Brooks also noted last year. Mr. Jones did not seem to fully appreciate his current situation and the impact it will have on his life. Though he is aware he has been sentenced to life plus 20 years, he maintained that his lawyer had told him he would be released in 20 years, at age 40, which was incorrect. At the first meeting he was upset about the additional charges against him; at the second session he seemed relaxed and nonchalant about their potential impact on his situation and the serious trial he may be facing. It was not clear if this was an issue of maturity, as adolescents often do

(continued)

(*continued*)

not comprehend the lifelong impact of things (he has been incarcerated since age 17 and remains immature), or if his apparent disconnection from the seriousness of his situation is rooted in a personality or mental disorder.

At the present time, Mr. Jones's mental disorder appears to be fairly well-controlled with psychotropic medication. He demonstrated an ability to discuss his present situation articulately and constructively. He clearly had a rational and factual knowledge of legal proceedings in general, and had a factual understanding of the charges against him. His rational understanding of the charges was less clear, but did not appear to be impaired to the point that he could not confer with defense counsel effectively. Two particular concerns were his occasionally inappropriate emotional expression, and it was not clear if his difficulty with appreciating long-term consequences will have an impact on his ability to effectively participate in the preparation of his defense.

Mr. Jones has an unequivocal history of minimizing the symptoms and impact of his mental disorder, and has remarked at how he can present himself in a falsely positive light while on medication. His competence to stand trial may fluctuate based on his medication compliance and mental state, and it may not be abundantly clear when this defendant loses his ability to attend and make appropriate decisions on his behalf. Mr. Jones expressed his understanding that a finding of incompetence will not result in dropped charges, but would only postpone the

inevitable. He maintained that he has no desire to postpone the matter in question.

There are times when evaluations of defendants do not produce clear-cut, affirmative answers to the referral question. This is one of those cases. Based on the current evaluation and available information, it is my opinion that Mr. Jones had the capacity to understand the proceedings against him and to assist his attorney at the time he was evaluated. This condition has the potential to change based on his medication compliance and the effectiveness of his treatment. As noted in previous evaluations, his mental condition clearly has the potential to deteriorate, and if his hearings or trial are postponed or lengthy, the issue of competence may need to be revisited at any point during the process. His current attorney appears to be sensitized to his condition and able to work with him. Future requests for competency evaluations, if necessary, may promote early intervention if Mr. Jones's condition begins to deteriorate. This would decrease the length of time necessary to restabilize him if indeed he has decompensated.

In order to maintain his current level of functioning, it is imperative that he complies with treatment recommended by his psychiatrist and that he receives consistent mental health care.

Respectfully submitted,
Jane Smith, Psy.D., ABPP
Diplomate in Forensic Psychology
Licensed Clinical Psychologist

Once a competency evaluation has been completed and the written report submitted, the court may schedule a hearing. Such a hearing may not be necessary, however, if both the defense and the prosecution accept the findings and recommendations of the evaluator. For defendants found incompetent, either the trials are postponed until competency is regained or the charges are dismissed. But it is the disposition of incompetent defendants that is perhaps the most problematic area in competency procedures.

Prior to 1972, there was no legal direction on how long an incompetent defendant can be held, and some were held indefinitely. But in that same year came the case of *Jackson v. Indiana* in which the U.S. Supreme Court held that defendants committed solely on the basis of incompetency "cannot be held more than the reasonable period of time necessary to determine whether there is a substantial probability that he will attain that capacity in the foreseeable future" (p. 738). The Court did not specify how long a period of time would be reasonable nor did it indicate how progress toward the goal of regaining competency could be assessed.

At the present time the length of commitment of incompetent defendants varies from state to state, with some states having specific time limits while other states base length of treatment on a proportion of the length of sentence that would have been given if the defendant had been convicted. While in the psychiatric hospital most defendants receive psychotropic medication, although some jurisdictions have established treatment programs designed to increase understanding of the legal process or that confront problems that hinder a defendant's ability to participate in their defense (Davis, 1985).

The question of competence in juveniles, especially adolescents has proven to be an important one in forensic psychology. The MacArthur Foundation Research Network interviewed 1,400 individuals aged 11–24 both in juvenile detention centers and in the community at large to determine whether teens differed from young adults (aged 18–24) in their abilities relevant for competence to stand trial. Youth were interviewed in Philadelphia, Los Angeles, northern Florida, and Virginia. Using a standard assessment tool (MacArthur Competence Assessment Tool—Criminal Adjudication (MacCAT-CA)), the study first gauged the functional abilities defined in the existing legal concept of *competence to proceed*—the ability to understand the purpose and nature of the trial process; the capacity to provide relevant information to counsel and to process that information; and the ability to apply information to one's own situation in a manner that is neither distorted nor irrational (Grisso et al., 2003). The youngest group was nearly three times more likely than youth older than 15 to be significantly impaired in reasoning and understanding, two important components of legal competence. In other words, nearly one-third of 11 to 13-year-olds and one-fifth of 14 to 15-year-olds had deficits that courts might see as serious enough to question their ability to proceed in a trial. These patterns varied little by race, ethnicity, gender, socioeconomic status, or region of the country.

Can Competency be Restored against a Defendant's Will?

In most circumstances, people are free to refuse unwanted medical treatment, even when such treatment may be in their best medical interests. This can include declining blood transfusions, refusing extreme measures to sustain life (e.g., mechanical resuscitation), not accepting lifesaving cancer treatments, and not vaccinating their children.

But in the criminal justice system, incarcerated individuals—even those who are simply awaiting trial—have a reduced right to refuse unwanted medical treatment. The courts have generally held that in prisons the rights of the state must be balanced with the prisoner's right to refuse treatment. Thus, the state often puts forth various medical and legal reasons to forcibly administer medical treatment to a prisoner. These may include the need to halt the spread of disease within the prison, to ensure the physical safety of prisoners and prison personnel; and to "restore" competency to an incompetent defendant so that he may stand trial or even be executed. It is this last class that is the most troubling from a legal standpoint.

There are two general scenarios involving restoration of competency of incarcerated individuals. The first is where an incompetent criminal defendant awaits trial and, without restoration of competency, may be incarcerated indefinitely until competency returns. The second is where a defendant is sentenced to death but later deemed incompetent to be executed, and the state seeks to restore competency through forced medication—solely to then execute the prisoner.

In *Riggins v. Nevada* (1992), the Court was faced with the issue of involuntarily medicating a mentally ill prisoner who had not yet been convicted. The trial court refused to allow Riggins to discontinue his medication despite his arguments that its continuation would affect both his demeanor at trial and his ability to meaningfully assist in his own defense. As in *Harper*, the Supreme Court recognized the serious and sometimes fatal side effects associated with the administration of antipsychotic medications. In this case, however, the Court held that the nonconvicted defendant could not be involuntarily medicated absent any showing by the state that less intrusive means were available to restore his competency and that he was a danger to himself or others—which had not ever been made.

In 2001 a federal court established a legal precedent for forcibly administering medication to restore competency in a case of a federal Capitol crime. The decision was based on the events of July 24, 1998, when Russell Eugene Weston, armed with a .38 caliber revolver forced his way past security checkpoints at the U.S. Capitol. He shot and killed Capitol police officers Jacob Chestnut and John Gibson. He also shot and seriously wounded capitol police officer Douglas McMillan. Weston, himself seriously wounded in the gunfight, was arrested at the scene. The government indicted Weston on two counts of murdering a federal law enforcement officer, one count of attempting to murder a federal law enforcement officer, and three counts of using a firearm in a crime of violence (*United States v. Weston*, 2001).

The government wanted to try Weston for these crimes but was initially unable to do so because the district court found him incompetent to stand trial. The district court accepted the conclusion of a court-appointed forensic psychiatrist that Weston suffered from paranoid schizophrenia, and that the severity of his symptoms rendered him incapable of understanding the proceedings against him and assisting in his defense, as required by a federal statute for bringing a defendant to trial (*18 U.S.C.* § 4241(a)). After two administrative hearings and two district court hearings, the government obtained an order authorizing it to administer antipsychotic medication against Weston's will.

May the Federal Government Administer Antipsychotic Drugs Involuntarily to a Mentally Ill Criminal Defendant in order to Render that Defendant Competent to Stand Trial for Serious, but Nonviolent, Crimes?

Sell v. United States (2003)

In 1997, the federal government charged Dr. Charles Sell with submitting fictitious insurance claims for payment. Although Sell has a long history of mental illness and was initially found competent to stand trial for fraud and attempted murder, a federal magistrate judge ordered his hospitalization to determine whether he would attain the capacity to allow his trial to proceed. Subsequently, the magistrate authorized forced administration of antipsychotic drugs. The district court affirmed the magistrate's decision and concluded that medication was the only viable hope of rendering Sell competent to stand trial and was necessary to serve the federal government's interest in obtaining an adjudication of his guilt or innocence. The court of appeals affirmed this decision as well. On the fraud charges, the appellate court found that the federal government had an essential interest in bringing Sell to trial, that the treatment was medically appropriate, and that the medical evidence indicated that Sell would fairly be able to participate in his trial. The case was appealed to the U.S. Supreme Court.

In this case the Court was asked to clarify the circumstances in which a court may order the involuntary administration of antipsychotic medication to a criminal defendant who is incompetent to stand trial, but who is competent to make medical decisions on his own behalf (including the decision to refuse antipsychotic medication) and who is not dangerous to himself or others.

The American Psychological Association, in a filed *amicus* brief took the position that, although such involuntary administration of antipsychotic medication is not flatly forbidden by the Constitution, its use must be carefully limited to those circumstances where no less intrusive approach will be effective, the specific identified medication is substantially likely to be effective at restoring the individual to competency, and the medication is not likely to result in serious adverse side effects.

In a 6–3 opinion delivered by Justice Stephen G. Breyer, the Court held that the Constitution allows the federal government to administer antipsychotic drugs, even against the defendant's will, in limited circumstances. The Court reasoned that such conditions include if the treatment is medically appropriate, is substantially unlikely to have side effects that may undermine the trial's fairness, and, taking account of less intrusive alternatives, is necessary significantly to further important governmental trial-related interests. Finding that the district court and court of appeals' findings did not satisfy these conditions, however, the Court vacated the lower court's judgment.

The Court further clarified (at pp. 12–13) that (1) in determining whether the government has an important interest in bringing a defendant to trial, a trial court must consider the possibility that the defendant will be civilly committed, or has already been detained for a lengthy period; (2) the government must show that the medication is substantially likely to render the defendant competent to stand trial; (3) the court must find that no alternative, less intrusive (e.g., nondrug) alternative approach is likely to achieve substantially the same result of restoring a defendant to competency; and (4) the particular medication must be in the patient's best interest, taking into account both efficaciousness and side effects (pp. 12–13).

A further important point is that the Court made clear that, before ordering involuntary administration of drugs to restore a defendant to competency, a trial court should first consider whether involuntary medication would be justified to address the defendant's dangerousness to himself or others (pp. 14–15). The Court's analysis showed support with involuntary drug treatment on grounds of dangerousness rather than with such drug administration solely for restoration of competency. The Court specifically remarked that, although involuntary administration of drugs solely for trial competence may be permitted in certain instances, "those instances will be rare" (p. 12).

CRIMINAL RESPONSIBILITY AND INSANITY

Trial competence is different from **criminal responsibility**. The former refers to current ability to understand and participate in the trial process. Criminal responsibility (the "insanity defense") refers to one's state of mind at the time of the alleged crime. The distinction sounds relatively straightforward, but the two are frequently confused. For example, a person could be psychotic and not responsible when assaulting someone in 2007, but be non-psychotic and fully competent for his trial in, say, 2008. Similarly (but less commonly), a person could be mentally capable of (and thus responsible for) intending to rob a bank in 2007 but be unable to understand the trial process a year later (perhaps because of decompensating psychiatric illness or head trauma).

It is a common misconception that *insane* is a psychiatric or psychological term, but its origins and present usages are legal not medical. However, insanity has always been juxtaposed with mental illness and even with dangerousness. This is evidenced by the old legal maxim of *insanus est qui, abjecta ratione, omnia cum impetus et furore facit*—he is insane who, reason being thrown away, does everything with violence and rage (Black, 1990). But under most present law the term *insanity* refers to "... a condition which renders [an] affected person unfit to enjoy liberty of action because of the unreliability of his behavior [which can include] concomitant danger to himself or others" (Black at 794).

In the criminal justice system legal insanity is most pertinent to the conception of punishment. The English and American systems of justice are based on the assumption that people are free agents and make rational decisions concerning their actions. Accordingly, individuals are held accountable for their actions. Insanity is thought to interfere with free and rational decision making. Therefore, an insane person cannot form the necessary "criminal intent" or "guilty mind" (i.e., *mens rea*) to be considered culpable.

The Historical Basis of the Insanity Defense

As indicated in chapter 1 of this text, in the thirteenth century, the English Lord Bracton established the principle of mental deficiency in human behavior. He said that some people simply do not know what they are doing and act in a manner "as to be not far removed from the brute" (Menninger, 1968). From that concept, "insanity" came to mean that a person lacks the awareness of what he/she is doing and therefore cannot form an intent to do wrong.

From the fourteenth through sixteenth centuries in England, in order to be found guilty of an offense, an individual had to understand the difference between good and evil. Because the capacity to freely choose evil behavior was "restrained in children, in fools, and in the witless," the witless were sometimes found to be without guilt (Pratt & Diamond, 1966). In the 1724 case of *Rex v. Arnold*, jurors were instructed to acquit the defendant (who had wounded a British lord in an assassination attempt) if they found him to be "totally deprived of his understanding and memory, and doth not know what he is doing, no more than a brute or a wild beast." This revised instruction meant that insanity had become less a moral failing (good versus evil) and more a cognitive failing—that is, a mental deficiency involving "understanding and memory" (p. 109). More than a century later, in the 1840 case of *Regina v. Oxford*, the standard shifted even further. In that case, it was held that, because of a "diseased mind," the defendant was "quite unaware of the nature, character, and consequences of the act he was committing" (p. 525).

The M'Naughten Rule

One of the most important cases in the history of the insanity defense concerns that of Daniel M'Naughten who shot and killed the British Prime Minister's secretary in 1843 and attempted to assassinate the prime minister himself. M'Naughten believed that the prime minister was the architect of the numerous of personal and financial misfortunes that had befallen him. During his trial, nine witnesses testified to the fact that he was insane, and the jury acquitted him, finding him "**not guilty by reason of insanity**."

Queen Victoria was not happy with this outcome, and requested that the House of Lords review the verdict with a panel of judges, and pass new laws to protect the public from "the wrath of madmen who could now kill with impunity" (Eule, 1978). The judges reversed the jury verdict, and the formulation that emerged from their review—that a defendant should not be held responsible for his actions if he could not tell that his actions were wrong at the time he committed them—became the law governing legal responsibility in cases of insanity in England.

This new **M'Naughten Test** as embraced by American courts, required clear proof that the individual was, at the time he/she committed the offense, operating under defect of reason from a disease of the mind and that such a defect resulted in the individual's not being able to recognize the nature and quality of his actions, or not knowing that such actions were wrong. This became the insanity standard until the mid-twentieth century. In 1998, 25 states plus the District of Columbia still used versions of the M'Naughten Rule to test for legal insanity (Huckabee, 2000). But the nineteenth century was to see other cases that set the stage for further changes in the legal definition of insanity.

On Sunday, February 27, 1859 Congressman Daniel Sickles saw Phillip Barton Key (a member of Washington, DC's social elite and the son of Francis Scott Key, author of *The Star Spangled Banner*) attempting to call up to a second story window where Sickles' wife slept. Having suspected that his wife and Key were having an affair, Sickles grabbed two handguns from his bedroom. He dashed into the street where several pedestrians were walking. He ran up to Key screaming: "You must die! You must die!" Without further provocation, he fired several shots at Key, striking him in the leg and thigh. Key fell back against a fence and pled for his life: "Please don't kill me!" Sickles pointed a handgun at the victim's chest and fired point blank killing Key.

At his trial for first degree murder his attorney said that Sickles could not be held responsible because he was driven insane by the knowledge his wife was having an affair with Phillip Key. Sickles was acquitted of the charges and in the process became one of the first defendants in American history to utilize an insanity defense.

The confusion regarding mental illness and insanity in the criminal justice system had not changed much by 1881 when Charles Guiteau was charged with the assassination of President James Garfield.

Guiteau was a strange and at times bizarre individual who exhibited many of the symptoms of paranoid schizophrenia. One of his delusions was that he should be appointed as ambassador to France because he wrote a speech for President Garfield that he imagined helped get Garfield elected in 1880. In reality the speech was never used and Guiteau became angry and resentful over this "betrayal" by the president. After stalking the president for almost a month, he managed to shoot Garfield in the back in Washington, DC. The president died from his wounds three months later.

Guiteau reported that God told him to kill Garfield for political reasons (Knappman, 1994). He was found guilty or murder on January 13, 1882. Upon hearing the verdict Guiteau jumped to his feet and screamed "You are all low, consummate jackasses!" (p. 190). While on the gallows he recited an incoherent poem in a child's voice before being hung. This case illustrated the misunderstanding regarding legally significant mental illness and the need for change in the way the criminal justice system dealt with insanity.

The Durham Test: Irresistible Impulse

Many critics of the M'Naughten Test noted that cognition is only part of "insanity" and maybe not even the most important part. In an effort to capture the volitional aspect of insanity, some states added the term *irresistible impulse* to their definitions of insanity. The revised M'Naughten Test allowed an insanity defense to be raised on the grounds that the person may have known the nature and quality of his actions and knew it was wrong, but the person's mental disability resulted in an overpowering impulse or compulsion which did not allow the individual to resist the actions he undertook. The rationale here was that such a powerful compulsion made the prospect of criminal punishment ineffective as a deterrent and, thus, persons should not be held accountable for their actions. Or stated another way, a defendant could be acquitted if "his reasoning powers were so far dethroned by his diseased mental condition as to deprive him of willpower to resist the insane impulse to perpetrate the deed, though knowing it to be wrong" (*Smith v. United States*, 1929). The federal circuit court in the District of Columbia adopted this "Durham Test" in the 1954 case of *Durham v. United States*. But the test never received wide acceptance in the United States and was rejected by thirty states and five federal circuits.

The Model Penal Code: Turning Responsibility to the Jury

In 1962, the American Law Institute ("ALI") drafted the **Model Penal Code** test in an attempt to solve problems of earlier insanity tests. This rule says that a defendant is not responsible for criminal conduct where he/she, as a result of mental disease or defect, did not possess "substantial capacity either to appreciate the criminality of his conduct or to conform his conduct to the requirements of the law." This new rule was based on the District of Columbia Circuit's decision in the federal appellate case of *United States v. Brawner* (2007). In comparison to the M'Naughten Test (knowing right from wrong), the Model Penal Code lowered the insanity standard to a "substantial incapacity" to appreciate the difference between right and wrong; thereby recognizing degrees of incapacity. This standard is very vague and leaves a number of factors up to the jury to determine, given the facts of a case and the testimony of experts. About half the states have adopted the Model Penal Code rule for insanity.

Not Guilty by Reason of Insanity (NGRI) v. Guilty but Mentally Ill (GBMI)

Some of the beliefs of the general public concerning the insanity defense are that criminals often claim insanity; many of these criminals are set free by juries; those found NGRI are released back into society after the trial; and such persons present a threat to society due to their dangerousness and being "back on the street." The reality of the insanity defense is much different than the public generally believes. The insanity defense is employed in only about 1 out of every 200 criminal cases. Of these, it is successful less than 1% of the time (Wrightsman, 1994). Kirschner and Galperin (2001) examined all defendants who were indicted for felonies and who raised any type of psychiatric defense in New York County from

1988 to 1997 and found that psychiatric defenses were only used for 16% of all indicted defendants during this time.

But even when successful, an NGRI verdict is not grounds for immediate release back into society. Rather, the offender found NGRI is confined to a mental hospital for an indeterminate length of time. It is rare that such offenders are released from the hospital short of several years, and many remain there for most (if not all) of their lives. The criteria for release in these cases are far more restrictive than for other cases of commitment. In fact, it is not uncommon for an insanity acquittee to serve more time in a psychiatric hospital than he/she would have served in prison had the jury returned a guilty verdict. The typical NGRI acquitte is a seriously disturbed (and often psychotic) marginalized member of society who is most often an unemployed white male in his late 20s or early 30s with a history or previous hospitalizations and/or arrests (Wrightsman, Nietzel, & Fortune, 1994).

Nevertheless, when John Hinckley was found not guilty by reason of insanity on June 21, 1982 for attempting to assassinate President Reagan, there was great pressure for reform of the insanity defense. Within a month of the trial's conclusion, committees of the House and Senate held hearings regarding use of the insanity defense. During the three years following the Hinckley acquittal, Congress and half of the states enacted changes in the insanity defense, all limiting use of the defense. Congress and nine states limited the substantive test of insanity; Congress and seven states shifted the burden of proof to the defendant, and one state, Utah, abolished the defense outright.

Twelve states in the aftermath of the Hinckley trial established a completely separate verdict of "guilty but mentally ill" (GBMI). The primary difference with regard to the GBMI verdict concerns the finding of guilty rather than not guilty and the defendant is still considered fully culpable for the crime. In states allowing for a finding of GBMI, the defendant generally pleads insanity, but the jury has the option of finding him or her GBMI rather than NGRI. In such cases the defendant is sentenced for the crime committed, but spends the sentence in a hospital until sanity is restored. If and when such a time arrives that the defendant is perceived to have regained his/her sanity, the person is transported to prison to serve the remainder of the sentence. Time in the hospital is not credited as good time spent toward earlier parole.

The GBMI verdict has not escaped criticism, the major one being that it confuses jurors and offers a shortcut verdict that enables them to avoid the difficult issues surrounding the insanity defense. In addition, most jurors do not understand that the mental illness of a defendant found GBMI does not insure that he/she will receive additional treatment in prison. One of the more common criticisms of the insanity defense as a whole concerns its reliance on expert testimony. More specifically, in cases in which insanity is an issue, jurors may be unduly influenced by the expressed opinions of experts whose testimony, although influential, may have little basis in scientific accuracy. This is especially true since psychologists and psychiatrists usually have little if any training in legal matters.

Some of these issues have been addressed in the Insanity Defense Reform Act of 1984, which was the first comprehensive federal legislation governing the insanity defense and the disposition of individuals suffering from a mental disease or defect who are involved in the criminal justice system. The Act requires the defendant to prove, by "clear and convincing evidence," that "at the time of the commission of the acts constituting the offense, the defendant, as a result of a severe mental disease or defect, was unable to appreciate the nature and quality or the wrongfulness of his acts." This is generally viewed as a return to the "knowing right from wrong" standard. The Act also restricted the scope of expert testimony by saying that "No expert witness testifying with respect to the mental state or condition of a defendant in a criminal case may state an opinion or inference as to whether the defendant did or did not have the mental state or condition constituting an element of the crime charged or a defense thereto. Such ultimate issues are for the trier of fact alone" (Title 18, U.S. Code, § 17).

Can a Mentally Incompetent Person Be Executed?

Panetti v. Dretke (2007)

On September 8, 1992, Scott Louis Panetti, dressed in camouflage military fatigues and donning a recently shaved head, fired a sawed off shotgun at his parents-in-law at close range inside their Texas home while his wife and daughter watched in terror. At trial, Panetti appeared in an old-fashioned cowboy outfit, shouted incomprehensible ramblings at the judge and jury, and applied to subpoena more than 200 witnesses, including Pope John Paul II, John F. Kennedy, and Jesus Christ. Panetti also blamed the shootings on "Sarge," one of his multiple personalities whom he claimed was responsible for the killings. The jury found him guilty of murder and sentenced him to death.

Panetti, however, suffers from a long history of mental illness including schizoaffective disorder. Although he understands that he killed two people and he knows that the state's stated reason for his execution is because of the murders, he believes that the state actually intends to execute him in order to carry out a satanic conspiracy against him. The U.S. District Court and the U.S. Court of Appeals for the Fifth Circuit upheld Panetti's execution on the grounds that he is "aware" of his death sentence and its stated purpose. But Panetti argued that "awareness" is not enough and that a prisoner must also have a "rational understanding" of the connection between his crime and the punishment.

The U.S. Supreme Court accepted the case in order to determine whether executing a mentally ill prisoner who lacks "rational understanding" of the reasons for his execution would violate the Eighth Amendment. In making their decision, the Supreme Court conducted a thorough analysis of English and American common law as well as contemporary normative standards. The court found that the common law tradition has prohibited executing the mentally ill because it lacks a retributive purpose, finding that civilized societies possess a "natural abhorrence" toward killing a prisoner who lacks the "capacity to come to grips with his own conscience or deity," and that this value "is still vivid today" (p. 409).

Although the Court did not establish a standard to determine a requisite level of insanity that a prisoner must display in order to have his death sentence repealed, Justice Powell addressed this issue in a concurring opinion. Powell noted that the death penalty can only be effective in punishing a prisoner if he understands its "existence and purpose." (p. 421). If the prisoner is capable of understanding "the connection between his crime and punishment" then the underlying retributive goal of the criminal law would be satisfied (p. 422). If the prisoner is unaware of the punishment and the reason for it, however, then executing him would be cruel and unusual in violation of the Eighth Amendment.

CIVIL COMMITMENT

The total number of persons involuntarily committed on any given day in the United States is approximately 39,868 (Parry, 2005).

History and Rationale

In colonial America incompetent persons was not considered a matter of government responsibility and were left to their families for care. Mentally disabled persons without family support often joined wandering bands drifting from town to town. If such a person became violent, he/she might be punished as a criminal. If not, the person was subjected to restraint and perhaps whipping; no treatment was provided, since none existed. It was not until Benjamin Franklin and others authorized the establishment of general hospitals to receive and cure mental illness as well as the sick and poor in the mid-eighteenth century that government and society accepted responsibility for care and treatment of mentally ill individuals (Parry, 1994). It was not until 1773 in Williamsburg, Virginia, when the first hospital devoted exclusively to the mentally disabled was constructed. Also during this period, state legislatures began enacting statutes that expressly provided authority for confining the mentally disabled in community institutions.

Civil commitment and the inpatient treatment of the mentally ill faced a major transformation in the mid-1950s with the advent of psychotropic medications. These drugs offered, for the first time, an inexpensive, relatively quick treatment that could be made available to a large number of mentally ill people. Hospital beds could be emptied at a faster rate, allowing more admissions but also, in the long run, reducing the overall population. At the same time as the medication revolution, came the community treatment movement. In 1963, Congress passed the **Community Mental Health Centers Act**, which provided funding for the establishment of outpatient treatment centers. The CMHC Act was representative of a widespread effort to move the locus of treatment from isolated hospitals to the patients' communities.

Beginning in the 1970s, commitment proceedings became reformed resulting in more constitutional rights for the mentally ill together with the ability to resist compulsory commitment. The 1975 case of *O'Connor v. Donaldson*, discussed elsewhere in this chapter, held, among other things, that mental illness and a need for treatment alone were insufficient justifications for involuntarily committing mentally ill persons who were not dangerous. Limits on involuntary hospitalizations have been upheld by the Supreme Court in cases such as *Foucha v. Louisiana* (1992) where the Court held that an individual who is not mentally ill cannot be involuntarily committed for civil purposes, and that the standard for commitment should be mental illness and dangerousness to self or others (or a grave lack of ability to care for oneself) rather than mental illness alone.

Types of Civil Commitment

There are today three places of commitment for persons with mental illness: "inpatient" commitment (to an institution); "outpatient" commitment (to the community with close monitoring by a government agency, private agency, or individuals); and "criminal" commitment, that is, where a person is either found not guilty of criminal responsibility, yet mentally ill and in need of care and treatment, or found guilty and mentally ill and who will receive psychiatric services in a prison (Stavis, 1995).

INPATIENT CIVIL COMMITMENT   In line with *Foucha v. Louisiana*, as of this writing, the inpatient commitment statutes of every state and the District of Columbia require some combination of mental illness and dangerousness. For two examples, the reader is directed to Virginia's Involuntary Commitment Statute (VA Code § 37.2: 800–809), and Illinois's Commitment Statute (405 ILL. COMP. STAT. 5/1–119), both of which require some degree of mental illness and an imminent danger to self or others for involuntary commitment.

OUTPATIENT CIVIL COMMITMENT   According to the Treatment Advocacy Center (TAC), and its founder Dr. E. Fuller Torry, there are over 3 million individuals with schizophrenia and manic–depressive illness (bipolar disorder) in the United States, and approximately 800,000 of them who, would have been in state hospitals before "deinstitutionalization" began in the 1970s. Almost 40% of these individual are not under treatment at any one time. Many are homeless or in jail, or arguably responsible for increasing episodes of violence. Due to the lack of awareness of their illness, these individuals deny they are sick and refuse to take medication (Torrey, 2008). In response to this observation, many jurisdictions have instituted what is called **assisted outpatient treatment**.

According to its proponents, assisted outpatient treatment ("AOT") is designed to help people adhere to a treatment plan, prevent psychological decompensation, and assist them in functioning successfully out of the hospital. The TAC points to studies in Arizona, Hawaii, Iowa, New York, North Carolina, and other states that demonstrated that assisted outpatient treatment works. For example, in New York, during the course of court-ordered treatment when compared to the three years prior to participation in the program, assisted outpatient treatment (AOT) recipients experienced far less hospitalization, homelessness, arrest, and incarceration.

One of the more recent incarnations of AOT is **Kendra's Law**. The law was originally introduced by then New York State Governor George E. Pataki as a response to two similar incidents occurring in 1999 on the New York subway system. In one incident a man diagnosed with schizophrenia pushed Edgar Rivera into the path of an oncoming train severing his legs. In the other incident, Andrew Goldstein, age 29, pushed 32-year-old Kendra Webdale on the tracks, killing her. Both men were schizophrenic and had been dismissed by psychiatric facilities with little or no medication (Haroules, 2005).

It should be noted that the increasing use of AOT has not gone without criticism. The most frequent criticism is that such procedures represent an inappropriate infringement on civil liberty. More specifically, it is contended that outpatient commitment (a) abandons the dangerousness criteria for civil commitment, (b) promotes unwarranted inpatient commitment of those who do not meet civil commitment criteria, and (c) undermines important individual liberties by diluting the right to refuse treatment. Despite, these serious and fundamental doubts about outpatient commitment, its practice seems to be growing, and 42 states and the District of Columbia have some kind of assisted outpatient treatment laws in place (Prentky et al., 2006; Zander, 2005).

SEXUALLY VIOLENT PREDATOR COMMITMENT This type of civil commitment has become increasingly more prevalent since the mid-1990s, and involves confining sex offenders deemed too dangerous to release from prison. The first **sexually violent predator law** in the United States was the Community Protection Act of 1990 passed in the state of Washington. As of this writing there are 17 states with such a law that calls for dangerous sex offenders to be confined in a treatment center or psychiatric hospital after they've served their prison sentences. Despite some state-to-state variation, all sexually violent predator ("SVP") laws share four basic elements. To be committed, an individual must (a) have some mental disorder or abnormality that (b) causes or is associated with (c) an elevated risk of future sexual misconduct. In addition, all SVP laws profess that (d) a purpose of commitment is treatment. The law gives an inmate the right to a jury trial. A judge has the ultimate say over whether a sex offender is confined to the state facility, released outright or released with constant monitoring (Lieb & Gookin, 2005).

The first test case involving SVP was ***Kansas v. Hendricks*** (1997), which is described in more depth below. This case arose from a 1993 incident involving the rape and murder of a University of Kansas student by Leroy Hendricks, a five-time convicted child molester who had been in and out of prisons for nearly 40 years. The Kansas Legislature passed their SVP law in reaction to this crime. The law provided for the civil commitment of certain sexually violent felons who were considered too dangerous to be released back into the community.

SVP laws have also met with criticism from some in the psychological community who feel that it is scientifically impossible to predict whether a convicted sex offender will reoffend. In *Kansas v. Hendricks* the defendant made it clear that he would not be able to resist committing further sex crimes upon release from prison. In fact, he asserted that the only way to absolutely prevent him from molesting another child was for him to die. He felt that he was a pedophile and that his condition was not treatable. But such an open admission is usually not the case, and courts look to psychological and psychiatric experts for judgments regarding the likelihood of future violent sexual acts—judgments that may be difficult to make. It is indeed possible that some decisions by courts regarding sexually violent predators are based more on moral grounds than on hard scientific evidence. The deprivation of liberty and imposition of treatment resulting from such SVP commitments may, according to some, rest on "bad science," which misrepresents, and selectively reports findings from scientific articles (Bilbrey, 1999).

FORENSIC PSYCHOLOGY IN THE SPOTLIGHT

Is an *Absolute* lack of Self-Control Necessary before a Sexually Violent Predator can be Civilly Committed?

Kansas v. Hendricks (1997) *and Kansas v. Crane* (2002)

At issue in the 2002 case of *Kansas v. Crane* was whether the Kansas Sexually Violent Predator Act (SVPA) was constitutional in that the defendant, Michael Crane *could* exercise some control over his inclination to commit sexually violent acts. Previously, in the 1997 case of *Kansas v. Hendricks*, the Kansas SVPA had been found to be constitutional by the U.S. Supreme Court with regard to Ex Post Facto, Double Jeopardy, and Substantive Due Process challenges. That case involved an individual, Leroy Hendricks, who was unable to control his urges to commit future acts of sexual violence. The Kansas SVPA survived the ex post facto and double jeopardy challenges in *Hendricks* because the Court interpreted the SVPA's intention to be primarily civil in nature rather than criminal, and as such, these constitutional protections did not apply to SVPA proceedings. The Court found that in order to be one of the "narrow circumstances" in which a state may physically restrain someone due to their inability to control their behavior, a danger to society must be posed.

In *Crane* the Court had to decide if, in addition to a showing of mental illness or mental abnormality and dangerousness, a showing of a complete "lack of control" on the part of the civilly committed defendant was necessary in order for the SVPA to be constitutional. Is a lesser degree of volitional control or other impairments specified by SVP laws, such as emotional impairments allowable under the constitution?

The Court held the Kansas SVPA constitutional because it was sufficiently narrowly tailored so that it restricted the freedom of a small subclass of severely dangerousness mentally ill patients without infringing on the freedom of the dangerous, nonmentally ill. The due process analysis previously announced in *Hendricks* does not require a showing of a complete "lack of control" (in addition to mental illness or mental abnormality). A showing of *some degree* of volitional impairment is constitutional. The Supreme Court has consistently upheld involuntary commitment statutes that detain people who are unable to control their behavior and thereby pose a danger to the public health and safety, provided the confinement takes place pursuant to proper procedures and evidentiary standards.

The Kansas SVPA was specifically upheld because it unambiguously requires a precommitment finding of dangerousness either to one's self or to others, and links that finding to a determination that the person suffers from a mental abnormality or personality disorder.

Summary

The first American hospital for the exclusive care of people with mental disorders was established in 1773, in Williamsburg, Virginia. During the next 180 years these "asylums" became "warehouses" for individuals with mental disorders (and others) without sufficient procedural safeguards. From 1955 to 1975, with the advent of psychotropic medication and the proliferation of the community mental health movement, treatment of the mentally ill moved from the institution to the community.

The issue of **competency** is relevant in both the civil and criminal justice systems. In the civil justice system this may involve making a contract, understanding the terms of a will, deciding medical treatment, consenting to participation in research, and the need for appointing legal guardians and conservators. In the criminal justice system competency is involved in the capacity to comprehend legal proceedings, communicate with an attorney, and to understand and waive certain rights. The overriding principle that makes the issue of competence so important is that a person who cannot understand the nature and purpose of criminal proceedings should not be the subject of such actions against him or her.

There is no psychiatric diagnosis that always renders a defendant incompetent to stand trial or waive constitutional rights. Even the presence of psychosis is not sufficient by itself for such a finding. People with schizophrenia or bipolar illness are not incompetent per se, and those with less serious diagnoses are not necessarily competent. In order for a court to make a determination on the competency issue, a forensic evaluation and subsequent report are often required. The drafting of a forensic report requires the examiner to organize, weigh, and integrate data from various sources. At the minimum, reports should include the circumstances of the referral, nature of clinical contacts, collateral data sources, relevant personal background information, clinical findings, and conclusions.

For a defendant found incompetent to stand trial, either the trial is postponed until competency is regained or the charges may be dismissed. But the Supreme Court established in the case of *Jackson v. Indiana* that a defendant committed solely on the basis of incompetency cannot be held more than the reasonable period of time necessary to determine whether there is a substantial probability that he will attain that capacity in the foreseeable future. Presently, the length of time allowed for the commitment of incompetent defendants varies from state to state. The Supreme Court has ruled that in most cases a nonconvicted defendant cannot be involuntarily medicated unless a showing can be made that less intrusive means are not available to restore competency and that the defendant is a danger to himself or others. And in the 2001 case of *United States v. Weston* a federal court established a legal precedent for forceably administering medication to restore competency in a case of a federal capitol crime.

Trial competence is different from criminal responsibility. The former refers to current ability to understand and participate in the trial process. Criminal responsibility (sanity) refers to one's state of mind at the time of the alleged crime. The primary test of insanity up until the mid-1950s in this country was the M'Naughten Test, which required proof that the individual was, at the time he/she committed the offense, under defect of reason resulting from a disease of the mind and that such a defect resulted in the individual's not being able to recognize the nature and quality of his/her actions (or not knowing that such actions were wrong). Most states adhere to the M'Naughten Test or the American Law Institute's Model Penal Code (substantial capacity) test for insanity defenses.

A majority of the states allow for a verdict of not guilty by reason of insanity (NGRI) or guilty but mentally ill (GBMI). As a result of the Insanity Defense Reform Act of 1984, the federal insanity defense requires that a defendant prove, by clear and convincing evidence, that at the time of the commission of the acts constituting the offense, the defendant, as a result of a severe mental disease or defect, was unable to appreciate the nature and quality or the wrongfulness of his acts. The Act also restricted the scope to expert testimony in sanity determinations.

Key Terms

Assisted outpatient treatment *244*
Criminal responsibility *226*
Competence to stand trial *225*
Competency *222*

Conservatorship *223*
Dusky v. United States 226
Guardianship *223*
Informed consent *223*
Kansas v. Hendricks 245
Model Penal Code *241*

M'Naughten Test *240*
Not guilty by reason of insanity *240*
O'Connor v. Donaldson 228
Parens patriae 225
Right to treatment *228*

Sexual violent predator law *245*
Testamentary capacity *223*
Testator *223*
Washington v. Harper 229
Wyatt *v.* Stickney *228*

Review Questions

1. In the middle ages, what was thought to be the cause of mental disorders?
2. Who were responsible for caring for the mentally ill in colonial America?
3. Why did the population in mental institutions begin to drop in the mid-1950s?
4. How is the issue of competency relevant in the civil and criminal justice system?
5. When should a court consider appointing a guardian and/or a conservator?
6. What does the Sixth Amendment guarantee to a criminal defendant?
7. How is the "right to liberty" relevant to patients in state confinement?
8. How is the competency standard for pleading guilty related to that for standing trial?
9. Is a psychiatric diagnosis alone sufficient for rendering a defendant incompetent?
10. What are some of the important points to cover in a forensic psychological report?
11. For how long can a defendant be committed due to incompetency to stand trial?
12. Under what circumstances can a defendant receive medication against his will?
13. How is trial competence different from criminal responsibility?
14. What does the M'Naughten Rule for insanity hold?
15. What does the Modal Penal Code say in reference to insanity?
16. What is the difference between "not guilty by reason of insanity" and "guilty but mentally ill"?

Chapter Resources on the World Wide Web

American Bar Association Committee on Mental and Physical Disability Law
http://www.abanet.org/disability/home.html

American Psychological Association Amicus Briefs
http://www.apa.org/psyclaw/issues.html

American Psychological Association Ethics Code
http://www.apa.org/ethics/

Civil Commitment of Sexually Violent Predators
http://www.mobar.org/journal/1999/novdec/bilbrey.htm.

Disability Issues in Psychology
http://www.apa.org/pi/disability/

History and Overview of Forensic Psychology
http://faculty.ncwc.edu/toconnor/psy/psylect01.htm

National Survey of Involuntary Civil Commitments
http://www.abanet.org/disability/docs/statebystate.pdf

New York State's Assisted Outpatient Treatment (AOT) Program
http://www.nyclu.org/aot_program_tstmny_040805.html

The Law and Society Home Page
http://www.lawandsociety.org/

Treatment Advocacy Center
http://www.treatmentadvocacycenter.org/GeneralResources/index.htm

For Further Reading

Cohen, B. J., McGarvey, E. L., Pinkerton, R. C., & Kryzhanivska, L. (2004). Willingness and competence of depressed and schizophrenic inpatients to consent to research. *Journal of the American Academy of Psychiatry Law, 32,* 134.

Costanzo, M. (2004). *Psychology applied to law.* Belmont, CA: Wadsworth/Thompson Learning.

Davis, D. L. (1985). Treatment planning for the patient who is incompetent to stand trial. *Hospital and Community Psychiatry, 36,* 268.

Kirschner, S. M., & Galperin, G. J. (2001). Psychiatric defenses in New York County: Pleas and results. *Journal of the American Academy of Psychiatry and the Law, 29*(2), 194.

Kitaeff, J. (2007). *Malingering, lies, and junk science in the courtroom.* Youngstown, NY: Cambria Press.

Morse, S. J. (1994). Culpability and control, *142 University of PA Law Review,* 1587.

Roesch, R., Grisso, T., & Poythress, N. G., Jr. (1986). Training programs, courses, and workshops in psychology and law. In M. F. Kaplan (Ed.). *The impact of social psychology on procedural justice.* Springfield, IL: Thomas.

Schopp, R. F. (2001). *Competency, condemnation, and commitment.* Washington, DC: American Psychological Association Press.

Reisner, R., Slobogin, C., & Rai, A. (2004). *Law and the mental health system: Civil and criminal aspects.* St. Paul, MN: Thomson West.

Prentky, R. A., Janus, E. S., Barbaree, H., Schwartz, B. K., & Kafka, M. (2006). Sexually violent predators in the courtroom: Science on trial. *Psychology, Public Policy, and Law, 12,* 4.

CHAPTER 12

Juries and the Courtroom

CHAPTER OBJECTIVES

After reading this chapter you would:

- Know the relevance of the Sixth Amendment to the Constitution.
- Understand the effects of jury size on jury decision making.
- Know how *voir dire* is used to determine juror bias.
- Understand "challenge for cause" and when it is used in court.
- Understand "peremptory challenge" and when it is used in court.
- Know under what circumstances a change of venue might be called for.
- Understand the importance of the Supreme Court case of *Batson v. Kentucky*.
- Know the juror personality attributes that can affect jury verdicts.

INTRODUCTION

Prior to any discussion on the relevance of forensic psychology, and the impact of psychological principles on juries and court proceedings, certain fundamental legal principles must be laid down.

As discussed in the previous chapter, the Sixth Amendment to the U.S. Constitution states, "In all criminal prosecutions, the accused shall enjoy the right to a speedy and public trial, by an impartial jury of the State and district wherein the crime shall have been committed." (U.S. Const. Amend. VI). In 1968, the Supreme Court, in *Duncan v. Louisiana*, reaffirmed the long-standing legal view that not all criminal prosecutions require a jury trial. Such cases would include those the Court classified as petty for purposes of the right to a trial by jury.

Exactly what *petty* meant was tested in *Baldwin v. New York* in 1970, when the Court held that "no offense can be deemed 'petty' for purposes of the right to trial by jury where imprisonment for more than six months is authorized." Regardless of the nature of the crime or the possible sentence, under federal law, a jury trial is considered the standard mode of adjudication, and waiver of this right requires agreement of the judge, the prosecutor, as well as the defendant. A jury trial in federal court can sometimes be had at the behest of the prosecutor alone, even over the defendant's objection. But at the state level, the general view is that the jury is primarily a protection to the defendant, and the defendant has the last word as to whether the trial will be held before a judge or a jury. For example, in Virginia there is an absolute right to a jury trial in criminal cases, and a jury trial even in civil cases should be considered "sacred under Virginia law" (Article 1, § 11, Virginia Constitution).

Size of the Jury

Since the Supreme Court's decision in *Thompson v. Utah* in 1898, it's been the law of the land that in federal criminal cases, a jury must have 12 members. In 1970, the Court ruled that criminal trials in state courts can use as few as six jurors. Specifically, the Court in *Williams v. Florida* (1970) held that a state six-person felony jury did not violate the Sixth Amendment, reversing the common law tradition and federal law requiring 12 jurors. The Court in *Williams* expressed that a group of six citizens were as well equipped as a dozen to interpose their common-sense judgment between the defendant and the state to determine guilt or innocence. Six jurors is a large enough number "to promote group deliberation, free from outside attempts at intimidation, and to provide a fair possibility for obtaining a representative cross section of the community . . . especially if the requirement of unanimity is retained. And, certainly the reliability of the jury as a fact finder hardly seems likely to be a function of its size" (*Williams v. Florida*, 1970).

Research conducted in the 1970s consistently indicated that effectiveness in jury decision making decreased with decreasing size. In one study participants were placed into juries ranging from 6 to 12 members, shown a videotaped trial, and asked to deliberate until a verdict. The results indicated that although smaller-sized groups fostered behavior that would be beneficial for some purposes, most of the advantages relevant specifically to jury decision making favored larger groups. In smaller groups, members did participate more equally in discussions, found the deliberations more satisfying, and were more cohesive. But larger groups debated more vigorously, collectively recalled more evidence from the trial and made more consistent and predictable decisions. This latter finding suggests that as juries grow smaller, in criminal cases they will make more errors of acquitting the guilty and convicting the innocent. And, in civil cases, not only will the rate of erroneous verdicts rise, but juries may render damage awards that are more unpredictable from case to case despite similarities in plaintiffs' losses (Saks, 1977).

The classic research on conformity behavior also supports the use of larger juries. Because larger groups increase the likelihood that a dissenter will have at least one ally, individuals in the minority in larger juries will be better able to resist social pressure. Larger juries are also more likely than smaller juries to contain members of minority groups, spend more time deliberating, and reach fewer erroneous decisions. Furthermore, one of the basic principles of tests and measurements is that reliability and validity increase (up to a point) as the judging group increases in size (Clearly, 2005; Saks & Marti, 1997).

In 1978, the Court drew the line on the constitutionally permissible size of a felony jury by holding in *Ballew v. Georgia* that five jurors are too few and is a violation of the Sixth Amendment. In making its decision, the Court relied on a number of psychological studies on group dynamics and jury functioning, indicating that as the size of a jury decreases from 12 to 6 or less jurors, the likelihood of convicting an innocent person rises (Davenport, 2005).

Voting Requirement of Jury and Burden of Proof

As mentioned at various points in this text, the **burden of proof** in criminal cases is beyond a reasonable doubt, and this is the highest possible burden of proof. The burden of proof in civil cases is a preponderance of the evidence where the plaintiff must only prove that it is more likely than not that the defendant is liable. In certain types of civil cases (such as those involving fraud), there may be a higher burden of proof called clear and convincing evidence.

The common law requires a unanimous jury verdict in criminal trials. The origins of this rule are shrouded in obscurity, although it was in the latter half of the fourteenth century that the rule appeared, and it became a standard part of the common law by the eighteenth

TABLE 12.1 Burden of Proof and Unanimity Requirements in Jury Trials

Type of Trial	Burden of Proof	Unanimity
Criminal	Beyond a reasonable doubt	Can never be less than six members (*Ballew v. Georgia*) and if six members, must be unanimous (*Williams v. Florida*; *Burch v. Louisiana*). Can be by 11–1 or 10–2 in 12-person juries (*Burch v. Louisiana*)
Civil	Clear and convincing evidence, or preponderance of the evidence	Must be unanimous in federal courts, can be less than unanimous in state courts

century (Davenport, 2005; Thayer, 1892). But in 1972 the Court considered, in *Apodaca v. Oregon*, the constitutionality of a state law that permitted criminal defendants to be convicted by less-than-unanimous votes. (Oregon allowed convictions on 10 to 2 votes.) The Court upheld the state law reasoning that there was no significant difference between a unanimous jury and a jury voting by 10 to 2 or 11 to 1. Thus, the Oregon law did not violate the Sixth Amendment right to a jury trial.

The Supreme Court visited the issue of jury size and unanimity for the final time in 1979. In *Burch v. Louisiana*, the Court found Louisiana's law that allowed misdemeanor convictions on 5 to 1 votes by a six-person jury violated the Sixth Amendment right of defendants to a trial by jury. If a jury is to be as small as six, the Court reasoned, the verdict must to be unanimous. In a civil case in the federal courts, a jury's decision also needs to be unanimous, unless instructed otherwise by the court. In some states, such as Virginia, all jury verdicts must be unanimous (see Table 12.1).

Requirement for a Nonbiased Jury

The Sixth Amendment guarantees an impartial jury, but how can a totally impartial jury ever really be guaranteed? Impartiality of juries requires (1) that a jury be a representative cross-section of the community and (2) that jurors chosen are unbiased, that is, willing to decide the case on the basis of the evidence presented. A violation of a defendant's right to an impartial jury occurs, for example, when the jury or any of its members is subjected to pressure or influence that could impair freedom of action, or is exposed to possibly prejudicial material or communications (*Brown v. Allen*, 1953; *Lockhart v. McCree*, 1986; *Taylor v. Louisiana*, 1975; *Williams v. Florida*, 1970).

Most potential jurors are unaware of their biases. This is supported by psychological research finding that individuals may not be consciously aware of attitudes that influence their decision-making and behavior. To make matters worse, the effects of stereotypic and dogmatic beliefs on behavior increases when individuals are pressured from such factors as time limitations, other jurors, exhaustion, or the need to incorporate complex information and make sound decisions (Bodenhausen, 1990; Gilbert & Hixon, 1991).

During the process of jury selection (***voir dire***), potential jurors may at times distort and confabulate (mix old and new information) in their reports of past experiences. This is due to memory failure or embarrassment over revealing what they consider to be socially undesirable information. During court proceedings and deliberations they may also feel pressure to conform to the views of other jurors. Jurors may also unconsciously screen or interpret evidence in a manner that matches their preexisting beliefs (Anderson, Lepper, & Ross, 1980; Swan & Read, 1981). There is also research suggesting that when groups make judgments, their level of performance does not rise to the level of the highest functioning group member, rather, when particularly difficult decisions have to be made, groups typically perform at the level of their average member (Laughlin, VanderStoep, & Hollingshead, 1991). Accordingly, even the placement of one biased juror on a jury panel can have significant implications.

JURY SELECTION

Selecting an unbiased, impartial jury involves two steps. First, a jury pool is selected from among eligible jurors in the community. To accomplish this, a county or city usually compiles a master jury list (also called a **jury wheel**) of eligible jurors from among the citizenry. From this list, a jury pool (or **venire**) is selected and summoned to appear for jury service. The Federal Jury Selection Act of 1968 guaranteed that jury pools be made up of a representative cross-section of the community. This is attained by supplementing voter lists as a source of eligible jurors with drivers' license lists, city or telephone directories, and the use of statistical methods to ensure unbiased selection.

To be eligible for jury service in the federal system, an individual must be a U.S. citizen; be at least 18 years of age; reside primarily in the judicial district for one year; be able to read, write, and speak the English language with sufficient mastery; be physically and mentally capable of service; not be currently subject to felony charges; and never have been convicted of a felony unless their civil rights have subsequently been legally restored. The following three groups are exempt from federal jury service: (1) members of the armed forces on active duty; (2) members of professional fire and police departments; and (3) "public officers" of federal, state, or local governments who are actively engaged full time in the performance of public duties. Persons belonging to these groups may not serve on federal juries, even if they so desire. Also, under federal law, a person cannot be required to serve on jury duty more often than once every two years.

In federal court, a juror biographical report is prepared consisting of the following information: name, city and zip code, date of birth, gender and race, occupation and employer, education, marital status and spouse's occupation, and number of children. This list is provided to the attorneys. However, anonymous juries are used in cases involving notorious criminal defendants with a history of violence or intimidation against witnesses or jurors.

After an initial jury pool is chosen, actual jurors in a case are selected in a process known as *voir dire* to eliminate jurors with overt or potential biases. It is the function of the *voir dire* process to give the defense and the prosecution the opportunity to inquire into, or have the trial judge inquire into, any bias or prejudice that would make it inappropriate for any potential juror to serve on the jury. In such instances, the proper standard for exclusion of a juror is "whether the juror's views would prevent or substantially impair the performance of his duties as a juror in accordance with his instructions and his oath" (*Wainwright v. Witt*, 1985, p. 424).

Challenges for Cause

Challenges for cause can be used to remove a perspective juror who (1) is ineligible to serve due to statutory requirements (e.g., he/she is not a resident of the local jurisdiction, not a U.S. citizen, below the mandated age requirement, or does not speak English); (2) has a mental or physical disability that would interfere with his/her ability to serve on a jury; (3) had recently served on a jury; (4) had previous felony convictions; (5) had a relationship with or is related to one of the parties in the case or their attorneys; or (6) may be impartial or biased (e.g., have preconceived judgments in the matter before the court, be prejudiced for or against a party in the matter, or exposed to excessive media coverage of the case.) All these factors are relevant for attempting to excuse a perspective juror "for cause" but it is the issue of impartiality or bias that is usually the basis for attorneys' objections to an individual serving on the jury.

Although prejudicial factors are vitally important, they are also notoriously difficult to ascertain as jurors may be deceptive to avoid admitting publically that they hold certain biases. Lieberman and Sales (2007) cite that another problem with jurors misrepresenting their attitudes and experiences during *voir dire* questioning is that some jurors simply fail to respond to questions posed to them. If for example, jurors in groups are asked to respond by raising their hands, jurors may simply remain silent during questioning. To overcome the possibility that jurors may not reveal their intentional or unconscious biases, questioning often focuses on other factors that may be related to more subtle biases that could affect the verdict decision. Jurors may be questioned about demographics such as their race, religion, marital status, number of children, and occupation. They may be asked about their hobbies, interests, what books or magazines they read, what television shows they watch, and what organizations they belong to. They may also be questioned about attitudes they may hold toward the legal system. These could include factors such as the presumption of innocence, burden of proof, and attitudes toward the death penalty.

Jury selection consultants (who may or may not be psychologists) can help to identify potentially biased jurors by conducting community surveys (or telephone surveys) to interview people who met the same eligibility standards of prospective jurors. Questions concerning biographical information and general beliefs and attitudes about the defendant, which may influence their verdict, can then be posed. This practice, particularly common in the 1970s, involved presenting interviewees with a brief description of the case and questioning as to how they would vote if they were part of the jury. Such surveys help to identify demographic, personality, or attitudinal variables of potential jurors, which would incline them to vote guilty or not guilty in a particular case (Kovera et al., 2003). Psychologists and consultants from other disciplines sometimes also develop jury questionnaires that are presented to the entire jury pool prior to the actual *voir dire*.

Peremptory Challenges

In addition to unlimited challenges for cause, both sides in a criminal trial have a limited number of **peremptory challenges** that, with important exceptions, do not have to be based on any identifiable reason. In criminal cases, the defense will typically receive the same or a greater number of peremptory challenges than is allocated to the prosecution. In felony criminal cases tried in federal court, six peremptory challenges are provided to the prosecution and 10 to the defense; however, more can be awarded depending on the circumstances of the case (Bureau of Justice Statistics, 1998). When there is a large degree of pretrial publicity surrounding a case, the number of peremptory challenges allotted to each side is generally increased. For example, in the criminal trial of O. J. Simpson, the prosecution was awarded 20 peremptory challenges (Wrightsman, Greene, Nietzel, & Fortune, 2002).

Pretrial Publicity

In *Irvin v. Dowd* (1961), Irvin was convicted of committing multiple murders in a rural area of Indiana. The crimes understandably generated extensive media coverage in this small rural town where such crime had been unheard of. When the case reached the Supreme Court, Irvin argued that the **pretrial publicity** prevented him from receiving a fair trial due to the impartiality of the jury. The Court agreed, noting that 8 of the 12 jurors who heard the case admitted they had decided that Irvin was guilty before the trial began. But despite these admissions, the trial judge accepted as conclusive the jurors' statements that they would be able to render an impartial verdict. The Court held that it was reversible error for the trial judge to determine that the substantial publicity surrounding the case would not impair juror impartiality. In its decision, the Court set down a basic rule that when pretrial publicity is substantial, a trial court should not necessarily accept a juror's assertion of impartiality, and that such cases raised a presumption of **juror bias**.

The presumed prejudice of a jury seemed evident in the notorious trial of Dr. Samuel Sheppard (*Sheppard v. Maxwell*, 1966). This case was made even more famous by the television series and movie *The Fugitive*, which was loosely based upon it. The case arose when Marilyn Sheppard, Dr. Sam Sheppard's pregnant wife, was brutally bludgeoned to death in their home in 1954. Dr. Sheppard was the main suspect in the investigation from the onset, and he was eventually arrested and charged with murder.

Local officials allowed Sheppard's murder trial to degenerate into a media circus. The media heavily publicized the case before the trial and even disrupted control of the court during the trial. The jurors were exposed to intense media coverage of the case until the time they began their deliberations. Following deliberations, Sheppard was convicted of murder. Sheppard spent ten years in prison before the Supreme Court, utilizing a "totality of the circumstances" approach regarding pretrial publicity, ruled that the excessive publicity had deprived him of a fair trial. Sheppard was acquitted at his second trial. The *Sheppard* case brought national attention to the problem of pretrial publicity. Trial judges attempted to address this problem by imposing gag orders on the press, preventing the reporting of pretrial information. The press resisted this approach and was supported by the 1976 Supreme Court decision in *Nebraska Press Association v. Stuart* in which the Court held that a trial judge's "**gag order**" was an unconstitutional prior restraint on the press.

Following the Court's decision in *Nebraska Press Association*, some trial courts attempted to close criminal trials to the public, including the press. The Court limited such activities by declaring that the right of access to criminal trials is guaranteed by the First and Fourteenth Amendments (*Richmond Newspapers v. Virginia*, 1980). Closure of a trial, according to the Court, can only be permitted if there is an overriding interest, such as ensuring a defendant's right to a fair trial. In this and subsequent cases, the Court has continued to make it very difficult to justify such closure.

Twenty-five years after the *Sheppard* case, the Court again confronted the issue of pretrial publicity in *Mu'min v. Virginia* (1991), where the Court held that the Due Process Clause of the Fourteenth Amendment does not mandate that prospective jurors be asked in *voir dire* examinations about specific information concerning the case that they have seen or heard in the media. The Sixth Amendment's impartial jury requirement will adequately be satisfied when jurors do not admit during *voir dire* that they have been prejudiced by pretrial publicity. As a result of *Mu'Min*, judges are not constitutionally required to allow defendants to inquire into the content of publicity to which jurors have been exposed, thereby making the jurors' own assertions of impartiality dispositive. In most cases, this precludes any further inquiry.

Does Pretrial Publicity Effect Juror Bias?

Ruva, Mcevoy, and Bryant (2007)

Participants in this study were informed that they might read crime stories related to a trial that they were about to view and then be asked to make a verdict. They were told that, like actual jurors, they were not to use any of this prior information when making decisions about the defendant's guilt; that they must only use the evidence presented during the trial.

To simulate pretrial publicity, participants in the exposed pretrial publicity (PTP) group were given media packets containing news articles about crimes that were taken from a web-based archive of an actual local newspaper known for its reporting of murder investigations and trials. These news stories contained general information about the case (e.g., victim, when and where the crime took place, description of the crime) as well as information that was not presented at trial and that could have a biasing effect on juror verdicts.

Participants in the nonexposed PTP group received packets containing actual news articles involving an unrelated crime in which a woman was accused of embezzling child support funds. These articles were similar in composition to the news articles in the exposed condition (i.e., both packets contained nine separate news articles of approximately the same length and consisted of 10 pages of text).

The trial was then presented via television and VCR. The researchers utilized stimulus materials consisting of a real videotaped criminal trial of a man who was accused of murdering his wife. In the video the defendant pled not guilty and claimed that his wife accidentally shot herself when he tried to prevent her from committing suicide by shooting herself in the head.

Immediately following the viewing of the trial, each juror was given a verdict form and asked for their verdicts (not guilty, hung, or guilty), how confident they were in these verdicts (guilt ratings), and to specify the length of the prison sentence (from a given range of 30–45 years) they would suggest if they found the defendant guilty.

The results indicated that negative pretrial publicity about a defendant had an extremely biasing effect on juror decision making. Those who were exposed to negative pretrial publicity were significantly more likely to misattribute information contained in the negative media packets to the trial.

Jurors who were exposed to negative PTP also perceived the defendant as being less credible than did nonexposed jurors, suggesting that negative PTP may cause jurors to form a negative impression of the defendant. These impressions may then influence jurors'

interpretations of trial evidence and hence their verdicts. These jurors also tended to perceive the prosecution's story of the case as more plausible, while jurors who were not exposed to the negative PTP were more likely to find both stories plausible and so were more likely to find the defendant not guilty because of the reasonable doubt instructions that all of the jurors received.

The researchers conclude that in a case where there is a lot of negative pretrial publicity about the defendant, it may be impossible for that defendant to get a fair trial. Even if jurors are instructed not to use information contained in the PTP to make decisions about guilt, they may be unable to do so because of source memory errors or negative impressions they have formed about the defendant.

Courts have developed several ways of overcoming prejudicial **pretrial publicity**. One such way is by permitting extensive juror questionnaires that give both sides the chance to identify persons who have been exposed to pretrial publicity and who have already made up their minds about the guilt or innocence of the defendant. A court also may sequester the jury during the course of the trial. Another method is to postpone the trial until publicity decreases. In rare cases a court will change the venue of the trial to a location less affected by the pretrial publicity.

Challenges Based on Race and Gender

In the 1880 case of *Strauder v. West Virginia*, the Supreme Court decided that "the State denies a black defendant equal protection of the laws when it puts him on trial before a jury from which members of his race have been purposefully excluded." (p. 100). That decision laid the foundation for the Court's unceasing efforts to eradicate racial discrimination in the procedures used to select juries. In *Strauder*, the Court explained that exclusion of black citizens from service as jurors is an example of the kind of injustice the Fourteenth Amendment was specifically designed to eradicate. The Court has subsequently repeatedly affirmed that a person's race simply "is unrelated to his fitness as a juror" (*Thiel v. Southern Pacific Co.*, 1946, p. 328) and that by denying a person participation in jury service on account of race the state unconstitutionally discriminates against the excluded juror (see, e.g., *Carter v. Jury Commission of Greene County*, 1970; *Neal v. Delaware*, 1880).

Despite the Supreme Court's rulings extending back to 1880, up until 1986 an attorney could excuse a juror using a peremptory challenge without offering any reason whatsoever. The attorney's reasons could be based on any factors including race or gender. But the 1986 Supreme Court decision in **Batson v. Kentucky** changed this scenario forever. In *Batson*, a prosecutor used his peremptory challenges to strike all four black persons on the venire so Batson, a black man, was tried by an all white jury for burglary. Setting specific standards for peremptory challenges, the Court ruled that attorneys in both criminal and civil trials could no longer use peremptory challenges to remove potential jurors on the basis of race. The use of peremptory challenges on the basis of gender, however, took longer to be addressed by the Court.

Traditionally, the long-standing prohibition against allowing women to serve on juries was based on the English common law, which excluded women from juries under the doctrine of *propter defectum sexus*; literally, the "defect of sex" (*U.S. v. DeGross*, 1992). In this country, supporters of the exclusion of women from juries tended to couch their objections in terms of the ostensible need to protect women from the ugliness and depravity of trials. One court declared that

"Criminal court trials often involve testimony of the foulest conduct, the use of filthy and loathsome words, references to intimate sex relationships, and other elements that would prove humiliating, embarrassing, and degrading to a lady" (*Bailey v. State*, 1949, p. 428). But it was not until 1994 in *J.E.B. v. Alabama ex rel.* that the Supreme Court ruled that jurors could not be excluded on the basis of gender.

J.E.B. was a paternity suit by the state on behalf of T.B., the mother of a minor child. After challenges for cause, only 10 of 33 jurors were male; the state then used nine of its ten peremptory strikes to remove male jurors; petitioner used all but one of his strikes to remove female jurors. As a result, all the selected jurors were female. The Court upheld J.E.B.'s contention that the pattern of striking male jurors by the state, solely on the basis of gender, constituted the kind of purposeful discrimination that violated the Equal Protection Clause. To excuse male or female jurors by the use of peremptory challenges solely on the basis of their gender assumes men and women "hold particular views simply *because* of their gender" (pp. 138–140). (Italics added). The Court expressed the idea that such stereotypes reflect and reinforce patterns of historical discrimination that are contrary to the equal protection clause of the Constitution.

Beyond race and gender, several jurisdictions have dealt with the issue of peremptory challenges based on religion. The 2004 case of *State v. Fuller* was one in which the defendant was charged with first-degree armed robbery. During jury selection, the prosecutor used four of his first five peremptory challenges to excuse African-Americans.

When defense counsel objected, the prosecutor responded that two of the potential jurors (including the non-African-American) were excused not because of their race but because they were "demonstrative about their religions." The "demonstrativeness" apparently consisted of the white juror stating that he worked as a missionary, and the African-American juror wearing black garb and a skullcap, from which the prosecutor inferred that he was "obviously Muslim." Neither juror indicated that his religious beliefs would interfere with his serving fairly on the jury. The trial court overruled the objection, and the jury convicted the defendant on both counts. The New Jersey Appellate Division affirmed, based on the majority's distinction between excluding members of cognizable religious groups—which would constitute impermissible discrimination—and excluding individuals who merely appeared to be religious. The New Jersey Supreme Court subsequently overruled the appellate court, finding that the prosecutor's belief concerning religious jurors was reflective of the very stereotypes that had been used in the past to justify a policy of blanket exclusion that is contrary to law (*State v. Fuller*, 2004).

JURORS' ATTRIBUTES AND RESULTING VERDICTS

The famous trial attorney Melvin Belli (1982) felt that married people made better jurors for criminal defendants because they are more forgiving. Clarence Darrow (1936) argued that wealthy jurors are conviction prone, except when the defendant is on trial for a white-collar crime.

Fulero and Penrod (1990) expressed that ethnicity, race, gender, wealth, social status, occupation, age, religion, marital status, hobbies, interests, reading and television, organizations, demeanor, and appearance are always important factors in jury selection but that every case needs to be individually analyzed to determine the kind of jurors you want and don't want.

Renowned litigator Seymour Wishman (1986) suggested that attorneys avoid any juror whose face one does not like, because "chances are he doesn't like yours either" (pp. 72–73). He also expressed the opinion that a preference for certain baseball teams can (and has) been used to guide jury selection decisions. Who then do we want on a jury? Wishman provided the example of an African-American accused of a violent crime. In such a case, the prosecutor would likely prefer a juror who is a "middle-class housewife who was once mugged, while the defense doesn't because studies have suggested that such a juror is most likely to convict in such a case. Wishman reported on several trials in which defense lawyers hired psychologists to conduct detailed juror studies before selection. He expressed the belief that guilt or innocence may have less of an effect on the verdict than whether or not the jurors find the accused "their kind of guy" (p. 72).

Physical and Demographic Juror Attributes

AGE   Some legal authorities have suggested that defense attorneys exclude older jurors, but others have expressed that the elderly are more lenient and should be included in a jury (Appleman, 1952). Yet other studies failed to find any relationship between age and verdict (Moran & Comfort, 1982; Simon, 1967).

Generally speaking, prosecutors are more likely to peremptorily challenge younger jurors (between 30 and 34 years old), whereas defense attorneys are more likely to challenge somewhat older jurors (between 40 and 44). The effects of age on civil trial decision making are likewise mixed. Some research has shown that middle-aged jurors are more plaintiff-oriented than either younger or older jurors in liability decisions (Denove & Imwinkelried, 1995), and that older jurors are more likely to believe there are too many illegitimate lawsuits and that damage awards are too high (Hans & Lofquist, 1994).

GENDER   Darrow (1936) believed that attorneys representing criminal defendants should avoid female jurors. However, Belli (1982) suggested that women are desirable jurors from the perspective of criminal defendants, with the exception being if the defendant is an attractive woman. In addition, well-known attorney F. Lee Bailey advised that if a witness against a defendant is female, the attorney should choose women for the jury because women are "somewhat distrustful" of other women (Bailey & Rothblatt, 1971).

Biskind (1954) argued that women should be avoided when seeking large damage awards, and Wagner (1989) added that this was particularly true for suburban housewives. Heyl (1952) advocated that plaintiffs' attorneys should select male jurors if the plaintiff is female, but defense attorneys should select women if the plaintiff is male. As was presented as true for criminal trials, Wagner also noted that women have a tendency to dislike other women who are attractive or successful and these should be avoided when representing an attractive female plaintiff.

Some research with mock jurors have indicated that gender was correlated with verdicts for mock jurors in an insanity defense case, with females more likely to convict than males. Similar findings were obtained in a trial involving a drug trafficking charge and child sexual abuse cases (Cutler, Moran, & Narby, 1992; Kovera, Gresham, Borgida, Gray, & Regan, 1997; Kovera, McAuliff, & Hebert, 1999). In cases involving women accused of killing men who had repeatedly battered them, female jurors were less conviction prone than their male counterparts (Schuller & Hastings, 1996). Similar findings have been obtained in death penalty studies (Fitzgerald & Ellsworth, 1984). Finally, Hahn and Clayton (1996) found that juror gender interacted with attorney gender, with attorneys being more successful when presenting their case (either an assault or robbery case) to mock jurors of the same sex. In addition, male attorneys were most successful when they presented their case to male jurors using an aggressive presentation style. Female jurors were not influenced by presentation style.

OCCUPATION   It is an old legal axiom to never accept a juror whose occupation begins with the letter "P." This would include plumbers, painters, poets, physicians, psychiatrists, psychologists, pimps and prostitutes, among others. Although lacking empirical support (or much common sense), this advice has been heeded by trial attorneys for decades. Some legal authors recommend excluding jurors with the same occupation as the opposing party in civil trials. Others have more specific recommendations. For example, Appleman (1952) argues that farmers have a tendency to be generous when rendering civil damages. Jacobs (2007) asserts that although nurses may claim to be concerned about people who have experienced injuries, they will actually be intolerant of pain and suffering because of their occupation, as will people who work in social welfare services.

Using similar logic, some authors indicate that police officers would not be sympathetic to a plaintiff's pain and suffering. It has also been proposed that jurors with occupations that expose them to a variety of aspects of life (e.g., creative people such as artists and writers) are less likely to be shocked by the details of a crime, and as a result, are more preferable jurors for the defense in criminal cases (Bailey & Rothblatt, 1971). In criminal cases, higher socioeconomic status has been found to be associated with a greater conviction rate, however, the opposite has also been found (Visher, 1987). As far as education level, the research is also inconsistent. Some research has shown that less educated people are more conviction prone (e.g., Wiener & Stolle, 1997), while others (e.g., Simon, 1967), found that when education was used along with occupation level to identity a juror's socioeconomic status, higher status was related to a greater degree of being conviction prone. All in all, there are relatively few controlled studies that have shown occupation to be a significant predictor of jury verdicts. The research that has been done, however, suggests that occupation may be indirectly related to jury verdicts in that jurors with high status jobs are more likely to emerge as jury forepersons and to influence the opinions of others (Bonazzoli, 1998).

ETHNICITY AND RACE Among the general public and media, unpopular jury verdicts are frequently attributed to racial composition (Cowan & Fairchild, 1997; Reynolds, 1996). Yet much of the historical assumptions relating to race and jury verdicts are anecdotal, not derived from empirical research, and overly stereotypic. Nevertheless, there have been many such assumptions that continue to affect the psychology of courtroom behavior. These assumptions are roughly based on two factors.

The first factor is referred to as "**emotionality**," or the ability to empathize with the pain and suffering of others particularly in a legal context (e.g., with the plaintiff in a personal injury suit) (Sannito & McGovern, 1993). Goldstein (1935) ranked the following groups on emotionalism from high to low: Irish, Jewish, Italian, French, Spanish, Slavic, and Nordic. Hispanics and African-Americans have subsequently been added to the list of high emotionality, pro-plaintiff individuals (Lane, 1984; Wagner, 1989).

A number of more recent studies also show a link between ethnicity and emotions. For example, Consedine and Magai (2002) found that African-Americans and Jamaicans reported greater joy and less negative affect than European-Americans or Russian–Ukrainian immigrants. Vrana and Rollock (2002) similarly found that African-Americans expressed more positive emotions and fewer negative emotions than whites, and that African-American men exhibited higher blood pressure in emotional contexts than whites. Asian-Americans, in particular Japanese-Americans and Indians, have been shown to have lower levels of positive emotions and higher levels of negative emotion than Europeans and Hispanics (Scollon, Diener, Oishi, & Biswas-Diener, 2004).

The second rationale for considering the impact of race and ethnicity on jury verdicts is the fundamental principle that prospective jurors relate to those with similar characteristics, backgrounds, or experiences (Blue, 2007). Some research supports this assertion and demonstrates that jurors are more lenient to defendants who share their background, and more punitive toward defendants with different backgrounds, particularly for racial characteristics. The general finding in the literature is that white jurors are more punitive toward black defendants than they are toward white defendants (King, 2007). However, this only seems to be the case when there is not racially charged trial content (Sommers & Ellsworth, 2000, 2001). The authors suggest that race-relevant trial content makes many white jurors uncomfortable about possibly being perceived as prejudiced.

Is a racially diverse jury better able to make decisions than a racially homogeneous one? The answer appears to be yes but only to an extent (Sommers, 2006). Whereas mixed race juries may show increased performance in the form of generating more creative and feasible ideas, there is also the increased risk of interpersonal conflict and low morale (McLeod, Lobel, & Cox, 1996; Moreland, Levine, & Wingert, 1996).

There is also the reality that certain groups have had historical conflicts with each other, and trial lawyers are often cautioned to be cognizant of such factors when selecting a jury. Despite the fact that attorneys are prohibited from making purely race-based peremptory challenges, race and ethnicity still appear to be a factor used by attorneys (Baldus et al., 2001).

PHYSICAL ATTRACTIVENESS   Research has indicated that physical attractiveness plays an undeniable role in the socialization process. Beckham, Spray, and Pietz (2007) report that adults more frequently excuse physically attractive children for aggressive behavior than they do unattractive children. Attractiveness also seems to be relevant in education. There is research indicating that attractive college students receive less punishment when caught cheating, and that physically attractive people tend to enjoy greater mental health and psychological well-being (Umberson & Hughes, 1987; Berger, Webster, Ridgeway, & Rosenholtz, 1986), and greater chances of success in personnel selection (Shannon, Stark, & Patrick, 2003).

In the courtroom setting, there is evidence that attractiveness can also influence verdicts and sentences in court cases. Beckham et al. (2007) reviewed studies indicating that in personal injury suits, jurors generally awarded more money to attractive plaintiffs than to unattractive plaintiffs, and that attractive defendants charged with killing pedestrians while driving intoxicated received more lenient sentences than did unattractive defendants. But attractiveness can be a two edged sword if jurors perceive that a defendant is trying to "take advantage" of his/her good looks.

Personality Attributes

AUTHORITARIANISM   Originally developed by Adorno in the 1950s, the personality construct of **authoritarianism** refers to an individual's desire for order, well-defined rules, and an authoritative leadership structure. As discussed elsewhere in this text, individuals who score high on measures of authoritarianism typically conform to conventional norms and exhibit a desire to punish individuals who deviate from those norms (Adorno, Frenkel-Brunswik, Levinson, & Sanford, 1950b). Authoritarianism has also been linked to prejudicial attitudes and hostility towards groups such as Jews, communists, and other minorities (Narby, Cutler, & Moran, 1993).

Interest in authoritarian personalities began with scales designed in an effort to understand the origins of mass support of the Nazis. Authoritarianism is typically measured using a scale (originally called the "F" or "Fascism" scale) comprised of questions that asks individuals to rate their level of agreement with a variety of behaviors related to authoritarian attitudes (e.g., "It would be best for everyone if the proper authorities censored magazines and movies to keep trashy material away from the youth," "There is nothing sick or immoral in somebody being a homosexual," "One reason we have so many troublemakers in our society nowadays is that parents and other authorities have forgotten that good old-fashioned physical punishment is still one of the best ways to make people behave properly") (Lieberman & Sales, 2007, pp. 80–82).

The presence of an **authoritarian personality** seems to be modestly related to individuals' likelihood to vote for conviction in criminal cases (Narby et al., 1993). According to the theory, this would make sense because authoritarians have a strong belief in the legitimacy of conventional authority and are driven to punishing deviates from that authoritarian norm. To these people, criminal defendants represent individuals who have rejected the rules of society (Bray & Noble, 1978; Moran & Comfort, 1982).

But this conviction-propensity seems stronger for what is referred to as *legal authoritarianism* in contrast to *traditional authoritarianism*. Legal authoritarianism refers to a belief that a defendant generally did indeed commit the crime with which he is charged and that the arrest was justified. This form of juror bias is often measured by the Juror Bias Scale (Kassin & Wrightsman, 1983). Traditional authoritarianism refers to a belief in more governmental authority, and increased punitive measures generally (Christie, 1991, 1993). This form of juror bias is frequently assessed by the Right Wing Authoritarianism Scale (Altemeyer, 1981), which is a 24-item scale assessing an orientation toward acceptance of established authority and law, acceptance of law as a basis for morality, and punitive attitudes toward legitimate targets.

LOCUS OF CONTROL   **Locus of control** (Rotter, 1966) refers to an individual's belief in the source of outcomes in life. More specifically, are events that occur in a person's life the result of a person's actions or of outside forces beyond his/her control? *Internal locus of control* reflects the belief that an individual is responsible for his/her outcomes through his/her skills or efforts. In short, one is in control of one's own destiny. *External locus of control* refers to the tendency to attribute outcomes to factors beyond one's control, such as luck, fate, or the actions of others (Phares & Wilson, 1972).

Rotter developed the *Internal–External Locus of Control Scale* to measure individual differences on this personality dimension. The scale contains a series of paired statements, and respondents are required to select which of the two statements in the pair best reflects their attitudes. For example, respondents must choose between "As far as world affairs are concerned, most of us are the victims of forces we can neither understand, nor control" and "By taking an active part in political and social affairs the people can control world events," or between the statements "Many of the unhappy things in people's lives are partly due to bad luck" and "People's misfortunes result from the mistakes they make" (Lieberman & Sales, 2007, pp. 88–89).

As an example of internal versus external locus of control in the jury setting, Sosis (1974) found that individuals classified as internals recommended more severe punishment for a defendant in a drunk driving case than did externals or a group of moderates whose scores on the scale fell in the middle of the range. In addition, internals viewed the defendant as more responsible for his actions than externals did. In a civil trial, when a victim's contribution is often considered by jurors, it is possible that individuals high in locus of control could attribute greater responsibility to a victim and be more lenient to a defendant. In addition, it should be noted that studies on conformity show internals are more resistant to conformity pressures than externals. As a result, the locus of control personality dimension may be related to the dynamics of deliberations and may indirectly be of some use to attorneys.

Is there a Relationship between Jurors' Locus of Control and Defendants' Attractiveness on Verdicts?

Beckham, Spray, and Pietz (2007)

Beckham et al. (2007) had 98 participants complete Rotter's (1966) I–E Scale, which measures an individual's degree of internal versus external locus of control.

In the study, participants then viewed one of four photographs, read a murder vignette, and endorsed a sentence on a sentencing form. Each case vignette was attached to the sentencing form along with a picture of either (a) an attractive Caucasian man, (b) an unattractive Caucasian man, (c) an attractive African-American man, or (d) an unattractive African-American man. The vignette was a description of an actual murder case, with names and dates changed for the purposes of the study.

The case described in the vignette involved a male defendant convicted of premeditated first-degree murder. The vignette indicated that the defendant beat the victim to death with a jackhammer, and that the defendant said he had murdered the victim because the victim had stolen money from a mutual landlord, had gotten into a conflict with the defendant's father, and had spread false rumors

about the defendant's deceased's sister. The vignette also mentioned that the defendant confessed to the crime to a friend while under the influence of marijuana.

The authors selected 38 photographs of nonsmiling men taken from the shoulder up. Thirty-six individuals of varying sex, age, race, educational status, and socioeconomic status served as peer raters for the photographs and rated each photograph on a 5-point scale from 1 (least attractive) to 5 (most attractive). Of the 38 original photographs, four were used in this study: the two photographs of Caucasian men that the peer raters deemed most attractive and least attractive, and the two photographs of African-American men that the peer raters deemed most attractive and least attractive.

All participants read the same murder case, but viewed only one of the four photographs, which was placed at the top of the murder vignette. Participants were asked to study the defendant's picture for 10 seconds before they read the murder vignette. After participants finished reading the vignette, they were asked to choose a sentence for the defendant: either life in prison or the death penalty.

The results of the study did not support the contention that unattractive defendants would receive the death penalty more often than would attractive defendants. The authors suggested the possible explanation that a defendant's attractiveness may only operate as an advantage for certain crimes, that is, those less severe than murder. The results also did not reveal any significant difference in harshness of punishment as a factor of internal or external locus of control. Again, the authors suggest that the severity of the crime may have been too great to allow an effect.

However, the results did indicate that a jurors' age and gender may influence sentencing regardless of the attractiveness of the defendant. More specifically, it was shown that young men are less likely to recommend the death penalty than are young women or middle-aged men. It is suggested this may be because the defendants and the jurors were of similar age, thereby making it difficult for jurors to elect the death sentence. More specifically, if jurors are more able to identify with the defendant, they will be more likely to impose a lenient sentence.

Closely related research suggests that jurors are more likely to believe the testimony of persons who are like themselves. Following this theory, lawyers often seek to impanel jurors who most resemble their clients and principal witnesses, and to exclude jurors who might be the counterparts of the opposing party or significant adverse witnesses (Lubet, 1997).

JUST WORLD BELIEFS   **Just world beliefs** refer to the attitude that people get what they deserve in life. This concept is generally based on principles of equity. Individuals who believe in a just world tend to believe that good things will happen to good people and bad things will happen to bad people (or that if something bad happens to someone, he/she probably did something that instigated it). For example, if a person who believes in a just world hears a report on the news about a carjacking, although he may feel some sympathy for the victim, he/she may also believe that the victim did something that encouraged the crime to occur (e.g., the victim should not have put expensive rims on his/her car, or should not have driven the car in a high-crime area (Lerner, 1980; Montada & Lerner, 1998).

Believing in a just world is not a rare phenomenon. A survey conducted in England found that 33% of respondents agreed that women who were victims of rape are usually responsible for the attack (Wagstaff, 1982a). By making such attributions, perceivers can believe that if they alter their behavior they can avoid succumbing to the same fate. As a result, just world beliefs create a buffer against the anxiety related to perceptions that the world is a random place where negative events can befall us or our loved ones at any time, or that actions in the world are outside of our control.

Belief in a just world is typically measured using a self-report scale (Furnham, 1998). For example, Rubin and Peplau (1975) used a Just World Scale that required respondents to indicate their level of agreement with items that reflect a just world (e.g., "By and large people deserve what they get") and items that reflect a random world where outcomes are not predictable (e.g., "Careful drivers are just as likely to get hurt in traffic accidents as careless ones"). Using this measure, belief in a just world has been shown to correlate with a wide variety of factors, including locus of control beliefs, authoritarianism, religiousness, admiration of political leaders, and negative perceptions of underprivileged classes (Furnham, 1998).

ATTITUDES TOWARD THE DEATH PENALTY   The Supreme Court decision in *Witherspoon v. Illinois* (1968) established a standard for excusing individuals from the penalty phase of a trial in a capital case. According to the Court in Witherspoon, a juror can be constitutionally excused when he/she would never vote for the death penalty or when his/her opposition to the death penalty prevents him or her from being impartial in the penalty phase. In 1985, the Supreme Court clarified the death qualification standard in *Wainwright v. Witt* by stating that jurors can be constitutionally excused if their opposition to the death penalty would prevent or substantially impair the performance of their duties during the sentencing phase of the trial. Courts currently balance these interests by allowing parties to exclude for cause only those jurors whose attitude toward the death penalty is so strong, either for or against, that it would "prevent or substantially impair the performance of [their] duties as a juror" (*Wainwright v. Witt*, 1985, p. 424).

A juror's attitude towards the death penalty does not affect jury voting in a straightforward fashion (Lieberman & Sales, 2007). Research by O'Neil, Patry, and Penrod (2004) indicate that attitudes may have a direct, unmediated effect on verdicts, where the effect of attitudes is independent of the effect of the evidence in the case. Attitudes may also be mediated by jurors' findings of aggravating and mitigating factors (i.e., attitudes may affect how jurors interpret the evidence). Lastly, attitudes may influence the weight that jurors assign to any aggravating and mitigating factors; that is, there may be interactions between attitudes and aggravating and mitigating factors. But the primary affect of attitudes toward the death penalty are direct, in other words, supporters of the death penalty were more likely to sentence the defendant to death. Such individuals believe the death penalty is a deterrent, irrespective of their findings of aggravating and mitigating factors.

In fact, the effect of general support of the death penalty was greater than the effect of any manipulation of evidence or of aggravating or mitigating factors. Similarly, positive attitudes toward the use of the death penalty have been shown to be associated with positive attitudes toward police and prosecutors and less favorable attitudes toward defense attorneys and due process factors in death penalty cases.

When selecting a jury, probably the most important things for a lawyer to keep in mind regarding death penalty attitudes is how they seem to be related to demographic and personality factors. For example, Lieberman and Sales (2007) report research showing that individuals who are white, male, married, of upper income levels, and with authoritarian and conservative personalities are only generally most likely to favor the death penalty. In summarizing the research on the relationship between death penalty attitudes and verdicts, Lieberman and Sales (2007) in their book *Scientific Jury Selection*, conclude that this relationship "is best characterized as weak or moderate" (Lieberman & Sales, 2007, p. 97).

SCIENTIFIC JURY SELECTION

DEFINITION AND HISTORY Scientific jury selection can generally be defined as the application of behavioral and social scientific principles to the selection of jurors most sympathetic to a particular side in a court case (Clearly, 2005). Beginning in the 1970s, social scientists began seriously applying scientific jury selection to certain high profile cases. These included the Angela Davis trial, the Wounded Knee trials, trials stemming from the Attica prison riots, the trial of Mark David Chapman (John Lennon's assassin), Vietnam Veterans against the War, Vietnam Veterans against the Manufacturers of Agent Orange, the trials of Attorney General John Mitchell, and at least one defendant in the "Watergate" trials (Cutler, 1990; Lieberman & Sales, 2007).

One of the most notorious early cases to which scientific jury selection was applied was the 1971 trial of Philip Berrigan and six other antiwar activists known collectively as the "Harrisburg Seven" (Clearly, 2005). The group had been accused, among other things, of conspiring to obtain and destroy the selective service records of American men and kidnap then-Secretary of State Henry Kissinger. The social scientists who applied scientific jury selection in this case did so because they believed in the activists' cause and suspected that the prosecutor (in this case, the government) had selected Harrisburg, Pennsylvania, as the venue for the trial because of its rampant political conservatism.

Because a jury biased in favor of the defense would not have been likely in that venue, the defense team set as their goal the procurement of a jury that would at least be *fair* to the defendants. Securing such a fair jury required extraordinary effort since the attitudes held by Harrisburg residents indicated that a local jury would not be favorable for their side. Pretrial polling suggested that 8 out of 10 registered voters held views unfavorable to the defense

(Kressel & Kressel, 2002). A survey of over 1,000 Harrisburg residents, together with follow-up interviews, resulted in a demographic profile of individuals most and least likely to sympathize with the defense. This profile was used to guide jury selection. The defense achieved a victory: the jury hung on most charges, delivering only a minor conviction (for smuggling letters out of prison).

Also in the 1970s, social scientists participated in jury selection in the Joan Little criminal trial. A team of social scientists led by John McConahay, a Duke University psychology professor, assisted the defense in first being granted a change of venue (Little was an African-American woman, and surveys revealed that the North Carolina county where the trial was to be held was anti-African-American) and then in jury selection by constructing a profile of the ideal juror for the defense. The jury acquitted Little of all charges after barely an hour of deliberations.

Nearly 30 years after the Harrisburg Seven case, the issues of community hostility, pretrial publicity, and change of venue exploded in New York City in the shooting death of a 23-year-old West African immigrant named Amadou Bailo Diallo.

In the early morning of February 4, 1999, Diallo was standing near his building after returning from a meal. Police officers Edward McMellon, Sean Carroll, Kenneth Boss, and Richard Murphy passed by in a Ford Taurus when they thought Diallo matched the description of a (since-captured) serial rapist and approached him. The officers were in plain clothes. The officers claimed that they loudly identified themselves as NYPD officers and that Diallo ran up the outside steps toward his apartment house doorway at their approach, ignoring their orders to stop and "show his hands." As the suspect reached into his jacket, Carroll believed Diallo was drawing a firearm and yelled "Gun!" to alert his colleagues. The officers opened fire on Diallo and during the burst McMellon fell down the steps, appearing to be shot. The four officers fired 41 shots, hitting Diallo 19 times. The investigation found no weapons on Diallo's body; the item he had pulled out of his jacket was not a gun, but a wallet.

The officers were all indicted on charges of second-degree murder and reckless endangerment by a grand jury. For the trial, the New York appellate court granted a defense motion for a change of venue to Albany, New York, stating that pretrial publicity had made a fair trial in New York City impossible. On February 25, 2000, after two days of deliberations, a jury unanimously voted to acquit the officers of all charges. Diallo's death, the change of venue, and the verdict sparked massive demonstrations against "police brutality" and "racial profiling" resulting in more than 1,700 arrests over the course of many weeks. Charges against the protesters were later dropped. In 2001, the Justice Department announced that it would not charge the officers with having violated Diallo's civil rights.

Diallo's mother and stepfather filed a $61,000,000 ($20 million plus $1 million for each shot fired) lawsuit against the city of New York and the officers, charging gross negligence, wrongful death, racial profiling, and other violations of Diallo's civil rights. They later accepted a $3,000,000 settlement, which was one of the largest settlements against the city of New York for a single man with no dependents under New York State's restrictive wrongful death law, which limits damages to pecuniary (money) loss by the decedent's next of kin.

The consequences of intense media attention and community hostility were again dramatically brought to light in the case of *The People of the State of California v. Scott Peterson* in 2004.

Laci Peterson of Modesto California, eight months pregnant, was last seen alive on December 23, 2002. On April 13, 2003, the decomposed body of a late term male fetus, his umbilical cord still attached, was found on the San Francisco Bay shore north of Berkeley. One day later, the body of a recently pregnant woman washed to shore 1 mile away from where the baby's body was found. The woman's cause of death was impossible to discern; due to decomposition, the body was decapitated, armless, and legless. DNA tests verified they were the bodies of Laci Peterson and her son.

Laci's husband Scott Peterson was arrested on April 18, 2003, in La Jolla, California, and he was charged with murder. Due to increasing community hostility towards Peterson in the Modesto area, the judge allowed a change of venue to Redwood City, California, on January 20, 2004. The trial began in June of the same year and was followed closely by the media. After being found guilty of first-degree murder, Peterson's defense team requested yet another change of venue and a change of jurors, this time for the penalty phase of the trial. Saying there was no location in California the trial could be moved to that had not been saturated by press coverage of the case, the judge ruled that moving the trial to another location would accomplish nothing.

During the last three decades, the industry of trial consulting has continued to grow in size and number (Cutler, 1990). Consulting firms use academic, behavioral, and social psychological principles to accomplish their goals. They also rely on market research and advertising strategies. The trial consulting industry generally uses any techniques that will give their clients the upper hand in a trial. This can include in-court assessments, change of venue surveys, mock trials, shadow juries, witness preparation, attorney communication assessments, evidence preparation, focus groups, and even pretrial investigations of prospective jurors.

The goal of a **focus group** is to represent a cross-section of the community. This means that the demographic characteristics of participants in the focus group should be similar to those in the jury pool or on the actual jury. Such a group is assembled to test specific components and strategies of an attorney's case, in much the same way that a focus group might test a product about to be introduced to the market (Strier, 1999).

Pretrial investigations of prospective jurors is similar in many ways to background investigations that might be performed on law enforcement applicants. It consists of contacting prospective jurors' coworkers or neighbors, or people in the community who are affiliated with the same school, house of worship, or club as a prospective juror. Surveillance includes drive-by observations and photograph-taking of a prospective juror, and checking public records of each prospective juror, such as those of voter registration, court proceedings, and property holdings. It is no shock that these techniques have met with charges of privacy invasion (Strier, 1999). **Mock trials** attempt to duplicate the conditions of a real trial and use shadow juries to evaluate evidence and testimony (Diamond & Zeisel, 1974).

Regardless of our opinions of **trial consultants** and their strategies, they are likely here to stay. Trial consulting is estimated to be a $400 million industry, with over 400 firms and over 700 practitioners (Strier, 1999). This is reasonable when one considers that the stakes of a jury trial can be extremely high, whether it involves capitol murder or a corporation that stands to lose millions or even billions of dollars in a civil suit.

FORENSIC PSYCHOLOGY IN THE SPOTLIGHT
Does "Gruesome" Evidence Increase the Likelihood of Conviction?

Bright (2007)

Research utilizing mock trials strongly suggests that jurors presented with gruesome evidence, such as descriptions or images of torture and mutilation, are up to five times more likely to convict a defendant than jurors not privy to such evidence.

In a 2004 study at the University of New South Wales, participants read a transcript of a hypothetical trial involving a defendant charged with his estranged wife's murder. Participants were assigned to one of two evidence conditions: a gruesome or a nongruesome evidence condition. In the nongruesome version, the victim was

stabbed in the chest. In the gruesome version, the victim was "brutally tortured" for over 30 minutes, as numerous incisions were made to her body with a sharp instrument. The victim's face was "obliterated beyond recognition" and cuts were made to almost every part of her body. After her death, an attempt was made to decapitate the corpse.

After reading witness examinations by the prosecution and the defense, mock jurors read the judge's instructions outlining the role of jurors, the elements of the crime of murder and the definition of reasonable doubt—instructions identical to those administered by judges in similar cases in the criminal courts in New South Wales. Participants who reviewed gruesome evidence were more than twice as likely to find the defendant guilty (34.4%) than were participants who did not review gruesome evidence (13.9%).

In a 2006 study, researchers found that mock jurors who saw gruesome photographs, compared with those who saw no photographs, reported experiencing significantly more intense emotional responses, including greater anger at the defendant. The conviction rate was significantly higher among jurors who witnessed visual evidence in the form of gruesome (41.2%) or neutral photographs (38.2%) compared to the conviction rate among those without photographic evidence (8.8%).

In another 2006 study, researchers randomly assigned participants to one of four groups: verbal gruesome, verbal nongruesome, color photographs and black-and-white photographs. The gruesome version contained detailed descriptions of the wounds to the victim's neck. These detailed descriptions were omitted from the verbal nongruesome trial excerpts. Participants in the two photograph groups viewed 20 photographs from a real murder case tried in New South Wales in color or black and white, selected to include both neutral and differentially gruesome photographs (such as a close-up of a victim's neck wound versus blood-stained clothing).

The study indicated that photographic evidence, irrespective of whether this evidence is neutral or gruesome, can increase the likelihood of conviction. According to the researchers, "Admitting gruesome photographic evidence appears to increase the incriminating value that jurors ascribe to prosecutorial evidence by influencing jurors' emotional state." The researchers concluded that the prejudicial influence of gruesome evidence on decision making occurs at an unconscious level, and that jurors appear to be unaware of the extent to which they are susceptible to prejudice as a result of exposure to this type of evidence.

As examples of these gruesome prejudicial factors, the researchers cite actual criminal cases from New South Wales. For example, in the criminal trial of *R v. Bowhay* (1998), the judge explained his admission of postmortem photographs into evidence, saying: "In this day and age where people see "blood and guts" on the television and on the movie screen day after day and week after week, I fail to see how it could be expected the jury would misuse this evidence".

In the 1996 trial of convicted serial killer, Ivan Milat, for the "backpacker murders" Milat's defence team challenged the admissibility of photographs of one of the victim's skeletal remains (*R v. Milat*, 1996). However, prosecutors argued that to connect the murder to other murders and to implicate Milat as the perpetrator, the photographs should be admitted to demonstrate the savagery and cruelty of the murders. The chief justice ruled the photographs admissible, quoting from an earlier case to support his decision:

> If a photograph is of a particularly horrific nature, a question will no doubt arise as to whether its prejudicial shock effect is so great as to outweigh its probative value . . . It is important . . . (to consider) whether its prejudicial effect outweighs its probative value, not merely whether it merely accompanies such probative value. . . . The mere horrific nature of the photograph is not by itself a ground for its rejection. (*R v. Allen*, 1992, p. 6)

The researchers concede that horrific details are unlikely to be excluded from evidence so long as they have "probative value." Australian law tends (like American law) to assume the probative value of postmortem photographs usually outweighs any prejudicial impact on jurors.

Summary

The Sixth Amendment to the Constitution guarantees that in all criminal prosecutions, the accused shall have the right to a speedy and public trial with an impartial jury. In all criminal cases a unanimous jury decision is required. In civil trials in federal courts, a jury's decision also must be unanimous. The Supreme Court, *Burch v. Louisiana* (1979) held that verdicts made by a six-person jury in a misdemeanor case must also be unanimous, although states may alter this for their own courts. In order to be eligible for jury service in federal and state courts, an individual must meet certain requirements. In federal court an individual must, among other things, be a U.S. citizen; be at least 18 years of age; be able to read, write, and speak English; and be a nonfelon.

During the process of *voir dire*, the judge (or trial lawyers) question jurors in an attempt to determine if they meet the qualifications for service or have biases that could interfere with their service on the jury. Such challenges "for cause" can be due to, among other things, a juror not meeting certain statutory requirements, is not a U.S. citizen, does not speak English, reveals a bias, et cetera. Under most circumstances an unlimited number of challenges are allowed.

In addition to unlimited challenges for cause, both sides in a criminal trial have a limited number of peremptory challenges that, with very important exceptions, do not have to be based on any identifiable reason. The only exception to this rule is that such challenges may not be based solely on race (*Batson v. Kentucky*) or on gender (*J.E.B. v. Alabama ex rel.*).

There has been unsupported as well as some empirical support for demographic factors being relevant in jury decision making. These include such things as juror age, occupation, ethnicity, and physical attractiveness. In addition, there are personality variables that also seem to be related to how jurors vote. These include authoritarianism, locus of control, "just world beliefs" and attitudes toward the death penalty. When factors such as excessive pretrial publicity or community hostility are present, a change of venue may be requested where the trial is moved to another location.

Trial consulting has become a booming industry in the United States. Their ranks include psychologists, lawyers, sociologists, and organizational and marketing experts, and their main task is usually to help pick a jury best suited to a particular side of a case. Trial consultants use psychological principles, focus groups, behavioral analyses, pretrial investigations, and mock juries in their work. The industry is largely unregulated and concerns over privacy issues and other matters are frequently expressed.

Key Terms

Authoritarian personality *259*

Batson v. Kentucky 255

Burden of proof *250*

Challenge for cause *252*

Emotionality *258*

Focus group *264*

Gag order *254*

Juror bias *253*

Jury wheel *252*

Just world beliefs *261*

Locus of control *259*

Mock trial *264*

Peremptory challenge *253*

Pretrial publicity *253*

Scientific jury selection *262*

Trial consultants *264*

Venire *252*

Voir dire 251

Review Questions

1. What are the general requirements of the Sixth Amendment?
2. What are the requirements for service on a federal jury?
3. How many challenges for cause are allowed in a trial?
4. On what basis may a challenge for cause be made?
5. What was the holding of the Supreme Court in *Batson v. Kentucky*?
6. How many peremptory challenges are generally permitted in a trial?

7. Under what circumstances is a unanimous jury verdict required?
8. What are some ways that juror bias can be eliminated or reduced?
9. What are some of the possible effects of negative pretrial publicity?
10. Is it permissible for a judge to issue a "gag order" on the press?

Chapter Resources on the World Wide Web

Bureau of Justice Statistics Homepage
http://www.ojp.usdoj.gov/bjs

Scientific Jury Selection: History, Practice, and Controversy
http://www.publications.villanova.edu/Concept/2005/
jury_selection.pdf

CourtTVnews: The Amadou Diallo Shootings
http://www.courttv.com/trials/diallo/

League of Women Voters of the United States
http://www.lwv.org/AM/Template.cfm?Section=Home

Science Daily Home Page
http://www.sciencedaily.com/

CNN.com/Crime
http://www.cnn.com/CRIME/

Oyez Project: Pretrial Publicity
http://www.oyez.org/issues/criminal-procedure/pretrial-publicity/

For Further Reading

Adler, S. J. (1994). *The jury: Trial and error in the American courtroom.* New York: Times Books.

Bruschke, J., & Loges, W. E. (2003). *Free press v. fair trials: Examining publicity's role in trial outcomes.* Mahwah, NJ: Lawrence Erlbaum Associates.

Christie, R. (1991). Authoritarianism and related concepts. In J. P. Robinson, P. R. Shaver, & L. S. Wrightsman (Eds.), *Measures of personality and social psychological attitudes.* San Diego, CA: Academic Press.

Davenport, A. U. (2005). *Basic criminal law: the United States constitution, procedure and crimes.* Upper Saddle River, NJ: Pearson Prentice Hall.

Dimitrius, J., & Mazzarella, M. (1999). *Reading people: How to understand people and predict their behavior—anytime, anyplace.* New York: Ballantine Books.

Hastie, R. (Ed.). (1993). *Inside the juror: the psychology of juror decision making.* New York: Cambridge University Press.

Kressel, N. J., & Kressel, D. F. (2002). *Stack and sway: the new science of jury consulting.* Boulder, CO: Westview Press.

Lieberman, J. D., & Sales, B. D. (2007). *Scientific jury selection.* Washington, DC: American Psychological Association.

Lubet, S. (1997). *Modern trial advocacy* (2nd ed.). Notre Dame, IN: NITA.

Montada, L., & Lerner, M. J. (Eds.). (1998). *Responses to victimization and belief in a just world.* New York: Plenum Press.

Ruva, C., Mcevoy, C., & Bryant, J. B. (2007). Effects of pre-trial publicity and jury deliberation on juror bias and source memory. *Applied Cognitive Psychology, 21,* 45–67.

Saks, M. J. (1977). *Jury verdicts: the role of group size and social decision rule.* Lexington, MA: D.C. Heath.

Wagner, W. (1989). *The art of advocacy: Jury selection.* New York: Matthew Bender.

Wishman, S. (1986). *Anatomy of a jury: the system on trial.* New York: Times Books.

CHAPTER 13

Repressed Memories and Novel Syndromes

CHAPTER OBJECTIVES

After reading this chapter you would:

▪ Understand the definition of false memories and confabulation.

▪ Know the meaning of repression and dissociation in the memory context.

▪ Understand the implications of repressed memories.

▪ Understand the significance of the McMartin preschool case.

▪ Appreciate the roles of the judge and the jury in evaluating syndrome evidence.

▪ Understand homosexual panic, black rage, and road rage.

▪ Be aware of the issues associated with the polygraph technique.

▪ Understand how expert witnesses can be evaluated and dealt with in trials.

INTRODUCTION

In 1943 the psychoanalyst Leo Kanner first identified "autism," and suggested its cause may be related to a "genuine lack of maternal warmth" exhibited by mothers who are obsessive and "mechanical" in the way they relate to their children (Kanner, 1943). In fact, in a 1960 article, Kanner bluntly described both parents of autistic children as "just happening to defrost enough to produce a child" (Kanner, 1960). As discussed in chapter 1, Bruno Bettelheim embraced this theory and championed the notion that autism was the product of mothers who were cold, distant and rejecting, thus depriving their children of the chance to "bond properly" (Bettelheim, 1950, 1954, 1962). Bettelheim referred to these mothers as "refrigerator moms." But all this was based on unsupported theoretical and psychoanalytical concepts with no scientific or empirical validation.

Regardless of the validity of their theories, psychologists as well as psychiatrists during the last two centuries have still generally been advocating for increased involvement in the courtroom and the legal system as a whole. In 1906, Sigmund Freud stated as part of a lecture to a law class,

There is a growing recognition of the untrustworthiness of statements made by witnesses, at present the basis of so many judgments in Courts of Law; and this has quickened in all of you, who are to become judges and advocates, an interest in a new method of investigation, the purpose of which is to lead the accused person to establish his own guilt or innocence objectively. This method is of a psychological and experimental character and is based upon psychological research; it is closely connected with certain views which have only recently been propounded in medical psychology. (Freud, 1906).

As previously discussed in other parts of this text, Hugo Münsterberg (the "father of forensic psychology") advocated for psychology's increased involvement in the courts and legal system, and criticized the legal profession for its failure to apply psychological principles to the evaluation of testimony in the courtroom (Münsterberg, 1909).

But others, such as psychologist Margaret Hagen, warned about the increased "business" of unsubstantiated and non-scientifically derived expert testimony and its abuses in the American legal system (Salerno, 2005).

REPRESSED AND FALSE MEMORIES

A false memory is a memory that is a distortion of an actual experience or a confabulation of an imagined one. Many false memories involve confusing or mixing fragments of memory events, some of which may have happened at different times but which are remembered as having occurred together. Many false memories involve an error in source memory. Some involve treating dreams as if they were playbacks of real experiences. Still other false memories are believed to be the result of the prodding, leading, and suggestions of psychologists, psychiatrists, counselors, and other "therapists."

A **confabulation** is a fantasy that has unconsciously emerged as a factual account in memory. A confabulation may be based partly on fact or be a complete construction of the imagination. Perfectly healthy individuals make up stories all the time. Psychologist Helen Phillips at Lund University has recently demonstrated this point in a relatively simple yet telling experiment.

Subjects were shown pairs of cards with pictures of faces on them and asked to choose the most attractive. Unbeknownst to the subject, the person showing the cards was a magician and routinely swapped the chosen card for the rejected one. The subject was then asked why they picked this face. Often the swap went completely unnoticed, and the subjects came up with elaborate explanations about hair color, the look of the eyes, or the assumed personality of the substituted face. Clearly people routinely confabulate under conditions where they cannot know why they made a particular choice (Phillips, 2006).

It seems that confabulation is not just a deficit of memory, it is something anybody might do, even people with perfectly fine memories and healthy brains. We know that children and many adults confabulate when encouraged to talk about things of which they have no knowledge. We certainly know that eyewitnesses can be influenced by suggestive inquiries to confabulate (Hirstein, 2005).

Source memory involves a memory that is accurate and often detailed in every way, except that the source is mistaken. For example, in the 1980 presidential campaign, Ronald Reagan repeatedly told a heartbreaking story of a World War II bomber pilot who ordered his crew to bail out after his plane had been seriously damaged by an enemy hit. His young belly gunner was wounded so seriously that he was unable to evacuate the bomber. Reagan could barely hold back his tears as he uttered the pilot's heroic response: "Never mind. We'll ride it down together." But this story was an almost exact duplicate of a scene from the 1944 film *A Wing and a Prayer*. Reagan had apparently retained the facts but forgotten their source (Schacter, 1996, p. 287).

An even more dramatic case of source amnesia (also called **memory misattribution**) is that of Tom Kessinger, a mechanic at Elliott's Body Shop in Junction City, Kansas, who gave a detailed description of two men he said had rented a Ryder truck like the one used in the Oklahoma City bombing of the Alfred P. Murrah Federal Building. He reported that one of the men looked just like Timothy McVeigh. The other man wore a baseball cap and a T-shirt, and had a tattoo above the elbow on his left arm. That was Todd Bunting, who had rented a truck the *day before* McVeigh. Kessinger mixed the two memories but was absolutely certain the two came in together.

Despite the ease with which memory can be manipulated, and the common errors in memory and recall, many lay people, as well as some psychological theorists, still hold that there are presently hundreds of thousands, or even millions, of women struggling with the question of whether in the distant past they were the victims of incest and that such memories can be restored with the proper therapeutic intervention. Indeed, the leading self-help book on the topic *The Courage to Heal* (Bass & Davis, 1994), has sold close to a million copies. Tens of thousands have confronted their fathers, often in their therapist's offices, and a thousand or more have brought civil lawsuits. Advocates of the theory of repressed and recovered memories of childhood sexual abuse view such trauma as resulting in amnesia for these memories that are simply too upsetting to be consciously accessible (Terr, 1991; Van der Kolk, 1994a).

Hypothesized mechanisms for this amnesia include **repression** and **dissociation**. Repression a psychological defense mechanism whereby distressing thoughts, memories, or impulses that may give rise to anxiety are excluded from consciousness and left to operate in the unconscious. Dissociation refers to the abnormal integration of thoughts, feelings, and experiences into the stream of consciousness and memory so that traumatic memories can be split off from conscious awareness (Bernstein & Putnam, 1986).

The case of the **McMartin preschool** in 1987 is a glaring example of what can happen when false memories, overzealous experts, and a fad-desensitized media collide to form a perfect storm of hysteria. The school was founded by Virginia McMartin, who lived in the small oceanfront community of Manhattan Beach, California, just south of Los Angeles. She had opened the school and hired members of her family and church to help build and run it. Her daughter, Peggy Buckey, was the administrator. The school was considered so exemplary that the town of Manhattan Beach had given Virginia an award for educational excellence.

But all that changed when one vindictive parent made allegations that her son was sexually abused by staff members at the school. Before long the school was called a "sexual house of horrors" by the media, and the prosecutor claimed that the defendants in the case were not just a danger to the children at the school, but to the community as a whole.

One of the allegations against the school was that it procured young children for adult sexual pleasures. An assistant DA insisted that there were *millions* of pornographic photographs that could be produced into evidence, but none were ever produced. The prosecution's case rested on the results of interviews conducted at Children's Institute International (CII) at UCLA. One doctor, William E. Gordon, testified that the photographs did indeed show evidence of abuse. He was reported to be an "expert" who had previously testified in some 300 trials on the same issue. But he admitted he was not a certified pediatrician, but a professor, and had no formal education in psychiatric diagnoses or in the evaluation of sexual abuse.

What was particularly disturbing about this case was that the charges of physical and sexual horrors were based on no real evidence other than stories "retrieved" from some of the children. In fact, almost anything that was reported by the children was construed as a sign of child abuse even if concrete evidence refuted it (Earl, 1995).

In the end, 360 children were diagnosed at CII as having been abused at the McMartin preschool. It was the longest and most expensive legal proceeding in American history. But after seven years from the first accusations, no one was convicted. It had cost the community almost $16 million and had cost many parents their reputations and peace of mind (Showalter, 1997).

Another example of the deleterious effects of false memories and overzealous experts is the case of Gary Ramona of Napa Valley, California, who lost his marriage, his children, his reputation, and his career as a result of the occurrences of 1994. All it took was his daughter, Holly, her psychiatrist, and a family therapist to uncover "repressed memories" and accuse him of sexually abusing her when she was a little girl.

"Repressed memory syndrome" purports to involve forgetting a painful experience that can then be remembered through a therapeutic intervention. Often, the "revealed" experiences conveniently give rise to civil lawsuits against those included in the newly restored memories, usually parents or relatives. The remembered events range from child abuse to witchcraft, demonic rituals, alien abductions to murder. The major problem with many of these recalled events is that the one doing the remembering is not the patient but rather the therapist.

In the Ramona case, when Gary Ramona took his daughter's psychiatrist and family therapist to court, home movies shown during the 1994 trial revealed family vacations, graduations, and numerous scenes of a cheerful, happy Holly Ramona. From where, then, did the accusations come? It turned out that the real source of Holly's memories of sexual abuse was her psychiatrist, Richard Rose, and therapist, Marche Isabella.

When Holly first consulted Isabella, the idea of sexual abuse was nowhere in her mind. She sought treatment for bulimia. But early in her treatment, Isabella planted the idea of sexual abuse by telling Holly that 70% to 80% of bulimia patients had been sexually abused. Isabella also cited sexual abuse as a possible explanation for Holly's fear of snakes. And when Holly pointed to her long history of urinary infections, Isabella reportedly had a ready diagnosis—sexual abuse. Indeed, when Holly told Isabella that her dad had once glanced at her in what might be construed as a suggestive way, Isabella labeled her father's conduct as "emotional incest" (a stylish diagnosis of the sexual abuse genre, found nowhere in legitimate psychiatry).

Even with all this assistance, Holly's "memories" of sexual abuse did not come as easily to her as they did to her psychiatrist and therapist. After several months of psychiatric treatment, Holly was still uncertain about the meaning of her "visions" and whether they were real or imaginary. When placed under sodium amytal, she claimed to recall incidents of abuse, although even then she admitted the details were vague and that she could not see her father's face clearly.

Can alleged sexual abuse occurring over a 12-year period be so traumatic as to be expelled from conscious memory? Can such repressed memories be reliably recovered through the administration of a **sodium amytal** ("truth serum") and hypnotherapy? The answer to these questions was an (at least in this case) unfortunate "yes," and Gary Ramona was charged with repeated rape and sexual abuse of his daughter—including anal intercourse and forced copulation with the family dog.

It turns out that the psychiatrist who administered sodium amytal to Holly (which some erroneously believed to guarantee the truthfulness of her recollections) had been the subject of five prior medical malpractice claims. Soon after the filing of *Ramona v. Isabella*, the psychiatrist moved to Hawaii, giving up the practice of medicine entirely. Jurors in the case were shocked that the amytal interview was not taped and that no medical notes were taken by the treating therapists. Mr. Ramona was awarded half a million dollars in civil damages due to negligence by Holly's therapist. The court ruled that Mr. Ramona was a *de facto* client of Ms. Isabella and that she consequently owed him a duty of care (*Ramona v. Isabella*, 1994; Brown, Scheflin, & Hammond, 1998).

In her 1997 book about the Ramona case, author Moira Johnston expressed the view that recovered memories are the modern equivalent of "the invisible manifestations of the devil that had condemned Salem's innocent [women] as witches." The Salem trials ended only when a judge finally banned such "spectral evidence" from the courtroom (Johnston, 1997).

In another case, Patricia Burgus had been undergoing psychotherapy for severe postpartum depression from 1986 to 1992. Drugs and hypnosis helped her to "recall" that she had been part of a satanic cult, had been abused by numerous men, had abused her own children, had had sex with John F. Kennedy, and had even cannibalized people. At one point, her husband brought in some hamburger meat from a family picnic, and the therapists agreed to test the meat to see if it was human.

Burgus eventually realized that she has not been an abused devil-worshipping cannibal or a child abuser. She sued her former therapists, and the case was settled on the day that the trial was expected to commence, six years after the case had been filed, for $10.6 million. The medical center agreed to pay approximately $3 million, and the psychiatrists agreed to pay the remainder.

Soon after the Burgues settlement, a federal grand jury in Houston, Texas, returned an indictment against the administrator and four caregivers at the former Spring Shadows Glen Hospital. The criminal charges accused the mental health professionals (psychologists, psychiatrists, psychotherapists) of exaggerating diagnoses and overstating the need for expensive treatment in order to unjustly collect insurance payments. The accusations were that the clinicians convinced patients that they had participated in satanic cults and that as a result they had multiple personality disorder (MPD). The indictment stated, "It was further part of the conspiracy that the defendants and others would and did fraudulently treat the insured patients for MPD caused by unsubstantiated and unrealistic allegations and abuses, including satanic ritual abuse and cult activity, while at the same time creating medical records to substantiate such treatment" (*United States v. Peterson* et al., 1993).

These were not isolated events in the 1990s and likely still occur. A study by Poole, Lindsay, Memon, and Bull (1995) found that large numbers of certified psychotherapists were using subjective, highly influential techniques such as hypnosis, dream analysis, and guided imagery to "uncover" repressed memories of childhood sexual abuse. In a 1995 study by Michael Yapko, more than 1,000 members of the American Association of Marriage and Family Therapy reported believing that "hypnosis can be used to recover memories from as far back as birth." One-third of the members agreed with the statement that "the mind is like a computer, accurately recording events that actually occurred." And one-fourth of them agreed that "someone's feeling certain about a memory means the memory is likely to be correct" (Lilienfeld, Lynn, & Lohr, 2003; Poole et al., 1995).

All told, there seems to be a large class of cases in which people share a desperate desire to be a victim of "something," even if it's imaginary, and sometimes to assign blame to others for these events. Over the last fifteen years following the height of the "recovered memory" sensation, hundreds of accusers have retracted their claims, and many have switched from suing their parents to suing their therapists. Another effect of this fad is that, based on these precedents, many courts will no longer hear cases in which recovered memories are the primary evidence (Lutus, 2006).

NOVEL SYNDROMES

In 1978, Dan White and Harvey Milk were elected to the city council of San Francisco. Soon after the election White changed his mind about serving and impulsively resigned. But following the advice and encouragement of his supporters, White asked Mayor George Moscone to allow him to withdraw his resignation. The mayor refused. Infuriated, White obtained a handgun and entered City Hall through a back window to avoid the metal detectors at the main entrance. Once inside, he went directly to the mayor's office and shot Moscone dead. He then walked to the office of Harvey Milk, who he felt had been instrumental in convincing Moscone not to allow him to withdraw his resignation, and shot him dead as well.

The jury convicted White of only two counts of voluntary manslaughter instead of first-degree murder because they saw the killings as being "nonpremeditated." During the trial, there was testimony by a psychiatrist to the effect that White's eating habits had changed as a result of his manic–depressive syndrome and that his eating habits were cyclical, alternating with the manic and depressive phases of the illness. Accordingly, White would eat junk food to deal with his problems, which in turn made him feel worse, and so forth. The psychiatrist did not claim that White's bad eating habits caused him to commit the killings, but that they were caused by his mental illness. Dan White served a little more than five years for the double murder of Moscone and Milk. On October 22, 1985, a year and a half after his release from prison, White was found dead in a running car in his ex-wife's garage. He was 39 years old (Lindsey, 1985). But what will be remembered forever about White and the murders of Moscone and Milk was the notion of the "Twinkie Defense."

Even today there remain ideas about the effects of eating junk food, and in particular sugar, that are not based on scientific fact. Halpern Brooks, and Stephenson (2007) point out that although most people believed that eating large quantities of sugar and sweet food can cause children to be hyperactive, a review of the scientific literature reveals that no such relationship exists. Halpern notes that "[t]he belief that sugar consumption causes hyperactivity creates an expectancy, which can be strong and overrule the critical thinking process when it comes to formulating conclusions about experienced events, such as the relationship between sugar consumption and behavior." (p. 17).

The statements about sugar and junk food consumption and their effect on the behavior of Dan White were made by a psychiatrist, who would normally be regarded as an authoritative and trustworthy expert by a jury. But according to Halpern, the lack of critical thinking about scientific evidence in the courtroom often is the result of jurors automatically accepting the testimony of such "experts." "When an expert's testimony corroborates the beliefs of jurors, they are not motivated to seek disconfirming evidence." (p. 20).

Is applied psychology inordinately affected by "social fashion?" Are various forms of social activism presented to juries, the media, and the public in the guise of science? Do various "syndromes" presented by experts determine guilt or innocence? And how much is a jury swayed by fantasies or distorted memories of events that may not have even occurred?

A **syndrome** is a set of symptoms and signs that occur in a regular pattern from patient to patient, that collectively indicate or characterize a disease, psychological disorder, or other abnormal condition (Miller, 1998b). Psychological syndrome evidence is so important because it can put in the hands of the jury tremendous power to determine the credibility of a witness in a trial—the type of determination that an expert witness would never be permitted to make. For example, it is not permissible under the rules of evidence for an expert to testify whether a witness (or defendant) is telling the truth. But the jury, being the "lie detector in the courtroom" can make such a determination, and it can rely on "syndrome evidence" to do it (*United States v. Barnard*, 1973).

Some rules of evidence take an unduly optimistic view of the mental powers of juries, while other rules assume the jurors to be, as one law professor put it, "a group of low grade morons" (Damaska, 1997). In both civil and criminal cases, there has been a distinct trend to introduce various syndromes into evidence (battered woman syndrome [BWS], rape trauma syndrome [RTS], sexual addiction syndrome) to explain behavior unique to a victim or as a determination of whether a witness is telling the truth (Slovenko, 2002).

For example, using syndrome evidence, prosecutors may wish to explain why an alleged rape victim delayed in reporting that a rape had occurred (due to RTS) or why a victim of domestic abuse remained with her abusive husband (due to BWS). The problem is, that some syndromes are based on little or no empirical evidence, may be grounded in social activism rather than science, may not be applicable to the individual, or may not exist at all.

In the late 1970s, the first type of syndrome most people were aware of was the **Stockholm syndrome** in which hostages form an identification with their captors who had terrorized them. In these situations, bonding to one's captor is a survival strategy for victims that has been observed in a variety of hostage-taking situations. The Stockholm syndrome received its name after a hostage situation in a bank robbery in Stockholm, Sweden, in 1973. Three women and one man were held hostage for six days by two men. During this period, the four hostages and their captors "bonded," and the hostages even came to see their captors as protecting them from the police. Following the release of the hostages, one of the women became engaged to one of the captors; another of the hostage started a "defense fund." All this was done in the face of the fact that the hostages were bound with dynamite and mistreated.

Syndromes have been multiplying. The appellate court judge in *Werner v. State* described the dramatic increase by saying, "Today, we have the following labels: 'The Battered Wife Syndrome'; 'The Battered Child Syndrome'; 'The Battered Husband Syndrome'; 'The Battered Patient Syndrome'; 'The Familial Child Sexual Abuse Syndrome'; 'The Rape Trauma Syndrome'; 'The Battle Fatigue Syndrome'; 'The Vietnam Post-Traumatic Stress Syndrome'; 'The Policeman's Syndrome'; 'The Whiplash Syndrome'; 'The Low-Back Syndrome'; 'The Lover's Syndrome'; 'The Love Fear Syndrome'; 'The Organic Delusional Syndrome'; and 'The Holocaust Syndrome.' Tomorrow, there will probably be additions to the list, such as 'The Appellate Court Judge Syndrome' " (*Werner v. State*, 1986).

Battered Woman Syndrome

In 1967, while researching classical conditioning, an accidental discovery occurred. In the experiment, dogs were placed in harnesses so that they could not escape and then were presented with small electric shocks (Overmier & Seligman, 1967; Seligman & Maier, 1967). After this experience, these dogs as well as dogs who had not undergone the original harness studies were placed in a shuttle box that consisted of two sides both with independent electric grids on the floor.

Seligman and associates discovered a distinct difference between the dogs who had originally been harnessed and those who had not. For the latter, when a shock was presented, they almost immediately, after trying different methods of escape, jumped across the barrier to escape the uncomfortable shock. The previously harnessed dogs showed distress, as did the other dogs, but unlike the other dogs, failed to escape the shock and ultimately laid down on the grid and whimpered. These studies demonstrated that previous learning can result in a drastic change in behavior. When presented with a situation that allowed the dogs to control their experience, those who learned earlier that they had no control failed to escape the shock. Without this learning, escape was not only seen as a possibility, the behavior to escape was exercised in every case.

Considering these results, Seligman attempted to discover if similar effects would occur in humans. Experiments were designed presenting a loud irritating noise (rather than the original shock) to human subjects (Hiroto, 1974). In these experiments, subjects were presented with the noise and told that if they solved a puzzle the noise would turn off. By pressing a series of buttons, for example, one group learned that they had control over their environment. A second group, however, were presented with puzzles that had no solutions, resulting in an inability to turn off the irritating noise.

To test if the subjects' learning would generalize to other situations, these same subjects as well as new subjects were then presented with similar situations but with new types of problems to solve. The problems in this phase were identical, so each group had an equal chance of solving them. Those who were able to control their environment before did as well as new subjects; however, those in the unsolvable condition before, did significantly worse. Like the dogs in the original experiments, the human subjects also inaccurately generalized their **learned helplessness** to a new situation. Several replications of these experiments support the idea that we can learn to be helpless in an environment that actually offers us control (Peterson, Maier, & Seligman, 1993). This realization has since been applied to many aspects of human behavior and does well to explain why people in certain situations accept their uncomfortable or negative situation despite the ability to change it. Ten years after Seligman's original learned helplessness experiments, the phenomenon was applied to the cycle of battering and an adaptation seen in cases of domestic violence.

The term **battered woman syndrome** was introduced into the psychological lexicon by psychologist **Lenore Walker**, who from 1978 to 1981 conducted interviews with 435 women in the Rocky Mountain Region of Colorado, each of whom had been, or were at the time, victims of domestic violence. These interviews were conducted with a view to identifying key sociological and psychological factors that made up the proposed battered woman syndrome. The syndrome denotes a set of distinct psychological and behavioral symptoms that result from prolonged exposure to situations of intimate partner violence (Craven, 2003).

Walker identified three distinct periods within the course of a battering cycle.

1. *The Tension-Building Stage.* This stage is characterized by a series of minor verbal and physical battering events that precede an acute battering incident. Typical characteristics of this stage include (a) increases in the frequency and severity of the battering incidents, (b) decrease in the effectiveness of strategies used by the women to placate their batterers, and (c) feelings of responsibility on part of the women because they have been unable to control the batterer's behavior.

2. *The Acute Battering Stage.* During the tension-building stage, tension builds and is ultimately released in an acute battering incident or series of incidents. The characteristics of this stage are (a) uncontrollable rage and destructiveness on the part of the batterer, which usually does not end until the victim is severely beaten; (b) the triggering of rage by some external event or the internal state of the batterer, as opposed to the behavior of the victim; and (c) an acute battering incident that is briefer in duration than either the tension-building stage or the period of contrite and loving behavior.

3. *Contrite and Loving Behavior.* This is a period of unusual calm that typically follows the acute battering incident, during which the batterer attempts to make up for the abusive behavior. Characteristics associated with this stage are said to be (a) admission of wrongdoing on the part of the batterer, accompanied by apologies and the batterer's assurances that the abusive behavior will not happen again; (b) intensive effort on the part of the batterer to "win back" the victim through gifts, enlistment of other family members, and appeals to the victim's guilt over the adverse consequences the batterer will suffer if the victim leaves; (c) victim's capitulation from anger, fear, hurt, and loneliness to happiness and confidence; and (d) a strengthening of the bond between the batterer and victim as they both come to believe, through reinforcement, that their relationship can be made to work (Dutton, 1993).

BWS has been the subject of expert testimony in a variety of cases, including the defense of accused battered women who have killed their partners.

Originally, the plea in such cases was not guilty by reason of insanity (NGRI) and was the functional equivalent to post-traumatic stress disorder (PTSD), but some theorists and activists regarded NGRI as a stigma that often resulted in psychiatric commitment, so the defense shifted to self-defense (Slovenko, 2002). Expert testimony is now allowed in these cases to explain the lower threshold of self-defense as a result of the abuse (e.g., *State v. Kelly*, 1984).

Another reason that BWS has become admissible evidence presented by experts in many courts is that many jurors have inaccurate, stereotypic ideas about battered women, and facts about battering relationships have been considered beyond the ken of the jury (see, e.g., *Arcoren v. U.S.*, 1992; *Smith v. State*, 1981; *State v. Allery*, 1984; *State v. Borelli*, 1993; *State v. Gallegos*, 1986).

By 1993, BWS gained legal acceptance in all state courts to assist the jury in evaluating the reasonableness of a defendant's belief of being in mortal or imminent danger (Blowers & Bjerregaard, 1994). But the BWS construct has typically not been permitted as a means of allowing experts to testify about a defendant's state of mind at the time of the killing (e.g., *People v. Erikson*, 1997). Hagen (1997) notes that when the BWS defense to murder has been allowed into court, it was usually successful. In one-third of all cases where the defense has presented a BWS defense, the defendant was acquitted. In 100% of the cases where the court excluded this defense, the defendants were convicted.

Since the publication of Hagen's book (*Whores of the Court: The Fraud of Psychiatric Testimony and the Rape of American Justice*) in 1997, the defense of BWS has come under increased scrutiny. There is a distinct paucity of research establishing BWS as a bona fide reliable condition, which undercuts the claim that the condition exists as a distinct diagnostic entity (Dixon & Dixon, 2003). The defense of BWS is not raised now as often as it was in the 1990s. Instead, the defense is now more commonly offered as a variant of PTSD.

The effects of battering and abusive relationships have been studied using a variety of methods, including clinical interviews, surveys, and the administration of psychological tests. National surveys have attempted to document the prevalence of abuse using large representative samples, but have failed to provide meaningful descriptions of the experience of battered women. Clinical interviews provide detailed information about battered women's experiences, but because these are typically small, selective samples, the degree to which they are representative of, and generalizable to, all battered women is questionable. In fact, the clinical characteristics of the BWS do not appear consistently among women who have experienced long-term abuse. Because learned helplessness does not appear universally (as evidenced by the wide range of coping efforts among different battered women and the cyclical nature of violence in domestic relationships), questions have been raised about the reliability with which the syndrome can be identified across various cases. Schuller and Rzepa (2002) challenged both the notion that domestic violence is cyclical and that women who are battered always or usually experience "learned helplessness." Their conclusion is that there is no *single profile* of the battered woman (p. 237). In addition, the research regarding the BWS has been directly attacked for methodological flaws including (1) failure to employ an appropriate control group, (2) failure to employ appropriate statistical tests, and (3) failure to employ controls to guard against researcher bias. A review of the literature on learned helplessness (the theoretical underpinning of BWS) found several studies in which battered women took action to end their abuse and employed a wide range of coping skills in their relationships.

These self-help measures, however, conflict with learned helplessness theory, which would predict that battered women would not take positive action to change their situations (Faigman, 1986; Faigman & Wright, 1997). Because BWS has not been adopted as a formal diagnosis, many courts permit experts to testify about research findings but often restrict them from offering opinions regarding whether a defendant exhibits the syndrome (Schuller & Vidmar, 1992).

Insanity or Self-Defense?

Is the BWS based on insanity or self-defense? This is a vitally important question as each has different requirements, implications, and consequences under the criminal law. Insanity is an *excuse*. Self-defense is a *justification*. The syndrome has most often been offered as a claim of *self-defense*, meaning that the woman (or man) was "justified" in killing of an abusive spouse as a means of preventing imminent death or extreme bodily harm. This would be equivalent to using a (legally possessed) handgun to shoot an assailant who is about to impale you with a large knife with the apparent intent of killing you. A claim of *insanity* means that the woman (or man) was not able to distinguish right from wrong or to conform her or his behavior to the law due to a mental disease or defect (Cross, 1982).

Consider the facts in *State v. Norman* (1988). Norman was beaten by her husband for years. He would demand that she bark like a dog, eat dog or cat food, and sleep on the cold concrete floor. If she refused he would hit her with whatever was handy: his fist, a flyswatter, a baseball bat, a shoe, an ashtray, all of which left scars. Two days before the killing, he took her to a truck stop and forced her to prostitute herself, something he had done on numerous other occasions. He also assaulted her, for which he was arrested. Upon returning from jail the next day, he beat her continuously, and Norman, apparently in distress, took an overdose of tranquilizers. When emergency personnel arrived to treat her, the husband tried to interfere, stating, "Let the bitch die. . . . She ain't nothing but a dog. She don't deserve to live." Then next day, the day of the shooting, the husband again beat Norman all day, kicking her in the head, smashing food in her face, and putting a cigarette out on her chest. When he decided to take a nap, Norman took her daughter's baby, whom she had been babysitting, to her mother's house so her husband would not wake up from the crying. At her mother's, Norman picked up a gun, returned home, and killed her husband while he lay sleeping.

Norman's self-defense claim based on BWS failed. Would the result have been the same if an insanity defense had been utilized? Claims such as those made in *Norman* are likely better characterized as claims of insanity or diminished responsibility that focus on inner pathological states (i.e., an "excuse") rather than on the manner in which the woman's relationship with the batterer makes her actions reasonable (a "justification"). This is likely the case despite the insistence of some writers that the excuse characterization is demeaning to women (Schneider, 1986).

Rape Trauma Syndrome

Burgess and Holmstrom coined the term **rape trauma syndrome** (RTS) in 1974, referring to the acute phase and long-term reorganization process that is said to occur as a result of forcible rape or attempted forcible rape (Burgess & Holmstrom, 1974). The authors studied 92 patients who presented to the emergency room at Boston City Hospital during a one-year period with the complaint of rape. According to this study, rape victims generally go through a two-phase reaction—an *acute phase* and a *long-term reorganization phase.*

In the acute phase, lasting several weeks after the rape, victims are said to experience physical trauma from the rape, skeletal muscle tension manifesting in headaches, sleep disturbances, and an elevated startle reaction, gastrointestinal disturbances, as well as intense fear and self-blame. In the long-term phase, victims experience disorganization in their lives and must go through a "reorganization process," which is marked by increased motor activity, nightmares, phobic reactions to the circumstances of the rape, and the fear of being alone or in crowds.

In the criminal trial for rape, evidence of RTS is usually introduced to put the victim's actions into context and make her more credible. For instance, the prosecution may present an expert on RTS to explain the victim's actions around the time of her alleged rape especially if they seem inconsistent with the expected behavior of someone who has just been raped (e.g., returning to the scene of the rape as a gesture of defiance, lack of exhibited fear, continuing to have contact with the assailant following the assault, delaying reporting of the assault to police) (Ritchie, 1998; Stefan, 1994). At other times testimony regarding RTS may be introduced to support the prosecution's contention that the victim did not consent to intercourse, or to show that intercourse did, in fact, take place (see, e.g., *State v. Huey*, 1985; *State v. Marks*, 1982; *State v. Saldana*, 1982).

Evidence of RTS has also been offered by the defense to argue that if the victim had actually been raped she would exhibit symptoms of RTS. That is, the absence of RTS has actually been used as a defense for rape (see, e.g., *Henson v. State*, 1989).

But in the overwhelming majority of cases where RTS has been proffered, it has been by the prosecution to help explain inconsistent and contradictory statements and behaviors by the alleged victim (see, e.g., *People v. Taylor*, 1990). During the last 25 years, an increasing number of jurisdictions have allowed RTS admitted into evidence for this reason. Although RTS testimony is not admitted as substantive evidence that the victim was, *in fact*, raped, many states' decisions could arguably be interpreted as doing just that. In *State v. Allewalt* (1986) the Maryland Supreme Court held that it was not an abuse of discretion to admit testimony of an expert who testified about PTSD and his belief that the witness suffered from PTSD as a result of the rape in question.

A 1992 review of case law found that a frequent concern regarding RTS was the problem in recognizing a single syndrome given the broad range of symptoms and responses exhibited by different victims (Frazier & Borgida, 1992). Burgess and Holmstrom's original work, as well as other early studies of RTS, have been criticized as suffering serious methodological flaws, such as lack of a control groups, problems with sample size and sample characteristics, failure to operationalize important definitions and concepts, potential selection bias, inconsistent interviewing methods, and inadequate long-term follow-up of victims.

The characteristics of RTS are not universal in all rape victims, accordingly, the syndrome cannot be validated as a definitive sign that a rape did or did not occur. Not all rape survivors respond to rape in this way; some have none of these symptoms, and others experience only some of the symptoms (Brownmiller, 1975). Although it is likely that a person who presents with all or many of the symptoms of RTS has been raped, it is far from definitively so. Likewise, it cannot be assumed that a person who claims to have been raped, has not in fact been raped merely because she presents with few, or none, of the symptoms of the RTS.

The Automatism Syndrome

"Death Driver Walks Free due to Automatism Condition." This was a recent lead story in a London newspaper describing how an 89-year-old retired businessman was driving his Jaguar at least 76 mph in a 30 mph speed zone, when he smashed head on into a couple's car, killing them both. The driver, according to medical experts, may not have known what he was doing due to a blocked blood vessel in his brain (transient ischemic attack), resulting in confusion and disorientation. Explaining why the charges were being dropped, the prosecutor stated that he could not disprove the defense of "noninsane automatism."

In Britain, automatism is an absolute defense. As has been observed by Lord Denning in the case of *Bratty v. A-G* in 1936, "No act is punishable if it is done involuntarily: and an involuntary act in this context—some people nowadays prefer to speak of it as 'automatism'—means an act which is done by the muscles without any control by the mind, such as a spasm, a reflex action or a convulsion; or an act done while suffering from concussion or whilst sleep-walking." The defense is not so straight forward or absolute in this country.

As discussed in Chapter 3 of this text, every crime (except strict liability offenses such as traffic offenses, selling liquor to a minor, statutory rape) consists of at least two elements: (1) the physical conduct associated with the crime (known as the *"actus reus"*) and (2) the mental state, or level of intent, associated with the crime (known as the *"mens rea"*). To convict an individual of a particular crime, the state must prove beyond a reasonable doubt that the defendant committed the *actus reus* with the requisite *mens rea* for that crime.

The concept of automatism is directly related to the concept of *actus reus*. For example, if Zach pushes Sarah's arm into Daniel, Sarah cannot be convicted of assault even though her arm committed the actual touching, because Sarah's act was not voluntary. Another way of looking at it is that Sarah did not "intend" to commit the assault and thus did not have the *mens rea* for the crime. But a distinction is usually made between an act over which there is no conscious control and a conscious action with unintended consequences. The previous example is of the first type of act. An example of the latter situation would be if Sarah, in purposefully tapping Daniel on her own accord, meant only to frighten him but instead killed him; her act would be voluntary, but she would not have the *mens rea* for murder. (Reisner et al., 1999, p. 565).

The **automatism** (or "unconsciousness") defense recognizes that some criminal acts may be committed involuntarily, even though no third party (like Zach in the example above) is involved. The classic example of the "automaton" is the person who commits an offense while sleepwalking; courts have held that such an individual does not have conscious control of his/her physical actions and therefore acts involuntarily. Therefore, in *People v. Lisnow* (1978) the court held that a Vietnam veteran who struck a maitre d' in a restaurant for "no apparent reason" and then went into the parking lot and engaged in other "acts of violence" while in a "dreamlike" state was entitled to a jury instruction on the automatism defense. Other situations would include crimes occurring during a state of unconsciousness induced by medical conditions such as epilepsy, hypoglycemia, or a severe head injury. In fact, hypoglycemia (low blood sugar) one of the most dangerous side effects of diabetes providing it can be proved to have been present at the time of the offence, is a valid defense acceptable in most jurisdictions in the civilized world.

Most American courts have held that for the automatism defense to prevail, a person claiming to be effected by a medical condition at the time of the offense must show that the disability had not been experienced on previous occasions, that is, that reasonable steps could not have been taken to prevent the occurrence. Thus, if a person who knows he is subject to epileptic seizures, loses control of a car because of a seizure, and kills someone in the process, he may not be able to take advantage of the defense (*People v. Decina*, 1956).

Factitious Disorder by Proxy

Factitious disorder by proxy, commonly referred to as **Munchausen syndrome by proxy** (MSBP) derives from the adult form of Munchausen syndrome in which the patient fabricates and/or induces his own symptoms and presents himself for treatment. The description of Munchausen syndrome by proxy was first made in 1977, after British pediatrician Roy Meadow recognized that mothers of two children in his practice were engaging in dissimulations that put their children in the patient role, using the children as proxies. Meadow began a crusade against parents who willfully harm or kill their children. He was knighted for these works. He endorsed the dictum, "One sudden infant death is a tragedy, two is suspicious and three is murder, until proved otherwise," in his book, *ABC of Child Abuse* (1997); this became known as "Meadow's Law" and at one time was widely adopted by social workers and child protection agencies in Britain (Taylor, 2003).

Munchausen-type symptoms were first incorporated into the *Diagnostic and Statistical Manual of Mental Disorders* (DSM-III) in 1980 as one of the factitious disorders. In addition to production of factitious physical symptoms, factitious psychological symptoms were recognized. Factitious psychological symptoms have been held to include factitious PTSD, factitious psychosis, factitious depression, factitious rape, and factitious bereavement (Rand, 2007).

Jones et al. (1986) presented what they considered to be the warning signs of MSBP, which included persistent or recurrent illnesses for which a cause cannot be found, discrepancies between history and clinical findings, signs and symptoms that do not occur when a child is away from the mother, unusual or bizarre symptoms, failure of the child to respond to treatment despite repeated hospitalizations, and frequent comparisons of the child's medical problems to those of the parents. The DSM-IV-TR (2000) continues to include Munchausen-type symptoms under factitious disorders. *Factitious Disorder with Predominantly Psychological Signs and Symptoms* (300.16) includes ". . . the intentional production or feigning of psychological symptoms that are suggestive of a mental disorder [where the goal] is apparently to assume the 'patient' role. . . ." (p. 514). It is further noted that "the victim is often a young child and the perpetrator is the child's mother" (p. 782).

Any diagnostic recognition of factitious disorder by proxy presents many problems from a scientific and evidentiary perspective. The empirical basis for factitious disorder by proxy is questionable, given that only a small number of preliminary controlled studies exist. Furthermore, most of the literature on this condition is based on clinical observations, rather than systematic studies. Critics of MSBP cite that when children suffer complex, controversial, or confusing illnesses, or when symptoms are amorphous or vague, parents can be unjustly accused, and that worldwide, there have been thousands of very sick children forcibly removed from mothers because these women have insisted, often correctly, that their children are ill (Allison & Roberts, 1998). It is further maintained that MSBP has served as a catchphrase for disadvantaged mothers with chronically ill children who share nothing beyond an ability to confuse and eventually antagonize their physicians.

Homosexual Panic

On March 6, 1995, Scott Amedure appeared with Jonathan Schmitz on the *Jenny Jones Show*. On the show he revealed that he had a secret crush on Schmitz. But Schmitz was not flattered; rather, he felt embarrassed and humiliated. Three days after the taping, Schmitz withdrew money from his savings account, purchased a shotgun, drove to Amedure's trailer, and shot him twice through the heart, killing him instantly. He then left the trailer, dialed 911, and confessed to the shooting (*People v. Schmitz*, 1998). The resulting murder trial is perhaps the most infamous case in which a defendant asserted the **homosexual panic defense** (HPD). This defense is now more commonly referred to as the *gay panic defense*. Schmitz's counsel argued that the humiliation of being identified by Amedure as an object of his homosexual affections drove Schmitz to kill. In essence, Schmitz blamed Amedure's sexuality as being an indirect cause of his own actions. In doing so, he asked the jury to understand and sympathize with his reaction to being the object of a homosexual crush. The jury did sympathize, and found Schmitz guilty of the lesser offense of second-degree murder.

Homosexual panic was first described in 1920 by Dr. Edward Kempf as an intense form of anxiety, tension, and rage, experienced by an individual with latent homosexual tendencies, and brought about by the mere presence or sight of homosexuals. Such individuals are usually precariously psychologically balanced with fragile egos (Chuang & Addington, 1988; Slovenko, 2002). Neither homosexual or gay panic appear in the DSM-IV-TR.

The HPD has been attempted in various cases as a justification for the behavior of defendants who murder gay individuals (*People v. Milner*, 1988; *State v. Escamilla*, 1994). In these cases, testimony on homosexual panic was not allowed, while in others (e.g., *Parisie v. Greer*, 1983) it was. In the 1980s, the HPD proved unsuccessful in a Louisiana case in which the defendant claimed that when the victim touched his leg, it unleashed his "excessive hostility toward and fear of homosexuals." It was likewise unsuccessful in a 1988 Minneapolis case by a defendant who claimed that his "revulsion from the deceased's homosexual advances elicited a heat-of-passion response." But in Toronto, in 1992, a 19-year-old was acquitted of fatally stabbing his boss, claiming he was both in fear for his life and was also operating out of homosexual panic (Slovenko, 2002).

Can gay panic challenge a person's sexuality in such a disruptive fashion that it can lead to taking another person's life? Are the merits of a gay panic defense at all credible? Should evidence of it be permitted in a criminal trial? Does allowing the gay panic defense in court allow a defendant to blame the victim for the offender's behavior? Gay panic certainly does not constitute mental illness under an insanity defense, and it does not allow a defense of self-defense or provocation, as those defenses are based on the behavior expected of a "reasonable person" (Slovenko, 2002). Perhaps it is most appropriate, as some have suggested (e.g., Chuang & Addington, 1988) that legal defenses in gay panic cases be construed as hate crimes based on phobic beliefs about homosexuality. Homosexual (or gay) panic does not have wide acceptance in the scientific community, and recent trends suggest it is not likely to be deemed admissible as a defense any time soon.

Black Rage

The origins of **black rage syndrome** used as a defense can be traced back to the 1925 case of Dr. Ossian Sweet. The events surrounding this case, as well as the historical backdrop, are illustrated in detail in famed defense attorney Clarence Darrow's book, *Clarence Darrow's Two Greatest Trials: Reports of the Scopes Anti-Evolution Case and the Dr. Sweet Negro Trial* (Darrow, 1927).

As a young boy in Polk County, Florida, Ossian Sweet once saw a crowd of 5,000 white people pouring kerosene over a young black boy and setting him on fire. Hidden and terrified, he watched the crowd turn the whole occasion into a Roman holiday and, once their victim was dead, get drunk. This obviously made a profound impression on the mind and heart of the young sensitive boy. Hearing accounts of lynching incidents were also not uncommon at the time. Sweet became a physician, and on September 8, 1925, he and his family moved into a house in a Detroit neighborhood that was unfortunately rampant with racism, white mob activity, and the Ku Klux Klan. The events of that day are recounted in vivid detail in Clarence Darrow's book and that source should be consulted. Suffice it to say, the Sweets were attacked in their home by an angry mob apparently intent on killing the family. Shots were fired from within and from without the house. The police came and arrested the Sweets. It was at the police station that they learned for the first time that a man had been killed and a boy wounded. Later that afternoon, they were formally indicted for the murder of Leon Breiner and for assault with intent to kill one Eric Houghberg.

The National Association for the Advancement of Colored People (NAACP) recruited **Clarence Darrow** and renowned civil liberties lawyer Arthur Garfield Hays for the defense along with three local African-American attorneys, Cecil Rowlette, Charles Mahoney, and Julian Perry. This legal team employed a traditional rationale as their defense strategy with a racial twist. The common law rule in a self-defense case is that one can only use deadly force if one has a reasonable belief that serious bodily harm or death is imminent. The defense could not meet this burden since Sweet had fired before the crowd ever attacked. To circumvent this requirement, evidence was presented of the history of white mobs beating and killing black people, especially in the context of attempts to move into segregated white neighborhoods. Following a hung jury, the case was retried, and the jury acquitted Sweet; all charges were dismissed against the other ten defendants (Harris, 2001).

But the black rage defense, while resulting in an acquittal in the Sweet case, has not met with much success in other cases. This is essentially because in any black rage defense, one must establish the particular, concrete interplay between the defendant and the oppression he/she faced. General evidence of racism, sexism, and poverty that is not tied into the facts will not suffice. Accordingly, in most cases, such a defense is used in conjunction with such defenses as insanity or diminished capacity, rather than self-defense alone. There is also little scientific support for a distinct diagnosis of black rage. No proof exists for the reliability or validity of this diagnostic construct (Goldklang, 2003; Harris, 1997).

One of the most infamous cases involving the black rage defense was *People v. Ferguson* (1998). Colin Ferguson is the man who shot and killed six commuters on the Long Island Railroad. His lawyer was William Kuntsler, famous for his defense of radical causes. Mr. Kuntsler explained to the press and the public that his client, as a result of 200 years of racial prejudice and injustice by whites against African-Americans, had lost control of himself and had gone berserk. But Mr. Ferguson was not African-American at all, but rather Jamaican and had lived in the United States only a short time, but these facts seemed to have had no influence on Mr. Kuntsler's trial strategy. But the defense never got its day in court, because Ferguson fired his attorney and elected to defend himself. Ferguson's defense was simply that he wasn't the person who had done the shooting. He was convicted on all counts.

Four years prior to the Ferguson trial, attorney Erik M. Sears introduced the term *early Arab trauma* in defense of his client Rashid Baz. In March 1994, Baz had opened fire with an automatic weapon on a group of Jewish children on their way to Yeshiva in Brooklyn, New York. But this was no explosive or impulsive act. Baz stationed himself on the Brooklyn Bridge meticulously timing the arrival of the bus. Due to the moving nature of the target, however, he was only able to kill one of the innocent children. The defense portrayed the killer as the "victim" because he had spent the first 18 years of his life in Lebanon and could not be held responsible for his murderous acts due to the psychological scarring he had received during those years. The jury felt otherwise and sentenced Baz to 141 years in prison without the chance of parole.

Road Rage

Road rage is another popular term that has received considerable attention in the media as a syndrome or pattern of aggressive behavior, for which scientific and legal recognition is being sought. Typically, road rage involves impulsive acts of violence committed against people whose driving incurs the wrath of the perpetrator. The victim may be a pedestrian, bicyclist, or other driver, and the offender's behavior may include rude conduct, obscene gestures, aggressive retaliatory maneuvers, physical confrontation, and property damage.

Recently there have been some attempts to define road rage as **displaced aggression**. Displaced aggression occurs when a person is provoked, is unwilling or unable to retaliate against the original provocateur, and subsequently aggresses against a seemingly innocent target (Dollard, Doob, Miller, Mowrer, & Sears, 1939; Hovland & Sears, 1940). For example, a woman may insult her husband for no apparent reason after having been bereted previously by her boss. Oftentimes, the target provides no justification or instigation to warrant a retaliatory response from the aggressor. However, on other occasions the "innocent" target may provide a trivial and ambiguous instigation ("a trigger") to aggress. For instance, in the previous example, the wife may perceive her husband as being hostile and subsequently display a disjunctively escalated aggressive response toward him.

There is research which supports the notion that displaced aggressive is related to behavioral inhibition. One key feature of behavioral inhibition that may account for this relationship is the finding that inhibited individuals are punishment aversive (Carver & White, 1994). It appears that when confronted with provocations, individuals who inhibit their feelings are likely to initially inhibit retaliatory responses while continuing to dwell angrily and plot revenge. Such data are consistent with research linking behavioral inhibition with other forms of rumination (Leen-Felder, Zvolensky, Feldner, & Lejuez, 2004) and negative affect. Denson, Pedersen, and Miller (2006) presents data linking trait displaced aggression with road rage, domestic abuse, and laboratory displaced aggression. Such data is consistent with the notion that individuals high in trait displaced aggression may initially inhibit aggressive behavior when provoked yet subsequently take it out on others (spouses, fellow drivers, or fellow students).

Although road rage has appeared tangentially in some legal cases, the concept remains a behavioral descriptor, rather than a formal diagnosis. As such, expert testimony in cases involving instances of road rage should rely on generally accepted diagnostic categories such as personality disorders, substance abuse, and other relevant conditions.

Sexual Addiction Syndrome

Some researchers and clinicians have compared compulsive sexual behavior with substance addiction, the latter of which is included in the DSM-IV-TR as a mental disorder (American Psychiatric Association, 2000). However, **sexual addiction** can be conceptualized as a compulsive need to engage in sexual behavior or to become sexually aroused. Moreover, sexual addiction is often viewed as encompassing excessive sexual behavior, failed efforts to reduce such behavior, and interference with important activities (e.g., work and productivity, family, and relationships) despite knowledge of the detrimental effects of the behavior.

Nevertheless, Gold and Hefner (1998) noted that the literature on sexual addiction consists largely of theories that are based on clinical observation and that there is little research to support its validity. The lack of such research suggests that expert testimony on sexual addiction would fail under most legal standards for admissibility.

There are simply no valid and reliable studies available at this time to show that sexual addiction syndrome can be effectively distinguished from other disorders, that individuals with sexual addiction produce reliable and reproducible patterns of responses on psychological testing, and that the course, family patterns, and outcomes of sexual addiction can be predicted with any degree of accuracy.

Sexual addiction has not fared much better in the courts. For example, in *United States v. Romualdi* (1996), the defendant attempted to utilize sexual addiction as a defense to federal charges of possession of child pornography. A psychologist's report concluded that time in jail would be counterproductive for the defendant as it would only serve to increase his sense of psychological isolation. The psychologist recommended probation and group therapy for "sexually addictive individuals" (p. 3). Even if there were such a viable diagnosis as sexual addiction, the facts of this case indicated that the defendant had fantasies only and had not actually engaged in sexual activities with children, pointing to a diagnosis of paraphilia and not any possible "sexual addiction." In addition, another result of the case was clarification that expert testimony in criminal cases should always be based on recognized diagnoses rather than pseudo-scientifically derived labels that have been fashionably designed to complement a criminal defense.

So is there such thing as a "sexual addiction?" In his chapter "Are Sexual Offenses the Result of an Addictive Pattern?" in *Malingering, Lies, and Junk Science in the Courtroom* (Kitaeff, 2007), clinical psychologist Stanton Samenow debunks the myth that holds that when a person repeatedly chooses a certain type of behavior, it is the result of an addiction. Samenow points out how there is increasing excitement during every phase of a sex offense. These phases include fantasizing about the act, pursuing the object, the actual commission of the act, and the aftermath. Some offenders report experiencing pangs of regret, but these are fleeting and are of little value in deterring future misconduct. These men know the horrible consequences of their actions, but according to Samenow they have a "chilling capacity" to remove these thoughts from their consciousness while they pursue their objectives. Any possible feelings of guilt are similarly brushed aside (p. 577).

The main point here according to Samenow, is that people make choices in how they behave sexually. Behaving in a manner which victimizes other people is freely chosen by these individuals who seek excitement. Sex offenders are not suffering from a "disease" or an "addiction." "They [sex offenders] are not helpless in the face of irresistible impulses which they cannot control, rather, they choose not to control their impulses. Sex offenders make choices, if the consequences of their behavior become unbearable, they are free to make other choices that are more responsible" (p. 584).

So how are the courts to deal with unscientifically-grounded or questionable expert testimony and techniques? The first way is through the effective use of the rules of evidence. As mentioned previously, the two major standards for judging the admissibility of expert testimony are the "general acceptance" test outlined in *United States v. Frye* (1923) and the relevant, helpful, and reliable standard outlined in the *Federal Rules of Evidence* and expanded upon in *Daubert v. Merrell Dow Pharmaceuticals, Inc.* (1993). Although the *Federal Rules of Evidence* is a federal standard, many state courts have adopted it for determining the admissibility of expert testimony.

Because state courts are not bound to follow the rulings of federal courts, unless there is a state law that violates individual rights or privileges guaranteed by the U.S. Constitution, there may be considerable variability in legal standards not only across states but also between federal and state jurisdictions within the same state. Trial judges in *Frye* jurisdictions for example, should insure general acceptance by the relevant scientific community before admitting evidence or expert testimony. Judges in federal courts, and those jurisdictions who have adopted the Federal Rules of Evidence or the *Daubert* standard, must aggressively assume the role of gatekeeper and examine the relevance and reliability of all proffers of expert testimony.

The other ways of dealing with questionable techniques and testimony is through the investigation and cross examination of experts themselves and their qualifications. For example, in a review of the use of expert witnesses in criminal cases, Prince William County Virginia, Assistant Commonwealth Attorney Sandra R. Sylvester presents the example of an "expert" who claimed that he was obtaining a baccalaureate and master's degree combination from "Columbia State University." The following exchange occurred regarding his formal education during a hearing in the case of *Commonwealth v. Billy Leon Smalls* and *Commonwealth v. Jennifer Nicole Talley*.

QUESTION: You have no formal education, yet; isn't that correct? You have no degrees?

ANSWER: Well . . . I have formal education. I do not have a degree of yet.

QUESTION: [W]here did you do the course work that prepared you for the BA/MA degree you anticipate receiving?

ANSWER: That's at Columbia State University.

QUESTION: Where is that, sir?

ANSWER: That is in Louisiana. (pp. 46–48)

An investigation into Columbia State University discovered that it was not an academic institution, but rather a diploma mill. The Louisiana attorney general had obtained evidence that it was a mail drop in Orange County, California, and filed injunctions against the bogus university (Sylvester, 2007). Another expert claimed to have "police experience" and to have "investigated burn cases." But an investigation revealed that his police experience was limited to patrolling parking lots at mental health facilities, and that he had investigated only one burn case—that of a psychiatric patient who suffered a cigarette burn (p. 368). All in all, it is up to attorneys themselves "to distinguish between charlatans and Nobel Prize winners" (Holmgren, 2001).

FORENSIC PSYCHOLOGY IN THE SPOTLIGHT

Can False Memories be "Implanted?"

Loftus and Pickrell (1995); *Porter, Yuille, and Lehman* (1999); *Mazzoni, Loftus, and Kirsch* (2001)

Loftus and Pickrell (1995) contacted subjects' parents to confirm that each subject had never been lost in a mall. They then told subjects that their parents said this event did happen to them, along with three true events. Using these methods, 25% of subjects were able to be led to believe that they were in fact lost in a mall. And these subjects could even provide details about what they remembered.

Porter, Yuille, and Lehman (1999) were able to implant false memories of various events in their subjects, including having a serious medical procedure as a child, being lost for an extended period, being seriously hurt by another child, and experiencing a serious outdoor incident.

Mazzoni, Loftus, and Kirsch (2001) were able to implant a traumatic implausible event (witnessing demonic possession) by having people read accounts of how often demonic possession happened and giving subjects a personalized suggestion that they witnessed a possession. Subjects were initially chosen because they rated demonic possession as a highly implausible event and they also rated it as highly traumatic. Subjects were then asked to read an article about the prevalence of demonic possession. The article convinced 18% of the skeptics to say that they had witnessed a demonic possession.

Summary

Psychologists and psychiatrists during the last two centuries have been advocating for their increased involvement in the courtroom and the legal system. This has resulted in a "parade of experts" seeking to testify regarding all manner of psychological phenomenon and syndromes, some of which are unsupported by scientific research. Psychologists and mental health professionals have been injecting their expertise into the criminal justice system in such matters as repressed and recovered memories of childhood sexual abuse. The case of the McMartin preschool in 1987 is an example of what can happen when things like "recovered memories" are claimed by experts, memories which are not only "recovered" but are actually implanted by the experts themselves.

There have been many novel syndromes during the last 30 years—some of which are based on scientific data and are useful; many of which are based on questionable research and developmental methods and are of no value. The latter is particularly true when a "syndrome" is initially developed for the purpose of establishing a legal defense. In addition, there is evidence that applied psychology is inordinately affected by "social fashion" and that social activism is presented to the courts and the public is the guise of science.

A syndrome is a set of symptoms and signs that occur in a regular pattern from patient to patient, that collectively indicate or characterize a disease, psychological disorder, or other abnormal condition. Psychological syndrome evidence is extremely important because it can put in the hands of the jury tremendous power to determine the credibility of a witness in a trial (a determination that an expert witness would not be permitted to make), thereby allowing such evidence into testimony "through the back door."

The battered woman syndrome has been introduced in criminal trials for the defense of accused battered women who have killed their partners. By 1993 battered woman syndrome gained legal acceptance in all state courts to assist the jury in evaluating the reasonableness of a defendant's belief of being in mortal or imminent danger (i.e., self defense). Rape trauma syndrome has also been used primarily as an aid to prosecutors in explaining apparently inconsistent behavior exhibited by a rape victim.

The automatism syndrome in which bodily movements occur in the absence of conscious control (e.g., an epileptic seizure occurring while driving a car, or sleepwalking) is a valid defense acceptable in most jurisdictions in the world. Most American courts have held that for the automatism defense to prevail, however, a person claiming to be effected by a medical condition at the time of the offense must show that the disability had not been experienced on previous occasions.

Other syndromes that have been used as a form of defense in criminal trials include factitious disorder by proxy (Munchausen syndrome by proxy), homosexual panic (or "gay panic"), black rage, road rage, and sexual addiction syndrome.

Key Terms

Automatism *278*
Battered woman
   syndrome *274*
Black rage syndrome *280*
Clarence Darrow *281*
Displaced aggression *282*

Dissociation *270*
Factitious disorder by
   proxy *279*
False memory *269*
Homosexual panic *280*
Learned helplessness *274*

Lenore Walker *274*
McMartin preschool *270*
Munchausen
   syndrome by proxy *279*
Rape trauma syndrome *277*
Repression *270*

Road rage *281*
Sexual addiction
   syndrome *282*
Sodium amytal *271*
Stockholm syndrome *273*
Syndrome *273*

Review Questions

1. Within the context of memory, what is the meaning of repression and dissociation?
2. Why is the issue of false memories so important in the legal system?
3. What are the implications of the McMartin preschool case?
4. How can false memories be "implanted" in human subjects?
5. What is a syndrome, and why are psychological syndromes so important?
6. According to Lenore Walker, what are the phases of the battered woman syndrome?

7. How does the battered woman syndrome circumvent the typical requirement for a claim of self-defense?
8. How is the issue of "excuse" versus "justification" implicit in the battered woman syndrome?
9. What are the essential elements of the rape trauma syndrome?
10. What is the legal reasoning behind a defense of "automatism"?
11. What are the essential ingredients of a black rage defense?
12. For what reasons is a "sexual addiction" not considered a true addiction?

Chapter Resources on the World Wide Web

The Skeptics Dictionary: False Memory
http://skepdic.com/falsememory.html

Famous American Trials
http://www.law.umkc.edu/faculty/projects/ftrials/sweet/background.htm

The Price of Bad Memories
http://faculty.washington.edu/eloftus/Articles/price.htm

Battered Woman Syndrome
http://www.austdvclearinghouse.unsw.edu.au/

Stokholm Syndrome
http://www.geocities.com/kidhistory/trauma/stockhol.htm

Munchausen Syndrome by Proxy
http://www.ipt-forensics.com/journal/volume2/j2_2_4.htm.

A Society of Victims
http://www.arachnoid.com/psychology/victimhood.php

American Psychological Association: Battered Woman Syndrome
http://www.apa.org/psyclaw/hawthorne.html

For Further Reading

Bass, E., & Davis, L. (1994). *The courage to heal*. New York: Harper Collins.

Darrow, C. (1927). *Clarence Darrow's two greatest trials: Reports of the scopes anti-evolution case and the Dr. Sweet Negro*. Gerard, KS: Haldeman-Julius Co.

Halpern, D. F., Brooks, A., & Stephenson, C. (2007). How science by media creates false certainties and resistance to conceptual change. In J. Kitaeff (Ed.), *Malingering, lies, and junk science in the courtroom*. Youngstown, NY: Cambria Press.

Johnston, M. (1997). *Spectral evidence*. Boston, MA: Houghton Mifflin Company.

Salerno, S. (2005). *SHAM*. New York: Crown.

Samenow, S. Are sexual offenses the result of an addictive pattern? In J. Kitaeff (Ed.), (2007). *Malingering, lies, and junk science in the courtroom*. Youngstown, NY: Cambria Press.

Thoennes, N., & Pearson, J. (1988). Summary of findings from the sexual abuse allegations project. In E. B. Nicholson (Ed.), *Sexual abuse allegations in custody and visitation cases* (pp. 1–36). Washington, DC: American Bar Association.

CHAPTER 14

Forensic Psychology and the Workplace

CHAPTER OBJECTIVES

After reading this chapter you would:

- Know the implications of the Age Discrimination in Employment Act.
- Understand how the Americans with Disabilities Act affects employment practices.
- Be aware of basic case law in employment discrimination.
- Understand the concepts of negative stereotyping and stigmatization in discrimination.
- Understand the concepts of psychological discomfort and paternalism in discrimination.
- Know the various types of work-related sexual harassment.
- Know how psychologists can help ameliorate the effects of sexual harassment.
- Understand what workplace violence is, and know how it can be prevented.

INTRODUCTION

Psychology as applied to the workplace has traditionally been the province of Industrial and Organizational (I-O) Psychology. I-O psychologists work in a wide variety of settings applying psychological principles, providing consultation, and offering strategies in the following areas, among others:

(1) performing job analyses, (2) selecting and hiring employees, (3) developing and implementing training programs for workers, (4) conducting leadership and job satisfaction studies, and (5) promoting job satisfaction and favorable working conditions for employees.

In their professional work, I-O psychologists insure that all hiring, salary, and promotion practices follow relevant legal guidelines and statutory requirements. I-O psychologists are also involved in issues of preventing sexual harassment and consulting with management after an incident has occurred. There can be considerable overlap in training and experience between industrial/organizational psychologists and forensics psychologists. But it is usually forensic psychologists, because of their knowledge and training in personality theory, psychopathology, assessment, criminology, and the law, who are most involved with those aspects of the work environment such as employment discrimination, sexual harassment, and work environment violence.

EMPLOYMENT DISCRIMINATION

Theories of discrimination in employment are based on the predicate of what is and is not "fair." The answer to the question, "What is fair?" is based on the theory of **distributive justice**. Distributive justice refers to how available rewards are distributed or divided up among members of a group or a society, or the relationship between the contributions that people make and what they get back. In American society, distributive justice is based mostly on "equity." More specifically, the rewards that people receive ought to be distributed in proportion to each person's contributions (Sampson, 1975). But there is no single method for determining the value of different contributions, and the fair allocation of rewards is a substantially subjective phenomenon. Most employment litigation is an attempt to restore perceived fairness and restore equity to the domain of employment.

Since the enactment of Title VII of the Civil Rights Act, the Age Discrimination in Employment Act, and the Americans with Disabilities Act, many other issues related to the employment relationship have been considered by the federal courts. These have ranged from the employment application process, to terms and conditions of employment such as salary inequities, benefits issues, promotions, demotions, discipline, and discharges. In the decision-making process in these issues, courts have analyzed whether any of the federal civil rights laws have been implicated and violated.

Originating mostly in the 1960s with the advent of the civil rights movement, courts have often considered whether educational qualifications, such as requiring a high school education for an unskilled laborer job, adversely affected the employment opportunities of minority applicants. Gender issues, such as dress and appearance codes and whether different standards could apply to men versus women, appeared in the courts in the 1970s concurrently with the women's rights movement. In the 1980s, affirmative action issues were the focus of attention, and in the 1990s, controversies arose over how the equal employment opportunity laws applied to undocumented aliens and whether English-only policies resulted in national origin discrimination. Retaliation lawsuits increased, with innumerable decisions concluding that while no evidence of discrimination existed, an employers' responses to charges of discrimination resulted in unlawful retaliation.

Employment discrimination generally can be broken down to the following elements: race, sex and gender, age, religion, disability, national origin, and sexual orientation. There are several major sources of federal legislation that impose equal employment opportunity obligations on employers. These include (1) Title VII of the Civil Rights Act of 1964, (2) the Americans with Disabilities Act, (3) the Age Discrimination in Employment Act, (4) the Equal Pay Act, (5) the Civil Rights Acts of 1866 and 1871, and (6) the Civil Rights Act of 1991. However, state equal opportunity laws apply concurrently with federal equal employment opportunity laws, meaning that although an employer may be in compliance with state law, it may not be in compliance with federal laws and could face federal liability. Accordingly, employers must be diligent in their compliance with all applicable laws.

Title VII of the Civil Rights Act

Title VII of the Civil Rights Act (42 U.S.C. § 2000e et seq.), as amended, prohibits an employer from discriminating against an individual on the basis of race, color, sex, national origin, or religion with respect to hiring, discharge, compensation, promotion, classification, training, apprenticeship, referral for employment, or other terms, conditions, and privileges of employment. The Act includes in its definition of sex discrimination employment decisions made because of, or on the basis of, pregnancy, childbirth, or related medical conditions. What follows are examples of lawsuits filed under Title VII.

In *DiCarolo v. Potter* (2004), the Sixth Circuit held that an Italian-American former employee had presented direct evidence of national origin discrimination where his supervisor called him a "dirty wop" and complained about there being too many "dirty wops" working at the facility. In reaching this holding, the court emphasized that it was the employee's supervisor and a decision maker who made such statements and that the hate speech occurred three weeks prior to the employee's termination.

Bellaver v. Quanex Corp. (2000) was a case where a female employee claimed that she was discharged because her employer disapproved of her aggressive and sometimes abrasive interpersonal skills, while tolerating the same characteristics in male employees. Although the employer contended that the plaintiff was terminated in a reduction in force, the court still heard the case. The employee presented evidence that males who had problems with interpersonal communication were not criticized as severely. The jury concluded that this female employee was terminated because she did not behave in a way her employer deemed appropriate for "women."

In *Frank v. United Airlines, Inc.* (2000), flight attendants brought a class action suit alleging sex and age discrimination when the airlines, using a weight table produced by an insurance company, established a weight maximum for women corresponding to the medium body frame category on height and weight, as opposed to the large frame category used for men. Such practice resulted in female flight attendants having to weigh 14–25 pounds less than their male colleagues of the same height and age. The court held that the airline's weight policy constituted unlawful discrimination against women and was not justified as a bona fide occupational qualification in that no evidence was presented by the airline that a requirement that female flight attendants be disproportionately slimmer than males bore a relation to their ability to greet passengers, push carts, move luggage, or provide assistance in emergencies.

In *Olsen v. Marriott International, Inc.* (1999), a federal district court found no bona fide occupational qualification defense available when a hotel rejected a male applicant for a massage therapist position. The hotel asserted that it needed to hire primarily women due to its predominately female clientele, who preferred a woman masseuse to a male. The court ruled that the practice was discriminatory, in that customer preference was not a legitimate basis upon which to discriminate in favor of female versus male applicants.

In *Griggs v. Duke Power Company* (1971), a company requirement that persons applying for manual labor jobs have high school degrees was found to be discriminatory. Although the policy had been applied to all employees, its result was that an inordinate number of African-American applicants were excluded because a greater number of them in that geographic area had not graduated from high school, and the high school requirement was not validly related to the duties of such manual labor jobs.

In *Nichols v. Azteca Restaurant Enterprises, Inc.* (2001), the Ninth Circuit held that a male employee who was repeatedly teased for female mannerisms and referred to as "she" or "her" had stated a viable cause of action under Title VII. The court reasoned that the severe and pervasive hostile work environment the plaintiff was forced to endure was the result of gender stereotypes of how a male restaurant server "should" behave.

The Americans with Disabilities Act

Title I of the **Americans with Disabilities Act** (ADA) (42 U.S.C. § 12101 et seq.) prohibits both public and private employers from discriminating in employment against persons with physical or mental disabilities (which may include "intellectual" impairments). The EEOC and the Department of Justice enforce the ADA. The ADA requires employers to make reasonable accommodation to the needs of disabled applicants and employees, as long as such accommodation do not result in undue hardship to the employer's operations. The following are examples of ADA lawsuits.

Karraker v. Rent-A-Center, Inc. (2005) in which the Karraker brothers worked for Rent-A-Center, a chain of stores that offers household goods on a rent-to-own basis. To be eligible for promotion, employees were required to take the "APT Management Trainee-Executive Profile," which is a set of nine tests designed to measure math, language skills, interests, and personality traits. The test battery was intended to indicate whether a person would be comfortable working in a fast-paced office setting. But part of the Management Trainee-Executive Profile included the *Minnesota Multiphasic Personality Inventory (MMPI)*, which is a clinical test that reveals confidential and diagnostic formulations about an individual such as the existence of possible psychosomatic concerns, depression, paranoia, mania, and other mental disorders. The defense claimed, however, that the results of the MMPI were never evaluated by a psychologist nor was a psychological interview part of the process. Based on their scores, the Karrakers were not considered for promotion. They sued, contending that the use of a test that reveals the presence of psychopathology and personality disorders violated the ADA. The district court dismissed the suit. The Karrakers appealed. In reversing the trial court, the appeals court ruled that the administration of the *MMPI* conducted as part of a management test was an inappropriate and invasive "medical examination" that violated the ADA even though the employer did not have the test results interpreted by a psychologist. But since the test was originally designed to reveal mental illness and personality disorders, the likelihood of an employee with a mental disability being promoted would have been affected by the results of the test.

In *Petzold v. Borman's, Inc.* (2000), Petzold suffered from a neurological disorder known as Tourette Syndrome. The major symptom of this disorder is the involuntary shouting of obscene words, racial epithets, and other offensive words in social situations. Petzold worked as a bagger at a grocery store, during which he would, at times piercingly scream obscenities and racial slurs directly in the presence of customers, some of whom complained to the manager. Petzold's supervisor informed him that these outbursts could not be tolerated in a work environment and at customers. But he could not control this behavior, and he was later terminated. He sued for disability discrimination and won. The employer appealed. The appeals court ruled that although Petzold was disabled, his use of offensive language on a daily basis in the presence of customers, children, and other employees, made him unfit for his job as a bagger and furthermore constituted misconduct under the employer's work rules prohibiting "abusive language to any employee, supervisor, or customer."

The Age Discrimination in Employment Act

The Age Discrimination in Employment Act (ADEA) (29 U.S.C. §§ 621-634) prohibits discrimination on the basis of age against employees 40 or older. Presented here are samples of ADEA lawsuits.

Rachid v. Jack in the Box, Inc. (2004), where a 52-year-old employee sued his former employer for allegedly terminating him because of his age. The court held that the employee had established a *prima facie* (on its face) case of age discrimination by presenting evidence that his supervisor repeatedly made ageist comments to and about him such as stating that his absence from a meeting was due to the fact that "he's probably in bed or he's sleeping by [now] because of his age." The employee had voiced concerns to human resources that the supervisor was going to fire him because of his age, and the employee's replacement was five years younger.

Western Air Lines, Inc. v. Criswell (1985), the Supreme Court found that Western Airlines violated the ADEA by refusing to allow flight captains 60 years of age and over to switch to the position of flight engineer, and requiring flight engineers to retire at age 60. The Court held that the restriction was not a bona fide occupational qualification, since it was not reasonably necessary to ensure safe transport of passengers.

The Equal Pay Act

The Equal Pay Act (29 U.S.C. §§ 201-219) is part of the Fair Labor Standards Act, as amended. The act provides for equal pay for equal work performed by both sexes working in the same establishment. The act prohibits discrimination on the basis of sex with respect to wages paid for equal work on jobs that require equal skill, effort, and responsibility, performed under similar working conditions. The following are examples of Equal Pay Act lawsuits.

EEOC v. Outback Steakhouse (2001), in which a former employee alleged that the restaurant chain discriminated against her by paying a male counterpart a significantly larger salary and then firing her after she complained. The jury awarded the plaintiff $27,000 for the difference in earnings, $36,800 in back pay, $50,000 in compensatory damages for emotional pain and suffering, and $2.1 million in punitive damages.

In *Lavin-McEleney v. Marist College* (2001), the plaintiff Ms. Lavin was hired in 1976 as an assistant professor at Marist College. She was denied tenure in six years but promoted to associate professor three years after that. However, she never received a full professorship and was also paid less than her male colleagues in equivalent positions, about which she complained to college administrators with no results. In 1994, she filed a request to have her salary officially reviewed for gender disparity but the college president determined that she was fairly paid. She sued under the Equal Pay Act and Title VII. At the trial, expert testimony was presented indicating that women generally were paid less than men in comparable positions. The jury agreed. Lavin was awarded back pay, damages, and attorney fees for a total of $118,000. Marist appealed but the lower court's decision was affirmed by the appeals court reaffirming that the plaintiff had presented sufficient statistical evidence to show that male professors of similar rank, years of service, and background were paid more, and that such gender disparities were evident college-wide.

Quinones v. Houser Buick (2006) was a case in which Quinones worked as a technician for Houser Buick. He was always under the supervision of O'Connor, the collision repair manager. Quinones asked to be paid on a flat rate pay scale rather than on an hourly basis. He learned that his pay of $30,000 per year compared poorly with that of another employee, Barnes, who was paid a flat rate of $52,000 per year. He sued, contending that the reason for the pay difference was based on his Hispanic origin. Houser defended the suit asserting that the flat rate system is complex and allows employees who are highly productive to earn much more as pay is computed for each specific repair job completed. Quinones worked slowly; Barnes worked quickly and did high-quality work. The district court held that Houser offered a nondiscriminatory reason for the pay differential and held for defendant. Quinones appealed. The appeals court affirmed the lower court's decision holding that Houser Buick offered a legitimate rationale for its action, that is, different employees work at different speeds and abilities. Their pay is based on measures of their work output. The court saw this as a nondiscriminatory reason for the pay differential which was more than a mere pretext for the alleged discrimination.

Must a Woman Lawyer Wear Make Up and Walk Femininely?

Price Waterhouse v. Hopkins (1989)

Plaintiff Ann Hopkins was an associate with the law firm of Price Waterhouse, but despite all her efforts could not make partner. The firm admitted that Hopkins was qualified to be considered for partnership and probably would have been admitted; however, a number of the partners sharply criticized her interpersonal skills and specifically accused her of being abrasive, cold, or acting "masculine." One partner suggested that she could improve her chances for partnership by walking, talking, and dressing more femininely. Hopkins sued the firm in federal district court alleging sex discrimination in violation of Title VII.

The question before the court was whether the "interpersonal skills rationale" constituted a legitimate nondiscriminatory basis on which to deny Hopkins partnership, or was it merely being used as a pretext to disguise sex discrimination. The court required Price Waterhouse to show by clear and convincing evidence that the denial of partnership would have occurred regardless of the alleged discrimination. Price Waterhouse failed to meet this burden. However, they won the case on appeal due to a technical legal issue. Ms. Hopkins appealed to the U.S. Supreme Court.

The American Psychological Association submitted an *amicus* brief (friend of the court) arguing that (1) sex stereotyping exists as demonstrated by the empirical research; (2) stereotyping under certain conditions can create discriminatory consequences, especially where they shape perceptions about women's typical and acceptable roles in society; and (3) the conditions that promote stereotyping were present at Price Waterhouse. The Supreme Court reversed the DC Circuit and held that the plaintiff did not need to show that the discriminatory factor was the only reason for the firm's action, but that the unlawful motive was a "substantial" factor in the adverse employment action.

WHAT CAN PSYCHOLOGY CONTRIBUTE?

On September 11, 2003, the Eleventh Circuit Court of Appeals ruled in the case of *Garrett v. Board of Trustees of Univ. of Alabama* that individuals can sue a state agency for money damages under Section 504 of the Rehabilitation Act. The court made clear that people with disabilities have federal recourse against state employment discrimination and that Title I of the ADA prescribes standards applicable to the states.

The Paralyzed Veterans of America, National Organization on Disability, National Mental Health Association, and National Alliance for the Mentally Ill filed an *amicus* brief in Support of Garrett to the Supreme Court. The brief addressed some of the fundamental underpinnings of discrimination. Although these concepts were written about mental disabilities, they are, in some part, relevant to racial, religious, ethnic, and gender discrimination. The relevant concepts underlying all forms of discrimination as seen by the above-referenced advocacy groups include stereotyping, stigmatization, psychological discomfort, and paternalism.

Negative stereotyping refers to the belief that most or all members of a group subject to disability-related discrimination share certain negative characteristics and that the mere fact of having a disability is believed by society to generalize to a person's potential and limitations in many areas that extend far beyond the disability itself.

Stigmatization is a distrust, fear, embarrassment, and even avoidance of persons with mental disabilities. It tends to deny them access to resources and opportunities such as jobs and housing. Such stigmatization is often psychologically harmful and leads to low self-esteem, isolation, and hopelessness, as well as loss of dignity and the chance to fully participate in society (see U.S. Public Health Service: Report of the Surgeon General, 1999).

Psychological discomfort consists of feelings of disgust or repugnance that some people experience when interacting with or even being in the proximity of persons with disabilities. There is psychological research indicating for example, that persons encountering people with disabilities frequently experience psychological uneasiness and show inhibited behavior (Kleck, 1968; Kleck et al., 1966). Testimony before Congress during enactment of the ADA provided many tragic but true examples of the discomfort that people feel around persons with disabilities and the barriers that prevented disabled people from full participation in society. One woman who used a wheelchair due to polio she contracted as a child recounted how an attempt was made to remove her and a disabled friend from an auction house because they were "disgusting to look at." In another case, a woman with severe arthritis was denied a job because college administrators thought that "normal students shouldn't see her." In yet another instance, zoo employees in New Jersey refused admittance to a group of children with Down's because they were afraid the children would "upset the chimpanzees" (Bruyère & O'Keeffe, 1994, p. 3). Closely linked to psychological discomfort are the concepts of *paternalism* and *pity*, which are means utilized by society to express profound and sincere sympathy toward certain groups while simultaneously subordinating them economically. People with disabilities are seen as helpless dependent children who are best kept out of sight (Hahn, 1982).

Psychologists should be encouraged to conduct research which illuminates the nature, classification, and causes of discrimination, as well as the various ways discrimination presents itself both in the work setting and in society as a whole. More specifically, at its very basic level, discrimination of all sorts can manifest itself in three basic forms: overt, subtle, and covert (Samuel, Kaspar, & Wickrama, 2007; Swim, Ferguson, & Hyers, 1999); Williams, Neighbors, & Jackson, 2008).

Overt discrimination refers to discrimination that is readily apparent, visible, and observable and can be easily documented. This can be expressed by harassment, language and jokes, and even physical violence and other criminal acts. It can also be seen in unequal treatment in the family, employment, politics, religion, and other institutional sectors. *Subtle discrimination* refers to the unequal and harmful treatment of people that may be visible but often not noticed because members of the discriminated group have somehow "internalized" these negative attitudes and behavior as somehow being "normal." Subtle sex discrimination is particularly difficult to overcome because such behavior and comments are often not even seen as discriminatory because they have become accepted through tradition and custom. *Covert discrimination* refers to the harmful treatment of members of certain groups that is hidden and very difficult to prove or document. Because subtle and covert discrimination are more difficult to see, document, and remedy, they may last longer than overt discrimination and be more resistant to change. Overall, psychologists should be encouraged to be involved in research that illuminates the nature and causes, classification, and remedies of discrimination in its various forms (e.g., racism, sexism, ageism, homophobia, and discrimination against people with physical and mental disabilities).

SEXUAL HARASSMENT

Sexual harassment is defined by the Equal Employment Opportunity Commission (EEOC) as follows:

> Unwelcome sexual advances, requests for sexual favors, and other verbal or physical conduct of a sexual nature . . . when (1) submission to such conduct is made either explicitly or implicitly a term or condition of an individual's employment, (2) submission to or rejection of such conduct by an individual is used as the basis for employment decisions affecting such individual, or (3) such conduct has the purpose or effect of unreasonably interfering with an individual's work performance or creating an intimidating, hostile, or offensive working environment. (Equal Employment Opportunity Commission, 1980, Title VII, § 703).

Sexual harassment is generally of two types: (1) **quid pro quo sexual harassment**, which refers to situations in which the employment of persons is made contingent upon their complying with sexual demands, and harassment involves an implicit or explicit bargain whereby the harasser promises a reward or threatens punishment, depending on the victim's response, and (2) **hostile work environment sexual harassment**, which describes circumstances in which remarks, insults, or intimidation create an abusive atmosphere and make the work environment intolerable. In the United States sexual harassment is illegal under antidiscrimination legislation, but the statutory definitions and implications of sexual harassment have been changing since the 1960s.

Development of Sexual Harassment Law through Litigation and Statute

1964   Title VII of the Civil Rights Act, which prohibits discrimination at work on the basis of race, color, religion, national origin, and sex.

1976   *Williams v. Saxbe* (Washington, DC) recognized quid pro quo sexual harassment as discrimination.

1977   *Alexander v. Yale University* (Connecticut) ruled that quid pro quo sexual harassment constitutes sex discrimination in education.

1977   *Barnes v. Costle* (U.S. Court of Appeals for the Second District) ruled that when a female employee was retaliated against for rejecting the sexual advances of her boss, such retaliation constituted a violation of Title VII.

1980   *Brown v. City of Guthrie* (Oklahoma) established a legal precedent for hostile environment sexual harassment claims.

1981   *Bundy v. Jackson* (Washington, DC) sustained the definition of hostile environment sexual harassment, holding that employers can be liable for sexual insults and propositions even if the worker did not lose any job benefits as a result.

1985   *McKinney v. Dole* (U.S. Court of Appeals for the DC Circuit) ruled that physical violence, even if it is not overtly sexual, can be sexual harassment if the unwelcome conduct is based on the victim's gender.

1986   *Meritor Savings Bank v. Vinson* (U.S. Supreme Court) held that hostile environment sexual harassment is a form of sex discrimination that is actionable under Title VII, and that such a claim need not lead to "economic" or "tangible" harassment, but that a noneconomic injury can also violate Title VII. The Court also ruled that the severity and pervasiveness of the hostile work environment must be proven both subjectively and objectively. That is, there must be consideration of whether the victim in question found the behavior hostile or abusive (i.e., it caused psychological harm, fear, anxiety, or humiliation to the victim) and whether a "reasonable person" would have agreed with this assessment. (p. 67).

1991   Civil Rights Act of 1991 is passed by Congress to amend and strengthen the Civil Rights Act of 1964. It provided for, among other things, increased damages in cases of intentional employment discrimination.

1991   *Ellison v. Brady* (U.S. Court of Appeals for the Ninth Circuit) changed analysis of conduct from a "reasonable person" to a "reasonable women" test when determining whether actionable sexual harassment occurred.

1993   *Harris v. Forklift Systems, Inc.* (U.S. Supreme Court) held that to be actionable as hostile environment harassment, conduct need not seriously affect an employee's psychological well-being or lead the plaintiff to suffer injury. The Court held that the "totality of circumstances" must be taken into account to determine if a work environment has been made hostile or abusive, and psychological harm is but one of the considerations. In their decision, the Court stated, "Title VII comes into play before the harassing conduct leads to nervous breakdown" . . . [and] that "[a] discriminatorily abusive work environment, *even one that does not seriously affect employees' psychological well-being*, can and often will detract from employees' job performance, discourage employees from remaining on the job, or keep them from advancing in their careers" (pp. 21–22) (emphasis added).

1998   *Faragher v. City Of Boca Raton* (U.S. Supreme Court) held that an employer is vicariously liable for actionable discrimination caused by a supervisor.

1998   *Burlington Industries, Inc. v. Ellerth* (U.S. Supreme Court) held that under Title VII, an employee who refuses the unwelcome and threatening sexual advances of a supervisor, yet suffers no adverse, tangible job consequences, may recover against the employer without showing the employer is negligent or otherwise at fault for the supervisor's actions.

1998   *Oncale v. Sundowner Offshore Services, Inc.* (U.S. Supreme Court) held that sex discrimination consisting of same-sex sexual harassment is actionable under Title VII, and that Title VII protects men as well as women.

A survey by the federal government of 20,000 federal employees found that 42% of female workers had experienced at least one incident of sexual harassment at work during the previous two years (Brownmiller & Alexander, 1992). A 1993 study found that one-half of working women have experienced some sort of sexual harassment (Fitzgerald & Shulman, 1993). Another study conducted in 1994 found that 40% of women in large law firms endorsed being touched inappropriately, called "honey," and being sexually harassed in one form or another, and that these numbers are even higher in the armed forces reaching a high of 64% of females in 1995 in the U.S. Marine Corps (McAllister, 1995).

Despite these high figures, few harassed women (only 5–15%), actually make formal reports of harassment to their employers or fair employment agencies. Women are sometimes reluctant to make allegations of sexual harassment for a number of reasons, including fear of losing their jobs or otherwise hurting their careers, fear of not being believed, the belief that nothing can or will be done about the harassment, and embarrassment or shame at being harassed. In addition, victims of sexual harassment who do file formal complaints must endure a legal discovery process in which intimate details of their personal lives are often publicized in open court and their characters are questioned.

In recent years as women gained more power in the corporate workforce, men have also become the victims of sexual harassment. A question that has arisen, however, is whether same-sex harassment can qualify as sexual harassment. As previously mentioned, this matter was addressed by the U.S. Supreme Court in *Oncale v. Sundowner Offshore Services, Inc.* (1998). Specifically, the Court had to answer the question, does the prohibition against sex discrimination, set out in Title VII of the Civil Rights Act of 1964, apply to "same-sex" sexual harassment?

The facts in *Oncale* were relatively straight forward. In late October 1991, Joseph Oncale was working as part of an eight-man crew for Sundowner Offshore Services on a Chevron U.S.A., Inc., oil platform in the Gulf of Mexico. On several occasions, Oncale was forcibly subjected to sex-related, humiliating actions against him by two of the crew members in the presence of the rest of the crew. He was also physically assaulted in a sexual manner by the two men and threatened with rape. Oncale complained to supervisory personnel but received no assistance; in fact, the company's safety compliance clerk told him that the two crew members in question "picked [on] him all the time too" and called him a name suggesting homosexuality. Oncale eventually quit and asked that his pink slip reflect that he "voluntarily left due to sexual harassment and verbal abuse." He later stated in a deposition that "I felt that if I didn't leave my job, that I would be raped or forced to have sex."

Oncale filed a complaint against Sundowner in the U.S. District Court for the Eastern District of Louisiana, alleging that he was discriminated against in his employment because of his sex, but the district court held that "Mr. Oncale, a male, has no cause of action under Title VII for harassment by male co-workers." An appeals court agreed with the district court's ruling, and Mr. Oncale appealed to the Supreme Court.

The Court considered **Title VII of the Civil Rights Act of 1964** which provides, in relevant part, that "[i]t shall be an unlawful employment practice for an employer . . . to discriminate against any individual with respect to his compensation, terms, conditions, or privileges of employment, because of such individual's race, color, religion, sex, or national origin" (78 Stat. 255, as amended, 42 U.S.C. § 2000e-2(a)(1)).

The Court pointed to previous decisions in which it held that in formulating Title VII Congress intended to strike at the entire spectrum of disparate treatment of men and women in employment. For example, in *Newport News Shipbuilding & Dry Dock v. EEOC* (1983), the Court had already established that laws such as the Pregnancy Discrimination Act applied to male spouses of pregnant female employees as well as to the women themselves. And in *Castaneda v. Partida* (1977), the Court stated, "Because of the many facets of human motivation, it would be unwise to presume as a matter of law that human beings of one definable group will not discriminate against other members of that group" (p. 499). Of special note was the Court's reference to the need for determining the "objective severity" of harassment, which should be judged from the perspective of a reasonable person considering "all the circumstances."

In *Oncale*, the justices expressed in essence, that in same-sex (as in all) harassment cases, inquiry requires careful consideration of the social context in which particular behavior occurs and is experienced by its target. A professional football player's working environment is not severely or pervasively abusive, for example, if the coach smacks him on the buttocks as he heads onto the field, even if the same behavior would reasonably be experienced as abusive by the coach's secretary (male or female) back at the office. The real social impact of workplace behavior often depends on a constellation of surrounding circumstances, expectations, and relationships that are not fully captured by a simple recitation of the words used or the physical acts performed. In reversing the judgment of the court of appeals, the Supreme Court in *Oncale*, found no justification for a categorical rule excluding same-sex harassment claims from the coverage of Title VII.

Personality and Harassers

Some social psychologists describe male sexual harassment behavior as being of two types. For example, Fiske and Glick (1995) argued that these two "core" types of harassment consist of the *benevolent* kind (characterized by a genuine desire for lasting heterosexual intimacy), and the *hostile* kind (primarily expressing a desire for male dominance). Such hostile motives for harassment are often seen in males who believe in male superiority, view women as inferior, and maintain a desire to dominate women sexually. Benevolent motives for harassment include protectiveness, favorable attitudes toward women in traditional roles, and a desire for intimacy.

There has been some research linking the personality trait of *authoritarianism* with sexual harassment (Begany & Milburn, 2007). Some research has even suggested that authoritarianism is often a predictor of battering and sexually aggressive behavior (Ou, 1996; Petty & Dawson, 1989; Walker, Rowe, & Quinsey, 1993). As discussed elsewhere in this text, as originally developed by Adorno, Frenkel-Brunswik, Levinson, and Sanford (1950a, 1950b), the authoritarian personality shows rigid adherence to cultural traditions and traditional gender roles. Such individuals may exhibit self-righteousness, vindictively envious attitudes, and see the world as dangerous place. Males with such a personality orientation may also exhibit a form of "hypermasculinity," which is an excessive and rigid overidentification with the stereotypical male role model (Altemeyer, 1988). According to the general theory, authoritarianism develops as a result of harsh, punitive child rearing and the consequential displacement of negative emotions into the world.

Utilizing self-report instruments measuring authoritarianism, together with the Likelihood to Sexually Harass (LSH) Scale, which measures an individual's likelihood of sexual harassment based on a subject's responses to ten scenarios, researchers have found that authoritarianism predicts the likelihood that a man will endorse a greater likelihood of engaging in sexual harassment (Begany & Milburn, 2007; See also, Pryor, Giedd, & Williams, 1995).

Psychosexual Consequences of Sexual Harassment

Researchers have shown convincing evidence that sexual harassment often has serious and negative effects on women's physical and emotional health, and the more intense the harassment, the more severe the reactions. These reactions frequently include anxiety, depression, sleep disturbance, weight loss or gain, loss of appetite, and headaches (Schneider, Swann, & Fitzgerald, 1997). Fitzgerald et al. (1997) have found symptoms of post-traumatic stress disorder (PTSD) associated with continued sexual harassment. The same authors have used the "Sexual Experiences Questionnaire" (SEQ) to measure harassment in the form of unwanted sexual attention, and sexual coercion expressed through crude words, acts and gestures conveying hostile and misogynist attitudes. As indicated in this section, such attitudes and behaviors have been linked to depression, anxiety and stress-related physical problems, especially when the harassment is severe and frequent. Indeed, Richman (1999) has documented "[i]ncreased alcohol consumption (also referred to as "escape drinking"), drinking to intoxication, and prescription drug use" as also being associated with sexual harassment. (p. 361).

But sometimes a victim of sexual harassment may exhibit behaviors that are difficult for a jury to understand. It is frequently up to the forensic psychologist to offer expert testimony explaining these reactions. For example, the forensic expert may explain how victims often remain silent in the face of harassment out of financial necessity, fear of retaliation, intimidation, a sense of powerlessness, self-blame, denial, emotional numbing and dissociation (as are often seen in PTSD), and embarrassment. Absent such a psychological understanding, the victim herself may face further harassment in the form of incriminations and doubts about her veracity. It may be helpful in such situations to perform psychological evaluations, testing, or explorations of the psychological dynamics of the workplace including the interpersonal relationships at play as well as overt and covert psychological stressors (Drukteinis, 2007).

Since many sexual harassment claims are based on the "reasonable woman" standard delineated in *Ellison v. Brady*, a common defense tactic is to present testimony that would suggest to the jury that the claimant is not a reasonable woman of normal sensitivity but rather an individual with inflated sensitivities or needs, or even one suffering from a personality disorder known to cause interpersonal conflicts, excessive sensitivity, irritability, suspicion, flamboyance, perfectionism, manipulation, retaliation, poor reality contact or sexually suggestive behavior. In this way, what was perceived as sexual harassment and victimization by the plaintiff is presented as actually being the product of her own psychopathology. Of course, of the thousands of sexual harassment cases during the last 50 years, it is only reasonable to assume that some have bound to have been affected by such personality inclinations, psychopathology, or even by vengeful motives, retaliatory maneuvers, or lies.

For example, in *Ramirez v. Kelly* (1997), the plaintiff and the defendant (who was one of her supervisors) had an ongoing, voluntary sexual relationship. After the plaintiff found out that the defendant was married, she sued him for sexual harassment, claiming that she was raped and coerced to carry on the sexual relationship. Adequate evidence was presented by defense experts that she fit the diagnostic criteria for borderline personality disorder. In *Sudtelgte v. Reno* (1994), the plaintiff complained of being, among other things, persistently "picked on" by coworkers and supervisors. Expert testimony was admitted at trial, however, concerning the fact that the plaintiff suffered from a paranoid personality disorder. The court held that although the plaintiff may have felt subjectively harassed, it was the result of her abnormal sensitivity caused by her personality disorder. In other words, she could not show that a "reasonable woman" would have been similarly affected or offended.

It is very reasonable to expect an employer who is a defendant in a sexual harassment lawsuit to utilize a forensic psychologist or other mental health expert to testify as to the preexisting and present mental state and personality abnormalities of the plaintiff. The question we face is on what scientific and empirical evidence will the expert rely? For example, there is no credible scientific evidence that "hypersensitivity" or "personality disorders" are routinely characteristic of bogus sexual harassment plaintiffs. Indeed, there is little known about the personality characteristics of women filing valid sexual harassment suits altogether (Borgida, Rudman & Manteufel, 1995; Des Rosier, Feldthusen, & Hankivsky, 1998; Fitzgerald, 1999; Streseman, 1995).

Must a Sexual Harassment Plaintiff Prove Serious Psychological Injury?

Harris v. Forklift Systems, Inc. (1993)

In 1986, Teresa Harris, who was employed as a rental manager with Forklift Systems, Inc., complained about comments and behaviors directed to her by Forklift's president, Charles Hardy. She claimed that Hardy's sexually harassing conduct caused her to suffer PTSD-like symptoms and that she was ready to resign when Hardy apologized and claimed he was only kidding. After concluding that the harassment would not stop, however, she left Forklift and filed her complaint with the EEOC. Later, the district court concluded that Hardy was crude and vulgar, that Harris was the subject of a continuing pattern of sex-based derogatory conduct by Hardy, that Harris had been offended by the conduct, and that the conduct would have offended a reasonable manager. Nevertheless, the court concluded that Harris did not suffer *serious psychological injury* and therefore, Hardy's conduct did not create a hostile work environment. Based on this finding, the case was dismissed. The Sixth Circuit Court of Appeals affirmed the district court, and Harris appealed to the U.S. Supreme Court.

(continued)

(continued)

Along with the appeal, the American Psychological Association filed an *amicus* brief in which it related that men and women perceive sexual harassment behavior differently, and to insist on psychological "injury" would undermine the purposes of Title VII and deter reporting of severe sexual harassment. The Supreme Court, in a unanimous decision, held that "Title VII comes into play *before* the harassing conduct leads to a nervous breakdown" (p. 21) (emphasis added). Title VII can be enforced even if the harassment produces no tangible effects. Accordingly, a plaintiff alleging sexual harassment need not demonstrate any concrete psychological harm to prevail. This was a clear victory for plaintiffs and victims of sexual harassment. But the Court rejected the "reasonable woman" standard proposed by some lower courts and the EEOC, and stated that the harassing behavior must be sufficient to create an *objectively hostile or abusive* work environment in order for there to be a sufficient case. This portion of the Court's decision was clearly a victory for employers and defendants charged with sexual harassment.

But the main victory of the case was for employees and plaintiffs. When a plaintiff becomes dysphoric (sad), tearful, or fearful, this may suffice in proving she is clinically depressed. There would be no need for expert psychological testimony to establish, support, or confirm her level of discomfort or depression. It will not take an expert psychological witness to testify in the matter. This is of vital importance since hitherto in sexual harassment cases, once of the primary defenses open to employers or defendants was to challenge the plaintiff's level of suffering and to compare it to her general state of emotional well being both pre and post the alleged harassment. As a result of *Harris*, it may now be legally sufficient in such cases to rely only on the testimony of the plaintiff herself supported by testimony from her spouse, family members, friends and coworkers who knew her well both pre and post the alleged harassment.

The situation would be different of course, as in any case, if an employee or plaintiff herself calls her treating mental health professional to testify about the "nature and extent" of mental harm present. In this case, she thereby places her mental condition in controversy and the employer or defendant can attack such testimony with their own experts.

Additional ways Psychologists can Contribute

Psychologists can further assist in cases of sexual harassment by performing mediation. **Mediation** is the intervention into a dispute or negotiation of an acceptable, impartial and neutral third party who has no decision-making authority. The objective of this intervention is to assist the parties in voluntarily reaching an acceptable resolution of issues in dispute. Mediation is useful in highly-polarized disputes where the parties have either been unable to initiate a productive dialogue, or where the parties have been talking and have reached a seemingly insurmountable impasse. A mediator makes primarily procedural suggestions regarding how parties can reach an agreement. Occasionally, a mediator may suggest some substantive options as a means of encouraging the parties to expand the range of possible resolutions under consideration.

A mediator often works with the parties individually or in groups, to explore acceptable resolution options or to develop proposals that might move the parties closer to resolution. A psychologist-mediator may also have a particular understanding of the dynamics of sexual harassment. Whether the mediator is a psychologist or not, mediation gives both parties the opportunity to hear the opposing party's point of view and to settle despite disagreements with the other side's perspective (Gazeley, 1997; Stamato, 1992).

WORKPLACE VIOLENCE

Men do not discard their personal qualities when they go to work. Into the job they carry their intelligence, skill, habits of care and rectitude. Just as inevitably they take along also their tendencies to carelessness and camaraderie, as well as emotional make-up. In bringing men together, work brings these qualities together, causes frictions between them, creates occasions for lapses into carelessness, and for fun-making and emotional flare-up. . . . These expressions of human nature are incidents inseparable from working together. They involve risks of injury and these risks are inherent in the working environment. (*Hartford Accident & Indemnity Co. v. Cardillo*, 1940, p. 15)

—Mr. Justice Rutledge

Almost 2 million workers are victims of violent crime each year in the United States, and 18% of all violent crime takes place at the workplace. These crimes include 1.3 million simple assaults, 325,000 aggravated assaults (where a weapon of some sort is utilized), 36,500 rapes and sexual assaults, 70,000 robberies, and 900 homicides. Police officers are the most likely occupational group to be the victims of duty-related violence, followed by correctional officers, taxicab drivers, private security workers, and bartenders. But no occupational group, and certainly no work setting is immune. In 2007, 10% of male students and 5% of female students reported experiencing a threat or injury with a weapon on school property, and about a third (32%) of public and private school students, ages 12–18, reported that they have been bullied at school within the past six months (U.S. Department of Justice, Bureau of Justice Statistics, 2009).

Violence committed in the workplace itself is generally perpetrated by five categories of people (Bensimon, 1994; Burgess, Burgess, & Douglas, 1994; Catalano, Dooley, & Novaco, 1993). These include (1) criminals who see the workplace as a target of opportunity, (2) terrorists and those committing hate crimes, (3) employees who impulsively get into arguments and fights, (4) angry and resentful employees or customers who kill for revenge, and (5) stalkers who harm (or attempt to harm) another employee or an estranged partner. The first three groups are generally covered elsewhere in this book, so vengeful attacks and stalking will be discussed in the following sections.

The Resentful and Disgruntled Type of Employee

As briefly discussed in the chapter on mass murders and serial killers, the typical disgruntled workplace killer is in his 30s or 40s (Bensimon, 1994). He is usually about to be fired or laid off (or believes that this will be fired or laid off). Whereas an employee in his 20s can usually find other work at an entry level, a middle-aged man may find himself suddenly unemployed at a time he is "expected" to be at the peak of his career. This is one of the reasons job layoffs commonly precipitate depression, feelings of low self-esteem, alcohol abuse, and a desire to "get even." Frequently, it is actually the dehumanizing manner in which layoffs occur that is more upsetting to these people than the actual layoff itself (Bensimon, 1994).

The workplace killer usually identifies strongly with his job. He may be a loner with few outside interests or friends who isolates himself from coworkers and lacks supportive family. His job may be his only source of self-esteem and stability. Such workers often file grievances and are chronic complainers. They are likely to have difficulty accepting authority. They may threaten violence directly or in a veiled manner. In addition to the other personal and social stressors the workplace killer may be experiencing, the additional burden of facing a layoff or being fired can be the final straw that broke the camel's back. But it may be a slow process before they finally "snap" and go on a rampage. Such killers, it has been said, "spiraled down a long, slow slide, mentally and emotionally" before they actually kill (Burgess, Burgess, & Douglas, 1994, p. 14). If their job loss is preceded by another particularly high risk factor such as a home foreclosure or divorce, the time to the breaking point may be even less.

The disgruntled violent-prone employee may show other warning signs which exhibit themselves long before his actual rampage but should not be ignored. These include (1) difficulty accepting criticism from either supervisors or peers; (2) brooding over a recent humiliating life event where he was unfairly treated; (3) poor interpersonal skills, especially in conflict solving; (4) a past history of violence, impulsivity, or making threats; (5) a tendency to raise his voice, intimidate, or lose his temper with coworkers; and (6) a history of domestic violence, legal difficulties, conflict with coworkers, and making unwelcome sexual advances (Lewinski, 2007). Although these are all red flags, it is important to realize that many individuals who have or have had one or more of these behaviors may never hurt anyone either inside or outside the workplace.

The relationship between the assailant and the victim is also an important determinant in all types of workplace violence. For example, it may be a stranger with no legitimate relationship to the worker or workplace who enters the premises to commit a robbery or other violent act. It may be a current or former employee. It may also be a customer, client, or patient, perhaps predisposed to violence, or perhaps not, who lashes out in frustration over delays in receiving, or denial of, services. Or it may be anyone who has a personal relationship with an employee such as a former spouse or partner who enters the workplace to threaten, injure or kill an employee with whom he/she has a personal dispute. There has been no shortage of examples of violence committed by disgruntled employees.

SEPTEMBER 14, 1989 Joseph Wesbecker entered the printing plant where he had worked in downtown Louisville, Kentucky. He killed 8 coworkers and injured 12 others with a semiautomatic assault rifle. He then killed himself with a pistol. He had been described by coworkers as a "disgruntled" employee who believed that management had "done him dirty." He claimed that he had been injured by the chemicals he breathed at work. He filed a grievance and later a discrimination complaint against the company, and also threatened violence for several months prior to the shootings; this was common knowledge among some of his coworkers and supervisors.

MARCH 14, 1994 Tuan Nguyen, 29, recently fired from a Santa Fe Springs, California, electronics factory, used a still-valid security code to gain access to the building and shoot three people to death before killing himself.

APRIL 3, 1995 James Simpson, 28, a former employee at a refinery inspection station in Corpus Christi, Texas, shot and killed the owner of the company, his wife, and three workers before shooting himself to death.

JUNE 5, 1997 Daniel S. Marsden, a plastics factory employee in Santa Fe Springs, California, fatally shot two coworkers and wounded four others after an argument at work, then killed himself less than 2 hours later.

SEPTEMBER 15, 1997 Arthur Hastings Wise, 43, allegedly opened fire at an Aiken, South Carolina, parts plant, killing four and wounding three others. Wise had been fired two months earlier from his job at the plant.

OCTOBER 7, 1997 Charles Lee White, 42, opened fire with a rifle at the San Antonio paging company where his ex-girlfriend worked, killing her and another woman before shooting himself to death.

DECEMBER 18, 1997 Arturo Reyes Torres, 43, walked into a maintenance yard in Orange, California, with an AK-47 and killed his former boss and three others. Torres, who blamed the supervisor for getting him fired, is later shot by police.

MARCH 6, 1998 Matthew Beck, 35, a Connecticut Lottery Corporation accountant involved in a pay dispute, fatally shot the lottery president and three of his supervisors before killing himself.

DECEMBER 26, 2000 Armed with a rifle, a shotgun, and a pistol (which he had hidden the day before), 42-year-old software tester Michael McDermott, rose from his chair at Edgewater Technology in Wakefield, Massachusetts, and stormed through the office killing seven coworkers. Police found McDermott seated in the lobby and ordered him to disarm, to which he replied, "I don't speak German." A search of his work area revealed 28 boxes of ammunition, a bayonet, another rifle, and a demand letter from the IRS.

JULY 8, 2004 Several Lockheed-Martin employees were shot at the Lockheed-Martin manufacturing plant near Meridian, Mississippi. A factory worker known to be a racist and who had talked about murdering others opened fire with a shotgun and a rifle at the plant killing four

African-Americans and one white coworker before fatally shooting himself. Later that year Bryan Uyesugi walked into a meeting at his Xerox office building in Hawaii and killed seven employees. He had previously undergone anger management counseling, and was described as being very normal and mild mannered. His father said he knew of only one time when Bryan had lost his temper at work during his 15 years with Xerox. In his only angry outburst, he kicked an elevator door.

The Stalker Type of Violent Employee

Workplace violence that involves **stalking** is similar in many ways to a sexual obsession. Sexual obsession is sometimes called love obsession or "romantic stalking", and usually involves a spurned ex-lover or spouse whose primary motivation is revenge, or a severely disturbed individual who experiences unrealistic fantasies or even a delusional disorder where he firmly believes that the victim is in love with him. A subtype of such a disorder is the *erotomanic* type, in which the stalker engages in continuing efforts to contact the object of her affection despite his apathy and even hostility. Clinically, most individuals with this disorder are females, however, forensically – those that enter the criminal justice system – most are males. In the more common situation, the victim has clearly communicated something like "I wouldn't go out with you if you were the last man on Earth", but the offender simply refuses to give up, and his behavior often fits the diagnosis of dependent personality disorder or oven borderline personality disorder.

Personality Differences and Workplace Aggression

STATE ANGER v. TRAIT ANGER   There are generally two categories of anger: state and trait. **State anger** is an emotional response to a particular event, whereas **trait anger** is a disposition to experience anger over time and across context (Speilberger, 1996). Whereas state anger is generally a temporary or transitory emotional response, trait anger is more akin to a stable personality trait. Some people experience higher intensities of state anger than do other people, and the thematic and degree of environmental stimuli required to elicit the angry response will differ as well. High-trait-anger individuals are also likely to respond aggressively to particular situations than are low-trait-anger individuals. They also perceive a wider range of situations (or themes) as anger provoking than do low-trait-anger individuals, and their anger may be of greater intensity and last longer as well. An interesting metaphor for high-trait-anger versus low-trait-anger individuals would be a comparison between domestic and "killer" bees. The former group get angry less easily and less frequently and their anger is not likely to last long. But the latter group responds violently with minimal amounts of provocation and it takes a much longer time for their anger to dissipate.

Attitude toward Revenge

People who view aggressive behavior as acceptable or justifiable are more likely to engage in aggression than people who view aggressive behavior as unacceptable or unjustifiable (Bulatao & VandenBos, 1996). When people engage in aggressive behaviors for purposes of revenge, which refers to the infliction of harm in return for perceived harm (Stuckless & Goranson, 1992), they view their behavior as acceptable and justifiable (Turner & Cashdan, 1988). Thus, the desire to seek revenge may be related to the incidence of aggressive behavior.

In the workplace context, the desire for "revenge" is often associated with employee theft (Terris & Jones, 1982). Similarly, employees who perceive that they were treated unfairly by the employing organization were more likely to engage in organizational retaliatory behaviors than when they perceive that they were treated fairly by the employing organization (Skarlicki & Folger, 1997). And this relationship between perceptions of fairness and organizational retaliatory behaviors is more intense in employees who experience high levels of internal distress ("negative affectivity").

Negative Affectivity

Negative affectivity refers to a general disposition toward subjective distress (Watson, 1988; Watson & Clark, 1984). People who exhibit high negative affectivity perceive themselves as in distress, are highly sensitive to negative events, and have a generally pessimistic view of themselves, their surroundings, and the world. People who exhibit low negative affectivity perceive their world as less stressful, are less reactive to negative events, and are more optimistic about themselves and their surroundings (Mangan, Quartermain, & Vaughan, 1960; Watson, 1988). There seems to be a positive relationship between negative and depressing affectivity and the projection of negative and hostile motives to the workplace, and consequently the incidence of aggression in the workplace (Andersson & Pearson, 1999; Martinko & Zellars, 1998).

Self-Control

The literature on self-control (e.g., Block, 1977; Buss, 1961; Sarchione, Cuttler, Muchinsky, & Nelson-Gray, 1998) suggests that the incidence of workplace aggression may be related to the inability of individuals to manage and inhibit their emotions and frustration levels. Whereas individuals who possess higher levels of self-control are likely to remain calm during provocative situations, individuals who possess lower levels of self-control are likely to respond aggressively to provocative situations and react offensively to minimal provocations (Baron & Richardson, 1994).

Attributional Style

Various conceptualizations of the dynamics associated with anger and aggression indicate that a person's cognitive appraisal of negative outcomes may predict anger and subsequent aggression. Specifically, the psychological literature suggests that the likelihood of individuals responding aggressively to negative situations depends in part on their judgments of causality (i.e., to what they attribute the cause of the negative situations) (Greenberg & Alge, 1998; Mack et al., 1998; Martinko & Zellars, 1998; Neuman & Baron, 1998). Moreover, within the workplace context, Martinko and Zellars (1998) proposed that when individuals exhibit tendencies to attribute negative workplace outcomes to *other persons* or the employing organization (i.e., external attributions) and believe that these outcomes were controllable, intentional, and stable and that there were no mitigating circumstances, anger and subsequent aggression are more likely to be demonstrated than if individuals exhibit tendencies to attribute the causes to factors that are *internal*, uncontrollable, unintentional, or unstable.

Location of Workplace Violence

Most violence occurring in taxicabs, liquor stores, and convenience stores are associated with robbery and crimes of opportunity committed by customers rather than between employees. These venues are also likely to encounter customers who are intoxicated or under the influence of drugs. Health care facilities may be particularly predisposed to anger and potential violence due to perceived lack of care, administrative gridlocks, insurance payment frustrations, and prolonged waiting times for care. Furthermore, the very reason for a person coming to a health care facility, particularly an emergency room, may be associated with violence (e.g., intoxication, drug overdose, mental illness, spousal abuse, stabbings and gunshot wounds). In such circumstances the presenting problem is medical as well as criminal and a patient may be the victim of a crime, a witness or even a prisoner. Even an unassuming component of a hospital such as a newborn nursery can be a breeding ground for difficulties when, for example, someone claiming to be the father of a child is denied access to the visiting area. In pediatric units there may be intense and emotional issues regarding alleged child abuse or neglect. Violence in these settings may also be associated with family members of patients who are fearful, agitated, and stressed.

Business and government offices are prime targets for acts of revenge built on feelings of frustration and perceived neglect of one form or another. In restaurants customers expect good service, value for their money, and to get it quick. And the fast-food industry generally consists of low-end, low-wage, time-consuming, stressful jobs that are demeaning and degrading. These kinds of establishments are breeding grounds for harassment, specifically coworker harassment. In addition, management and supervision are typically lax, unskilled, and often part of the ongoing harassment dynamic. The tremendous turnover rate in personnel also supports the bringing in of new, psychologically unscreened applicants.

THE EFFECTS OF WORKPLACE VIOLENCE

Violence impacts organizations in many ways that go beyond the tragedy of dead or seriously injured employees. When there is a lingering threat of violence against an organization, the consequences can be a decrease in moral and productivity. Employees do not function well when they are frightened, anxious or disturbed by violent incidents or threats of violence. Should the victim be a key employee or important executive, day-to-day operations can be seriously disrupted. Employees who lose confidence in the ability of the organization to protect them may look to other venues for employment. In addition, the negative attention brought on by a violent incident can have far-reaching ramifications for a business. Customers may be frightened away, business associates may not wish their names linked to the violence, and recruiting new employees can be difficult.

Liability is almost certain to be an issue in instances of workplace violence, especially where an employee was the cause of injury to others. Legal claims will be made under a theory of negligence in that the organization knew or should have known of a particular individual's propensity for violence and failed to act. Issues of **negligent hiring, negligent retention**, lack of due care, and inadequate supervision will be raised. Claims will be made that the violence, whether caused by an employee or outsider, was foreseeable and could have been prevented with effective and proactive management.

In one such early negligent retention case, *Carr v. William Crowell Co.* (1946), a state court ruled that the employer was responsible for an employee's intentional action that arose from the workplace. In this case an employee attacked another employee with a hammer, an act the court ruled was not due to personal malice, because the victim and attacker were strangers outside of work. The court said the injury was the result of the workplace setting itself.

Another landmark case in negligent hiring came in 1979 in *Vining v. Avis Rent-a-Car Systems, Inc.*, with a $750,000 award against Avis Rent-Car. In this case Avis management failed to check the application of a man before hiring him. The employee subsequently raped a coworker. Had Avis checked, it would have discovered that during the time the applicant listed as being in high school and college, he was actually serving a three-year prison sentence on a robbery conviction.

In the 1986 case of *Malorney v. B&L Motor Freight, Inc.*, the Illinois Appellate Court awarded $4,000,000 to a woman who was raped by an employee of B&L Motor Freight. His employment application indicated he had no prior criminal convictions, while in reality he had. The court ruled that the employer had a general duty to check criminal records for employees who will interface with the public, or who could have a foreseeable opportunity to commit a violent sex crime against someone in the course of their employment. In another case, an Amtrak employee shot and seriously wounded his supervisor. The court awarded the supervisor $3.5 million from Amtrak. The action, *Smith v. Amtrak* (1987) was brought because of Amtrak's alleged failure to discipline the employee for previous actions that indicated violent tendencies. Because the employee had attacked other employees, the court ruled that the violence was foreseeable and held Amtrak responsible for negligent retention.

THE CONTRIBUTIONS OF PSYCHOLOGISTS

Psychologists can utilize their particular expertise to prevent workplace violence by (1) using effective preemployment screening, (2) developing policies and procedures on how to deal with threats, (4) implementing risk-reduction programs and therapeutic interventions for problem employees, and (5) crisis management.

Preemployment Screening

In chapter 7, the necessity of performing pre-employment psychological screening on applicants for law enforcement positions was stressed. But it is also recommended that prior to extending an offer of employment in many other career fields, the following should be checked as part of a thorough background screening: references, educational credentials, employment history and performance, professional licenses or certification (if relevant), motor vehicle history, and criminal background.

If psychological testing instruments are used (and are legally defensible), they must possess certain psychometric properties. These include reliability, validity, and utility. Reliability refers to the consistency of a test to yield the same results when administered at different times. Statistically, reliability refers to the ability of a test to yield equivalent results if given at different times to the same person or to two different people with identical capacities and interests.

There are various kinds of validity, but they all essentially relate to the ability of an assessment instrument to accurately measure what it was designed to measure. Validity therefore relates to the ability of the test to predict real life outcomes. Utility refers to the usefulness and incremental value of the test results within the context of the entire selection battery. A test will have utility if it is reliable, if it provides real life predictability (validity), if its predictability is better than that of other procedures alone (such as interview), and if it is practical and relatively inexpensive to administer.

The types of personality characteristics that are most important when making a hiring decision depend on the nature of the job and the needs of the employer. Some of the most frequently assessed areas include intelligence and problem-solving skills, judgment, honesty and integrity, attitudes toward supervision and authority, presence or absence of bias, team orientation, history of alcohol or drug abuse, and stress tolerance.

When performing preemployment screening, it must be insured that clinical diagnoses or psychiatric labeling of candidates be avoided and that any tests that are administered are not considered "medical tests" within the framework of the ADA. Any testing instrument that could result in revealing a disability is illegal, unless the testing is administered after a conditional job offer is made and the nature of the job necessitates the use of such medically oriented psychological tests (e.g., police work, nuclear power plant personnel, federal law enforcement). For the purpose of general **preemployment screening** however, the following testing instruments are most appropriate:

1. Personnel Assessment Form (PAF)
2. Employee Screening Questionnaire (ESQ)
3. Guilford–Zimmerman Temperament Survey (GZTS)
4. Sixteen Personality Factor Questionnaire (16 PF)
5. Millon Index of Personality Styles Revised (MIPS-R)

Clinicians should assure that no items are offensive, invasive, or deal with religious preferences or sexual orientation. And finally, federal law prohibits employment practices that discriminate on grounds of race, color, religion, sex, and national origin. Any testing regimen selected must be shown not to have an adverse impact on any race, sex, or ethnic group.

Developing Policies and Procedures

It is always preferable for employers to be prepared ahead of time for potentially violent employees and crisis situations. A psychological consultant may help by developing a formal workplace violence program. As part of the workplace violence program, organizations should train employees at all levels to recognize and report the danger signals that often precede incidents of violence, and on how to report threats using the chain of command. It is helpful to have policies on when to recommend discipline or dismissal, voluntary therapy, mandatory medical leave, psychiatric evaluation, and mandatory drug screens.

Both *instrumental* support and *informational* support are important in situations where workplace violence has occurred. Instrumental support is support received from coworkers, supervisors, and management following the experience of aggression or violence (e.g., "My coworkers provide support when I experience an aggressive or violent situation at work"). Informational support is the training received on how to deal with aggressive or threatening acts. Both instrumental support and informational support tend to moderate the effects of workplace violence on emotional well-being, somatic heath, and job-related emotions (Schat, Kelloway, & Kevin, 2003). Generally, the negative consequences of workplace violence can be mitigated by training and interventions that enhance the availability of both these support mechanisms.

Risk Reduction Programs and Interventions

Despite any amount of support and proactive measures that may be taken, employees will always have to be disciplined. Psychologists can also assist in these situations. For example, a model of employee discipline called *Discipline Without Punishment* (DWP), developed by Grote (1995, 2006), treats each worker like an adult who is worthy of respect. The discipline procedure is kept on a mature and professional level, which does not foster defensiveness or safe-facing behavior. The focus of the DWP procedure is not on the employee but rather on the problem to be solved, and the responsibility for solving the problem or correcting the behavior is placed squarely on the shoulders of the employee. With this system, the discipline process, at least in the early stages, is less like punishment and more like coaching. If needed, a psychologist (employed by the company or contracted) can be brought into the disciplinary meeting as either a facilitator or intermediary who can guide the process in a safe and fair manner.

If an employee must be terminated, a psychologist or other trained mental health professional can act as a buffer between the supervisor and the employee. This can help to defuse a potentially violent termination. When the employee is uncooperative and termination looks like the only alternative, the psychologist may work as a mediator and go-between and help explain the risk of termination to the employee.

If an incident occurs and a potentially violent employee has been detected, a plan should be developed to help reduce the risk of an actual violent episode. In such a plan, the clinician should determine which risk factors are static and which are dynamic (Resnick & Kausch, 1995). Static factors such as demographics and age are not changeable. Dynamic factors such as current stress level and possible depression are amenable to treatment. Because disgruntled employees are often isolated persons without social support, it is important in the social history to explore the individual's pattern of social interactions. Does the employee now have supportive family or friends to help him or her cope with stress? Does the employee have a pattern of acting impulsively, talking out problems, or holding them inside and building up resentment?

It is particularly important to obtain a detailed history of alcohol and drug use when evaluating an employee for potential violence. For example, PCP is the hallucinogen most associated with violence (Budd & Lindstrom, 1982). Stimulants, such as amphetamines increase the risk of violence due to disinhibition, grandiosity, and a tendency toward paranoia (Honer, Gewirtz, & Turey, 1987). Referral to an onsite Employee Assistance Program (EAP) or an outside clinician might be appropriate when significant risk factors are present or suspected.

A weapons history assessment is likely to provide vital information about any plans for violence. The employee should be asked if he/she has ever owned a gun. If so, what particular weapons? Did he/she ever threaten or injure a person with a weapon? How recently was the weapon acquired? Does he/she keep a loaded gun? If an employee has moved a weapon recently, it may be an indicator of potential violence out of a perceived need for self-protection.

The need to have a policy in place for warning potential victims is of paramount importance. In the landmark case of *Tarasoff v. Regents of the University of California* (1976), the California Supreme Court determined that when a therapist determines, or according to the standard of his profession should determine, that his patient presents a serious danger of violence to another, he incurs an obligation to use reasonable care to protect the intended victim from danger. Some state courts have applied the Tarasoff doctrine only to identifiable victims, whereas others have included broader categories of potential victims. Most states have adopted some form of a Tarasoff-like statute.

Crisis Management

The ideal **Crisis Management** Team should consist of a member of executive management along with a management member from human resources, security, and risk management. There should also be a legal advisor, a psychologist, and possibly an employee representative. This group is charged with developing workplace violence policies and should be the decision making body when workplace violence issues arise or incidents occur. The Crisis Management Team should report directly to the organization's highest executive officer. Team members should have a working knowledge of the organization as a whole and should be experienced experts in their respective disciplines. They must be able to fully comprehend the complex issues surrounding workplace violence and be prepared to offer viable solutions to problems affecting their particular area of responsibility.

The Crisis Management Team should meet regularly. Once a workplace violence program is developed and in place, it must undergo continuous review. Regular meetings permit the team to keep current on the daily operations of the organization and assist them in identifying and evaluating potential problems. Activation of the team only after problems occur puts them at a serious disadvantage in maintaining an effective program. A proactive approach not only aids the team in monitoring and managing the program; it also puts the organization in a much better position to defend itself should an incident occur and litigation result. The team should also be tasked with contingency planning. When an employee is thought to be "at risk," the organization must take immediate action. Responsibility for evaluating the risk and developing a response plan should be coordinated through the Crisis Management Team. Should an incident occur, there must be a response plan in place to deal with it, trying to develop a plan under fire virtually guarantees failure (Resnick & Kausch, 1995).

As indicated above, in the immediate aftermath of a workplace violence incident, available personnel must demonstrate concern and caring for those who have been harmed by the trauma. Workers must know that management will do everything possible to care for those affected. Following the immediate and short-term crisis interventions, a post-trauma mental health team can return to the workplace on a periodic basis to counsel and debrief employees as needed. Prompt and appropriate psychological care of traumatized employees can reduce the number of stress claims and the amount of settlements, because it makes a positive statement about the commitment of management to employee well-being.

Brom and Kleber (1989, 1989b) have developed a program that avoids the singling out of individuals who may need assistance following a traumatic event. In their model, assistance of traumatized employees is standardized and all involved personnel participate. Assistance is formulated as an official program within the organization, with a clear delineation of staff and responsibilities. The clinician's function is solely to support the traumatized employees immediately after the event and in the longer-term recovery period. Organizations develop clear policies and procedures with regard to the temporary absence of traumatized employees and, if necessary, the transfer of an employee to another position within the organization without penalty or stigmatization. With proper intervention, employees are less likely to develop substance abuse problems, somatization, or PTSD.

FORENSIC PSYCHOLOGY IN THE SPOTLIGHT

How Important is the Role of Supervisors and Leadership Styles on the Emotional Experiences and Well-Being of Employees?

Bono, Foldes, Vinson, & Muros (2007)

The researchers sought to investigate to what extent supervisors and managers affect the emotions of their employees in the work setting. The authors theorized three main reasons for understanding why many employees may naturally feel uneasy and anxious when interacting with their supervisors. The first is that supervisors directly evaluate their performance. The second is that employees (like most people) have a need for autonomy, which is often limited in the work environment. Close interaction with supervisors means that employees are vulnerable to observation, which may be a catalyst for feeling that their autonomy is monitored and controlled (George & Zhou, 2001; Ryan & Deci, 2000). The third is that the presence and expectations of supervisors may lead employees to overly constrain their emotional responses in a manner known as **emotional regulation** (Diefendorff & Richard, 2003). Although emotional regulation may have a positive sound to it (i.e., the ability to regulate ones' emotions), it is far from positive. Instead, emotional regulation refers to a form of emotional phobia where an individual's feelings are perceived as invalid and something to run away from (Baugh, 2006; Schore, 2003). It is acting without authenticity (Little, 2000). Emotional regulation can leave one feeling stilted, blunted, unhappy, and depressed. The suppressing of emotions in this manner also has physiological and cognitive costs, including cardiovascular activation, decreased memory, somatic symptoms, depersonalization, and "burnout" (Gross, Richards, & John, 2006; Schaubroeck & Jones, 2000).

But this is not the case with all employees. Ashforth and Humphrey (1993) suggested that employees who identify with their work are more likely to feel authentic even when conforming to role expectations, such as demands for emotional regulation. This is where leadership can play a role. In both lab and field studies, Bono and Judge (2003) demonstrated that managers' transformational leadership behaviors can influence employees' identification with their work. They also found that **transformational leadership** was a positive predictor of the extent to which employees felt that their work activities were self-congruent and consistent with their own interests and values.

A transformational leader is someone who has vision and passion and believes he/she can achieve great things by injecting this same kind of enthusiasm and energy into their subordinates and employees. They are people-oriented and believe that success comes through deep and sustained commitment, and they model this for their employees (Bass, 1985, 1990). Transformational leaders are typically characterized as empathetic, and the behavioral dimension of individualized consideration explicitly describes such leaders as attending to and supporting the individual needs of followers. Such leaders may be able to help employees cope with emotional regulation in more effective and less psychologically draining ways by helping employees to understand why and how positive emotional expressions contribute to work goals (Shamir, House, & Arthur, 1993). Because they engender trust, transformational leaders are also uniquely positioned to assist employees in coping with emotional labor.

Participants in the present study were employees of an ambulatory health care organization. Paper surveys were used to gather general job satisfaction and stress data. Participants were also trained in the use of a personal digital assistant (PDA). For the experience sampling surveys, participants were signaled four times each day, Monday through Friday, for two weeks. The signal intervals were modified to accommodate participants' regular working hours (e.g., 7 A.M. to 3 P.M. or 8 A.M. to 4 P.M.). Participants were signaled once during each 2-hour segment of their 8-hour workday. Participants were given 10 minutes to respond to each signal, after which the survey was no longer available. They were told to respond to the surveys based on the emotions and attitudes they were experiencing "immediately before the beep went off." The researchers assessed momentary job satisfaction by asking participants to rate their agreement with the statement "At this very moment, I am fairly satisfied with my job" on a 5-point scale (1 = *strongly disagree*, 5 = *strongly agree*). Immediately after being signaled by the PDA, participants were asked to report whether they were currently at work (*yes* or *no*). Next, they responded to the following question: "When the beep went off, were you interacting with any of the following?" 1 (*supervisor*), 2 (*coworker*), 3 (*customer/client*), 4 (*family/friends*), 5 (*no one*), 6 (*other*).

(continued)

(*continued*)

A measure of general job satisfaction was obtained using five Brayfield–Rothe items (e.g., "Most days I am enthusiastic about my work".) (See Bono & Judge, 2003; Brayfield & Rothe, 1951). Distinguishing between felt emotions and the act of emotional regulation, participants were also asked about faking (i.e., expressing an emotion they did not feel); the three positive emotions (happiness, enthusiasm, and optimism); hiding (i.e., feeling an emotion they were not expressing); and the three negative emotions (anxiety, irritation, and anger). Responses for these items were evaluated on a 7-point scale (1 = *none at all*, 7 = *an intense amount*) for feeling, hiding, and faking. The researchers assessed momentary stress by asking participants to respond to the statement "At this very moment, I am experiencing stress." Three positive (happiness, enthusiasm, and optimism); and three negative (anxiety, anger, and irritation) work-relevant emotions were selected for the study. Participants reported the degree to which they felt the six selected emotions at each signal.

The leadership behaviors of participants' supervisors were measured using the 20-item Multifactor Leadership Questionnaire (MLQ—Form 5x) (Avolio, Bass, & Jung, 1995). The MLQ is the most frequently used measure of transformational leadership and has exhibited high reliability and validity. Responses were evaluated on a 5-point scale ranging from 1 (*not at all*) to 5 (*frequently, if not always*). Consistent with other researchers whose interest is the general construct of transformational leadership behaviors, items were combined to form a single score for each supervisor (Lim & Ployhart, 2004).

The direct effects of supervisors' transformational leadership behaviors on employees' momentary emotional experiences was assessed and quantified. This tested the theory that transformational leaders influence employee emotions. In this analysis the supervisor's typical leadership behaviors were linked to employees' emotions across all interactions, including those with customers and coworkers.

The results showed that employees who work for supervisors rated high on transformational leadership style reported experiencing more positive emotions throughout the course of their workday. Employees experience less optimism, happiness, and enthusiasm when they interact with supervisors than when they interact with customers, clients, and coworkers. But this effect is greatly modified when employees report to supervisors who engage in transformational leadership behaviors, compared with those who do not.

Managers' transformational leadership behaviors may have broad, deep, and long-lasting effects on individual employees and the organization as a whole. Beyond their immediate effects on employee mood, the positive emotions elicited by transformatioal leaders have the potential to influence the overall work climate and customer satisfaction. Employees who are optimistic are more likely to invest the time to help others (Lee & Allen, 2002) and can be expected to persist in work tasks—even in the face of difficulty (Seligman & Schulman, 1986). In the same vein, research by Pugh (2001) linked positive emotional displays by employees to customer evaluations of service quality.

The main results from this study is that managers may be able to help employees more by reducing or eliminating the need for emotional regulation (perhaps by encouraging and supporting authenticity) rather than attempting to buffer them from the negative effects of emotional regulation after it occurs. Supervisors and their managerial styles are extremely important in the emotional experiences of their employees, and this effect may reach beyond the workplace.

Summary

Distributive justice refers to how available rewards are distributed or divided up among members of society. Employment litigation and discrimination lawsuits are in many ways based on perceived unfairness in a society's distributive justice scheme. Employment discrimination can generally be broken down to factors of race, sex and gender, age, religion, disability, national origin, and sexual orientation.

The most important sources of federal legislation that impose equal employment opportunity obligations on employers are Title VII of the Civil Rights Act, the Americans with Disabilities Act, the Age Discrimination in Employment Act, and the Equal Pay Act.

Title VII of the Civil Rights Act prohibits an employer from discriminating against individuals on the basis of race, color, sex, national origin, or religion with respect to hiring, discharge, compensation, promotion, classification, training, apprenticeship, referral for employment, or other terms, conditions, and privileges of employment. Title I of the Americans with Disabilities Act (ADA) prohibits both public and private employers from discriminating in employment against persons with physical or mental disabilities. The Age Discrimination in Employment Act (ADEA) prohibits discrimination on the basis of age against employees aged 40 or older.

Sexual harassment is generally of two types. The first is quid pro quo harassment in which employment or promotion of persons is made contingent upon their complying with sexual demands. The second is hostile work environment harassment in which remarks, insults, or intimidation operate to create an abusive atmosphere in the workplace. There has been some research suggesting that the personality trait of authoritarianism is linked with those who sexually harass. One way psychologists can help ameliorate the effects of sexual harassment is by performing mediation between parties.

More than 1.5 million workers are victims of violent crime each year in the United States. Such violence is usually committed by resentful or disgruntled employees or by employee who stalk other employees. Employers who do not take affirmative and proactive actions to reduce the likelihood of workplace violence can be held legally liable for negligent hiring, negligent retention, and lack of due care and inadequate supervision. Psychologists can utilize their particular expertise to prevent workplace violence by conducting preemployment screening, helping to develop policies and procedures on how to deal with threats, implementing risk-reduction programs, and performing crisis management.

Key Terms

Age Discrimination in
     Employment Act *290*
American with Disabilities
     Act *289*
Crisis management *306*
Emotional regulation *307*
Equal Pay Act *290*

Distributive justice *287*
*Harris v. Forklift Systems,
     Inc. 294*
Hostile work
     environment *293*
Mediation *298*
Negligent hiring *303*

Negligent retention *303*
Preemployment
     Screening *304*
*Price Waterhouse v.
     Hopkins 291*
Quid pro quo sexual
     harassment *293*

State Anger v. Trait
     Anger *301*
Transformational
     leadership *307*
Stalking *301*
Title VII of the Civil
     Rights Act of 1964 *295*

Review Questions

1. What is the meaning of "distributive justice"?
2. What kinds of practices are prohibited by Title VII of the Civil Rights Act of 1964?
3. Describe the basic provisions of the Age Discrimination in Employment Act.
4. How does the Americans with Disabilities Act affect employment practices?
5. What is meant by negative stereotyping and by stigmatization?
6. How is psychological discomfort and paternalism related to discrimination?
7. What is quid pro quo sexual harassment?
8. How is authoritarianism related to sexual harassment?
9. What are some of the psychological and financial affects of sexual harassment?
10. What are some ways in which workplace violence can be prevented?

Chapter Resources on the World Wide Web

Society of Industrial and Organizational Psychology
http://www.siop.org/Instruct/IOIntro/sld003.aspx

U.S. Equal Employment Opportunity Commission (EEOC)
http://www.eeoc.gov/

EEOC Sexual Harassment Statistics
http://www.eeoc.gov/stats/harass.html

Monitor on Psychology: Sexual Harassment
http://www.apa.org/monitor/oct03/harass.html

Psychological Opinions in Sexual Harassment Claims
http://www.psychlaw.com/LibraryFiles/SexualHarassment.html

Dealing with Workplace Violence
http://humanresources.about.com/od/healthsafetyandwellness/a/workviolence_3.htm

Sigma Assessment Systems, Inc.
http://www.sigmaassessmentsystems.com/selection/default.asp

For Further Reading

Adorno, T. W., Frenkel-Brunswik, E., Levinson, D. L., & Sanford, R. N. (1950). *The authoritarian personality*. New York: Norton.

Altemeyer, R. (1988). *Enemies of freedom: Understanding right-wing authoritarianism*. San Francisco: Jossey-Bass.

Kelleher, M. (1997). *Profiling the lethal employee: Case studies of workplace violence*. Westport: Praeger.

Koch, W. J., Douglas, K. S., Nicholls, T. L., & O'Neill, M. L. (2006). *Psychological injuries*. New York: Oxford University Press.

Lane, I. M., & Siegel, L. (1982). *Personnel and organizational psychology*. Georgetown, Ontario: Richard D. Irwin, Inc.

Lowman, R. L. (1993). *Counseling and psychotherapy of work dysfunctions*. Washington, DC: American Psychological Association.

Stefan, S. (2002). *Hollow promises: Employment discrimination against people with mental disabilities*. Washington, DC: American Psychological Association.

CHAPTER 15

Forensic Psychology Applied to Children and Families

CHAPTER OBJECTIVES

After reading this chapter you would:

- Understand the difference between child abuse and child neglect.
- Know the three main types of child abuse.
- Know the definition of pedophilia and how it is assessed.
- Understand neuroimaging and how it is related to sexual offenders.
- Explain how online sexual predators operate.
- Understand the various motives for filicide.
- What is gendercide? How is it frequently religiously motivated?
- Understand child sexual abuse accommodation syndrome.

INTRODUCTION

Government statistics indicate that approximately 2.6 million reports of possible child maltreatment are made to child-protective service agencies each year (U.S. Department of Health and Human Services, 2004). These statistics are likely underestimated given that many cases go unreported. And when they are reported, they may not be investigated, as evidenced by reports that only 26% of the cases of seriously injured and moderately injured children were fully investigated by child-protective service agencies. In addition, many children experience more than one form of victimization (Runyon et al., 2006). Tragically, about 1,300 children die of maltreatment each year, and most of these children are younger than age three (Gosselin, 2005).

TYPES OF MALTREATMENT

There are two broad categories of child maltreatment: neglect and abuse.

Child Neglect

Child neglect is demonstrated by a failure to provide for a child's basic needs; it is an act of omission rather than one of commission. Examples would include failing to provide adequate supervision or failure to provide necessary food, shelter, medical, or dental care. Neglect may also include failure to educate a child or attend to special education or emotional needs.

According to U.S. Department of Health and Human Services data, children in the United States experience neglect at the rate of 7.2 victims per 1,000 children. Compared with abusive parents, neglectful parents are more likely to have difficulties with anger control, low self-esteem, and psychopathology (Bath & Haapala, 1993; Brown, Cohen, Johnson, & Salzinger, 1998). Other factors associated with parental neglect include violence in the marriage, lack of a social support network, parental alcohol abuse, unemployment, and a history of **child abuse** in the mothers (Dubowitz, 1999; Zuravin & DiBlaso, 1992).

Child neglect can have tremendous long-lasting physical and psychological implications for children who are victims. This can include both "internalizing" problems such as apathy, withdrawal, and low self-esteem and "externalizing" problems such as conduct disorders and verbal and physical aggression (Gosselin, 2005; Hildyard & Wolfe, 2002). An extensive research review by Law and Conway (1992) revealed that neglect also has deleterious effects on children's language development with associated delays ranging from six to nine months. These delays include greater difficulty in verbal comprehension, articulation, and cognitive development. Furthermore, relative to physically abused children, neglected children revealed greater cognitive and academic deficits; scored lower on standardized math, language, and reading tests than their peers; and were ranked low by their teachers in peer acceptance and overall emotional health (Hildyard & Wolfe, 2002).

Child Abuse

Physical child abuse is anything that may cause physical injury (e.g., punching, beating, kicking, biting, shaking, throwing, stabbing, choking, burning, or hitting). About 19% of maltreatment victims experience physical abuse. *Emotional child abuse* is any behavior that impairs a child's emotional development or sense of self-esteem or worth and may include such things as constant criticism or rejection. This accounts for at least 8% of cases (Gosselin, 2005). *Sexual child abuse* can include molestation (indecent touching of the child or forcing the child to touch the perpetrator on the genitals or breasts), rape (the insertion of any object into any orifice for sexual gratification), voyeurism (looking at the victim in various stages of undress), exhibitionism (exhibiting his/her genitalia to a child), pornography (indecent filming or videotaping of children), and forced prostitution (engaging in prostitution at the instruction of an adult) (McDonald, 2004; Rennison & Welchans, 2000).

Approximately 80% of perpetrators of sexual child abuse are parents. Other relatives account for about 7%, and unmarried partners of parents account for 3%. The remaining perpetrators include persons such as camp counselors, school employees, coaches, or individuals with an unknown relationship to the victim (Gosselin, 2005). When a blood relative perpetrates sexual abuse, it is known as "incest." If the sexual relationship is between a parent and child, the power position of the parent identifies the perpetrator. Parental child incest is the type that is most commonly reported, but sibling incest may actually be the most frequent form (Sgroi, 1984).

A national survey by Finkelhor, Ormrod, Turner, and Hamby (2005) of children and adolescents between the ages of 2 and 17 found that approximately 1 in 12 reported being sexually abused in the study year. In the survey, parents responded for younger children. From an international standpoint, Finkelhor (1994) reviewed international surveys of adults (which unfortunately employed differing survey methodology) from 19 countries. The average rate of childhood sexual abuse recalled was approximately 20% for women and 10% for men. Across these international surveys, females were more likely to have been sexually abused than males, females were more likely to have been abused by relatives than males, and the perpetrators were usually male.

Indicators of Child Sexual Abuse

Pullins and Jones (2006) report a number of studies suggesting that certain behavioral patterns are strongly suggestive, but by no means conclusive of **child sexual abuse**. Prominent among these is an unusual degree of sexual knowledge or sexual behavior for the child's age. This would include early sexual intercourse, having older partners, experience with numerous sexual partners, more frequent intercourse, and having exchanged sex for money (Luster & Small, 1997). The impact of such abuse can range from no apparent effects to very severe ones. The severe effects can include depression, anxiety, guilt, fear, sexual dysfunction, withdrawal, acting out behavior, and post-traumatic stress disorder. Effects may also include regressive behaviors (e.g., bet-wetting), sleep disturbances, eating problems, and performance problems at school (Seto, 2008). In addition, children who are the victims of sexual abuse are also often exposed to a variety of other stressors and difficult circumstances in their lives, including parental substance abuse.

Many parents mistakenly regard childhood symptoms of fear, depression, withdrawal, and oppositional behavior as always suggesting sexual abuse. These symptoms are certainly of concern, and as mentioned, can result from sexual abuse; however, they are not exclusive to childhood sexual abuse. In fact, Kendall-Tackett, Williams, and Finkelhor (1993) estimated that approximately 20–30% of sexually abused children show no emotional symptoms at all. Adults who were sexually abused as children commonly experience depression. Additionally, high levels of anxiety in these adults can result in self-destructive behaviors, such as alcoholism or drug abuse, anxiety attacks, situation-specific anxiety disorders, and insomnia. Many victims also encounter problems in their adult relationships and in their adult sexual functioning.

PEDOPHILIA

Pedophilia is discussed separately because (1) it potentially crosses the boundaries between physical, emotional, and sexual abuse; (2) it is a disorder of sexual desire involving considerable fantasy and behavior upon which sexual gratification depends; (3) it is not synonymous with sexual offending against children, though these concepts are often used interchangeably in public, political, and media accounts; and (4) it often leads to criminal activity. Pedophilia is listed in the *Diagnostic and Statistical Manual of Mental Disorders* (DSM-IV-TR) as one of the paraphilias.

A **paraphilia** is a condition in which a person's ability for sexual arousal and gratification is based upon fantasizing about and engaging in sexual behavior that is atypical and usually extreme (Nathan, Gorman, & Salkind, 1999). A paraphilia can center around certain objects (shoes, underwear, animals, children) or around specific behaviors (inflicting pain, exposing oneself). Paraphilias are generally more common in men than in women. A paraphilia is much more than a mere preoccupation because one's sexual gratification is completely dependent on that object or act.

Some examples of paraphilias include *pedophilia* (sexual activity with a child usually 13 years old or younger), *exhibitionism* (exposure of genitals to strangers), *voyeurism* (observing private—usually sexual—activities of unaware victims), *frotteurism* (rubbing against a nonconsenting person, usually in a crowded and constrained space such as an elevator), and *fetishism* (use of inanimate objects). Much less common paraphilias include *sexual masochism* (being humiliated or forced to suffer), *sexual sadism* (inflicting humiliation or suffering), *transvestic fetishism* (cross-dressing), *asphyxiophilia* (self-induced asphyxiation almost to the point of unconsciousness, also known as autoerotic asphyxiation), *coprophilia* (handling or eating feces), *necrophilia* (sex with the dead or someone pretending to be dead), *urophilia* (being urinated on), and *zoophilia* (engaging in sex with nonhuman animals) (Seto, 2008). Some of these behaviors are illegal, and those who may be receiving treatment for such paraphilias are likely under legal requirements (i.e., court order) to do so.

The *modus operandi* of pedophiles is usually to first gain the trust and even friendship of their intended victims. They may work in schools, camps, or other areas that would allow close contact with children. Direct sexual contact is more likely to be by fellatio or cunnilingus than by forced sexual intercourse. Some pedophiles prefer fondling or touching their victims. In cases where pedophiles do actually engage in intercourse, the victim is more likely to be older. For the most part pedophiles prefer female rather than male victims (Bogaert, Bezeau, Kuban, & Blanchard, 1997).

If the victim is a female, the offender is more likely to be a relative, and the offense will probably occur in the victim's residence. In contrast, if the pedophile chooses a male victim, the perpetrator is more likely to be a stranger and the offense occurs outside of the residence (Murray, 2000; Greenberg, Bradford, & Curry, 1995).

Hebephilia is a term closely related to pedophilia and is used to describe the sexual preference for pubescent children. Unlike pedophiles, hebephiles are attracted to children who show some signs of secondary sexual development, such as the emergence of pubic hair and the initial development of breasts in girls. Unlike pedophilia, however, hebephilia is not listed in the DSM-IV-TR.

Methods of Assessing Pedophilia

There are various methods for the measurement of pedophilic tendencies and severity. **Clinical interviews** usually allow for pedophiles or sexual offenders to be asked questions about sexual thoughts and behaviors, especially with regard to children. Men who have committed sexual offenses against children are asked about the details of these crimes. Pedophilia can be diagnosed with interviews after a careful consideration of the person's entire sexual history. For example, the DSM-IV-TR criteria for pedophile would likely be met by someone who acknowledges having frequent and intense fantasies about having sex with children, collects and masturbates to media depicting children, and engages in repeated sexual acts involving children.

During interviews, the individual's social contacts with children should also be explored. Such contact may be through family, friends, social and religious organizations, neighbors, and any employment or volunteer activity that involves close proximity to children. Men who have limited social and sexual contacts with adults and a high level of emotional and social affinity for children are more likely to be pedophiles (Finkelhor & Araji, 1986). It appears that the number of adults with whom a man has had sexual contacts is inversely related to the amount of sexual arousal he exhibits to stimuli depicting children in the laboratory, suggesting as well that pedophiles have fewer meaningful or even purely sexual contacts with adults. Indeed, many self-identified pedophiles have never been married, and those who are married report having poor sexual relationships with their spouses (Finkelhor & Araji, 1986).

The weakness of interviews of course is that respondents often lie. This is certainly more likely to be the case when endorsing fantasies of behaviors that may be both embarrassing and illegal, when reporting having actually engaged in these behaviors, or when they may be facing criminal charges (Kennedy & Grubin, 1992).

Self-report questionnaires have also been used to assess pedophilia. One of these is the *Multiphasic Sex Inventory* (Nichols & Molinder, 1984), which contains 300 questions divided into 20 scales, including validity scales. The clinical scales assess sexual behaviors and thoughts dealing with sexual deviance, atypical sexual behavior, sexual dysfunction, and general knowledge and attitudes about sex and attraction. The inventory has been successful in differentiating between sexual offenders and nonoffenders. The *Clarke Sexual History Questionnaire* consists of 24 scales that differentiate "erotic desire" from "disgust" for a variety of sexual behaviors. The scales have been found to correctly classify 45–90% of subjects and to discriminate between clinically relevant groups and controls in research studies (Paitich, Langevin, Freeman, Mann, & Handy, 1977).

The *Wilson Sexual Fantasy Questionnaire* (Wilson, 1978) consists of 40 items describing a number of sexual fantasies and subsequent attitudes about sexual fantasies. The questionnaire is organized into four fantasy areas: intimate, exploratory, impersonal, and sadism–masochism. These themes involve sexual activity with a consenting partner, sexual activity with multiple partners, sexual activity with strangers, and sexual activity with partners who have not given consent, respectively. The questionnaire also contains items about sexual fantasies involving sex with children under the age of 12. Respondents report interests on a scale of 0 to 5. A similar self-report device is the *Sexual Interest Cardsort Questionnaire* (Abel & Becker, 1979), which contains 75 items differentiating somewhat successfully normal from abnormal sexual interests and behaviors.

It should be noted that questionnaires, like interviews, are vulnerable to self-report biases, and there are no studies on the predictive validity of these questionnaires. There are also a number of other, more recent similar types of questionnaires in clinical use today. These include the *Static 99* (Hanson & Thornton, 1999), the *Sex Offender Risk Appraisal Guide* (Quinsey, Rice, & Harris, 1995), the *Minnesota Sex Offender Screening Tool—Revised* (Epperson, Kaul, & Hesselton, 1998), and the *Violence Risk Scale-Sexual Offender Version* (Oliver & Wong, 2006).

Neuroimaging

As discussed in the chapter on mass murders and serial killers, **neuroimaging** is a technique that measures mental activity and brain patterns. There is research suggesting that such neuroimaging can be used to measure sexual interest and arousal (Dolan, Millington, & Park, 2002; Mendez, Chow, Ringman, Twitchell, & Hinkin, 2000; Sumich, Kumari, & Sharma, 2003).

As early as the 1960s, research was being carried out which began to reveal differences in patterns of neural activity that could be detected when presenting sexual versus nonsexual stimuli to male participants (e.g., Begleiter & Platz, 1969). Kopell, Wittner, Lunde, Wolcott, and Tinklenberg (1974) found that both men and women showed differences in electroencephalogram readings for their preferred sex compared with their nonpreferred sex, and Cohen, Rosen, and Goldstein (1985) found relatively higher electroencephalogram activation in the right temporal region of the brain when men were presented with sexual stimuli. Other studies (e.g., Karama et al., 2002), employing higher-resolution neuroimages, have reported different areas of relatively higher brain activation when individuals were exposed to sexual versus neutral stimuli.

DreBing et al., (2001) used a case study design employing functional magnetic resonance imaging to detect differential activation of the anterior cingulate gyrus and right orbitofrontal cortex of a 33-year-old pedophile who preferred boys compared with men who preferred adult women. The pedophile showed differential activation of the anterior cingulate gyrus when he looked at pictures of boys in swimsuits but not when he looked at pictures of adult women in swimsuits; the other men showed the same pattern of activation when presented with pictures of adult women in swimsuits, but not with pictures of boys in swimsuits. The pedophile also differed from the normal controls in not showing left hemispheric activation during the stimulus presentations. These results suggest in part that the same areas of the brain are involved in processing of sexual stimuli by pedophiles and nonpedophiles. Similarly, researchers have identified specific brain regions that are selectively activated by seeing faces or body parts (Grill-Spector, 2004). It is possible that neuroimaging methods could eventually reveal the brain structures involved in processing of sexual stimuli, thus allowing clinicians to detect the likelihood for reoffending with greater discriminative and predictive ability.

Is There Neurobehavioral Evidence of Orbitofrontal Brain Dysfunction in Sex Offenders?

Spinella, White, Frank, & Schiraldi (2006)

The goal of this study was to determine if sex offenders exhibit neurological prefrontal brain dysfunction in contrast to normal controls, as evidenced by four behavioral measures sensitive to orbitofrontal dysfunction.

There has been prior research demonstrating such dysfunction in criminal populations, and it is associated with increased aggression and impulsive behavior (Brower & Price, 2001; Raine, Meloy, Bihrle, Stoddard, & LaCasse, 1998). More specifically, orbitofrontal damage usually results in alterations in personality, poor decision making, insensitivity to consequences, and deficits in empathy (Bechara, Damasio, & Damasio, 2000). The present study presupposes that child molesters also show deficits of empathy, which is also linked to orbitofrontal dysfunction.

(continued)

(*continued*)

The voluntary participants in this study were 21 sex offender males, enrolled in an outpatient treatment program. The behavioral measures consisted of the following: (1) *Go/No-Go Tapping*, where the participant imitated a standardized sequence of taps (either 1 or 2 taps) performed by the examiner; (2) *Antisaccades*, requiring the participant to look in the direction opposite the visual target, presented in randomized order; (3) *Delayed Spatial Alternation*, where the participant was shown two opaque cups and told a penny was underneath one of them. A movable screen prevented the subject from seeing the placement of the penny, and a felt board underneath minimized extraneous auditory cues. Both cups were baited with pennies for the first trial, and on every successive trial, the cup opposite the subject's last choice was baited. The task involved 25 trials, with 24 possible alternations. The participant was thus required to correctly remember the placement of the penny on the last trial and alternate his response on each successive trial, and (4) the *Alberta Smell* Test, where eight scented markers were presented monorhinally (one nostril at a time) and blindly to the participants. After each stimulus item, they were asked to open their eyes and choose from a list of the eight possible scents.

The results indicated that sex offenders performed worse than controls on all of the measures given, with the exception of one, and the measures on which they differed are measures that involve response modulation, more specifically behavioral measures that require a person to change and adapt his responses as he acquires a new rule and to respond appropriately based on changing rules. In other words, the sex offenders in this study showed an impaired ability to alter behavior on tasks that require altering one's behavior in accordance with learned rules.

Although there were limitations to this study (e.g., the study does not explain why all people with prefrontal injuries do not proceed to become sex offenders and that sexual behavior also involves interaction with the limbic system), there is neuropsychological evidence provided that supports the idea of behavioral indicators in the form of orbitofrontal dysfunction in sex offenders. The authors discuss the possible implications of the results for the treatment of sex offenders. The greatest of these is empirical support for treatment programs focusing on teaching techniques for impulse control and response modulation, as do many programs at the present time.

Child Sexual Abuse Accommodation Syndrome

In 1983, psychiatrist Roland Summit introduced the formal concept of **child sexual abuse accommodation syndrome (CSAAS)**. In his article, he outlined for clinicians why child victims of intra-family sexual abuse may be reluctant to disclose their experiences. Summit's model included five behavioral components. The first was *secrecy*, whereby the abuser forces the child to keep the abuse secret and often threatens physical harm or the complete breakup of the family, which would be the child's fault. The second was *helplessness*, where the child needed the abuser for provision of resources or felt a complete sense of powerlessness to do anything about the abuse. This would lead to a sense of passive acceptance. The third was *entrapment*, in which the child simply felt trapped by circumstances and unable to escape. The fourth was feelings of being *conflicted* over the right thing to do. The fifth reason why child victims did not disclose their abuse according to Summit was the delayed and *unconvincing disclosures* that had already been made. Summit maintained that children who have been sexually abused may show self-blame and self-doubt and be afraid of their abuser and the consequences of disclosure. Accordingly, to survive sexual abuse by a trusted family member, children were thought to make accommodating efforts to accept the abuse and keep it secret. He also maintained that in those instances where children did reveal their abuse, they would be prone to recant their revelations out of fear, only to reveal them again in the future.

Testimony of CSAAS has been used to explain seemingly inconsistent or illogical behavior on the part of child victims of sexual abuse, including delayed reporting, the lack of witnesses or physical evidence, and retraction by the victim. Summit asserted that the testimony of social science experts may be critical in clarifying such seemingly illogical behavior and to overcome the jury's misconceptions about the claims of child victims. But more often than not, CSAAS testimony is misleading and confusing to juries since its application is often used not only to explain the reactions of child victims, but also to prove that sexual abuse occurred at all. Moreover, and equally confusing, is that behaviors characterizing the syndrome have been noted in children who have never been sexually abused (Levy, 1989).

CSAAS is also resistant to being "disproved" because the defining features are contradictory. More specifically, if a child claims victimization at any time, CSAAS provides an explanation; if that same child recants, CSAAS explains that behavior as well, thus making claims of child sexual abuse almost impossible to disprove or defend against. For example, in *United States v. Bighead* (1997) an expert testified at trial but had not actually examined the alleged victim. The child had not reported the abuse at the time it allegedly occurred, and the expert's testimony was offered to explain why this actually made sense under a theory of CSAAS in which delayed reporting can be common among those who have experienced sexual abuse.

Critics of CSAAS point to the devastating effects making false accusations based on CSAAS can have on families. Schultz (1989) reported that such mistakes hurt not just the accused but the child as well. The falsely accused adult is likely to suffer emotional and physical trauma, family disruption, and financial ruin. His relationship with his child may also be irretrievably damaged. The nonabused child may have been indoctrinated into the victim role and been exposed to unnecessary information and scenarios regarding explicit and deviant sexual behavior. And unfortunately, allegations of sexual abuse have been used to gain the legal advantage in custody situations. Thoennes and Pearson (1988) estimate that accusations of sexual abuse were found in 2–10% of contested custody cases, but note that the actual numbers may be much higher. Other such critics have identified studies revealing, contrary to CSAAS theory, that most children do disclose abuse within the first or second interview. Only a small minority of these children recant their abuse reports (London et al., 2005). In fact, in almost every relevant study in the area, children disclosed abuse when directly asked.

Finally, when courts are confronted with CSAAS testimony, they have traditionally been lax in scrutinizing its scientific basis. Instead, they have relied on the unsubstantiated testimony of experts or the acceptance of CSAAS by other courts (see, e.g., *State v. Edelman*, 1999). But under *Daubert v. Merrell Dow Pharmaceuticals, Inc.* (1993), *General Electric Co. v. Joiner* (1997), *Kumho Tire Company Ltd. v. Carmichael* (1999), and the Federal Rules of Evidence, trial judges need to consider factors such as error rates, peer-reviewed publications, and general acceptance by the relevant scientific community in their evaluation of such testimony.

Online Sexual Predators

Certainly, the Internet and online computer exploration and communication have opened a world of possibilities for children. Unfortunately, there are individuals who will take advantage of this and attempt to lure and sexually exploit children through the use of online services. Thirty-nine percent of children say they trust the people they meet on the Web; yet one in five children has received an online solicitation for sex (Wolak, Finkelhor, & Mitchell, 2004).

Some online **sexual predators** gradually seduce children by giving them attention and showing affection and kindness. In this "soft sell" approach, such individuals often devote considerable amounts of time, money, and energy in their efforts. They pretend to care and empathize with children's problems, and they are often aware of the latest music, hobbies, and interests of children. Sexual content is slowly introduced into the context of conversations after children's trust has been obtained and their inhibitions are lowered.

Some individuals immediately engage in sexually explicit conversation with children; they collect and trade child-pornographic images, while others seek face-to-face meetings with children via online contacts. Children, especially adolescents, are sometimes interested in and curious about sexuality and sexually explicit material. Most online sex offenders targeting such children are patient enough to use and exploit these needs and develop relationships with their intended victims. In addition, these predators are often able to move these relationships offline.

The needs and vulnerabilities of older children and adolescents sometimes make it less necessary for adult offenders to even hide their adult status. In fact, in many cases, victims are actually aware they are conversing online with adults. These offenders may not even deceive victims about their sexual interests. Sex may be discussed online, and some victims who meet offenders face to face go to such meetings expecting to engage in sexual activity. Some victims even profess love or close feelings for offenders.

It is important to note that many child sex offenders operating online target young adolescents, not young children; accordingly, they do not fit the clinical profile of pedophiles, who, by definition, are sexually attracted to prepubescent children. For various reasons, it would be difficult for pedophiles to utilize the Internet to directly target young children. For one thing, young children are simply not as accessible in the online environment as adolescents. They use the Internet less for communicating with friends or talking in chat rooms, and they are more closely supervised by parents (Rideout, Roberts, & Foehr, 2005; Wang, Bianchi, & Raley, 2005). And of course, due to their young age, children are less interested in pursuing relationships than are adolescents. However, adult men who pursue adolescent girls and boys are still a significant problem, especially since studies have found that such men are more likely to have criminal histories, less education, feelings of inadequacy, and arrested psychosocial development (Hines & Finkelhor, 2007).

INFANTICIDE

> I understand too well the dreadful act
> I'm going to commit, but my judgment
> can't check my anger, and that incites
> the greatest evils human beings do.
>
> —Euripides, *Medea*

Infanticide is the deliberate killing of a newborn (Resnick, 1969). Unfortunately this practice has not been uncommon throughout much of human history. Infanticide of newborns was not a crime in Europe 2,000 years ago. As head of the household, a father had the right of deciding whether to raise a child or allow the child to die. As in most other parts of the world, Europeans practiced infanticide for many reasons, including lack of economic resources and to eliminate illegitimate children. All this started to change in the seventeenth century in Europe when England enacted the Act to Prevent the Destroying and Murthering of Bastard Children in 1623. This law punished with death any unmarried woman who concealed the death of her "bastard" child. To avoid prosecution, the burden was on the woman to prove that she had intended to care for the child but that it was stillborn (O'Donovan, 1984). In fact, the mother needed to produce a witness that the child was stillborn. By the end of the seventeenth century the laws in England against the murder or concealment of the children of unmarried women became less severe. Women could now defend themselves based on temporary insanity, and in 1803, the burden of proving live birth was placed with the prosecution. In 1828, an act of parliament reformed the law so that all women, not just unmarried women, were equally liable for prosecution for these crimes.

In the research and clinical literature, **neonaticide** refers to the killing of a newborn within the first 24 hours. There are two forms of neonaticide: *Active neonaticide* is the killing of a newborn as a direct result of violence, and *passive neonaticide* is the killing of a newborn due to negligence directly following the birth. An example of active neonaticide would be the violent shaking of the newborn during a fit of rage, helplessness, or panic. An example of passive neonaticide would be allowing the newborn to fall into a toilet and then failing to take action to prevent his/ her drowning. Another case would be leaving a newborn outside, exposed to the elements, to die. The term **filicide** is reserved for killing of a child older than 24 hours (Resnick, 1970).

An estimated 1,200–1,500 young children are murdered each year by a parent or other person (Emery & Laumann-Billings, 1998). From 1976 to 2005, of all children under age five murdered 31% were killed by fathers, 29% were killed by mothers, 23% were killed by male acquaintances, 7% were killed by other relatives, and 3% were killed by strangers. Of those children killed by someone other than their parent, 81% were killed by males (U.S. Bureau of Justice Statistics, 2007).

What are the motives behind these horrific behaviors? Stern (1948) used the term *Medea complex* to refer to maternal hatred for a child. The name originates from Greek mythology, describing the situation of intense love turning to intense hate in which the mother harbors death wishes for her offspring. There have been case studies suggesting at least five traits exhibited by mothers who committed filicide. These include (1) coolness and detachment during childhood from their own mothers, (2) suicidal thoughts or attempts, (3) substantial feelings of personal inadequacy, (4) actual mental illness, and (5) feelings that their child was somehow defective (Tuteur & Glotzer, 1959).

A comprehensive analysis of 131 case studies worldwide from 1751 through 1967 (Resnick, 1969, 1970) revealed several distinct motivational patterns of mothers who kill their children. One motive is called *filicide associated with suicide* in which the parent (usually the mother) desires to commit suicide but does not want to abandon the child when she kills herself. She is fearful that nobody will be available to care for her child after her death. Another motive, *filicide to relieve suffering*, is where the parent kills a child (or children) to relieve real or imagined suffering. Alder and Polk (2001) report a father who killed his ailing daughter because "well, if she's dead—she's all right, nothing can happen to her . . . I wouldn't have to worry about [her] anymore" (p. 47).

A closely aligned motivation to filicide associated with suicide, which appears repeatedly in the psychological literature, is **misguided altruism**, in which the parent believes that the killing is actually in the best interests of the children. Parents who may have always regarded themselves as responsible and caring people (and may have been seen this way by others in the community) may lose a job and their savings and feel incapable of taking care of the family anymore. They kill their families in a misguided effort to spare them the hardships and humiliation. Most altruistic killers kill themselves as well.

Yet another motive according to Resnick (1969, 1970), is *acutely psychotic filicide* where parents kill due to psychosis, active hallucinations, and delusions. In these kinds of cases the mothers' delusional belief system is so great that the filicide seems rational to them (Stanton, Simpson, & Wouldes, 2002). Mentally ill mothers who commit filicide are usually in their late 20s or early 30s and often married (Stanton & Simpson, 2002). Schizophrenia, bipolar illness, and severe personality disorders are a common diagnosis in such instances. In addition, postpartum psychotic depression has become a diagnosis associated with neonaticide, and infanticide in particular.

Postpartum depression reportedly affects 10–22% of adult women within the first year after the baby's birth (Gold, 2001). The psychotic form of postpartum depression is characterized by command hallucinations to kill the infant or delusions that the infant is possessed. Postpartum psychosis this severe seems to occur in from 1 in 500 to 1 in 1,000 deliveries, and the risk of psychotic episodes is increased for women who have experienced prior postpartum mood episodes. One of the most notorious and emotionally excruciating cases of psychotic filicide occurred on June 20, 2001, when Andrea Pia Yates methodically drowned each of her five children, one by one in the bathtub.

Upon their marriage in 1993, she and Russell Yates announced that they were planning on having "as many babies as nature allowed," which was a central teaching of their newly shared religious belief system. But by 1999, after three children and one miscarriage, Andrea was already showing signs of serious depression and had one psychiatric hospitalization. Although advised by her psychiatrist to have no more children, she became pregnant with her fifth child one month after her discharge from the psychiatric unit. Soon after the birth of her fifth child in November 2000, Yates again became seriously depressed, and six months later was again hospitalized. While in the hospital she was treated with antidepressant and antipsychotic medication.

On June 20, 2001, after her husband left for work at 9:00 A.M., Yates filled the bathtub with water and proceeded to drown her three youngest sons, Luke, Paul, and John, placing their bodies next to each other on a bed, an arm of one of the children was placed around another. The infant, Mary, was the fourth victim. The oldest, Noah, attempted to flee but was caught and then drowned next to his sister's body.

Yates took Mary's body into the other room, laid it next to the first three, and covered all four with a sheet. Noah was forgotten in the tub. Andrea then called 9-1-1 and calmly asked for a police officer to come, asking for an ambulance only after it was suggested by the operator. Yates then called her husband at work saying, "You need to come home . . . it is time." Rusty asked her if anyone was hurt and she replied "Yes." He then asked who and she replied "It's the children . . . all of them." Andrea received the officers at the door, telling them she had just killed her children. She led them to the master bedroom where they found the four youngest children covered with a sheet, lying face up on the bed and the fifth still floating lifeless in the bathtub (Ramsland, 2005).

Upon being interviewed by the police, Yates again confessed to ceremonial killings of the children one by one. During the next few days she told the evaluating psychiatrist that she realized about six weeks ago that two of her children had become "retarded" due to her improper manner of home schooling. She reported hearing growling noises coming from the walls and was convinced that it was Satan chastising her. She also claimed that evil cartoon characters on television would tell her what a bad mother she was and that her children were not righteous and would perish in the fires of hell if they were not saved (Lezon, 2006).

Yates was convicted of first-degree murder in 2002 and sentenced to life in prison with parole possible after 40 years. On January 6, 2005, the Texas Court of Appeals reversed the convictions, because a psychiatrist and prosecution witness admitted he had given materially false testimony during the trial. On January 9, 2006, Yates again entered pleas of not guilty by reason of insanity. On February 1, 2006, she was granted release on bail on the condition that she be admitted to a mental health treatment facility, and on July 26, 2006, after three days of deliberations, Yates was found not guilty by reason of insanity, as defined by the state of Texas. She was committed to the North Texas State Hospital but was later transferred to a low-security state mental hospital in Kerrville, Texas. It should be noted that many experts disagree that Yates was "insane" at the time of the murders and that she does not belong in the category of psychotic filicide. It is contended that she knew exactly what she was doing, planning the murders meticulously and executing them methodically, that she knew right from wrong and was aware of the wrongfulness of her actions, and that she anticipated being tried and punished for what she had done (Setrakian, 2006).

Under Resnick's categorical system, the motive in many cases of *unwanted child filicide* is where the child is seen as a burden, preventing one or both parents from reaching their goals in life. A graphic example within the context of neonaticide is the case of Brian Peterson and Amy Grossberg.

Grossberg and Peterson grew up in an affluent suburb of Wyckoff, New Jersey. During the entire nine months of her pregnancy Amy managed to keep the situation hidden from her parents, and she refused to get an abortion because she believed this would guarantee discovery by them. Amy was additionally concerned that she no longer looked thin and sexy and felt badly that the pregnancy interfered with her sex life. She allegedly told her boyfriend, "As soon as everything gets better, I'll be my sweet, normal self" (Charen, 1998).

On November 12, 1996, 18-year-old Grossberg and 19-year-old Peterson checked into a Comfort Inn and delivered the unnamed child. They wrapped him in a garbage bag and disposed of him in a dumpster. The bloody sheets were discovered by a cleaning woman, who immediately contacted police. K-9 Police dogs found the body in the dumpster. Upon returning to school, Grossberg became very ill, and it became clear to the medical personnel at the hospital that she had recently given birth yet had no baby. The police were notified and interviewed both Grossberg and Peterson. Their story was that they believed the infant was stillborn when they disposed of it, but an autopsy proved differently. The autopsy indicated that the baby was born alive and that the cause of death was multiple skull fractures apparently cause by blunt trauma and shaking.

At their trial in December 1996, Peterson asserted that it was Grossberg's decision to dispose of the baby. Grossberg claimed that Peterson acted alone in placing the baby into the dumpster. Although a first-degree murder charge with the possibility of the death penalty was threatened by the prosecutors in Delaware, a plea bargain for manslaughter was accepted by all parties. Amy Grossberg received a 30-month sentence but was released from prison for good behavior after having served just 22 months. Brian Peterson received a two-year sentence and was released in 18 months.

A very similar but much older case with a different outcome was *People v. Campbell* (1895). In *Campbell*, although both father (John Campbell) and mother (Nancy Cook) were indicted for the killing of their newborn child, only Campbell was tried and sentenced (Schwartz & Isser, 2000). Campbell's conviction was based solely on Cook's testimony that she had not seen the baby but had delivered a live premature child. She also testified, however, that she did not witness Campbell dispose of the child. No body or remains were discovered. Campbell's conviction was later reversed on appeal on the ground that corroboration of Cook's testimony was required. Although the trial court's decision was reversed, this case demonstrated that a baby's death could at times be established by circumstantial evidence alone.

Historically, in most cases similar to those just described, for a charge of murder to be maintained, "the state must demonstrate *beyond a reasonable doubt* that the baby was alive and that it had an independent circulation" (*Shedd v. State*, 1934, p. 78). But such a required determination is often difficult if not impossible to make, as the only witness may be the defendant, there was no medical supervision, and the pathologist's testimony is often inconclusive (Schwartz & Isser, 2000). And finally, in these situations, we are dealing with "the most commonplace and natural event in human history"—childbirth (Oberman, 1996, p. 80).

In response to public and media attention regarding instances where infants have been discarded in public places and left to die, every state has adopted some sort of legislation that offers a legal and safe means for mothers to relinquish newborn babies. Commonly referred to as "**Safe Haven Infant Protection Acts**," "Abandoned Infant Protection Acts," or "Safe Surrender Laws," these laws allow a parent under most circumstances to surrender a newborn anonymously without the fear of criminal prosecution. The intent of these statutes is to encourage mothers, who might otherwise discard their children, to go to an emergency room, police station, fire house, or other safe place to drop off their infants.

For example, under the New York State Abandoned Infant Protection Act, parents, guardians, or other legally responsible persons who are unable to care for their newborn infants may anonymously and safely leave their infant in the care of a responsible person at a hospital, police station, fire station or a responsible person at another safe location. The Abandoned Infant Protection Act also creates an *affirmative defense* to prosecution for abandonment of a child under Penal Law § 260.00, providing that the parent, guardian, or other legally responsible person (1) intended that the child be safe from physical injury and cared for in an appropriate manner, (2) left the child with an appropriate person or in a suitable location, and (3) promptly notified an appropriate person of the child's location.

Another dramatic case of unwanted child filicide, but this time involving nonneonates (over two months of age), and an adult married mother, is that of Susan Smith. On October 25, 1994, 23-year-old Smith reported that she had been carjacked by an African-American man who drove away with her sons still in the car. Smith made tearful pleas on television for the rescue and return of her children. But nine days later she confessed to letting her vehicle roll into John D. Long Lake, drowning her children inside. When confessing, she reportedly said that she was very ashamed for what she had done and asked the sheriff for his gun so that she could kill herself (Rekers, 1995).

In her confession, Smith wrote that she had driven off Highway 49 and onto the road leading to John D. Long Lake because she wanted to commit suicide. She believed that her children would be better off with her and with God than if they were left without a mother and alone. But she exited the vehicle before it plunged headfirst into the lake. The prosecution's case was based on the theory that Susan wanted to escape her loneliness, unhappiness, and the stresses in her life by establishing an exciting, intimate relationship with her wealthy boyfriend.

To live this new life Smith would need to free herself of her children and the demands of motherhood. The defense team's psychiatrist diagnosed her as having a "dependent personality disorder" with needs for constant attention. He also expressed that her family tree had a genetic predisposition for depression and alcoholism.

Closing arguments were given on July 22, 1995. After deliberating for more than 2 hours, the jury returned a verdict of guilty of two counts of murder. The jury rejected the prosecution's request for a sentence of death for Smith and decided instead that she should spend the rest of her natural life in prison. She was sentenced to 30 years to life in prison. Smith will be eligible for parole in 2025; she will be 53 years old.

Parental Alienation Syndrome

Parental alienation syndrome (PAS) has been described as the intense rejection of a parent by children after divorce (Gardner, 1987). Another characteristic of this syndrome is exaggerated criticism by one parent of the other parent that is expressed to the children. In a longitudinal study of 700 highly conflicted divorce cases followed over 12 years, Clawar and Rivlin (1991) described four criteria for PAS. These are as follows: (1) *Access and Contact Blocking* in which there is active blocking of access or contact between the child and the absent parent; (2) *Unfounded Abuse Allegations* where false or unfounded accusations of abuse against the absent parent are made; (3) *Deterioration in Relationship since Separation*, which has to do with the existence of a positive relationship between the minor children and the now absent or nonresidential parent prior to the marital separation and a substantial deterioration of it since then; and (4) *Intense Fear Reaction by Children*, which refers to an obvious fear reaction on the part of the children of displeasing or disagreeing with the potentially alienating parent with regard to the absent or potential target parent.

But the assumption that a child's disdain for one parent is unjustified and pathologically attributable to denigration on the part of the "alienating" parent is not universally accepted. It is certainly possible (and at times likely) that parents will undermine each other's relationships with their children following separation. Indeed, many state statutes actually include a "friendly parent" rule, a preference for awarding custody to the parent who will be more likely to promote the children's relationship with the other parent; however, the scientific status of PAS generally remains questionable. The syndrome has also been attacked, in cases involving allegations of domestic violence, parental substance abuse, and child sexual abuse (Dunne & Hedrick, 1994).

RELIGIOUSLY MOTIVATED FILICIDE AND "GENDERCIDE"

Dena Schlosser was an intensely religious mother. But she severed her infant daughter's arms in submission to a charismatic preacher based on a verse in the Bible stating, "And if thy right hand offend thee, cut it off, and cast if from thee" (Matthew 5:30). Another mother, Deanna Laney, bashed in the heads of her six- and eight-year-old sons with a rock in response to divine signs (Rapaport, 2006). On October 4, 2005, in Pakistan, Jaffer Hussain, in response to "God's orders," slit the throat of his eight-year-old son. He even told his wife the night before the killing that he wanted to make a gift of his children to God. In the same year, also in Pakistan, Muhammad Arshad murdered his nine-year-old son, Muhammad Akram, on the orders of his spiritual leader, to ward off evil times.

In yet another case, 16-year-old Aqsa "Axa" Parvez was the victim of what appeared to be a religiously inspired **honor killing** in Mississauga, Ontario, Canada. Honor killings can be defined as acts of murder in which a woman is killed for her actual or perceived immoral behavior (Taylor, 1999). Many of the victims of honor killings are women who do not accept her family's tribal and Islamic traditions, refuse forced marriages, marry according to their will, or live independently. They are murdered by their family members to save the "honor" of the family. In this instance, Axa's father, Muhammad Parvez, was accused of strangling Axa after she refused to wear the hijab, a traditional Islamic headscarf for women, and expressed her desire to dress like other Western girls. Growing up in a Muslim family of Pakistani origin, Parvez was required to wear a hijab while out of the house. However, Parvez's friends claimed that she refused to wear the veil and would often change her clothing once she got to school and then would change back before going home. Her friends also claimed that she was drawn to Western culture though her family adhered to a devout form of Islam and that she was not getting along well with her family. A week before her death, she had moved in with her friend Lubna Tahir to escape tension with her family. One student reported that her father was threatening her, causing her to fear for her life. Her father allegedly strangled her, causing her to die from neck compression.

Another honor killing likewise motivated by religious and cultural fanaticism was the 1989 slaying of 16-year-old Palestina Isa by her father, Zein Isa. This killing was particularly disturbing in that it was inadvertently audio recorded from beginning to end by the Federal Bureau of Investigation. This was because Zein Isa, a member of the Abu Nidal Organization, was under surveillance in connection with alleged terrorist activities. In this grizzly 8-minute audio sequence, Zein stabbed his daughter 13 times as his wife held the girl down. In the tape Zein can be heard shouting "Die! Die quickly! Die quickly!" (Harris, 1995).

Honor killers often expect light sentences (if any) based on the defense that they were merely following the directives set down in their Islamic beliefs as stated in the Koran. Although most honor killings occur in Muslim countries, such killings have been reported in Bangladesh, Britain, Brazil, Ecuador, Egypt, India, Israel, Italy, Jordan, Pakistan, Morocco, Sweden, Turkey, Uganda, Afghanistan, Iran, and preliberation Iraq (Nebehay, 2000). Pakistan is probably the worst offender, where such killings are known as *karo-kari*.

In addition to honor killings, the barbaric tradition of family members killing female babies and young girls (referred to as **gendercide**) has been going on for centuries. In Greece prior to 200 B.C.E. "the murder of female infants was so common that among 6,000 families living in Delphi no more than 1% had two daughters" (Rummel, 1997, pp. 65–66). This practice has been particularly noted in India and China (Kishor, 1993). The practice of gendercide was greatly reduced during the 1950s, 1960s, and 1970s in China probably as a result of the establishment of the People's Republic in 1949 (Coale & Banister, 1994). However, there are signs that it is being reinstitutionalized due to the "one-child policy" introduced by the Chinese government in 1979 to control China's excessive population growth (Johansson & Nygren, 1991). This imbalance between the sexes is now to the point where there are 111 million men in China who will not be able to find a wife.

ELDER ABUSE AND NEGLECT

Elder abuse can be defined as any knowing, intentional, or negligent act by a caregiver or any other person that causes harm or a serious risk of harm to a vulnerable adult (Thompson & Priest, 2005). Between 1 and 2 million Americans age 65 or older are injured, exploited, or otherwise mistreated every year by someone on whom they depend for care or protection. However, there are various data suggesting that this is an extremely low estimate. For example, Pillemer and Finkelhor (1988) report that only 1 in 14 incidents, excluding incidents of self-neglect, ever come to the attention of authorities. It is quite likely that many older victims of abuse decide not to disclose mistreatment because they fear abandonment, institutionalization, or severe repercussions from the abuser (Cyphers, 1999). These trends seem to be increasing. A 2004 Survey of State Adult Protective Services showed a 19.7% increase from 2000 to 2004 in the total number of reports of elder abuse and neglect. In 20 of the states surveyed, more than two in five victims were age 80 or over. And most alleged perpetrators were adult children (32.6%) or other family members (21.5%). The revelation that adult children are the most frequent abusers of the elderly has been a consistent finding during at least the last ten years (National Center on Elder Abuse, 2005).

Older people who are ill, frail, disabled, mentally impaired, or depressed are at the greatest risk of abuse. Households that experience family discord as a result of the older person's presence and that have a history of violent interactions within the family and poor stress tolerance contribute to the likelihood of elder abuse. This is especially true if family members are socially isolated, lack care-giving skills, are financially burdened, abuse alcohol, are depressed, or were themselves victims of abuse as children (Thompson & Priest, 2005). In addition, caregivers and relatives who were dependent on the victim, especially for financial support or housing, were at a greater risk of becoming abusive (Wolf, 1998). Poor health, Alzheimer's, depression, and cognitive impairment on the part of an older person also increased the likelihood of abuse (Cyphers, 1999; Quinn & Tomita, 1997).

Types of Abuse or Neglect

Physical abuse accounts for 15% of the substantiated cases of elder mistreatment in the United States (National Center on Elder Abuse (NCEA), 1998). This kind of abuse includes the use of force against an elderly person that results in physical pain, injury, or impairment. Such abuse includes hitting, shoving, pinching, burning, or biting. In addition, the inappropriate use of drugs, restraints, or confinement would constitute physical abuse.

Emotional abuse consists of the infliction of psychological anguish, pain, or suffering. Examples include insults, threats, humiliation, intimidation, harassment, name calling, humiliation and ridicule, and ignoring or isolating the elderly person (Thompson & Priest, 2005). Abusers may also threaten to institutionalize the victim or deny access to their grandchildren.

Neglect or abandonment is by far the most common type of elder mistreatment, accounting for 55% of all substantiated cases. Abandonment occurs when an older person is deserted by his/her caregiver who previously had assumed responsibility for providing care for that individual. Neglect refers to the refusal or failure of a person to uphold obligations to care for an older person. This often involves the failure to provide an elderly person with basic necessities such as water, food, shelter, safety, hygiene, and medications. In addition, social isolation of the elderly can be accomplished by taking mail and denying access to the telephone, Internet, and the outside world.

Sexual abuse is defined as "non-consensual sexual contact of any kind with an elderly individual" (NCEA, 1998, p. 11). Examples of sexual abuse would include unwanted touching, rape, sodomy, coerced nudity, showing an elderly person pornographic material, forcing the person to watch sex acts, or forcing the elder to undress.

Financial exploitation represents about 12% of substantiated abuse cases and refers to misuse of an elder's funds, fraud, taking money under false pretenses, forgery, forced property transfers, purchasing expensive items with the older person's money without the older person's knowledge, denying the older person access to his/her own funds or home, the improper use of legal guardianship, powers of attorney, or conservatorships, and embezzlement. Financial exploitation also includes scams perpetrated by sales people for health-related services, by mortgage companies, and by financial managers (NCEA, 1998).

Health care fraud and abuse is usually carried out by unethical doctors, nurses, hospital personnel, and other health care providers. Examples include charging for care that was not provided, double billing for services, overmedicating or undermedicating, and Medicaid fraud (Pillemer & Finkelhor, 1988).

Intervention Strategies and Ageism

It is unfortunate that some elderly victims encounter a form of *ageism* in their interactions with law enforcement and the court system. This is demonstrated when these institutions do not take victims seriously or simply fail to understand their situation (Lisae, 2002). **Ageism** itself can be defined as "any attitude, action, or institutional structure which subordinates a person or group because of age or any assignment of roles in society purely on the basis of age" (Traxler, 1980, p. 4).

There is no shortage of empirical evidence supporting the concept that ageist attitudes are prevalent in American society. These include studies of ageism as expressed in the media, and ageist attitudes in children and young adults (Mitchell, Wilson, Revicki, & Parker, 1985; Weinberger & Millham, 1975). Even psychologists and other mental health professionals are not immune to ageist attitudes. Ray, McKinney, and Ford (1987) examined the ratings of clinical psychologists toward clinical vignettes where the age of the clients was varied. Significant differences were found with older clients rated less ideal and given significantly poorer prognoses than younger clients. Interestingly, older psychologists rated older clients much more favorably.

Some of the intervention strategies for elder abuse are known to include (1) the creation of residential shelters for victims with a staff attorney available to provide direct legal services and a designated social worker and nurse experienced with victims of abuse, (2) elder abuse detection and prevention strategies initiated in the community, (3) training and outreach programs for law enforcement and other community-based professionals and individuals (Lisae, 2002), and (4) a combination of individual therapy, family therapy, and relationship counseling that focuses on behavioral skills training, cognitive restructuring, and emotional control (Papadopolous & LaFontaine, 2000). For example, abusive caregivers must learn to understand that their behaviors are not caused by the victim. Rather, inappropriate behaviors are learned and therefore can be unlearned and replaced with more appropriate behaviors (Quinn & Tomita, 1997), and (5) the building of social support networks for both caregivers and elders, which provide an outlet for the relief of tension and frustration (Kosberg & Garcia, 1995).

FORENSIC PSYCHOLOGY IN THE SPOTLIGHT

Mercy Killing or Murder? The Case of Tracy Latimer

R. v. Latimer, (2001) 1 S.C.R. 3, 2001 SCC 1.

Tracy Latimer was born on November 23, 1980, in a rural farming area in Canada. An interruption in her supply of oxygen during the birthing process (perinatal asphyxia) resulted in severe cerebral palsy. As a result, Tracy was quadriplegic, bedridden, suffered seizures and intense pain, and was mentally disabled. In court testimony, Tracy's orthopedic surgeon described Tracy's condition as one of the worst forms of cerebral palsy in that it involved her entire body. "She was in severe pain, which could only be controlled using powerful drugs that would interact with the anticonvulsant and antiepileptic she was already taking to control her seizures. The combining of these drugs put her at risk for aspirating, pneumonia, and depression of her respiratory system's functioning. . . ." (p. 1).

On October 24, 1993, Tracy's father (Robert William Latimer) killed Tracy by placing her in the cab of his Chevy pickup and running a hose from the exhaust to the cab. He said he loved his daughter and could not bear to watch her suffer any longer. He stated that his actions were motivated by love for Tracy and a desire to end her pain. He described the medical treatments Tracy had undergone and was scheduled to undergo as "mutilation and torture" (Depalma, 1997).

The court transcript presented the case against Tracy's father on October 24, 1993:

The accused was charged with first degree murder following the death of [Tracy], his 12-year-old daughter who had a severe form of cerebral palsy. [Tracy] was quadriplegic and her physical condition rendered her immobile. She was said to have the

(*continued*)

(continued)

mental capacity of a four-month-old baby, and could communicate only by means of facial expressions, laughter and crying. [Tracy] was completely dependent on others for her care. She suffered five to six seizures daily, and it was thought that she experienced a great deal of pain. She had to be spoon-fed, and her lack of nutrients caused weight loss. There was evidence that [Tracy] could have been fed with a feeding tube into her stomach, an option that would have improved her nutrition and health, and that might also have allowed for more effective pain medication to be administered, but the accused and his wife rejected this option. After learning that the doctors wished to perform additional surgery, which he perceived as mutilation, the accused decided to take his daughter's life. He carried [Tracy] to his pickup truck, seated her in the cab, and inserted a hose from the truck's exhaust pipe into the cab. [Tracy] died from the carbon monoxide. The accused at first maintained that [Tracy] had simply passed away in her sleep, but later confessed to having taken her life. (File No. 26980, p. 1.)

Mr. Latimer's defense in the killing of his daughter was "necessity" in that his actions of filicide were necessary and merciful. But as is apparent in the charges stated above, the Crown prosecutor presented a different interpretation. There was evidence that Tracy could have been fed with a feeding tube into her stomach, an option that would have improved her nutrition and health and that might also have allowed for more effective pain medication to be administered. The Latimers rejected the feeding-tube option as being intrusive and as representing the first step on a path to preserving Tracy's life artificially. Although Tracy had a serious disability, she was not terminally ill. Her doctors anticipated that she would have to undergo repeated surgeries, her breathing difficulties had increased, but her life was not in its final stages. And her life was not without pleasure or joy. Tracy enjoyed music, bonfires, being with her family, and the circus. She liked to play music on a radio, which she could use with a special button. Tracy could apparently recognize family members, and she would express joy at seeing them. She also loved being rocked gently by her parents (court transcript, Sections 7, 8, and 9). The Crown granted that through her life, Tracy at times suffered considerable pain and the quality of her life was limited by her severe disability. "But the pain she

suffered was not unremitting, and her life had value and quality."

On November 16, 1994, a jury convicted Latimer of second-degree murder. But the Supreme Court ordered a new trial when it was learned that the Royal Canadian Mounted Police (RCMP), acting on orders from the Crown, had possibly tainted the case by questioning potential jurors on their views on religion, abortion, and mercy killing. Latimer stood trial again in October 1997 and was convicted, again, of second-degree murder. Nearly a year later, in November 1998, the Saskatchewan Court of Appeal heard the case. One justice drew a distinction between what he called Latimer's "compassionate filicide" and cold-blooded murder and favored granting Mr. Latimer a constitutional exemption from the minimum sentence for second-degree murder (25 years with no chance of parole for 10 years). The justice expressed that the law recognizes the wide range of moral culpability in murder and that Tracy Latimer's murder was a ". . . rare act of homicide that was committed for caring and altruistic reasons . . ."

But on January 18, 2001, the Supreme Court of Canada upheld his conviction and original life sentence. In rejecting Latimer's defense of necessity, the Court stated,

The defense of necessity is narrow and of limited application in criminal law. The accused must establish the existence of the three elements of the defense. First, there is the requirement of imminent peril or danger. Second, the accused must have had no reasonable legal alternative to the course of action he or she undertook. Third, there must be proportionality between the harm inflicted and the harm avoided. Here, the trial judge was correct to remove the defense from the jury since there was no air of reality to any of the three requirements for necessity. The accused did not himself face any peril, and [Tracy's] ongoing pain did not constitute an emergency in this case. [Tracy's] proposed surgery did not pose an imminent threat to her life, nor did her medical condition. It was not reasonable for the accused to form the belief that further surgery amounted to imminent peril, particularly when better pain management was available. Moreover, the accused had at least one reasonable legal alternative to killing his daughter: he could have struggled on, with what was unquestionably a difficult situation, by helping [Tracy] to live and by minimizing her pain as much as possible or by permitting an institution to do so. Leaving open the question of whether the proportionality requirement could be met in a homicide situation, the harm inflicted in this case was immeasurably more serious than the pain resulting from [Tracy's] operation which the accused sought to avoid. Killing a person—in order to relieve the suffering produced by a medically manageable physical or mental condition—is not a proportionate response to the harm represented by the non-life-threatening suffering resulting from that condition. (File No: 26980, p. 1)

Latimer's first attempt for day parole was originally denied in December 2007, reportedly because he still denied any wrongdoing. However, that decision was overturned two months after the Supreme Court of Canada's verdict, and Latimer was released for day parole on March 13, 2008.

Summary

There are two broad categories of child maltreatment: neglect and abuse. Neglect is demonstrated by a failure to provide for a child's basic needs; it is an act of omission. Abuse is an act of "commission" and can be physical, emotional, or sexual in nature. The impact of sexual abuse on children can range from no apparent effects to very severe ones. The severe effects can include depression, anxiety, guilt, fear, sexual dysfunction, withdrawal, acting out, behavior, and posttraumatic stress disorder. Adults who were the victims of sexual abuse as children commonly experience depression, high levels of anxiety, relationship difficulties, and self-destructive behaviors such as alcoholism and drug abuse.

A paraphilia is a condition in which a person's ability for sexual arousal and gratification is upon fantasizing about and engaging in sexual behavior that is atypical and usually extreme. Paraphilias can center around specific objects, such as shoes or underwear, or around specific behaviors, such as inflicting pain or exposing oneself. Pedophilia is one type of paraphilia that crosses the boundaries between physical, emotional, and sexual abuse. It is a disorder of sexual desire involving fantasy and gratification-seeking behavior related to children, but it is not synonymous with sexual offending against children, although it can lead to extremely abusive and criminal activity.

Methods of assessing pedophilia include clinical interviews, self-report questionnaires, and neuroimaging. Researchers have identified specific brain regions that are selectively activated when people see faces or body parts. Neuroimaging methods could eventually reveal the brain structures involved in the processing of sexual stimuli, thus allowing for more efficient reoffending detection and greater discriminative and predictive validity.

Child sexual abuse accommodation syndrome attempts to explain why children who are sexually abused by family members are often reluctant to disclose the abuse. Forced secrecy by the abuser, as well as helplessness, and feeling trapped and conflicted by the victim, all contribute to nondisclosure. Testimony regarding this syndrome is often confusing to jurors in that the "syndrome" is used to explain why children don't report abuse and at the same time to prove that the behaviors associated with the syndrome indicate that abuse has occurred.

Online sexual predators have been known to immediately engage in sexually explicit conversation with children in the online environment, or they may deceive victims about their sexual intent. Sex may be discussed online, and some victims who meet offenders face to face go to such meetings expecting to engage in sexual activity. Some victims even profess love or close feelings for offenders.

Infanticide is the deliberate killing of a newborn. When the killing occurs within 24 hours after birth, it is called neonaticide. Some of the motives associated with neonaticide and filicide include filicide associated with suicide, filicide to relieve suffering, acutely psychotic filicide. In response to public and media attention regarding instances where infants have been discarded in public places and left to die, every state has adopted some sort of legislation that offers a legal and safe means for mothers to relinquish newborn infants. Another type of filicide is referred to as "gendercide" in which girls are killed simply for being girls. In some instances this behavior has societal approval. A final type of filicide is religiously motivated and sometimes called "honor killings." Usually restricted to radical Muslim cultures, girls are killed by family members for bringing dishonor to the family.

Elder abuse can be defined as any knowing, intentional, or negligent act by a caregiver or any other person that causes harm or a serious risk of harm to a vulnerable adult. Such abuse can be physical, emotional, neglectful, sexual, financial, or fraudulent.

Key Terms

Ageism *325*

Child abuse *312*

Child sexual abuse *312*

Child sexual abuse accommodation syndrome *316*

Elder abuse *323*

Filicide *319*

Gendercide *323*

Honor killings *323*

Infanticide *318*

Misguided altruism *319*

Neonaticide *318*

Neuroimaging *315*

Paraphilia *313*

Parental alienation syndrome *322*

Postpartum depression *319*

Safe Haven Infant Protection Acts *321*

Sexual predator *317*

Review Questions

1. What are the various types of child maltreatment?
2. How is child abuse different from child neglect?
3. What is the parental alienation syndrome?
4. What are the various types of child abuse?
5. What are some of the indicators of child sexual abuse?
6. What is the definition of pedophilia?
7. What is a paraphilia?

8. What is the logic behind the child sexual abuse accommodation syndrome?
9. Who are online sexual predators, and how do they operate?
10. What is filicide? How is it differentiated from neonaticide?
11. What are some of the motives in cases of filicide?
12. What is "gendercide"?

Chapter Resources on the World Wide Web

American Psychological Association
http://www.apa.org/releases/sexabuse/homepage.html.

The Clarke SHQ: A clinical sex history questionnaire for males
http://www.springerlink.com/content/v3g80h32r8558730/.

Bureau of Justice Statistics
http://www.ojp.usdoj.gov/bjs/homicide/children.htm.

Federal Bureau of Investigation
http://www.fbi.gov/publications/pguide/pguidee.htm.

Gendercide Watch
http://www.gendercide.org/case_honour.html.

Growing sex imbalance shocks China. *The Guardian*
http://www.guardian.co.uk/world/2002/may/13/gender.china.

National Abandoned Infants Assistance Resource Center
http://aia.berkeley.edu/publications/fact_sheets/boader_defs.php.

Supreme Court of Canada: Official Decisions
http://scc.lexum.umontreal.ca/en/1997/1997rcs1-217/1997rcs1-217.html

The murder of Tracy Latimer
http://www.normemma.com/indxadvo.htm#Tracy

For Further Reading

Brower, M. C., & Price, B. H. (2001). Neuropsychiatry of frontal lobe dysfunction in violent and criminal behaviour: A critical review. *Journal of Neurology, Neuro-surgery, & Psychiatry, 71*(6), 720–726.

Emery, R. E., Otto, R. K., & O'Donohue, W. T. (2005). A critical assessment of child custody evaluations limited science and a flawed system. *Psycho-Logical Science in the Public Interest, 6*, 1.

Gosselin, D. (2005). *Heavy hands.* Upper Saddle River, NJ: Pearson Prentice-Hall.

Kosberg, J. I., & Garcia, J. L. (1995). *Confronting the Maltreatment of Elders by Their Family* Thousand Oaks, GA: Sage.

Rekers, G. (1995). *Susan Smith: Victim or Murderer* (pp. 144–146). Lakewood, CO: Glenbridge Publishing.

Rummel, R. J. (1997). *Death by government.* Piscataway, NJ: Transaction Publishers.

Seto, M. C. (2008). *Pedophilia and Sexual Offending Against Children.* Washington, DC: American Psychological Association.

CHAPTER **16**

Treatment and Rehabilitation in Forensic Psychology

CHAPTER OBJECTIVES

After reading this chapter you would:

- Understand the function of mental health courts.
- Know the functioning of alternative dispute resolution.
- Understand the various methods used for treatment of child abuse.
- Know the treatment methods available for child sexual abuse offenders.
- Understand the treatment techniques for domestic violence.
- Know the various modes of treatment available for post-traumatic stress disorder (PTSD) in prisons.
- Know the major treatment approaches for terrorism-induced psychological disturbances.
- Understand the methods for restoring competency to stand trial.

INTRODUCTION

In 2000 the *Washington Post* reported the story of Ellene Price, a homeless person who had been sleeping on the streets of Chicago for 28 consecutive days when she decided that she had had enough. But she knew that she could not return to a homeless shelter because she had been thrown out of several due to her strange behavior. And the mental hospital where she had been actively hallucinating discharged her after a week. With nowhere else to turn, and the weather turning cold, Price decided to get arrested so she could sleep indoors at the Cook County Jail.

To be arrested Price grabbed another woman by the neck and threw her to the ground. After pleading guilty to battery she was sentenced to a year in jail—thereby joining a quarter of a million mentally ill people incarcerated in the country's various prisons and jails. She saw jail as a relief: she had a clean uniform, three meals a day, a shower, and a roof over her head. In other words, "three hots and a cot." The Cook County Jail has become the county's largest institutionalized population of mentally ill people. And this statistic is slowly becoming the norm across the country.

Price served less than one-quarter of her sentence. Officials from Thresholds, a national psychiatric rehabilitation center based in Chicago, went to her sentencing judge and got her early release. As a member of the program, she received intensive one-on-one counseling as well as assistance in meeting her daily needs and help finding affordable housing. She was visited by

Thresholds staff members at least once a day and given her medication. She was helped with shopping and doing her laundry. She and other members went on group outings to the beach, baseball games, and restaurants. Caseworkers were on call 24 hours a day and would look for her or any member if necessary. The criminalization of people with mental illness is just one of the areas in which forensic psychology can have input.

People with mental illness frequently fall through the cracks of this country's social service and mental health systems and land instead in the criminal justice system. These individuals tend to be overlooked, turned away because of their symptoms, or intimidated. They end up disconnected from community supports and alone.

A 2003 report by the U.S. Department of Health and Human Services indicates that about 12 out of every 1,000 children are victims of maltreatment each year and that child-protective services agencies received about 2,672,000 reports of *possible* maltreatment in 2001 alone (APA, 2007). In another area, in 2001, more than half a million American women were victims of nonfatal violence committed by an intimate partner (Bureau of Justice Statistics, 2003). They accounted for 85% of intimate partner violence (588,490 total), and men accounted for approximately 15% of the victims (103,220 total). Women are five to eight times more likely than men to be victimized by an intimate partner, and such violence makes up 20% of all violent crimes against women. In a related area of social concern, at least one out of five adult women and one out of ten adult men report having been sexually abused as children. Lastly, the National Institute of Mental Health reports that approximately 3.6% of the adults in the United States between the ages of 18–54, or approximately 5.2 million people, have symptoms of PTSD during the course of any given year.

The field of forensic psychology offers therapeutic interventions, direct treatment, and rehabilitation services aimed at the amelioration of these problems as well as others. This chapter will review the use of mental health courts as a means of addressing the inordinately large number of mentally ill inmates in this county's prisons. We will also look at alternate dispute resolution as a viable solution to human conflict and disputes without the cost and emotional stress of litigation. Treatment techniques for domestic violence, child abuse, child sexual abuse, and terrorism-induced psychological disturbances will also be addressed. Finally, we will examine the psychological methods employed for restoration of competency to stand trial.

ALTERNATIVE INTERVENTIONS

Mental Health Courts

Contact with the criminal and juvenile justice systems can be doubly traumatic for people with mental illnesses, and the resulting criminal record can impede their later access to housing and mental health services. The increasing "criminalization" of the mentally ill is representative of the underlying issue of the need for basic services and supports that public systems have failed to deliver in meaningful ways. This concern has led a number of communities to establish some form of **mental health courts** to process criminal cases involving people with serious mental illnesses. These specialty courts strive to reduce the incarceration and recidivism of people with mental illness by linking them to the mental health services and supports that might have prevented their arrest in the first place.

Mental health courts straddle the worlds of criminal law, mental health, and psychology, requiring collaboration from practitioners in each field. There are today 25–30 of these courts, depending on the definition used, and more are being planned. In 2000, Congress passed the America's Law Enforcement and Mental Health Project Act, which makes federal funds available to local jurisdictions seeking to establish or expand mental health specialty courts and diversion programs. Such courts are designed to promote court-imposed treatment as a substitute for incarceration. They also have an obligation under the Americans with Disabilities Act (ADA) to accommodate individuals with mental illnesses.

Lawmakers have been concerned about the high percentage of jail and prison inmates who have mental illnesses, the incarceration of people with mental illnesses typically for much longer periods than other offenders, the fact that while incarcerated these inmates become especially vulnerable to assault and other forms of intimidation by other inmates, and the awareness that psychological and psychiatric treatment in prison is not successful in ameliorating the mental health conditions caused by incarceration itself. The Bureau of Justice Statistics reports that (1) approximately a quarter million individuals with severe mental illnesses are incarcerated at any given moment—about half arrested for nonviolent offenses, such as trespassing or disorderly conduct; (2) 16% of state and local inmates suffer from a mental illness and most receive no treatment beyond medication; and (3) during street encounters, police officers are almost twice as likely to arrest someone who appears to have a mental illness. A Chicago study of thousands of police encounters found that 47% of people with a mental illness were arrested, while only 28% of individuals without a mental illness were arrested for the same behavior.

Two rationales underlie the therapeutic court approach: to protect the public by addressing mental illness issues that contributed to criminal acts in the first place and to recognize that criminal sanctions alone have limited effectiveness on rehabilitation or punishment when mental illness is a significant cause of criminal activity. Therefore, the goals of mental health courts can be summarized as follows: (1) to break the cycle of mental deterioration and criminal behavior that begins with the failure of the community mental health system and (2) to provide effective treatment options instead of the usual criminal sanctions for offenders with mental illnesses.

According to the Bazelon Center, breaking the cycle of repeated contact with the criminal or juvenile justice systems must start with expanded and more focused community-based services and supports. Improving access to meaningful services and supports will inevitably reduce the number of incidents between individuals with mental illnesses and the law enforcement and justice systems. Furthermore, such access is critical to the effectiveness of any diversion program directed toward people who have mental illnesses, including mental health courts.

To reduce recurrent involvement with the criminal justice (arrests and repeated incarcerations) by individuals suffering from mental illness, communities across the country would benefit greatly by developing programs that create choices for diversion and alternative disposition. Effective police diversion programs that replace arrests for minor offenses with access to services and community supports are the first step in this constructive direction. Various effective strategies should also be put into place for mentally ill individuals who have committed more serious offenses. This should include reintegration programs back into the community following time served in jail or prison. One of the major roles of courts and the judiciary in these areas is to address the needs of those who cannot, because of the nature of their offense, be diverted to a community program without being arrested. Programs can be initiated at prebooking or arraignment for those individuals with mental illness for whom punishment through incarceration is not appropriate.

The use of mental health courts or their equivalent does not happen overnight. There are certain requirements that are important for their operation. These include (1) training in how to deal with the mentally ill for judges, prosecutors, and defense attorneys; (2) voluntary participation in transfer to a mental health court so as not to violate the equal protection clause of the Fourteenth and Sixth Amendments, which guarantee a trial by jury, or the requirement of the ADA; (3) permission of defendants to withdraw and have their cases heard in criminal court without prejudice; (4) the presence of a defense counsel who have a background in mental health issues; (5) the continuing jurisdiction over a defendant while the defendant is receiving therapeutic services; and (6) a service plan signed by the defendant detailing what action will be taken in response to failure to comply with its requirements.

Alternate Dispute Resolution

Alternative dispute resolution (ADL) refers to a variety of processes available for the resolution of disputes other than through traditional litigation. ADL differs fundamentally from the adversarial system in that it seeks a mutually satisfactory process rather than victory of one side over the other. There are numerous advantages of ADL, including speed of resolution, flexibility, increased responsiveness to personal issues, and less expense. The primary components of ADL include negotiation, mediation, and arbitration (Schneider, 2000).

Negotiation is also used to resolve disputes. **Mediation** is one form of negotiation that involves the use of a third party to facilitate reaching a settlement. **Arbitration**, on the other hand, is an adjudicatory process by which a third party decides the outcome of the dispute. For serious problems and psychological stressors faced by couples and others, mediation can rightly be referred to as a form of "treatment." Mediation can also provide the therapeutic benefits of face-to-face conversation between parties in a safe and controlled environment. Numerous studies have shown that participants are happier with the mediation process than with litigation (Guthrie & Levin, 1998). But the implementation of therapeutic jurisprudence techniques such as alternate dispute resolution, is fundamentally dependant upon efforts by law schools to teach these approaches.

TREATMENT

Treating Victims of Domestic Violence

The National Institute of Justice and the Centers for Disease Control and Prevention have found that women are more often the recipients of intimate partner violence than are men. Twenty-two percent of surveyed women versus seven percent of surveyed men reported in 1996 that they were physically assaulted by a current or former spouse, cohabiting partner, boyfriend or girlfriend, or date in their lifetime. Approximately 1.3 million women and 835,000 men are physically assaulted by an intimate partner annually in the United States (Tjaden & Thoennes, 2000).

A victim of physical or psychological abuse often experiences feelings of intimidation, loss of control, hopelessness, and recurrent and intrusive thoughts and psychological *reliving* of the abuse (Miller & Veltkamp, 1996). Yet a victim of prolonged abuse may unconsciously deny the abuse and refuse efforts to constructively respond to the situation. This often results in stagnation, feelings of entrapment, and *accommodation* to the abusive situation. Treatment of both the abused individual and the perpetrator is usually the most effective approach, and is likely to require a multidisciplinary team involvement. In physical and sexual abuse cases of children by a parent, it is often helpful to involve siblings, as they have often been exposed to the same family themes as the victim, and in many cases, the siblings may have been abused themselves. They may also feel guilty that they had not attempted to intervene and stop the abusive pattern (Miller & Veltkamp, 1989).

It is not uncommon for women (or men) to initially turn to informal help sources such as family and friends when there are issues of domestic violence. But more commonly they turn to formal sources such as the police, health care professionals, religious leaders, and the social service system (Sullivan, 2006). Community resources that could be helpful to victims and clinicians if available include safe-shelter environments and 24-hour crisis phone lines. The safe shelters should provide a place where victims can seek refuge from perpetrators, as well as participate in support groups and programs for children (Sullivan, 2006). The hotlines should be available anytime, day or night, for counseling, information, referrals, and screening to help find a safe environment.

Berk, Newton, and Berk (1986) reported that for women who were actively attempting other strategies at the same time, a stay at a shelter dramatically reduced the likelihood of further violence. But this is not universal. Although shelters receive high effectiveness ratings in general by their residents, not all women feel that shelters are options for them, and some are distrustful of the experiences they might have there. Lesbian women, for example, are much more likely to have negative shelter experiences and to believe that shelters are for heterosexual women only. Some women of color, regardless of sexual orientation, also hesitate to use shelters for various reasons. One of these reasons is that many shelters are staffed primarily by white women who may be unaware of or insensitive to the needs and issues of other cultures (Sullivan, 2006).

Batterers often use finances as a means of controlling their victims during and after the relationship. Some batterers deny their victims access to money or prevent them from working outside the home. Others harass their victims at work until they are fired, or they damage their homes, causing them to be evicted. One result of these tactics is that some battered women either have no credit or their credit is so badly marred that it represents too large a risk to landlords. As a result, these women are unable to obtain and keep permanent, affordable housing independent of their abusers. **Transitional housing programs** for survivors of domestic violence were designed to offer an important alternative to living with an abusive partner and are a resource for many battered women.

Women often turn to hospitals or health care providers for help with symptoms related to the stress of being abused by a partner. Researchers and practitioners have outlined interventions health care providers can implement to assist survivors of intimate partner violence. These interventions include providing emotional support and mental health counseling, safety planning, education, legal advise, referral to community services, and consistent documentation of abuse history (Campbell & Lewandowski, 1997).

Legal advocacy programs provide a legal advocate to act as a liaison between the victim of domestic violence, whether residing at a shelter or in the house, and the court system. Communities are encouraged to implement programs within police stations and prosecutors' offices to reach women in need of legal assistance. A novel strategy for providing free legal advocacy to survivors of intimate partner violence has been to locate such services within law schools. Over 40 law schools now have programs staffed primarily by law students working as legal advocates, and the number is growing. Utilizing law students not only increases the likelihood of survivors being paired with especially knowledgeable advocates but also serves to educate future lawyers about the many barriers facing battered women and men (Schneider, 2000).

Another intervention involves providing advocacy and support at the time the violence occurs in the form of a first response team, which can be, but does not necessarily need to be, housed within the criminal justice system. First response teams generally consist of trained advocates or social workers who either accompany police officers on domestic violence calls or are called to the scene after an arrest has been made.

Corcoran, Stephenson, Ferryman, and Allen (2001) surveyed 219 police officers in a locale that used a first response team; 79% of the officers found the team to be useful. Although a first response team can provide immeasurable assistance to women after the police have been called, such help is limited if the police, prosecutors, judges, and probation officers are not cooperative in holding perpetrators accountable for their behavior.

Finally, *Perpetrator's Counseling Programs* can provide perpetrators themselves with alternatives to physical, psychological, and other abusive behaviors that are often part of the profile. Most such programs that already exist comply with specific state standards, collaborate with victim service programs to insure victims' safety, and utilize well-established, usually cognitive–behavioral clinical regimens (Gondolf, 1991; Pence & Paymar, 1993). Most abusers in these programs have been mandated by the court.

Treating Perpetrators of Domestic Violence

Given the personality traits and behavioral attributes of perpetrators of domestic violence, the word "psychopath" is the diagnostic category that comes to mind. Psychopaths, or more accurately, individuals with **antisocial personality disorder** are generally described as showing a constellation of affective, interpersonal, and behavioral characteristics, including egocentricity; impulsivity; irresponsibility; shallow emotions; lack of empathy, guilt, or remorse; pathological lying; manipulativeness; and the persistent violation of social norms and expectations (Cleckley, 1988; Hare, 1996).

Psychopaths have traditionally been regarded as untreatable (Hare, 1996). And there is evidence to support this contention. Although psychopaths often volunteer for various prison treatment programs, and may even show "improvement," their goal is usually to impress therapists, prison officials, and parole boards that they are model prisoners and have changed for the better. Upon release, however, it usually does not take long for them to return to their old patterns of behavior. Rice et al. (1992) presented evidence suggesting, that psychopaths who participate in therapy are actually *more* likely to engage in violent crime following treatment than psychopaths who did not receive such treatment. Sherman (2000) reviewed a series of studies documenting programs that attempted to provide therapeutic interventions for antisocial personalities. One of the studies compared 176 criminals who participated in a "personality-disordered offenders program" and received intensive group and individual therapy, with 146 who were not treated. The rate of violent offending decreased in the nonpsychopaths receiving treatment, but increased among treated psychopaths when compared with psychopaths who received no treatment.

Another study of more than 300 offenders receiving social skills training and anger management therapy found that one-year reconviction rates were significantly higher in treated than in nontreated psychopaths. Yet another study found that the sex offenders most likely to reoffend were those with strong psychopathic tendencies who were rated as "good risks" by psychological personnel because of their "insight" into their problems. In other words, recidivism occurred most often in psychopaths who had the ability to convince their therapists they had made good progress in treatment, but in reality, therapy helped these individuals sharpen their skills at conning others (Hare, 1996).

Treating Victims of Violent Crime

Certain traumas do much more than injure us physically and even psychologically. They violate our very sense of safety, stability, and what theorists refer to as "ontological security." Ontological security is a stable mental state derived from a sense of continuity with regard to the events in one's life. It is a sense of order and absence of chaos and anxiety that gives meaning to a person's life. Events such as being the victim of a violent crime is not consistent with the meaning of an individual's life; this tends to threaten that individual's sense of ontological security.

More than traumas such as hurricanes, train accidents, and plane crashes, violence intentionally caused by other people and aimed directly at us, robs us of our sense that the world can ever be a safe place again. Victim services are helpful in this regard, are available in all 50 states, and are particularly useful for sexual assault victims, domestic violence victims, and children. One such victim service entity is the National Organization for Victim Assistance (NOVA), which has developed a generic model of victim services that contains three major components: (1) emergency response at the time of the crisis, (2) victim stabilization in the days following the trauma, and (3) resource mobilization in the aftermath of the crime (Young, 1988).

Miller (1998a) offers some very common sense suggestions for first responders who must deal with the victims of crime. The responder's first concern is to see that serious injuries get treated. It is vitally important that a first responder (police officer, fire fighter, crisis worker, medic, or mental health professional) introduce him/herself to the victim as well as bystanders. Regardless of any uniform that the first responder may be wearing, it may be necessary to repeat the introduction several times. The victim should be heard by the first responder in an understanding, sympathetic, and nonjudgmental fashion. There is no need to press for details regarding the crime as there will be sufficient time for this later by local or federal authorities. Instilling a sense of safety, comfort, and trust is much more important at this point.

The importance of trauma counseling and psychological intervention cannot be overstated. Kilpatrick et al. (1998) reported that 19% of rape victims attempt suicide, 44% report suicidal ideation, and 16% say that they had "a nervous breakdown" following the rape. But the degree of susceptibility to developing actual stress-related disorders such as PTSD varies from person to person and seems to depend on psychological, social, demographic, and environmental factors. Demographic factors include ethnic background, religious beliefs, socioeconomic status, gender, age, and most importantly, the presence of supportive relationships. Psychological factors include coping mechanisms, self-confidence and self-esteem, emotional stability, and resiliency. Environmental factors include the degree of violence involved in the incident and the location of the crime or attack. For example, victims who are attacked in an environment they had formerly perceived as being "safe" tend to experience more negative reactions than those attacked in "unsafe" locations (Markesteyn, 1992).

The psychological reactions to violent crime can include minor sleep disturbances, irritability and worry, depression, anxiety disorders, alcohol and drug abuse, suicidal thoughts and attempts, and PTSD. PTSD symptoms include intense fear, feelings of helplessness or horror, agitation, persistent reexperiencing of the traumatic event in the form of flashbacks, increased arousal, avoidance of stimuli associated with the trauma, emotional numbing, and clinically significant distress or impairment in social, occupational, or other important areas of functioning (American Psychiatric Association, 2000, p. 463). Most of the research on PTSD indicates that treatment is most effective when begun soon after the traumatic event and should consist of some combination of pharmacotherapy and cognitive behavioral therapy. But it is important for PTSD survivors to know that recovery is still possible even if treatment is not received immediately (McCann & Pearlman, 1990; Shalev, 1996, 2007).

Although it may not always be a comfortable experience, psychotherapy for PTSD often involves facing the memories and images of trauma head on. For example, Miller (1998b) points out that there is a time in the treatment of the PTSD patient where the psychologist must take the patient back to the original traumatic event and have him/her discuss it in step-by-step detail. The goal, according to Miller, is to "counteract maladaptive avoidance tendencies and to diminish the chance that they will congeal into longstanding patterns of behavior" (p. 33). Miller cautions, however, that sometimes it is necessary to work through the patient's other "peripheral issues" before the traumatic event can be adequately explored (Miller, 1998b; McCann & Pearlman, 1990). Therapy should increase adaptive defense mechanisms and allow a patient to reenter normal life and reassume normal social roles with the understanding that problems along the way are not signs of regression but merely necessary bumps in the road to recovery (Miller, 1998b).

For victims of violent crimes who decide to press charges and testify in court, the recovery process from PTSD can seem even longer than with noncriminal traumatic events, or where no charges are pressed. This is because of the time it takes for the criminal justice system to run its course, cross-examinations by defense counsel, et cetera. Studies have shown, for example, that the prevalence of PTSD is higher among victims who wade through the criminal justice system than among crime victims in general (Freedy et al., 1994). But if the decision has been made to proceed through the criminal justice system, it may be somewhat therapeutic for victims of violent crimes to file a request for *restitution* as part of the sentence as well as a *victim impact statement*. The assistance of a mental health professional during these times to help prevent a replay of the original traumatizing effects is highly recommended (Miller, 1998a, 1998b).

Treating Child Abuse Offenders

When reviewing the psychological literature on evidence-based interventions for stopping child abuse, one of the most common treatment approaches of parents who physically abuse their children was found to be psychoeducational in nature (Chaffin & Schmidt, 2006). Parenting classes, or parent support groups, are psychoeducational groups that help teach parents nonphysical behavior management techniques. Such groups have been found to be helpful in teaching anger management and alternative methods of discipline (Wolfe, 1993, 1994; Wolfe, Wekerle, & McGee, 1992). Often, in these parenting classes, parents are presented with educational materials, and there is group discussion about parenting practices. This often results in an increase in knowledge of alternatives to physical punishment and knowledge of normal child development (Hughes & Wilson, 1988). As previously mentioned, anger management therapy has been found to be particularly beneficial for parents who have physically abused their children (Golub, Espinosa, Damon, & Card, 1987).

Parent–child interaction therapy (PCIT) is a coached behavioral parent training protocol that trains parents on criteria of specific behavioral parenting skills using live sessions. PCIT teaches skills such as use of praise and reflection, and a specific timeout protocol for compliance training. Controlled studies have shown that PCIT is highly effective in decreasing child behavior problems, that treatment effects generalize to nontreated siblings and to other environmental settings, and that improvements are maintained over time (Eisenstadt et al., 1993; McNeil et al., 1991).

Cognitive–behavioral therapy (CBT) and family therapy (FT) approaches have also been used for physically abusive parents. CBT addresses such things as views on violence and physical punishment, parents' attributional style and expectations, self-management, and child behavior management skills. FT focuses on parent–child interactions and the teaching of parent–child problem-solving routines. On the basis of children's reports, studies have shown that families utilizing FT and CBT protocols had less parent-to-child violence than families receiving routine community services across measures. But some researchers report that the effectiveness of these programs is very limited except when they are reinforced by structured home visits (Cohn & Daro, 1987). These models utilize volunteers as well as professionals to provide case management, referral services, and social support directly in the home. They also include family support programs, parenting classes, informational programs, case management programs, mutual aid programs, parent–infant nurturing programs, and programs for teen mothers.

Treating Child Sexual Abuse Offenders

As discussed in the chapter on forensic psychology applied to children and families, child sexual abuse is the exploitation of a child or adolescent for another person's sexual and control gratification (Whitcomb, Hook, & Alexander, 2000). Sexual abuse in childhood produces long-term psychological problems. These include severe depression, guilt, substance abuse, anxiety, sleep problems, fears and phobias, and even suicide. Children often feel responsible for the abuse they experienced, especially if no obvious force was used by the adult.

In the 1950s treatment for child sexual abuse was essentially the same as treatment for the paraphilias such as fetishism. The treatment of choice was in the form of aversive conditioning (Seto, 2008). Using a classical counterconditioning paradigm, these techniques include the pairing of noxious stimuli such as mild electric shock or ammonia odors with repeated presentations of sexual stimuli depicting children. These examples utilize **overt sensitization** where the aversive stimuli is applied *in vivo* or in real life. A variation of this procedure is called **covert sensitization** in which the aversive stimulus is imagined by the subject *in vitro*. For example, the subject may be asked to imagine being discovered by family members while engaging in sexual behavior involving children.

Using the behavioral technique of *satiation*, the treatment participant masturbates to ejaculation while verbalizing aloud variations of his pedophilic fantasies. After ejaculating, and throughout the refractory period, he is instructed to continue masturbating to the same fantasies over several long sessions. Masturbatory reconditioning involves associating sexual arousal with adults.

In the techniques of *thematic shift*, the participant masturbates to a pedophilic sexual fantasy until the point of orgasm, then switches to a sexual fantasy about an adult. The research suggests that these kinds of behavioral techniques can have an effect on changing sexual arousal patterns, but it is less clear how long these changes are maintained (Barbaree, Bogaert, & Seto, 1995; Barbaree & Seto, 1997).

The method most often used to determine whether a particular treatment modality for child sexual abuse is successful is the measure of **recidivism**. Recidivism is considered the best measure of treatment efficacy since the primary goal of sex-offender treatment is the reduction of future victimization (Prentky & Burgess, 1990). There is some research to suggest that treatment does indeed reduce recidivism among sex offenders. Marshall, Fernandez, Hudson, & Ward (1998) reviewed data from over 30 sex-offender treatment programs in different settings and for different offender populations worldwide. They concluded that despite the diversity of settings and clients, most programs operate from a cognitive–behavioral perspective and include relapse prevention as the connective theme running throughout the various treatment components.

Most cognitive–behavioral programs begin with the requirement that participants acknowledge at least some portion of their offense. But intervention also includes activities to increase victim empathy, change distorted thinking patterns such as justifications and minimizations, improve social skills, teach self-control, and develop lifelong self-management strategies. Treatment also may include behavioral interventions to reduce deviant sexual arousal. Patients develop detailed plans for avoiding behavioral relapse and managing potentially risky situations and urges.

McGrath, Cumming, Livingston, and Hoke (2003) examined the recidivism rates of 195 adult male sex offenders who were referred to a prison-based cognitive–behavioral treatment program. Out of this sample, 56 of the offenders completed treatment, 49 entered treatment but did not complete, and 90 refused treatment services. After approximately six years, the sexual reoffense rate for the completed treatment sample was 5.4% as compared with 30.6% for the partial treatment, and 30% for the no-treatment groups. Those participants who had aftercare treatment and correctional supervision services in the community had even lower recidivism rates. In a comprehensive study on the effectiveness of sex-offender treatment, Alexander (1997) conducted a meta-analysis of 81 sex-offender treatment studies involving 11,350 subjects. The results overwhelmingly showed that sex offenders who received treatment while in prison had a lower rate of recidivism than those offenders who did not receive treatment. Among the sex offenders who received treatment in prison, 9.4% reoffended, whereas those offenders who did not receive treatment had a reoffense rate of 17.6%.

More recently, Laws (2003) has indicated that the relapse-prevention model incorporated in cognitive–behavioral sex-offender treatment is not well suited to some types of sex offenders. Cognitive–behavioral sex-offender treatment operates under the uncertain assumption, according to Laws that there is only a single model of relapse, relapse is usually triggered by negative emotions or events, that all offenders are attempting to avoid offending, and that offending was the result of skills deficits. Ward and Hudson (1998, 2000) presented a self-regulation model for relapse prevention in sex offenders that took into account the individual differences in offenders; for example, some offenders are not triggered by a negative event, but rather plan and seek out offensive sex. Some offenders are not affected or influenced by a lack of social skills, and this would therefore not be an appropriate focus of their sex-offender treatment program. Regardless of the relapse prevention model utilized, a cognitive-behavioral approach addressing cognitive distortions, victim empathy, and deviant sexual arousal are still critical components of almost any sex-offender treatment.

Drug treatments and medical interventions have also been attempted to reduce sexual behavior directed toward children by targeting the hormones or neurotransmitters underlying sexual drive, arousal, and sexual response. **Antiandrogens** interfere with the action of testosterone. The most commonly prescribed medications are cyproterone acetate (CPA) and edroxyprogesterone acetate (**DepoProvera**). The former is not approved for use in the United States, while the latter is. But neither drug is specifically approved by regulatory bodies. Gijs and Gooren (1996) reviewed the literature evaluating the effects of CPA and DepoProvera, focusing on methodologically strong studies, that is, those using double-blind procedures, placebo conditions, and random assignments. They identified four controlled studies of CPA and six such studies of DepoProvera. All four studies of CPA reported that treated men had a significant reduction in sexual response, whereas only one of the six DepoProvera studies showed an effect. Cooper, Sandhu, Losztyn, and Cernovsky (1992) tested both DepoProvera and CPA over 28 weeks. Both drugs appeared to reduce sexual thoughts, fantasies, and behavior (frequency of masturbation and frequency of erections on awakening), and there also appeared to be an effect on penile responding, assessed phallometrically (the measurement of changes in penile circumference).

Central hormonal agents such as the Gonadotropin releasing hormone (GnRH), which inhibit the production of testosterone by overriding pituitary regulation, have shown some success in decreasing sexual thoughts and behavior. Similar results have been found using carbamazepine (an anticonvulsant and mood stabilizing drug used primarily in the treatment of epilepsy and bipolar disorder) and clonazepam (a benzodiazepine used in the treatment of anxiety) (Varela & Black, 2002).

Surgical castration permanently reduces sexual response by removal of the testes. This results in the near complete elimination of the production of androgens (the adrenal glands produce a small amount). Although it is rarely performed now, surgical castration was performed on hundreds of convicted sex offenders in the Netherlands and in Germany in the past (Wille & Beier, 1989). It continues to be performed occasionally in Germany, the Czech Republic, and Switzerland. Surgical castration is an option for some sex offenders in the United States, with the passage of legislation in nine states since 1996 requiring chemical (antiandrogen) or surgical castration for sex offenders who want to be paroled and released into the community. Physical castration is permitted as an alternative to antiandrogens in four states, and it is the only option available in Texas. Five states permit castration only for offenders against victims under 13 or 14 years of age (Seto, 2008). The procedure does appear to be effective at reducing sexual desire and the chances of reoffending (Hansen & Lykke-Olsen, 1997; Wille & Beier, 1989).

Treatment of Post-traumatic Stress Disorder—in Prison

Rates of PTSD are particularly high in prison inmates. Gibson et al. (1999) report the rate of PTSD among male inmates to be 21%. Zlotnick (1997) reports a 48% occurrence among female inmates, and Ovaert, Cashel, and Sewell (2003) have found a rate as high as 65% for male juvenile offenders. Treatment modalities for inmates generally fall into one of three areas: exposure and desensitization, cognitive and cognitive–behavioral, and skills based.

Exposure and Desensitization Treatments

Eye movement desensitization and reprocessing (EMDR) was introduced in1989 by Shapiro as a treatment for trauma-related disorders, specifically PTSD. EMDR is an exposure treatment that involves cognitive restructuring. Two main distinguishing factors of EMDR are short exposure times and eye movements. Clients simultaneously focus on both the traumatic material (exposure) and an external stimulus using saccadic (quick movements) of the eye alternating bilateral stimulation (e.g., following the therapist's hand movements from side-to-side with the eyes). They are also taught to identify and cognitively restructure problematic beliefs related to the traumatic event(s) in order to process the traumatic affect and produce more adaptive thinking. These procedures are repeated until there is a low level of distress associated with remembering the traumatic event. A meta-analysis reported by Davidson and Parker in 2001 found EMDR to be more efficacious in treating PTSD than nonexposure treatments or no treatment conditions and to be equally as effective as other exposure treatments.

Automatic Incident Reduction

Another exposure approach that has been studied in the correctional setting is automatic incident reduction (TIR), first introduced by Gerbode in 1984. TIR is a sensitization procedure using repetitive guided imagery of the traumatic event. The session ends when the client no longer experiences stress associated with the trauma, and cognitive distortions have been restructured (Gerbode, 1989). According to the theory underlying TIR, once the specific trauma is processed, symptoms are assumed to resolve. Valentine and Smith (2001) examined the clinical efficacy of TIR for reducing the symptoms of trauma in 123 female prisoners who had experienced interpersonal violence. The intervention condition included a pretest, a joining session, a 3–4 hour TIR session, an exit interview and debriefing followed by a post-test, and then a three-month follow-up. The results indicated a decrease in depression, anxiety, avoidance, and intrusive thoughts.

Cognitive Treatments

A study using cognitive–behavioral and expressive therapies (CBET) for male juveniles with PTSD consisted of check-in, psychoeducation, relaxation training, and trauma-related art therapy (McMackin, Leisen, Cusack, LaFratta, & Litwin, 2002). In addition to participant satisfaction, individual therapists reported that participants openly discussed their feelings in individual therapy and improved their understanding of how trauma resulted from their offending. Participants who received relaxation training also reported improved coping skills, sleeping, and anger management. This type of treatment has also been found to be effective in treating rape victims in the community (Resick & Schnicke, 1992, 1993).

Skills-Based Approaches

Najavitis et al., (1998) developed an integrated therapeutic approach emphasizing self-control strategies called "seeking safety." Zlotnick, Najavitis, Rohsenow, and Johnson (2003) performed an uncontrolled study of seeking safety with 18 incarcerated women who were enrolled in a residential substance abuse treatment program in a prison's minimum security wing. The women attended an average of 14, 90-minute group sessions (range 6–24 sessions) over 12 weeks. There was a significant decrease in their PTSD symptoms from pre- to post-treatment as measured by a clinician-administered PTSD Scale.

Heckman et al., (2007) describes another skills-based intervention utilized by Salerno (2005) with six female prisoners with PTSD. The intervention consisted of 10, 2-hour sessions that occurred weekly and focused on the development and practice of a variety of cognitive–behavioral skills as well as hypnotic skills such as relaxation, safe place, containment, affect modulation, age progression and regression. Outcomes included participant and facilitator impressions: group cohesion, comfort in sharing personal experiences, active demonstration of coping and conflict-resolution skills, and rating the group as more useful, innovative, stimulating, and meaningful than other groups (Salerno, 2005).

TERRORISM-INDUCED PSYCHOLOGICAL DISTURBANCES

Only in the last 20 years has terrorism become a significant fact of life for Americans. Accordingly, the body of clinical psychological literature on terrorism has lagged behind that of other types of traumatic events. Unfortunately, these events have been increasing in frequency, and many experts maintain that the worst is yet to come.

Terroristic attacks, such as those on Oklahoma City and the World Trade Center, combine features of a criminal assault, a disaster, and an act of war (Hills, 2002). Accordingly, many of the treatment approaches combine what we know from treating victims of criminal assault, grief, natural and manmade disasters, riots, war, workplace violence, and school shootings (Miller, 2002a, 2002b, 2002c).

The most distressing effect on survivors of terrorist attacks is the shattering of their fundamental beliefs about themselves (e.g., invulnerability and immortality); the world (e.g., predictability, controllability, safety); and other people (e.g., trust, safety, and isolation) that had previously shaped their lives. Many survivors feel isolated from other people who could not possibly understand what they had gone through. Concerns about death and questions about the meaning and purpose of their lives may haunt them (Difede et al., 1997).

A study cited by Miller (2002a) of the more devastating 2001 World Trade Center attack found that 11% of all New Yorkers showed symptoms of PTSD two months following the incident, which is almost three times the national average. An additional finding was that the degree of PTSD distress was most strongly related to the amount of TV coverage watched. This suggests that potentially vulnerable victims may have attempted to use information gathering via television as a coping mechanism but instead ended up retraumatizing themselves.

Following a terror attack many survivors experience a type of "pan phobia" accompanied by a heightened sense of vulnerability and an avoidance of anything related to the trauma. Survivors may have frequent nightmares of the imagined horrifying death of a victim they have known, or wish-fulfillment fantasies of rescuing the victim. Their grief may be compounded by guilt if they feel they should have foreseen the attack or done more to keep their loved one safe (Miller, 2002a; Ressler et al., 1988; Sprang & McNeil, 1995).

Immediate Psychological Interventions

As with other violent crimes, the first responder on the scene of a terrorist attack may be a police officer, emergency medical technician, firefighter, or mental health crisis counselor. Miller (2002) recommends that such people should obtain as much information as possible from the victim about the terrorist crime itself and begin a plan for aiding other potential victims. Collaborative work with other first responders is essential to ensure that investigators obtain valuable data while victims receive optimal care. First responders should avoid empty statements such as "Everything will be all right" and instead offer more concrete and realistic information such as "We're going to take you to a safe hospital." A victim's wishes should be accommodated as much as reasonably possible, if, for example, the victim wants a family member or friend to remain during treatment or questioning. Victims should be allowed to talk and express their emotions even if they may seem somewhat digressive or rambling. First responders should provide basic, understandable education about the onset and course of possible post-traumatic symptoms, and attempt to normalize the traumatic stress experience while discouraging a sense of an inevitable severe stress-related disability to come.

Outreach programs in the community should be identified, around which psychological care can be organized. Identifying high-risk groups is one of the most important aspects of any disaster consultation (Ursano, Fullerton, & Norwood, 1995). If possible, help to identify the remains of loved ones. Although this may shatter any hope that he/she may still be alive, the actual sight of the deceased often provides a strange sort of reassuring confirmation that the victim's death agonies may have fallen short of the survivor's imagined horrors, and even if not, that the physical presence of the body at least means that the victim's suffering is finally over (Rynearson, 1996). Outcome studies of mourners of a death from natural causes report shorter periods of denial and higher total recall of the deceased in those who were able to view the body prior to burial (Sprang & McNeil, 1995). When no definitive remains are found, symbolic remains may serve as a surrogate. For example, an urn of ashes from Ground Zero was offered by the city of New York to each family of a missing person (Miller, 2002a).

Individual Psychotherapy

Sprang and McNeil (1995) have presented a phased treatment model originally designed for survivors of murder victims that can productively be applied to the treatment of survivors of terrorist homicide.

An initial evaluation and debriefing phase occurs immediately following the traumatic event and focuses on crisis intervention and stabilization of the individual's emotional, social, and physical environment. At this stage, the individual's defenses should not be challenged. Instead, the intervention should include empathic support, validation, and normalization of the patient's reaction to the traumatic loss. Survivors should be prepared for the emotional, financial, practical, and social losses that follow the terrorist killing of a family member. Therapists should encourage a graded and dosed ventilation of emotion and provide necessary support.

Then, therapists should gradually begin to educate family members as to what they can expect and try to dispel unrealistic expectations. Other aspects of this educative process include providing concrete information about such victim resources as the Red Cross, National Organization for Victim Assistance, Crime Victims Compensation Fund, employee assistance programs, and so on. At each step, the therapist should monitor patients' reactions to avoid overwhelming them with too much information too quickly. When trust and therapeutic rapport have developed, relaxation training, biofeedback, desensitization, and cognitive–behavioral techniques can be applied for symptom management. Opportunities should be provided, arranged, or planned for patients to take back some control of their lives, for example, by helping and educating other victims or running support groups.

The patient should be helped to reduce self-blame through the use of cognitive or existential therapeutic approaches. Psychological mastery over the traumatic bereavement can be encouraged by asking patients to describe the future: "If you were not struggling with your grief anymore, what would you be doing?" A related process involves helping the patient say a psychological goodbye to the slain loved one, realizing that there will always be painful memories but that the survivors have a right to continue their own lives.

A productive therapeutic approach involves validating the survivors' pain while supporting their strengths and helping them to live as normalized a life as possible, albeit a life that will be radically different from the one they led before. For such patients, Spungen (1998) recommends that they keep a daily diary or journal and write down their thoughts and feelings about the murder or terror attack and about their deceased loved one. This notebook should be portable enough to carry around so that patients can jot down their thoughts as they occur. Another suggestion is to tape record thoughts into a portable recorder; these can later be transcribed, if desired. Even if the survivor never reads the diary again, the act of writing itself can be therapeutic; clinicians will recognize this as the technique of *journaling* or *narrative therapy*. Spungen has found that some individuals may create several volumes of such notes before they realize they have made progress. The only caveat is that this exercise should not become a prolonged obsessive preoccupation to the exclusion of other therapeutic strategies and participation in life generally.

By simply asking what the victim saw, heard, felt, touched, or tasted, the clinician opens additional channels of information and facilitates additional narrative working-through. Hanscom (2001) described a treatment model that emerged from her work with survivors of torture and that may be applied to victims of terrorism, especially incidents involving abduction, hostage taking, and abuse. In this model, an essential condition of healing of torture and trauma survivors is the reestablishment of the experience of trust, safety, and the ability to have an effect on the world. This relearning relies less on particular therapeutic techniques and procedures than on the compassionate human interaction and therapeutic alliance between the survivor and a counselor who is willing and able to listen effectively.

A **"HEARTS" model** to deal with the aftermath of terror has been suggested by Miller (2002a, 2002b;), Hanscom (2001), and others. HEARTS is an acronym for:

H = *Listening to the* **history**. This includes providing a gentle environment, listening with body language, attending the flow of speech, hearing the voice and tone of the speaker, observing the speaker's movements and reactions, looking at facial expressions, remaining quietly patient, and listening compassionately. Clinicians will recognize this as a basic description of *active listening*.

E = *Focusing on* **emotions** *and reactions*. This involves using reflective listening, asking gentle questions, and naming the emotions.

A = **Asking** *about symptoms*. This involves using one's personal and therapeutic style to investigate current physical symptoms, current psychological symptoms, and suicidal tendencies.

R = *Explaining the* **reason** *for symptoms*. This includes showing how the symptoms fit together, describing how the body reacts to stress and trauma, explaining the interaction between the body and mind, and emphasizing that these are normal symptoms that normal people have to a very abnormal event.

T = **Teaching** *relaxation and coping skills*. This involves instructing the patient in relaxation skills, such as abdominal breathing, meditation, prayer, imagery, visualization, and others, and discussing coping strategies (e.g., recognizing how they have coped in the past, reinforcing old and healthy strategies, and teaching new coping skills).

S = *Helping with* **self-change**. This involves discussing the person's world view—the original view and any changes, adaptations, or similarities—and recognizing the positive changes in the self.

Family Therapy

Whether it is a single family member who is hurt or killed in a terrorist attack, or a mass terrorist casualty incident where hundreds of families are killed, injured, or displaced, family members can act as both exacerbating and mitigating factors to one another in their efforts to cope with trauma. Accordingly, a key therapeutic task often involves turning vicious cycles of recrimination and despair into positive cycles of support and hope.

Family therapists have long recognized that the effects of successive traumas are often cumulative (Alarcon, 1999; Catherall, 1998; Figley, 1998). Accordingly, therapy for terrorist bereavement may have to deal with unresolved traumatic material from the past, which will almost certainly be reevoked by the more recent trauma of the murder. In addition, other aspects of life cannot automatically be put on hold when the death occurs, so therapy must address coexisting issues such as school and job problems, marital conflict, substance abuse, or other preexisting family stresses.

Therapists should inquire about individual family members' private perceptions of death. Nihilism and despair are common early responses, and helping patients and families to recover or develop sustaining spiritual or philosophical beliefs or actions can buffer the destabilizing and disintegratory effects of the murder. Therapeutic measures may involve exploring the family members' concepts of life and death, as well as encouraging both private meditative and socially committed activities, such as support groups or political or religious antiterrorism activities (Rynearson, 1996). Many Oklahoma City and World Trade Center survivors started or joined various charitable or social service foundations as a way of memorializing their slain loved ones.

Pictures and other mementos of the deceased family member can serve as comforting images for survivors. In looking at family picture albums together, therapists and survivors can bring up positive imagery that may counterbalance the grotesque recollections of the terror attack. Similar memorializing activities include writing about the deceased or creating a scrapbook, but as previously cautioned, these activities should never be part of an unhealthy obsessive preoccupation (Spungen, 1998).

Community Responses

By definition, mass-casualty terrorist disasters are community events, and there is much that community leaders can do to offer support and increase therapeutic and social morale. Commendations and awards to professional first responders, volunteer rescue workers, service providers, and others who have distinguished themselves are important components of the community recovery process. Memorials to the victims of the terrorist disaster are part of the healing process and should be encouraged. Leaders are powerful symbols in and of themselves. Local and regional leaders should be encouraged to set an example of expressing their own grief in a healthy and mature way, to lead the community in recognizing the appropriateness of constructive mourning (Ursano, Fullerton, & Norwood, 1995).

STRESS ASSOCIATED WITH MILITARY DEPLOYMENT

According to a recent report by the American Psychological Association (APA), deployment can be a complex and overwhelming process. Deployment means extended separations and the uncertainty of having a loved one in a combat zone. The situation creates an environment in which the development of significant emotional problems for military personnel and their families is a real possibility (APA, 2007).

According to the APA report, military personnel and their families are reporting increasingly high levels of emotional problems resulting from deployment stress, and more than 30% of all soldiers meet the criteria for a mental disorder but less than half (23–40%) of those with mental health concerns actually seek help.

There are certain risk factors that seem to exacerbate stress on military personnel and their families. These include families with a preexisting history of problems, young families experiencing their first military separation, and families who recently moved to a new duty station. Additionally, families with foreign-born spouses, service members without a unit affiliation or those serving in the National Guard or Reserves are more likely to experience higher stress levels.

The APA report also identified serious barriers to accessing quality mental health care for military personnel and their families. A 40% vacancy rate of active duty psychologists contributes to the increased stress and diminished morale among the other mental health and medical providers in the military care system. This shortage leads to high attrition rates for psychologists and necessitates an overflow of referrals to civilian psychologists who may not have as much training as military psychologists on issues related to the military and deployment.

Long waiting lists for mental health and medical care and limited clinic hours at hard-to-reach locations also make it difficult for returning military personnel and their families to get help. Further, according to the report, stigma and negative attitudes within the military about obtaining mental health treatment often prevent those in need of care from seeking it. Children of military families are also dealing with the effects of deployment. Currently, 700,000 children in the United States have at least one parent deployed overseas for military duty. Having a child's primary caretaker in a war zone can be one of the most stressful events a child can experience.

To help reduce the stressful impact of military deployment on families, certain preventive actions can be taken. These include (1) educating military leadership about the importance of mental health issues on active duty personnel and their dependants; (2) taking measures to reduce the stigma often associated with seeking mental health services, such as by making certain mental health services mandatory upon return from military combat to screen for PTSD, traumatic brain injuries, and similar conditions; (3) undertake more research on mental health issues related to deployment policies and treatment plans for service members and their families; and (4) increase recruitment efforts to attract and retain qualified psychologists (APA, 2007).

Is Psychotherapy Useful in Treating Post-traumatic Stress Disorder in the Early Stages?

Shalev (2007)

A research team headed by Dr. Arieh Shalev, chair of the Department of Psychiatry and founding director of the Center for Traumatic Stress at Hadassah University Hospital in Jerusalem, performed a study to assess whether survivors of a psychologically traumatic event improved significantly with psychotherapy during the early stages of the traumatic event and to determine which forms of treatment given soon after the traumatic event can prevent the development of chronic PTSD.

The researchers studied 248 adults with early symptoms of **post-traumatic stress disorder (PTSD)** following a traumatic event that had occurred no more than four weeks earlier. From a diagnostic point of view, PTSD cannot be diagnosed until four weeks after the precipitating event, however, by ameliorating these symptoms prior to the end of this four week period, subsequent PTSD or other trauma-related disorders may be prevented.

Patients were treated for 12 weeks with cognitive therapy (techniques that help change harmful ways of thinking), cognitive behavioral therapy (techniques that help alter ways of interpreting events, in addition to desensitizing their reactions to traumatic memories), antidepressant medication (selective serotonin reuptake inhibitors or "SSRI"), all known to be helpful in treating chronic PTSD, a placebo, or no intervention.

The results indicated that patients receiving cognitive therapy and cognitive–behavioral therapy showed significantly less severe symptoms at the end of three months than patients who were receiving medication, placebo, or no treatment. The researchers noted that other studies have indicated that both cognitive–behavioral therapy and medication, or a combination of each, can be effective for PTSD in the first three months, and therefore the effectiveness of pharmacological interventions for early treatment of PTSD should continue. It is important, note the researchers, that PTSD survivors know that recovery is still possible even if treatment is not received immediately. However, it is best for survivors to be treated as early as possible.

RESTORING PSYCHOLOGICAL COMPETENCY

Polling of directors of forensic facilities throughout the United States indicate that less than half of their patients who had been adjudicated incompetent to stand trial were provided treatment differing from other patients in the facility (Siegel & Elwork, 1990). There is data to suggest, however, that this may be changing. Restoration based on educational programs is more commonly encountered now than it was previously, and clinicians have been increasingly attending to specific competence restoration interventions for persons committed to their facilities as incompetent to stand trial (Pinals, 2005).

One of the programs for defendants judged incompetent to stand trial that has been growing in use utilizes actual models of courtrooms and competence-based problem-solving instruction. Such regimens have met with some success. Bertman et al. (2003) found substantial improvement utilizing a treatment protocol that educated incompetent defendants on their individualized legal rights, such as the meaning of the charges against them and the potential consequences related to their alleged offenses. The authors concluded that such "individualized treatment" combined with group treatment may be useful in the restoration process.

Mental retardation can also be a significant factor in judicial findings of incompetence to stand trial (Golding, 1992). Mental retardation is manifested by low intellectual abilities and impairment in functioning in major areas of life (such as communication, self-care, interpersonal skills, health, and safety). According to one review, 6% of adult defendants in studies comparing competent and incompetent defendants were diagnosed as mentally retarded (Nicholson & Kugler, 1991). Another study found mental retardation as the clinical factor at hand in 16% of cases involving a clinical opinion that a defendant was incompetent to stand trial (Warren et al., 1991). Persons with mental illness may also have mental retardation and vice versa, but they do not always coexist. Accordingly, mental retardation or mental illness alone, or a combination of both, may be at issue for any given incompetent defendant.

In *Sell v. United States* (2003), the Supreme Court ruled that *forced medication* for incompetent defendants to restore their competence could be permitted, but only in limited circumstances. Medication is certainly a key component of restoration, but courts have still been concerned about the impact of forced medication on the legal best interests of individual defendants.

Pinals (2005) thoughtfully points out that from a policy standpoint, without restoration efforts for mentally disordered offenders, the question of "warehousing" untreated individuals could become a significant concern. Indeed, if very large numbers of mentally disordered defendants can avoid trial (and thus legal culpability) by virtue of having a mental disability that is not being addressed or treated, society would fail at integrating them into the social requirements of other citizens. This unfortunate consequence can be avoided to a great extent if ongoing efforts are made to accurately assess defendants' capacities, rather than simply presuming incompetence based on the presence of a mental disorder (Geller & Appelbaum, 1985; Ladds & Convit, 1994).

FORENSIC PSYCHOLOGY IN THE SPOTLIGHT

Can Trauma have Long-Term Effects on the Brains of Healthy Individuals?

Ganzel et al. (2007)

Twenty-two healthy adults viewed fearful and calm faces while undergoing functional magnetic resonance imaging (fMRI) to measure their bilateral amygdala activity (the brain structure which indicates emotional intensity, and forms and stores emotional memories) between three and half and four years after September 11, 2001.

All of the participants had some level of exposure to the events of September 11. The authors wanted to determine whether close physical proximity to a traumatic event—in this case the World Trade Center attack—sensitized parts of the brain to emotional stimuli 41 and 48 months after the terrorist attacks. Eleven of the participants were within 1.5 miles of the World Trade Center on September 11, 2001. The control group—those participants living at least 200 miles from New York on 9/11/01—subsequently moved to the New York metropolitan area at the time of the MRI scanning.

Results indicated that participants who were within 1.5 miles of the World Trade Center on 9/11 had significantly higher bilateral amygdala activity to fearful versus calm faces compared with those who were living more than 200 miles away. These results suggest that exposure to traumatic events in the past was associated with emotional responses several years later in people who were close to the initial trauma. Yet, the participants did not meet the criteria for a diagnosis of PTSD, depression, or anxiety at

time of imaging. All the participants were screened for psychiatric, medical, and neurological illnesses.

This finding suggests that a heightened amygdala reactivity following high-intensity trauma exposure may be slow to recover and can be responsible for heightened reactions to everyday emotional stimuli. Furthermore, the group closest to the World Trade Center on 9/11 reported more current symptoms and more symptoms at the time of the trauma than the group living further from ground zero on 9/11. These symptoms included increased "arousal" (e.g., difficulty sleeping, irritability, hypervigilance); "avoidance" (e.g., not wanting to go downtown when they used to enjoy doing so); and "intrusion" (e.g., recurrent and distressing memories or dreams). Furthermore, those who reported 9/11 as the worst and most intense trauma experienced in their life time also had more brain activity when viewing fearful faces.

The researchers point out that there may be long-term neurobiological correlates of trauma exposure, even in people who appear resilient. Since these effects were observable using mild, standardized emotional stimuli (not specific trauma reminders), they may extend further into everyday life than previously thought. "We have known for a long time that trauma exposure can lead to subsequent vulnerability to mental health disorders years after the trauma. This research is giving us clues about the biology underlying that vulnerability. Knowing what's going on will give us a better idea how to help" (p. 238).

Summary

Mental health courts are designed to promote court-imposed treatment as a substitute for incarceration. Such courts are designed to break the cycle of mental deterioration and criminal behavior associated with the failure of the community mental health system and to provide effective treatment options instead of the usual criminal sanctions for offenders with mental illnesses. The concepts of therapeutic jurisprudential and alternate dispute resolution serve to treat interpersonal conflict and encourage effective communication without the stress of litigation. The success of such techniques is greatly dependent upon efforts by law schools to teach these approaches.

A victim of domestic violence experiences physical or psychological abuse, often producing feelings of intimidation, loss of control, hopelessness, and recurrent thoughts of the abuse. Domestic violence can be treated by utilizing shelters, counseling, legal and medical advocacy programs, and community interventions. For parents who physically abuse their children, the most common treatments are psychoeducational therapy and parenting classes, individual psychotherapy, cognitive–behavioral therapy, anger management training, and support groups.

Child sexual abuse offenders are often treated using classical counterconditioning paradigms such as the pairing of noxious stimuli with repeated presentations of sexual stimuli in either an overt sensitization mode (live) or a covert sensitization mode (imagined). Cognitive–behavioral programs and interventions aimed to increase empathy, change distorted thinking patterns, improve social skills, and teach self-control are also utilized. Drugs such as *Antiandrogens* (e.g., DepoProvera), which interfere with the action of testosterone, and hormonal agents such as the Gonadotropin are means of "chemical castration" and are used to decrease or eliminate sexual drive. In rare cases, actual surgical castration is used for the same purpose.

Treatments for post-trauamtic stress disorder in prison are usually behavioral (exposure and desensitization, EMDR); cognitive–behavioral; or skills based. Symptoms of post-traumatic stress disorder occur outside of prison from criminal assault, homicidal bereavement, natural and manmade disasters, war, political violence and terrorism, workplace homicide, and school shootings. Immediate (first-responder) psychological interventions are designed to calm victims and express understanding of their symptoms. This is often followed by individual therapy, possible family therapy, and community interventions.

Programs designed to restore competency to stand trial usually involve structured classes, groups, modeling and role playing, videos, and trips to courthouses. Many more individuals who are currently adjudicated as incompetent to stand trial could be restored to competency if appropriate and research-based techniques are utilized.

Key Terms

Review Questions

1. What roles do mental health courts play in the criminal justice system?
2. What is alternate dispute resolution, and when could it be employed?
3. What are some of the current techniques for the treatment of child abuse?
4. What are the methods used for the treatment of child sex offenders?
5. What are the various therapeutic approaches for dealing with domestic violence?
6. How is post-traumatic stress disorder dealt with in prison settings?
7. What are the methods used for treating terrorism-induced psychological trauma?
8. What kinds of programs are employed to restore competency to stand trial?

Chapter Resources on the World Wide Web

Bureau of Justice Assistance Home Page
http://www.ojp.usdoj.gov/BJA/index.html

The Bazelon Center Home Page
http://www.bazelon.org

Journal of the American Academy of Psychiatry and the Law Online
http://www.jaapl.org/

American Academy of Family Physicians Home Page
http://www.aafp.org/online/en/home.html

American Psychological Association: Psychology and the Prison System
http://www.apa.org/monitor/julaug03/prisontoc.html

American Psychological Association Monitor: New Hope for Sex Offender Treatment
http://www.apa.org/monitor/julaug03/newhope.html

Center for Offender Management
http://www.csom.org/pubs/mythsfacts.html

National Center for Children Exposed to Violence Home Page
http://www.nccev.org/index.html

Cornell University: Program for Anxiety and Trauma Stress Studies
http://www.patss.com

Psychiatric Times
http://www.psychiatrictimes.com

For Further Reading

Figley, C. R. (Ed.). (1998). *Burnout in families: The systemic costs of caring*. Boca Raton, FL: CRC Press.

Lutzker, J. R. (Ed.). (2006). *Preventing violence*. Washington, DC: American Psychological Association.

Marshall, W. L., Fernandez, Y. M., Hudson, S. M., & Ward, T. (Eds.). *Sourcebook of treatment programs for sexual offenders*. New York: Plenum Press.

Resick, P. A., & Schnicke, M. K. (1993). *Cognitive processing therapy for rape victims: A treatment manual*. Newbury Park: Sage.

Seto, M. C. (2008). *Pedophilia and sexual offending against children. Theory, assessment, and intervention*. Washington, DC: American Psychological Association.

Sprang, G., & McNeil, J. (1995). *The many faces of bereavement: The nature and treatment of natural, traumatic, and stigmatized grief*. New York: Brunner/Mazel.

Spungen, D. (1998). *Homicide: The hidden victims, a guide for professionals*. Thousand Oaks, CA: Sage.

GLOSSARY

Actuarial judgments: statistically based assessments relying on validated relationships between measurable predictor and outcome variables and ultimately determined by fixed, or mechanical, and explicit rules. *Actuarial* variables are defined as variables that are "static or historical" and do not change.

Actus reus: the "guilty act." The physical aspect of a crime which renders the actor criminally liable if combined with a guilty mind.

Affective aggression: hostile, impulsive, or thoughtless aggression driven by anger with the ultimate goal of harming another.

Affray (common law): the mutual combat of two or more persons in a public place.

Aggression: behavior that has as its goal the infliction of harm upon another person who is in turn motivated to avoid the harm.

Alternative dispute resolution: a variety of processes available for the resolution of disputes other than through traditional litigation. It differs fundamentally from the adversarial system in that it seeks a mutually satisfactory conclusion rather than victory for one side over the other.

Americans with Disabilities Act ("ADA"): a federal statute put into law in 1990 that prohibits employers, employment agencies, and labor unions from discriminating against qualified individuals with disabilities in job application procedures, hiring, firing, advancement, compensation, job training, and other terms, conditions, and privileges of employment. The ADA covers employers with 15 or more employees, including state and local governments.

Amygdala: one of the structures of the brain thought to be implicated in aggression.

Antisocial personality disorder: a personality disorder marked by lying, unreliability, irresponsibility, manipulativeness, disregard for the rights of others and the standards of society, lack of remorse, and physical aggressiveness. Individuals with this disorder may appear to be charming at times, but their ability to form and maintain deep and long-lasting relationships is severely impaired.

Appellant: the person filing a formal appeal demanding appellate review.

Appellate brief: a written argument filed with an appellate ("reviewing") court on why a trial (initial decision-making court) acted correctly or incorrectly.

Appellee: the person filing a response to a formal appeal demanding appellate review.

Arbitration: an adjudicatory process by which a third party decides the outcome of a dispute.

Arson (common law): the malicious burning of the dwelling of another.

Assault: an attempt or threat to inflict harm (battery) upon a person, or an intentional placing of another person in apprehension of being harmed.

Assisted outpatient treatment: a form of civil commitment whereby the individual is treated on an outpatient basis, primarily with medication, and pursuant to a court order. Usually such individuals do not meet the requirements for inpatient civil commitment. Kendra's Law is one example of this form of commitment.

Authoritarianism: set of personality traits strongly associated with (1) an aversion to differences in people, (2) a desire for conformity to prevailing social norms and proper authority, (3) strict morality, (4) political and social intolerance, (5) an aversion to ambiguity, (6) and a desire for clear and unambiguous authority.

Automatism: a legal defense that recognizes that some criminal acts may be committed involuntarily, even though no third party is involved. The classic example of the "automaton" is the person who commits an offense while sleepwalking.

Battered Woman Syndrome ("BWS"): a psychological syndrome denoting a set of distinct psychological and behavioral symptoms that result from prolonged exposure to situations of intimate partner violence. BWS has successfully been used in a limited number of cases as a defense to a murder charge when the abused victim kills her abuser partner. The legal rationale in these instances is "self-defense."

Battery: the unlawful application of force to the person of another or to an extension of the other.

Black rage syndrome: a psychological syndrome holding that a defendant's past exposure to racism in general suffices as a defense to violent criminal acts. Lacking in success, this defense has been most recently used in conjunction with such defenses as insanity or diminished capacity, rather than self-defense alone.

Breach of duty: a violation or omission of a preestablished duty.

Burgher Guard: the nation's first police force, established in 1657 in New Amsterdam (New York City).

Burglary (common law): the breaking and entering of the dwelling of another in the nighttime with the intent to commit a felony therein.

Challenges for cause: removing a potential juror from a jury panel who (1) is ineligible to serve due to statutory requirements (e.g., he/she is not a resident of the local jurisdiction, not a U.S. citizen, below the mandated age requirement, or does not speak English); (2) has a mental or physical disability that would interfere with his/her ability to serve on a jury; (3) had recently served on a jury; (4) had previous felony convictions; (5) had a relationship with or is related to one of the parties in the case or their attorneys; or (6) may be impartial or biased (e.g., have preconceived judgments in the matter before the court, be prejudiced for or against a party in the matter, or exposed to excessive media coverage).

Child sexual abuse accommodation syndrome: the psychological syndrome used to explain why child victims of intra-family sexual abuse may be reluctant to disclose their experiences.

Clinical judgments: assessments using human (versus statistical or mechanical) decision-making processes, that take into account *clinical* variables which are subject to change.

Coerced-compliant false confessions: confessions made despite the knowledge of one's innocence, due to extreme methods of police interrogations.

Coerced-internalized false confessions: confessions made under pressure by innocent individuals who come to believe that they have indeed committed a crime.

Cognitive scripts: learned ways of responding that are stored in a person's memory and are used as guides for behavior and social problem solving.

Common law rape: unlawful sexual intercourse with a female without her consent.

Competence to stand trial: a defendant's ability to function in a meaningful fashion in a legal proceeding.

Competency: appearing in the laws of evidence, contract law, wills and estates, domestic and family law, as well as criminal law. In the most general of terms, a competent person is one who has sufficient mental or physical capacity, or has legitimate authority to engage in some legally significant act.

Confabulation: filling in the gaps in one's memory with irrelevant facts or information. This is often seen in hypnotized and intoxicated individuals.

Confirmation bias: a type of selective thinking whereby one tends to notice and look for what confirms one's beliefs, and to ignore, not look for, or undervalue the relevance of what contradicts one's beliefs.

Conservatorship: a court-appointed relationship in which the conservator becomes the surrogate decision maker for matters concerning the property and/or income of a person deemed incapable of administering his/her own financial affairs because of physical, mental, or other incapacity.

Countermeasures: in reference to the polygraph, these are measures used by examinees to deceive the machine and the examiner.

Critical incident: any event that has a stressful impact sufficient to overwhelm the usually effective coping skills of an individual. Such events often lie outside the realm of normal human experience and could be expected to produce significant emotional reactions in a normal person. The term is frequently associated with stressful events occurring in police work.

Critical Incident Stress Debriefing ("CISD"): a program to help police officers deal with symptoms resulting from exposure to trauma. Such a program allows the officer to process the event, ventilate emotions, and talk about its impact. CISD may occur on an individual or group basis.

Custody: a momentary physical control over a thing or a person which is subject to the right of another person to regain physical control at any time.

Dactyloscopy: the study of fingerprint patterns for the purpose of making identifications.

Dehumanization: the process by which only positive characteristics are attributed to members of a terrorist group and only negative characteristics are attributed to members of any other group.

Demonization: the social psychological conditioning process whereby group members become convinced that the enemy is in league with the devil or represents some kind of cosmic evil.

Demonstrative evidence: not a "real thing" but tangible material used for explanatory or illustrative purposes only, such as a visual aid, an anatomical model, a chart, a diagram, a map, a film, et cetera.

Depluralization: the process whereby terrorist recruits give up all their former ties and affiliations.

Depraved heart killing: complete indifference to the life of others; a legal creation whereby a defendant may be guilty of murder, if he acts in a manner that creates an unusually high risk of death, and that actually results in death. Driving over 100 miles per hour in a school zone while young children are present, for example, would be depraved heart killing if someone is killed because of the driver's actions.

Dichotomous thinking: a cognitive distortion where people are seen as either totally good or totally bad but never in between (see "splitting").

Diffusion of responsibility: the tendency for people to feel less responsible (or less culpable) when, either in the presence of, or on behalf of a group, they engage in harmful or even heinous behavior. In this way the individual mitigates his own culpability by maintaining that he acted under the mandate of some authority.

Disciple killer: a killer who follows the dictates of a charismatic leader.

Disgruntled employee killer: a former employee who may have been counseled, disciplined, or dismissed, then retaliates for this perceived injustice by going to the place where he once worked and killing his former employer and/or former fellow employees either randomly or selectively.

Disinhibition hypothesis: the theory that aggression is more likely to occur when a person's normal inhibitions are reduced, such as when one is under the effects of alcohol, or any substance which weakens the brain mechanisms that normally restrain impulsive behaviors.

Displaced aggression: an unexpected and disproportionate expression of aggression, occurring when a person is provoked. This is usually the result of one's unwillingness or inability to retaliate against the original provocateur, and subsequently aggresses against a seemingly innocent target. This has been used to explain "road rage."

Distributive justice: a theory of how available rewards are distributed in a society. In American society, distributive justice is based mostly on "equity." More specifically, the rewards that people receive are thought to be distributed in proportion to each person's contributions.

Documentary evidence: usually a writing, sound or video recording. It may be the transcript of a telephone conversation, et cetera. Authentication of such evidence is usually required before it can be accepted by a court.

Doll Test: designed by psychologists Kenneth Bancroft Clark and his wife, Mamie Phipps Clark, the test illustrated the harmful psychological effects of segregation on black children.

Durham test: a test for insanity stating that a defendant could be acquitted if his reasoning powers were so far dethroned by his diseased mental condition as to deprive him of willpower to resist the insane impulse to perpetrate the deed, though knowing it to be wrong. This is also known as the "irresistible impulse" test.

Duty: a legal or moral responsibility, an obligation of some sort.

Ecoterrorism: the use or threatened use of violence by an environmentally oriented group. These acts may be symbolic expressions of an environmentally based agenda.

Elder neglect/abandonment: a type of elder mistreatment whereby an older person is deserted by his/her caregiver who previously had assumed responsibility for providing care for that individual. Elder neglect can also include the refusal or failure of a person to uphold obligations to care for an older person. This can include behaviors such as failure to provide an elderly person with basic necessities such as water, food, shelter, safety, hygiene, and medications. Forced social isolation, such as taking mail and denying access to the telephone, Internet, and outside world, are also examples of neglect/abandonment.

Embezzlement: the fraudulent conversion of tangible personal property of value from another person after the wrongdoer has already obtained lawful possession.

Emotional child abuse: anything of a nonphysical nature done to a child that may impair his/her emotional development, self-esteem, or self-worth. This can include behaviors such as constant criticism or rejection.

Encoding: the first stage in memory building, it is the acquisition of new information.

English common law: a derivation from the medieval theory that the law as administered by the King's courts represented the common custom of the realm, as opposed to the custom of local jurisdictions that was applied in local or "manorial" courts.

Estimator variables: attributes of the person and the environment that affect memory (e.g., stress, cross-race versus within-race identifications, fatigue, and lighting).

Ethology: the zoological study of animal behavior.

Expert witness: someone who has *special* knowledge or skill gained by education, training, or experience, and is considered more knowledgeable than ordinary citizens. Some of the common expert witnesses that testify in criminal proceeding are professionals in the medical, psychological, or forensic fields.

Exposure therapy: a behavioral approach to traumatic stress that treats PTSD symptoms through a combination of imagined "reliving" of traumatic events, and live confrontations with triggers in the outside world. By repeatedly pairing such exposure with relaxation and feelings of safety, anxiety begins to subside.

Externalization: a primitive psychological defense mechanism usually found in individuals with narcissistic and borderline personality disturbances, where blame is externalized onto the outside world.

Eye Movement Desensitization and Reprocessing ("EMDR"): a form of therapy used to treat the victims of trauma. In EMDR the client is instructed to focus on an image, negative thought or body sensations associated with the traumatic event while simultaneously moving his or her eyes back and forth following the therapist's fingers as they move across the client's field of vision for intervals of 20–30 seconds or more.

Family annihilator: a person who kills an entire family at one time.

Felony murder rule: first-degree murder committed during the commission or attempted commission of a felony (a crime punishable with death or life imprisonment).

Filicide: the killing of a child older than 24 hours.

First-degree murder: murder committed with deliberatively premeditated malice aforethought, or with extreme atrocity or cruelty.

Fitness-for-duty evaluation: an ordered evaluation performed by a psychologist or psychiatrist on a current police officer to determine his or her present suitability for law enforcement functioning (e.g., to carry a weapon).

Foils (or fillers): nonsuspects used to fill in a lineup for comparison purposes.

Forensic accounting: the study and interpretation of accounting evidence.

Forensic anthropology: the identification of skeletal remains through the application of standard anthropological techniques.

Forensic economics: the study and interpretation of economic damage evidence such as lost earnings, the lost value of a business, lost profits, lost value of household service, replacement labor costs and future medical care costs.

Forensic engineering: the branch of engineering that determines the causes of failure of devices, structures, or why components or structures fail to operate as intended.

Forensic odontology: the branch of dentistry dealing with dental evidence and remains.

Forensic psychology: the application of scientific and professional psychology to questions and issues relating to the law and the legal system.

Forensic science: the study and practice of applying natural, physical and social science to the resolution of social and legal issues.

Forensic toxicology: the analyses of tissues and fluids from deceased persons to identify toxic substances that might have caused their death.

Foreseeability: the ability to see or know in advance; the physical injury of a person does not automatically equate to liability if the actor, as a person of ordinary intelligence and prudence, could not have reasonably anticipated danger to others created by his negligent acts.

Frustration–aggression hypothesis: a theory that aggression results from the frustration, that is, when environmental or internal circumstances interfere with a desired goal response.

Frye rule: holds that the requirement for expert opinion to be admitted into evidence is that such evidence be based on a scientific technique that is "generally accepted" as being reliable in the relevant scientific community.

Gendercide: the killing of female babies or young girls by family members. Such acts are most often culturally determined.

Glioblastoma: a type of brain tumor that has been associated with violent impulses in both animals and humans.

Guardianship: a legal relationship between a competent adult or "guardian" and a person who is no longer able to make responsible decisions. A minor child under legal guardianship appointed by a court is referred to as a ward of the court.

Hebephilia: closely related to pedophilia, hebephilia is a sexual preference for recently pubescent children.

Hedonistic: a type of serial killer who gains pleasure from the pure act of killing. Based on their primary motive, hedonistic killers may be further classified as lust, thrill, or comfort killers.

Homicide: the killing of a human being caused by another person, a neutral term under the law.

Homosexual panic: also referred to as "gay panic," this is an intense form of anxiety, tension, and rage, experienced by an individual (usually with latent homosexual tendencies), and brought about by the mere presence or sight of homosexuals. Such individuals are usually precariously psychologically balanced with fragile egos. Homosexual panic has been periodically used as a criminal defense when someone kills a gay person.

Honor killings: acts of murder in which a woman or girl is killed for her actual or perceived immoral behavior. Such acts are usually culturally determined.

Hostile work environment sexual harassment: circumstances in which remarks, insults, or intimidation create an abusive atmosphere and make the work environment intolerable.

Hydraulic model: a theory used to explain instinctive behavior, stating that certain human actions, such as aggression, are the result of the discharge of accumulated energy.

Hypnoinvestigations: interrogations and interviews using hypnosis as a memory aid.

Immunity: absolute freedom from civil liability for anything said on the witness stand. Many expert witnesses are granted such immunity from civil claims as they are considered to be friends of the court in their expert capacity.

Infanticide: the deliberate killing of a newborn.

Informed consent: the process by which a fully informed patient can participate in choices about his or her health care. Some of the elements involved in informed consent include the patient's understanding of the proposed treatment or intervention, reasonable alternatives to the proposed intervention, and the risks and benefits of the intervention.

Instincts: genetically programmed behaviors.

Instrumental aggression: the use of aggression as a premeditated means of obtaining some goal other than just to harm the victim.

Interrogative suggestibility: the susceptibility of an individual to interrogations due to various factors such as socially isolation, high anxiety levels during interrogations, generalized poor self-esteem, unassertiveness, and especially low levels of intelligence.

Involuntary manslaughter: an unintentional homicide, committed without malice, which is neither justified nor excused. The two principal types of involuntary manslaughter are: criminal negligence manslaughter and unlawful act manslaughter. Examples would include a camper who leaves a campfire burning, which later burns down a home, killing the occupants. Many traffic deaths also fall into this category, although some states have special categories of offenses called vehicular homicide.

JD: juris doctorate.

Junk Science: fanciful and unsupported theories, often in the form of syndromes, placed into the American legal system by faddists and others with less than adequate scientific credentials.

Just world beliefs: the attitude that people get what they deserve in life. This concept is generally based on principles of equity. Individuals who believe in a just world tend to believe that good things happen to good people and bad things happen to bad individuals.

Larceny: the trespassory taking and carrying away of the tangible personal property of another with the intent of depriving the other person of the property permanently or for an unreasonable period of time.

Lay witness: someone who has *personal* knowledge of the underlying facts of a case and can only testify to perceptions, facts, and data, grounded in their own experience. Lay witnesses are prohibited from testifying as to their opinions.

Learned helplessness: based on the animal research by Martin Seligman, and later extended to humans, this theory helps to explain why certain people accept their negative life situations, i.e., they have come to believe that they are helpless to make changes in their life Learned helplessness is the basis for the Battered Women Syndrome.

Locus of control: an individual's belief in the source of outcomes in life. More specifically that events that occur in a person's life are the result of a person's actions or of outside forces beyond his or her control.

Malum in se: acts that are crimes because they are inherently dangerous to life or health.

Malum Prohibitum: acts that are made crimes by statute.

Mass murder: the killing of three or more persons at a single location with no cooling-off period between the killings.

Maximization: where an interrogator tries to frighten a suspect by exaggerating the evidence available, the legal consequences, or stating that the interrogator knows the suspect is guilty, in the hope of eliciting a confession.

Mediation: a form of negotiation that involves the use of a third party to facilitate reaching a resolution.

Mens rea: the *intent* of a person, the mental or internal ingredient of a crime.

Mental health court: courts used to process criminal cases involving people with serious mental illnesses. These specialty courts strive to reduce the incarceration and recidivism of people with mental illnesses by linking them with mental health services and supports that might prevent future arrests.

Militia movement: in the United States, a right-wing extremist movement consisting of armed paramilitary groups, both formal and informal, with an antigovernment, conspiracy-oriented ideology.

Minimization: where an interrogator offers some moral justification for a suspect's actions, minimizes the seriousness of the situation, or shifts blame on to others, with the hope of eliciting a confession.

Misguided altruism: in the context of filicide, when a parent believes that killing his or her child is actually in the best interests of the child.

Mission-oriented: a type of serial killer who is not psychotic, but feels a powerful need to rid the world of those people he regards as loathsome, immoral or unworthy.

M'Naughten test: a test for insanity that requires clear proof that the individual was, at the time he or she committed the offense, operating under defect of reason from a disease of the mind and that such a defect resulted in the individual's not being able to recognize the nature and quality of his actions, or not knowing that such actions were wrong.

Modeling: the acquisition and maintenance of responses, including aggression, through observation and reinforcement.

Modus Operandi ("MO"): types of offender behavior at a crime scene that represent the functional components that are necessary for an offender to commit the crime. These can include factors such as time of day, location, type of victim, points or techniques for gaining entry, as well as tools used for committing the crime.

Munchausen syndrome by proxy: derived from the adult form of Munchausen syndrome in which patients fabricate and/or induce symptoms and present themselves for treatment, this syndrome involves (usually mothers) who intentionally place their children in the patient role, sometimes by actually inducing illness, thereby using the children as proxies for their own psychological needs.

Murder: the unlawful killing of a human being by another committed with malice aforethought, either express or implied.

Narcissistic personality disorder: a personality disorder marked by a sense of entitlement, exaggeration of abilities or accomplishments, lack of empathy, exploitation of others, envy, and an arrogant and haughty attitude. Individuals with this disorder are grandiose and require extreme amounts of admiration from others.

Necrophagia: cannibalizing one's victims.

Necrophilia: sex with the dead or with someone pretending to be dead.

Negative stereotyping: refers to the belief that most or all members of a group subject to disability-related discrimination share certain negative characteristics, and that the mere fact of having a disability generalizes to a person's potential and limitations in many areas that extend far beyond the disability itself.

Negligent hiring: in the context of law enforcement, the failure of a police department to properly select police officers, thus creating a liability of negligence by employing individuals who possess personality attributes or prior conduct that create an undue risk of harming others in carrying out his or her official responsibilities.

Neonaticide: the killing of a newborn within the first 24 hours of life.

Neuroimaging: a technique that measures mental activity and brain patterns. It has been used to measure reactions to sexual stimuli as well as arousal in other areas.

Obedience: an unquestioning deference to authority.

Pan-phobia: a "fear of everything" that begins to take over some people following a terrorist attack.

Paraphilia: a psychological condition in which a person's ability for sexual arousal and gratification is based upon fantasizing about and engaging in sexual behavior that is atypical and usually extreme.

Parens patriae: the governmental power to operate as the general guardian of all those who cannot care for themselves. Originally reserved for "infants, idiots and lunatics" (i.e., children, the mentally retarded and the insane), this power deals with the safety and needs of the individual rather than with society as a whole.

Parental alienation syndrome: the intense rejection of a parent by one or more children after a divorce, which is usually encouraged by the custodial parent.

Parent–Child Interaction Therapy ("PCIT"): a coached behavioral parent training protocol that trains parents to criteria on specific behavioral parenting skills using live sessions. PCIT teaches skills such as the use of praise and reflection and a specific timeout protocol for compliance training.

Pedophilia: sexual activity with a child usually 13 years old or younger.

Peremptory challenge: the right to challenge a juror without articulating, or being required to articulate, a reason for the challenge. In most jurisdictions each party to an action, both civil and criminal, is allowed a specified number of such challenges.

Petitioner: a person who seeks an appeal that is, a ruling by a higher court that it hear a case resulting from the decision of a lower court.

PhD: doctor of philosophy.

Physical child abuse: anything done to a child that may cause physical injury. This can include behaviors such as punching, beating, kicking, biting, shaking, throwing, stabbing, choking, or burning.

Polygraph: an instrument that simultaneously records changes in physiological processes such as heartbeat, blood pressure, respiration and electrical resistance (galvanic skin response, or GSR). The underlying theory of the polygraph is that when people lie they also get measurably nervous about lying. The heartbeat increases, blood pressure goes up, breathing rhythms change, perspiration increases, etc.

Possession: the legal right to control an object physically for a reasonably long period of time.

Postpartum depression: a depressive episode in women appearing within the first year after a baby's birth. It is estimated that between 10–22% of adult women have experienced postpartum depression. The psychotic form of postpartum depression is characterized by command hallucinations to kill the infant or delusions that the infant is possessed. Postpartum psychosis this severe seems to occur in from 1 in 500 to 1 in 1,000 deliveries, and the risk of psychotic episodes is increased for women who have experienced prior postpartum mood episodes.

Preemployment psychological screening: the use of psychological testing and interviews to "screen out" individuals found to be psychological inappropriate for a certain type of job (such as police work), and to "screen-in" positive characteristics, attitudes, and traits related to the job.

Premeditation: in the case of homicide, a killer acts with a cool mind, and reflects, at least for a short period of time (in some cases a matter of seconds), before the actual act of killing.

Pseudo commando killer: a killer who is preoccupied with weaponry, and who kills, usually after a long period of planning, in a military-like manner often using automatic weapons. He may kill to "teach the world a lesson."

Psychoactive drugs: drugs used to treat psychological and psychiatric disorders.

PsyD: doctor of psychology.

Punitive damages: a type of damages awarded by a court to "punish" an individual or agency for wrongdoings. Such damages also act as an example to possible future wrongdoers.

Quid pro quo sexual harassment: situations in which the employment of persons is made contingent upon their complying with sexual demands, and harassment involves an implicit or explicit bargain whereby the harasser promises a reward or threatens punishment, depending on the victim's response.

Rampage killer: an individual who sets out, typically with an arsenal of guns, to kill as many people as he can, sometimes randomly and sometimes against those with whom he has a grievance.

Rape Trauma Syndrome ("RTS"): a psychological syndrome used to help explain why many women who have been raped behave in certain predictable yet seemingly contraindicated fashions (e.g., fail to report the rape, continue a relationship with the alleged rapist, etc.). The syndrome refers to the acute and long-term reorganization process that is said to occur as a result of forcible rape or attempted forcible rape. RTS has been used by the prosecution in trials for rape to explain apparently inconsistent behaviors by the alleged victim.

Real evidence: a "real thing" that is relevant and material to a case, such as the actual murder weapon, not a mere example of a weapon of the type said to have been used in the alleged crime. Real evidence can also be a written contract, fingerprints, an automobile, etc.

Redline view: the rule holding that the felony-murder doctrine does not apply where one of two or more cofelons is killed by the police. The legal reasoning is that murder cannot be based upon a shooting that constitutes a justifiable homicide (where, for example, the police officer

or felony victim shoots the felon to prevent his escape or to prevent the commission of a felony).

Respondent: the person who must respond to a petition of appeal from a lower court.

Retrieval: the final stage in the memory process, it involves the recall of information stored in memory.

Retroactive memory falsification: the process proposed by Albert Von Schrenck-Notzing, holding that factors such as pretrial publicity can result in witnesses not being able to distinguish between what they actually saw and what they had read in the press. These were also referred to as "perceptual errors."

Revised frustration-aggression hypothesis: the theory holding that frustration does not inevitably result in aggression but creates only a "readiness" for aggressive acts. The actual expression of the aggression depends on some eliciting event in the environment.

Revolutionary terrorists: those who seek the complete abolition of a political system and engage in destructive acts to accomplish this mission.

Ritual: types of offender behavior that are a combination of fantasy and motivational factors that are psychologically based and fulfill a need of the offender. Ritual may be indicated at a crime scene with bindings of the victim, posing of victims, unique markings on victims, or any other symbolic behaviors.

Robbery (common law): larceny from a person by violence or intimidation.

Safe haven infant protection acts: laws that allow a parent under most circumstances to surrender a newborn anonymously without fear of criminal prosecution. The intent of these statutes is to encourage mothers, who might otherwise discard their children, to go to an emergency room, a police station, a fire house, or other safe place to drop off their infants.

Second-degree murder: generally, any murder that is not first-degree murder. Included in this category are: (1) a killing with malice aforethought, but without premeditation and deliberation; (2) a killing that results from an act done with intent to do great bodily harm (regardless of whether done with premeditation and deliberation); (3) a killing that results from an act done with a wanton and willful disregard of an unreasonable human risk, and (4) in some jurisdictions, a murder committed in the course of a felony not listed under first-degree felony murder (e.g., embezzlement, larceny).

Sequential presentation: in lineups or photo spreads, suspects are presented one at a time. The eyewitness compares each member in turn to his or her memory of the perpetrator and, on that basis, decides whether any person in the lineup or photo spread is the individual who committed the crime. Judgments are absolute and not relative as they are in simultaneous lineups.

Serial murder: incidents in which an individual (or individuals) separately kills a number of people (usually a minimum of three) over time. The cooling-off period for serial killers may be days or weeks but more likely months or years.

Serotonin: a neurotransmitter that has been implicated in human aggression.

Set-and-run killers: killers usually motivated by a need for revenge or profit, who employ techniques to allow their escape before their deadly act occurs. For example, a set-and-run killer might plant a bomb in a building, setting a time device so that he is far away from the crime scene when the explosion occurs.

Signature: a type of offender behavior at a crime scene that goes beyond what is necessary to commit the crime, to the fulfillment of a psychological need of the offender. Signature aspects are symbolic and hold special significance to the offender. Such behaviors are also known as "calling cards."

Simultaneous presentation: in lineups or photo spreads, all suspects are presented at the same time. Eyewitnesses report which person or photo looks most like the culprit *relative to* other members of the group. Judgments are relative and not absolute as they are in sequential presentations.

Sodium amytal: a psychoactive drug erroneously believed to induce information from an unwilling individual. These so-called "truth serums" also include sodium pentothal, ethanol, scopolamine, and temazepam.

Somatotyping: the classification of body and physique as a way of understanding behavior, including criminal behavior.

Splitting: a primitive psychological defense mechanism seen in individuals whose self-concept have failed to integrate the good and bad parts of the self. Such individuals often need an outside enemy to blame for their own inadequacies and weaknesses, and they view other people as being either "all good" or "all bad" (see dichotomous thinking).

Spree killing: the killing of three or more individuals without a cooling-off period, usually at two or three different locations.

Staging: the purposeful alteration of a crime scene prior to the arrival of the police, usually done in order to obscure the underlying motive for the crime.

State anger: a situational and temporary angry emotional response to a particular event.

Statutory law: laws enacted by authorized powers of the state such as legislatures.

Statutory rape: having sexual intercourse with a female or male under statutory age of consent which may be 16, 17, or 18 years of age depending on the state statute.

Stigmatization: a distrust, fear, embarrassment, and even avoidance of persons with mental disabilities. It tends to deny such people access to resources and opportunities such as jobs and housing. Such stigmatization is often psychologically harmful and leads to low self-esteem, isolation, and hopelessness, as well as loss of dignity and the chance to fully participate in society.

Storage: the second step in building memory, it is the maintaining of new information after it has already been encoded.

Suicide by cop: making it necessary for police to use deadly force as a means of ending one's life.

Super males: men who were thought to be prone to violence by virtue of an extra Y, or male sex chromosome.

Surgical castration: removal of the testes in order to reduce or eliminate the production of androgens and thereby reduce sexual response. This procedure has occasionally been used to treat sex offenders.

Syndrome: a set of symptoms and signs that occur in a regular pattern from patient to patient, that collectively indicate or characterize a disease, psychological disorder, or other abnormal condition. Psychological syndrome evidence is important because it can put in the hands of the jury tremendous power to determine the credibility of a witness in a trial.

System variables: attributes of the criminal justice system that affects memory (e.g., the manner in which eyewitnesses are interviewed by police and how they are instructed prior to viewing a lineup).

Tarasoff duty: the duty established in *Tarasoff v. Regents of the University of California* limiting the confidentiality of communication between patient and mental health professional (and requiring third-party notification) when a threat has been made against an outside party who could be clearly identified.

Testator: a person making a will.

Testimonial evidence: evidence that comes to court through witnesses speaking under oath or affirmation. They could be testifying about something they saw (eyewitnesses), something they heard (hearsay witnesses), or something they know (character, habit, or custom witnesses).

Title: legal ownership.

Title VII of the Civil Rights Act: a federal statute (42 U.S.C. § 2000e et seq.) that prohibits employers from discriminating against people on the basis of race, color, sex, national origin, or religion with respect to hiring, discharge, compensation, promotion, classification, training, apprenticeship, referral for employment, or other terms, conditions, and privileges of employment.

Tort: a private or civil wrong committed by an individual or group against another individual or group.

Trait anger: a disposition to experience anger over time and across contexts, such that it is akin to a personality trait.

Transformational leadership: a leadership style characterized by vision and passion that inspires similar enthusiasm and energy in subordinates and employees. Such leaders are people-oriented and empathic; they believe that success comes through deep and sustained commitment and they model this for their employees.

Visionary: a type of serial killer who is psychotic. He often hears voices or sees visions and is driven to kill by these hallucinations or delusions.

Voir dire: literally to speak the truth. This denotes the preliminary examination of jurors to determine their qualification and suitability to serve as jurors.

Voluntary false confessions: self-incriminating statements purposefully offered in the absence of pressure by the police.

Voluntary manslaughter: an intentional homicide under extenuating circumstances that mitigate, but do not justify or excuse, the killing. The element of malice aforethought (necessary for murder) is not present. The most common type of voluntary manslaughter involves the intentional killing of another while in the heat of passion caused by an adequate provocation; that is, a provocation that would cause a reasonable person to lose their normal self-control.

Weapons effect: the tendency of the presence of a weapon to distract attention away from other aspects in a situation where an eyewitness is making an identification. In addition, the mere presence of weapons in pictures or in the natural environment tends to increase aggressive behavior in both angered and nonangered adults.

Wild beast test: formulated in 1256 by the English Judge Henry de Bracton, this refers to not holding insane people morally accountable for their actions due to the fact that they were "beast-like."

Yerkes-Dodson law: a description of the effects of arousal on learning. Under extremely low levels of external stress, a person may be so relaxed and un-alert that little learning takes place. On the other hand, if a person is facing an excessively stressful situation, perception is narrowed, information is funneled, and less learning occurs than under mild levels of stress. Performance on many tasks is best when the level of arousal is moderate enough to ensure adequate attention but not so high as to disrupt accuracy.

REFERENCES

A Profile of Older Americans. (1998). American Association of Retired Persons (AARP) A quantitative review of comparative research. *Psychological Bulletin, 109*, 355.

Aamodt, M. G. (2004). *Research in law enforcement selection.* Boca Raton, FL: Brown Walker Press.

ABAnet. *Litigation.* Retrieved August 8, 2007, from http://abanet.org/litigation/tips/.

Abdollahi, M. K. (2002). Understanding police stress research. *Journal of Forensic Psychology Practice, 2*(2), 1–24.

Abel, G. G., & Becker, J. V. (1979). *The sexual interest card sort.* Unpublished manuscript.

Abelson, R. P. (1982). The psychological status of the script concept. *American Psychologist, 36*, 715–712.

Abshire, J., & Bornstein, B. H. (2003). Juror sensitivity to the cross-race effect. *Law and Human Behavior, 27*(5), 471–480.

Acton, R. G., & During, S. M. (1992). Preliminary results of aggression management training for aggressive parents. *Journal of Interpersonal Violence, 7*, 410–417.

Adelmann, H. (1966). *Marcello Malpighi and the evolution of embryology.* Ithaca, NY: Cornell.

Adorno, T., Frenkel-Brunswik, E., Levinson, D., & Sanford, N. (1950a). The adults: A review of social scientific research. *Aggression & Violent Behavior, 12*, 300–314.

Adorno, T., Frenkel-Brunswik, E., Levinson, D., & Sanford, N. (1950b). *The authoritarian personality.* New York: Harper.

Akhtar, S. (1999). The psychodynamic dimension of terrorism. *Psychiatric Annals, 29*(6), 350–355.

Akiskal, H. S., Kilzieh, N., Maser, J. D., Clayton, P. J., Schettler, P. J., Shea, M. T., et al. (2006). The distinct temperament profiles of bipolar I, bipolar II, and unipolar patients. *Journal of Affective Disorders, 92*, 19–33.

Alarcon, R. D. (1999). The cascade model: An alternative to comorbidity in the pathogenesis of posttraumatic stress disorder. *Psychiatry, 62*, 114–124.

Albrecht, S. (1996). *Crisis management for corporate self-defense.* New York: Amacom.

Albrecht, S. (1997). *Fear and violence on the job: Prevention solutions for the dangerous workplace.* Durham, NC: Carolina Academic Press.

Alder, C., & Polk, K. (2001). *Child victims of homicide.* Cambridge, England: Cambridge University Press.

Alexander, M. A. (1997). Sex offender treatment probed anew. In B. A. Arrigo & S. L. Shipley (Eds.), *Forensic psychology* (pp. 391–395). Burlington, MA: Elsevier Academic Press.

Alexander, Y., & Brenner, E. H. (Eds.). (2001). *Terrorism and law.* Ardsley, NY: Transnational.

Ahlers, M. (2006, May 23). *Malvo: Muhammad 'made me a monster' Younger man cross-examined by former mentor in sniper trial.* CNN. Retrieved July 17, 2007, from http://www.cnn.com/2006/LAW/05/23/sniper.trial/index.html.

Allen, C. (2003). A treatment for PTSD? *Psychology Today.* Retrieved July 7, 2007, from http://psychologytoday.com/articles/pto-20031027-000002.html

Allen, J. J. B. (2002). The role of psychophysiology in clinical assessment: ERPs in the evaluation of memory. *Psychophysiology, 39*, 261–280.

Allen, J. J. B., & Iacono, W. G. (2001). Assessing the validity of amnesia in dissociative identity disorder: A dilemma for the DSM and the courts. *Psychology, Public Policy, and Law, 7*, 311–344.

Allen, R. F., & Pilnick, S. (1973). Confronting the shadow organization: How to detect and defeat negative norms. *Organizational Dynamics, 1*, 2–18.

Allen, S. G. (1983). How much does absenteeism cost? *Journal of Human Resources, 18*, 379–393.

Allison, D. B., & Roberts, M. S. (1998). *Disordered mother or disordered diagnosis? Munchausen by proxy syndrome.* Hillsdale, NJ: Analytic Press.

Allison, R. B. (1984). Difficulties diagnosing the multiple personality syndrome. *The International Journal of Clinical and Experimental Hypnosis, 32*(2), 102–117.

Alpert, J. (Ed.). (1995). *Sexual abuse recalled: Treating trauma in the era of the recovered memory debate.* Northvale, NJ: Jason Aronson.

Altemeyer, B. (1981). *Right Wing Authoritarianism.* Winnepeg: University of Manitoba Press.

Altemeyer, R. A. (1988). *Enemies of freedom: Understanding right-wing authoritarianism.* San Francisco, CA: Jossey-Bass.

Altemeyer, R. A. (1998). The other "authoritarian personality." In M. P. Zanna (Ed.), *Advances in experimental social psychology* (Vol. 30, pp. 47–91). New York: Academic Press.

American Academy of Pediatricians. Policy statement. Retrieved October 21, 2008, from http://aappolicy.aappublications.org/cgi/content/full/pediatrics;104/2/341

American Board of Forensic Psychology. (home page). Retrieved February 6, 2008, from http://www.abpp.org

American Psychiatric Association. (2000). *Diagnostic and statistical manual of mental disorders* (4th ed., text revision). Washington, DC: American Psychiatric Association.

American Psychological Association. (1978). Report of the task force on the role of psychology in the criminal justice system. *American Psychologist, 33*, 1099–1113.

American Psychological Association. (2007). *Graduate study in psychology, 2007.* Washington, DC: Author.

American Psychological Association. (2002). *Ethical principles of psychologists and code of conduct.* Retrieved February 26, 2008, from http://www.apa.org/ethics/code2002.html

Ammerman, R. T., & Hersen, M. (1991). *Case studies in family violence.* New York: Plenum.

American Psychological Association of Graduate Students (APAGS). *Home Page.* Retrieved August 15, 2009, from http://www.apa.org/apags/

An assessment of the Aldrich H. Ames espionage case. Abstract of report of investigation. Retrieved March 2, 2007, from http://nsi.org/Library/Espionage/Hitzreport.html.

Ancheta, A. N. (2006). *Scientific evidence and equal protection of the law.* Piscataway, NJ: Rutgers University Press.

Andersen, S. M., & Zimbardo, P. G. (1984, Fall/Winter). On resisting social influence. *Cultic Studies Journal, 1*(2), 196–219.

Anderson, C. A., Benjamin, A. J., & Bartholow, B. D. (1998). Does the gun pull the trigger? Automatic priming effects of weapon pictures and weapon names. *Psychological Science, 9*, 308–314.

Anderson, C. A., Lepper, M. R., & Ross, L. (1980). Perseverance of social theories: The role of explanation in the persistence of discredited information. *Journal of Personality and Social Psychology, 39*, 1037–1049.

Andersson, L. M., & Pearson, C. M. (1999). Tit for tat? The spiraling effect of incivility in the workplace. *Academy of Management Review, 24*, 452–471.

Anfang, S., & Appelbaum, P. S. (1996). Twenty years after Tarasoff: Reviewing the duty to protect. *Harvard Review of Psychiatry, 4*(2), 67–76.

Anshel, M. (2000). A conceptual model and implications for coping with stressful events in police work. *Criminal Justice and Behavior, 27*, 375–400.

Anson, R. H., & Bloom, M. E. (1988). Police stress in occupational context. *Journal of Police Science and Administration, 16*, 229–233.

Anti-Defamation League. (2007). New Black Panther Party for Self-Defense. Retrieved February 11, 2009, from http://www.adl.org/learn/ext_us/ Black_Panther.asp?LEARN_Cat=Extremism&LEARN_SubCat= Extremism_in_America&xpicked=3&item=Black_Panther.

APA online. Elder abuse and neglect: In search of solutions. Retrieved March 11, 2008, from http://www.apa.org/pi/aging/eldabuse.html.

Appleman, J. (1952). Successful jury trials, A symposium. In *Trial advocacy.* Retrieved August 15, 2009, from http://law.uark.edu/documents/ Orientation_(Trial_Advocacy).pdf

Arbisi, P. A., & Butcher, J. N. (2004). Psychometric perspectives on detection of malingering of pain: Use of the Minnesota Multiphasic Personality Inventory-2. *Clinical Journal of Pain, 20*, 383–391.

Archer, J. (1991). The influence of testosterone on human aggression. *British Journal of Psychology, 82*, 1–28.

Arito, H., Sudo, A., & Suzuki, Y. (1981). Aggressive behavior of the rat induced by repeated administration of cadmium. *Toxicology Letters, 7*, 457–461.

Aronson, E., Wilson, T. D., & Akert, R. M. (2002). *Social psychology: The heart and the mind.* New York: Harper Collins.

Arrigo et al. at 103, citing Taylor, A. J. W. (2002). Coping with catastrophe: Organising psychological first-aiders. *New Zealand Journal of Psychology, 31*(2), 104–109.

Arrigo, B. A., & Garsky, K. (1997). Police suicide: A glimpse behind the badge, In R. G. Dunham & G. P. Alpert (Eds.), *Critical issues in policing: Contemporary readings* (3rd ed.). Prospect Heights, IL: Waveland Press, 609–626.

Arrigo, B. A., & Shipley, S. L. (2000). *Forensic psychology.* Burlington, MA: Elsevier Academic Press.

Arrigo, B. A., & Shipley, S. L. (2005). *Forensic psychology* (2nd ed., pp. 391–395). Burlington, MA: Elsevier Academic Press.

Asch, S. E. (1956). Studies of independence and conformity: A minority of one against a unanimous majority. *Psychological Monographs, 70*, 416.

Ash, P., Slora, K. B., & Britton, C. F. (1990). Police agency officer selection practices. *Journal of Police Science and Administration, 17*(4), 258–269.

Ashbaugh, S. (1999). *Quantitative-qualitative friction ridge analysis: An introduction to basic and advanced ridgeology.* Boca Raton, Florida, CRC Press, 11–19.

Ashforth, B. E., & Humphrey, R. H. (1993). Emotional labor in service roles: The influence of identity. *Academy of Management Review, 18*, 88–115.

Åström, P. (2007). The study of ancient fingerprints. *Journal of Ancient Fingerprints, 1*, 2–3. At the annual conference of the British Psychological Society, Brighton, England.

Austin, E. J., & Deary, I. J. (2000). The "four As": A common framework for normal and abnormal personality? *Personality and Individual Differences, 28*, 977–995.

Autopsy shows teen died from "neck compression." (2007, December 12). *CTV.ca.* Retrieved March 21, 2009 from http://www.ctv.ca/servlet/ ArticleNews/story/CTVNews/20071211/muslim_dad_071212/200712 12?hub=TopStories.

Avolio, B. J., Bass, B. M., & Jung, D. I. (1995). *Multifactor leadership questionnaire technical report.* Redwood City, CA: Mind Garden.

Azevedo, A. D., Hilton, S. M., & Timms, R. J. (1980). The defense reaction elicited by midbrain and hypothalamic stimulation in the rabbit. *Journal of Physiology, 301*, 56–57.

Bachman, R. (1994). *National crime victimization survey: Violence and theft in the workplace* (Tech. Rep. No. NCJ-148199). Washington, DC: U.S. Department of Justice.

Bacon, F. (1939). Novum organum. In E. A. Burtt (Ed.), *The English philosophers from Bacon to Mill* (pp. 24–123). New York: Random House. (Original work published 1620.)

Baddeley, A. (1990). *Human memory: Theory and practice.* Boston, MA: Allyn & Bacon.

Bagby, R. M., Quilty, L. C., & Ryder, A. (2008). Personality and depression. *Canadian Journal of Psychiatry, 53*, 14–25.

Bailey, F. L., & Rothblatt, H. B. (1971). *Successful techniques for criminal trials.* Rochester, NY: Lawyers Cooperative.

Bailey, F. L., & Rothblatt, H. B. (2007). Successful techniques for criminal trials. In J. D. Lieberman & B. D. Sales (Eds.), *Scientific jury selection* (pp. 65–70). Washington, DC: American Psychological Association.

Baker, T., & Baker, J. (1996). Preventing police suicide. *FBI Law Enforcement Bulletin, 65*(10), 24–27.

Baldus, D. C., Woodworth, G., Zuckerman, D., Weiner, N. A., & Broffitt, B. (2001). The use of peremptory challenges in capitol murder trials: A legal and empirical analysis. *University of Pennsylvania Journal of Constitutional Law, 3*, 1–172.

Baldwin, J. (1993). Police interview techniques: Establishing truth or proof? *The British Journal of Criminology, 33*, 325–352.

Bandura, A. (1990). Mechanisms of moral disengagement. In W. Reich (Ed.), *Origins of terrorism: Psychologies, ideologies, theologies, states of mind.* Cambridge: Cambridge University Press, 161–191.

Bandura, A. (1998). Personal and collective efficacy in human adaptation and change. In J. G. Adair, D. Belanger, & K. L. Dion (Eds.), *Advances in Psychological Science* (pp. 51–72). East Sussex, UK: Psychology Press Ltd.

Bandura, A., Ross, D., & Ross, S. (1961). Transmission of aggression through imitation of aggressive models. *Journal of Abnormal and Social Psychology, 63*, 375–382.

Bandura, A., & Walters, R. H. (1959). *Adolescent aggression.* New York: Ronald Press.

Barbaree, H. E., Bogaert, A. F., & Seto, M. C. (1995). Sexual reorientation therapy for pedophiles: Practices and controversies. In L. Diamant & R. D. McAnulty (Eds.), *The psychology of sexual orientation, behavior, and identity: A handbook* (pp. 357–383). Westport, CT: Greenwood Press.

Barbaree, H. E., and Seto, M. C. (1997). Pedophilia: Assessment and treatment. *Sexual Deviance: Theory, Assessment, and Treatment*, 175–193.

Bardsley, M., Bell, R., & Lohr, D. (n.d.). *The BTK story.* TruTV. Retrieved October 30, 2008, from http://www.trutv.com/library/crime/ serial_killers/unsolved/btk/15.html

Barland, G. H. (1988). The polygraph use in the USA and elsewhere. In A. Gale (Ed.), *The polygraph test: Lies, truth and science.* London: Sage.

Barland, G. H., & Raskin, D. C. (1976). *Validity and reliability of polygraph examination of criminal suspects* (Contract No. 75-N1-99-0001). Washington, DC: National Institute of Justice, Department of Justice.

Barling, J. (1996). The prediction, experience, and consequences of workplace violence. In G. R. VandenBos & E. Q. Bulatao (Eds.), *Violence on the job: Identifying risks and developing solutions* (pp. 29–49). Washington, DC: American Psychological Association.

Baron, R. A., & Richardson, D. R. (1994). *Human aggression* (2nd ed.). New York: Plenum.

Barrick, M. R., & Mount, M. K. (1991). The big five personality dimensions and job performance: A meta-analysis. *Personnel Psychology, 44*, 1–26.

Barrick, M. R., & Mount, M. K. (2005). Yes, personality matters: Moving on to more important matters. *Human Performance, 18*, 359–372.

Barrick, M. R., Mount, M. K., & Judge, T. A. (2001). The FFM personality dimensions and job performance: A meta-analysis of meta-analyses. *International Journal of Selection and Assessment, 9*, 9–30.

Bartol, C. R. (1991a). *Criminal behavior.* Upper Saddle River, NJ: Prentice Hall.

Bartol, C. R. (1991b). Predictive validation of the MMPI for small-town police officers who fail. *Professional Psychology Research and Practice, 22*, 127–132.

Bartol, C. R., & Bartol, A. M. (2004). *Introduction to forensic psychology* (pp. 84–87). Thousand Oaks, CA: Sage.

Bass, B. M. (1985). *Leadership and performance beyond expectation.* New York: Free Press.

Bass, B. M. (1990). From transactional to transformational leadership: Learning to share the vision. *Organizational Dynamics* (Winter), 19–31.

Bass, E., & Davis, L. (1994). *The courage to heal.* New York: Harper Collins.

Bath, H. L., & Haapala, D. A. (1993). Intensive family preservation services with abused and battered women syndrome and expert testimony. *Vanderbilt Law Review, 35*, 753.

Baugh, M. (2006). *Emotional regulation skills.* DBTSF. Retrieved May 6, 2008, from http://www.dbtsf.com/emotional-regulation.htm

Baumgartner, J. V., Scalora, M. J., & Huss, M. T. (2002, January). Assessment of the Wilson sex fantasy questionnaire among child molesters and nonsexual forensic offenders. *Sex Abuse, 14*(1), 19–30.

Beavan, C. (2001). *Fingerprints: The origins of crime detection and the murder case that launched forensic science.* New York: Hyperion.

Beaver, H. (1999). *Client violence against professional social workers: Frequency, worker characteristics, and impact on worker job satisfaction, burnout, and health.* Doctoral dissertation, University of Arkansas, 1999. Dissertation Abstracts International 60(06).

Bechara, A., Damasio, H., & Damasio, A. R. (2000). Emotion, decision making and the orbitofrontal cortex. *Cerebral Cortex, 10*, 295–307.

Beck, A. T. (2002). Prisoners of hate. *Behavior Research and Therapy, 40*(3), 209–216.

Beckham, C. M., Spray, B. J., & Pietz, C. A. (2007). Jurors' locus of control and defendants' attractiveness in death penalty sentencing. *The Journal of Social Psychology, 147*(3), 285–298.

Bedau, H. A., & Putnam, C. (1996). False confessions and other follies. In D. S. Connery (Ed.), *Convicting the innocent* (pp. 69–83). Cambridge, MA: Brookline Books.

Beecher-Monas, E., & Garcia-Rill, E. (2003). Danger at the edge of chaos: Predicting violent behavior in a post-Daubert world. *Cardozo Law Review, 24*.

Begany, J. J., & Milburn, M. A. (2007). Psychological predictors of sexual harassment: Authoritarianism, hostile sexism, and rape myths. *Psychology of Men & Masculinity, 3*, 2.

Begleiter, H., & Platz, A. (1969). Evoked potentials: Modifications by classical conditioning. *Science, 166*(3906), 769–771.

Beirich, H., & Potok, M. (2009). USA: Hate groups, radical-right violence, on the rise. *Policing, 3*(3), 255–263.

Bekerian, D. A., Dennett, J. L., Reeder, C., Slopper, K., Saunders, H., & Evans, L. (1994, April). *The influence of the cognitive interview technique on attributions of memory.* Paper presented at the annual conference of the British Psychological Society, Brighton, England.

Bell, B., Rose, C. L., & Damon, A. (1972). The normative aging study: An interdisciplinary and longitudinal study of health and aging. *Aging & Human Development, 3*(1), 5–17.

Bell, B. E., & Loftus, E. F. (1985). Vivid persuasion in the courtroom. *Journal of Personality Assessment, 49*(6), 659–664.

Belli, M. (1982). *Modern trials.* St. Paul, MN: West Publishing.

Bem, D. J. (1966). Inducing belief in false confessions. *Journal of Personality and Social Psychology, 3*, 707–710.

Bem, D. J. (1967). When saying is believing. *Psychology Today, 1*(2), 21–25.

Bennell, C., & Jones, N. J. (2005). Between a ROC and a hard place: A method for linking serial burglaries using an offender's modus operandi. *Journal of Investigative Psychology and Offender Profiling, 2*, 23–41.

Bennett, R. J., & Robinson, S. L. (2000). Development of a measure of workplace deviance. *Journal of Applied Psychology, 85*, 349–360.

Benokraitis, N. V., & Feagin, J. R. (1986). *Modern sexism: Blatant, subtle, and covert discrimination.* Englewood Cliffs, NJ: Prentice Hall.

Ben-Shakhar, G., & Dolev, K. (1996). Psychophysiological detection through the guilty knowledge technique: The effects of mental countermeasures. *Journal of Applied Psychology, 81*, 273–281.

Bensimon, H. F. (1994, January). Violence in the workplace. *Training and Development, 48*, 26–28.

Berger, J., Webster, M., Ridgeway, C., & Rosenholtz, S. (1986). Status cues, expectations and behavior. *Advances in Group Processes, 3*, 1–22.

Berk, R. A., Newton, P. J., & Berk, S.F. (1986). What a difference a day makes: An empirical study of the impact of shelters for battered women. *Journal of Marriage and the Family, 48*, 481–490.

Berkowitz, L. (1962). *Aggression: A social psychological analysis.* San Francisco, CA: Jossey-Bass.

Berkowitz, L. & LePage, A. (1967). Weapons as aggression-eliciting stimuli. *Journal of Personality and Social Psychology, 7*, 202–207.

Berlinger, J. (Producer & Director). (1992). *My brothers' keeper* [Motion picture]. USA: Wellspring Media.

Bernstein, E. M., Laney, C., Morris, E. K., & Loftus, E. F. (2005). False memories about food can lead to food avoidance. *Social Cognition, 23*, 11–34.

Bernstein, E. M., & Putnam, F. W. (1986). Development, reliability, and validity of a dissociation scale. *Journal of Nervous and Mental Disease, 174*, 727–735.

Berry, C. M., Ones, D. S., & Sackett, P. R. (2007). Interpersonal deviance, organizational deviance, and their common correlates: A review and meta-analysis. *Journal of Applied Psychology, 92*, 410–424.

Bertman, L. J., Thompson, J. W., Waters, W. F., Estupinan-Kane, L., Martin, A., & Russell, L. (2003). Effects of an individualized treatment protocol on restoration of competency in pretrial forensic inpatients. *Journal of the American Academy of Psychiatry and the Law, 31*, 27–35.

Bettelheim, B. (1962). *Dialogues with Mothers.* Glencoe, IL: The Free Press.

Bettelheim, B. (1950). *Love is Not Enough.* New York: The Free Press.

Bettelheim, B. (1954). *Symbolic Wounds.* Glencoe, IL: The Free Press.

Bettelheim, B. (1960). *The Informed Heart.* New York, NY: Alfred A. Knopf.

Bettelheim, B. (1955). *Truants from Life.* Glencoe, IL: The Free Press.

Bettencourt, B. A., Tally, A., Benjamin, A. J., & Valentine, J. (2006). Personality and aggressive behavior under provoking and neutral conditions: A meta-analytic review. *Psychological Bulletin, 132*, 751–777.

Bianchini, K. J., Greve, K. W., & Glynn, G. (2005). On the diagnosis of malingered pain-related disability: Lessons from cognitive malingering research. *The Spine Journal, 5*, 404–417.

Bies, R. I., Tripp, T. M., & Kramer, R. M. (1997). At the breaking point: Cognitive and social dynamics of revenge in organizations. In R. A. Giacalone & J. Greenberg (Eds.), *Antisocial behavior in organizations* (pp. 18–36). Thousand Oaks, CA: Sage.

Bilbrey, R. (1999, November–December). *Civil commitment of sexually violent predators: A misguided attempt to solve a serious problem.* The Missouri Bar Journal. Retrieved February 6, 2009 from, http://www.mobar.org/1182129e-7fb6-4d16-a1e8-318a8b493f10.aspx

Binet, A. (1900). *La suggestibilite´* [On suggestibility]. Paris: Schleicher.

Biskind, E. L. (1954). *How to prepare a case for trial.* Englewood Cliffs, NJ: Prentice Hall.

Black, H. C. (1990). *Black's law dictionary.* St. Paul, MN: West Publishing Co.

Black, J. (2000). Personality testing and police selection: Utility of the "Big Five." *New Zealand Journal of Psychology, 29*, 2–9.

Blasi, A. (1980). Bridging moral cognition and moral action: A critical review of the literature. *Psychological Bulletin, 88*, 1–45.

Blau, T. H. (1994). *Psychological services for law enforcement.* New York: Wiley.

Blau, T. H., Super, J. T., & Brady, L. (1993). The MMPI good cop/bad cop in identifying dysfunctional law enforcement personnel. *Journal of Police and Criminal Psychology, 9*(1), 2–4.

Block, R. (1977). *Violent crime.* Lexington, MA: Lexington Books.

Bloom, H., Eisen, R. S., Pollock, N., & Webster, C. D. (2000). *WRA-20 Workplace risk assessment: A guide for evaluating violence potential, Version 1.* Toronto: Workplace.calm inc.

Bloom, D., & Kleber, R. J. (1989). *Crisis management for corporate self-defense.* New York: Amacom.

Blowers, A. N., & Bjerregaard, B. (1994, Winter). The admissibility of expert testimony was most prevalent in homicide cases. *Journal of Psychiatry and Law, 22,* 527–560.

Blue, L. A. (2007). Identifying and addressing juror bias in voir dire. In J. D. Lieberman & B. D. Sales (Eds.), *Scientific jury selection.* Washington, DC: American Psychological Association.

Bodenhausen, G. V. (1990). Stereotypes as judgmental heuristics: Evidence of circadian variations in discrimination. *Psychological Science, 1,* 319–322.

Boer, D. P. (2006). Sexual offender risk assessment strategies: Is there a convergence of opinion yet? *Sexual Offender Treatment, 1,* 1–4.

Boer, D. P., Hart, S. D., Kropp, P. R., & Webster, C. D. (1997). *Manual for the Sexual Violence Risk – 20: Professional guidelines for assessing risk of sexual violence.* Vancouver, B.C.: The Mental Health, Law, and Policy Institute.

Bogaert, A. F., Bezeau, S., Kuban, M., & Blanchard, R. (1997). Birth order, sexual orientation, and pedophilia. *Journal of Abnormal Psychology, 106,* 331–335.

Bohl, N. (1995). Professionally administered critical incident debriefing for police officers. In M. I. Kurke & E. M. Scrivner (Eds.), *Police psychology into the 21st century.* Hillsdale, NJ: Lawrence Erlbaum.

Bonazzoli, M. J. (1998). Jury selection and bias: Debunking invidious stereotypes through science. *Quinnipiac Law Review, 18,* 247–305.

Bono, J. E., Foldes, H. J., Vinson, G., & Muros, J. P. (2007). The role of supervision and leadership. *Journal of Applied Psychology, 92*(5), 1357–1367.

Bono, J. E., & Judge, T. A. (2003). Self concordance at work: Toward understanding the motivational effects of transformational leaders. *Academy of Management Journal, 46,* 554–571.

Booth, A. D., & Osgood, W. (1993). The influence of testosterone on deviance in adulthood: Assessing and explaining the relationship. *Criminology, 31*(1), 93–117.

Borchard, E. (1932). *Convicting the innocent: Errors of criminal justice.* New Haven, CT: Yale.

Boren, R. W. (2000). The hillside strangler trial. *Loyola of Los Angeles Law Review, 33,* 705.

Borgida, E., Rudman, L. A., & Manteufel, L. L. (1995). On the courtroom use and misuse of gender stereotyping research. *Journal of Social Issues, 51,* 181–192.

Borman, W. C., White, L. A., Pulakos, E. D., & Oppler, S. H. (1991). Models of supervisor job performance ratings. *Journal of Applied Psychology, 76,* 863–872.

Bothwell, R. K., Deffenbacher, K. A., & Brigham, J. C. (1987). Correlation of eyewitness accuracy and confidence: Optimality hypothesis revisited. *Journal of Applied Psychology, 72,* 691–695.

Bouchard, T. J. (2004). Genetic influence on human psychological traits: A survey. *Current Directions in Psychological Science, 13,* 148–151.

Boyle, K. (2004). *Arc of justice: A saga of race, civil rights, and murder in the jazz age.* New York: Henry Holt.

Boyle, G. J., Richards, L. M., & Baglioni, A. J., Jr. (1993). Children's motivation analysis test (CMAT); An experimental manipulation of curiosity and boredom. *Personality and Individual Differences, 15,* 637–641.

Braid, J. (2008). *Neurypnology or the rationale of nervous sleep: Considered in relation with animal magnetism.* Whitefish, MT: Kessinger Publishing. (Original work published 1843.)

Brakel, S. J., & Rock, R. S. (Eds.). (1971). *The mentally disabled and the law* (p. 36). Chicago: University of Chicago Press.

Brand, C. (1987). The importance of general intelligence. In S. Modgil & C. Modgil (Eds.), *Arthur Jensen: Consensus and controversy* (pp. 251–265). Philadelphia, PA: Falmer Press.

Brandon, R., & Davies, C. (1973). *Wrongful imprisonment.* London, England: Allen and Unwin Brothers Ltd.

Brandt, D. (2002). *Mind control and the secret state.* New dawn magazine. Retrieved November 2, 2008 from, http://www.newdawnmagazine.com/Articles/Mind%20Control%20and%20the%20Secret%20State.html

Braverman, M. (1999). *Preventing workplace violence: A guide for employers and practitioners.* Thousand Oaks, CA: Sage.

Bray, R. M., & Noble, A. M. (1978). Authoritarianism and decisions of mock juries: Evidence of jury bias and group polarization. *Journal of Personality and Social Psychology, 36,* 1424–1430.

Brayfield, A. H., & Rothe, H. F. (1951). An index of job satisfaction. *Journal of Applied Psychology, 35,* 307–311.

Breuer, J., & Freud, S. (1955). Studies on hysteria. In J. Strachey (Ed.), *The standard edition of the complete psychological works of Sigmund Freud* (Vol. 2, pp. 21–319). London: Hogarth Press. (Original work published 1895.)

Bright (2007, November 26). Grisly court evidence makes juries more likely to convict. *Science Daily.* Retrieved February 24, 2008 from http://www.sciencedaily.com/releases/2007/11/071119100343.htm

British Government of Ireland Act (1920). EconomicExpert.com. Retrieved August 26, 2009, from http://www.economicexpert.com/a/Government:of:Ireland:Act:1920.html

Britton, P. (1997). *The jigsaw man.* London: Bantam Press.

Brophy, J. (1966). *The meaning of murder.* London: Whiting & Wheaton.

Brough, P. (2005). A comparative investigation of the predictors of work-related psychological well-being within police, fire and ambulance workers. *New Zealand Journal of Psychology, 34,* 127–134.

Brower, M. C., & Price, B. H. (2001). Neuropsychiatry of frontal lobe dysfunction in violent and criminal behaviour: A critical review. *Journal of Neurology, Neurosurgery, & Psychiatry, 71*(6), 720–726.

Brown, C. W., & Ghiselli, E. E. (1947). Factors related to the proficiency of motor coach operators. *Journal of Applied Psychology, 31,* 477–479.

Brown, D., Scheflin, A. W., & Hammond, D. C. (1998). *Memory, trauma, treatment and the law.* New York: Norton.

Brown, T. A. (2007). Temporal course and structural relationships among dimensions of temperament and DSM–IV anxiety and mood disorder constructs. *Journal of Abnormal Psychology, 116,* 313–328.

Brownmiller, S. (1975). *Against our will: Men, women and rape.* New York: Simon & Schuster.

Bruschke, J., & Loges, W. E. (2003). *Free press vs. fair trials: Examining publicity's role in trial outcomes.* Mahwah, NJ: Lawrence Erlbaum Associates.

Bruyère, S. M., & O'Keeffe, J. O. (1994). *Implications of the Americans with disabilities act for psychology.* Washington, DC: American Psychological Association & Springer.

Bryant, R. A., Sackville, T., Dang, S. T., Moulds, M., & Guthrie, R. (1999). Treating acute stress disorder: An evaluation of cognitive behavior therapy and supportive counseling techniques. *American Journal of Psychiatry, 156,* 1780–1786.

Buckhout, R. (1974). Eyewitness testimony. *Scientific American, 231,* 23–31.

Buckhout, R. (1980). Nearly 2000 witnesses can be wrong. *Bulletin of the Psychonomic Society, 16*(4), 307–310.

Budd, R. D., & Lindstrom, D. M. (1982). Characteristics of victims of PCP-related deaths in Los Angeles country. *Journal of Clinical Toxicology, 19*, 997–1004.

Bulatao, E. Q., & VandenBos, G. R. (1996). Workplace violence: Its scope and issues. In G. R.VandenBos & E. Q.Bulatao (Eds.), *Violence on the job* (pp. 1–23). Washington, DC: American Psychological Association.

Bureau of Justice Statistics. (1998). *Compendium of federal justice statistics.* Retrieved February 17, 2008, from http://www.ojp.usdoj.gov/bjs/abstract/cfjs98.htm

Burgess, A. W., Burgess, A. G., & Douglas, J. E. (1994). Examining violence in the workplace. *Journal of Psychosocial Nursing, 32*, 14.

Bushman, B. J., & Baumeister, R. F. (1998). Threatened egotism, narcissism, self-esteem, and direct and displaced aggression: Does self-love or self-hate lead to violence? *Journal of Personality & Social Psychology, 75*, 219–229.

Buss, A. H. (1961). *The psychology of aggression.* New York: Wiley.

Buss, A. H. (1963). Physical aggression in relation to different frustrations. *Journal of Abnormal and Social Psychology, 67*, 1–7.

Butler, L. D., Duran, R. E., Jasiukaitis, P., Koopman, C., & Spiegel, D. (1996). Hypnotizability and traumatic experience: A diathesis-stress model of dissociative symptomatology. *American Journal Psychiatry, 153*(7), 42–63.

Caine, S., Smrkovski, L., & Wilson, M. (1990). *Voiceprint identification.* Forensic tape analysis, Inc. Retrieved October 19, 2008, from http://www.forensictapeanalysisinc.com/Articles/voice_id.htm

Canadian of Pak origin kills his daughter for not wearing veil. *The Times of India* (2007, December 11). Retrieved August 1, 2008, from http://barbadosfreepress.wordpress.com/2007/12/11/canadian-father-murders-teenage-daughter-over-refusal-to-wear-muslim-headscarf-hijab/

Campbell, J., & Lewandowski, L. (1997). Mental and physical health effects of intimate partner violence on women and children. *The Psychiatric Clinics of North America, 20*, 353–374.

Cantor, B. J. (2009). *Cross-examanination.* Expert article library. Retrieved June 28, 2008, from http://expertpages.com/news/cross_examination.htm

Cantor, D. (1994). *Criminal shadows.* London: HarperCollins.

Cantor, D. (1995). Psychology of offender profiling. In R. Bull & D. Carson (Eds.), *Handbook of psychology in legal contexts* (pp. 343–355). New York: Wiley.

Cantor, D. (2000). Offender profiling and criminal differentiation. *Legal and Criminological Psychology, 5*, 23–46.

Canter, D. V., Alison, L. J., Alison, E., & Wentink, N. (2004). The organized/disorganized typology of serial murder: Myth or model? *Psychology, Public Policy, and Law, 10*, 293–320.

Carbone, J. (2007). Into the wonderland of clairvoyance: Faulty science and the prediction of future dangerousness. In J. Kitaeff (Ed.), *Malingering, lies, and junk science in the courtroom.* Youngstown, NY: Cambria Press.

Carlan, P. E., & Nored, L. S. (2008, June). An Examination of Officer Stress: Should Police Departments Implement Mandatory Counseling? *Journal of Police and Criminal Psychology, 23*(1), 8–15.

Carroll, D. (2005). How accurate is polygraph lie detection? In L. S. Wrightsman & S. M. Fulero (Eds.), *Forensic psychology* (2nd ed., pp. 95–101). Belmont, VA: Wadsworth.

Carroll, J. B. (1961). The nature of the data, or how to choose a correlation coefficient. *Psychometrika, 26*, 347–372.

Carroll, J. B. (1993). *Human cognitive abilities: A survey of factor-analytic studies.* New York: Cambridge University Press.

Carroll, R. T. (2007). *Confirmation bias.* The skeptic's dictionary. Retrieved October 15, 2008, from http://skepdic.com/confirmbias.html

Carroll, R. T. Polygraph (lie detector). *The skeptic's dictionary.* Retrieved November 21, 2007, from http://www.Skepdic.com

Carter, D., & Radelet, L. (1999). *The police and the community* (6th ed.). New York: Prentice-Hall.

Carver, C. S., & White, T. L. (1994). Behavioral inhibition, behavioral activation, and affective responses to impending reward and punishment: The BIS/BAS Scales. *Journal of Personality and Social Psychology, 67*, 319–333.

Catalano, R., Dooley, D., & Novaco, R. (1993). Using ECA survey data to examine the effects of job layoffs on violent behavior. *Hospital and Community Psychiatry, 44*, 874–879.

Catharsis reconsidered. Retrieved June 9, 2007, from http://robertmasters.com/Work_Section/catharsis.htm

Catherall, D. R. (1998). Treating traumatized families. In C. R. Figley (Ed.), *Burnout in families: The systemic costs of caring* (pp. 187–215). Boca Raton, FL: CRC Press.

Cattell, J. M. (1895). Measurements of the accuracy of recollection. *Science, 2*, 761–766.

Cattell, R. B. (1970). A factor analytic system for clinicians. 1. The integration of functional and psychometric requirements in a quantitative and computerized diagnostic system. In A. R. Mahrer (Ed.), *New approaches to personality classification.* New York: Columbia University Press.

Cattell, R. B. (1971). Estimating modulator indices and state liabilities. *Multivariate Behavioral Research, 6*, 7–33.

Cattell, R. B. (1969). The profile similarity coefficient, rp, in vocational guidance and diagnostic classification. *The British Journal of Educational Psychology, 39*, 131–142.

Cattell, R. B., & Jaspers, J. (1967). A general plasmode (No. 30–10–5–2) for factor analytic exercises and research. *Multivariate Behavioral Research Monographs, 67*(3), 1–212.

Cattell, R. B., & Vogelmann, S. (1977). A comprehensive trial of the scree and KG criteria for determining the number of factors. *Multivariate Behavioral Research, 12*, 289–325.

Ceci, S. J., & Bruck, M. (1993). Suggestibility of the child witness: A historical review and synthesis. *Psychological Bulletin, 113*(3), 403–439.

Chaffin, M., & Schmidt, S. (2006). An evidence-based perspective on interventions to stop or prevent child abuse. In J. R. Lutzker (Ed.), *Preventing Violence: Research and Evidence-Based Intervention Strategies* (pp. 49–68). Washington, DC: American Psychological Association.

Chapman, W. P. (1960). Depth electrode studies in patients with temporal lobe epilepsy. In E. R. Ramey & S. O'Doherty (Eds.), *Electrical studies on the unanesthetized brain* (pp. 334–350). New York: Hoeber.

Charen, M. (1998, July 15). Feelings, not morality, rule. *Jewish World Review.* Retrieved March 30, 2008, from http://www.jewishworldreview.com/cols/charen071598.html

Chassell, C. (1935). *The relation between morality and intellect.* New York: Teachers College Press.

Chibnall, J. T., & Detrick, P. (2003). The NEO-PI-R, inwald personality inventory, and MMPI in the prediction of police academy performance: A case for incremental validity. *American Journal of Criminal Justice, 27*, 233–248.

Christie, R. (1991). Authoritarianism and related constructs. In J. P. Robinson, P. R. Shaver, & L. S. Wrightsman (Eds.), *Measures of personality and social psychological attitudes.* San Diego, CA: Academic Press.

Christie, R. (1993). Some experimental approaches to authoritarianism: I. A retrospective on the Einstellung (rigidity?) Paradigm. In W. F. Stone, G. Lederer, & R. Christie (Eds.), *Strength and weakness: The authoritarian personality today.* New York: Springer-Verlag.

Chuang, H. T., & Addington, D. (1988). Homosexual panic: A review of its concept. *Canadian Journal of Psychiatry, 33*, 613–617.

City of New York agrees on $3 million settlement to family of Amadou Diallo. CourtTVnews. Retrieved February 25, 2008, from http://www.courttv.com/trials/diallo/010604_settlement_ap.html

Church, R., & Robertson, N. (1999). How state police agencies are addressing the issue of wellness. *Policing: An International Journal of Police Strategies and Management, 22*, 304–312.

Clark, L. A. (2005). Temperament as a unifying basis for personality and psychopathology. *Journal of Abnormal Psychology, 114*, 505–521.

Clark, L. A. (2007). Assessment and diagnosis of personality disorder: Perennial issues and an emerging reconceptualization. *Annual Review of Psychology, 58*, 227–257.

Clawar, S. S., & Rivlin, B. V. (1991). Children held hostage: Dealing with programmed and brainwashed children. Chicago, IL: American Bar Association.

Clearly, A. (2005). *Scientific jury selection: History, practice, and controversy.* Retrieved February 3, 2008, from http://www.publications.villanova.edu/Concept/2005.html

Cleckley, H. M. (1988). *The mask of sanity: An attempt to clarify some issues about the so-called psychopathic personality* (5th ed.). Augusta, GA: E.S. Cleckley.

Clifford, B. R. (1983). Memory for voices: The feasibility and quality of earwitness evidence. In S. A. Lloyd-Bostock & B. R. Clifford (Eds.), *Evaluating witness evidence* (pp. 189–218). New York: Wiley.

Clifford, B. R., Rathborn, H., & Bull, R. (1981). The effects of delay on voice recognition accuracy. *Law and Human Behavior, 5*, 201–208.

Coale, A. J., & Banister, J. (1994, August). Five decades of missing females in China. *Demography, 31*(3), 472.

Cochrane, C. N. (1929). *Thucydides and the science of history.* London: Oxford University Press.

Cocozza, J., & Steadman, H. (1976). The failure of psychiatric predictions of dangerousness. *Rutgers Law Review, 29*, 1084, 1096–1099.

Cohn, A., & Daro, D. (1987). Is treatment too late: What ten years of evaluative research tell us. *Child Abuse & Neglect, 11*, 433–442.

Cohen, A. S., Rosen, R. C., & Goldstein, L. (1985). EEG hemispheric asymmetry during sexual arousal: Psychophysiological patterns in responsive, unresponsive, & dysfunctional men. *Journal of Abnormal Psychology, 94*(4), 580–590.

Cohen, B. J., McGarvey, E. L., Pinkerton, R. C., & Kryzhanivska, L. (2004). Willingness and competence of depressed and schizophrenic inpatients to consent to research. *Journal of the American Academy of Psychiatry Law, 32*, 134–143.

Cohn, A. H., & Daro, D. (1987). Is treatment too late: What ten years of evaluative research tell us. *Child Abuse & Neglect, 11*, 433–442.

Cole, S. A. (2001). *Suspect identities: A history of fingerprinting and criminal identification* (pp. 60–61). Cambridge, MA: Harvard University Press.

Cole, S. A. (2005). More than zero: Accounting for error in latent fingerprint identification. *Journal of Criminal Law & Criminology, 95*(3), 985–1078.

Cole, S. A. (2006). The prevalence and potential causes of wrongful conviction by fingerprint evidence. *Golden Gate University Law Review, 47*, 49–105.

Comrey, A. L. (1978). Common methodological problems in factor analytic studies. *Journal of Consulting and Clinical Psychology, 46*, 648–659.

Connor, W. R. (1984). *Thucydides.* Princeton: Princeton University Press.

Connors, E., Lundregan, T., Miller, N., & McEwan, T. (1996). *Convicted by juries, exonerated by science: Case studies in the use of DNA evidence to establish innocence after trial.* Alexandria, VA: National Institute of Justice.

Consedine, N. S., & Magai, C. (2002). The uncharted waters of emotion: Ethnicity, trait emotion, and emotion expression in older adults. *Journal of Cross-Cultural Gerontology, 17*, 71–100.

Conti, R. P. (1999).The psychology of false confessions. *The Journal of Credibility Assessment and Witness Psychology, 2*(1), 14–36.

Cook, P. E., & Hinman, D. L. (1999). Serial murder in lethal violence: A sourcebook on fatal domestic, and acquaintance violence. Boca Raton, FL: CRC Press.

Cooke, G. (1969). The court study unit: Patient characteristics and differences between patients judged competent and incompetent. *Journal of Clinical Psychology, 25*, 140–143.

Cooper, A. J., Sandhu, S., Losztyn, S., & Cernovsky, Z. (1992). A double-blind placebo controlled trial of medroxyprogesterone acetate and cyproterone acetate with seven pedophiles. *Canadian Journal of Psychiatry, 37*(10), 687–693.

Copes, H. (2005). *Policing and stress.* Upper Saddle River, NJ: Pearson.

Copson, G. (1995). *Coals to Newcastle: A study of offender profiling.* London: Home Office.

Cortina, J. M., Doherty, M. L., Schmitt, N., Kaufman, G., & Smith, R. G. (1992). The "Big Five" personality factors in the IPI and MMPI: Predictors of police performance. *Personnel Psychology, 45*, 119–140.

Costa, P. T., Jr., & McCrae, R. R. (1992). *Revised NEO personality inventory (NEO PI-R) professional manual.* Odessa, FL: Psychological Assessment Resources.

Court transcript. Examination—in—cheif of Dr. Anne K. Dzus. Retrieved February 6, 2008, from http://robertlatimer.net/documents/page110.htm

CourtTVnews. (2002, April 1). *Workplace shooting suspect accused of killing seven victims in seven minutes.* Retrieved July 13, 2007, from http://www.courttv.com/trials/mcdermott/background.html

Cowan, G., & Fairchild, H. H. (1997). Introduction to the issue. *Journal of Social Issues, 53*, 409–415.

Craven, Z. (2003). *Battered women syndrome.* Australian Domestic and Family Violence Clearinghouse. Retrieved November 21, 2007, from http://www.austdvclearinghouse.unsw.edu.au/.

Crimes of honor. Stop! The killing of our own blood. Retrieved March 23, 2008, from http://www.karokari.com/index.html

Cross, J. (1982).The expert as educator: A proposed approach to the use of battered women syndrome and expert testimony. *Vanderbilt Law Review, 35*, 753.

Crouse, J., & Stalker, D. (2007). Do right-wing authoritarian beliefs originate from psychological conflict? *Psychoanalytic Psychology, 24*(1), 25–44.

Cullen, M. J., & Sackett, P. (2003). Personality and counterproductive workplace behavior. In M. A. Barrick & A. M. Ryan (Eds.), *Personality and work* (pp. 150–182). San Francisco, CA: Jossey-Bass.

Cutler, B. L. (1990). Introduction: The status of scientific jury selection in psychology and law. *Forensic Reports, 3*, 227–232.

Cutler, B. L., Dexter, H. R., & Penrod, S. D. (1990). Nonadversarial methods for improving juror sensitivity to eyewitness evidence. *Journal of Applied Social Psychology, 20*, 1197–1207.

Cutler, B. L., Moran, G., & Narby, D. J. (1992). Jury selection in insanity cases. *Journal of Research in Personality, 26*, 165–182.

Cutler, B. L., & Penrod, S. D. (1988). Improving the reliability of eyewitness identification: Lineup construction and presentation. *Journal of Applied Psychology, 73*, 281–290.

Cutler, B. L., & Penrod, S. D. (1995). *Mistaken identifications: The eyewitness, psychology, and the law.* New York: Cambridge University Press.

Cutler, B. L., Penrod, S. D., & Dexter, H. R. (1989). The eyewitness, the expert psychologist, and the jury. *Law and Human Behavior, 13*, 311–332.

Cutler, B. L., Penrod, S. D., & Dexter, H. R. (1990). Jury sensitivity to eyewitness identification evidence. *Law and Human Behavior, 14*, 185–191.

Cutler, B. L., Penrod, S. D., & Martens, T. K. (1987). The reliability of eyewitness identifications. The role of system and estimator variables. *Law and Human Behavior, 11*, 223–258.

Cutler, B. L., Penrod, S. D., & Stuve, T. E. (1988). Jury decision making in eyewitness identification cases. *Law and Human Behavior, 12*, 41–56.

Cyphers, G. C. (1999). Out of the shadows: Elder abuse and neglect. *Policy and Practice of Public Human Services, 570*, 25–30.

Dabbs, J. M., Jr. (1991). Salivary testosterone and cortisol among late adolescent male offenders. *Journal of Abnormal Child Psychology, 19*(4), 469–478.

Dahmer, L. (1994). *A father's story.* New York: William Morrow & Co.

Dalal, R. S. (2005). A meta-analysis of the relationship between organizational citizenship behavior and counterproductive work behavior. *Journal of Applied Psychology, 90*, 1241–1255.

Daley, R. (1981). *Prince of the city.* New York: Berkeley.

Damaska, M. R. (1997). *Evidence law adrift.* New Haven: Yale University Press, quoting professor Edmund Morgan, p. 34.

Darley, J. M., & Latane, B. (1968). Bystander intervention in emergencies: Diffusion of responsibility. *Journal of Personality and Social Psychology, 8*, 377–383.

Darrow, C. (1927). *Clarence Darrow's two greatest trials: Reports of the Scopes anti-evolution case and the Dr. Sweet Negro.* Gerard, Kansas: Haldeman-Julius Co.

Darrow, C. (1936, May). Attorney for the defense. *Esquire, 5*, 36.

Darrow, C. (2007). Attorney for the defense. In J. D. Lieberman & B. D. Sales (Eds.), *Scientific jury selection.* Washington, DC: American Psychological Association.

Darwin, C. (1899). *The expression of emotions in man and animals.* London: John Murray.

Davenport, A. U. (2005). *Basic criminal law: The United States constitution, procedure and crimes* (p. 112). Upper Saddle River, NJ: Prentice Hall.

Davidson, P. R., & Parker, K. C. (2001). EMDR: A meta-analysis. *Journal of Consulting and Clinical Psychology, 69*, 305–316.

Davis, D. L. (1985). Treatment planning for the patient who is incompetent to stand trial. *Hospital and Community Psychiatry, 36*, 268–271.

Davis, R. C. (1961). Physiological responses as a means of valuating information. In A. D. Biderman & H. Zimmer (Eds.), *The manipulation of human behavior.* New York: Wiley.

Davis, R. D., & Rostow, C. (2003). Relationship between cognitive ability and background variables and disciplinary problems in law enforcement. *Applied H.R.M. Research, 8*(20), 77–80.

Davis, S. F., Armstrong, S. L., & Huss, M. T. (1993). Shock-elicited aggression is influenced by lead and/or alcohol exposure. *Bulletin of the Psychonomic Society, 31*(5), 353–421.

Davis, S. F., Arb, J. D., & Huss, M. T. (1995). Chronic cadmium exposure influences aggressive responding and partial reinforcement extinction performance. *Psychological Record, 45*(4), 565–575.

Dawes, R. M., Faust, D., & Meehl, P. E. (1989). Clinical versus actuarial judgment. *Science, New Series, 243*, 1668–1674.

De Fruyt, F., McCrae, R. R., Szirmák, Z., & Nagy, J. (2004). The five-factor personality inventory as a measure of the five-factor model: Belgian, American, and Hungarian comparisons with the NEO-PI-R. *Assessment, 11*, 207–215.

Death driver walks free due to automatism condition. *London Evening Standard.* Retrieved November 30, 2007, from http://www.thisislondon.co.uk/news/.

Deaton, W. L. (1992). Review of the Shipley Institute of Living Scale. In J. J. Kramer & J. C. Conoley (Eds.), *Mental measurements yearbook* (11th ed., pp. 822–824). Lincoln, NE: Buros Institute of Mental Measurements.

Decicco, D. A. (2000, December). Police officer candidate assessment and selection. *FBI Law Enforcement Bulletin (00145688), 69*(12), 1–8.

Deffenbacher, K. A., Bornstein, B. H., Penrod, S. D., & McGorty, E. K. (2004). A meta-analytic review of the effects of high stress on eyewitness memory. *Law and Human Behavior, 28*, 687–706.

Deffenbacher, K. A., Cross, J. F., Handkins, R. E., Chance, J. E., Goldstein, A. G., Hammersley, R., et al. (1989). Relevance of voice identification

research to criteria for evaluating reliability of an identification. *Journal of Psychology, 123*, 109–119.

Deffenbacher, K. A., & Loftus, E. F. (1982). Do jurors share a common understanding concerning eyewitness behavior? *Law and Human Behavior, 6*, 15–30.

DeNeve, K. M., & Cooper, H. (1998). The happy personality: A meta-analysis of 137 personality traits and subjective well-being. *Psychological Bulletin, 124*, 197–229.

Denning, D. E. (2000). *Cyberterrorism.* Retrieved August 15, 2009, from http://www.cs.georgetown.edu/~denning/infosec/cyberterror-GD.doc.

Denove, C. F., & Imwinkelried, E. J. (1995). Jury selection: An empirical investigation of demographic bias. *American Journal of Trial Advocacy, 19*, 285–336.

Denson, T. F., Pedersen, W. C., & Miller, N. (2006). The displaced aggression questionnaire. *Journal of Personality and Social Psychology, 90*(6), 1032–1051.

Depalma, A. (1997, December 1). Father's killing of Canadian girl: Mercy or murder? *The New York Times.* Retrieved October 21, 2008, from http://query.nytimes.com/gst/fullpage.html?res=9A0CE7D81E3AF932A35751C1A961958260&sec=health&spon=&pagewanted

DePaulo, B. M., Lindsay, J. J., Malone, B. E., Muhlenbruck, L., Charlton, K., & Cooper, H. (2003). Cues to deception. *Psychological Bulletin, 129*, 74–112.

Dershowitz, A. (1969, February). The psychiatrist's power in civil commitment. *Psychology Today, 2*, 43–47.

Dershowitz, A. (1974). The origins of preventive confinement in Anglo-American law, part 1: The American experience. *University of Cincinnati Law Review, 43*, 1.

Des Rosier, N., Feldthusen, B., & Hankivsky, O. A. R. (1998). Legal compensation for sexual violence: Therapeutic consequences and consequences for the judicial system. *Psychology, Public Policy, and Law, 4*, 433–451.

D'Souza, D. (2002, May 1). Sell USA's virtue to Muslim world. *USA Today Home Page.* Retrieved August 30, 2009, from http://www.usatoday.com/news/opinion/2002/05/02/ncguest2.htm%20; www.jihadwatch.org/archives/015034.php

Detrick, P., & Chibnall, J. T. (2006, November). NEO PI-R personality characteristics of high-performing entry-level police officers. *Psychological Services, 3*(4), 274–285.

Detrick, P., & Chibnall, J. T. (2002). Prediction of police officer performance with the Inwald personality inventory. *Journal of Police and Criminal Psychology, 17*(2), 9–17.

Detrick, P., Chibnall, J. T., & Luebbert, M. C. (2004). The revised NEO personality inventory as predictor of police academy performance. *Criminal Justice and Behavior, 31*, 676–694.

Dhossche, D. M. (1999). Aggression and recent substance abuse: Absence of association in psychiatric emergency room patients. *Comprehensive Psychiatry, 40*(5), 343–346.

Diagnostic and statistical manual of mental disorders (4th ed., text revision). (2000). Washington, DC: American Psychiatric Association.

Diallo Case. *Washingtonpost.com.* Retrieved February 25, 2008, from http://www.washingtonpost.com/wp-dyn/nation/specials/aroundthenation/nypd/

Diamond, S. S., & Zeisel, H. (1974). A courtroom experiment on juror selection and decision-making. *Personality and Social Psychology Bulletin, 1*, 276–277.

Diefendorff, J. M., & Mehta, K. (2007). The relations of motivational traits with workplace deviance. *Journal of Applied Psychology, 92*, 967–977.

Diefendorff, J. M., & Richard, E. M. (2003). Antecedents and consequences of emotional display rule perceptions. *Journal of Applied Psychology, 88*, 284–294.

Dietz, M. (1983). *Killing for profit.* Chicago: Nelson-Hall.

Dietz, P. (1986). Mass, serial and sensational homicides. *Bulletin of the New York Academy of Medicine, 62*(5), 477–491.

Dietz, P. E., & Hazelwood, R. R. (1982). Atypical autoerotic fatalities. *Medicine and Law, 1*, 301–319.

Difede, J., Apfeldorf, W. J., Cloitre, M., Spielman, L. A., & Perry, S. W. (1997). Acute psychiatric responses to the explosion at the World Trade Center: A case series. *Journal of Nervous and Mental Disease, 186*, 519–522.

Digman, J. M. (1996). The curious history of the five-factor model. In J. S. Wiggins (Ed.), *The five-factor model of personality: Theoretical perspectives* (pp. 1–20). New York: Guilford.

Dilchert, S., Ones, D. S., Davis, R. D., & Rostow, C. D. (2007). Cognitive ability predicts objectively measured counterproductive work behaviors. *Journal of Applied Psychology, 92*(3), 616–627.

Dixon, J. W., & Dixon, K. E. (2003, summer). Gender-specific clinical syndromes and their admissibility under the federal rules of evidence. *American Journal of Trial Advocacy, 27*, 25.

Dobbert, D. L. (2004). *Halting the sexual predators among us: Preventing attack, rape, and lust homicide.* Westport, CT: Greenwood.

Dobson, V., & Sales, B. (2000). The science of infanticide and mental illness. *Psychology, Public Policy, and Law, 4*, 1098–1112.

Dodson, C. S., & Krueger, L. E. (2006). I misremember it well: Why older adults are unreliable witnesses. *Psychonomic Bulletin & Review, 13*(5), 770–775.

Dolan, M., Millington, J., & Park, I. (2002). Personality and neuropsychological function in violent, sexual and arson offenders. *Medical Science and the Law, 42*(1), 34–43.

Dollard, J., Doob, L. W., Miller, N. E., Mowrer, O. H., & Sears, R. R. (1939). *Frustration and aggression.* Oxford, England: Yale University Press.

Douglas, J. E. (2003, February). Violent crime scene analysis: Modus operandi, signature, and staging. *Crime & clues.* Retrieved August 30, 2008, from http://www.crimeandclues.com/92feb003.html

Douglas, J. E., & Olshaker, M. (1999). *The anatomy of motive.* New York: Scribner.

Douglas, J. E., & Burgess, A. W. (1986). Criminal profiling: A viable investigative tool against violent crime. *FBI Law Enforcement Bulletin, 55*(12), 9–13.

Douglas, J. E., Burgess, A. W., Burgess, A. G., & Ressler, R. K. (1992). *Crime classification manual: A standard system for investigating and classifying violent crimes.* San Francisco, CA: Jossey-Bass.

Douglas, J. E., & Munn, C. (1992, February). Violent crime scene analysis: Modus operandi, signature, and staging. *FBI Law Enforcement Bulletin, 71*(1), 1–10.

Douglas, K. S., Yeomans, M., & Boer, D. P. (2005). Comparative validity analysis of multiple measures of violence risk in a sample of criminal offenders. *Criminal Justice and Behavior, 32*, 479–510.

Douglas, S., & Martinko, M. J. (2001). Exploring the role of individual differences in the prediction of workplace aggression. *Journal of Applied Psychology, 86*, 4.

Drebing et al. (2001). Homosexuelle pädophile und funktionelle netzwerke–fMRI-Fallstudie [Homosexual pedophilia and functional networks–An fMRI case report and literature review]. *Fortschritte der Neurologie, Psychiatrie, und ihrer Grenzgebiete, 69*, 539–544.

Drizin, S., & Leo, R. (2004, March). The problem of false confessions in the post-DNA world. *North Carolina Law Review, 82*(3).

Dror, I. E. (2005). Perception is far from perfection: The role of the brain and mind in constructing realities. *Brain and Behavioural Sciences, 28*(6), 763.

Dror, I. E. (2006). Why experts make errors. *Journal of Forensic Identification, 56*(4), 600–616.

Dror, I. E. & Charlton, D. (2006). Why experts make errors. *Journal of Forensic Identification, 56*(4), 600–656.

Drukteinis, A. M. (1992). Contemporary psychiatry: Serial murder–the heart of darkness. *Psychiatric Annals, 22*, 532–538.

Drukteinis, A. M. (2007). *Psychological opinions in sexual harassment claims.* Retrieved July 11, 2007, from http://www.psychlaw.com/LibraryFiles/SexualHarassment.html

Dubner, S. J. (1992). Portrait of a serial killer. *New York, 25*, 82–87.

Dubowitz, H. (Ed.). (1999). *Neglected children: Research, practice, and policy.* Thousand Oaks, CA: Sage.

Dunder, J. (2003). The free information society. Retrieved August 26, 2009, from http://www.freeinfosociety.com/viewprofile.php?profile=1.

Dunne, J., & Hedrick, M. (1994). The parental alienation syndrome: An analysis of sixteen selected cases. *Journal of Divorce and Remarriage, 21*, 21–38.

Dutton, M. A. (1993). Understanding women's responses to domestic violence: A redefinition of battered woman syndrome. *Hofstra Law Review, 21*, 1191, 1205–1206.

Duwe, G. (2000). Body-count journalism: The presentation of mass murder in the news media. *Homicide Studies, 4*, 364–399.

Dysart, J. E., Lindsay, R. C. L., MacDonald, T. K., & Wicke, C. (2002). The intoxicated witness: Effects of alcohol on identification accuracy from showups. *Journal of Applied Psychology, 87*, 170–175.

Earl, J. (1995). The dark truth about the dark tunnels of the McMartin. *Issues in Child Abuse Accusations, 7*(2), 76–131.

Echeburua, E., de Corral, P., Sarasua, B., & Zubizaretta, I. (1996). Treatment of acute posttraumatic stress disorder in rape victims: An experimental study. *Journal of Anxiety Disorders, 10*, 185–199.

Edwards, K. A. (2008). *Informed consent. Ethics in medicine.* University of Washington school of medicine. Retrieved April 23, 2008, from http://depts.washington.edu/bioethx/topics/consent.html

EEOC. *Sexual harassment charges: EEOC & FEP as combined: FY 1992–FY 1999.* Retrieved August 15, 2008, from http://www.eeoc.gov/stats/harass.html

Egger, M. D., & Flynn, J. P. (1963). Effects of electrical stimulation of the amygdala on hypothalamically elicited attack behavior in cats. *Journal of Neurophysiology, 26*, 705–720.

Egger, S. A. (2002). *The killers among us. An examination of serial murder and its investigation.* Upper Saddle River, NJ: Prentice Hall.

Ehlers, A., Clark, D. M., Hackmann, A., McManus, F., Fennell, M., Herbert, C., et al. (2003). A randomized controlled trial of cognitive therapy, self-help, and repeated assessment as early interventions for PTSD. *Archives of General Psychiatry, 60*, 1024–1032.

Eisenstadt, T. H., Eyberg, S. M., McNeil, C. B., Newcomb, K., & Funderburk, B. (1993). Parent–Child interaction therapy with behavior problem children: Relative effectiveness of two stages and overall treatment outcome. *Journal of Clinical Child Psychology, 22*, 42–51.

Elaad, R. (2003). Effects of feedback on the overestimated capacity to detect lies and the underestimated ability to tell lies. *Applied Cognitive Psychology, 17*, 349–363.

Helpguide.org. *Elder abuse.* Retrieved March 20, 2008, from http://www.helpguide.org/mental/elder_abuse_physical_emotional_sexual_neglect.htm

Elder mistreatment: Abuse, neglect and exploitation in an aging America. (2003). *National Research Council Panel to Review Risk and Prevalence of Elder Abuse and Neglect.* Retrieved April 23, 2009, from http://www.ncea.aoa.gov/NCEAroot/Main_Site/pdf/publication/FinalStatistics050331.pdf

Ellis, H. D., Shepherd, J. W., Flin, R. H., Shepherd, J., & Davies, G. M. (1989). Identification from a computer-driven retrieval system compared with traditional mugshot album search: A new tool for police investigations. *Ergonomics, 32*, 167–177.

Ellsworth, I. C. (1989). Are twelve heads better than one? *Law and Contemporary Problems, 52*, 205–224.

Emery, R. E., & Laumann-Billings, L. (1998). An overview of the nature, causes, and consequences of abusive family relationships. *American Psychologist, 53*, 121–135.

Epperson, D. L., Kaul, J. D., Huot, S., Goldman, R., & Alexander, W. (2003). Minnesota sex offender screening tool-revised (MnSOST-R) technical paper: Development, validation, and recommended risk level cut scores. *Unpublished Manuscript.* St. Paul, MN: Iowa state university and Minnesota department of corrections.

Epstein, R. A. (1995). *Cases and materials on torts* (6th ed., pp. 523–524). New York: Aspen Publishers.

Erdelyi, M. W. (1994). The empty set of hypermnesia. *International Journal of Clinical and Experimental Hypnosis, 42,* 379–390.

Estabrooks, G. H. (1972, April). Hypnosis comes of age. *Science Digest,* pp. 44–50.

Eule, J. (1978). The presumption of sanity: Bursting the bubble. *UCLA Law Review, 25,* 637–699.

Everly, G. S. (2003). Psychological counterterrorism. *International Journal of Emergency Mental Health, 5*(2), 57–59.

Ewing, C. P., & McCann, J. T. (2006). *Minds on trial: Great cases in law and psychology.* New York: Oxford University Press.

Fabrigar, L. R., Wegener, D. T., MacCallum, R. C., & Strahan, E. J. (1999). Evaluating the use of exploratory factor analysis in psychological research. *Psychological Methods, 4,* 272–299.

Faigman, D. L. (1986). The battered woman syndrome and self-defense: A legal and empirical dissent. *Virginia Law Review, 72,* 619.

Faigman, D. L., & Wright, A. (1997). The battered woman in the age of science. *Arizona Law Review, 39,* 67.

False confessions by adults. *False confessions.* Retrieved June 9, 2007, from http://www.justicedenied.org/false.htm

Famous american trials. Retrieved November 29, 2007, from http://www.law.umkc.edu/faculty/projects/ftrials/sweet/background.htm

Farkas, G. M. (1986). Stress in undercover policing. In J. T. Reese & H. A. Goldstein (Eds.), *Psychological services for law enforcement* (pp. 443–440). Washington, DC: U.S. Government Printing Office.

Federal Bureau of Investigation (2008, July 7). *National center for the analysis of violent crime critical incident response group.* Retrieved July 14, 2008, from http://www.fbi.gov/page2/july08/serialmurder_070708.html

Federal Bureau of Investigation. *A parent's guide to internet safety.* Retrieved March 18, 2008, from http://www.fbi.gov/publications/pguide/pguidee.htm

Feldman, S., & Stenner, K. (1997). Perceived threat and authoritarianism. *Political Psychology, 18*(4), 741–770.

Ferdoff, J. P. (1995). Antiandrogens vs. serotonergic medications in the treatment of sex offenders: A preliminary compliance study. *Canadian Journal of Human Sexuality, 4,* 111–122.

Festinger, L., Pepitone, A., & Newcomb, T. (1952). Some consequences of de-individuation in a group. *Journal of Abnormal and Social Psychology, 47,* 382–389.

Feyerick, D., & Steffen, S. (2009). 'Sexting' lands teen on sex offender list. *CNN.com.* Retrieved August 15, 2009, from http://www.cnn.com/2009/CRIME/04/07/sexting.busts/index.html.

Fido, M. & Skinner, K. (1999). *The official encyclopedia of Scotland yard.* London: Virgin Books.

Fiedler, K., Schmod, J., & Stahl, T. (2002). What is the current truth about polygraph lie detection? *Basic and Applied Social Psychology, 24,* 313–324.

Figley, C. R. (1998). Burnout as systemic traumatic stress: A model for helping traumatized family members (pp. 15–28). In C. R. Figley (Ed.), *Burnout in families: The systemic costs of caring.* Boca Raton, FL: CRC Press.

Filipczak, B. (1993, July). Armed and dangerous at work. *Training, 30,* 40.

Final report on the status of assisted outpatient treatment. *New York state office of mental health.* Retrieved August 15, 2007, from http://www.omh.state.ny.us/omhweb/Kendra_web/finalreport/.

Finkelhor, D. (1994). The international epidemiology of child sexual abuse. *Child Abuse & Neglect, 18,* 409–417.

Finkelhor, D., & Araji, S. (1986). Explanations of pedophilia: A four factor model. *Journal of Sex Research, 22,* 145–161.

Finkelhor, D., Ormrod, R., Turner, H., & Hamby, S. L. (2005). The victimization of children and youth: A comprehensive, national survey. *Child Maltreatment, 10,* 5–15.

Fisher, R. P., Geiselman, R. E., & Raymond, D. S. (1987). Critical analysis of police interview techniques. *Journal of Police Science and Administration, 15,* 177–185.

Fiske, S., & Glick, P. (1995). Ambivalence and stereotypes cause sexual harassment: A theory with implications for organizational change. *Journal of Social Issues, 51,* 97–115.

Fitzgerald, D. R., & Ellsworth, P. C. (1984). Due process vs. crime control: Death qualification and jury attitudes. *Law and Human Behavior, 8,* 31–51.

Fitzgerald, L. F. (1993). Sexual harassment: Violence against women in the workplace. *American Psychologist, 48,* 1070–1072.

Fitzgerald, L. F. (1999). Junk logic: The abuse defense in sexual harassment litigation. *Psychology, Public Policy, and Law, 5*(3), 730–759.

Fitzgerald, L. F., Drasgow, F., Hulin, C. L., Gelfand, M. J., & Magley, V. J. (1997). Antecedents and consequences of sexual harassment in organizations: A test of an integrated model. *Journal of Applied Psychology, 82,* 578–589.

Fitzgerald, L. F., & Shulman, S. L. (1993). Sexual harassment: A research analysis and agenda for the 1990s. *Journal of Vocational Behavior, 32,* 152–175.

Fitzgerald, L., Shullman, S., Bailey, N., Richards, M., Swecker, J., Gold, Y., et al. (1988). The incidence and dimensions of sexual harassment in academia and the workplace. *Journal of Vocational Behavior, 32,* 152–175.

Flaherty, T. (Ed.). (1993). *Compulsion to kill.* Alexandria, VA: Time-Life Books.

Flint, C. (2003). *Spaces of hate: Geographies of Discrimination and intolerance in the U.S.A.* New York, NY: Routledge.

Foa, E. B., & Rothbaum, B. O. (1998). *Treating the trauma of rape: Cognitive-behavioral therapy for PTSD.* UK: Guilford Press.

Foa, E. B., Rothbaum, B. O., Riggs, D. S., & Murdock, T. B. (1991). Treatment of posttraumatic stress disorder in rape victims: A comparison between cognitive-behavioral procedures and counseling. *Journal of Consulting and Clinical Psychology, 59,* 715–723.

Ford, J. K., MacCallum, R. C., & Tait, M. (1986). The application of exploratory factor analysis in applied psychology: A critical review and analysis. *Personnel Psychology, 39,* 291–314.

Fortmann, K., Leslie, C., & Cunningham, M. (2002). Cross-cultural comparisons of the Reid integrity scale in Latin America and South Africa. *International Journal of Selection and Assessment, 10,* 98–108.

Foster, H. H. (1969). Confessions and the station house syndrome. *Depaul Law Review, 18,* 683–701.

Fox, J. A., & Levin, J. (1998). Multiple homicide: Patterns of serial and mass murder. In C. R. Bartol & A. M. Bartol (Eds.), *Introduction to forensic psychology.* Thousand Oaks, CA: Sage.

Fox, J. A., & Levine, J. (1994). *Overkill: Mass murder and serial killing exposed.* New York: Plenum.

Fox, J. A., & Levin, J. (2005). *Extreme killing: Understanding serial and mass murder.* Thousand Oaks, CA: Sage.

Fox, J. A., Levin, J., & Quinet, K. (2005). *The will to kill.* Upper Saddle River, NJ: Pearson.

Francis galton and fingerprints. Francis galton: fingerprinter. Retrieved October, 7, 2008, from http://galton.org/fingerprinter.html

Frank, J., & Frank, B. (1957). *Not guilty.* London: Gallanez.

Frazier, P., & Borgida, E. (1992). Rape trauma syndrome: A review of case law and psychological research. *Law and Human Behavior, 16,* 301.

Freedy J. R., Saladin, M. E., Kilpatrick, D. G., Resnick, H. S., & Saunders, B. E. (1994). Understanding acute psychological distress following natural disaster. *Journal of Trauma Stress, 7*, 257–273.

Freud, S. (1930). *Civilization and its discontents* (pp. 59–145). London: Hogarth Press.

Freud (1906–1908). *The standard edition of the complete works of Sigmund Freud.* Londone: Hogarth Press.

Fried, I. (1997). Syndrome E. *The Lancet, 350*, 1845–1847.

Fried, J. (2001, September 9). Following up. *The New York Times.* Retrieved November 29, 2007, from http://topics.nytimes.com/top/reference/timestopics/people/b/rashid_baz/index.html

Fromm, E. (1973). *The anatomy of human destructiveness.* Austin, TX: Holt, Rinehart & Winston.

Fulero, S. M., & Penrod, S. D. (1990). Attorney jury selection folklore: What do they think and how can psychologists help? *Forensic Reports, 3*, 233–259.

Funder, D. C., & Block, J. (1989). The role of ego-control, ego-resiliency, and IQ in delay of gratification in adolescence. *Journal of Personality and Social Psychology, 57*, 1041–1050.

Furnham, A. (1998). Measuring the beliefs in a just world. In Montada, L., & Lerner, M.J., (Eds.,). *Responses to victimization and belief in a just world* (p. 141). New York: Plenum Press.

Galton, F. (2006). *Finger prints.* Amherst, NY: Prometheus Books. (Original work published 1892.)

Ganzel, B., Casey, B. J., Glover, G., Voss, H. V., & Temple. E. (2007). The aftermath of 9/11: Effect of intensity and recency of trauma on outcome. *Emotion, 7*(2), 227–238.

Gardner, R. A. (1987). *The parental alienation syndrome and the differentiation between fabricated and genuine sexual abuse.* Cresskill, NJ: Creative Therapeutics.

Garrido, E., Masip, J., & Herrero, C. (2004). Police officers' credibility judgments: Accuracy and estimated ability. *International Journal of Psychology, 39*, 254–275.

Gass, R. (1979). The psychologist as expert witness: Science in the courtroom. *Maryland Law Review, 38*, 539, 544–554.

Gazeley, B. J. (1997). Venus, mars and the law: On mediation of sexual harassment cases. *Williamette Law Review, 33*, 605–633.

Geberth, V. J. (1990). *Practical Homicide Investigation* (2nd ed). New York: Elsevier.

Geberth, V. J. (1996). *Practical homicide investigation: Tactics, procedures and forensic techniques* (3rd ed.). New York: CRC Press.

Geberth, V. J., & Turco, R. N. (1997). Antisocial personality disorder, sexual sadism, malignant narcissism, and serial murders. *Journal of Forensic Sciences, 42*, 49–60.

Geen, R. G. (1990). *Human aggression.* Pacific Grove, CA: Brooks/Cole.

Geide, K. (1996). Economic espionage: Looking ahead. In T. Sarbin (Ed.), *Vision 2021: Security Issues for the Next Quarter Century.* Proceedings of conference sponsored by Defense Personnel Security Research Center and Security Policy Board Staff, June 25, 1996. Monterey, CA: Defense Personnel Security Research Center.

Geiselman, R. E., & Fisher, R. P. (1985). *Interviewing victims and witnesses of crime* (p. 1). Washington, DC: National Institute of Justice.

Geiselman, R. E., Fisher, R. P., Firstenberg, I., Hutton, L. A., Sullivan, S. J., Avetissian, I. V., et al. (1984). Enhancement of eyewitness memory: An empirical evaluation of the cognitive interview. *Journal of Police Science and Administration, 12*, 74–79.

Geiselman, R. E., Fisher, R. P., MacKinnon, D. P., & Holland, H. L. (1985). Eyewitness memory enhancement in the police interview: Cognitive retrieval mnemonics versus hypnosis. *Journal of Applied Psychology, 70*, 401–412.

Geiselman, R. E., Fisher, R. P., MacKinnon, D. P., & Holland, H. L. (1986). Enhancement of eyewitness memory with the cognitive interview. *American Journal of Psychology, 99*, 385–401.

Geller, J. L., & Appelbaum, P. S. (1985). Competency to stand trial: Neuroleptic medication and demeanor in court. *Hospital & Community Psychiatry, 36*, 6.

Gelles, M. (n.d.). *Exploring the mind of the spy.* Naval Criminal Investigative Service. Retrieved March 26, 2007, from http://www.da.usda.gov/ocpm/Security%20Guide/Treason/Mind.htm

Gendercide watch: Case study: Honour killings and blood feuds. Retrieved March 23, 2008, from http://www.gendercide.org/case_honour.html

George, J. M., & Zhou, J. (2001). When openness to experience and conscientiousness are related to creative behavior: An interactional approach. *Journal of Applied Psychology, 86*, 513–524.

Gerbode, F. (1989). *Beyond psychology: An introduction to meta-psychology.* Palo Alto, CA: IRM Press.

Giannangelo, S. (1996). *The psychopathology of serial murder.* Westport, CT: Praeger.

Gibson, E., Holt, J. C., Fondacaro, K. M., Tang, T. S., Powell, T. A., & Turbitt, E. L. (1999). An examination of antecedent traumas and psychiatric comorbidity among male inmates with PTSD. *Journal of Traumatic Stress, 12*, 473–484.

Giddens, A. (2005) *Modernity and self-identity: Self and society in the late modern age.* Stanford, CA: Stanford University Press.

Gijs, L., & Gooren, L. (1996). Hormonal and psychopharmacological interventions in the treatment of paraphilias: An update. *The journal of Sex Research, 33*, 273–290.

Gilbert, D. T., & Hixon, J. G. (1991). The trouble of thinking: Activation and application of stereotypic beliefs. *Journal of Personality and Social Psychology, 50*, 509–517.

Gilbert, J. N. (2007). *Criminal investigation* (7th ed., p. 108). Upper Saddle River, NJ: Prentice Hall.

Girgis, A. (2006). *Violence from self-love: Narcissism and aggression in the face of ego threat.* Retrieved January 8, 2007, from http://digitalcommons.trinity.edu/psychtheses/4

Glossary of fingerprint terms. Crime scene forensics, LLC. Retrieved October 7, 2008, from http://www.crimescene-forensics.com/Fingerprint_terms.html

Gold, L. H. (2001). Clinical and forensic aspects of postpartum disorders. *Journal of the American Academy of Psychiatry and Law, 29*, 344–347.

Gold, S. N., & Heffner, C. L. (1998). Sexual addiction: Many conceptions, minimal data. *Clinical Psychology Review, 18*, 367–381.

Goldberg, L. R. (1992). The development of markers for the big-five factor structure. *Journal of Personality and Social Psychology, 59*(6), 1216–1229.

Goldberg, L. R. (1993). The structure of phenotypic personality traits. *American Psychologist, 48*, 26–34.

Golding, S. L. (1992). Studies of incompetent defendants: Research and social policy implications. *Forensic Reporter, 5*, 77.

Goldklang, D. L. (2003). Post-traumatic stress disorder and black rage: Clinical validity, criminal responsibility. In S. O. Lilienfeld, S. J. Lynn, & J. M. Lohr (Eds.), *Science and pseudoscience in clinical psychology* (p. 96). New York: The Guilford Press.

Goldstein, I. (1935). *Trial technique.* Chicago: Callaghan.

Golub, J. S., Espinosa, M., Damon, L., & Card, J. (1987). A videotape parent education program for abusive parents. *Child Abuse & Neglect, 11*, 255–265.

Gondolf, E. W. (1991). A victim-based assessment of court-mandated counseling for batterers. *Criminal Justice Review, 16*, 214–226

Goodwin, R. J., & Gurulé, J. (1997). *Criminal and scientific evidence* (p. 5). Charlottesville, VA: MICHIE Law Publishers.

Goscinski, I., Kwiatkowski, S., Polak, J., Orlowiejska, M., & Partyk, A. (1997). The Kluver-Bucy syndrome. *Journal of Neurosurgical Science, 41*(3), 269–272.

Gosselin, D. (2005). *Heavy hands.* Upper Saddle River, NJ: Pearson Prentice-Hall.

Gottfredson, M. R., & Hirschi, T. (1990). *A general theory of crime.* Stanford, CA: Stanford University Press.

Gottfredson, S. D., & Moriarty, L. J. (2006, September). Clinical versus actuarial judgments in criminal justice decisions: Should one replace the other? *Federal Probation Newsletter, 70*, 2.

Gotz, M.J., Johnstone, E.C., & Ratcliffe, S. G. (1999). Criminality and antisocial behaviour in unselected men with sex chromosome abnormalities. *Psychological Medicine, 29*, 953–962.

Graham, J. (2006, August 20). Experts-see-red-flags-in-confession. *Chicago Tribune.* State and Regional News, at C-3.

Green, P., & Iverson, G. L. (2001). Effects of injury severity and cognitive exaggeration on olfactory deficits in head injury compensation claims. *NeuroRehabilitation, 16*(4), 237–243.

Greenberg, D. M., Bradford, J. M. W., & Curry, S. (1995). Infantophilia – A new subcategory of pedophilia? A preliminary study. *Bulletin of the American Academy of Psychiatry and Law, 23*, 63–71.

Greenberg, D. M., Bradford, J. M. W., Curry, S., & O'Rourke, A. (1996). A comparison of treatment of paraphilias with three serotonin reuptake inhibitors: A retrospective study. *Bulletin of the American Academy of Psychiatry and the Law, 24*, 525–532.

Greenberg, I., Perna, F., Kaplanm, M., & Sullivan, M. A. (2005). Behavioral and psychological factors in the assessment and treatment of obesity surgery patients. *Obesity Research, 13*, 244–249.

Greenberg, J. (1990). Employee theft as a reaction to underpayment inequity: The hidden cost of pay cuts. *Journal of Applied Psychology, 75*, 561–568.

Greenberg, J., & Alge, B. J. (1998). Aggressive reactions to workplace injustice. In R. W. Griffin, A. O'Leary-Kelly, & J. M. Collins (Eds.), *Dysfunctional behavior in organizations: Violent and deviant behavior* (pp. 83–117). Stamford, CT: JAI Press.

Greenstone, J. L. (1995). Hostage negotiations team training for small police departments. In M. I. Kurke & E. M. Scrivner (Eds.), *Police psychology into the 21st century.* Hillsdale, NJ: Lawrence Erlbaum.

Grill-Spector, K. (2004). Using multiple functional criteria to define high-level human visual areas in the lateral occipital and temporal lobes. *Journal of Vision, 4*(8), 90.

Gross, J. J., Richards, J. M., & John, O. P. (2006). Emotion regulation in everyday life. In D. K. Snyder, J. A. Simpson, & J. N. Hughes (Eds.), *Emotion regulation in couples and families: Pathways to dysfunction and health* (pp. 13–39). Washington, DC: American Psychological Association.

Grisso, T., Styeinberg, L., Woolard, J., Cauffman, E., Scott, E., Graham, S., et al. (2003). Juveniles' competence to stand trial: A comparison of adolescents' and adults' capacities as trial defendants. *Law and Human Behavior, 27*, 333–363.

Grossman, D. (1995). *On killing: The psychological cost of learning to kill in war and society.* Boston: Little, Brown.

Grote, D. (2006). *Discipline without punishment* (2nd ed.). New York, NY: AMACOM.

Grove, D. (1995). *Discipline without punishment: The proven strategy that turns problem employees into superior performers.* New York: Amacom.

Grove, D., & Harvey, E. L. (1983). *Discipline without punishment.* New York: McGraw-Hill.

Grove, W. M., & Meehl, P. E. (1996). Comparative efficiency of informal (subjective, impressionistic) and formal (mechanical, algorithmic) prediction procedures: The clinical–statistical controversy. *Psychology, Public Policy, and Law, 2*, 293–323.

Guthrie, C., & Levin, J. (1998). A 'Party Satisfaction' Perspective on a Comprehensive Mediation Statute. *Ohio State Journal on Dispute Resolution, 13*, 885–907.

Gruys, M. L., & Sackett, P. R. (2003). Investigating the dimensionality of counterproductive work behavior. *International Journal of Selection and Assessment, 11*, 30–42.

Gruzelier, J. (2000). Redefining hypnosis: Theory, methods, and integration. *Contemporary Hypnosis, 17*, 51–70.

Gudjonsson, G. H. (1991). The application of interrogative suggestibility to police interviewing. In J. F. Schumaker (Ed.), *Human suggestibility: Advances in theory, research, and application* (pp. 279–288). New York: Routledge.

Gudjonsson, G. H. (1992). *The psychology of interrogations, confessions, and testimony.* London: Wiley.

Gudjonsson, G. H. (1999). The making of a serial false confessor: The confessions of Henry Lee Lucas. *The Journal of Forensic Psychiatry, 10*, 416–426.

Gudjonsson, G. H., & Clark, N. (1986). Suggestibility in police interrogation: A social psychological model. *Social Behaviour, 1*, 83–104.

Gudjonsson, G. H., & MacKeith, J. A. C. (1990). A proven case of false confession: Psychological aspects of the coerced-compliant type. *Medicine, Science, and the Law, 30*, 329–335.

Guidelines for child custody evaluations in divorce proceedings. (home page). Retrieved April 15, 2009, from http://www.apa.org/practice/childcustody.html

Gustafson, R. (1993) Alcohol-related expected effects and the desirability of these effects for Swedish college students measured with the Alcohol Expectancy Questionnaire (AEQ). *Alcohol and Alcoholism, 28*, 469–475.

Guttmacher, M. S. (1933, April). Psychiatry and the courts. *American Journal of Orthopsychiatry, 161.*

Guttmacher, M. S. (1955). The status of adult court psychiatric clinics. *Crime and Delinquency, 1*, 97–104.

Hagen, M. A. (1997). *Whores of the court: The fraud of psychiatric testimony and the rape of American justice.* New York: Regan Books.

Hahn, H. (1982). Disability and rehabilitation policy: Is paternalistic neglect really benign? *Public Administration Review, 42*, 385–388.

Hahn, P. W., & Clayton, S. D. (1996). The effects of attorney presentation style, attorney gender, and juror gender on juror Decisions. *Law and Human Behavior, 20*, 533–554.

Hakstian, A. R., Rogers, W. T., & Cattell, R. B. (1982). The behavior of number-of-factors rules with simulated data. *Multivariate Behavioral Research, 17*, 193–219.

Hale, R. (1993). The application of learning theory to serial murder or "You too can learn to be a serial killer."' *American Journal of Criminal Justice, 17*, 37–45.

Halpern, D. F., Brooks, A., & Stephenson, C. (2007). How science by media creates false certainties and resistance to conceptual change. In J. Kitaeff (Ed.), *Malingering, lies, and junk science in the courtroom* (pp. 16–18). Youngstown, NY: Cambria Press.

Hans, V. P., & Lofquist, W. S. (1994). Perceptions of civil justice: The litigation crisis attitudes of civil jurors. *Behavioral Science & the Law, 12*, 181–196.

Hanscom, K. L. (2001). Treating survivors of war trauma and torture. *American Psychologist 56*(11), 1032–1039.

Hansen, M. (2000). Experts are liable, too: Client suits against "friendly experts" multiplying, succeeding. *American Bar Association Journal, 86*, 17.

Hanson, R. (1997). *Development of a brief actuarial risk scale for sexual offense recidivism.* Department of the Solicitor General of Canada. Public Works and Government Services Canada. Cat. No. J54-1/1997-E, ISBN: o-662-26207-7.

Hanson, R. K., & Harris, A. (2001). A structured approach to evaluating change among sex Offenders. *Sexual Abuse: A Journal of Research and Treatment, 13*(2), 105–122.

Hanson, R. K., & Thornton, D. (1999). *Static 99: Improving actuarial risk assessments for sex offenders* (User Report 99–02). Ottawa, Ontario, Canada: Department of the Solicitor General of Canada.

Hanson, R. K., & Thornton, D. (2003). *Notes on the development of the static 2002* (Report # 2003-01). Ottawa, Canada: Public Safety and Emergency Preparedness Canada.

Hare, R. D. (2003). *Manual for the Hare Psychopathy Checklist-Revised (2nd ed.)*. Toronto, ON: Multi-Health Systems.

Hare, R. D. (1991). Manual for the Psychopathy-Checklist-Revised. Toronto: Multi Health Systems.

Hare, R. D. (1996). Psychopathy: A clinical construct whose time has come. *Criminal Justice and Behavior*, 23, 25–54.

Hargrave, G. E., & Hiatt, D. (1987). Law enforcement selection with the interview, MMPI, and CPI: A study of reliability and validity. *Journal of Police Science and Administration*, 15(2), 25–28.

Haroules, B. (2005, April 8). New York State's assisted outpatient treatment (AOT) program. *Statement before the assembly standing committee on mental health, mental retardation and developmental disabilities, and the assembly standing committee on codes*. Retrieved August 15, 2007, from http://www.nyclu.org/aot_program_tstmny_040805.html

Harris, C. W. (1967). On factors and factor scores. *Psychometrika*, 32, 363–379.

Harris, E. (1995). *Guarding the secrets: Palestinian terrorism and a father's murder of his too-American daughter*. Chicago, Ill: Scribner.

Harris, P. (1997). *Black rage confronts the law*. New York: New York University Press.

Harris, P. (2001). The black rage defense. *Connecticut Public Interest Law Journal*, 1(1).

Hartigan, J. A., & Wigdor, A. K. (Eds.). (1989). *Fairness in employment testing: Validity generalization, minority issues, and the general aptitude test battery*. Washington, DC: National Academy Press.

Haward, L. R. C. (1988). Hypnosis by the police. *British Journal of Experimental and Clinical Hypnosis*, 5, 33–35.

Haward, L., & Ashworth, A. (1980, March). Some problems of evidence obtained by hypnosis. *Criminal Law Review*, 469–485.

Hazelwood, R. R. (2001). Analyzing the rape and profiling the offender. In R. R. Hazelwood & A. W. Burgess (Eds.), *Practical aspects of rape investigation* (3rd ed.). Boca Raton, FL: CRC Press.

Hazelwood, R. R., & Warren, J. (1990, February). The criminal behavior of the serial rapist. *FBI Law Enforcement Bulletin*, 71(1), 11–16.

Heatherington, M., Stanley-Hagan, M., & Anderson, E. R. (1989). Marital transitions: A child's perspective. *American Psychologist*, 44(2), 303–312.

Heckman, C. J., Cropsey, K. L., & Olds-Davis, T. (2007). Posttraumatic stress disorder treatment in correctional settings: A brief review of the empirical literature and suggestions for future research. *Psychotherapy: Theory, Research, Practice, & Training*, 44(1), 46–53.

Hellkamp, D. T., & Lewis, J. E. (1995). The consulting psychologist as an expert witness in sexual harassment and retaliation cases. *Consulting Psychology Journal: Practice and Research*, 47, 3.

Henig, M. S. (1927). Intelligence and safety. *Journal of Educational Research*, 16, 81–87.

Henke, E. (1838). *Handbuch des Cnminalrechts und der Criminalpolitik*. Berlin: Vierter Theil.

Hennig, J., Reuter, M., Netter, P., Burk, C., & Landt, O. (2005). Two types of aggression are differentially related to serotonergic activity and the ATT9C TPH polymorphism. *Behavioral Neuroscience*, 119, 16–25.

Herndon, J. (1998, October). *Correlates of MMIP-2 L scale: Elevations in an LEO selection test battery*. Paper presented at the 27th annual meeting of the Society of Police and Criminal Psychology, Portland, OR.

Herrnstein, R. J., & Murray, C. (1994). *The bell curve: Intelligence and class structure in American life*. New York: Free Press.

Heskin, K. (1984). The psychology of terrorism in Ireland. In A. Yonah & A. O'Day (Eds.), *Terrorism in Ireland* (pp. 88–105). New York: St. Martin's Press.

Heyl, C. (1952). Selection of the jury. *Illinois Bar Journal*, 40, 328–341.

Hiatt, D., & Hargrave, G.E. (1988). MMPI profiles of problem police officers. *Journal of Personality Assessment*, 52(4), 722-731.

Hibbard,W. S., & Worring, R. W. (1981). *Forensic hypnosis: The practical application of hypnosis in criminal investigation*. Springfield, IL: Charles C. Thomas.

Hickey, E. W. (1997). *Serial killers and their victims*. Belmont, CA: Wadsworth.

Hickey, E. W. (2005). *Sex crimes and paraphilia*. Upper Saddle River, NJ: Prentice-Hall.

Hicks, S. J., & Sales, B. D. (2006). *Criminal profiling: Developing an effective science and practice*. Washington, DC: American Psychological Association.

Higham, P. A., & Roberts, W. T. (1996). Measuring recall performance. *Psycholoqy*. Retrieved February 26, 2009, from http://ftp.princeton.edu/pub/harnad/psycoloquy/1996.volume.7/psyc.96.7.38witness-memory.13.higham

Hildyard, K. L., & Wolfe, D. A. (2002). Child neglect: Developmental issues and outcomes. *Child Abuse and Neglect*, 26, 679–695.

Hills, A. (2002). Responding to catastrophic terrorism. In L. Miller (Ed.), *Psychological interventions*. Hills, CA: Sage.

Hindu approaches to handling crisis. Retrieved June 9, 2007, from http://www.beliefnet.com/story/60/story_6041_1.html

Hines, D., & Finkelhor, D. (2007). Statutory sex crime relationships between juveniles and adults: A review of social scientific research. *Aggression & Violent Behavior*, 12, 300–314.

Hiroto, D. S. (1974). Locus of control and learned helplessness. *Journal of Experimental Psychology*, 102, 187–193.

Hirstein, W. (2005). *Brain fiction: Self-deception and the riddle of confabulation*. Cambridge, MA: MIT Press.

History of fingerprinting. The thin blue line information section. Retrieved September 30, 2008, from http://www.policensw.com/info/fingerprints/finger01.html

Hoffer, T. B., Hess, M., Welch, Jr., V., & Williams, K. (2007). *Doctorate Recipients from United States Universities: Summary Report 2006*. Chicago: National Opinion Research Center.

Hogan, J., & Hogan, R. (1989). How to measure employee reliability. *Journal of Applied Psychology*, 74, 273–279.

Hogan, R. (1973). Moral conduct and moral character: A psychological perspective. *Psychological Bulletin*, 79, 217–232.

Hogan, R., Hogan, J., & Roberts, B. W. (1996). Personality measurement and employment decisions: Questions and answers. *American Psychologist*, 51(5), 469–477.

Hoge, S. K., Bonnie, R. J., Poythress, N., & Monahan, J. (2006). Attorney-client decision-making in criminal cases: Client competence and participation as perceived by their attorneys. *Behavioral Sciences and the Law*, 10, 385–394.

Hoge, S. K., Bonnie, R. J., Poythress, N., Monahan, J., Eisenberg, M., & Feucht-Haviar, T. (1997). The MacArthur adjudicative competence study: Development and validation of a research instrument. *Law and Human Behavior*, 21, 141–179.

Holmes, O. W. (1881). *The common law*. Mineola, NY: Dover Publications.

Holmes, R. M. (1986). *Acts of war: The behavior of men in battle*. New York: Free Press.

Holmes, R. M., & DeBurger, J. (1985). Profiles in terror: The serial murderer. *Federal Probation*, 39, 29–34.

Holmes, R. M., & DeBurger, J. (1988). *Serial murder*. Newbury Park, CA: Sage.

Holmes, R. M., & Holmes, S. T. (1996). *Profiling violent crimes: An investigative tool*. Thousand Oaks, CA: Sage.

Holmes, R. M., & Holmes, S. T. (1998). *Serial murder* (2nd ed). Thousand Oaks, CA: Sage.

Holmes, R. M., & Holmes, S. T. (2001). *Murder in America*. Thousand Oaks, CA: Sage.

Holmes, S. T., & Holmes, R. M. (2002). *Sex crimes: Patterns and behavior* (2nd ed.). Thousand Oaks, CA: Sage.

Holmgren, B. K. (2001) Prosecuting the shaken infant case. In S. Lazoritz, & V. J. Palusci (Eds.), *The shaken baby syndrome: A multidisciplinary approach* (pp. 275–331). New York: Hawthorne Maltreatment and Trauma Press.

Holusha, J. (1984, July 21). Mass killer is recalled as a gun-loving youth. *New York Times*, p. 8. Retrieved March 08, 2007, from http://proquest. umi.com.

Honer, W. E., Gewirtz, E., & Turey, M. (1987). Psychosis and violence in cocaine smokers. *Lancet, 1*, 451.

Honts, C. R., Kircher, J. C., & Raskin, D. C. (2002). The scientific status of research on polygraph techniques: The case for polygraph tests. In D. L. Faigman, D. Kaye, M. J. Saks, & J. Sanders (Eds.), *Modern scientific evidence: The law and science of expert testimony* (pp. 446–483). St. Paul, MN: West.

Honts, C. R., & Perry, M. V. (1992). Polygraph admissibility: Changes and challenges. *Law and Human Behavior, 16*, 357–379.

Honts, C. R., & Raskin, D. C. (1988). A field study of the validity of the directed lie control question. *Journal of Police Science and Administration, 16*, 56–61.

Horowitz, S. W., Kircher, J. C., Honts, C. R., & Raskin, D. C. (1997). The role of comparison questions in physiological detection of deception. *Psychophysiology, 34*, 108–115.

Horvath, F., Jayne, B., & Buckley, J. (1994). Differentiation of truthful and deceptive criminal suspects in behavior analysis interviews. *Journal of Forensic Sciences, 39*, 793–807.

Hoskins, R. K. (1990). *Vigilantes of Christendum*. Lynchburg, VA: Virginia Publishing Company.

Hough, L. M. (2001). I/Owes its advances to personality. In B. W. Roberts & R. Hogan (Eds.), *Personality psychology in the workplace* (pp. 19–44). Washington, DC: American Psychological Association.

Hough, L. M., & Ones, D. S. (2001). The structure, measurement, validity, and use of personality variables in industrial, work, and organizational psychology. In N. Anderson, D. S. Ones, H. S. Kepir, & C. Visweswaran (Eds.), *Handbook of industrial, work, and organizational psychology: Vol. 1. Personnel psychology* (pp. 233–237). London, England: Sage.

Hovland, C., & Sears, R. (1940). Minor studies in aggression: VI. Correlation of lynchings with economic indices. *Journal of Psychology, 9*, 301–310.

Howe, M. D. (Ed.). (1963). *Oliver Wendell Holmes, the common law*. MA: Harvard University Press. (Original work published 1881.)

Hubbard, D. G. (1971). *The skyjacker: His flights of fantasy*. New York: Macmillan.

Hubbard, D. G. (1983). The psychodynamics of terrorism. In Y. Alexander, T. Adeniran, & R. A. Kilmarx (Eds.), *International violence* (pp. 45–53). New York: Praeger.

Huckabee, H. M. (2000). *Mental disability issues in the criminal justice system*. Springfield, IL: Charles C. Thomas Publisher Ltd.

Hudson, R. A. (1999). *The Sociology and Psychology of Terrorism: Who Becomes a Terrorist and Why?* Retrieved June 20, 2007, from http://www.loc.gov/rr/frd/

Huff, R., Rattner, A., & Sagarin, E. (1986). Guilty until proven innocent. *Crime and Delinquency, 32*, 518–544.

Hunter, J. E., & Schmidt, F. L. (2000). Racial and gender bias in ability and achievement tests: Resolving the apparent paradox. *Psychology, Public Policy, and Law, 6*, 151–158.

Hunter, J. E., & Schmidt, F. L. (2004). *Methods of meta-analysis*. Thousand Oaks, CA: Sage.

Horwitz, S., & Ruane, M. (2004). *Sniper: Inside the Hunt for the Killers Who Terrorized the Nation*. New York, NY: Random House.

Hyman, I. E., Husband, T. H., & Billings, F. J. (1995). False memories of childhood experiences. *Applied Cognitive Psychology, 9*, 181–197.

Iacono, W. G. (2008, October). Effective policing: Understanding how polygraph tests work and are used. *Criminal justice and behavior, 35*(10), 1295–1308.

Iacono, W. G., & Lykken, D. T. (1997). The validity of the lie detector: Two surveys of scientific opinion. *Journal of Applied Psychology, 82*, 426–433.

Iacono, W. G., & Patrick, C. J. (1999). Polygraph ("lie detector") testing: The state of the art. In A. K. Hess & I. B. Weiner (Eds.), *The handbook of forensic psychology*. New York: John Wiley.

Inbau, F. E., & Reid, J. E. (1967). *Criminal interrogation and confessions*. (2nd ed.). Baltimore: Williams & Wilkins.

Inbau, F. E., Reid, J. E., & Buckley, J. P. (1986). *Criminal interrogation and confessions* (3rd ed.). Baltimore: Williams & Wilkins.

Inbau, F. E., Reid, J. E., Buckley, J. P., & Jayne, B. C. (2001). *Criminal interrogation and confessions* (4th ed.). Gaithersberg, MD: Aspen.

Innocence Project. (2001). (home page). Retrieved June 10, 2007, from http://www.innocenceproject.org/

Federal Bureau of Investigation. *Integrated automated fingerprint identification system*. Retrieved October 8, 2008, from http://www.fbi.gov/hq/cjisd/iafis.htm

Inwald, R. (1992). *Inwald personality inventory technical manual* (Rev. ed.). New York: Hilson Research.

Inwald, R. E., & Shusman, E. J. (1984, March). IPI (Inwald Personality Inventory) and MMPI (Minnesota Multiphasic Personality Inventory) as Predictors of Academy Performance for Police Recruits. *Journal of Police Science and Administration, 12*(1),1–11.

Isely, D. (1994). *One hundred and one botanists* (pp. 68–70). Ames, IA: Iowa State University Press.

Jackson, J. L., Van Koppen, P. J., & Herbrink, C. M. (1993). *Does the service meet the needs? An evaluation of consumer satisfaction with specific profile analysis and investigative advice as offered by the scientific research advisory unit of the National Criminal Intelligence Division (CRI)* (NISCALE Report NSCR 93-05). Amsterdam: NSCR.

Jacobs, J. E. (1988). Euripides medea: A psychodynamic model of severe divorce pathology. *American Journal of Psychotherapy, 42*(2), 308–319.

Jacobs, S. K. (2007). Jury selection tips. In J. D. Lieberman & B. D. Sales (Eds.), *Scientific jury selection*. Washington, DC: American Psychological Association.

Janus, J. (2005, May 13). *Now go out and kill!!! The truth seeker*. Retrieved, November 2, 2008, from http://www.thetruthseeker. co.uk/article.asp?ID=57.

Jansz, J., & Van Drunen, P. (2003). *A social history of psychology* (pp. 207–209). Malden, MA: Wiley-Blackwell.

Jasper, H. H. (1937). The relation between morality and intellect: A compendium of evidence contributed by psychology, criminology, and sociology [Book review]. *American Journal of Psychology, 49*, 159.

Jayaratne, S., Vinokur-Kaplan, D., Nagda, B., & Chess, W. (1996). A national study on violence and harassment of social workers by clients. *Journal of Applied Social Sciences, 20*(1), 1–14.

Jensen, A. R. (1998). *The g factor: The science of mental ability*. Westport, CT: Praeger.

Johansson, S., & Nygren, O. (1991, March). The missing girls of china: A new demographic account. *Population and Development Review, 17*(1), 40–41.

John, O. P. (1990). The "big five" factor taxonomy: Dimension of personality in the natural language and in questionnaires. In: L. A. Pervin (Ed.), *Handbook of personality*. New York: Guilford.

Johnston, M. (1997). *Spectral evidence*. Boston, MA: Houghton Mifflin Company.

Jones, J. G., Butler, H. L., Hamilton, B., Perdue, J. D., Stem, H. P., & Woody, R. C. (1986). Munchausen syndrome by proxy. *Child Abuse & Neglect, 10*, 3340.

Jones, J. W. (2006). *The psychological roots of religious terrorism.* Retrieved June 20, 2007, from http://home.att.net/pcr-aar/2005/jones.htm

Jordon, K. (2003). What we learned from the 9/11 first anniversary. *Family Journal of Counseling and Therapy for Couples & Families, 11*(2), 110–116.

Jordan, L. (2002). Elder abuse and domestic violence: Overlapping issues and legal remedies. *American Journal of Family Law, 15*, 149.

Juergensmeyer, M. (2000). *Terror in the mind of God.* Berkeley: University of California Press.

Justice Denied. Retrieved June 8, 2007, from http://www.justicedenied.org/false.htm

Kamisar, Y., LaFave, W. R., Israel, J. H., & King, N. J. (2003). *Modern criminal procedure* (10th ed.). St. Paul, MN: West Publishing.

Kanner, L. (1943). *Autistic disturbances of affective contact.* Nervous Child, 2: 217–50

Kanner, L. (1949). Problems of nosology and psychodynamics in early childhood autism. *American Journal of Orthopsychiatry, 19*(3): 416–26.

Kanner, L. (1960, July 25). The child is father. TIME. Retrieved July 29, 2008, from http://www.time.com/time/magazine/article/0,9171,826528,00.html.

Kaplan, J., & Weisberg, R. (1991). *Criminal law: Cases and materials* (2nd ed., p. 248). Boston, MA: Little, Brown.

Kanner, L., & Eisenberg, L. (1956). Early infantile autism 1943–1955. *American Journal of Orthopsychiatry* 26: 556–66.

Karama, S., et al. (2002). Areas of brain activation in males and females during viewing of erotic film excerpts. *Human Brain Mapping, 16*(1), 1–13.

Kassin, S. M. (2002, November 1). False confessions and the jogger case. *New York Times*, p. A31.

Kassin, S. M. (2008). Commonsense myths and misconceptions. *Criminal Justice and Behavior, 35*(10), 1309–1322.

Kassin, S. M., & Fong, C. T. (1999). "I'm innocent!" Effects of training on judgments of truth and deception in the interrogation room. *Law and Human Behavior, 23*, 499–516.

Kassin, S. M., & Gudjonsson, G. H. (2004). The psychology of confessions: A review of the literature and issues. *Psychological Science in the Public Interest, 5*(2), 35–69.

Kassin, S. M., & Kiechel, K. L. (1996). The social psychology of false confessions: Compliance, internalization, and confabulation. *Psychological Science, 7*, 125–128.

Kassin, S. M., & Sukel, H. (1997). Coerced confessions and the jury: An experimental test of the "harmless error" rule. *Law and Human Behavior, 21*(1), 27–46.

Kassin, S. M., & Wrightsman, L. S. (1983). The construction and validation of a juror bias scale. *Journal of Research in Personality, 17*(4), 423–442.

Kassin, S. M., & Wrightsman, L. S. (1985). Confession evidence. In S. M. Kassin & L. S. Wrightsman (Eds.), *The psychology of evidence and trial procedure* (pp. 67–94). London: Sage.

Kebbell, M. R., & Milne, R. (1998). Police officers' perception of eyewitness factors in forensic investigations. *Journal of Social Psychology, 138*, 323–330.

Kebbell, M. R., & Wagstaff, G. F. (1998). Hypnotic interviewing: The best way to interview eyewitnesses? *Behavioral Sciences and the Law, 16*, 115–129.

Kelleher, M. (1997). *Profiling the lethal employee: Case studies of workplace violence.* Westport: Praeger.

Kendall-Tackett, K. A., Williams, L. M., & Finkelhor, D. (1993). Impact of sexual abuse on children: A review and synthesis of recent empirical studies. *Psychological Bulletin, 113*, 164–180.

Kennedy, H. G., & Grubin, D. H. (1992). Patterns of denial in sex offenders. *Psychological Medicine, 22*, 191–196.

Kennedy, L. (1985). *The airman and the carpenter.* New York: Viking.

Kennedy, T. D., & Haygood, R. C. (1992). The discrediting effect of eyewitness testimony. *Eyewitness testimony.* Cambridge, MA: Harvard University Press. Keppel, R. D., & Birnes, W. J. (1997). *Signature killers: Interpreting the calling cards of the serial murderer.* New York: Pocket Books.

Kernberg, O. (1975). *Borderline conditions and pathological narcissism.* New York: Jason Aronson.

Kershaw, A. (2004, June 5). Spain and U.S. at odds on mistaken terror arrest. *New York Times*, p. A1.

Killeen, P. R., & Nash, M. R. (2003). The four causes of hypnosis. *International Journal of Clinical and Experimental Hypnosis, 51*, 195–231.

Kim, J.-O., & Mueller, C. W. (1978). *Factor analysis: Statistical methods and practical issues (Quantitative applications in the social sciences No. 14).* Thousand Oaks, CA: Sage.

King, N. J. (2007). Postconviction review of jury discrimination: Measuring the effects of juror race on jury decisions. In J. D. Lieberman & B. D. Sales (Eds.), *Scientific jury selection.* Washington, DC: American Psychological Association.

Kinney, J., & Johnson, D. L. (1993). *Breaking point: The workplace violence epidemic and what to do about it.* Washington, DC: U. S. Department of Health and Human Services.

Kilpatrick, D. G., Resnick, H. S.,Saunders, B. E., & Best, C. L. (1998). Rape, other violence against women, and posttraumatic stress disorder: Critical issues in assessing the adversity-stress-psychopathology relationship. In B.P. Dohrenwend (Eds.), *Adversity, stress, & psychopathology*, New York: Oxford University Press, 161–176.

Kircher, J. C., & Raskin, D. C. (2000). Computer methods for the psychophysiological detection of deception. In M. Kleiner (Ed.), *Handbook of polygraph testing.* San Diego, CA: Academic Press.

Kirschner, S. M., & Galperin, G. J. (2001). Psychiatric defenses in New York county: Pleas and results. *Journal of the American Academy of psychiatry and the law, 29*(2), 194–201.

Kishor, S. (1993, April). May God give sons to all: Gender and child mortality in India. *American Sociological Review, 58*, 2, 262.

Kitaeff, J. (1972). The diction of cognizance. *The American Journal of Psychoanalysis, 32*(2), 216.

Kitaeff, J. (2006). Psychological assessment services for law enforcement. In J. Kitaeff (Ed.), *Selected readings in forensic psychology.* Upper Saddle River, NJ: Pearson.

Kleck, R. (1968). Physical stigma and nonverbal cues emitted in face-to-face Interaction. *Human Relations, 21*, 26–27.

Kleck, R. E., Ono, H., & Hastorf, A. H. (1966). The effects of physical deviance upon face-to-face interaction. *Human Relations, 19*, 433–435.

Kleinfield, N. R. (2007, April 22). Before deadly rage, a life consumed by troubling silence. *The New York Times.* Retrieved May 22, 2007, from http://www.nytimes.com/2007/04/22/us/22vatech.html?ex=1179979200?en=9d7a5ca43a5

Kleinhauz, M., Horowitz, I., & Tobin, T. (1977). The use of hypnosis in police investigation: A preliminary communication. *Journal of the Forensic Science Society, 17*, 77–80.

Klüver, H., & Bucy, P. C. (1939). Preliminary analysis of functions of the temporal lobes in monkeys. *Arch Neurology and Psychiatry, 42*, 979–1000.

Knapp, S., VandeCreek, L., & Fulero, S. (1993). The attorney—psychologist—client privilege in judicial proceedings. *Psychotherapy in Private Practice, 12*, 1–15.

Knappman, E. W. (1994). *Great American trials* (p. 190). Detroit, MI: Visible Ink Press.

Knight, Z. G. (2006). Some thoughts on the psychological roots of the behavior of serial killers as narcissists: An object relations perspective.

Social Behavior and Personality: An International Journal, 34, 1189–1206.

Knight, Z. G. (2007, March). Sexually motivated serial killers and the psychology of aggression and "evil" within a contemporary psychoanalytical perspective. *Journal of Sexual Aggression, 13,* 21–35.

Kocsis, R. N., and Hayes, A. F. (2004). Believing is seeing? Investigating the perceived accuracy of criminal psychological profiles. *International Journal of Offender Therapy and Comparative Criminology, 48*(2), 149–160.

Koenig, B. E. (1986). Spectrographic voice identification: A forensic survey. *Journal of the Acoustical Society of America, 79,* 2088–2090.

Kolko, D. J. (1996). Individual cognitive-behavioral treatment and family therapy for physically abused children and their offending parents: A comparison of clinical outcomes. *Child Maltreatment, 1,* 322–342.

Kopell, B. S., Wittner, W. K., Lunde, D. T., Wolcott, L. J., & Tinklenberg, J. R. (1974). The effects of methamphetamine and secobarbital on the contingent negative variation amplitude. *Psychopharmacology, 34*(1), 55–62.

Kosberg, J. I., & Garcia, J. L. (1995). *Confronting the maltreatment of elders by their family.* Thousand Oaks, GA: Sage.

Kovera, M. B., Dickinson, J. J., & Cutler, B. L. (2003). Voir dire and jury selection. In *Handbook of psychology: Forensic psychology,* (pp. 161-175), New York, NY: John Wiley & Sons.

Kovera, M. B., Gresham, A. W., Borgida, E., Gray, E., & Regan, P. C. (1997). Does expert testimony inform or influence juror decision-making? A social cognitive analysis. *Journal of Applied Psychology, 82,* 178–191.

Kovera, M. B., McAuliff, B. D., & Hebert, K. S. (1999). Reasoning about scientific evidence: Effects of juror gender and evidence quality on juror decisions in a hostile work environment case. *Journal of Applied Psychology, 84,* 362–375.

Kraft-Ebing, R. (1998). *Psychopathia sexualis—The complete english language translation.* New York: Arcade Publishing.

Krapohl, D.J. (2002). The polygraph in personnel selection. In M. Kleiner (Ed.), *Handbook of polygraph testing.* San Diego, CA: Academic Press.

Krauss, D. & Lee, D. (2003). Deliberating on dangerousness and death: Jurors' ability to differentiate between expert actuarial and clinical predictions of dangerousness. *International Journal of Law and Psychiatry, 26,* 113–137.

Kressel, N. J., & Kressel, D. F. (2002). *Stack and sway: The new science of jury consulting.* Boulder, CO: Westview Press.

Kretschmer, E. (1921). *Korperban und charakter* (26th ed). Berlin: Springer Verlag.

Krzywinski, M. (2008). *Lexical analysis of 2008 US presidential and vice-presidential debates.* Retrieved December 28, 2008, from http://mkweb.bcgsc.ca/debates/

Kuch, K. (1989). A treatment for post-traumatic phobias and PTSD after car accidents. In P. A. Keller & S. R. Heyman (Eds.), *Innovations in clinical practice: A source book* (pp. 263–271). Sarasota, FL: Professional Resource Exchange.

Kunc, N. (2001). Robert Latimer and the dread of disability. *Professional Development for Human Services.* Retrieved March 29, 2008, from http://www.normemma.com/indxadvo.htm#Tracy

Kurtz, P. D., Gaudin, J. M., Wodarski, J. S., & Howing, P. T. (2006). Maltreatment and the school-aged child: School performance consequences. In J. R. Lutzker (Ed.), *Preventing violence.* Washington, DC: American Psychological Association.

La Barre, W. (1964). Confession as cathartic therapy in American Indian tribes. In A. Kiev (Ed.), *Magic, faith, and healing: Studies in primitive psychiatry today* (pp. 36–49). New York: Free Press.

Laci Peterson's remains identified; husband arrested (2003, April 18). *CNN.* Retrieved February 26, 2008, from http://en.wikipedia.org/wiki/Laci_Peterson

Ladds, B., & Convit, A. (1994). Involuntary medication of patients who are incompetent to stand trial: A review of empirical studies. *Bulletin of the American Academy of Academic Psychiatry and Law, 22,* 519–527.

Lane, B., & Gregg, W. (1994). *The encyclopedia of serial killers.* Emeryville, CA: Diamond/Charter.

Lane, B., & Gregg, W. (2004). *The encyclopedia of mass murder.* New York, NY: Carroll & Graf.

Lane, F. (1984). *Lane's Goldstein trial techniques* (3rd ed.). Wilmette, IL: Callaghan.

Langenburg, G. (2002, September 30). *The detail.* Retrieved October 9, 2008, from http://www.clpex.com/Articles/TheDetail/1-99/The Detail60.htm

Langevin, R., & Paitich, D. (2002). *Clarke Sex History Questionnaire for Males-Revised (SHQ-R).* North Tonawanda, NY: MHS Inc.

Langsley, D. (1980, September 19). Viewpoint, a commentary by APA's President. *Psychiatric News,* p. 25, col. 1.

Larson, J. A. (1969). *Lying and its detection: A study of deception and deception tests.* Montclair, NJ: Patterson Smith.

Latent dactyloscopy: The science of fingerprinting. *The thin blue line information section.* Retrieved September 30, 2008, from http://www.policensw.com/info/fingerprints/finger01.html

Latent print section. *West Virginia State Police.* Retrieved October 7, 2008, from http://www.wvstatepolice.com/crime/latent.pdf

Lau, V. C. S., Au, W. T., & Ho, J. M. C. (2003). A qualitative and quantitative review of antecedents of counterproductive behavior in organizations. *Journal of Business and Psychology, 18,* 73–99.

Laufer, B. (1912). History of the finger-print system. *The Print, 16*(2), 1–13.

Laughlin, P. R., VanderStoep, S. W., & Hollingshead, A. B. (1991). Collective versus individual induction: Recognition of truth, rejection of error, and collective information processing. *Journal of Personality and Social Psychology, 61,* 50–67.

Law, J., & Conway, J. (1992). Effect of abuse and neglect on the development of children's speech and language. *Developmental Medicine and Child Neurology, 34,* 943–948.

Laws, R. D. (2003, March).The rise and fall of relapse prevention. *Australian Psychologist, 38*(1), 22–30.

Layton, D. (1998). *Seductive poison: A Jonestown survivor's story of life and death in the people's temple.* New York, NY: Anchor.

Leach, A.-M., Talwar, V., Lee, K., Bala, N., & Lindsay, R. C. (2004). "Intuitive" lie detection and children's deception by law enforcement officials and university students. *Law and Human Behavior, 28,* 661–685.

LeBlanc, M. M., & Kelloway, E. K. (2002). Predictors and outcomes of workplace violence and aggression. *Journal of Applied Psychology, 87,* 444–453.

LeBlanc, V. R., Regehr, C., Jelley, R. B., & Barath, I. (2008). The relationship between coping styles, performance and responses to stressful scenarios in police recruits. *International Journal of Stress Management, 15*(1), 76–93.

Lee, K., & Allen, N. J. (2002). Organizational citizenship behavior and workplace deviance: The role of affect and cognitions. *Journal of Applied Psychology, 87,* 131–142.

Leen-Felder, E. W., Zvolensky, M. J., Feldner, M. T., & Lejuez, C. W. (2004). Behavioral inhibition: Relation to negative emotion regulation and reactivity. *Personality and Individual Differences, 36,* 1235–1247.

Lefebvre, C. D., Marchand, Y., Smith, S. M., & Connolly, J. F. (2007). Determining eyewitness identification accuracy using event-related brain potentials (ERPs). *Psychophysiology, 44,* 894–904.

Legge, G. E., Grosmann, C., & Pieper, C. M. (1984). Learning unfamiliar voices. *Journal of Experimental Psychology: Learning Memory, and Cognition, 10,* 298–303.

Leo, R. A. (1996). Miranda's revenge. Police interrogations as a confidence game. *Law and Society Review, 30,* 259–288.

Leo, R. A., Drizin, S., Neufeld, P., Hall, B., & Vatner, A. (2006). Bringing reliability back in: False confessions and legal safeguards in the twenty-first century. *Wisconsin Law Review, 2006,* 479–539.

Leo, R. A., & Ofshe, R. J. (1998). The consequences of false confessions: Deprivations of liberty and miscarriages of justice in the age of psychological interrogation. *Journal of Criminal Law and Criminology, 88,* 429–497.

Lerner, M. J. (1980). *The belief in a just world: A fundamental delusion.* New York: Plenum Press.

Levi, A. M. (2002). Lineup size, the modified sequential lineup, and the sequential lineup. *Cognitive Technology, 7,* 39–46.

Levine, F. J., & Tapp, J. L. (1973). The psychology of criminal identification: The gap from Wade to Kirby. *University of Pennsylvania Law Review, 121,* 1079–1131.

Levitt, R. E., Aronoff, G., Morgan, C. D., Overley, T. M., & Parrish, M. J. (1975). Testing the coercive power of hypnosis: Committing objectionable acts. *International Journal of Clinical and Experimental Hypnosis, 23,* 59–67.

Levy, R. (1989, April 21). *Using "scientific" testimony to prove child sexual abuse.* Inaugural lecture at the University of Minnesota Law School for the Dorsey & Whitney Professor of Law, Minneapolis, MN.

Lewinski, B. (2007, April 24). The lethal employee. *PoliceOne.Com.* Retrieved July 13, 2007, from http://www.policeone.com/writers/columnists/ForceScience/articles/1239206/.

Leyton, E. (2005). *Hunting humans: The rise of the modern multiple murderer.* Toronto, Canada: McClelland & Stewart Ltd.

Lezon, D. (2006). *Yates not 'grossly psychotic' before drownings, Dietz testifies.* Houston http://www.chron.com/disp/story.mpl/special/drownings/4044790.html

Lieb, R., & Gookin, K. (2005, March). *Involuntary commitment of sexually violent predators: Comparing state laws.* Retrieved August 14, 2007, from www.wsipp.wa.gov/rptfiles/05-03-1101.pdf

Lieberman, J. D., & Sales, B. D. (2007). *Scientific jury selection.* Washington, DC: American Psychological Association.

Lilienfeld, S. O., Lynn, S. J., & Lohr, J. M. (Eds.). (2003). *Science and pseudoscience in clinical psychology.* New York: The Guilford Press.

Lim, B. C., & Ployhart, R. E. (2004). Transformational leadership: Relations to the five-factor model and team performance in typical and maximum contexts. *Journal of Applied Psychology, 89,* 610–621.

Lindesmith, A. R., & Dunham, H. W. (1941). Some principles of criminal typology. *Social Forces, 19,* 307–314.

Lindsay, R. C. L., Lea, J. A., & Fulford, J. A. (1991). Sequential lineup presentation: Technique matters. *Journal of Applied Psychology, 76,* 741–745.

Lindsay, R. C. L., Lea, J. A., Nosworthy, G. J., Fulford, J. A., Hector, J., LeVan, V., et al. (1991). Biased lineups: Sequential presentation reduces the problem. *Journal of Applied Psychology, 76,* 796–802.

Lindsay, R. C. L., Lim, R., Marando, L., & Cully, D. (1986). Mock-juror evaluations of eyewitness testimony: A test of metamemory hypotheses. *Journal of Applied Social Psychology, 16,* 447–459.

Lindsay, R. C. L., & Wells, G. L. (1985). Improving eyewitness identifications from lineups: Simultaneous versus sequential lineup presentations. *Journal of Applied Psychology, 70,* 556–564.

Lindsey, R. (1985, October 22). Dan White, killer of San Francisco mayor, a suicide. *The New York Times,* p. A18.

Linn, R. L. (1968). A Monte Carlo approach to the number of factors problem. *Psychometrika, 33,* 37–72.

Lippit, A. M. (1997). Martin Arnold's memory machine. In: Afterimage. *The Journal of Media Arts and Cultural Criticism, 24*(6), 8–10.

Lipton, J. P. (1977). On the psychology of eyewitness testimony. *Journal of Applied Psychology, 62,* 90–95.

Lisae, J. (2002). Elder abuse and domestic violence: Overlapping issues and legal remedies. *American Journal of Family Law, 15,* 149.

Little, B. R. (2000). Free traits and personal contexts: Expanding a social ecological model of well-being. In W. B. Walsh & K. H. Craik (Eds.), *Person–environment psychology: New directions and perspectives* (2nd ed., pp. 87–116). Mahwah, NJ: Erlbaum.

Litwack, T. R. (2001). Actuarial Versus Clinical Assessments of Dangerousness. *Psychology, Public Policy, and Law, 7*(2), 409–443.

Litwack, T. R., & Schlesinger, L. B. (1999). Dangerousness risk assessments: Research, legal and clinical considerations. In A. K. Hess & I. B. Weiner (Eds.), *Handbook of forensic psychology* (pp. 171–217). New York: Wiley.

Loftus, E. F. (1979). *Eyewitness testimony.* Cambridge, MA: Harvard University Press.

Loftus, E. F. (1998). The price of bad memories. *Skeptical Inquirer.* Retrieved November 17, 2007, from http://faculty.washington.edu/eloftus/Articles/price.htm

Loftus, E. F., & Ketcham, K. (1994). *The myth of repressed memory.* New York: St. Martin's Press.

Loftus, E. F., & Pickrell, J. (1995). The formation of false memories. *Psychiatric Annals, 25*(12), 720–725.

London, K., Bruck, M., Ceci, S. J., & Shuman, D. W. (2005). Disclosure of child sexual abuse: What does the research tell us about the ways that children tell? *Psychology, Public Policy, and Law, 11*(1), 194–226.

Lorenz, K. (1966). *On aggression.* New York: Harcourt, Brace and World.

Los Angeles Police Department. (home page). Retrieved October 21, 2009, from http://www.lapdonline.org

Love, K. G., Vinson, J., Tolsma, J., & Kaufmann, G. (2008). Symptoms of undercover police officers: A comparison of officers currently, formerly, and without undercover experience. *International Journal of Stress Management, 15*(2), 136–152.

Lu, C. (2004). Agents, structures and evil in world politics. *International Relations, 18,* 498–509.

Lubet, S. (1997). *Modern trial advocacy: Analysis and practice.* Notre Dame, IN: National Institute for Trial Advocacy.

Lubinski, D. (2000). Scientific and social significance of assessing individual differences: "Sinking shafts at a few critical points." *Annual Review of Psychology, 51,* 405–444.

Luster, T., & Small, S. A. (1997). Sexual abuse history and number of sex partners among female adolescents. *Family Planning Perspectives, 29,* 204–211.

Lutus, P. (2006). How to whine your way to sympathy. *A society of victims.* Retrieved November 11, 2007, from http://www.arachnoid.com/psychology/victimhood.php

Luus, C. A. E., & Wells, G. L. (1991). Eyewitness identification and the selection of distracters for lineups. *Law and Human Behavior, 15,* 43–57.

Lykken, D. T. (1974). Psychology and the lie detector industry. *American Psychologist, 29,* 725–739.

Lykken, D. T. (1988). The case against polygraph testing. In A. Gale (Ed.), *The polygraph test: Lies, truth and science* (pp. 111–125). London: Sage.

Lykken, D. T. (1991). What's wrong with psychology anyway? In D. Cicchetti & W. M. Grove (Eds.), *Thinking clearly about psychology: Vol. 1. Matters of public interest* (pp. 3–39). Minneapolis: University of Minnesota Press.

Lykken, D. T. (1998). *A tremor in the blood: Uses and abuse of the lie detector.* New York: Plenum.

Lyman, M. D. (2008). *Criminal investigation: The art and the science.* Upper Saddle River, NJ: Prentice Hall.

Lynam, D., Moffitt, T. E., & Stouthamer-Loeber, M. (1993). Explaining the relation between IQ and delinquency: Class, race, test motivation, school failure, or self-control? *Journal of Abnormal Psychology, 102,* 187–196.

Maaga, M. M., & Wessinger, C. (1998). *Hearing the Voices of Jonestown,* Syracuse, NY: UniversityPress.

Macdonald, J. M. (1969). *Psychiatry and the criminal* (2nd ed.). Springfield, IL: Charles C. Thomas.

Macdonald, J. M., & Michaud, D. L. (1987). *The confession: Interrogation and criminal profiles for police officers.* Denver, CO: Apache.

Mack, D., Shannon, C., Quick, J., & Quick, J. (1998). Stress and the preventive management of workplace violence. In R. W. Griffin, A. O'Leary-Kelly, & J. M. Collins (Eds.), *Dysfunctional behavior in organizations: Violent and deviant behavior* (pp. 119–141). Stamford, CT: JAI Press.

MacLeod, A. D. (1995). Undercover policing: A psychiatrist's perspective. *International Journal of Law and Psychiatry, 18,* 239–247.

MacLeod, M. D. (1995, November). The psychology of identification parades. *NLJ Expert Witness Supplement, 1740*–1746.

MacLeod, M. D. (2007). Charles Whitman. Retrieved May 25, 2008, from http://www.crimelibrary.com/notorious_murders/mass/whitman/index_1.html

Major, B., & Gramzow, R. H. (1999). Abortion as stigma: Cognitive and emotional implications of concealment. *Journal of Personality and Social Psychology, 77,* 735–745.

Malpass, R. S., & Devine, P. G. (1981). Eyewitness identification: Lineup instructions and the absence of the offender. *Journal of Applied Psychology, 66,* 482–489.

Mangan, G. L., Quartermain, D., & Vaughan, G. M. (1960). Taylor MAS and group conformity pressure. *Journal of Abnormal and Social Psychology, 61,* 146–147.

Mann, J. J. (1999). Role of the serotonergic system in the pathogenesis of major depression and suicidal behavior. *Neuropsychopharmacology, 21*(2), 995–1055.

Manning, J. (2000). The Tylenol murders. *The Eighties Club.* Retrieved July 7, 2008, from http://eightiesclub.tripod.com/id298.htm

Mantwill, M., Köhnken, G., & Aschermann, E. (1995). Effects of the cognitive interview on the recall of familiar and unfamiliar events. *Journal of Applied Psychology, 80,* 68–78.

Marcus, B., & Schuler, H. (2004). Antecedents of counterproductive behavior at work: A general perspective. *Journal of Applied Psychology, 89,* 647–660.

Marcus, B., Schuler, H., Quell, P., & Hümpfner, G. (2002). Measuring counterproductivity: Development and initial validation of a German self-report questionnaire. *International Journal of Selection and Assessment, 10,* 18–35.

Margolin, J. (1977). Psychological perspectives in terrorism. In Y. Alexander & S. M. Finger (Eds.), *Terrorism: Interdisciplinary perspectives.* New York: John Jay.

Mark, V. H., Ervin, F. R., & Sweet, W. H. (1972). Deep temporal lobe stimulation in man. In B. E. Eleftheriou (Ed.), *The neurobiology of the amygdala* (pp. 207–240). New York: Plenum Press.

Markesteyn, T. (1992). *The psychological impact of nonsexual criminal offenses on victims.* Ottawa: Ministry of the Solicitor General of Canada.

Marshall, W. L., Fernandez, Y. M., Hudson, S. M., & Ward, T. (1998). Conclusions and future directions. In W. L. Marshall, Y. M. Fernandez, S. M. Hudson, & T. Ward (Eds.), *Sourcebook of treatment programs for sexual offenders* (pp. 477–478). New York: Plenum Press.

Marshall, W. L., Hamilton, K., & Fernandez, Y. (2001). Empathy deficits and cognitive distortions in child molesters. *Sex Abuse, 13,* 123–130.

Mart, E. G. (2002). *Munchausen's syndrome by proxy.* Manchester, NH: Bally Vaughan Publishing.

Martens, W. H. J. (2004). Terrorist with antisocial personality disorder. In R. Borum (Ed.), *Psychology of terrorism.* Tampa: University of South Florida.

Martinko, M. J., & Zellars, K. L. (1998). Toward a theory of workplace violence: A cognitive appraisal perspective. In R. W. Griffin, A. O'Leary-Kelly, & J. M. Collins (Eds.), *Dysfunctional behavior in organizations: Violent and deviant behavior* (pp. 1–42). Stamford, CT: JAI Press.

Marzuk, P. M., Nock, M. K., Leon, A. C., Portera, L., & Tardiff, K. (2002). *American Journal of Psychiatry, 159,* 2069–2071.

Mazzoni, G. A. L., Loftus, E. F., & Kirsch, I. (2001). Changing beliefs about implausible autobiographical events: A little plausibility goes a long way. *Journal of Experimental Psychology: Applied, 7,* 51–59.

McCann, I. L., & Pearlman, L. A. (1990). Vicarious traumatization: A framework for understanding the psychological effects of working with victims. *Journal of Traumatic Stress, 3,* 131–149.

McCaslin, S. E., Rogers, C. E., Metzler, T. J., Best, S. R., Weiss, D. S., Fagan, J. A., et al. (2006). The impact of personal threat on police officers' responses to critical incident stressors. *Journal of Nervous Mental Disorders, 194,* 591–597.

McCauley, C. R., & Segal, M. E. (1987). Social psychology of terrorist groups. In C. Hendrick (Ed.), *Group processes and intergroup relations: Annual review of social and personality psychology.* Beverly Hills: Sage.

McConkey, K. M., & Roche, S. M. (1989). Knowledge of eyewitness memory. *Australian Psychologist, 24,* 377–384.

McConkey, K. M., & Sheehan, P. W. (1996). *Hypnosis, memory, and behavior in criminal investigation.* New York: Guilford.

McCord, D. (1997). Syndromes, profiles and other mental exotica: A new approach to the admissibility of nontraditional psychological evidence in criminal cases. In R. J. Goodwin & J. Gurulé (Eds.), *Criminal and scientific evidence.* Charlottesville, VA: Michie Law Publishers.

McCrae, R. M., & John, O. P. (1992). An introduction to the five-factor model and its applications. (PDF). *Journal of Personality, 60*(2), 175–175.

McCrae, R. R., & Costa, P. T. (1983). Joint factors in self-reports and ratings: Neuroticism, extraversion and openness to experience. *Personality and Individual Differences, 4*(3), 245–255.

McCrae, R. R., & Costa, P. T. (2004, February). A contemplated revision of the NEO Five-Factor Inventory. *Personality and Individual Differences, 36*(3), 587–596.

McCrae, R. R., Costa, P. T., Jr., del Pilar, G. H., Rolland, J. P., & Parker, W. D. (1998). Corss-cultural assessment of the five-factor model: The revised NEO Personality Inventory. *Journal of Cross-Cultural Psychology, 29,* 171–188.

McCrae, R. R., Costa, P. T., Jr., Lima, M. P., Simões, A., Ostendorf, F., Angleitner, A., et al. (1999). Age differences in personality across the adult life span: Parallels in five cultures. *Developmental Psychology, 35,* 466–477.

McDermott, M. C., Owen, T., & McDermott, F. M. (1996). *Voice identification: The aural/spectrographic method.* Owl Investigations, Inc. Retrieved October 1, 2008, from http://www.owlinvestigations.com/forensic_articles/aural_spectrographic/fulltext.html

McDonald, W. (2004). *Child maltreatment 2002.* Washington, DC: Department of Health and Human Services.

McElhaney, J. W. *Picking a jury.* Retrieved February 20, 2008, from http://www.uchastings.edu/site_files/faculty_webs_adjunct/chengSecondVoirDire.pdf

McGarry, A. L. (1965). Competency for trial and due process via the state hospital. *American Journal of Psychiatry, 122,* 623.

McGehee, F. (1937). The reliability of the identification of the human voice. *Journal of General psychology, 17,* 249.

McGrath, R. J., Cumming, G., Livingston, J. A., & Hoke, S. E. (2003). Outcome of a treatment program for adult sex offenders: From prison to community. *Journal of Interpersonal Violence, 18*(1), 3–17.

McHenry, J. J., Hough, L. M., Toquam, J. L., Hanson, M. A., & Ashworth, S. (1990). Project A validity results: The relationship between predictor and criterion domains. *Personnel Psychology, 43,* 335–354.

McKenzie, I. K. (1994). Regulating custodial interviews: A comparative study. *International Journal of the Sociology of Law, 22,* 239–259.

McLeod, P. L., Lobel, S. A., & Cox, T. H., Jr. (1996). Ethnic diversity and creativity in small groups. *Small Group Research, 27,* 248–264.

McMackin, R. A., Leisen, M. B., Cusack, J. F., LaFratta, J., & Litwin, P. (2002). The relationship of trauma exposure to sex offending behavior among male juvenile offenders. *Journal of Child Sexual Abuse, 11,* 25–40.

McMains, J. T. (1995). Law enforcement applications for critical incident stress teams. In M. I. Kurke & E. M. Scrivner (Eds.), *Police psychology into the 21st century.* Hillsdale, NJ: Lawrence Erlbaum.

McMains, M. J. & Mullins, W. C. (2006) *Crisis negotiations. Managing critical incident and hostage situations in law enforcement and corrections* (3rd ed.). Dallas, TX: Anderson Publishing.

McNeil, C. B., Eybert, S. M., Eisenstadt, T. H., Newcomb, K., & Funderburk, B. W. (1991). Parent-child interaction therapy with behavior problem children: Generalization of treatment effects to the school setting. *Journal of Clinical Child Psychology,* 20, 140–151.

Meadow, R. (1997, May). *ABC of child abuse.* London: BMJ books.

Meehl, P. E. (1970). Nuisance variables and the ex post facto design. In M. Radner & S. Winokur (Eds.), *Minnesota studies in the philosophy of science: Vol. V. Analyses of theories and methods of physics and psychology* (pp. 373–402). Minneapolis: University of Minnesota Press.

Meehl, P. E. (1978). Theoretical risks and tabular asterisks: Sir Karl, Sir Ronald, and the slow progress of soft psychology. *Journal of Consulting and Clinical Psychology,* 46, 806–834.

Meissner, C. A, & Brigham, J. C. (2001a). A meta-analysis of the verbal overshadowing effect in face identification. *Applied Cognitive Psychology,* 15, 603–616.

Meissner, C. A., & Brigham, J. C. (2001b). Thirty years of investigating the own-race bias in memory for faces: A meta-analytic review. *Psychology, Public Policy, and Law,* 7, 3–35.

Mello, E. W., & Fisher, R. P. (1996). Enhancing older adult eyewitness memory with the cognitive interview. *Applied Cognitive Psychology,* 10, 403–418.

Meloy, J., Reid, A., Hempel, G., Mohandie, K., Shiva, A., & Gray, B. (2001). Offender and offense characteristics of a nonrandom sample of adolescent mass murderers. *Journal of the American Academy of Child and Adolescent Psychiatry,* 40(6), 719–728.

Melton, G. B., Petrila, J., Poythress, N. G., & Slobogin, C. (1997). *Psychological evaluations for the courts: A handbook for mental health professionals and lawyers.* New York: The Guilford Press.

Melton, G. B., Petrila, J., Poythress, N. G., & Slobogin, C. (2007). *Psychological evaluations for the courts: A handbook for mental health professionals and lawyers* (3rd ed.). New York: The Guilford Press.

Melville, J. D., & Naimark, D. (2002). Punishing the insane: The verdict of guilty but mentally ill. *Journal of the American Academy of Psychiatry and the Law,* 30(4), 553–555.

Memon, A., & Higham, P. A. (1999). A review of the cognitive interview. *Psychology, Crime and Law,* 5, 177–196.

Memon, A., Hope, L., & Bull, R. (2003). Exposure duration: Effects on eyewitness accuracy and confidence. *British Journal of Psychology,* 94, 339–354.

Mendez, M. F., Chow, T., Ringman, J., Twitchell, G., & Hinkin, C. H. (2000). Pedophilia and temporal lobe disturbances. *Journal of Neuropsychiatry and Clinical Neurosciences,* 2(1), 71–76.

Menninger, L. (2005, September). Proof of qualification for commitment as a mentally disordered sex offender. *American Journal of Proof of Facts,* 51(3), 299.

Menninger, K. (1968). *The crime of punishment.* New York: The Viking Press.

Mental health history of Seung Hui Cho: A report to the Governor. Retrieved July 6, 2008, from http://www.governor.virginia.gov/tempContent/techPanelReport-docs/8%20CHAPTER%20IV%20LIFE%20AND%20MENTAL%20HEALTH%20HISTORY%20OF%20CHOpdf.pdf

Merriam-Webster on Line. Retrieved November 18, 2007, from http://www.m-w.com/dictionary/repression

Metchik, E. (1999). An analysis of the "screening out" model of police officer selection. *Police Quarterly,* 2, 79–95.

Meyer, G. J., Finn, S. E., Eyde, L. D., Kay, G. G., Dies, R. R., Eisman, E. J., et al. (2002). Amplifying issues related to psychological testing and assessment. *American Psychologist,* 57, 140–141.

Miles, D. R., & Carey, G. (1997). Genetic and environmental architecture of human aggression. *Journal of Personality and Social Psychology,* 72, 207–217.

Milgram, S. (1963). Behavioral study of obedience. *Journal of Personality and Social Psychology,* 67, 371–378.

Milgram, S. (1974). *Obedience to authority.* New York: Harper & Row.

Miller, L. (2002a). Psychological interventions for terroristic trauma: Symptoms, syndromes, and treatment strategies. *Psychotherapy: Theory, Research, Practice, Training,* 39(4), 283–296. Miller, L. (1998a). Psychotherapy of crime victims: Treating the aftermath of interpersonal violence. *Psychotherapy: Theory, Research, Practice, Training,* 35, 336–345.

Miller, L. (2002b). Law enforcement responses to youth violence: Psychological dynamics and Intervention strategies. In R.S. Moser, & C.E. Franz (Ed.), Shocking violence II: Violent disaster, war, and terrorism affecting our youth (pp. 165–195). New York: Charles C Thomas.

Miller, L. (2002c). Posttraumatic stress disorder in school violence: Risk management lessons from the workplace. *Neurolaw Letter,* 33, 36–40.

Miller, L. (2006). *Practical police psychology.* Springfield, IL: Charles C. Thomas.

Miller, L. (1998b). *Shocks to the system.* New York: W.W. Norton & Company.

Miller, R. D. (2003). Hospitalization of criminal defendants for evaluation of competence to stand trial or for restoration of competence: Clinical and legal issues. *Behavioral Science and the Law,* 21, 369.

Miller, T. W., & Veltkamp, L. J. (1989). Assessment of child sexual abuse: Clinical use of fables. *Child Psychiatry and Human Development,* 20(2), 123–133.

Mison, R. B. (1992). Comment, homophobia in manslaughter: The homosexual advance defense as insufficient provocation. *California Law Review,* 80, 133, 136, 167.

Mitchell, J. T. (1983). When disaster strikes: The critical incident debriefing process. *Journal of Emergency Medical Services,* 8, 36–39.

Mitchell, J. T., & Everly, G. S., Jr. (1993). *Critical incident stress debriefing (CISD).* Ellicot City, MD: Chevron.

Mitchell, J., Wilson, K., Revicki, D., & Parker, L. (1985). Children's perceptions of aging: A multidimensional approach to differences by age, sex, and race. *The Gerontologist,* 25, 182–187.

Mitchell, K. J., Livosky, M., & Mather, M. (1998). The weapon focus effect revisited: The role of novelty. *Legal and Criminological Psychology,* 3, 287–303.

Moffitt, T. E., Gabrielli, W. F., Mednick, S. A., & Schulsinger, F. (1981). Socioeconomic status, IQ, and delinquency. *Journal of Abnormal Psychology,* 90, 152–156.

Moffitt, T. E., & Silva, P. A. (1988). IQ and delinquency: A direct test of the differential detection hypothesis. *Journal of Abnormal Psychology,* 97, 330–333.

Monahan, J. (1981). *Predicting violent behavior: An assessment of clinical techniques.* Beverly Hills, CA: Sage.

Monahan, J., & Walker, L. (1986). Social authority: Obtaining, evaluating, and establishing social science in law. *University of Pennsylvania Law Review,* 134(3), 477–516.

Monahan, J., & Walker, L. (1987). Social frameworks: A new use of social science in law. *Virginia Law Review,* 73, 559–598.

Monahan, J., & Walker, L. (1998). *Social science in law. Cases and materials* (4th ed.). Westbury, NY: Foundation.

Mones, P. (1995). *Stalking justice: The dramatic true story of the detective who first used DNA testing to catch a serial killer.* New York: Simon & Schuster.

Monitor on Psychology. Sexual harassment too often leads to humiliation for victims. Retrieved July 8, 2007, from http://www.apa.org/monitor/oct03/harass.html

Montada, L., & Lerner, M. J. (Eds.). (1998). *Responses to victimization and belief in a just world.* New York: Plenum Press.

Montaldo, C. (2006, May 25). *Malvo Outlines Snipers' Plan of Terror.* About.com. Retrieved July, 17, 2007, from http://crime.about.com/b/a/256952.htm.

Montaldo, C. (2004, November 22). Peterson judge denies change of venue. *About.com: Crime/punishment.* Retrieved February 26, 2007, from http://crime.about.com/od/news/a/scott041122.htm

Moran, G., & Comfort, J. C. (1982). Scientific jury selection: Sex as a moderator of demographic and personality predictors of impaneled felony juror behavior. *Journal of Personality and Social Psychology, 43,* 1052–1063.

Moran, G., & Comfort, J. C. (2007). Neither "tentative" nor "fragmentary": Verdict preference of impaneled felony jurors as a function of attitude toward capital punishment. In J. D. Lieberman & B. D. Sales (Eds.), *Scientific jury selection* (p. 80). Washington, DC: American Psychological Association.

Moreland, R. L., Levine, J. M., & Wingert, M. L. (1996). Creating the ideal group: Composition effects at work. In E. H. Witte & J. H. Davis (Eds.), *Understanding group behavior: Vol. 2. Small group processes and interpersonal relations* (pp. 11–35). Mahwah, NJ: Erlbaum.

Morgan, C. A., Hazlett, G., Doran, A., Garrett, S., Hoyt, G., Thomas, P., et al. (2004). Accuracy of eyewitness memory for persons encountered during exposure to highly intense stress. *International Journal of Law and Psychiatry, 27,* 265–279.

Morgan, E. (2007, January 8). *Types of forensic science.* Retrieved August 9, 2008, from http://ezinearticles.com/?Types-of-Forensic-Science&id=410614

Morgan, S. J. (2001). *The mind of a terrorist fundamentalist: The psychology of terror cults.* Cincinnati, OH: Awe-Struck E-Books.

Mossman, D. (1999). Hired guns, whores, and prostitutes: Case law references to clinicians of ill repute. *Journal of the American Academy of Psychiatry and the Law, 27*(3), 416–425.

Moston, S., Stephenson, G. M., & Williamson, T. M. (1992). The effects of case characteristics on suspect behaviour during police questioning. *British Journal of Criminology, 32,* 23–40.

Mount, H. (2006, June 25). *The sniper's plan: kill six whites a day for 30 days.* Telegraph. Retrieved July 17, 2007, from http://www.telegraph.co.uk/news/worldnews/northamerica/usa/1519411/The-snipers-plan-kill-six-whites-a-day-for-30-days.html

Mueller, C. B., & Kirkpatrick, L. C. (1998). *Federal rules of evidence.* New York: Aspen.

Münsterberg, H. (1909). *On the witness stand.* Garden City, NY: Doubleday.

Murphy, K. R. (1993). *Honesty in the workplace.* Belmont, CA: Brooks/Cole.

Murray, G., Goldstone, E., & Cunningham, E. (2007). Personality and the predisposition(s) to bipolar disorder: Heuristic benefits of a two-dimensional model. *Bipolar Disorder, 9,* 453–461.

Murray, J. B. (2000). Psychological profile of pedophiles and child molesters. *The Journal of Psychology, 134*(2), 211–224.

Murray, J. P. (2001). TV violence and brainmapping in children. *Psychiatric Times,* p. 18.

Muthen, B. (1978). Contributions to factor analysis of dichotomous variables. *Psychometrika, 43,* 551–560.

Muthen, B. (1984). A general structural equation model with dichotomous, ordered categorical, and continuous latent variable indicators. *Psychometrika, 49,* 115–132.

Narby, D. J., Cutler, B. L., & Moran, G. (1993). A meta-analysis of the association between authoritarianism and jurors' perceptions of defendant culpability. *Journal of Applied Psychology, 78,* 34–42.

Nathan, P. E., Gorman, J. M., & Salkind, N. J. (Eds.). (1999). *Treating mental disorders: A guide to what works.* New York: Oxford University Press.

Najavitis, L. M., Weiss, R. D., Shaw, S. R., & Muenz, L. (1998). "Seeking safety": Outcome of a new cognitive-behavioral psychotherapy for women with posttraumatic stress disorder and substance dependence. *Journal of Traumatic Stress, 11,* 437–457.

National Abortion Federation. *Violence Statistics.* Retrieved July 5, 2007, from http://www.prochoice.org/about_abortion/violence/violence_statistics.html

National Center for PTSD. *Department of veterans affairs.* Retrieved July 6, 2007, from http://www.ncptsd.va.gov/ncmain/index.jsp

National Center on Elder Abuse (1998). Retrieved February 6, 2009, from http://www.ncea.aoa.gov/NCEAroot/Main_Site/pdf/publication/Final Statistics050331.pdf

National clearinghouse on marital and date rape. (1998). Retrieved January 22, 2007, from http://members.aol.com/ncmdr/

National Organization for Victim Assistance. Home Page. Retrieved February 6, 2009, from http://www.trynova.org/

National Research Council. (2003). *The polygraph and lie detection.* Washington, DC: National Academy Press.

Nebehay, S. (2000, April 7). "Honor Killings" of women said on rise worldwide. *Reuters Dispatch.*

Neisser, U., Boodoo, G., Bouchard, T. J., Boykin, A. W., Brody, N., Ceci, S. J., et al. (1996). Intelligence: Knowns and unknowns. *American Psychologist, 51,* 77–101.

Nelson, J. R., Smith, D. J., & Dodd, J. (1990). The moral reasoning of juvenile delinquents: A meta-analysis. *Journal of Abnormal Child Psychology, 18,* 231–239.

Nemeth, C. P. (2001). *Law & evidence: A primer for criminal justice, criminology, law, and legal studies.* Upper Saddle River, NJ: Prentice-Hall.

Neuman, J. H., & Baron, R. A. (1997). Aggression in the workplace. In R. A. Giacalone & J. Greenberg (Eds.), *Antisocial behavior in organizations* (pp. 37–67). Thousand Oaks, CA: Sage.

Neuman, J. H., & Baron, R. A. (1998). Workplace violence and workplace aggression: Evidence concerning specific forms, potential causes, and preferred targets. *Journal of Management, 24,* 391–419.

New Jersey Safe Haven Infant Protection Act. (P.L. 2000, CHAPTER 58). Retrieved April 1, 2009, from http://www.njleg.state.nj.us/2000/Bills/al00/58_.pdf

New York Police Department. (home page). Retrieved October 21, 2009, from http://www.nyc.gov/html/nypd

New York State Office of Children and Family Services. (home page). http://www.ocfs.state.ny.us/main/safe/info.asp

Newhill, C., & Wexler, S. (1997). Client violence toward children and youth service workers. *Children and Youth Services Review, 19,* 195–212.

Newton, M. (2000). *The encyclopedia of serial murder.* New York: Checkmark Books.

Nichols, H. R. & Molinder, I. (1984). *Multiphasic Sex Inventory: Manual,* Tacoma, WA: Authors. Nicholson, R. A., & Kugler, K. W. (1991). Competent and incompetent criminal defendants: A quantitative review of comparative research. *Psychological Bulletin, 109,* 355.

Noon, E., & Hollin, C. R. (1987). Lay knowledge of eyewitness behaviour: A British survey. *Applied Cognitive Psychology, 1,* 143—153.)

Norris, J. (1988). *Serial killers.* New York: Anchor Books/Doubleday.

North, C. S. (2001). The course of post-traumatic stress disorder after the Oklahoma City bombing. *Military Medicine, 166,* 51–52.

Note (1953). Voluntary false confessions: A neglected area in criminal administration. *Indiana Law Journal, 28,* 374–392.

Oberman, M. (1996). Mothers who kill: Coming to terms with modern American infanticide. *American Criminal Law Review, 34*(1), 1–10.

O'Connell, C. N., Shor, R. E., & Orne, M. T. (1970). Hypnotic age regression: An empirical and methodological analysis. *Journal of Abnormal and Social Psychology, 76*(Monograph Suppl.), 1–32.

Odeh, M. S., Zeiss, R. A. & Huss, M. T. (2006). Cues they use: Clinicians' endorsement of risk cues in predictions of dangerousness. *Behavioural Sciences and The Law, 24,* 147–156.

O'Donovan, K. (1984). The medicalisation of infanticide. *Criminal Law Review,* 259–264.

Official versions of decisions and reasons for decision by the Supreme Court of Canada (S.C.R.), *R. v. Latimer*. (1997). 1 S.C.R. 217. Retrieved March 31, 2008, from http://scc.lexum.umontreal.ca/en/1997/1997rcs1-217/1997rcs1-217.html

Ofshe, R. J., & Watters, E. (1994). *Making monsters: False memories, psychotherapy, and sexual hysteria.* New York: Scribner.

Oksol, E. M., & O'Donohue, W. T. (2003). A critical analysis of the polygraph. In W. T. O'Donohue, & E. R. Levensky (Eds.), *Handbook of forensic psychology: Resource for mental health and legal Professionals.* San Diego, CA: Academic Press, 601–634.

Oleson, J. C. (1996). Psychological profiling: Does it really work? *Forensic Update, 46,* 11–14.

Oliver, M., & Wong, S. (2006). Psychopathy, sexual deviance, and recidivism among different types of sex offenders. *Sexual Abuse: A Journal of Research and Treatment, 18*(1), 65–82.

Olmstead v. L.C. ex rel. Zimring, 119 S.Ct. 2176 (1999).

Olsson, U. (1979). Maximum likelihood estimation of the polychoric correlation coefficient. *Psychometrika, 44,* 443–460.

O'Malley, M., & Wood, O. (2008, March 17). "Compassionate homicide:" The law and Robert Latimer. *CBC News Online.* Retrieved August 1, 2008, from http://www.cbc.ca/news/background/latimer/.

O'Neil, K. M., Patry, M. W., & Penrod, S. D. (2004, December). Exploring the effects of attitudes toward the death penalty on capital sentencing verdicts. *Psychology, Public Policy, and Law, 10*(4), 443–470.

Ones, D. S. (2002). Introduction to the special issue on counterproductive behaviors at work. *International Journal of Selection and Assessment, 10,* 1–4.

Ones, D. S., & Viswesvaran, C. (2001a). Integrity tests and other criterion-focused occupational personality scales (COPS) used in personnel selection. *International Journal of Selection and Assessment, 9,* 31–39.

Ones, D. S., & Viswesvaran, C. (2001b). Personality at work: Criterion-focused occupational personality scales used in personnel selection. In B. W. Roberts & R. Hogan (Eds.), *Personality psychology in the workplace* (pp. 63–92). Washington, DC: American Psychological Association.

Ones, D. S., & Viswesvaran, C. (2003). Personality and counterproductive work behaviors. In A. Sagie, S. Stashevsky, & M. Koslowsky (Eds.), *Misbehavior and dysfunctional attitudes in organizations* (pp. 211–249). Hampshire, UK: Palgrave/Macmillan.

Ones, D. S., Viswesvaran, C., & Dilchert, S. (2005). Cognitive ability in personnel selection decisions. In A. Evers, O. Voskuijl, & N. Anderson (Eds.), *Handbook of selection* (pp. 143–173). Oxford, UK: Blackwell.

Ones, D. S., Viswesvaran, C., & Schmidt, F. L. (1993). Comprehensive meta-analysis of integrity test validities: Findings and implications for personnel selection and theories of job performance. *Journal of Applied Psychology, 78,* 679–703.

Ones, D. S., Viswesvaran, C., & Schmidt, F. L. (2003). Personality and absenteeism: A meta-analysis of integrity tests. *European Journal of Personality, 17,* 519–538.

Onin. *History of fingerprinting.* Retrieved October 7, 2008, from http://onin.com/fp/

Oppenheimer, K., Primz, R. J., & Bella, B. S. (1990). Determinant of adjustment for children of divorcing parents. *Family Medicine, 22*(2), 107–111.

Oppler, S. H., McCloy, R. A., & Campbell, J. P. (2001). The prediction of supervisory and leadership performance. In J. P. Campbell & D. J. Knapp (Eds.), *Exploring the limits in personnel selection and classification* (pp. 389–409). Mahwah, NJ: Erlbaum.

Orne, M. T. (1962). On the social psychology of the psychological experiment: With particular reference to demand characteristics and their implications. *American Psychologist, 17,* 776–783.

Orne, M. T. (1966). Hypnosis, motivation, and compliance. *American Journal of Psychiatry, 122,* 721–726.

Orne, M. T. (1970). Hypnosis, motivation, and the ecological validity of the psychological experiment. In W. J. Arnold & M. M. Page (Eds.), *Nebraska symposium on motivation* (pp. 187–265). Lincoln: Nebraska Press.

Orne, M. T. (1971). The simulation of hypnosis: Why, how, and what it means. *International Journal of Clinical and Experimental Hypnosis, 19,* 183–210.

Orne, M. T., Whitehouse, W. G., Orne, E. C., Dinges, D. F., & Nadon, R. (1984, December). The forensic use of hypnosis. National Institute of Justice Reports. In J. N. Gilbert (Ed.), *Criminal investigation* (7th ed., p. 127). Upper Saddle River, NJ: Prentice Hall.

Ostroff, C. (1993). Comparing correlations based on individual-level and aggregated data. *Journal of Applied Psychology, 78,* 569–582.

Ostroff, C., & Harrison, D. A. (1999). Meta-analysis, level of analysis, and best estimates of population correlations: Cautions for interpreting meta-analytic results in organizational behavior. *Journal of Applied Psychology, 84,* 260–270.

Ou, T. Y. (1996). *Are abusive men different? And can we predict their behavior?* Unpublished honors thesis, Department of Psychology, Harvard–Radcliffe College, Cambridge, MA.

Ovaert, L. B., Cashel, M. L., & Sewell, K. W. (2003). Structured group therapy for PTSD in incarcerated male juveniles. *American Journal of Orthopsychiatry, 73,* 294–301.

Overmier, J. B., & Seligman, M. E. P. (1967). Effects of inescapable shock upon subsequent escape and avoidance responding. *Journal of Comparative and Physiological Psychology, 63,* 28–33.

Paitich, D., Langevin, R., Freeman, R., Mann, K., & Handy, L. (1977). The Clarke SHQ: A clinical sex history questionnaire for males. *Archives of Sexual Behavior, 6*(5), 421–436.

Paley, B., & Geiselman, R. E. (1989). The effects of alternative photospread instructions on suspect identification performance. *American Journal of Forensic Psychology, 7,* 3–13.

Palmer, E. J. (2003a). An overview of the relationship between moral reasoning and offending. *Australian Psychologist, 38,* 165–174.

Palmer, E. J. (2003b). *Offending behaviour: Moral reasoning, criminal conduct and the rehabilitation of offenders.* Devon, England: Willan.

Pankanti, S., Prabhakar, S., & Jain, A. K. (2002, August). On the individuality of fingerprints. *Transactions on Pattern Analysis and Machine Intelligence, 24*(8), 1010–1025.

Papadopolous, A., & LaFontaine, J. (2000). *Elder abuse: Therapeutic perspectives in practice.* Bicester, UK: Winslow.

Parker, G., Manicavasagar, V., Crawford, J., Tully, L., & Gladstone, G. (2006). Assessing personality traits associated with depression: The utility of a tiered model. *Psychological Medicine, 36,* 1131–1139.

Pärlklo, T. I. (2002). Anabolic androgenic steroids and violence. *Acta Psychiatrica Scandinavica, 106,* 125–128.

Parry, J. (1994). Involuntary civil commitment in the 90s. *Mental & Physical Disability Law Reporter, 18,* 320.

Parry, J. (2005). *National survey of adult involuntary civil and forensic commitments.* The American Bar Association's Commission on Mental and Physical Disability Law. Retrieved August 13, 2007, from http://www.abanet.org/disability/home.html

Parry, J., & Drogin, E. Y. (2007). Mental disability law, evidence and testimony. Chicago, IL: American Bar Association.

Pearlstein, R. M. (1991). *The mind of the political terrorist.* Wilmington, DE: Scholarly Resources.

Pearson, J., & Thoennes, N. (1990). Custody after divorce: Demographic and attitudinal patterns. *American Journal of Orthopsychiatry, 60*(2), 233–249.

Pecher, D., Zeelenberg, R., & Barsalou, L. W. (2003). Verifying different–modality properties for concepts produces switching costs. *Psychological Science, 14,* 119–125.

Pence, E., & Paymar, M. (1993). *Education groups for men who batter: The Duluth model.* New York: Springer.

Pennebaker, J. W. (1997). *Opening up: The healing power of expressing emotions.* New York: Guilford Press.

Pennebaker, J. W. (2002). Writing, social processes, and psychotherapy: From past to future. In S. J. Lepore & J. M. Smyth (Eds.), *The writing cure: How expressive writing promotes health and emotional well-Being* (pp. 281–291). Washington, DC: American Psychological Association.

Penrod, S., & Cutler, B. (1995). Witness confidence and witness accuracy: Assessing their forensic relation. *Psychology, Public Policy, and Law, 1,* 817–845.

Perkins, R. M., & Boyce, R. N. (1982). *Case materials on criminal law and procedure, 3d.* Eagan, MN: Foundation Press.

Peterson, C., Maier, S., Seligman, M. (1993). *Learned helplessness.* New York: Oxford University Press.

Petty, G. M., & Dawson, B. (1989). Sexual aggression in normal men: Incidence, beliefs, and personality characteristics. *Personality and Individual Differences, 10,* 355–362.

Phares, E. J., & Wilson, K. G. (1972). Responsibility attribution: Role of outcome severity, situational ambiguity, and internal-external control. *Journal of Personality, 40,* 392–406.

Phillips, L. (2006, October). Mind function: Why your brain tells tall tales. *New Scientist magazine,* pp. 32–36.

Pickel, K. L. (1998). Unusualness and threat as possible causes of "weapon focus." *Memory, 6,* 277–295.

Piedmont, R. L., & Weinstein, H. P. (1994). Predicting supervisor ratings of job performance using the NEO personality inventory. *Journal of Psychology: Interdisciplinary and Applied, 128,* 255–265.

Pillemer, K., & Finkelhor, D. (1988). The prevalence of elder abuse: A random sample survey. *The Gerontologist, 28,* 51–57.

Pinals, D. A. (2005). Where two roads meet: Restoration of competence to stand trial from a clinical perspective. Retrieved December 21, 2007, from http://www.nesl.edu/journal/vol31/1/PINALS.pdf

Pinizzotto, A. J. (1984). Forensic psychology: Criminal personality profiling. *Journal of Police Science and Administration, 12,* 32–40.

Pinizzotto, A. J., & Finkel, N. J. (1990). Criminal personality profiling: An outcome and process study. *Law and Human Behavior, 14,* 215–233.

Platt, A. M., & Diamond, B. L. (1965). The origins and development of the "wild beast" concept of mental illness and its relation to theories of criminal responsibility. *Journal of the History of the Behavioral Sciences. 1,* 355–367.

Poole, D. A., Lindsay, D. S., Memon, A., & Bull, R. (1995). Psychotherapy and the recovery of memories of childhood sexual abuse: U.S. and British practitioners' opinions, practices, and experiences. *Journal of Consulting and Clinical Psychology, 63,* 426–437.

Porter, S., Yuille, J. C., & Lehman, J. R. (1999). The nature of real, implanted, and fabricated childhood emotional events: Implications for the recovered memory debate. *Law and Human Behavior, 23,* 517–523.

Post, J. M. (1984). Notes on a psychodynamic theory of terrorist behavior. *Terrorism: An International Journal, 7*(3), 242–256.

Post, J. M. (1990). Current understanding of terrorist motivation and psychology: Implications for a differentiated antiterrorist policy. *Terrorism, 13*(1), 65–71.

Post, S., & Denny, S. (2003). The terrorists in their own words: Interviews with 35 incarcerated middle-eastern terrorists. *Terrorism and Political Violence, 15*(1), 171–184.

Potterat, J. J., Brewer, D. D., Muth, S. Q., et al. (2004, April). Mortality in a long-term open cohort of prostitute women. *American Journal of Epidemiology, 159*(8), 778–785.

Poythress, N. (1981). *Conflicting postures for mental health expert witnesses: Prevailing attitudes of trial court judges.* Ann Arbor, MI: Center for Forensic Psychiatry.

Poythress, N. G. (1983). Psychological issues in criminal proceedings: Judicial preference regarding expert testimony. *Journal of Criminal Justice and Behavior, 10*(2), 175–194.

Pratt, D. V. (1993). *Legal writing: A systematic approach* (2nd ed.). St. Paul, MN: West Publishing.

Prentky, R. A., & Burgess, A. (1990). Rehabilitation of child molesters: A cost benefit analysis. *American Journal of Orthopsychiatry, 60,* 108–117.

Prentky, R. A., Janus, E. S., Barbaree, H., Schwartz, B. K., & Kafka, M. (2006). Sexually violent predators in the courtroom: Science on trial. *Psychology, Public Policy, and Law, 12,* 4.

Probst, T. M., & Brubaker, T. L. (2001). The effects of job insecurity on employee safety outcomes: Cross-sectional and longitudinal explorations. *Journal of Occupational Health Psychology, 6*(2), 139–159.

Pryor, J. B., Giedd, J. L., & Williams, K. B. (1995). A social psychological model for predicting sexual harassment. *Journal of Social Issues, 51,* 69–84.

PsycLAW. *APA amicus briefs.* Amicus briefs American Psychological Association. Retrieved August 9, 2008, from http://www.apa.org/psyclaw/amicus.html

Pugh, S. D. (2001). Service with a smile: Emotional contagion in the service encounter. *Academy of Management Journal, 44,* 1018–1027.

Pullins, L. G., & Jones, J. D. (2006, December). Parental knowledge of child sexual abuse symptoms. *Journal of Child Sexual Abuse, 15*(4), 1–18.

Quinet, K. (2007, November). The missing missing: Toward a quantification of serial murder victimization in the United States. *Homicide Studies, 11*(4), 319–339.

"Question Mark" killer quietly seethed with rage. *Fox News Online.* Retrieved May 22, 2007, from http://www.foxnews.com/printer_friendly_story/0,3566,266523,00.html

Quinn, M. J., & Tomita, S. K. (1997). *Elder abuse and neglect.* New York: Springer.

Quinsey, V. L., Harris, G. T., Rice, M. E., & Cormier, C. A. (1999). *Violent offenders: Appraising and managing risk.* Washington, DC: American Psychological Association.

Quinsey, V. L., Rice, M. E., & Harris, G. T. (1995). Actuarial prediction of sexual recidivism. *Journal of Interpersonal Violence, 10,* 85–105.

Raine, A. (2002). Biosocial studies of antisocial and violent behavior in children and adults: A review. *Journal of Abnormal Child Psychology, 30*(4), 311–326.

Raine, A., Buchsbaum, M.S., & La Casse, L. (1997). Brain abnormalities in murderers indicated by positron emission tomography. *Biological Psychiatry, 42,* 495–508.

Raine, A., Meloy, J. R., Bihrle, S., Stoddard, J., LaCasse, L., (1998). Reduced prefrontal and increased subcortical brain functioning assessed using positron emission tomography in predatory and affective murderers. *Behavioral Science and the Law, 16*(3), 319–332.

Ramona v. Isabella. No. 61898 (Cal. Super. Ct. May 13, 1994).

Ramsland, K. M. (2005). *Inside the minds of mass murderers: Why they kill.* Westport, CT: Praeger Publishers.

Rand, D. C. (2007). Munchausen syndrome by proxy. *IPT Journal.* Retrieved December 1, 2007, from http://www.ipt-forensics.com/journal/volume2/j2_2_4.htm

Rapaport, E. (2006). Mad women and desperate girls: Infanticide and child murder in law and myth. *Fordham Urban Law Journal, 33,* 527.

Raskin, D. (1990). Polygraph techniques for the detection of deception. In D. C. Raskin (Ed.), *Psychological methods in criminal investigations and evidence* (pp. 247–296). New York: Springer.

Raskin, R., & Terry, H. (1988, May). A principal-components analysis of the Narcissistic Personality Inventory and further evidence of its construct validity. *Journal of Personality and Social Psychology, 54*(5), 890–902.

Ray, D. C., McKinney, K. A., & Ford, C. V. (1987). Differences in psychologist's ratings of older and younger clients. *The Gerontologist, 27*, 82–86.

Read, J. D., Yuille, J. C., & Tollestrup, P. (1992). *Recollections of a robbery: Effects of arousal readings in forensic psychology.* Upper Saddle River, NJ: Pearson.

Recording Industry of America (RIAA). Parental advisory logo standards. Retrieved October 21, 2006, from http://www.narm.com/RIAA/PAS.pdf

Redding, R. E., Floyd, M. Y., & Hawk, G. L. (2001). What judges and lawyers think about the testimony of mental health experts: A survey of the courts and bar. *Behavioral Sciences & the Law, 19*(4), 583–594.

Reed, D. (2001, July/August). Therapist's duty to protect third parties: Balancing public safety and patient confidentiality. *Community Mental Health Report, 1*(5), 72–74.

Regnier, T. (2003). Barefoot in quicksand: The future of "future dangerousness" predictions in death penalty sentencing in the world of Daubert and Kumho. *Akron Law Review, 37*, 469, 482.

Reiter, P. J. (1958). *Antisocial or criminal acts and hypnosis: A case study.* Springfield, IL: Charles C. Thomas.

Reinhardt, J. (1957). *Sex perversions and sex crimes.* Springfield, IL: Charles C. Thomas.

Reinhardt, J. (1962). *The psychology of strange killers.* Springfield, IL: Charles C. Thomas.

Reiser, M. (1980). *Handbook of investigative hypnosis.* Los Angeles: Lehi.

Reisner, R., Slobogin, C., & Rai, A. (1999). *Law and the mental health system.* St. Paul MN: Thomson-West.

Reisner, R., Slobogin, C., & Rai, A. (2004). *Law and the mental health system: Civil and criminal aspects* (p. 1076). St. Paul, MN: Thomson West.

Rekers, G. (1995). *Susan smith: Victim or murderer.* Lakewood, CO: Glenbridge.

Religion in China. *Chinese studies.* Retrieved June 9, 2007, from http://www.chinaknowledge.de/Literature/Religion/buddhism.html

Religious confession. *Confessions of faith.* Retrieved June 9, 2007, from http://mb-soft.com/believe/txo/confes.htm

Rennison, C. M., & Welchans, S. (2000). *Intimate partner violence* (NCJ 178247). Washington, DC: U.S. Department of Justice.

Report by Dr. Mike Gelles, *Naval criminal investigative service.* Retrieved March 26, 2007, from http://www.usda.gov/da/ocpm/Security%20Guide/Treason/Mind.htm

Resick, P. A., & Schnicke, M. K. (1992). Cognitive processing therapy for sexual assault victims. *Journal of Consulting and Clinical Psychology, 60*, 748–756.

Resick, P. A., & Schnicke, M. K. (1993). *Cognitive processing therapy for rape victims: A treatment manual.* Newbury Park: Sage.

Resnick, P. J. (1969). Child murder by parents: A psychiatric review of filicide. *American Journal of Psychiatry, 126*, 73–83.

Resnick, P. J. (1970). Murder of the newborn: A psychiatric review of filicide. *American Journal of Psychiatry, 126*, 58–63.

Resnick, P. J., & Kausch, O. (1995). Violence in the workplace: Role of the consultant. *Consulting Psychology Journal, 47*(4), 213–222.

Ressler, R. K., Burgess, A. W., & Douglas, J. E. (1988). *Sexual homicide: Patterns and motives.* New York: Lexington Books.

Ressler, R. K., & Shachtman, T. (1992). *Whoever fights monsters.* New York: St. Martin's Press.

Restatement (third) of torts: Liability for physical harm, affirmative duties, duty to third persons based on special relationship with person posing risk §41 (2005). *American Law Institute.* Retrieved August 30, 2009, from http://www.ali.org/index.cfm?fuseaction=publications.ppage&node_id=53

Rey, L. (1996). What social workers need to know about client violence. *Families in Society, 77*, 33–39.

Reynolds, G. A. (Ed.). (1996). *Race and the criminal justice system: How race affects jury trials.* Washington, DC: Center for Equal Opportunity.

Rhawn, J. (2008). Charles Whitman: The amygdala & mass murder. *Brain-Mind.com.* Retrieved May 26, 2008, from http://brainmind.com/Case5.html

Rhoton, W. W. (1980). A procedure to improve compliance with coal mine safety regulations. *Journal of Organizational Behavior Management, 2*, 243–249.

Ribton-Turner, C. J. (1887). The history of vagrants and vagrancy. *Political Science Quarterly, 3*(4), 704.

Rice, M. E., Harris, G. T., & Cormier, C. A. (1992). An evaluation of a maximum security therapeutic community for psychopaths and other mentally disordered offenders. *Law and Human Behavior, 16*, 399–412.

Rideout, V., Roberts, D. F., & Foehr, U. G. (2005). *Generation m: Media in the lives of 8-18 year-olds.* Menlo Park, CA: The Henry J. Kaiser Family Foundation.

Ringstad, R. (2005, October). Conflict in the workplace: Social workers as victims and perpetrators. *Social Work, 50*(4), 305–313.

Ripley, A. (2008, August 7). *Time.com.* The anthrax files. Retrieved August 15, 2009, from http://www.time.com/time/nation/article/0,8599,1830130,00.html

Ritchie, E. C. (1998). Reactions to rape: A military forensic psychiatrist's perspective. *Military Medicine, 163*, 505–509.

Ritchie v. Indiana, 468 N. E. 2d. 1369 (Ind. Sup. Ct. 1984).

Robbins, T. (1988). *Cults, converts, and charisma: The sociology of new religious movements.* Newbury Park, CA: Sage.

Roberts, B. W., & Hogan, R. (Eds.). (2001). *Personality psychology in the workplace.* Washington, DC: American Psychological Association.

Roberts, N. A., & Levenson, R. W. (2001, November). The remains of the workday: Impact of job stress and exhaustion on marital interaction in police couples. *Journal of Marriage and the Family, 63*(4), 1052–1067.

Robinson, S. L., & Bennett, R. J. (1995). A typology of deviant workplace behaviors: A multidimensional scaling study. *Academy of Management Journal, 38*, 555–572.

Rodriguez, M. L., Mischel, W., & Shoda, Y. (1989). Cognitive person variables in the delay of gratification of older children at risk. *Journal of Personality and Social Psychology, 57*, 358–367.

Roesch, R., & Golding, S. L. (1980). *Competency to stand trial.* Urbana: University of Illinois Press.

Roesch, R., Grisso, T., & Poythress, N. G., Jr. (1986). Training programs, courses, and workshops in psychology and law. In M. F. Kaplan (Ed.), *The impact of social psychology on procedural justice* (pp. 83–108). Springfield, IL: Thomas.

Roesch, R., Hart, S. D., & Zapf, P. (1996). Conceptualizing and assessing competency to stand trial: Implications and applications of the MacArthur treatment competence model. *Psychology, Public Policy, and Law, 2*, 96–113.

Roesch, R., & Ogloff, J. R. P. (1996). Settings for providing civil and criminal mental health services. In B. D. Sales & S. A. Shah (Eds.), *Mental health and law: Research, policy and services* (pp. 191–218). Durham, NC: Carolina Academic Press.

Roesch, R., Ogloff, J. R. P., & Golding, S. L. (1993). Competency to stand trial: Legal and clinical issues. *Applied and Preventative Psychology, 2*, 43–51.

Rogers, K., & Kelloway, E. K. (1997). Violence at work: Personal and organizational outcomes. *Journal of Occupational Health Psychology, 2*, 63–71.

Roizen, J. (1997). Epidemiological issues in alcohol-related violence. In M. Galanter (Ed.), *Recent developments in alcoholism* (pp. 7–40). New York: Plenum Press.

Rosen, J. B., & Schulkin, J. (1998). From normal fear to pathological anxiety. *Psychological Review, 105*(2), 325–350.

Rösler, A., & Witztum, E. (1998). Treatment of men with paraphilia with long-acting analogue of gonadotropin-releasing hormone. *New England Journal of Medicine, 338,* 416–422.

Rossmo, D. K. (2000). *Geographic profiling.* New York: CRC Press.

Roth, P. L., Bevier, C. A., Bobko, P., Switzer, F. S., & Tyler, P. (2001). Ethnic group differences in cognitive ability in employment and educational settings: A meta-analysis. *Personnel Psychology, 54,* 297–330.

Rotter, J. B. (1966). Generalized expectancies for internal vs. external control of reinforcement. *Psychological Monographs, 80*(1), 1–28.

Rubin, Z., & Peplau, A. (1975). Who believes in a just world? *Journal of Social Issues, 29,* 73–93.

Ruby, C. (2002). Are terrorists mentally deranged? *Analyses of Social Issues and Public Policy, 2*(1), 15–26.

Rummel, R. J. (1997). *Death by government.* Piscataway, NJ: Transaction Publishers.

Runyon, M. K., Kenny, M. C., Berry, E. J., Deblinger, E., & Brown, E. J. (2006). Etiology and surveillance in child maltreatment. In J. R. Lutzker (Ed.), *Preventing violence* (pp. 23–47). Washington, DC: American Psychological Association.

Ruva, C., Mcevoy, C., & Bryant, J. B. (2007). Effects of Pre-Trial Publicity and Jury Deliberation on Juror Bias and Source Memory. *Applied Cognitive Psychology, 21,* 45–67.

Ryan, R. M., & Deci, E. L. (2000). Self-determination theory and the facilitation of intrinsic motivation, social development, and well-being. *American Psychologist, 55,* 68–78.

Rynearson, E. K. (1996). Psychotherapy of bereavement after homicide: Be offensive. In session: Psychotherapy in practice, 2. In L. Miller, Psychological interventions for terroristic trauma: Symptoms, syndromes, and treatment strategies. *Psychotherapy: Theory, Research, Practice, Training, 39*(4).

Sackett, P. R., Burris, L. R., & Callahan, C. (1989). Integrity testing for personnel selection: An update. *Personnel Psychology, 42,* 491–529.

Sackett, P. R., & DeVore, C. J. (2001). Counterproductive behaviors at work. In N. Anderson, D. S. Ones, H. S. Kepir, & C. Viswesvaran (Eds.), *Handbook of industrial, work and organizational psychology: Vol. 1. Personnel psychology* (pp. 145–164). London, England: Sage.

Sackett, P. R., & Ostgaard, D. J. (1994). Job-specific applicant pools and national norms for cognitive ability tests: Implications for range restriction corrections in validation research. *Journal of Applied Psychology, 79,* 680–684.

Sadava, S., & McCreary, D. (1997). *Applied social psychology.* Upper Saddle River, NJ: Prentice Hall.

Saferstein, R. (2001). *Criminalistics: An introduction to forensic science* (7th ed.). Upper Saddle River, NJ: Prentice Hall.

Saks, M. J. (1977). *Jury verdicts: The role of group size and social decision rule.* Lexington, MA: Heath.

Saks, M. J., & Marti, M. W. (1997). A meta-analysis of the effects of jury size. *Law & Human Behavior, 21,* 451–467.

Salerno, N. (2005). The use of hypnosis in the treatment of post-traumatic stress disorder in a female correctional setting. *Australian Journal of Clinical & Experimental Hypnosis, 33,* 74–81.

Salerno, S. (2005). *SHAM.* New York: Crown.

Sales, B. D. (2007). *Scientific jury selection.* Washington, DC: American Psychological Association.

Salgado, J. F. (2002). The big five personality dimensions and counterproductive behaviors. *International Journal of Selection and Assessment, 10,* 117–125.

Saltzman, J. (2004, January 22). Judge sets bail in DNA case. *Boston Globe,* p. B4.

Samaha, J. (1999). *Criminal law.* Belmont, CA: Wadsworth.

Samenow, S. E. (2004). *Inside the criminal mind* (2nd ed.). New York: Crown.

Samenow, S. (2007a). Are sexual offenses the result of an addictive pattern? In J. Kitaeff (Ed.), *Malingering, lies, and junk science in the courtroom.* Youngstown, NY: Cambria Press.

Samenow, S. (2007b). *The myth of the out of character crime.* Santa Barbara, CA: Greenwood.

Sampson, E. E. (1975). On justice as equality. *Journal of Social Issues, 31,* 45–64.

Sampson, R., & Lamb, J. (1993). *Crime in the making: Pathways and turning points through life.* Cambridge: Harvard University Press.

Samuel, N., Kaspar, V., & Wickrama, K. A. (2007). Overt and subtle racial discrimination and mental health: Preliminary findings for Korean immigrants. *American Journal of Public Health, 97*(7), 1269–1274.

Sanders, C. E., Lubinski, D., & Benbow, C. P. (1995). Does the defining issues test measure psychological phenomena distinct from verbal ability? An examination of Lykken's query. *Journal of Personality and Social Psychology, 69,* 498–504.

Sanders, G. S., & Simmons, W. L. (1983). Use of hypnosis to enhance eyewitness accuracy: Does it work? *Journal of Applied Psychology, 68,* 70–77.

Sannito, T., & McGovern, P. J. (1993). *Courtroom psychology for trial lawyers.* Sarasota, FL: Professional Resource Exchange.

Sarchione, C. D., Cuttler, M. J., Muchinsky, P. M., & Nelson-Gray, R. O. (1998). Prediction of dysfunctional job behaviors among law enforcement officers. *Journal of Applied Psychology, 83,* 904–912.

Sarno, G. (2005, September). Mental of emotional disturbance as defense or mitigating factor in attorney disciplinary proceedings. *American Journal of Proof of Facts, 46*(2), 563.

Saslove, H., & Yarmey, A. D. (1980). Long-term auditory memory: Speaker identification. *Journal of Applied Psychology, 65,* 111–116.

Saxe, L., Dougherty, D., & Cross, T. (1985). The validity of polygraph testing: Scientific analysis and public controversy. *American Psychologist, 40,* 55–366.

Sayette, M. A. (1993). An appraisal—disruption model of alcohol's effectiveness on stress responses in social drinkers. *Psychological Bulletin, 114,* 459–476.

Schacter, D. L. (1996). *Searching for memory- the brain, the mind, and the past.* New York: Basic Books.

Schachter, S. (1977). Nicotine regulation in heavy and light smokers. *Journal of Experimental Psychology, 106,* 5–12.

Schachter, S., Silverstein, B., Kozlowski, L. T., Perlick, D., Herman, C. P., & Liebling, B. (1977). Studies of the interaction of psychological and pharmacological determinants of smoking. *Journal of Experimental Psychology: General, 106,* 3–40.

Schachter, S., Silverstein, B., Kozlowski, L. T., Perlick, D., Herman, C. P., & Schacter, D. L. (1996). *Searching for memory—the brain, the mind, and the past.* New York: Basic Books.

Schat, A. C., & Kelloway, E. K. (2000). The effects of perceived control on the outcomes of workplace aggression and violence. *Journal of Occupational Health Psychology, 4,* 386–402.

Schat, A., & Kelloway, E. K. (2003), Reducing the adverse consequences of workplace aggression and violence: The buffering effects of organizational support, *Journal of Occupational Health Psychology, 8,* 110–22.

Schaubroeck, J., & Jones, J. R. (2000). Antecedents of workplace emotional labor dimensions and moderators of their effects on physical symptoms. *Journal of Organizational Behavior, 21,* 163–183.

Schechter, H., & Everitt, D. (2006). *The A to Z encyclopedia of serial killers.* New York: Simon and Schuster.

Scheck, B., Neufeld, P., & Dwyer, J. (2000). *Actual innocence.* New York: Random House.

Schein, D. D. (1986). How to prepare a company policy on substance abuse control. *Personnel Journal, 65,* 30–38.

Schiff, H. B., Sabin, T. D., Geller, A., Alexander, L., & Mark, V. (1982). Lithium in aggressive behavior. *American Journal of Psychiatry, 139,* 1346–1348.

Schlesinger, L. B. (1998). Pathological narcissism and serial homicide: Review and case report. *Current Psychology, 17,* 212–221.

Schlesinger, L. B. (2000). Serial homicide: Sadism, fantasy and a compulsion to kill. In L. B. Schlesinger (Ed.), *Serial offenders: Current thought, recent findings* (pp. 3–22). New York: CRC Press.

Schmalleger, F. (1999). *Criminal justice today.* Upper Saddle River, NJ: Prentice Hall.

Schmalleger, F. (2002). *Criminal law today* (2nd ed.). Upper Saddle River, NJ: Prentice Hall.

Schmidt, F. L. (2002). The role of general cognitive ability and job performance: Why there cannot be a debate. *Human Performance, 15,* 187–211.

Schmidt, F. L., Viswesvaran, C., & Ones, D. S. (1997). Validity of integrity tests for predicting drug and alcohol abuse: A meta-analysis. In W. J. Bukoski (Ed.), *Meta-analysis of drug abuse prevention programs* (pp. 69–95). Rockville, MD: NIDA Press.

Schmidt, S. (2004, May 22). Oregon Lawyer's Status Remains Murky. *Washington Post,* p. A2.

Schmidt, S., & Harden, B. (2004, May 8). Lawyer's fingerprint linked to bombing bag, detonators found in stolen van in Spain. *Washington Post,* p. A3.

Schmitt, R. B., Tizon, T. A., & Rotella, S. (2004, May 22). Critics galvanized by Oregon lawyer's case. *Los Angeles Times,* p. A13.

Schneider, A. K. (2000). Shattering negotiation myths: Empirical evidence on the effectiveness of negotiation style. *Harvard Negotiation Law Review, 2002, 7,* 143–233.

Schneider, E. (2000). *Battered women and feminist lawmaking.* London: Yale University Press.

Schneider, E. M. (1986). Describing and changing women's self-defense work and the problem of expert testimony. *Women's Rights Law Reporter, 9,* 195.

Schneider, K. T., Swann, S., & Fitzgerald, L. F. (1997). Job-related and psychological effects of sexual harassment in the workplace: Empirical evidence from two organizations. *Journal of Applied Psychology, 82,* 401–415.

Schopp, R. F. (2003, March–June). Outpatient civil commitment: A dangerous charade or a component of a comprehensive institution of civil commitment? *Psychology and Public Policy Law, 9*(1–2), 33–69.

Schore, A. (2003). *Affect dysregulation and disorders of the self.* New York: Norton.

Schrenck-Notzing, A. V. (1914). *Materialisations-phenomene.* Munich: Ernst.

Schuller, R. A., & Hastings, P. A. (1996). Trials of battered women who kill: The impact of alternative forms of expert evidence. *Law and Human Behavior, 20,* 167–188.

Schuller, R., & Rzepa, S. (2002). The scientific status of research on domestic violence against women. In D. Faigman, et al. *Science in the Law: Social and Behavioral* Science Issues 206, 237.

Schuller, R. A., & Vidmar, N. (1992). Battered woman syndrome evidence in the courtroom. *Law and Human Behavior, 16,* 273.

Schultz, D. P., & Schultz, S. E. (2004). *A history of modern psychology* (8th ed.). Belmont, CA: Wadsworth.

Schultz, L. (1989). One hundred cases of unfounded child sexual abuse: A survey and recommendations. *Issues in Child Abuse Accusations, 1*(1), 29–38.

Schwarz, T. (1981). *The hillside strangler: A murderer's mind.* Garden City, NY: Doubleday.

Schwartz, L. L., & Isser, N. K. (2000). *Endangered children: Neonaticide, infanticide, and filicide.* Boca Raton, FL: CRC Press.

Sciolino, E. (2004, March 12). Ten bombs shatter trains in Madrid, killing 192. *New York Times,* p. A1.

Scoboria, A., Mazzoni, G., Kirsch, I., & Milling, L. S. (2002). Immediate and persisting effects of misleading questions and hypnosis on memory reports. *Journal of Experimental Psychology: Applied, 8,* 26–32.

Scollon, C. N., Diener, E., Oishi, S., & Biswas-Diener, R. (2004). Emotions across cultures and methods. *Journal of Cross-Cultural Psychology, 35,* 304–326.

Scott, C. L. (2002). Commentary: A road map for research in restoration of competency to stand trial. *Journal of the American Academy of Psychiatry, 31*(1), 36–43.

Scott, R. E., & Leslie, D. L. (1993). *Contract law and theory.* Charlottesville, VA: The Michie Company.

Sears, D. (1991). *To kill again.* Wilmington, DE: Scholarly Resources Books.

Seligman, M. E., & Maier, S. F. (1967). Failure to escape traumatic shock. *Journal of Experimental Psychology, 74,* 1–9.

Seligman, M. E., & Schulman, P. (1986). Explanatory style as a predictor of productivity and quitting among life insurance sales agents. *Journal of Personality and Social Psychology, 50,* 832–838.

Sellbom, M., Ben-Porath, Y. S., & Bagby, R. M. (2008). On the hierarchical structure of mood and anxiety disorders: Confirmatory evidence and elaboration of a model of temperament markers. *Journal of Abnormal Psychology, 117,* 576–590.

Senate Committee on Labor and Human Resources. (1989). Report on the Americans with Disabilities Act of 1989, S. Rep. No. 101–116, pp. 8–9.

Serial killer hit list. (home page). Retrieved August 15, 2008, from http://www.mayhem.net/Crime/serial.html

Seto, M. C. (2008). *Pedophilia and sexual offending against children. Theory, assessment, and intervention.* Washington, DC: American Psychological Association.

Sewell, J. D., Ellison, K. W., & Hurrell, J. J. (1988, October). Stress management in law enforcement: Where do we go from here? *The Police Chief, 55,* 94–98.

Sgroi, S. M. (1984). *Handbook of clinical intervention in child sexual abuse.* Lexington, MA: Free Press.

Shalev, A. (2007, December 9). Psychotherapy useful in treating post-traumatic stress disorder in early stages. *ScienceDaily.* Retrieved May 12, 2009, from http://www.sciencedaily.com.

Shalev, A. Y. (1996). Stress versus traumatic stress: From acute homeostatic reactions to chronic psychopathology. In B. A. van der Kolk, A. C. McFarlane, & L. Weisaeth (Eds.), Traumatic stress: The effects of overwhelming experience on mind, body, and society (pp. 77–101). New York: Guilford.

Shalif, Y., & Leibler, M. (2002). Working with people experiencing terrorist attacks in Israel: A narrative perspective. *Journal of Systemic Therapies, 21*(3), 61–70.

Shamir, B., House, R. J., & Arthur, M. B. (1993). The motivational effects of charismatic leadership: A self-concept based theory. *Organization Science, 4,* 577–594.

Shannon, M., Stark, L., & Patrick, C. (2003). The influence of physical appearance on personnel selection. *Social Behavior and Personality, 31*(6), 613–624.

Shapiro, F. (1989). Efficacy of the eye movement desensitization procedure: A new treatment for post-traumatic stress disorder. *Journal of Traumatic Stress, 2*(2), 199–223.

Shapiro, F. (2002). *EMDR as an integrative psychotherapy approach: Experts of diverse orientations explore the paradigm prism.* Washington, DC: American Psychological Association Books.

Shapiro, P., & Penrod, S. (1986). A meta-analysis of facial identification studies. *Psychological Bulletin, 100,* 139–156.

Sheldon, W. (1942). *The varieties of temperament: A psychology of constitutional differences.* New York: Harper.

Sheldon, W. (1954). *Atlas of men: A guide for somatotyping the adult male at all ages.* New York: Harper.

Sheldon, W. H., Dupertuis, C. M., & McDermott, E. (1954). *Atlas of men.* New York: Harper and Brothers.

Sherman, C. (2000). Treatment for psychopaths is likely to make them worse. *Clinical Psychiatry News, 28*(5), 38.

Showalter, E. (1997). *Hystories: Hysterical epidemics and modern media.* New York: Columbia University Press.

Shuman, D. W., & Greenberg, S. A. (2003). The expert witness, the adversary system, and the voice of reason: Reconciling impartiality and advocacy. *Professional Psychology: Research and Practice, 34,* 3.

Shusman, E. J., Inwald, R. E., & Knatz, H. F. (1987). A cross-validation study of police recruit performance as predicted by the IPI and MMPI. *Journal of Police Science and Administration, 15*(2), 162–169.

Shusman, E. J., Inwald, R. E., & Landa, B. (1984). Correction officer job performance as predicted by the IPI and MMPI: A validation and cross-validation study. *Criminal Justice and Behavior, 11*(3), 309–329.

Shusta, R. M., Levine, D. R., Wong, H. Z., & Harris, P. R. (2005). *Multicultural law enforcement.* Upper Saddle River, NJ: Prentice Hall.

Siegel, A. M., & Elwork, A. (1990). Treating incompetence to stand trial. *Law and Human Behavior, 14,* 57–65.

Siever, L. J. (2002). Neurobiology of impulsive-aggressive personality-disordered patients. *Psychiatric Times, 18,* 8.

Sigma Assessment Systems, Inc. (home page). Retrieved July 16, 2007, from http://www.sigmaassessmentsystems.com/selection/default.asp.

Simon, R. (1996). *Bad men do what good men dream: A forensic psychiatrist illuminates the darker side of human behavior.* Washington, DC: American Psychiatric Press.

Simon, R. J. (1967). *The jury and the defense of insanity.* Boston: Little, Brown.

Singlular, S. (2006). *Unholy messenger: The life and times of the BTK serial killer.* New York: Scribner.

Skarlicki, D. P., & Folger, R. (1997). Retaliation in the workplace: The roles of distributive, procedural, and interactional justice. *Journal of Applied Psychology, 82,* 434–443.

Skarlicki, D. P., Folger, R., & Tesluk, P. (1999). Personality as a moderator in the relationship between fairness and retaliation. *Academy of Management Journal, 42,* 100–108.

Slater, M., Antley, M., Davison, A., Swapp, D., Guger, C., et al. (2006). A Virtual Reprise of the Stanley Milgram Obedience Experiments. *PLoSone.* Retrieved August 26, 2009, from http://www.plosone.org/article/fetchArticle.action?articleURI=info%3Adoi%2F10.1371%2Fjournal.pone.0000039.

Slovenko, R. (1997). The psychotherapist-patient testimonial privilege. *Psychoanalytic Psychology, 24*(1), 24–27.

Slovenko, R. (2002). *Psychiatry in law: Law in psychiatry.* New York: Brunner-Routledge.

Smith, B. M. (1967). The polygraph. *Scientific American, 216,* 25–31.

Smith, D. J. (1996). *Legal research and writing.* New York: Delmar.

Smith, M. C. (1983). Hypnotic memory enhancement of witnesses: Does it work? *Psychological Bulletin, 94,* 387–407.

Smith, M., & Alison, L. (2001, March). *Barnum effects in offender profiles.* Paper presented at The Fifth Biannual Conference of Investigative Psychology, University of Liverpool, Liverpool, UK.

Smyth, J. M. (1998). Written emotional expression: Effect sizes, outcome types, and moderating variables. *Journal of Consulting and Clinical Psychology, 66,* 174–184.

Snook, B. (2008). The criminal profiling illusion: What's behind the smoke and mirrors? *Criminal Justice and Behavior, 35*(10), 1257–1276.

Snow, C. P. (1961, February). Either-or. *Progressive,* p. 24.

Society of Industrial and Organizational Psychology. (Home Page). Retrieved July 19, 2007, from http://www.siop.org/Instruct/IOIntro/sld003.aspx

Solomon, S. D., Gerrity, E. T., & Muff, A. M. (1993). Efficacy of treatments for posttraumatic stress disorder: An empirical review. *JAMA, 268*(5), 633–638.

Solomon, R. M., & Horn, J. H. (1986). Post-shooting traumatic reactions: A pilot study. In J. T. Reese & H. A. Goldstein (Eds.), *Psychological services for law enforcement officers* (pp. 383–393). Washington, DC: U.S. Government Printing Office.

Sommers, S. R. (2006). On racial diversity and group decision making: Identifying multiple effects of racial composition on jury deliberations. *Journal of Personality and Social Psychology, 90*(4), 597–612.

Sommers, S. R., & Ellsworth, P. C. (2000). Race in the courtroom: Perceptions of guilt and dispositional attributions. *Personality and Social Psychology Bulletin, 26,* 1367–1379.

Sommers, S. R., & Ellsworth, P. C. (2001). White juror bias: An investigation of racial prejudice against Black defendants in the American courtroom. *Psychology, Public Policy, and Law, 7,* 201–229.

Sosis, R. H. (1974). Internal-external control and the perception of responsibility of another for an accident. *Journal of Personality and Social Psychology, 30,* 393–399.

Specialty Guidelines for Forensic Psychologists (Committee on Ethical Guidelines for Forensic Psychologists. ("CEGFP", 1991). *Division 41 of the American Psychological Association.* Retrieved March 15, 2009, from http://www.ap-ls.org/links/currentforensicguidelines.pdf

Speilberger, C. D. (1996). *State–trait anger expression inventory, research edition: Professional manual.* Odessa, FL: Psychological Assessment Resources.

Spies, R. A., & Plake, B. S. (Eds.). (2005). *The sixteenth mental measurements yearbook.* Lincoln, NE: University of Nebraska Press.

Spinella, M. (2002). A relationship between smell identification and empathy. *International Journal of Neuroscience, 112,* 605–612.

Spinella, M., White, J., Frank, M. L., & Schiraldi, J. (2006). Evidence of orbitofrontal dysfunction in sex offenders. *International Journal of Forensic Psychology, 1*(3), 62–68.

Sporer, S. L. (1992, September). A brief history of the psychology of testimony. *Current Psychology, 2*(3), 323–339.

Sprang, G., & McNeil, J. (1995). *The many faces of bereavement: The nature and treatment of natural, traumatic, and stigmatized grief.* New York: Brunner/Mazel.

Spungen, D. (1998). *Homicide: The hidden victims. A guide for professionals.* Thousand Oaks, CA: Sage.

Stacey, R. B. (2004). A report on the erroneous fingerprint individualization in the Madrid train bombing case. *Journal of Forensic Identification, 54*(6), 706–710.

Stack, R. (1998). *Courts, counselors & correspondents: A media relations analysis of the legal system.* Littleton, CO: F.B. Rothman.

Stahelski, A. (2004, March). *Terrorists are made not born, creating terrorists using social psychological conditioning.* Retrieved June 18, 2007, from http://www.homelandsecurity.org/journal/Articles/stahelski.html

Stamato, L. (1992). Sexual harassment in the workplace: Is mediation an appropriate forum? *Mediation Quarterly, 10,* 167, 169.

Stanton, J., & Simpson, A. (2002). Filicide: A review. *International Journal of Law and Psychiatry, 25,* 1–14.

Stanton, J., Simpson, A., & Wouldes, T. (2002). A qualitative study of filicide by mentally ill mothers. *Child Abuse & Neglect, 24*(11), 1451–1460.

Staub, E. (2004). Understanding and responding to group violence: Genocide, mass killing, and terrorism. In F. M. Moghaddam, & A. J. Marsella (Eds.), *Understanding terrorism: Psychosocial roots, consequesnces and interventions* (pp. 151–168). Washington, DC: American Psychological Association.

Stavis, P. (1995, July 1). *Civil commitment: Past, present, and future.* An Address at the National Conference of the National Alliance for the Mentally Ill, Washington, DC. Retrieved August 11, 2007, from http://www.cqcapd.state.ny.us/counsels_corner/cc64.htm

Steblay, N. M. (1992). A meta-analytic review of the weapon focus effect. *Law and Human Behavior, 16,* 413–424.

Steblay, N. M., & Bothwell, R. K. (1994). Evidence for hypnotically refreshed testimony. *Law and Human Behavior, 18,* 635–651.

Stefan, S. (1994). The protection racket: Rape trauma syndrome, psychiatric labeling, and law. *Northwestern University Law Review, 88,* 1271–1345.

Stenner, K. (2005). *The authoritarian dynamic.* Cambridge: Cambridge Press.

Stephens, C., Long, N., & Miller, I. (1997). The impact of trauma and social support on post-traumatic stress disorder: A study of New Zealand police officers. *Journal of Criminal Justice, 25,* 303–314.

Stern, E. S. (1948). The Medea complex: The mother's homicidal wishes to her child. *Journal of Mental Science, 94,* 321–331.

Stern, W. (1910). Abstracts of blectures on the psychology of testimony and on the study of individuality. *American Journal of Psychology, 21,* 270–282.

Stinson, V., Devenport, J. L., Cutler, B. L., & Kravitz, D. A. (1996). How effective is the presence-of-counsel safeguard? Attorney perceptions of suggestiveness, fairness, and correctability of biased lineup procedures. *Journal of Applied Psychology, 81,* 64–75.

Stockholm syndrome. *Digital archive of psychohistory.* Retrieved November 28, from http://www.geocities.com/kidhistory/trauma/stockhol.htm

Stoney, D. A. (2001). Measurement of fingerprint individuality. In H. C. Lee & R. E. Gaensslen (Eds.), *Advances in fingerprint technology* (2nd ed.). Boca Raton, FL: CRC Press.

StopVAW. *Employer responsibilities: Sexual harassment policies, trainings and complaint procedures.* Retrieved July 10, 2007, from http://www.stopvaw.org/Employer_Responsibilities_Sexual_Harassment_Policies_Trainings_and_Complaint_Procedures.html?Type=B_BASIC&SEC=%7BBB8CC131-B0C6-41E5-8970-314DB06C8D34%7D.

Strachey, J. (Ed.). (1895). The standard edition of the complete psychological works of Sigmund Freud (Vol. 2, pp. 21–319). London: Hogarth Press. (Original work published.)

Streseman, K. D. (1995). Headshrinkers, manmunchers, moneygrubbers, nuts and sluts: Reexamining compelled mental examinations in sexual harassment actions under the Civil Rights Act of 1991. *Cornell Law Review, 80,* 1268–1330.

Strier, F. (1999). Whither trial consulting? Issues and projections. *Law and Human Behavior, 23,* 93–115.

Strous, R. D., Stryjer, R., Keret, N., Bergin, M., & Kotler, M. (2003). Reactions of psychiatric and medical inpatients to terror and security instability in Israel. *Journal of Nervous & Mental Disease, 19*(2), 126–129.

Stuckless, N., & Goranson, R. (1992). The vengeance scale: Development of a measure of attitudes toward revenge. *Journal of Social Behavior and Personality, 7,* 25–42.

Sullivan, C. M. (2006). Evaluating parenting programs for men who batter: Current considerations and controversies. In J. L. Edleson & O. Williams (Eds.), *Parenting by men who batter women: New directions for assessment and intervention.* New York, NY: Guilford Press.

Sumich, A. L., Kumari, V., & Sharma, T. (2003). Neuroimaging of sexual arousal: Research and clinical utility. *Hospital Medicine, 64*(1), 28–33.

Summit, R. C. (1983). The child sexual abuse accommodation syndrome. *Child Abuse & Neglect, 7,* 177–193.

Swan, W. B., Jr., & Read, S. J. (1981). Acquiring self-knowledge: The search for feedback that fits. *Journal of Personality and Social Psychology, 41,* 1119–1128.

Swim, J. K., Ferguson, M. J., & Hyers, L. L. (1999). Avoiding stigma by association: Subtle prejudice against lesbians in the form of social distancing. *Basic and Applied Social Psychology, 21.*

Sylvester, S. R. (2007). The cost of reasonable doubt. In J. Kitaeff (Ed.), *Malingering, lies, and junk science in the courtroom* (pp. 357–381). Youngstown, NY: Cambria Press.

Tajfel, H. (Ed.). (1982). *Social identity and intergroup relations.* Cambridge, England: Cambridge University Press.

Tardiff, K. (1998). Unusual diagnoses among violent patients. *Psychiatric Clinics of North America, 21*(3), 567–576.

Taylor, A.J. (2002). Coping with catastrophe: Organising psychological first-aiders. *New Zealand Journal of Psychology, 31*(2), 104–109.

Taylor, M. (2003, December 19). Cot death expert to face investigation. *The Daily Mirror.* Retrieved March 18, 2007, from www.mirror.co.uk

Taylor, P. (1999, September 22). *Pakistan/honor killings.* GlobalSecurity.org. Retrieved February 26, 2009, from http://www.globalsecurity.org/military/library/news/1999/09/990922-pak2.htm

Telegram & Gazette (Worcester, MA) (2008, August 8). Case closed; Anthrax legacy: Greater knowledge, better vaccines (Editorial). Retrieved August 15, 2009, from http://www.highbeam.com/doc/1G1-182518572.html

Tellegen, A. (1993). Folk concepts and psychological concepts of personality and personality disorder. *Psychological Inquiry, 4,* 122–130.

Templin, N. (1990, May 21). Johnson & Johnson wellness program for workers shows healthy bottom line. *Wall Street Journal at B1.*

Terman, L. M. (1916). *The measurement of intelligence.* Boston, MA: Houghton Mifflin.

Terr, L. (1991). Childhood trauma: An outline and overview. *American Journal of Psychiatry, 148,* 10–20.

Terris, W., & Jones, J. (1982). Psychological factors related to employees' theft in the convenience store industry. *Psychological Reports, 51,* 1219–1238.

Tewari, R. K., & Ravikumar, K. V. (2000). History and development of forensic science in India. *Journal of Postgraduate Medicine, 46,* 303–308.

Texas defender service, junk science, Texas justice and the death penalty 45. (mod. 22 May 2003), available at http://www.texasdefender.org

Texas defender service, overwhelmingly inaccurate predictions of future dangerousness, misleading Texas capital juries with false predictions of future dangerousness. Retrieved November 27, 2008, from http://www.texasdefender.org

Thayer, J. B. (1892). The jury and its development. *Harvard Law Review, 5,* 249, 261.

The clarke SHQ: A clinical sex history questionnaire for males. Retrieved April 27, 2008, from http://www.springerlink.com/content/v3g80h32r8558730/

The Paul Ingram Case. Retrieved June 9, 2007, from http://www.psych.umn.edu/courses/psy1001/resources/paul-ingram_case.pdf

The people's temple. Retrieved June 22, 2007, from http://www.religioustolerance.org/dc_jones.htm

The psychiatric prediction of Dangerousness. (1975). *University of Pennsylvania Law Review, 123,* 439, 440.

The skeptic's dictionary: False memory. Retrieved November 21, 2007, from http://skepdic.com/falsememory.html

The Unabomber: Headline archives. *Federal Bureau of Investigation Press Room.* Retrieved July 9, 2008, from http://www.fbi.gov/page2/april08/unabomber_042408.html

The United States District Court for the Eastern District of Virginia (May 16, 2001). *Criminal Case No. 01-188-A.* Retrieved March 9, 2007, from http://fl1.findlaw.com/news.findlaw.com/hdocs/docs/hanssen/ushanssen50902wfsub.pdf

Theonnee, N., & Tjaden, P. G. (1990). The extent, nature and validity of sexual theory with implications for organizational change. *Journal of Social Issues, 51,* 97.

Thoennes, N., & Pearson, J. (1988). Summary of findings from the sexual abuse allegations project. In E. B. Nicholson (Ed.), *Sexual abuse allegations in custody and visitation cases* (pp. 1–36). Washington, DC: American Bar Association.

Thomas, J. (2004, April 28). 'I was not the man who did this' cleared of shooting charge, Stephan Cowans looks back at six years lost in prison. *Boston Globe* at F1.

Thompson, H., & Priest, R. (2005). Elder abuse and neglect: Considerations for mental health practitioners. *Adultspan Journal, 4*(2), 116.

Thompson, J. (1993). Psychological impact of body recovery duties. *Journal of the Royal Society of Medicine, 86*, 628–629.

Thornton, J. L. (1983, March). Uses and abuses of forensic science. *ABA Journal, 69*, 289–292.

Toch, H. (2002). *Stress in policing*. Washington, DC: American Psychological Association.

Torrey, E. F. (2008). *The insanity offense: How America's failure to treat the seriously mentally ill endangers its citizens*. New York: W.W. Norton & Company.

Toufexis, A. (1995). Workers who fight firing with fire. In P. J. Resnick & O. Kausch (Eds.), Violence in the workplace: Role of the consultant. *Consulting Psychology Journal: Practice and Research, 47*(4), 213–222.

Tousignant, D. D. (1991, March). Why suspects confess. *FBI Law Enforcement Bulletin, 60*(3), 14–18.

Townsend, J., Phillips, J. S., & Elkins, T. J. (2000). Employee retaliation: The neglected consequences of poor leader-member exchange relations. *Journal of Occupational Health Psychology, 5*, 457–463.

Traxler, A. J. (1980). *Let's get gerontologized: Developing a sensitivity to aging, the multi-purpose senior center concept: A training manual for practitioners working with the aging*. Springfield, IL: Illinois Department of Aging.

Treatment Advocacy Center. *Briefing papers*. Retrieved August 15, 2007, from http://www.treatmentadvocacycenter.org/BriefingPapers/index.htm

Treatment advocacy center. Legal resources. Retrieved February 6, 2009, from http://www.treatmentadvocacycenter.org/LegalResources/Index.htm

TruTV Crime Library. Susan Smith: Child murderer or victim? Retrieved March 31, 2008, from http://www.crimelibrary.com/notorious_murders/famous/smith/index_1.htm

TruTV Crime Library. Andrea Yates: Ill or evil? Retrieved April 1, 2008, from http://www.crimelibrary.com/notorious_murders/women/andrea_yates/index.html

Tucker, L. R., Koopman, R. F., & Linn, R. L. (1969). Evaluation of factor analytic research procedures by means of simulated correlation matrices. *Psychometrika, 34*, 421–459.

Turco, R. (1990). Psychological profiling. *International Journal of Offender Therapy and Comparative Criminology, 34*, 147–154.

Tully, C., Kropf, N., & Price, J. (1993). Is field a hard hat area? A study of violence in field placements. *Journal of Social Work Education, 29*, 191–199.

Turner, C. B., & Cashdan, S. (1988). Perception of college students' motives for shoplifting. *Psychological Reports, 62*, 855–862.

Turtle, J. W., Lindsay, R. C. L., & Wells, G. L. (2003). Best practice recommendations for eyewitness evidence procedures: New ideas for the oldest way to solve a case. *Canadian Journal of Police and Security Services, 1*, 5–18.

Turvey, B. (1999). *Criminal profiling: An introduction to behavioral evidence analysis*. San Diego, CA: Academic Press.

Tuteur, W., & Glotzer, J. (1959). Murdering mothers. *American Journal of Psychiatry, 116*, 447–452.

Twenge, J. M., & Campbell, K. W. (2003). "Isn't it fun to get the respect that we're going to deserve?" Narcissism, social rejection, and aggression. *Personality and Social Psychology Bulletin, 29*, 261–272.

Umberson, D., & Hughes, M. (1987). The impact of physical attractiveness on achievement and psychological well-being. *Social Psychology Quarterly, 50*(3), 227–236.

Unclassified abstract of the CIA Inspector General's report on the Aldrich H. Ames case and the U.S. Senate Select Committee on Intelligence report. (1994, November 1). Retrieved March 2, 2007, from http://nsi.org/Library/Espionage/Hitzreport.html

UN General Assembly Resolution 54/109, 9 December 1999.

Ursano, R. J., Fullerton, C. S., Bhartiya, V., & Kao, T. C. (1995). Longitudinal assessment of posttraumatic stress disorder and depression after exposure to traumatic death. *Journal of Nervous and Mental Disease, 183*, 36–42.

Ursano, R. J., Fullerton, C. S., & Norwood, A. E. (1995). Psychiatric dimensions of disaster: Patient care, community consultation, and preventive medicine. *Harvard Review of Psychiatry, 3*, 196–209.

Ursin, H. (1960). The temporal lobe substrate of fear and anger. A review of recent stimulation and ablation in animals and humans. *Acta Psychiatrica Scandinavica, 35*(3), 378–396.

U.S. Department of Justice, FBI. Terrorism in the United States (1988, December 31). *Terrorist research and analytical center, counterterrorism section, criminal investigative division*, 34.

U.S. Department of Justice Office of Justice Programs, Bureau of Justice Statistics. Crime characteristics. Retrieved July 15, 2008, from http://www.ojp.usdoj.gov/bjs/cvict_c.htm#relate

U.S. Department of Justice, Office of Justice Programs, Bureau of Justice Statistics. Homicides trends in the U.S. Retrieved July 15, 2008, from http://www.ojp.usdoj.gov/bjs/homicide/relationship.htm

U.S. Department of Justice, Office of Justice Programs. National violence against women survey. Retrieved November 27, 2008, from http://www.ncjrs.gov/txtfiles1/nij/183781.txt

U.S. Department of Justice, Bureau of Justice Statistics. (2009). *Workplace violence*. Retrieved May 4, 2009, from http://www.ojp.usdoj.gov/bjs/cvict_c.htm

U.S. Office of Personnel Management. *Alternate dispute resolution resource guide*. Retrieved July 19, 2007, from http://www.opm.gov/er/adrguide

U.S. Department of Justice. (2004). *Crime in the United States*. Retrieved July 15, 2008, from http://www.fbi.gov/ucr/cius_04/offenses_reported/violent_crime/murder.html

U.S. Public Health Service, Dep't of Health & Human Services, *Mental Health: A Report of the Surgeon General* (1999).

Van der Kolk, B. A. (1994a). The body keeps score. *Memory and Psychiatry, 25*, 1–14.

Van der Kolk, B. A. (1994b). The body keeps score: Memory and the evolving psychobiology of posttraumatic stress. *Harvard Review of Psychiatry, 1*, 253–265.

Varela, D., & Black, D. W. (2002). Pedophilia treated with carbamazepine and clonazepam. *American Journal of Psychiatry, 159*, 1245–1246.

Victoroff, J. (2005). The mind of the terrorist: A review and critique of psychological approaches. *Journal of Conflict Resolution, 49*(1), 3–42.

Violanti, J., & Aron, F. (1994). Ranking police stressors. *Psychological Reports, 75*, 824–826.

Virginia killer's violent writings. The smoking gun. Retrieved January 1, 2009, from http://www.thesmokinggun.com/archive/years/2007/0417071vtech1.html

Visher, C. (1987). Juror decision making: The importance of evidence. *Law and Human Behavior, 11*, 1–7.

Viswesvaran, C., Schmidt, F. L., & Ones, D. S. (2005). Is there a general factor in ratings of job performance? A meta-analytic framework for disentangling substantive and error influences. *Journal of Applied Psychology, 90*, 108–131.

Vodanovich, S. J., Verner, K. M., & Gilbride, T. V. (1991). Boredom proneness: The relationship between positive and negative affect. *Psychological Reports, 69,* 113–146.

Vonderache, A. R. (1940). Changes in the hypothalamus on organic disease. *Journal of Nervous and Mental Disease, 20,* 689–712.

Vrana, S. R., & Rollock, D. (2002). The role of ethnicity, emotional content, and contextual differences in physiological, expressive, and self-reported emotional responses to imagery. *Cognition & Emotion, 16,* 165–192.

Vrij, A. (2008). *Detecting lies and deceit: Pitfalls and opportunities.* Chichester, UK: Wiley.

Vronsky, P. (2004). *Serial killers: The method and madness of monsters.* Berkley, CA: Penguin.

Vronsky, P. (2007). *Female serial killers: How and why women become monsters.* Berkley, CA: Penguin.

Vucetich, J. (2008). In Encyclopædia Britannica. Retrieved October 06, 2008, from Encyclopædia Britannica Online: http://www.britannica.com/EBchecked/topic/633397/Juan-Vucetich.

Wade, C. (Ed.). (2006). FBI handbook of forensic sciences. In S. J. Hicks & B. D. Sales (Eds.), *Criminal profiling: Developing an effective science and practice.* Washington, DC: American Psychological Association.

Wagner, W. (1989). *The art of advocacy: Jury selection.* New York: Matthew Bender.

Wagstaff, G. F. (1982a). Attitudes toward rape. The "just world" strikes again? *Bulletin of the British Psychological Society, 35,* 277–279.

Wagstaff, G. F. (1982b). Helping a witness remember—A project in forensic psychology. *Police Research Bulletin, 38,* 56–58.

Wagstaff, G. F. (1984). The enhancement of witness memory by hypnosis: A review and methodological critique of the experimental literature. *British Journal of Experimental and Clinical Hypnosis, 2,* 3–12.

Wagstaff, G. F. (1989). Forensic aspects of hypnosis. In N. P. Spanos & J. F. Chaves (Eds.), *Hypnosis: The cognitive behavioral perspective* (pp. 340–357). Buffalo, NY: Prometheus.

Walker, L. E. (1984). *The battered woman syndrome.* New York: Springer.

Walker, W. D., Rowe, R. C., & Quinsey, V. L. (1993). Authoritarianism and sexual harassment. *Journal of Personality and Social Psychology, 65,* 1036–1045.

Wall, P. M. (1975). Eyewitness identification in criminal cases. *Psychological science in the public interest, 3,* 11–24.

Waller, J. (2002). *Becoming evil: How ordinary people commit genocide and mass killing.* New York: Oxford University Press.

Wallerstein, J. S. (1984). Children of divorce: Preliminary report of a ten year follow-up of young children. *American Journal of Orthopsychiatry, 54*(3), 444–458.

Wang, R., Bianchi, S., & Raley, S. (2005). Teenager's internet use and family rules: A research note. *Journal of Marriage and Family, 67*(5), 1249–1258.

Ward, T., & Hudson, S. M. (1998). A model of the relapse process in sexual offenders. *Journal of Interpersonal Violence, 13*(6), 700–725.

Ward, T., & Hudson, S. M. (2000). A self-regulation model or relapse prevention. In B. A. Arrigo & S. L. Shipley (2005). *Forensic psychology* (p. 393). Burlington, MA: Elsevier Academic Press.

Warren, J. I., Burnette, M., South, S. C., Chauhan, P., Bale, R., & Friend, R. (2002). Personality disorders and violence among female prison inmates. *Journal of the American Academy of Psychiatry and the Law, 30,* 502–509.

Warren, J. I., Fitch, W. L., Dietz, P. E., & Rosenfeld, B. D. (1991). Criminal offense, psychiatric diagnosis, and psycholegal opinion: An analysis of 894 pretrial referrals. *Bulletin of the American Academy of Psychiatry and Law, 19*(1), 63–69.

Watson, D. (1988). The vicissitudes of mood measurement: Effects of varying descriptors, time frame, and response formats on measures of positive and negative affect. *Journal of Personality and Social Psychology, 55,* 128–141.

Watson, D., & Clark, L. A. (1984). Negative affectivity: The disposition to experience aversive emotional states. *Psychological Bulletin, 96,* 465–490.

Watson, D., Clark, L. A., & Tellegen, A. (1988). Development and validation of brief measures of positive and negative affect: The PANAS scales. *Journal of Personality and Social Psychology, 54,* 1063–1070.

Watson, D., Gamez, W., & Simms, L. J. (2005). Basic dimensions of temperament and their relation to anxiety and depression: A symptom-based perspective. *Journal of Research in Personality, 39,* 46–66.

Webert, D. R. (2003). Are the courts in a trance? Approaches to the admissibility of hypnotically enhanced witness testimony in the light of empirical evidence. *American Criminal Law Review, 40,* 1301–1327.

Webster, C. D., Harris, G. T., Rice, M., Cormier, C., & Quinsey, V. L. (1994). *The violence prediction scheme: Assessing dangerousness in high risk men.* Toronto, Canada: Centre of Criminology, the University of Toronto.

Webster, C. D., & Hucker, S. J. (2003). *Release Decision Making.* Hamilton: St. Joseph's Healthcare. Revised in 2007 for Chichester: Wiley.

Wecht, C. (1994). *Cause of death.* New York: Onyx Books.

Weinberger, L. E., & Millham, J. (1975). A multi-dimensional, multiple method analysis of attitudes toward the elderly. *Journal of Gerontology, 30,* 343–348.

Weiner, T. (1994, July 31). Why I Spied. *New York Times Magazine,* section 6, p. 16.

Wells, G. L. (1998). Eyewitness testimony. *Encyclopedia of psychology.* Washington, DC: American Psychological Association.

Wells, G. L. (1984). How adequate is human intuition for judging eyewitness testimony? In G. L. Wells & E. F. Loftus (Eds.), *Eyewitness testimony: Psychological perspectives.* New York: Cambridge University Press.

Wells, G. L. (1986). Expert psychological testimony: Empirical and conceptual analyses of effects. *Law and Human Behavior, 3,* 71–93.

Wells, G. L. (1993). What do we know about eyewitness identification? *American Psychologist, 48,* 553–571.

Wells, G. L., & Lindsay, R. C. (1980). On estimating the diagnosticity of eyewitness nonidentifications. *Psychological Bulletin, 88,* 776–784.

Wells, G. L., Memon, A., & Penrod, S. D. (2005). Eyewitness evidence: Improving its probative value. *Psychological Science in the Public Interest, 7*(2), 45–75.

Wells, G. L., Small, M., Penrod, S., Malpass, R. S., Fulero, S. M., & Brimacombe, C. (1998). Eyewitness identification procedures: Recommendations for lineups and photospreads. *Law and Human Behavior, 22,* 603–647.

Werner, P., & Meloy, J. (1992). Decision making about dangerousness in releasing patients from long-term hospitalization. *Journal of Psychiatry & Law, 20,* 25–47.

Wertham, F. (1954, May). Blueprints to Delinquency. *Reader's Digest,* p. 24.

Wessinger, C. (Eds.). (2000). *Millennialism, persecution and violence: Historical cases (religion and politics).* New York: Syracuse University Press.

Whitcomb, D., Hook, M., & Alexander, E. (2004). Child victimization. In C. R. Bartol & A. M. Bartol (Eds.), *Introduction of forensic psychology.* Thousand Oaks, CA: Sage.

Whitcomb D., Hook, M., & Alexander, E. (2000). Child victimization. In A. M. Seymour, A. Seymour, M. Murray, & J. Sigmon, et al. (Eds.), *National victim assistance academy textbook* (p. 30). Washington, DC: U.S. Department of Justice, Office for Victims of Crime.

White, E. K., & Honig, A. L. (1995). The role of the police psychologist in training. In M. I. Kurke & E. M. Scrivner (Eds.), *Police psychology into the 21st century.* Hillsdale, NJ: Lawrence Erlbaum.

White, J. L., Moffitt, T. E., & Silva, P. A. (1989). A prospective replication of the protective effects of IQ in subjects at high risk for juvenile delinquency. *Journal of Consulting and Clinical Psychology, 57,* 719–724.

Wiederman, M. W. (2002). Reliability and validity of measurement. In M. C. Seto (Ed.), *Pedophilia and sexual offending against children.* Washington, DC: American Psychological Association.

Wiener, R. L., & Stolle, D. P. (1997). Trial consulting: Jurors' and attorneys' perceptions of murder. *California Western Law Review, 34,* 226–243.

Wigdor, A. K., & Garner, W. R. (Eds.). (1982). *Ability testing: Uses, consequences, and controversies.* Washington, DC: National Academy Press.

Wille, R., & Beier, K. M. (1989). Castration in Germany. *Annals of Sex Research, 2,* 103–133.

Williams, A. N. (2004). Child adoption in the seventeenth century: Vignettes from Defoe and Pepys. *Journal of the Royal Society of Medicine, 97,* 37–38.

Williams, D. R., Neighbors, H. W., & Jackson, J. S. (2008). Racial/ethnic discrimination and health: Findings from community studies. *American Journal of Public Health, 98,* 29–37.

Williams, G. C. (1996). *Adaptation and natural selection.* Princeton, NJ: Princeton University Press.

Williams, H. W. (1940). Intelligence and delinquency. In G. M. Whipple (Ed.), *The thirty-ninth yearbook of the National Society for the Study of Education: Intelligence: It's nature and nurture: Vol. 1. Comparative and critical exposition* (pp. 291–297). Bloomington, IL: Public School.

Williams, P. L. (2007). *The day of Islam.* Amherst, NY: Prometheus Books.

Wilson, C., & Seaman, D. (1997). *The serial killers: A study in the psychology of Violence.* London: Virgin Publishing.

Wilson, G. D. (1978). *The secrets of sexual fantasy* (1st ed.), London, England: J.M. Dent & Sons Ltd.

Wilson, J. Q. (1997). *Moral judgment* (pp. 20–21). New York: Basic Books.

Wilson, J. Q., & Herrnstein, R. J. (1985). *Crime and human nature.* New York: Simon & Schuster.

Wilson, P. (2003). The concept of evil and the forensic psychologist. *International Journal of Forensic Psychology, 1,* 1–9.

Wilson, P. R., Lincoln, R., & Kocsis, R. N. (1997). Validity, utility and ethics of profiling for serial violent and sexual offenders. *Psychiatry, Psychology and Law, 4,* 1–12.

Wishman, S. (1986). *Anatomy of a jury: The system on trial.* New York: Times Books.

Wolak, J., Finkelhor, D., & Mitchell, K. J. (2004). Internet-initiated sex crimes against minors: Implications for prevention based on findings from a national study. *Journal of Adolescent Health, 35*(5), 424.

Wolfe, D. A. (1993). Intervention research with child abusive families: Policy implications. In D. Cicchetti & S. Toth (Eds.), *Child abuse, child development, and social policy* (pp. 369–397). New York: Ablex.

Wolfe, D. A. (1994). The role of intervention and treatment services in the prevention of child abuse and neglect. In G. B. Melton & F. Barry (Eds.), *Safe neighborhoods: Foundations for a new national strategy on child abuse and neglect* (pp. 224–303). New York: Guilford.

Wolfe, D. A., Wekerle, C., & McGee, R. (1992). Developmental disparities of abused children: Directions for prevention. In R. DeV. Peters, R. J. McMahon, & V. L. Quinsey (Eds.), *Aggression and violence throughout the lifespan* (pp. 31–51). Thousand Oaks, CA: Sage.

Wolraich, M. L., Wilson, D. B., & White, J. W. (1995). The effects of sugar on behavior or cognition in children: A meta-analysis. *Journal of the American Medical Association, 274,* 1617–1621.

Woodrow, H. (1938). The effect of practice on groups of different initial ability. *Journal of Educational Psychology, 29,* 268–278.

Woodward, M. (1955). The role of low intelligence in delinquency. *British Journal of Delinquency, 5,* 281–303.

Woody, H. (2005). The police culture: Research implications for psychological services. *Professional Psychology: Research and Practice, 36,* 525–529.

Wrightsman, L. S. (1972). *Social psychology in the seventies.* Belmont, CA: Brooks/Coole.

Wrightsman, L. S., & Fulero, S. M. (2005). *Forensic psychology.* Belmont, CA: Wadsworth.

Wrightsman, L. S., Greene, E., Nietzel, M. T., & Fortune, W. H. (2002). *Psychology and the legal system.* Belmonst, CA: Wadsworth.

Wrightsman, L. S., & Kassin, S. M. (1993). *Confessions in the courtroom.* Thousand Oaks, CA: Sage.

Wrightsman, L. S., Nietzel, M., & Fortune, W. (1994). *Psychology and the legal system* (3rd ed.). Pacific Grove, CA: Brooks/Cole.

Wu, K. D., & Watson, D. (2005). Relations between hoarding and obsessive-compulsive disorder. *Behaviour Research and Therapy, 43,* 897–921.

Wyatt v. Stickney, 325 F.Supp. 781, 784 (M.D.Ala.1971).

Yandrick, R. M. (1996). *Behavioral risk management: How to avoid preventable losses from mental health problems in the workplace.* San Francisco, CA: Jossey-Bass.

Yarmey, A. D., Yarmey, M. J., & Todd, L. (2008, April). Frances McGehee (1912–2004): The first earwitness researcher. *Perceptual and Motor Skills, 106*(2), 387–394.

Young, J. (1988). Risk of crime and fear of crime. In M. Maguire & J. Pointing (Eds.), *Victims of crime: A new deal,* Berkshire, UK: Open University Press.

Zabell, S. L.(2005). Fingerprint evidence. *Journal of Law and Policy,* 143–179. Retrieved, October 8, 2008, from http://www.brooklaw.edu/students/journals/bjlp/jlp13i_zabell.pdf

Zander, T. K. (2005). Civil commitment without psychosis: The law's reliance on the weakest link in psychodiagnosis. *Journal of Sexual Offender Civil Commitment: Science and the Law, 1,* 17–82.

Zimbardo, P. G. (1967). The psychology of police confessions. *Psychology Today, 1*(2), 17–27.

Zimbardo, P. G. (1969). The human choice: Individuation, reason, and order versus deindividuation, impulse, and chaos. *Nebraska Symposium on Motivation, 17,* 237–307.

Zimbardo, P. G. (1974). On obedience to authority. *American Psychologist, 29*(7), 566–567.

Zimbardo, P. G., & Andersen, S. (1993). Understanding mind control: Exotic and mundane mental manipulations. In M. Langone (Ed.), *Recover from cults: Help for victims of psychological and spiritual abuse* (pp. 104–125). New York: Norton.

Zimbardo, P. G., Haney, C., Banks, C. & Jaffe, D. (1974). The psychology of imprisonment: Privation, power, and pathology. In Z. Rubin (Ed.), *Doing unto others: Explorations in social behavior* (pp. 61–73). Englewood Cliffs, NJ: Prentice Hall.

Zlotnick, C. (1997). Posttraumatic stress disorder (PTSD), comorbidity, and childhood abuse among incarcerated women. *Journal of Nervous & Mental Disease, 185,* 761–763.

Zwick, W. R., & Velicer, W. F. (1982). Factors influencing four rules for determining the number of components to retain. *Multivariate Behavioral Research, 17,* 253–269.

Zwick, W. R., & Velicer, W. F. (1986). Comparison of five rules for determining the number of components to retain. *Psychological Bulletin, 99,* 432–442.

CASES CONSULTED

Alaska v. Coon, 974 P 2d 386 (1999).

Alexander v. Yale University, 631 F. 2d 178, 2nd Circuit (1980).

Almonte v. New York Medical College, 851 F. Supp. 34, 41 (D. Conn. 1994).

Almonte v. New York Medical College, 851 F. Supp. 34, 41 (D. Conn. 1994).

Anaya v. Crossroads Managed Care Systems, Inc., 195 E3d 584 (10th Cir. 1999).

Apodaca v. Oregon, 406 U.S. 404 (1972).

Arcoren v. U.S., 929 F.2d 1235 (8th Cir.).

Ashcraft v. Tennessee, 322 US 143 (1944).

Bailey v. State, 215 Ark. 53, 6, 219 S.W. 2d 424, 428 (1949).

Baldwin v. New York, 399 U.S.66 (1970).

Ballew v. Georgia, 435 U.S. 223 (1978).

Barefoot v. Estelle, 463 U.S. at 921(1983).

Barnes v. Costle, 561 F.2d 983, 987 (CADC 1977).

Batson v. Kentucky, 476 U.S. 79 (1986).

Bedder v. Director of Public Prosecutions, [1954] 1 W. L.R. 1119.

Bellah v. Greenson, 81 Cal. App.3d 614 (1978).

Bellaver v. Quanex Corp., 200 F.3d 485 (7th Cir. 2000).

Blackburn v. Alabama, 361 U.S. 199, 206 (1960).

Boro v. Superior Court, (1985) 163 Cal.App.3d 1224.

Boynton v. Burglass, 90 So.2d.466, 470 (1991).

Brady v. Hopper, 570 F. Supp. 1333 (D. Colo. 1983), aff'd, 751 F.2d 329 (10th Cir. 1984).

Bratty v. A-G, (Northern Ireland) (1963) AC 386.

Brown v. Allen, 344 US 443 (1953).

Brown v. Board of Education of Topeka, 347 U.S. 483 (1954).

Brown v. City of Guthrie, 22 FEP Cases 1627 (W.D. Okla. 1980).

Brown v. Mississippi, 297 U.S. 278 (1936).

Bundy v. Jackson, 205 U.S. App. D.C. 444, 641 F.2d 934 (1981).

Burch v. Louisiana, 441 U.S. 130 (1979).

Burlington Industries, Inc. v. Ellerth, 118 S. Ct. 2257 (1998).

Carr v. William C. Crowell Co., 28 Cal. 2d 652, 171 P.2d 5 (1946).

Carter v. Jury Comm'n of Greene County, 396 U.S. 329 (1970).

Castaneda v. Partida, 430 U.S. 482, 499 (1977).

Chambers v. Florida, 309 U.S. 277 (1940).

Chambers v. Florida, 309 U.S. 277 (1940).

City of Greenwood v. Dowler, 492. N.E.2d 1081 (Ind. Ct. App. 1986).

Commonwealth v. Cowans, 756 N.E.2d 622 (Mass. App. Ct. 2001).

Commonwealth v. Malone, 354 Pa. 180, 47 A.2d 445 (1946).

Commonwealth v. Redline, (1958) 391 Pa. 486, 508, 510, 137 A.2d 472, 482, 483.

Commonwealth v. Williams, 270 Pa.Super. 27, 410 A.2d 880 (1979).

Commonwealth of Virginia v. Billy Leon Smalls, CR44275, 44292, 44293 (1999).

Commonwealth of Virginia v. Jennifer Nicole Talley, CR 44276, 44294 (1999).

Conte v. Harcher, 365 N.E.2nd 567 (Ill. App. 1977).

Culombe v. Connecticut, 367 U.S. 568 (1961).

Daubert v. Merrell Dow Pharmaceuticals, Inc., 509 U.S. 579 (1993).

Davidson v. Time Warner, Inc., No. Civ. A.V.-94-006, 1997.

Davis v. State, 595, N.W.2d 520 (Minn, 1999).

Deborah S. v. Diorio, 612 N.Y.S.2d. 542, 542 (1st Dep't 1994).

DeFilippo v. National Broadcasting Co., 446 A.2d 1036 (R.I. 1982).

DiCarolo v. Potter, 358 F.3d 408, 415–16 (6th Cir. 2004).

Director of Public Prosecutions v. Smith, House of Lords, 3 All. E.R. 161 (1961).

Drope v. Missouri, 420 U.S. 162, (1975).

Duncan v. Louisiana, 391 U.S. 145.

Durham v. United States, 214 F.2d 862 (1954).

Dusky v. United States, 362 U.S. 402 (1960).

Edwards v. Arizona, 451 U.S. 477 (1981).

EEOC v. Outback Steakhouse, D. Colo., No. 06-cv-01935. (2001).

Ellison v. Brady, 924 F.2d 872, 875–76 (9th Cir.1991).

Everingim v. Good Samaritan Center of New Underwood, 552 NW2d 837, (SD 1996).

Ewing v. Goldstein, 120 Cal. App. 4th 807 (2004).

Ewing v. Northridge Hospital Medical Center, 120 Cal. App. 4th 1289 (2004).

Fair v. United States, 234 F.2d 288 (5th Cir. 1956).

Faragher v. City of Boca Raton, 524 U.S. 775 (1998).

Faretta v. California, 422 U.S. 806, 836.

Foucha v. Louisiana, 504 U.S. 71 (1992).

Frank v. United Airlines, Inc., 216 F.3d 845 (9th Cir. 2000).

Frye v. United States, 293 F. 1013 (D.C. Cir. 1923).

Garrett v. Univ. of Alabama, 193 F.3d 1214 (11th Cir. 1999), reversing 989 F. Supp. 1409.

General Electric Co. v. Joiner, 522 U.S. 136 (1997).

Getsinger v. Owens Corning Fiberglass Corp., 335 S.C. 77, 80, 515 S.E.2d 104, 105–06.

Gilbert v. California, 388 US 263 (1967).

Gilchrist v. Trail King Industries, 612 N.W.2d 10 (S.D. 2000).

Girouard v. State, (1991). 321 Md. 532, 583 A.2d 718.

Godinez v. Moran, 509 U.S. 389 (1993).

Gray v. Blight, C.C.A. Colorado, 112 F.2d 696.

Griggs v. Duke Power Co., 401 U.S. 424 (1971).

Hamman v. County of Maricopa, 161 Ariz. 58, 59. (1989).

Harris v. Forklift Systems, Inc., 510 U.S. 17 (1993).

Hartford Accident & Indemnity Co. v. Cardillo, 112 F.2d 11, 15 (1940).

Haynes v. Washington, 373 U.S. 503 (1963).

Henson v. State, 535 N.E. 2d 1189 (Ind. 1989).

Hicks v. Feeney, 770 E2d 375 (3d Cir. 1985).

Hopewell v. Adibempe, 415. A 2d 625. (Md. Ct Spec. App. 1980).

House v. State, 445 So. 2d 815, 826–27 (Miss. 1984).

In re Heidnik, 112 F.3d 105 (3rd Cir. 1997).

In re Heidnik, 720 A.2d 1016 (Pa. 1998).

Irvin v. Dowd, 366 U.S. 717, 81 S. Ct. 1639, 6 L. Ed. 2d 751 (1961).

J.E.B. v. Alabama ex rel. T.B., 511 U.S. 127 (1994).

Jablonski by Pahls v. United States, 712 F.2d 391 (1983).

Jackson v. Indiana, 406 U.S. 715 (1972).

Jaffee v. Redmond, 518 U.S. 1, 12 (1996).

Jenkins v. United States, 307 F.2d 637.

Johnson v. Noot, 323 N.W. 2d. 724, 728 (1982).

Johnson v. Transportation Agency, Santa Clara City, 480 U.S. 616 (1987).

Johnson v. ZerTost, 304 U.S. 458 (1938).

Jones v. State of New York, 267 App. Div. 254, 45 N.Y.S.2d 404 (1943).

Jones v. United States, 529 U.S. 848 (2000).

Jordan v. City of New London, 2000 U.S. App. Lexis 22195 (1st Cir. 8/23/2000), affirming 1999 U.S.Dist. Lexis 14289, 15 IER Cases (BNA) 919 (D. Conn. 1999).

K Mart Corp. v. Ponsock, 103 Nev. 39, 732 P.2d 1363, 1368.

Kansas v. Crane, 534 U.S. 407 (2002).

Kansas v. Hendricks, 521 U.S. 346 (1997).

Karraker v. Rent-A-Center, Inc., 411 F.3d 831 (7th Cir., 2005).

Kawakita v. United States, 343 U.S. 717 (1952).

Kennedy v. Williamsburg County, 242 S.C. 477, 480, 131 S.E.2d 512, 513 (1963).

Kirby v. Illinois, 406 US 682 (1972).

Kline v. Ford Motor Co., 523 F.2d 1067, 1069 (9th Cir. 1975).

Kumho Tire Company Ltd. v. Carmichael, 119 S. Ct. 1167, 1999 U.S. LEXIS 2189 (1999).

Larrimore v. American National Ins. Co., 184 Okla. 614, 89 P.2d 340 (1939).

Lavin-McEleney v. Marist College, 239 F.3d 476 (2d Cir. 2001).

Leo v. Workmen's Compensation Appeal Board, 537 A.2d 399 (2004, February).

Lindabury v. Lindabury, 552 So.2d. 1117, 1118 (1989).

Little v. Armontrout, 487 U.S. 1210 (1988).

Lockhart v. McCree, 476 U.S. 162 (1986).

Malorney v. B&L Motor Freight, Inc. 496 N.E.2d 1086 (Ill.spp. 1986).

Manson v. Braithwaite, 1977, 432 U.S. 98.

McDonough v. Workmen's Compensation Appeal Board, 470 A.2d 1099 (Pa. 1984).

McEleney v. Marist College, 239 F.3d 476 (2nd Cir., 2001).

McIntosh v. Milano, 403 A. 2d 500 (N.J. Sup. Ct. Law Div. 1979).

McKinney v. Dole, 765 F.2d 1129 (D.C. Cir. 1985).

McQueen v. Garrison, 814 F.2d 951, 958 (4th Cir.), *cert. denied*, 484 U.S. 944 (1987).

Meritor Savings Bank v. Vinson, 106 S. Ct. 2399 (1986).

Miller v. California, 413 U.S. 15 (1973).

Miller v. City of Springfield, 146 F.3d 612, 8 AD Cases (BNA) 321 (8th Cir. 1998).

Miranda v. Arizona, 384 U.S. 436 (1966).

Misskelley v. Arkansas, 915 S.W.2d 702.

Misskelley v. State, 323 Ark. 449, 478, 915 S.W.2d 702, 717 (1996).

Missouri ex rel. McBride v. Dalton, 834 S.W.2d 890 (Mo. Ct. App. 1992).

Missouri v. Davis, 464 U.S. 962 (1983).

Morrow v. Maryland, 443 A. 2d.108 (MD. Ct. App. 1982).

Mu'min v. Virginia, 500 U.S. 415, 111 S. Ct. 1899, 114 L. Ed. 2d 493 (1991).

NAACP v. Claiborne Hardware Co., 458 U.S. 886, 927 (1982).

Naidu v. Laird, 539 A.2d 1064 (Del. 1988).

Neal v. Delaware, 103 US 370 (1880).

Nebraska Press Association v. Stuart, 427 U.S. 539, 96 S. Ct. 2791, 49 L. Ed.

Neil v. Biggers, 409 US 188 (1972).

New York v. Ferber, 458 U.S. 747 (1982).

New York v. Quarles, 467 U.S. 649 (1984).

Newport News Shipbuilding & Dry Dock v. EEOC, 462 U.S. 669 (1983).

Newsome v. McCabe et al., 256 F.3d 747 (2002).

Nichols v. Azteca Restaurant Enterprises, Inc., 256 F.3d 864 (9th Cir. 2001).

Nitroglycerine Case, 82 U.S. 524 (1872).

NSW (*R. v. Valevski*, 2000, NSWCCA 445).

O'Connor v. Donaldson, 422 U.S. 563 (1975).

Oleszko v. State Comp. Ins. Fund, 243 F.3d 1154 (9th dr. 2001).

Olivia N. v. National Broadcast Co., 126 Cal. App. 3d 488, 178 Cal. Rptr. 888 (1981).

Olmstead v. L.C. ex rel. Zimring, 119 S.Ct. 2176 (1999).

Olsen v. Marriott International, Inc., 75 F. Supp. 2d 1052 (D. Ariz. 1999).

Oncale v. Sundowner Offshore Services, Inc., 523 U.S. 75 (1998).

Palsgraf v. Long Island R. R. Co., 248 N.Y. 339, 162 N.E. 99 (1928).

Panetti v. Dretke, 127 S. Ct. 852 (2007).

Parisie v. Greer, 705 F.2d 882 (7th Cir. 1983).

PBA L-319 v. Twp. of Plainsboro, #C-173-98 Middlesex Co. NJ Super.Ct. (Unrptd., 1998).

Pearson v. State, 441 N.E.2d 468, 471 (Ind. 1982).

People of the State of California v. Scott Peterson, No. 1056770 (CA, 2004).

People v. Beckford, 532 N.Y.S.2d 462, 465 (N.Y. Gen. Term 1988).

People v. Burnick, 552 So.2d. 1117, 1118 (1975).

People v. Campbell, 159 Ill. 9 (1895).

People v. Decina, 2 N.Y.2d 133, 157 N.Y.S.2d 558, 138 N.E.2d 799 (1956).

People v. Erikson, 67 Cal. Rptr. 740 (Cal. 1997).

People v. Ferguson, 248 A.D. 2d 725, 670 N.Y.S. 2d 327(N.Y. App. Div. 1998).

People v. Hughes, 59 N.Y.2d at 535, N.Y.S.2d (1983).

People v. John Mark Karr, Sonoma County Superior Court No. MCR-375385 (2006).

People v. Lisnow, 88 Cal.App.3d Supp. 21, 26–27, 151 Cal.Rptr. 621, 623 (1978).

People v. McDarrah, 175 Ill.App.3d 284, 124 Ill. Dec. 827, 529 N.E.2d 808 (1988).

People v. Milner, 45 Cal.3d 227, 753 P.2d 669 (Sup. Ct. of Cal. 1988).

People v. Schmidt, 110 N.E. (1915) at 949.

People v. Schmitz, 586 N.W.2d 766, 768 (Mich. Ct. App. 1998).

People v. Shirley, 31 Cal.3d 18, 181 Cal. Rptr. 243, 641 P.2d 775, cert denied, 103 S. Ct.

People v. Taylor, 552 N.E.2d 131 (N.Y. 1990).

Perreira v. State, 768 P.2d 1198 (Colo. 1989).

Petersen v. State, 671 P. 2d 230 (1983).

Petzold v. Borman's, Inc., 617 N.W.2d 394 (Ct. App., Mich., 2000).

Plessy v. Ferguson, 163 U.S. 537 (1896).

Police Department v. Mosley, 408 U.S. 92, 95 (1972).

Price Waterhouse v. Hopkins, 490 U.S. 288 (1989).

Quinones v. Houser Buick, 436 F.3d 284 (1st Cir., 2006).

R. v. Allen, December 1992, NSW CCA, p. 6.

R. v. Bowhay, 1998, NSWSC 782.

R. v. Milat, 1996 87 A Crim R 446.

R. v. Latimer, [1997] 1 S.C.R. 217.

R. v. Latimer, [2001] 1 S.C.R. 3, 2001 SCC 1.

Rachid v. Jack in the Box, Inc., 376 F.3d 305, 307 (5th Cir. 2004).

Ramirez v. Kelly, 1997 WL 223053 (N.D. Ill. 1997).

Ramona v. Isabella, No. 61898 (Cal. Super. Ct. May 13, 1994).

Ramona v. Isabella, No. 61898 (Cal. Super. Ct. May 13, 1994).

Regina v. Byrne, (1960) 3 ALL E. R. 1, 4.

Regina v. Oxford, 9 Carr., & P. 525 (1840).

Rex v. Arnold, 16 How. St. Tr. 695 (1724).

Richmond Newspapers v. Virginia, 448 U.S. 555, 100 S. Ct. 2814, 65 L. Ed.

Riggins v. Nevada, 504 U.S. 127 (1992).

Risner v. United States Department of Transportation, 677 F.2d 36 (8th Cir.1982).

Ritchie v. Indiana, 468 N. E. 2d. 1369 (Ind. Sup. Ct. 1984).

Rock v. Arkansas, 483 U.S. 44 (1987).

Roper v. Simmons, 543 U.S. 551 (2005).

Roth v. United States, 354 U.S.76 1957).

Russell v. United States, 471 U.S. 858 (1985).

Schall v. Martin, 463 U.S. 880, 921 (1984).

Sell v. United States, 539 U.S. 166 (2003).

Shaw v. Glickman, 45 Md. App. 718, 415 A. 2d 625 (1980).

Shedd v. State, 178 Ga. 653, 173 S.E. 847 (1934).

Shepard v. State, 957 P2.d 553 (1997).

Sheppard v. Maxwel, 384 U.S. 333 (1966).

Sheppard v. Rees, 909 F.2d 1234, 1236 (9th Cir. 1990).

Smith v. Amtrak, 865 F.2d 467 (2d Cir. 1987).

Smith v. State, 277 S.E. 2d 678 (Ga.1981).

Smith v. United States, 148 F.2d 665 (1929).

Smith v. United States, 507 U.S. 197 (1993).

Sovereign News Co. v. Falke, 448 F.Supp. 306, 394 (N.D. Ohio 1977).

Spades v. City of Walnut Ridge, #98-4119, 186 F.3d 897 (8th Cir. 1999).

Sprynczynatyk v. General Motors Corp., 771 F.2d 1112, 1123 (8th Cir. 1985).

State of Maryland v. Kirk N. Bloodsworth, 84-CR-3138 (Baltimore County 1984).

State v. Allery, 682 P.2d 312, 316 (Wash.1984).

State v. Allewalt (517 A.2d 741), Md. 1986.

State v. Baucom, 28 Oregon App. 757, 561 P.2d 641 (1977).

State v. Borelli, 629 A.2d 1105 (Conn. 1993).

State v. Bressman, 689 P.2d 901 (Kan. 1984).

State v. Bricker, 321 Md. 86, 581 A.2d 9 (1990).

State v. Chapple, 660 P.2d 1208 (Ariz. 1983).

State v. Edelman, 593 N.W.2d 419 (S.D. 1999).

State v. Escamilla, 245 Neb. 13, 511 N.W.2d 58 (Neb. 1994).

State v. Fuller, 862 A.2d 1130 (N.J., 2004).

State v. Gallegos, 719 P.2d 1268 (N.M. App. 1986).

State v. Huey, 699 P.2d 1290 (Ariz. 1985).

State v. Hurd, 432 A.2d 86, 93 (N.J. 1981).

State v. Kelly, 97 N.J. 178, 478 A.2d 364 (1984).

State v. Marks, 647 P.2d 1292 (Kan. 1982).

State v. McQuillen, 689 P.2d 822 (Kan. 1984).

State v. Norman, 89 N.C.App. 384, 366 S.E.2d 586 (1988), rev'd, 324 N.C. 253, 378.

State v. Saldana, 324 N.W. 2d 227 (Minn. 1982).

State v. Weston, 475 N.E.2d 805, 813 (Ohio App. 1984).

State v. Whaley, 305 S.C. 138, 406 S.E.2d 369 (1991).

State v. Zola, 112 N.J. 384, 548 A.2d 1022 (1988).

State v. Saldana, 324 N.W. 2d 227 (Minn. 1982).

Stimson v. Michigan Bell Tel. Co., 77 Mich.App. 361, 258 N.W.2d 227, 231.

Stovall v. Denno, 388 US 293 (1967).

Strauder v. West Virginia, 100 U.S. 303 (1880).

Sudtelgte v. Reno, 63 FEP Cases 1257 (W.D. Mo. 1994).

Swisher v. United States, 237 F.Supp. 921 (W.D. Mo. 1965).

Tarasoff v. Regents of the University of California, 529 P.2d 553, (Cal. 1974).

Tarasoff v. the Regents of the University of California, et al., 551 P.2d 334, (Cal.1976).

Tate v. Marks, 647 P.2d 1292, Kan. 1982.

Taylor v. Louisiana, 419 U.S. 522, 528 (1975).

The People of the State of California v. Scott Peterson, Superior Court for the State of California, Case No.1056770 (2004).

Thiel v. Southern Pacific Co., 328 U.S. 227 (1946).

Thompson v. County of Alameda, 27 Cal. 3d 741, 167 Cal. Rptr. 70, 614 P.2d 728 (1980).

Thompson v. Utah., 170 U.S. 343 (1898).

Turner v. Jordan, 957 S.W.2d 815, 818–19 (Tenn. 1997).

U.S. v. DeGross, 960 F. 2d 1433, 1438 (CA9 1992) (en banc).

U.S. v. Scheffer, 523 U.S. 303 (1998).

Underwood v. United States, 256 F.2d 92 (5th Cir. 1966).

United States v. Baller, 519 F.2d 463, (4th Cir. 1975).

United States v. Barnard, 490 F.2d 907, 912 (9th Cir. 1973).

United States v. Bighead, 128 F.3d 1329, 1330 (9th Cir. 1997).

United States v. Brawner, 471 F.2d 969 (1972).

United States v. De Gross, 960 F.2d 1433 (CA9 1992).

United States v. Downing, 753 F.2d 1224 (3d Cir. 1985).

United States v. Franks, 511 F.2d 25, (6th Cir. 1975).

United States v. Hall, 165 F.3d 1095 (7th Cir. 1999).

United States v. Haupt, D.C.III., 47 Supp. 836, 839 (1942).

United States v. Mafnas, 701 F.2d 83 (1983).

United States v. Maivia, 728 F. Supp. (District of Hawaii, 1990).

United States v. Peterson, et al., U.S. Dist. Ct., Southern District, Texas, No. H-97-237.

United States v. Playboy Entertainment Group, Inc., 529 U.S. 803, 818 (2000).

United States v. Robert Philip Hanssen, The United States District Court for the Eastern District of Virginia, Criminal No. 01-188-A (2001).

United States v. Rincon, 28 F.3d 921 (9th Cir. 1994).

United States v. Romualdi, 101 F.3d 971 (4rd Cir. 1996).

United States v. Scheffer, 523 U.S. 303 (1998).

United States v. Smithers, 212 F.3d 306, 311–12 (6th Cir. 2000).

United States v. Taddy Jackman, U.S. App. LEXIS 2083 (2007).

United States v. Tanya Smith, 869 F2d 348,354, (7th Cir. 1989).

United States v. Wade, 388 U.S. 218, 229–34 (1967).

United States v. Waksal, 539 F. Supp. 834, 838 (S.D. Fla. 1982), rev'd on other grounds, 709.

United States v. Weston, 134 F. Supp. 2d 115, 117 (D.D.C. 2001).

United States v. Williams, 583 F.2d 1194, (2d Cir. 1978).

Vining v. Avis Rent-a-Car Systems, Inc., 354 So.2d 54 (Fla. 1977).

Virginia v. Bobbitt, 756, 446 S.E.2d 898 (1994).

Wainwright v. Witt, 469 U.S. 412 (1985).

Walker v. Osbourne, 763 F.Supp. 1144 (M.D. Ga. 1991).

Ward v. Texas, 316 U.S. 547 (1948).

Washington v. Harper, 494 U.S. 210 (1990).

Weitz v. Lovelace Health, 10Cir. No. 98–2265 (2000).

Werner v. State, 711 S.W.2d 639 (Tex. Cr. App. 1986).

Western Air Lines, Inc. v. Criswell, 472 U.S. 400 (1985).

Whiteside v. W.C.A.B, 650 A.2d 1202 (Pa. Commw. 1994).

Wicker v. McCotter, 783 F.2d 487, 492–93 (5th Cir.).

Williams v. Florida, 399 U.S. 78 (1970).

Williams v. Saxbe, 413 F.Supp. 654 (1976).

Winters v. New York, 333 U.S. 507 (1948).

Witherspoon v. Illinois, 391 U.S. 510 (1968).

Wofford v. Eastern State Hosp., 795 P.2 516 (Okla. 1990).

Wood v. Laidlaw Transit, Inc., 77 N.Y.2d 79, 565 N.E.2d 1255, 564 N.Y.S.2d 704.

Wyatt v. Stickney, 325 F. Supp. 781, 784 (M.D.Ala.1971).

Youngberg v. Romeo, 457 U.S. 307 (1982).

Zamora v. Columbia Broadcasting System, 480 F. Supp. 199 (S.D. Fla. 1979).

CODES AND AUTHORITIES

Americans with Disabilities Act of 1990, 42 U.S.C. § 12101 et seq.

Ariz. Rev. Stat. Ann. § 12-2234.

Ark. Code Ann. § 16-41-101 Rule 503; Iowa Code Ann. § 622.10.

Article 3, U.S. Constitution

California Penal Code, § 203.

California Penal Code, § 273.8.

California Penal Code § 647 (f).

20 CFR. § 404.1520.

20 CFR. § 404.1510.

29 C.F.R. Part 1607, Uniform Guidelines on Employee Selection Procedures, § 1607.3.

Code of Federal Regulations Ch. XIV (7-1-00 Edition), Section 1604.11.

EEOC Enforcement Guidance: Vicarious Employer Liability for Unlawful Harassment by Supervisors No. 915.002, 11-18 (June 18, 1999).

English Statute of Treason (1350).

Equal Employment Opportunity Commission. (1980). The federal guideline on sexual harassment (Title VII, § 703). Washington, DC: EEOC.

Federal Jury Selection and Service Act of 1968, Pub. L. No. 90-274, 82 Stat. 53, 28 U.S.C. Sec. 1861 et seq.

Kansas Statute Annotated 59-29a02 (1994) amended in (1996).

405 Illinois Comp Statute 5/1-119.

Maryland Code Annotated, Cts. & Jud. Proc. § 9-108.

Model Penal Code § 251.4.

New York Criminal Code, § 120.16.

Qualifications of Nonmedical Psychologist to Testify as to Mental Condition or Competency, 72 A.L.R.Sth 579 (1999).

Restatement (Third) of Torts: Liability for Physical Harm, Affirmative Duties, Duty to Third Persons Based on Special Relationship with Person Posing Risk § 41 (2005).

Texas Criminal Code § 43.21(a).

Title IV, § 40001-40703 of the Violent Crime Control and Law Enforcement Act of 1994 HR 3355).

Title VI, 42 U.S. Code § 2000d et seq.

Title 18, U.S. Code, § 17.

Title 18, U.S. Code, § 1111.

18 U.S. Code § 793.

18 U.S. Code § 4241(a).

28 U.S. Code § 702.

29 U.S. Code §§ 621-634.

42 U.S. Code § 1983.

78 Stat. 255, as amended, 42 U.S.C.

UN General Assembly Resolution 54/109, 9 December 1999.

U.S. Constitution, Sixth Amendment (1791).

Virginia Code § 9.1-116.1.

Virginia Code § 18.2-51.2.

Virginia Code § 18.2-61.

Virginia Code § 18.2-60.3.

Virginia Code § 18.2-346.

Virginia Code § 18.2-372.

Virginia Code § 37.2: 800-809.

INDEX

Note: Page numbers in **bold** refer to definition of the term cited in text.